Handbook of
Clinical Gerontology
(PGPS-146)

Pergamon Titles of Related Interest

Lewinsohn/Teri CLINICAL GEROPSYCHOLOGY:
New Directions in Assessment and Treatment
Pinkston/Linsk CARE OF THE ELDERLY: A Family Approach
Rybash/Hoyer/Roodin ADULT COGNITION AND AGING:
Developmental Changes in Processing, Knowing and Thinking
Yost/Corbishley/Allender GROUP COGNITIVE THERAPY:
A Treatment Method for Depressed Older Adults

Related Journals

Free sample copies available upon request

EXPERIMENTAL GERONTOLOGY
CLINICAL PSYCHOLOGY REVIEW

PERGAMON GENERAL PSYCHOLOGY SERIES
EDITORS
Arnold P. Goldstein, *Syracuse University*
Leonard Krasner, *Stanford University and SUNY at Stony Brook*

Handbook of Clinical Gerontology

Laura L. Carstensen
Stanford University

Barry A. Edelstein
West Virginia University

PERGAMON PRESS

New York ● Oxford ● Beijing ● Frankfurt
São Paulo ● Sydney ● Tokyo ● Toronto

Pergamon Press Offices:

U.S.A.	Pergamon Press, Maxwell House, Fairview Park, Elmsford, New York 10523, U.S.A.
U.K.	Pergamon Press, Headington Hill Hall, Oxford OX3 0BW, England
PEOPLE'S REPUBLIC OF CHINA	Pergamon Press, Room 4037, Qianmen Hotel, Beijing, People's Republic of China
FEDERAL REPUBLIC OF GERMANY	Pergamon Press, Hammerweg 6, D–6242 Kronberg, Federal Republic of Germany
BRAZIL	Pergamon Editora, Rua Eça de Queiros, 346, CEP 04011, Paraiso, São Paulo, Brazil
AUSTRALIA	Pergamon Press Australia, P.O. Box 544, Potts Point, N.S.W. 2011, Australia
JAPAN	Pergamon Press, 8th Floor, Matsuoka Central Building, 1–7–1 Nishishinjuku, Shinjuku-ku, Tokyo 160, Japan
CANADA	Pergamon Press Canada, Suite No. 271, 253 College Street, Toronto, Ontario, Canada M5T 1R5

First printing 1987

Library of Congress Cataloging-in-Publication Data
Handbook of clinical gerontology.
(Pergamon general psychology series ; 146)
Includes index.
1. Geriatrics—Handbooks, manuals, etc.
2. Geriatric psychiatry—Handbooks, manuals, etc.
I. Carstensen, Laura L. 1953–   .II. Edelstein,
Barry A., 1945–   . III. Series. [DNLM:
1. Geriatrics. WT 100 H2328]
RC952.55.H38   1987   618.97   86–22561
ISBN 0–08–031947–5

Printed in Great Britain by Hazell Watson & Viney Limited, Aylesbury, Bucks

To my parents, with love and gratitude

L. C.

To Lee, Brian and Ronnie, with love

B. E.

Contents

Preface and Acknowledgements   xi

Part I. Normal Aging

1   The Cell Biology and Theoretical Basis of Human Aging   3
     Leonard Hayflick

2   Molar Aging: The Physiology and Psychology of Normal Aging   18
     Judy M. Zarit
     Steven H. Zarit

3   Environment and the Need Satisfaction of the Aging   33
     M. Powell Lawton

Part II. Psychiatric Disorders

4   Paranoid and Schizophrenic Disorders Among the Aging   43
     Felix Post

5   Alcohol Abuse Among the Elderly   57
     Sheldon Zimberg

6   The Sexual Behavior and Problems of the Elderly   66
     William T. O'Donohue

7   Affective Disorders Among the Aging   76
     Susan A. Gaylord
     William W. K. Zung

8   Dementia   96
     Thomas Crook

9   Depression and Dementia   112
     Linda Teri
     Burton V. Reifler

Part III. Common Medical Problems

10   Cancer Management Issues   123
     Jerome W. Yates
     Rosemary Yancik

11   Cardiovascular Disease   132
     John T. Santinga

12   Orthopedic Issues in the Elderly   144
     Robert R. Karpman

13   Drug Use in the Geriatric Patient   152
     Rubin Bressler

Part IV. Behavior Problems and Their Management

14   Wandering and Disorientation   177
     Richard A. Hussian

15   Pain Management in the Elderly   190
     Ellie T. Sturgis
     Jeffrey J. Dolce
     Patricia C. Dickerson

16   Dependence in Aging   204
     Margret M. Baltes
     HansWerner-Wahl

17   Age-related Changes in Social Activity   222
     Laura L. Carstensen

18   Sleep Disturbances   238
     Richard R. Bootzin
     Mindy Engle-Friedman

19   Urinary Incontinence: Behavioral Assessment and Treatment   252
     Kathryn L. Burgio
     Bernard T. Engel

20   Family Management of the Elderly   267
     Roger Patterson

21   Cognitive, Behavioral, and Psychological Sequelae of Cerebrovascular   277
     Accidents and Closed Head Injuries in Older Adults
     Robert J. McCaffrey
     Jerid M. Fisher

Part V. Social Issues

22   Social Support, Interpersonal Efficacy, and Health: A Life Course   291
     Perspective
     Toni C. Antonucci
     James S. Jackson

23   The Challenge of Bereavement   312
     Patricia A. Wisocki
     James R. Averill

24   Prevention of Age-related Problems   322
     Robert Kastenbaum

25   A Place to Call Home   335
     Graham D. Rowles

26   Clinical Issues for Assessment and Intervention with the Black Elderly   354
     Brenda F. McGadney
     Robin Goldberg-Glen
     Elsie M. Pinkston

27   Politics and Aging: The Gray Panthers   376
     Maggie Kuhn

28   Ethics and the Elderly   387
     William T. O'Donohue
     Jane E. Fisher
     Leonard Krasner

Author Index   401

Subject Index   423

About the Editors and Contributors   431

Preface and Acknowledgements

Throughout the 20th century our society has witnessed a tremendous growth in the size of the elderly population, and a concomitant increase in the need for health and social service delivery to the aged population. Today, 25 million people in the United States are over the age of 65. Of those who reside in the community, an estimated 10% to 25% suffer from significant mental health problems. Among the institutionalized, 80% exhibit some form of mental health impairment. Moreover, it is a minority of older persons who do not suffer from significant medical problems. But in spite of obvious demographic imperatives, the elderly remain sorely underserved by mental health and medical professionals.

In part, limited services reflect limited training currently available in schools of the social sciences and medicine. The elderly client often presents with a clinical picture that is not consistent with classic symptomatology. And only rarely will the behavioral problem of an elderly client be free of physical and social influences. Often psychological problems of the elderly are described as "making sense" and "less bizarre" than those of younger persons, yet consequences for the elderly are often much more severe. Institutionalization, for example, can be a very likely alternative to behavior management problems, such as forgetfulness or depression misdiagnosed as dementia. Often,

treatment is straightforward and effective, but a multidimensional understanding of the problem is essential and includes an examination of health, pharmacological, social, and psychological factors.

Gerontologists have long been aware of the confluence of physical and mental health impairment, and of the extraordinary challenge that the interdependence of psychological, behavioral, and physical problems poses to the clinician. Although there is general agreement that effective treatment requires a consideration of multiple factors, the task is an ominous one. Virtually every discipline has a geriatrics or gerontology subspecialty with an increasingly voluminous literature. To be expert in every arena is a practical impossibility.

This volume was designed for use by those interested in the treatment of medical and psychological problems that the elderly face. It is aimed at both the student of clinical gerontology and the seasoned professional. It will serve as a teaching tool to familiarize the student with the broad spectrum of problems that face an aging population. For the professional, it will function as a comprehensive resource on which one can rely for an up-to-date discussion of medical, social, or mental health problems, both within and outside one's specialty area.

The book contains chapters on normal aging processes, psychiatric disorders, medical disorders, behavior problems, and social issues. Part I provides a general background on normal aging processes. Together, the chapters in this section provide a discussion of normal aging from the cellular to the environmental level. Parts II, III, and IV include chapters on specific disorders chosen to represent the most common and debilitating physical, mental, and behavioral problems that elderly individuals experience. And last, Part V contains chapters that describe social factors relevant to the physical and psychological well-being of the aged population. Together, they provide the practitioner or researcher with a review of many social, psychological, and medical issues pertinent to the care of an aging patient or client.

As in all compendiums, space limitations precluded the inclusion of some topics. Others were not included for reasons that are highly significant. Conspicuous in its absence, for example, is a chapter on anxiety disorders among the aged, disorders that are assumed to be quite prevalent among the elderly, but about which very little has been written.

We were very fortunate to have the opportunity to bring together the work of scholars and scientists from the United States and Europe into a resource text that provides a wide array of information, spanning multiple disciplines. We are most appreciative of the obvious efforts of the contributing authors in this volume, both in the preparation of their chapters and for their extensive work in the study of aging. Without exception, the contributors to this volume are persons whose work has expanded significantly our knowledge base on aging and the aged.

The editors are deeply grateful for the secretarial assistance of Lana Fish and Claire Noel, and the technical assistance of Tracey Arndt. We also want to thank the staff of Pergamon Press, Inc., particularly Jerome Frank and Christina Lombardi, for their extensive efforts in bringing the book to fruition. Finally, LC gratefully acknowledges a grant from the National Institute on Aging (New Investigator Research Award R23 AG05592–01), which supported, in part, her work on this volume.

Part I

Normal Aging

It would be impossible to understand the disorders of aging without an understanding of normal aging. In this section, normal aging is reviewed from three levels—molecular, molar, and environmental. The aim of the section is to familiarize the reader with a theoretical model of aging, provide discussion of aging at the cellular level, review age-related physical and psychological changes that accompany normal aging, and discuss the effects of environmental factors on age-related changes.

Chapter 1

The Cell Biology and Theoretical Basis of Human Aging

Leonard Hayflick

The phenomenon of biological aging is generally believed to be a universal occurrence in all living things. It is a manifestation of the sum of a multitude of biological decrements that occur after sexual maturation. Yet this concept cannot be accepted without qualification.

There are animals in which aging is rare or has never been demonstrated. Some fish and amphibians that have an indeterminate size may also have an indeterminate life span (Comfort, 1979). Thus, the universality of aging, even in vertebrates, remains unproven. These animals are not immortal. Although normal age changes may not occur, they will die eventually of disease, predation, or accidents at an actuarially determined annual rate, which is not true aging.

In fact, the occurrence of aging arguably is restricted to humans and to the domestic and zoo animals that we choose to protect. The extreme manifestations of old age that are found to occur in humans simply do not occur in feral animals. If aging occurs at all in wild animals, its expression is brief because the physiological decrements of aging quickly make these animals vulnerable to disease and predation. Few feral animals live long enough after sexual maturation to experience old age. As soon as they incur even slight decrements in, say, running speed or jumping ability, they are culled by predators. Similarly, as soon as their immune system becomes less capable, they may die of disease, or what is more likely is that they will be culled by predators when disease has reduced their ability to elude capture. As a result, the likelihood is remote that evolution could have selected for the aging process. There are simply too few feral animals on which selective pressure could have been applied. Thus, aging cannot be viewed as an adaptation.

In developed countries, humans have been so successful in resolving causes of death attributable to acute diseases that their aging is expressed to an extreme unattainable by wild animals. Civilization has produced life expectations that were unknown in prehistoric times, revealing a plethora of physiological decrements that perhaps, teleologically, never were intended to be revealed. Aging may be an artifact of civilization or domestication because this "unnatural" circumstance has permitted the expression of aging that otherwise would not have occurred.

AGING AND DISEASE

Aging must be distinguished from disease. Biological changes attributable to aging are frequently referred to as "normal age changes," as if there was a category of "abnormal age changes." Age-related changes are not diseases—they are natural losses of function. Loss and graying of the hair, reduced exercise capacity and stamina, wrinkled skin, the menopause, presbyopia, loss of short-term memory, and hundreds of other similar decrements of old age are not diseases—they do not increase our vulnerability to death. Other "normal" decrements in vital organs do produce increased vulnerability to pathological change. For example, normal age-related decrements in immune-system functions increase vulnerability to diseases that in youth would be easily resolved, or antigens recognized as self in youth might be recognized by an aging immune system as nonself, thus producing many of the chronic autoimmune diseases of old age.

ETIOLOGY OF AGING

What is the cause of the aging phenomenon? This question, which is fundamental in the science of gerontology, might well be analogous to asking, "What is the cause of development?" Similarly, the frequently asked question, "How can aging be stopped or slowed?" is equivalent to asking, "How can development be stopped or slowed?"

There is no good reason why aging has to happen. The great German biologist August Weismann believed that aging occurs to benefit the species by removing less fit animals from an environment where limited space and other resources should be conserved for the young (Weismann, 1892). This is an illogical argument because if chronologically older animals continued to remain fit, their deaths would not benefit younger members. Thus, there would be no basis for an aging process to evolve in the first place. Weismann's notion can also be discredited because with few, or no, old feral animals surviving, there is little possibility that evolution could have selected for the aging process.

Furthermore, there is no selective advantage for a species to have its members live much beyond the age of sexual maturity and child rearing. For example, from the standpoint of simple survival of the species, there is no advantage for humans to live much beyond the age of, say 30. This would permit sufficient time for the production of new progeny and the rearing of that progeny to sexual maturation. Because life expectation at birth in prehistoric times was about 18 years, it is apparent that the human species has survived for a much

longer period of time with an 18-year life expectation than it has with the current 75 in developed countries. Thus, the human species has survived for a much longer period of time with few, or no, old members than it has with many old members.

Weissmann, however, was prescient on one major point: He surmised correctly that the ability of normal somatic cells to replicate and function was limited. The opposite was believed for decades, but this dogma was finally upset by Hayflick and Moorhead in 1961. Thus, the limited ability for normal human and animal cells to replicate and function may represent a fundamental reason why the lives of individual animals are finite. In fact, many of the multitude of functional decrements reported to occur in cultured normal human cells as they reach the end of their life span are identical to the changes that occur in humans as they age.

BIOGERONTOLOGY NEGLECTED

Despite the virtual universality of biological aging, the study of the phenomenon has been one of the most neglected areas of biological inquiry. The reasons for this are complex and are undoubtedly manifestations of the convergence of at least three separate phenomena.

First, the field has suffered more from a lunatic fringe than has, perhaps, any other area of biological research. Claims for increasing human longevity are probably as old as civilization itself. They have ranged from the more recent dietary fads and inoculations with monkey testicular extracts to the biblical admonition to King David, who "was old and stricken in years."

In an effort to increase his longevity "his servants said unto him: 'Let there be sought for my lord the king a young virgin; and let her stand before the king, and be a companion unto him . . . that the lord the king may get heat. . . .' So they sought for a fair damsel throughout all the borders of Israel . . . and brought her to the king. And the damsel was very fair; and she became a companion unto the king, and ministered to him; but the king knew her not" (Ezra & Nehemiah, 1944). Yet, as for modern yogurt eaters and recipients of monkey testicular extracts, " . . . the days of David drew nigh that he should die. . . . " (Ezra & Nehemiah, 1944). Modern scientists are loath to enter fields reputed to be dominated by charlatans and practitioners of the black arts. Young scientists would be foolhardy to attempt to begin a career against such odds, and established investigators would prefer not to risk a reputation made in a "legitimate" field in order to enter one held in disdain.

A second reason for the neglect of biogerontology has been the lack of a sufficient factual basis or testable theoretical foundation that could lead to the design of good experiments. This is, of course, the classic Catch-22, because without good science, the insufficient factual base and unimpressive theoretical underpinning will not improve. And because of this few scientists will willingly enter the field.

A third reason why biogerontology has been passed over by the mainstream of biological scientists is that little research funds have been available. The few people who have worked in the field have obtained financial support in the name of those basic disciplines that underlie biogerontology. These are biochemistry, physiology, cell biology, and, in fact, virtually any traditional field of basic biological science. This also holds, of course, for other multidisciplinary fields, such as embryology and developmental biology. But to identify oneself as an embryologist or a developmental biologist has been far more acceptable than to identify oneself as a gerontologist. Thus, what progress has been made in biogerontology has occurred by identifying the research with a basic field of biology but interpreting the results in a gerontological context. In this way, a few biogerontologists have learned how to obtain research support and maintain their scientific reputations while conducting research on aging. Even to this day many a biogerontologist would prefer to be identified as an immunologist, molecular biologist, biochemist, or cell biologist first and as a gerontologist second.

In the past decade, all of these circumstances have changed radically. Perhaps the most important reason for this was the establishment of the National Institute on Aging at the National Institutes of Health. The handful of gerontologists who dedicated themselves to the establishment of this institute resolved, virtually in one stroke, all of the aforementioned reasons for the lack of progress in the field. Gerontology suddenly became respectable and reasonably well funded. Instant gerontologists appeared, and even some established researchers in the field began to identify themselves publicly as gerontologists. Thus, the field probably has advanced more in the past decade than it has in the entire previous 100 years.

One of the major benefactors of this dramatic change has been the field of biogerontology, which holds that the cell is the main arena in which fundamental knowledge of the aging process is most likely to be found. I have named this discipline "cytogerontology" (Hayflick, 1974). What follows is an historical account of studies on the origins of the cell biology of aging and how the field has evolved to the present time.

FOUNDATIONS OF CYTOGERONTOLOGY

The origin of age changes in multicellular organisms can be attributed to only three possibilities, which are not mutually exclusive. Aging in metazoans can only result from (a) perturbations within individual cells, (b) changes in the extracellular matrix, or (c) influences of more highly organized cell hierarchies on other tissues or organs.

An essential element in considering the role of cells as the origin of age-related changes is whether or not they are capable of normal function, including division, for an indefinite period of time. That is, are normal somatic cells immortal?

Centennial of the Controversy

The controversy that arose in the course of efforts to answer this fundamental question actually began about 100 years ago. But even this fact has been brought to light only recently (Kirkwood & Cremer, 1982). In 1881 August Weismann proposed that the somatic cells of higher animals have a limited doubling potential. Although he provided no experimental evidence for his surmise, Weismann (1891) stated that " . . . death takes place because a worn-out tissue cannot forever renew itself, and because a capacity for increase by means of cell division is not everlasting but finite."

There are at least two ways in which the immortality of normal cells can be determined. First, vertebrate cells can be serially cultured in laboratory glassware, and second, similar cells, containing specific markers allowing them to be distinguished from host cells, can be serially transplanted in isogenic laboratory animals. The transplanted tissue is regrafted to a younger host when the previous host becomes old. The goal of such studies has been to answer this fundamental question: can normal vertebrate cells that function and replicate under ideal conditions escape from the inevitability of aging and death that is obligatory for the animal from which they were derived?

Immortal Heart Cells?

Of the studies undertaken in cell culture, before 1960, one stood out as the classic response to the question of cell immortality. In the early part of this century, Alexis Carrel, a noted cell culturist, surgeon and Nobel laureate, described experiments purporting to show that fibroblasts derived from chick heart tissue could be cultured serially indefinitely. The culture was voluntarily terminated after 34 years (Parker, 1961). Carrel's findings created worldwide interest not only in the scientific community but in the lay press as well.

Its importance to gerontologists was clear. If true, it strongly implied that cells released from in vivo control could divide and function normally for a period of time in excess of the life span of the species. Thus, either the types of cells cultured play no role in the aging phenomenon or aging results from changes in the intracellular matrix or at higher levels of cell organization. That is, aging could result from physiological interactions between cells only when they are organized as tissues or organs. In any case, Carrel's results and their interpretation were of vital concern to biogerontologists because they strongly suggested that aging is not the result of events occurring within individual cells.

In the years that followed Carrel's observations, support for his experimental results seemed to be forthcoming from many laboratories, where it was noted that several cell populations appeared to have the striking ability to replicate indefinitely. Immortal cell populations derived from a variety of human and animal tissues were reported to occur spontaneously in dozens of laboratories in the period from the early 1940s to the early 1960s. These cell populations, numbering in the hundreds, are best known by the prototype cell lines HeLa (derived from a human cervical carcinoma in 1952) and L cells (derived from mouse mesenchyme in 1943). They continue to flourish even to this day in cell-culture laboratories throughout the world.

Immortal cell populations still arise spontaneously from normal cell cultures by a mysterious process. However, now they can be created, albeit at low efficiency, by exposure to radiation, chemical carcinogens or certain oncogenic viruses. More recently, this process of "immortalization," as it has come to be called, can be accomplished routinely by fusing mortal antibody-producing lymphocytes to immortal myeloma cells. The resulting hybrid, known as a hybridoma, will continue to express specific antibody indefinitely (Kohler & Milstein, 1975). The use of this technique is one important cause of the current revolution in biotechnology.

Nevertheless, what seemed to be incontrovertible evidence for the existence of immortal cells soon gave way to new insights and a preponderance of opposing information.

AGING UNDER GLASS

Of central importance to the question of cell immortality as it relates to biogerontology is whether the cell populations studied in vitro are composed of normal or abnormal cells. Clearly the aging of animals occurs in normal cell populations. If we are to equate the behavior of normal cells in vivo with that of similar cells in vitro, then the latter must be shown to be normal as well. Twenty-five years ago Moorhead and I postulated that all immortal cell populations are abnormal in one or more important property (Hayflick & Moorhead, 1961). As such they are not proper subjects for the study of aging, and indeed they are not proper subjects for the study of many other biological phenomena for which they are frequently used. All immortal cell lines vary in chromosome number, morphology, or banding pattern from the original animal or human cells from which they were derived. Most, but not all, produce tumors when inoculated into experimental animals.

Aging is Inevitable

Moorhead and I described the finite replicative capacity of normal human fibroblasts and interpreted the phenomenon as aging at the cellular level (Hayflick & Moorhead, 1961). We demonstrated that when normal human embryonic cells are grown under the most favorable conditions, aging and death are the inevitable consequences after about 50 population doublings. We called this the *Phase III phenomenon*. We also showed that the death of our cultured normal human cells was not due to some trivial cause involving medium components or culture conditions but was an inherent property of the cells themselves (Hayflick, 1965; Hayflick & Moorhead, 1961).

This observation now has been confirmed in hundreds of laboratories, where variations in medium components and cultural conditions have been as numerous as the laboratories themselves.

Since 1961, when we had made our observation and interpretation, no normal human or animal cell population has been shown to be immortal. Immortality is defined as the continuous serial cultivation in vitro or in vivo in which at least 100 population doublings occur over a minimum of at least 2 years. Cultured or transplanted normal cells are defined as those having properties identical to the cells composing the tissue of origin.

All Immortal Cells are Abnormal

The widespread use of immortal abnormal cell populations for a variety of research purposes has created enormous problems in the interpretation of experiments in which these cells are used. It is virtually impossible to extrapolate results obtained with these abnormal cell populations to the behavior of normal cells in vivo. The failure to recognize this fundamental distinction is the reason why much of the effort in modern cancer biology is seriously flawed. The current widespread use of such abnormal cell lines as C3H, 3T3, and BHK 21 in efforts to understand the conversion of normal cells to cancer cells is indefensible. These cells are widely used as normal cells in order to determine whether various treatments will convert them to cancer cells. There is a little regard for the fact that these cells already have been proven to produce tumors when inoculated into laboratory animals (Boone, 1975; Boone, Takeichi, & Paranjpe, 1976). Even if they did not, the fact that they are chromosomally abnormal and are immortal should be sufficient reason not to use them for studies in which the use of normal cells is mandated.

This fundamental flaw in the conduct of much research in modern cancer biology can be circumvented by appreciating the fact that entirely normal cell populations can be cultured in vitro. Such cultures are normal in every respect if they are derived from normal tissue and, of course, have a finite capacity to replicate.

Conceptual Origins

Although there were many reports prior to ours that described the failure of most cultured cells to proliferate indefinitely, none characterized the cells as normal, ruled out artifacts as the cause, or suggested that the phenomenon might be associated with aging (Puck, Cieciura, & Fisher, 1957; Puck, Cieciura, & Robinson, 1958; Swim & Parker, 1957). In fact, the observation that cultured cells frequently failed to replicate indefinitely was probably made hundreds of times from the genesis of cell-culture techniques in the early 1900s to our report 60 years later.

Those prior failures went unreported because the existing dogma insisted that the failure of cells to proliferate indefinitely in vitro must be attributable to errors in the "art" required to keep cells dividing forever. That dogma was so well entrenched that our original manuscript (Hayflick & Moorhead, 1961) was rejected by the *Journal of Experimental Medicine* with the statement that "The largest fact to have come out from tissue culture in the last fifty years is that cells inherently capable of multiplying will do so indefinitely if supplied with the right milieu in vitro." That belief was tantamount to the belief that, given the right milieu in vivo, human beings also will live forever.

The finding that cultured normal cells have a finite capacity to replicate has had important implications in gerontological theory. But before these implications are considered, it will be necessary to discuss how Carrel was misled into believing that he had successfully cultured chick fibroblasts for 34 years.

ALEXIS CARREL AND THE MYTH OF HIS IMMORTAL CHICK CELLS

By the late 1960s it became apparent to me and others that Carrel's claim to have cultured chick fibroblast cells for 34 years was spurious (Hayflick, 1970; Hayflick, 1972). It had to be assumed that Carrel's chick cultures consisted of normal cells. This is so because until quite recently no one has ever found an immortal chick fibroblast population (Ogura, Fujiwara, & Namba, 1984). One of these immortal cell lines was produced by exposure of the chick cells to the carcinogen N-methyl-N'-nitro-N-nitrosoguanidine, and the other arose spontaneously. In both cases the immortal cells were shown to be abnormal and to produce retroviruses.

It has been 50 years since the voluntary termination of Carrel's alleged immortal chick fibroblasts, and the publication of Ogura, Fujiwara, and Namba is the first authentic report of a spontaneous transformation of normal chick fibro-blasts. The rarity of this event can be appreciated when one considers that chick tissue has been one of the most frequently cultured tissue in the past 50 years. Thus, the likelihood that Carrel had found such a population is remote, especially because, until now, all attempts to repeat his findings have been unsuccessful (Harris, 1957; Hay & Strehler, 1967; Lima & Macieira-Coelho, 1972; Ponten, 1970). Furthermore, even if his observation was legitimate, the immortal cells must have been abnormal and thus cannot be used as evidence that normal cells had escaped the inevitability of the Phase III phenomenon.

I have proposed one explanation for Carrel's findings, in which the method of preparation of the chick embryo extract, used as a source of nutrients for his culture, allowed for the introduction of new, viable fibroblasts into the so-called "immortal" culture at each feeding (Hayflick, 1972). Although we believed that Carrel was unaware of this artifact, Witkowski (1979, 1980, 1985), suggests otherwise in a lengthy study of Carrel's immortal cells.

INVERSE RELATIONSHIP BETWEEN DONOR AGE AND CELL POPULATION DOUBLINGS

In the decade that followed our first report (Hayflick & Moorhead, 1961), further evidence appeared from studies in cytogerontology that provided important new insights into cellular aging. In 1965 we reported that cultured fibroblasts derived from older humans replicated fewer times than those derived from embryos (Hayflick, 1965). Because the technique for determining population doublings was crude at that time, we were unable to establish a direct relationship between donor age and population doubling potential. Subsequently, studies done by others not only confirmed the principle that we had observed but extended it significantly.

Martin, Sprague, and Epstein (1970) derived cultures from human donors ranging from fetal age to 90 years. Although the data reveal considerable scatter, they observed a regression coefficient, from the first to the ninth decade, of −0.2 population doubling per year of life, with a standard deviation of .05 and a correlation coefficient of −.50. The scatter found is not unlike that reported to occur with virtually any age-related change that is

measured cross-sectionally and not longitudinally. Nevertheless, at least nine more studies have confirmed the finding that the number of population doublings of cultured human cells is inversely proportional to donor age. This inverse relationship has now been shown to occur in normal human cells derived from such diverse tissue as lung (Hayflick, 1965), skin (Goldstein, Moerman, Soeldner, Gleason, & Barnett, 1978; Martin et al., 1970; Schneider & Mitsui, 1976; Vracko & McFarland, 1980), liver (LeGuilly, Simon, Lenoir, & Bourel, 1973), arterial smooth muscle (Bierman, 1978), lens (Tassin, Malaise, & Courtois, 1979) and T-lymphocytes (Walford, 1982; Walford, Jawaid, & Naeim, 1981).

DIRECT RELATIONSHIP BETWEEN MAXIMUM SPECIES LIFE SPAN AND POPULATION DOUBLINGS OF THEIR CULTURED CELLS

More than a decade ago, we suggested that the population doubling potential of cultured fibroblasts from several animal species revealed a surprisingly good direct correlation with maximum species life span (Hayflick, 1973). In the years since, several other reports have appeared that have added substantially to this idea, especially the work of Rohme (1981). One report, in which several marsupial species were studied, does not support this finding; however, the authors did not determine population doublings by conventional means, nor is the maximum life spans of the species they studied known (Stanley, Pye, & MacGregor, 1975). Figure 1.1 shows the direct proportionality between different species maximum life spans and the population doubling potential of their cultured fibroblasts. Embryonic fibroblasts were used in nine of the ten species studied. Juvenile tissue was used in the study of the Galapagos tortoise.

If this relationship can be extended and confirmed, it suggests the presence of a chronometer or pacemaker within all normal cells that is characteristic for each specie and that dictates maximum cell doubling or functional capacity with an apparent evolutionary basis. The postulated chronometer may or may not be the same one that we suggest might control the inverse relationship between donor age and population doubling potential.

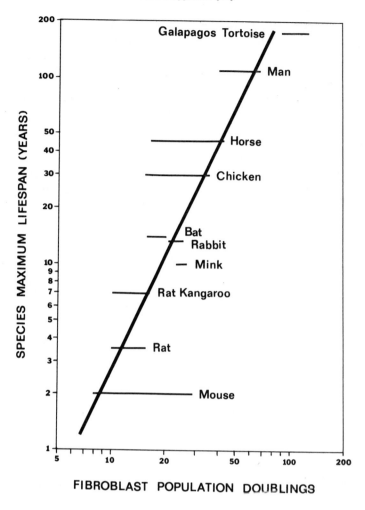

Figure 1.1. Fibroblasts from the embryos of ten different species multiply in culture to a maximum number of population doublings that is roughly proportional to the lifespan for that species. Galapagos tortoise cells were derived from a juvenile animal.

PROGERIA AND WERNER'S SYNDROME

Progeria, or Hutchinson–Gilford syndrome, is a human disorder leading to manifestations of age-changes in patients as young as 9 years of age (Reichel, Garcia-Bunuel, & Dilallo, 1971). A very rare disease, it is thought by many to represent a model for precocious aging, in which individuals at the end of the first decade of life manifest the physical signs of aging typical of their normal counterparts at the seventh decade of life. The Werner syndrome is similar to progeria in many ways, although its salient manifestations occur in later years. The full clinical picture shows early graying and loss of hair, short stature, juvenile cataracts, proneness to diabetes, atherosclerosis and calcification of the blood vessels, osteoporosis, and a high incidence of malignancy (Epstein, Martin, Schultz, & Motulsky, 1966).

If the Werner syndrome and progeria are examples of accelerated aging, when does aging occur in cultured fibroblasts taken from these donors? From 2 to 18 doublings were found to occur, whereas normal values would be between 20 and 40 (Goldstein, 1969; Goldstein, 1971; Goldstein et al., 1978). Others have reported decreased mitotic activity, DNA synthesis, and cloning efficiency of cultured progeria cells (Danes, 1971; Nienhaus, DeJong, & Tenkate, 1971).

THE MEMORY OF CULTURED NORMAL HUMAN CELLS

When we first established human diploid cell strains 25 years ago, it became apparent that their finite lifetime imposed a serious limit on the capacity to work with any single strain. We found that a strain derived from fetal tissue underwent 50 ± 10 population doublings over a period of about 1 year and was then lost (Hayflick, 1965; Hayflick & Moorhead, 1961). In order to circumvent this important limitation, we succeeded in freezing viable normal human cells at subzero temperatures (Hayflick & Moorhead, 1961). In this way it was possible to fully characterize a single human diploid cell strain and have it available for study for long periods of time. The potential yield of cells from a population capable of 50 population doublings is about 20 million metric tons (Hayflick, 1965).

In 1962 we developed, and placed into liquid nitrogen storage, several hundred ampules of our normal human diploid cell strain WI-38, which subsequently became the most completely characterized normal human cell population in the world. It is today the archetype normal human fibroblast and is used worldwide for applications in biological research, virus isolation and identification, and the production of several human virus vaccines.

WI-38 has been in cryogenic storage for 25 years, which represents the longest period of time that a viable normal human cell population has ever been stored. The ability to preserve normal cell strains has permitted experimentation directed toward answering a fundamental question in cytogerontology: If cells are frozen at various population doubling levels up to Phase III, how many population doublings will the cells undergo when they are thawed or reconstituted? Do they have a "clock" that is arrested in the cold at the population doubling level at which they were frozen? If so, then the total cumulative number of doublings both before and after freezing would be about 50 in the case of a fetal strain. Or does freezing reset the "clock" to zero or to some random number?

In the years since 1962 we have shown that WI-38 and other human cell strains have a remarkable

memory. Even after 25 years, WI-38 cells remember at which population doubling level they were frozen and, upon reconstitution, undergo the number of population doublings remaining from the time they were frozen to 50. More than 130 ampules have been reconstituted by us since 1962, and the memory of the cells is as accurate today as it was then.

FUNCTIONAL FAILURE AS CULTURED NORMAL HUMAN CELLS REACH PHASE III

The probability that animals age because one or more cell types lose the ability to proliferate is unlikely. It is more likely that decrements in physiological function that appear before cells lose their capacity to replicate are the true causes of age-related changes. In 1971 we reported the first functional decrement in a normal human cell population before its loss of proliferative capacity (Houck, Sharma, & Hayflick, 1971). We found that WI-38 cells lost much of their ability to synthesize collagen and to induce collagenolytic activity after almost 40 population doublings.

In the next decade almost 200 functional changes have been found to occur in cultured normal human cells prior to their loss of replicative capacity. A full tabulation is presented in a recent review (Hayflick, 1980). The changes reported to occur cover virtually all aspects of cell biochemistry, morphology, and behavior. They include changes in lipids, carbohydrates, amino acids, proteins, RNA, DNA, enzymes, cell cycle dynamics, cell size and morphology, synthesis, incorporation, and stimulation.

Mitotic Failure Does Not Cause Aging

It is more likely that functional changes, which herald the approaching loss of division capacity, play a central role in the expression of aging and result in the death of the individual animal well before its cells fail to divide.

Of great importance is the realization that many of these same changes that have been reported to occur in cultured normal human cells as they age in vitro are identical to changes that are known to occur in cells in vivo as humans age (Hayflick, 1980). This finding adds considerable weight to our contention that the Phase III phenomenon is indeed an expression of aging at the cellular level.

Clearly, there are several classes of cells that are incapable of division in mature animals, and it is just as likely, if not even more likely, that these cells play a greater role in the expression of age-related changes than those cells that are capable of dividing. Examples of nondividing cells would be neurons and muscle cells. It is important to emphasize that the cessation of mitotic activity is only one functional decrement whose genetic basis may be similar to those functional decrements known to occur in aging nondividing cells. We have proposed, therefore, that the same kind of gene action that results in physiological decrements in aging nondividing cells also occurs in aging cells that can still divide. It is not our belief that age-related changes result necessarily from the loss of the function to divide, but simply in the loss of any function characteristic of an aging cell. The basis for the loss of any of these functions is thought to be similar.

If these conclusions are accurate, an understanding of the mechanism by which normal cells lose their capacity to replicate could provide insights into the cause of decrements in other functional properties, such as those that occur in aging neurons or muscle cells.

THE FINITE LIFETIME OF NORMAL CELLS IN VIVO

As indicated at the outset of this discussion, there are two ways in which a determination of cell immortality can be made. The first method is to grow normal cells in culture. That has been discussed, and the conclusion is that under these conditions normal cells do have a finite capacity to replicate and function. The second way is to determine whether normal cells can proliferate indefinitely in vivo.

If all cell types were continuously renewed without loss of function or capacity for self-renewal, organs composed of such cells would be expected to function normally indefinitely, and their host would live forever. Regrettably, renewal of cell populations does not occur in most tissues, and when it does, cell proliferation is not indefinite.

Is it possible, then, to circumvent the death of normal animal cells resulting from the death of the host by transferring marked cells to younger animals seriatim? Such experiments would provide an in vivo counterpart to the in vitro experiments described above. If the analogy is accurate, we would predict that normal cells transplanted serially to proper inbred hosts would, like their in vitro counterparts, age. Such experiments would largely rule out objections to in vitro studies that are based on the artificiality of the in vitro environment. The question could be answered by serial orthotopic transplantation of normal somatic tissues to new, young, inbred hosts each time the recipient approaches old age.

Data reported from many different laboratories in which rodent mammary tissue (Daniel, deOme, Young, Blair, & Faulkin, 1968), skin cells (Krohn, 1962), and hematopoietic cells (Cudkowicz, Upton, Shearer, & Hughes, 1964; Ford, Micklem, & Gray 1959; Harrison, 1973; Harrison, 1975; Hellman, Botnick, Hannon, & Vigneulle, 1978; Siminovitch, Till, & McCulloch, 1964) were employed to demonstrate that normal cells serially transplanted to inbred hosts do not survive indefinitely. Studies done with hematopoietic cells to investigate this point actually number in the dozens (Hayflick, 1984).

The trauma of transplantation does not appear to influence the results, and in heterochronic transplants, survival time is related to the age of the grafted tissue (Krohn, 1962). Cancer cells, on the other hand, frequently can be transplanted indefinitely. Thus, the immortality of cancer cells in vitro is precisely mimicked in vivo.

Many grafts transplanted in vivo have been found to survive much longer than the life span of the host or donor species before aging and dying. This fact has been erroneously interpreted by some to mean that normal cells can replicate continuously for periods of time in excess of the species, known life span. However, grafted tissue behaves quite differently from cultured cells. The latter are usually kept in a state of continuous proliferation. The cells in grafted tissue are not dividing continuously, nor are the number of cells in the dividing pool as great as that in cell cultures. If fibroblasts in grafted tissue replicated to the extent that comparable cells do in vitro, the graft would quickly weigh more than its host. Thus, it is important to appreciate that long survival time is not equivalent to proliferation time or rounds of division. Cells in grafts have a very low reproductive turnover rate. This is analogous to holding normal cell cultures at room temperature, which extends calendar time for cell survival but does not result in increased population doublings.

THEORIES OF
BIOLOGICAL AGING

What, then, are the most likely causes of biological aging? The relative newness of the field of gerontology as a serious science, with the consequent lack of an extensive and reliable data base, has encouraged speculations about the theoretical underpinnings of the field. One reason for the plethora of biogerontological theories is that manifestations of biological changes over time affect virtually all components of living systems from the molecular level up to the level of the whole organism. These hierarchical changes have made it possible to construct theories of aging based on events that occur over time at the level of the molecule, cell organelle, cell, tissue, organ, or whole animal.

Often, a particular age-associated change within this hierarchy will be defended with great vigor and emotion by the theorist more on the basis of bias than fact. Nevertheless, most current theories of biological aging suffer from the criticism that they are, or may be, mere expressions of the effect of some more fundamental change. There is a common failure to recognize that changes more fundamental than the one observed may induce the effect that was chosen for study.

Because all fundamental life processes depend on genetic events, theories of aging that depend on these events have attracted the most attention.

The Genome as the Basis for Aging

A variety of age-related biological phenomena appear to be orchestrated by events that occur in the genetic apparatus. A number of these phenomena are so profound that, together, they provide the factual foundation for several genetically based theories of the cause of age-related changes in cell metabolism and function. Some of these phenomena are as follows:

1. The life spans of animal species are remarkably constant and species-specific. For example, the maximum life span for a fruit fly is about 1 month, for a mouse about 3 years, and for a human about 115 years.

2. In humans, for example, the mean difference in longevity between fraternal twins was found to be twice as great as that between identical twins (Kallman & Jarvik, 1959). The ancestors of nonagenarians and centenarians were found to have significantly greater longevity than the ancestors

of individuals not selected for great longevity (Pearl & Pearl, 1934).

3. In many animal species the female is more longevous than the male, but this is by no means true for all animal species (Comfort, 1979).

4. In the past decade it has become apparent that some single gene changes result in accelerated aging in humans, as in the case of progeria and the Werner syndrome. On the other hand, Down's syndrome is characterized by trisomy. In each of these conditions, several age-related phenomena appear to be accelerated. Polygenic changes are also thought to influence the rate and characteristics of age-associated changes in normal individuals.

5. Genotoxic effects, that is, the effects of mutagens, such as radiation, on longevity, are certainly the result of effects on the cell genome.

6. A direct correlation has been observed between the efficiency of certain kinds of DNA repair processes and species longevity. More long-lived species are found to have more efficient DNA repair capabilities (Hart & Setlow, 1974). However, DNA ligation is also associated with normal development.

7. Heterosis, or hybrid vigor, occurs when members of two different inbred strains are themselves mated. They produce F_1 hybrids having greater longevity than either parental strain. A phenomenon known as the Lansing effect suggests that in some animals, including humans, the progeny of older mothers have a shorter life expectation and this effect may extend through several generations (Comfort, 1979; Strehler, 1977).

8. In a study of inbred mouse strains, it has been estimated that half of the variance associated with longevity was due to genetic factors (Goodrick, 1975).

These observations have led many biogerontologists to the belief that the genetic apparatus plays the central role in effecting age changes. It is important, however, to emphasize that differences of opinion exist. Some of the nongenetic factors that may produce age-related changes include passive stochastic processes, such as the accumulation of damage or errors in important macromolecules (Hayflick, 1985).

The Somatic Mutation Theory

The somatic mutation theory of aging enjoyed its greatest popularity in the late 1950s and early 1960s as a derivative of burgeoning developments in the field of radiobiology. The central concept is that the accumulation of a sufficient level of mutations in somatic cells will produce physiological decrements characteristic of aging. If mutations are the fundamental cause of age changes, they must occur randomly in time and location (Maynard-Smith, 1962). Early champions of this idea were Szilard (1959) and Failla (1960). Failla postulated dominant mutations as the cause of aging. Szilard argued that aging was due to genes ("targets") being "hit" or "struck" by a mutational event, which he, unlike Failla, regarded as recessive. Thus, a pair of homologous genes must be hit at a particular rate and in a sufficient number of cells in order to achieve phenotypic expression.

Maynard-Smith (1962) pointed out that if Szilard was correct, inbred animals, homologous at most gene loci, would display the maximum species life span, because homozygous faults would be lethal and heterozygous faults would be few or nonexistent. Yet in mice and *Drosophila* inbreeding reduces the life span. Furthermore, Szilard's hypothesis would predict that diploid organisms would live longer than their haploid counterparts, who contain only one chromosome set. In the hymenopteran wasp, *Habrobracon*, haploid and diploid males have identical life spans. Haploid males are more sensitive to ionizing radiation than diploid male wasps, yet irradiation shortens the life span of diploids far more than that of haploids. These observations are inconsistent with the mutation theory. Although reduced life spans do occur in irradiated animals, extended life spans have also been observed (Sacher, 1963). Moreover, irradiated old animals should show accelerated age changes, as should animals treated with mutagenic agents, but they do not (Hayflick, 1985).

Curtis and Miller (1971), the last major advocates of the somatic mutation theory, based their conclusions on the frequency of abnormalities observed in the chromosomes of dividing cells in the livers of old mice. They found a higher frequency of abnormalities in the cells of short-lived strains than in those of long-lived strains. Curtis and Miller made similar findings in guinea pigs and dogs. Nevertheless, other comparisons between short- and long-lived strains were inconsistent with these findings, and hybrids between short- and long-lived strains did not yield the expected results. Neutron irradiation of dividing cells was found by Curtis and Miller to yield aberrations in up to 90% of the cells, yet the life span was unaffected.

In the past decade, few significant studies have been conducted on the role of somatic mutations in aging. In spite of the contrary evidence, there is an expectation among some researchers that the critical experiments should be redesigned using the technology of modern molecular biology.

The Error Theory

The error theory, to some extent a derivative of the somatic mutation theory, was first postulated by Medvedev (1961) and elaborated by Orgel (1963).

It has been suggested that the repeated DNA nucleotide sequences in the genome of eukaryotic organisms may be (a) a reserve of information for evolutionary change, (b) a means of increasing functional expression, and/or (c) a reserve mechanism for protecting vital information from random errors that may occur in functioning DNA sequences. Medvedev proposed that the loss of unique nonrepeated DNA sequences could produce age decrements and that selected reiterated sequences may be an evolved means for delaying the inevitability of the event by providing the redundancy necessary for the maintenance of vital information.

An outgrowth of the concept of error accumulation in reiterated DNA sequences is Orgel's hypothesis that the essential source of age-associated decrements in cell function is the occurrence of inaccuracies in protein synthesis. This hypothesis resulted in a flurry of experiments designed to learn whether an incorrect amino acid incorporated in a protein molecule could accelerate aging phenomena or whether misspecified proteins accumulated in old cells. Errors in enzyme molecules that processed information-containing molecules were thought to be the most important potential sources of important damage. A misspecified enzyme could produce a cascade of faulty molecules, with presumably profound effects, called an *error catastrophe*. One group has claimed to have obtained evidence in support of the error catastrophe theory, but most other studies have failed to do so. The idea is now in general disfavor despite the fact that altered proteins are frequently found in the cells of old organisms.

A correlate of error accumulation as a cause of age-associated changes is the effectiveness of those systems that repair genome damage. Evidence from the cultured cells of several different species has revealed that the efficiency of repair of ultraviolet damage to DNA is directly correlated to a species' life span (Hart & Setlow, 1974). Again, contrary evidence has also been reported, and the original finding remains equivocal (Hayflick, 1985).

The Program Theory of Aging

Adherents of the program theory of aging, unlike advocates of such stochastically based theories as errror accumulation, postulate a purposeful sequence of events written into the genome. This leads to age changes, much as similar instructions written into the genetic message lead to the orderly expression of developmental sequences.

The conceptual simplicity of this idea is part of its attractiveness, but attempts to test it experimentally have met with little success. The finding that cultured normal human and animal cells have a finite ability to replicate and function has provided the best evidence in support of the theory, but so does the fundamental fact that aging occurs naturally in intact animals (Hayflick & Moorhead, 1961). Programming assumes an orderly sequence of events, with which few would disagree, but it does not provide mechanistic details.

On the other hand, it has been argued effectively that although events occurring from conception to the full expression of adulthood may be programmed, postreproductive events or aging may not be purposely determined by the genome. That is, age-associated changes may be produced by a kind of freewheeling, non-genome-dependent continuation of the inertia developed from previously determined developmental events. Therefore, function declines or terminates in a more or less random fashion, like the eventual demise of a new automobile that is poorly repaired or maintained.

To complete the analogy, the manufacture of an automobile, like the growth of an individual animal, is predicated on the presence of accurate blueprints and their proper execution. What happens after the automobile is built or after the individual reaches sexual maturation is not governed by blueprints but occurs in most systems randomly and inevitably. Which system fails first and leads to the demise of the automobile or individual is, therefore, a random process with, nevertheless, a narrowly expressed "mean time to failure." This would be characteristic of the specific make of the automobile or the particular animal species.

Entropy and Aging

In terms of physics, a genetic program should succumb to the second law of thermodynamics, which states that a closed system tends to a state of equilibrium or of maximum entropy in which nothing more happens. That is, ordered systems tend to move to greater disorder. The initially well-organized genetic program, by increasing entropy, thus becomes disordered, producing those changes recognized as aging. Our mortality may, in this way, be decreed by the second law of thermodynamics. Although this may be a tenable hypothesis as it pertains to somatic cells or to individual members of a species, it seems to fly in the face of the enormous amount of evidence for biological evolution that superficially appears to be in conflict with the second law. Moreover, it seems to be in conflict with the apparent immortality of the germ plasm and certain immortal abnormal cancer-cell populations.

Delayed Expression of Deleterious Genes

Medawar (1957) has argued persuasively that the presence of deleterious genes in a species might be thwarted by a selection process that would postpone their manifestations if it were not possible to eliminate them. This strategy would result in the piling up of deleterious genes in the postreproductive period, when their expression would do less harm.

A variation on this theme is expressed by Williams (1957), who postulates pleiotropic genes having both favorable and unfavorable actions. If the favorable gene expression is able to increase fecundity, that gene might be selected even though it might express a deleterious action later in life. Deleterious age changes then would be the penalty paid by individuals for the expression of beneficial genes early in life. An accumulation of such late-acting genes in various organ systems would behave like late-programmed events and give rise to the entire constellation of age-associated changes.

Longevity Assurance Genes

Sacher (1968) is critical of the program theory of aging for what he believes to be errors in logic. He illustrates his point by comparing the life histories of annual plants and mammals. Annual plants are semelparous, that is, characterized by a single reproductive effort, completed at the end of the life span and frequently not until somatic cell death. The final step of the reproductive process, seed dispersal, depends on the death of the plant, and this requires that senescence be closely integrated with prior stages. The stages are known to be under the specific control of hormones and end with the formation of specific hydrolytic enzymes.

Sacher restricts programmed aging to cases such as this, where there is (a) specific control of onset either by internal or external signals; (b) the presence of a specific enzyme mechanism; and (c) a functional role for senescence and/or death in a specific temporal relationship with other life processes. The rapid aging and death of the Pacific salmon after spawning is a good example of this event occurring in animals.

Mammals, on the other hand, are examples of iteroparous reproduction, where reproductive success depends on producing a number of litters over an extended reproductive span. Sacher argues that this offers no functional role for senescence and death. On the contrary, he maintains that this would place a premium on the maintenance of physiological vigor and survival. Long life in mammals, therefore, is the result of selection for an extended period of assured physiological performance. A great whale that lives 30 times longer than a mouse has a million times more cells at risk for age-associated changes. Nevertheless, a comparable whale cell is more stable, by several orders of magnitude, than a mouse cell.

"It would be expected," says Sacher, "that the selective process acts on mechanisms for *increasing* the stability of the organism at all levels, from the molecular to the systemic." Sacher emphasizes the more evolutionary logical role of genetic systems that maintain life rather than theories that these systems might program age-associated changes. Until it can be shown that evolution selects for greater longevity, at least in mammals, the study of life maintenance systems or "longevity assurance genes" may be more productive that the current emphasis on a search for the causes of age-associated physiological decrements (Sacher, 1968).

The postulated longevity-assurance genes may be simply sets of genes that have evolved to express themselves at later times during an animal's development, in order to increase its survivability. These genes would not be directly involved with aging per se, but would serve, by their later expression, to delay age-associated changes. Aging, then, would be a secondary manifestation of earlier occurring developmental events. For example, natural selection in a species may favor individuals capable of reaching sexual maturity at a later time, in order to provide better opportunities for the survival of progeny. A secondary effect of this (not directly selected for) would be a concomitant delay in the expression of aging.

Why do we age? may be the wrong question. The right question could be, Why do we live as long as we do?

REFERENCES

Bierman, E. L. (1978). The effect of donor age on the in vitro lifespan of cultured human arterial smooth-muscle cells. *In Vitro, 14,* 951–955.

Boone, C. W. (1975). Malignant hemangioendotheliomas produced by subcutaneous inoculation of Balb/3T3 cells attached to glass beads. *Science, 188,* 68–70.

Boone, C. W., Takeichi, N., & Paranjpe, M. (1976). Vasoformative sarcomas arising from Balb/3T3 cells attached to solid substrates. *Cancer Research, 36,* 1626–1633.

Comfort, A, (1979). *The biology of senescence* (3rd ed.). London: Churchill Livingstone.

Cudkowicz, G., Upton, A. C., Shearer, G. M., & Hughes, W. L. (1964). Lymphocyte content and proliferative capacity of serially transplanted mouse bone marrow. *Nature, 201,* 165–167.

Curtis, H. J., & Miller, K. (1971). Chromosome aberrations in liver cells of guinea pigs. *Journal of Gerontology, 26,* 292–293.

Danes, B. S. (1971). Progeria: A cell culture study on aging. *Journal of Clinical Investigation, 50,* 2000–2003.

Daniel, C. W., deOme, K. B., Young, J. T., Blair, P. B., & Faulkin, L. J., Jr. (1968). The in vivo lifespan of normal and preneoplastic mouse mammary glands: A serial transplantation study. *Proceedings of the National Academy of Sciences of the U.S.A., 61,* 53–608.

Epstein, C. J., Martin, G. M., Schultz, A. L., & Motulsky, A. G. (1966). Werner's syndrome: A review of its symptomatology, natural history, pathologic features, genetics and relationship to the natural aging process. *Medicine, 45,* 177–221.

Ezra & Nehemiah; 5704 (1944). 1 Kings 1:1–4, 2:1. In *The holy bible.* Philadephia: The Jewish Publication Society of America.

Failla, G. (1960). The aging process and somatic mutations. In Strehler B. L. (Ed.), *The biology of aging* (Publication No. 6), (pp. 170–175). Washington, DC: American Institute of Biological Sciences.

Ford, C. E., Micklem, H. S., & Gray, S. M. (1959). Evidence of selective proliferation of reticular cell-clones in heavily irradiated mice. *British Journal of Radiology, 32,* 280.

Goldstein, S. (1969). Lifespan of cultured cells in progeria. *Lancet, 1,* 424.

Goldstein, S. (1971). The biology of aging. *New England Journal of Medicine, 285,* 1120–1129.

Goldstein, S., Moerman, E. J., Soeldner, J. S., Gleason, R. E., & Barnett, D. M. (1978). Chronologic and physiological age effect replicative lifespan of fibroblasts from diabetics, prediabetics, and normal donors. *Science, 199,* 781–782.

Goodrick, C. L. (1975). Life-span and inheritance of longevity in inbred mice. *Journal of Gerontology, 30,* 257–264.

Harris, M. (1957). Quantitative growth studies with chick myoblasts in glass substrate cultures. *Growth, 21,* 149–166.

Harrison, D. E. (1973). Normal production of erythrocytes by mouse marrow continuous for 73 months. *Proceedings of the National Academy of Sciences of the U.S.A., 70,* 3184–3188.

Harrison, D. E. (1975). Normal function of transplanted marrow cell lines from aged mice. *Journal of Gerontology, 30,* 279–285.

Hart, R. W., & Setlow, R. B. (1974). Correlation between DNA excision repair and and life-span in a number of mammalian species. *Proceedings of the National Academy of Sciences of the U.S.A., 71,* 2169–2173.

Hay, R. J., & Strehler, B. L. (1967). The limited growth span of cell strains isolated from the chick embryo. *Experimental Gerontology, 2,* 123–135.

Hayflick, L. (1965). The limited in vitro lifetime of human diploid cell strains. *Experimental Cell Research, 37,* 614–636.

Hayflick, L. (1970). Aging under glass. *Experimental Gerontology, 5,* 291–303.

Hayflick, L. (1972). Cell senescence and cell differentiation in vitro. In *Aging and development,* Academy of Science and Literature, Mainz, Germany. Stuttgart: F. K. Schattauer Verlag.

Hayflick, L. (1973). The biology of human aging. *American Journal of the Medical Sciences, 265,* 433–445.

Hayflick, L. (1974). Cytogerontology. In M. Rockstein (Ed.), *Theoretical aspects of aging.* New York: Academic Press.

Hayflick, L. (1980). Cell aging. In C. Eisdorfer (Ed.), *Annual review of gerontology and geriatrics.* New York: Springer.

Hayflick, L. (1985). Theories of biological aging. *Experimental Gerontology, 20,* 145–159.

Hayflick, L., & Moorhead, P. S. (1961). The serial cultivation of human diploid cell strains. *Experimental Cell Research, 25,* 585–621.

Hellman, S., Botnick, L. E., Hannon, E. C., & Vigneulle, R. M. (1978). Proliferative capacity of murine hematopoietic stem cells. *Proceedings of the National Academy of Sciences of the U.S.A., 75,* 490–494.

Houck, J. C., Sharma, V. K., & Hayflick, L. (1971). Functional failures of cultured human diploid fibroblasts after continued population doublings. *Proceedings of the Society of Experimental Biology and Medicine, 137,* 331–333.

Kallman, E. J., & Jarvik, L. F. (1959). Individual differences in constitution and genetic background. In Birren J. E. (Ed.), *Handbook of aging and the individual* (pp. 216–263). Chicago: University of Chicago Press.

Kirkwood, T. B. L., & Cremer, T. (1982). Cytogerontology since 1881: A reappraisal of August Weismann and a review of modern progress. *Human Genetics, 60,* 101–121.

Kohler, G., & Milstein, C. (1975). Continuous cultures of fused cells secreting antibody of predefined specificity. *Nature, 256,* 495–497.

Krohn, P. L. (1962). Review lectures on senescence: 2. Heterochronic transplantation in the study of aging. *Proceedings of the Royal Society of London* (Biology), *157,* 128–147.

LeGuilly, Y., Simon, M., Lenoir, P., & Bourel, M. (1973). Long-term culture of human adult liver cells: Morphological changes related to in vitro senescence and effect of donor's age on growth potential. *Gerontologia, 19,* 303–313.

Lima, L., & Macieira-Coelho, A. (1972). Parameters of aging in chicken embryo fibroblasts cultivated in vitro. *Experimental Cell Research, 70,* 279–284.

Martin, G. M., Sprague, C.A., & Epstein, C. J. (1970). Replicative lifespan of cultivated human cells: Effect of donor's age, tissue, and genotye. *Laboratory Investigation, 23,* 86–92.

Maynard-Smith, J. (1962). Review lectures on senescence: 1. The causes of aging. *Proceedings of the Royal Society of London (Biology),* Series B, *157,* 115–127.

Medawar, P. B. (1957). *The uniqueness of the individual.* London: Methuen.

Medvedev, Zh. A. (1961). Aging of the organism at the molecular level. *Uspekhi Sovremennoy Biologii, 51:* 299–314.

Nienhaus, A. J., DeJong, B., & Tenkate, L. P. (1971). Fibroblast culture in Werner's syndrome. *Humangenetik, 13,* 244–246.

Ogura, H., Fujiwara, T., & Namba, M. (1984). Establishment of two chick embryo fibroblastic cell lines. *Gann, 75,* 410–414.

Orgel, L. E. (1963). The maintenance of the accuracy of protein synthesis and its relevance to aging. *Proceedings of the National Academy of Sciences of the U.S.A., 49,* 517–521.

Parker, R. C. (1961). *Methods of tissue culture.* New York: Harper & Row.

Pearl, R., & Pearl, R. deW. (1934). *The ancestry of the long-lived.* London: Milford.

Ponten, J. (1970). The growth capacity of normal and Rous-virus-transformed chicken fibroblasts in vitro. *International Journal of Cancer, 6,* 323–332.

Puck, T. T., Cieciura, S. J., & Fisher, H. W. (1957). Clonal growth in vitro of human cells with fibroblastic morphology. *Journal of Experimental Medicine, 106,* 145–158.

Puck, T. T., Cieciura, S. J., & Robinson, A. (1958). Genetics of somatic mammalian cells: 3. Long-term cultivation of euploid cells from human and animal subjects. *Journal of Experimental Medicine, 108,* 945–956.

Reichel, W., Garcia-Bunwel, R., & Dilallo, J. (1971). Progeria and Werner's syndrome as models for the study of normal human aging. *Journal of the American Geriatrics Society, 19,* 369–375.

Rohme, D. (1981). Evidence for a relationship between longevity of mammalian species and life spans of normal fibroblasts in vitro and erythrocytes in vivo. *Proceedings of the National Academy of Sciences of the U.S.A., 78,* 5009–5013.

Sacher, G. A. (1963). Effects of X-rays on the survival of *Drosophila melanogaster. Physiological Zoology, 36,* 295–311.

Sacher, G. A. (1968). Molecular versus systemic theories on the genesis of aging. *Experimental Gerontology, 3,* 265–271.

Schneider, E. L., & Mitsui, Y. (1976). The relationship between in vitro cellular aging and in vivo human aging. *Proceedings of the National Academy of Sciences of the U.S.A., 73,* 3584–3588.

Siminovitch, L., Till, J. E., & McCulloch, E. A. (1964). Decline in colony-forming ability of marrow cells subjected to serial transplantation into irradiated mice. *Journal of Cellular and Comparative Physiology, 64,* 23–31.

Stanley, J. F., Pye, D., & MacGregor, A. (1975). Comparison of doubling numbers attained by cultured animal cells with the life span of species. *Nature, 255,* 158–159.

Strehler, B. L. (1977). *Time, cells and aging.* New York: Academic Press.

Swim, H. E., & Parker, R. F. (1957). Culture characteristics of human fibroblasts propagated serially. *American Journal of Hygiene, 66,* 235–243.

Szilard, L. (1959). On the nature of the aging process. *Proceedings of the National Academy of Sciences of the U.S.A., 45,* 30–45.

Tassin, J., Malaise, E., & Courtois, Y. (1979). Human lens cells have an in vitro proliferative capacity inversely proportional to the donor age. *Experimental Cell Research, 123,* 388–392.

Vracko, R., & McFarland, B. M. (1980). Lifespan of diabetic and non-diabetic fibroblasts in vitro. *Experimental Cell Research, 129,* 345–350.

Walford, R. L. (1982). Studies in immunogerontology. *Journal of the American Geriatrics Society, 30,* 617–625.

Walford, R. L., Jawaid, S. Q., & Naeim, F. (1981). Evidence for in vitro senescence of T-lymphocytes cultured from normal human peripheral blood. *Age, 4,* 67–70.

Weismann, A. (1891). *Essays upon heredity and kindred biological problems,* (2nd ed.). Oxford: Clarendon Press.

Weismann, A. (1892). *Aufsatze über Vererbung und verwandte biologische Fragen.* Jena: Verlag von Gustav Fischer.

Williams, G. C. (1957). Pleiotropy, natural selection, and the evolution of senescence. *Evolution, 11,* 398–411.

Witkowski, J. A. (1979). Alexis Carrel and the mysticism of tissue culture. *Medical History, 23,* 279–296.

Witkowski, J. A. (1980). Dr. Carrel's immortal cells. *Medical History, 24,* 129–142.

Witkowski, J. A. (1985). The myth of cell immortality. *Trends in Biochemical Sciences, 10,* 258–260.

Chapter 2

Molar Aging: The Physiology and Psychology of Normal Aging

Judy M. Zarit and Steven H. Zarit

Until quite recently, the concept of senescence included the idea that aging inevitably led to increased physical and mental disability that resulted in death. Only premature death from catastrophic illness or accident could interfere with the gradual diminishing of abilities beginning in the sixth or even fifth decade of life. It was commonly believed that everyone would become "senile" if he or she lived long enough. With the identification of specific disease processes that are responsible for cognitive decline and the discovery that the majority of older persons do not experience cognitive impairment, there has been an abrupt about-face regarding this issue.

Currently there is a growing body of literature identifying exceptionally healthy older persons—people who at 80, 90, or 100 are not only intact cognitively but are physiologically much younger than their chronological age. Such people as the 70-year-old woman weight-lifter, the 80-year-old marathoner, the 85-year-old cold-water swimmer, and the alert centenarian are no longer uncommon. Their numbers are continuously growing, although perhaps not for obvious reasons. The current rise in the number of people over 65 years

of age is due primarily to increased and better food supplies, improved sanitation, and the advent of medical treatments allowing individuals to survive heretofore fatal illnesses (McKeown, 1978).

The two trends in the public consciousness—that of the senile elder and that of the superhealthy older person—contribute to the difficulty in establishing what constitutes normal aging. They represent the two extremes but do little to clarify the critical issue: What constitutes normal aging and what is the result of disease, environmental insult, or accident? This fundamental question underlies the bulk of the gerontological literature as we attempt to define a normative population. While this sounds like a simple proposition, it is confounded by increased interindividual and intraindividual variability with age, large areas of overlap between normality and pathology, imprecise measurement, and the multiplicity of theories to explain the results of empirical studies on aging.

This chapter will first highlight some of the critical methodological issues that underlie current research on aging. Then it will provide an introduction to the literature that attempts to establish normative data on physiological aging, including changes in appearance and in the cardiovascular, respiratory, gastrointestinal, reproductive, and nervous systems. Finally, psychological aging will be explored, including sensation and perception, learning and memory, and intelligence and personality. There clearly *are* changes that occur with aging, and this chapter will present an approach to studying those changes within the existing methodological constraints.

METHODOLOGICAL ISSUES IN THE STUDY OF AGING

The interpretation of data on age-related physiological and psychological changes depends on understanding the advantages and limitations of particular research strategies. Three issues are particularly critical: (a) the confounding of aging and generational differences, (b) interindividual differences, and (c) the conditions under which the effects of aging are assessed. A fourth issue—the interaction of aging and disease—also plays a role.

Aging and Generational Differences

Most research on aging makes use of a cross-sectional design, that is, older people and younger people are compared to one another at one point in time. This approach has the advantage of providing considerable information about the relative differences between young and old without having to wait for a group of subjects themselves to age. As Schaie (1967) pointed out, however, cross-sectional studies confound the effects of aging and cohort or generational factors. While differences found between young and old in a cross-sectional study might be due to the aging process, cohort effects cannot be ruled out. Because findings from cross-sectional research cannot automatically be assumed to be related to the aging process, Schaie (1967) recommended referring to these results as showing *age differences* and to use the term *age change* for differences that are subsequently found to be due to aging rather than to a cohort or some other factor.

The usefulness of this distinction is illustrated by Kausler (1982). He notes the commonplace observation that young adults today are, on the average, taller than older adults, and although a certain amount of loss of height occurs with aging, most people would not conclude that aging is the primary cause of the observed difference. A more probable explanation is that better nutrition and improved infant care have led to more optimal growth rates in younger people. Kausler cites data summarized by Youmans (1982), which showed that recent Harvard undergraduates were 1.5 inches taller, on the average, than their fathers when they had attended college.

Although the role of cohort effects in this example is readily apparent, a reliance on cross-sectional studies can result in an underestimation of their influence on other physiological and psychological dimensions, where generational differences are not immediately obvious. Shock (1968) noted the importance of taking cohort factors into account in the study of physiological aging in humans. Changes in nutrition, life-style, medical care, and the environment have produced what demographers call *compression of mortality and morbidity*. As various health problems are prevented or delayed, death and disease-related impairments have increasingly become concentrated in old age. More people are surviving to old age than ever before, and they tend to be in better health (Crimmins, 1984). Cross-sectional studies of physiological functions conducted 20 or 40 years ago would provide a very different picture of aging than the studies conducted today on a cohort in relatively better health. Similarly, cohort differences in education and income, as well as other cultural changes, are likely to have an impact on many psychological variables. Some of these trends will be explored later in the chapter.

Other research designs can be used to differentiate between the effects of aging and those of cohort factors, but these approaches have certain limitations. Longitudinal studies, which follow a single cohort over time, have the advantage of actually measuring a particular intraindividual change rather than inferring it from a comparison of two age groups. This design, however, creates a potential confounding of age and period effects. Period effects are the historical events that occur during the time of the study. As an example, a study of the development of political views from adolescence to young adulthood conducted during the 1960s would not be able to differentiate the respective influences of age and the Vietnam War.

To compensate for these potential confounds, Schaie (1967) has proposed using sequential research strategies in which age, cohort, and period effects are controlled. Schaie and his associates (Baltes & Schaie, 1976; Schaie, Labouvie, & Buech, 1973; Schaie & Labouvie-Vief, 1974; Schaie & Stone, 1982) have used a cohort-sequential design in which several cohorts are followed over time in order to distinguish the probable effects of aging and generation on intelligence. Kausler (1982) summarizes other sequential research strategies and their relative advantages.

Longitudinal and sequential strategies both encounter a major methodological problem: a considerable dropout rate over time. Furthermore, there may be an interaction between subjects who drop out and major study variables. Generally, subjects who score lower on psychological tests are more likely to refuse to be retested at a later time. In an older sample, there will also be attrition due to mortality. The result is that subsequent samples in any longitudinal study constitute an ever more selective group, and the results may not be generalizable to the whole population. Schaie (1967) has suggested compensating for the effects of dropouts by bringing in new age-matched samples of subjects at each retesting interval in sequential studies. While considerable controversy exists over the interpretation of findings from longitudinal and sequential studies (Baltes & Schaie, 1976; Botwinick, 1977; Horn & Donaldson, 1976), findings from sequential studies indicate that cohort factors have a definite impact on at least some selected psychological abilities. Clearly, the potential confound of age and cohort needs to be considered.

Interindividual Differences in Aging

Another important factor in the evaluation of research on aging is that individual differences appear to be greater among older subjects. In virtually every study of psychological functioning, the standard deviation of the scores of older persons is greater than that of younger persons, and the same tendency is observed with respect to many physiological variables as well (Schonfield, 1974; Tobin, 1977). In other words, older people differ more among themselves than does a comparable sample of younger adults.

The significance of increased interindividual differences in the interpretation of research findings can be illustrated by a recent study that used the CAT scan to estimate cerebral atrophy across the adult age span (Takeda & Matsuzawa, 1985). In this study, subjects with diseases that generally lead to increased evidence of cerebral atrophy (e.g., Alzheimer's disease), were excluded in order to develop a normative estimate of brain volume. The results are summarized in Figure 2.1. One obvious finding is that there is an average differ-

ence between young and old subjects in the estimates of brain volume, with older subjects more likely to show increased atrophy. Indeed, the researchers concluded that aging is associated with increased atrophy. But an examination of Figure 2.1 also reveals that there is increased variability in the scores of older subjects and that some older subjects had little or no atrophy, when compared to younger adults. Because this study is cross-sectional, we do not know if the older subjects with little or no atrophy would have had greater brain volume at younger ages as well. Nonetheless, the implications of this research is clear. Age differences are not manifested to a similar degree by all older persons.

The finding that there is greater variation in the scores of older subjects in numerous studies raises questions about our conceptualization of the aging process. We often think of it as being a unitary phenomenon which is correlated with chronological age. A better explanation of these findings is that the mechanisms that lead to physiological and psychological changes are not strongly linked to chronological age, and that people do not experience the same decline at approximately the same age. Furthermore, there may be multiple mechanisms of aging, with both inter- and intraindividual differences in the rate of age-related change in various functions and abilities. Some individuals may manifest more changes than others, while a given individual may manifest different rates of change for various functions, including the possibility of improvements over time in some abilities (Baltes, 1984; Baltes, Dittman-Kohli, & Dixon, 1984). Rather than focusing solely on average differences between young and old, we need to consider possible sources of differences among older samples in order to understand the relationship between aging and various physiological functions and behavior. Another implication is that generalizations about older people that are based on mean scores for any function or ability can be misleading, underestimating the abilities of some individuals and overestimating those of others.

HOW ABILITIES ARE ASSESSED: NORMAL CONDITIONS AND TESTING THE LIMITS

In a series of studies, Baltes has proposed another important research dimension for estimating the effects of aging: the conditions under which abilities are assessed (Baltes, 1984; Baltes,

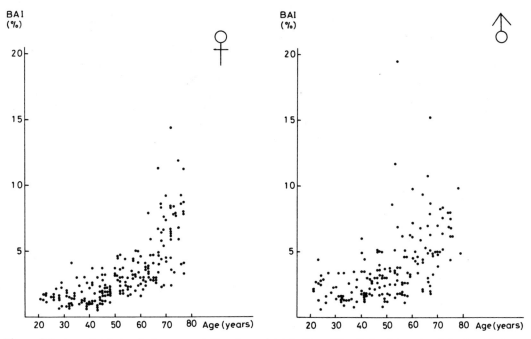

Figure 2.1. Age-related atrophy in women (left) and men (right). (From "Age-Related Atrophy: A Study with Computed Tomography" by S. Takeda and T. Matsuzawa, 1985, *Journal of Gerontology, 40*, p. 162. Copyright 1985 by the Gerontological Society of America. Reprinted by permission of the *Journal of Gerontology*.)

Dittmann-Kohli, & Dixon, 1984; Kliegl, Smith, & Baltes, 1986). When a function is measured under normal conditions, it is difficult to determine what effect is due to aging and what to other factors. If we were interested in studying walking, for example, we might discover that two individuals walk at the same rate while using very different levels of physical resources. For one person, the pace could be quite comfortable, with considerable reserve capacity remaining for additional activity, while for another person, walking at that pace might represent maximum effort.

According to Kliegl, Smith, and Baltes (1986), most research on aging has been conducted under normal conditions, without pushing individuals to their limits. By designing studies that test the limits of functioning, however, it is possible both to determine more precisely the restrictions that have occurred as a result of aging and to examine the potential for overcoming age-related deficits. In the example of walking and running, most likely there would be little or no age differences if we compared people at a comfortable rate of walking, but large differences if we compared them in running. Yet it is also possible to condition older persons for increased physical activity (deVries, 1970), which indicates a reserve capacity for

improved functioning. While older individuals who train themselves for running might never approach record times for particular events, such as the marathon, their ability to compete represents considerable reserve capacity.

Kliegl, Smith, and Baltes (1986) have applied this model to digit span. Using a classical mnemonic strategy, the method of loci, they have trained older and younger persons to learn long lists of numbers that greatly exceed ordinary memory span. This approach has demonstrated both reserve capacity and the limits of function due to aging. The ability of older persons to learn strings of 80 or 90 digits indicates considerable reserve capacity. The fact that the best older subjects learn at a slower pace than even the slowest younger subjects suggests the limits of aging. The implication is that estimates of normative performance under normal conditions may be misleading, failing to indicate clearly the restriction caused by aging or to reveal the potential for improvement.

NORMAL PHYSIOLOGICAL AGING

Aging is defined as "to cause to ripen or become mature over a period of time under fixed conditions" (*Webster's New World Dictionary*, 1970).

Biological aging has to do with why a particular organism has a finite life span (see Hayflick, Chapter 1, this volume). The most potent predisposing factors for longevity are heredity and environment. Some definitions of biological aging focus on deterioration, suggesting the existence of endogenous factors leading to inevitable decline, while others place emphasis on such exogenous factors as disease, leading to the optimistic belief that when medical science unlocks the mystery of disease there will be no limit to longevity. Birren and Zarit (1985) fashioned a comprehensive definition: "Biological aging, senescing, is the process of change in the organism, which over time lowers the probability of survival and reduces the physiological capacity for self-regulation, repair and adaptation to environmental demands."

Busse (1969) speaks of *primary* and *secondary* aging. Primary aging is the result of inherited biological processes that are time-dependent; secondary aging is caused by the decline in function because of chronic disease. Perlmutter and Hall (1985) make a similar distinction. They define primary aging as gradual age-related changes observed in all members of a species that may be the result of genetic programming, and secondary aging as changes resulting from disease, disuse, or abuse. The distinction between primary and secondary aging is clearer at a semantic level than the practical, however, since approximately 85% of those over 65 suffer from at least one chronic illness (Satariano & Syme, 1981); moreover, it is difficult to live for very long without experiencing adverse environmental effects.

There are two basic classes of theories of aging: one that views aging as genetically programmed and one that views it in terms of damage. Programmed theories are based on the idea that aging is genetically controlled. Theoretically, aging is programmed at birth, just as puberty is, with differences in life span inherited from the parents. Support for genetic theories comes from observations of the similarity in the life spans of identical twins and the tendency of the children of long-lived parents to outlive the children of short-lived parents (Jones, 1956), although longevity of the mother may be a stronger factor (Abbott, Murphy, Bolling, & Abbey, 1974). There are also a number of hereditary diseases that limit life span, such as Down's syndrome, progeria, and Werner's syndrome. Because the gene for these diseases is known to differ from the normal and the length of life is altered, it is a strong argument for the gene-

tic determination of longevity and aging. Walford, Weindruch, Gottesman, and Tam (1981) propose that it is the programmed deterioration of the immune system that leads to aging. This theory arises from similarities in changes observed in normal aging and in the process of transplant rejection: loss of hair, kidney and vascular disease, failure to thrive, and shortened life span (Walford, 1983).

Damage theories posit that throughout their lifetime individuals accumulate damage that limits the natural ability of their biological systems to repair themselves. This damage can be at the level of the DNA (Sinex, 1977), cross-linkage (Bjorksten, 1974), free radicals (Harman, 1968), or lipofuscin (Sanadi, 1977). Each theory explains one aspect of aging, but no one theory deals comprehensively with all aspects of normal aging, such as why some people age prematurely, why the immune system becomes less efficient with age, why cells are subject to the Hayflick limit, why biochemical changes occur, why fibers of connective tissue deteriorate with age, why the rate at which any species can repair damage to its own DNA is related to its maximum life span, or why almost all animals have a similar metabolic rate, using in a lifetime about the same amount of energy per pound of body weight (Perlmutter & Hall, 1985).

Despite the lack of knowledge about the causes of normal aging, the results are undisputable. Changes that begin at the genetic and cellular level ultimately make themselves felt at the system level. However, not all systems age at the same rate. Appearance, and the cardiovascular, respiratory, gastrointestinal, reproductive, and nervous systems can vary considerably in age effects within the same individual. An individual can be 75 years old chronologically but have a 65-year-old heart and an 85-year-old gastrointestinal system. As noted earlier, individual differences increase dramatically with age, making it difficult to make generalizations about normal aging.

Appearance

The most obvious age-related changes are in appearance. Hair, nails, skin, body composition, skeleton, and teeth all undergo changes with age. The graying of hair may be the result of lack of a particular enzyme or a reduction or malfunction of pigment-producing cells (Rossman, 1977; Selmanowitz, Rizer, & Orentreich, 1977). Some scalp hair is lost by both men and women during normal aging, but some men show pattern baldness, which is hereditary. Baldness can also be caused by disease or injury to hair follicles. Nail growth is influenced by environmental factors, including nutrition and disease, and by aging in other systems, such as the endocrine and circulatory systems.

Normal aging produces changes in the elastic fibers and collagen, making the skin less pliable. The skin becomes thinner and drier, the fat deposits directly beneath it diminish, and the muscles decrease in size. Wrinkles, however, are primarily the result of secondary aging. Sun, wind, and abrasion are responsible for much of the damage seen in older skin; tanning is directly related to wrinkling. Wrinkles are also use-related, occurring at an angle to the direction of muscle pull on the skin (Rossman, 1977). Pigment-containing cells (melanocytes) decrease in number but increase in size with age, producing so-called "age-spots." Other common skin disorders, like keratoses, occur in the elderly, but they are not part of the normal aging process.

The relationship between muscle atrophy and aging is currently being studied. Cross-sectional studies show increased atrophy with age; however, the older subjects are likely to have begun reducing physical activity from age 30 onward. It is likely that there is some decline in muscle strength with age, but the rate of change is uncertain. deVries (1983) found no difference in either endurance or muscle strength between 22-year-olds and 62-year-olds who worked in a machine shop. If adults continue vigorous exercise throughout their lifetime it may become possible to compare low- and high-exercise groups and then to extrapolate the effects of exercise from normal aging effects on muscle strength.

Small changes in height are normal with aging, usually no more than 1 inch in men and under 2 inches in women; this is due to altered posture, thinning of cartilage disks, and loss of water in the disks. Calcium loss from the bones is also observed, with women losing almost twice as much as men (Tonna, 1977). Osteoporosis, leading to increased fractures, also occurs about 4 times more often in postmenopausal women than in older men. The reason for this is not known, but hypothetical causes include diminished estrogen levels, lack of exercise, lactase calcium deficiency, and increased parathyroid secretion with decreasing calcium blood level (Tonna, 1977). Osteoarth-

ritis also increases with age and seems to be related to genetics, hormone levels, and nutrition.

Teeth wear down quite slowly and become less vulnerable to cavities with age. Within the tooth there is a gradual cell loss in the pulp, until by age 70 about half the cells are gone. The most common cause of tooth loss is periodontal disease leading to bone loss, which increases with age. Again, genetics, nutrition, and disease appear to be major factors in periodontal disease.

Cardiovascular System

Current thinking about the normal aging of the cardiovascular system mirrors that of other systems. It was previously thought that arteriosclerosis, atherosclerosis, and occlusions were the result of normal wear and tear on the cardiovascular system, but now they are believed to be linked with age-related diseases.

The appearance of the heart changes with age as lipofuscin accumulates within the heart, but this change is not related to any disease process or cardiac irregularity. The collagen surrounding the muscle fibers stiffens and becomes insoluble. Fat is gradually deposited on the heart surface, and there is a gradual increase in heart size; substantially larger increases are observed in individuals who have gained weight. Cardiac output decreases by about 1% per year beginning at age 20 owing in part to a drop in the amount of blood pumped with each contraction of the heart and in part to a decrease in the heart rate (Kohn, 1977).

Under conditions of stress, the aging heart may be less effective in its response. Stress causes an increase in the heart rate. In younger men who exercise vigorously the heart rate may rise to 200 beats per minute. By contrast, men between 70 and 90 years of age show heart rates no faster than 125 beats per minute under the same work load. It is not known why the maximum heart rate declines with age, but research with rats indicates that the older heart takes more time to contract and relax after each contraction (Shock, 1977).

Arterial changes that occur with aging include the redistribution of elastin in the arterial walls, calcium binding with the elastin, an increase in collagen content, and an accumulation of lipids within the arteries. Changes in connective tissue are probably part of normal aging, but according to current research findings, the other changes may be indicative of chronically inflamed tissue.

Because arterial disease is fairly common among older adults, it is difficult to separate normal aging from the deterioration caused by disease. The result, however, is predictable. As the arteries become constricted, blood pressure tends to rise. However, the blood pressure of some older persons is no higher than that of younger persons. Factors such as diet and methods of food preparation and preservation have been suggested as the causes. The late Nathan Pritikin, who promoted a diet high in fiber and low in saturated fats, at autopsy was said to have had the arteries of a young man. He had been diagnosed as having coronary artery disease when in his 50s and dramatically altered his life-style and eating habits for the last 20 years of his life. This finding lends credence to proponents of diet as the critical factor in the development of coronary artery disease. However, decreased blood flow to peripheral vessels also appears to be part of normal aging, along with the heart's lessened ability to diminish the rate of arterial blood flow through body tissues. The decrease is most noticeable in the kidneys, internal organs, fingers, and hands and least noticeable in the brain, heart, and skeletal muscles (Kohn, 1977).

Respiratory System

The most obvious age-related change in the respiratory system is shortness of breath. Again, it is difficult to separate the long-term effects of air pollution, smoking, and respiratory infections from normal age changes. As people age, the rib cage becomes increasingly rigid and muscle fibers become smaller and fewer in number. As a result, the chest wall does not expand as far with each breath, and less air is taken into the lungs. The appearance of the lung changes over the years as carbon particles adhere to it. Cartilage in the trachea and bronchial tubes calcifies, increasing rigidity. Narrowing of the alveoli begins around age 40, affecting more than 80% of people in their 80s (Klocke, 1977). The flow of air into the lungs decreases by about 20% to 30% in the period between young adulthood and old age. However, total lung capacity and rate of respiration remain the same. Vital capacity declines each year beginning in the 20s, decreasing about 40% between ages 25 and 85 (Norris, Mittman, & Shock, 1964).

The maximum lung capacity begins to decline at age 20, although the rate of change increases after age 40. Maximal oxygen uptake declines 30% by age 60, again with wide individual differences.

Lung disorders are more frequent in older people, but they are considered to be the result of secondary aging. Emphysema was once believed to be a part of normal aging, but studies have indicated it is primarily the result of smoking (Auerbach, Garfinkel, & Hammond, 1974). Bronchitis and pneumonia occur more frequently among older adults, perhaps secondary to other diseases that have weakened the immune response.

Gastrointestinal System

Aging intestines generally secrete the same enzymes as youthful systems, but in smaller amounts. Muscle tissue may atrophy, but without apparent effect on the intestine's ability to absorb nutrients. Constipation is a frequent complaint among older people, but it is most likely to have been caused by decreased fluid intake, insufficient bulk in the diet, and lack of exercise. The problem is exacerbated by laxative abuse and the use of drugs prescribed for other conditions.

After the age of 50, the liver may begin to shrink and become more sluggish, the structure of its cells may change, and the enzymes it produces may be less concentrated. However, the body uses only about 20% of the liver, so the above effects are usually relevant only to the ingestion of drugs that are metabolized in the liver, which typically should be prescribed in lower doses. Gall bladder problems increase with age, as do other generalized gastrointestinal complaints. However, these are all secondary to the aging process, and none are considered to be the result of primary aging.

Excretory System

There are significant changes in the bladder and kidneys that appear to be correlated with age. Bladder capacity decreases with age (Rockstein & Sussman, 1979), and urinary tract infections increase. Aging of the kidneys starts at about age 30, when they begin to shrink. By age 90, they will each have lost one third of their weight. The arteries supplying the kidneys show typical circulatory system changes consistent with the degree of vascular disorder present. The filtration rate begins to decline at age 21, decreasing by 31% by age 80.

Endocrine System

Aging can affect the endocrine system at a number of different levels. It could lead to reduced hormone secretion of the glands or to a lack of responsiveness to hormones in the receptors. There may be changes in the secondary messengers that transmit hormonal signals, or there may be changes in the level of enzymes necessary to carry out hormone-related activities.

There is no significant change in size and weight of the pituitary gland, although it shows characteristic signs of aging. The supply of blood reaching the gland decreases after the onset of puberty; there is an increase in connective tissue and a change in the distribution of cells within the gland. When the pituitary is removed from rats and its hormones subsequently supplied by injection, the animals do not age (Walford, 1983). There are no significant declines in the levels of growth hormone, thyroid-stimulating hormone, and adrenal-stimulating hormone.

The parathyroid does not decrease in size with age, nor does it reduce its hormone secretions. The thyroid, however, does undergo anatomical changes. Individual cells change and collagen fibers appear. The production of thyroid hormones decreases with age, yet their level in the blood remains constant.

The incidence of adult-onset diabetes among Caucasians doubles between the ages of 45 and 64. This is related to the body's declining ability to dispose of glucose efficiently. There is a characteristic delay in the release of glucose in comparison to younger adults and so less is released. There is controversy over whether this decreased tolerance is a sign of normal aging or a disorder. More than half of the adults past 65 show reduced glucose tolerance, but only about 10% exhibit signs of diabetes (Rockstein & Sussman, 1979).

PSYCHOLOGICAL AGING

Normal psychological aging encompasses changes in sensory and perceptual processes, and cognitive abilities, such as intelligence, learning, and memory. Primary biological changes are generally believed to be the source of changes in psychological functions, although the role of psychological and sociological factors should also be considered (Birren, 1959). In the psychological realm, the role of prior experience can mitigate or exaggerate biologically influenced changes. In complex learning situations, for example, an older person may be able to draw upon prior learning or may experience difficulty because of interference from prior learning. Sociological factors include age norms and expectations and, especially, the opportunity for meaningful social interaction. Although most current studies are descriptive—that is, they demonstrate the existence of age-related differences—it is possible to use experimental research paradigms to test hypotheses about biological, psychological, or social causes (Kausler, 1982).

As with biological theories, it is also important to distinguish between primary and secondary changes. Although the severe intellectual deterioration associated with senile dementia is often believed to be typical of old age, the diseases that cause dementia actually affect only a small proportion of the population. Estimates generally range between 5% and 7% (Mortimer, Schuman, & French, 1981). In the absence of dementia, psychological changes are much less pronounced, and there are even possibilities of improved function in some areas. Optimally healthy persons show the fewest changes, while those with even minimal degrees of illness have somewhat greater deficits (Birren, Butler, Greenhouse, Sokoloff, & Yarrow, 1963). As was pointed out earlier, with advancing age the distinctions between primary and secondary changes become increasingly blurred.

Sensation and Perception

All five senses decline in sensitivity with age. At younger ages, the decrement in one sense can often be compensated for by strength in another. With advancing age, the ability to compensate is diminished by the decline in all sense modalities.

Vision is the sense most heavily relied upon, and its impairment poses a threat to independence. Blindness is relatively rare among younger people; more than half of all cases of blindness develop after the age of 65 (Rockstein & Sussman, 1979). Normal eye changes include miosis (decrease in the size of the pupil), weakened muscles controlling dilation (Fozard, Wolf, Bell, McFarland, & Podolsky, 1977), slower pupillary adjustment in response to changes in illumination, yellowing of the lens, thickening of the lens with cells produced over a lifetime, and sensitivity to glare that results from the thickening. The result is that older people require almost 100 times as much illumination as people in their 20s to discern a target in the presence of glare (Fozard & Popkin, 1978). The eye's ability and speed of accommodation are also affected by these structural changes, as is visual perception, increasing the time needed to process visual information. Further, the pathological processes of glaucoma, cataracts, and macular degeneration are increasingly common in old age.

As would be expected, along with changes in sensory functions, there are also changes in visual perception. These include increased time for complete dark adaptation (McFarland, Domey, Warren, & Ward, 1960; McFarland & Fisher, 1955), decreased color sensitivity (Dalderup & Fredericks, 1969; Gilbert, 1957), poorer depth perception (Bell, Wolf, & Bernholz, 1972), and greater sensitivity to optical illusions (Comalli, 1970; Lorden, Atkeson, & Pollack, 1979).

Hearing begins to decline at around age 25. Pitch discrimination, in particular, deteriorates steadily until age 55, then drops off markedly in the higher frequencies (Corso, 1977). Significant hearing loss is estimated to occur in 2.8% of the population by age 55, and by age 75, 15% are deaf. The incidence to tinnitus rises from 3% in young adults to 9% in the middle-aged and 11% in those aged 65 to 74 (Rockstein & Sussman, 1979). Tinnitus often occurs in people exposed to military combat. It is also caused by tumors, middle-ear infections, bone growth in the middle ear, drugs, and allergies. Age-related damage to the inner ear is difficult to assess, especially because most Americans live in noisy environments where they are likely to accumulate insults to the hair cells and other cochlear structures.

Auditory perception is selectively affected for higher frequency tones. Older individuals show decreases both in the minimum intensity of stimuli that they are able to detect and in the ability to discriminate tones of difference frequencies (Corso, 1977; Kausler, 1982).

One consequence of the decline in auditory perception is difficulty in speech perception. Older persons are particularly disadvantaged in the perception of degraded speech, that is, speech in which sentences are interrupted or spoken more rapidly than normal, under poor acoustical conditions, or in the presence of background noise (Bergman, Blumenfeld, Cascardo, Dask, Levitt, & Margulies, 1976). Even under favorable conditions, however, age differences are apparent (Olsho, Harkins & Lenhardt, 1985).

Sensitivity to odors may decline with age as the olfactory bulbs in the nasal lining atrophy, a process that begins in childhood. For example, one study found that the ability to detect the smell of natural gas, for instance, declines with age, with 30% of those over 65 unable to discern the smell (Chalke, Dewhurst, & Ward, 1958); however, there were wide interindividual differences and overlap between young and old groups in the study. Sensitivity to odor may be a cultural or individually learned ability, related to the perceived pleasantness or unpleasantness of a particular smell.

Smell and taste are closely connected, and while the number of taste buds decreases slightly during adulthood, there is no evidence of significant changes before the age of 75 (Arvidson, 1979). Some studies show that for people past 60 a taste must be more concentrated for it to be discerned, but again the individual differences between subjects were considerable (Kare, 1975).

Contrary to folklore, there is no clear evidence that sensitivity to pain decreases with age (see Chapter 15, this volume). There is a decrease in the number of receptors, and their individual sensitivity does decline, although selectively. Adults in their 60s and 70s seem to be less sensitive to light pressure on the palms and fingers than younger persons (Kenshalo, 1977). The loss of sensitivity to vibration in the feet occurs in about 40% of those between the ages of 64 and 73 (Skre, 1972). Researchers have been unable as yet to establish conclusively whether sensitivity to pain increases, decreases, or stays the same within an individual.

The response style of older adults complicates the assessment of sensory and perceptual difficulties. Specifically, there is a tendency toward increased cautiousness with age, with older adults not responding when uncertain. In a test of auditory perception, Rees and Botwinick (1971) used a stimulus-detection paradigm in which older and younger adults were to indicate if a test had been played. The frequencies of the sounds had been previously determined to fall within the range that the subjects could perceive. Nonetheless, the older adults consistently made more errors of omission, failing to report a tone. There were no age differences in errors of commission or incorrect reporting of a tone when none was played. Errors of omission are also more common in cognitive tests (Botwinick, 1978) and are particularly pronounced among older adults who are depressed (Miller & Lewis, 1977; Whitehead, 1973), which sometimes creates the mistaken impression that they are suffering from dementia.

Other consequences of auditory and visual changes are not well understood. While anecdotal evidence and case studies suggest a relationship between sensory loss and adaptation, particularly that sensory-impaired individuals are more likely to experience feelings of depression and loneliness, few systematic studies have been conducted. One phenomenon that has been explored is the relationship between paranoid disorders with onset in later life and bilateral hearing loss. Hearing loss is not present in every case of late-life paranoia. Some incidences are related to altered brain function or the exacerbation of a long-standing personality disorder (Cooper, Kay, Curry, Garside, & Roth, 1974).

The possibility of improving hearing and vision should not be overlooked. Clinical examples show the effectiveness of visual aids, such as high-powered magnifying glasses, spectacle-mounted microscopes, or closed-circuit television systems in the treatment of deficits resulting from vision disorders (Genensky & Zarit, 1986). Similarly, hearing aids have proved helpful for many hearing-impaired individuals. A major obstacle to rehabilitation, however, is that Medicare currently does not reimburse the cost of hearing aids, nor does it cover the costs for training in the most effective use of the aids.

Intelligence and Aging

The most studied question in the psychology of aging is whether or not there are changes in intelligence. Although continuing controversies exist over how intelligence is measured and the validity of tests, current tests are useful for indicating how people carry out complex cognitive activities. Because of the sensitivity of these tests to discern evidence of brain damage, they are also useful for what they reveal about changes in the brain with age (Zarit, Eiler, & Hassinger, 1985).

Intelligence tests usually include verbal tasks (e.g., tests of information, vocabulary, abstract thinking, and nonverbal) or performance tasks, (such as assembling blocks to match a design). Cross-sectional studies have found age-related differences in both types of intelligence, with the highest scores shown by people in their 20s, and greater differences on nonverbal tests.

Using a sequential research design, Schaie and his associates (Baltes & Schaie, 1976; Schaie & Labouvie-Vief, 1974; Schaie, Labouvie, & Buech, 1973; Schaie & Stone, 1982) have demonstrated that generational differences account for a significant proportion of the apparent age-related decline observed in cross-sectional studies. They have followed samples of subjects over a period of 28 years, retesting them every 7 years. The measure of intelligence was the Primary Mental Abilities (PMA) test (Thurstone & Thurstone, 1949), which comprises five subtests measuring different factors of intelligence: verbal meaning, spatial abilities, reasoning, arithmetic abilities, and word fluency. Although there had been attrition in the sample, through deaths (especially in the older groups) and failure to locate subjects for retesting, the results were striking. If one considered only cross-sectional findings, that is, comparisons across age groups for one time of testing, the older subjects scored lower on all five subtests. But if one considered the scores over time, there was an age-related decline on only one subtest, word fluency. The results of other subtests of the PMA remained unchanged at least up to age 67; even at more advanced ages, many subjects had unchanged or improved scores between test intervals. The original cross-sectional differences between the cohorts remained stable over time (see Figure 2.1). The younger groups did not decline to the levels that characterized the older cohorts; rather their scores were stable or improved. This finding suggests that the cohort has considerable influence on intelligence, and in fact, may have a greater impact than aging.

Although Schaie and his associates have emphasized the more optimistic implications of these findings, criticisms on methodological and theoretical grounds have been made. As noted earlier, high attrition rates call into question the generalizability of the findings (Botwinick, 1977).

From a theoretical perspective, Horn (Horn & Cattell, 1967; Horn & Donaldson, 1976) has used a two-factor model of intelligence to propose a differential decline in more biologically based dimensions, that is, dimensions of intelligence that are relatively independent of learning and experience. Tests of familiar verbal material represent knowledge that is acquired during one's lifetime, or what he calls *crystallized intelligence*. As has been seen, these show little or no change. Nonverbal tasks and measures of pure reasoning, which are relatively free from the influence of prior learning, represent the ability to apply a generalized intellectual ability to new problems or situations.

Such tasks are called *fluid intelligence*. Because these tests are less likely to be influenced by prior exposure, they are believed to be a more accurate measure of biological potential. These are the types of tasks that show more decline with age. In short, this theory suggests that the mechanics of intelligence that facilitate acquisition of new knowledge and skills decline, previously acquired knowledge is not severely affected.

Several criticisms have been directed at this interpretation of intelligence test scores. Speed is usually a factor in many tests of fluid intelligence. Older persons may be at a disadvantage when they must respond quickly and within brief time limits. However, studies that have allowed more time have not found significant improvements in performance (Storandt, 1977). It has also been argued that the relative difference between crystallized and fluid measures is an artifact of scoring procedures. When more stringent scoring is applied to verbal tests, older persons show greater decline than younger ones (Botwinick, 1977; Zarit, Eiler, & Hassinger, 1985).

Another possibility is that the skills that underlie fluid tasks are not practiced by most people during adulthood, and with appropriate stimulation, functioning can be improved. Plasticity of fluid abilities was tested in a novel experiment by Willis, Blieszner, and Baltes (1981), who trained older persons for a fluid intelligence task. The outcome was measured both for the task for which the subjects were trained and for other measures of intelligence to determine if there was transfer of training to related tasks. Subjects improved both in the training task and in near-transfer tasks, that is, other measures of fluid intelligence that were conceptually related to the training task. Only minimal improvement was found on far-transfer tasks, which were measures of crystallized intelligence. Improvement was maintained at a 6-month follow-up. These findings suggest the possibility that older persons can compensate for age-related declines in fluid abilities.

Memory

Perhaps the most widely held belief about aging is that there is a decline in memory, but as with other abilities, the change is not as extensive as once thought. In part, the expectation of memory loss is the result of viewing dementia as the outcome of aging rather than as a disease. While there is substantial memory loss with dementia, changes in memory in a healthy older person are more benign.

The most significant age differences in memory involve the ability to acquire new information. Once material is learned, subsequent recall is the same or almost the same as in younger persons (Botwinick, 1978; Craik, 1977; Hulicka & Weiss, 1965). These age differences vary, depending on the testing conditions and the type of material to be remembered. In divided attention experiments, where subjects are distracted by competing stimuli, learning and memory are more disrupted for older persons than for younger ones (Broadbent & Gregory, 1965; Craik, 1977). Similarly, when the amount of material to be processed in working memory becomes too great, age deficits will be more pronounced (Light, Zelinski, & Moore, 1982). The pacing of material is also important. When older persons are given more time to respond during the test period, age differences are reduced (Canestrari, 1963; Monge & Hultsch, 1971). Another factor that affects age differences in memory is whether or not the information to be learned and remembered is meaningful. The performance of older persons is substantially poorer than that of younger persons when less meaningful material, such as nonsense syllables are used, but they score at or near the same levels when more familiar material is used (Hulicka, 1967). In everyday situations, hearing loss and vision loss are likely to impede the learning and remembering of information.

A common observation made by and about older persons is that they remember the past but cannot recall more recent events. Specific research on this issue is limited because of the difficulty in equating recent and past events. When an older person says she remembers the past like it was yesterday, she may be referring to major life events, such as marriage or the birth of a child, which have important personal significance. What happened in the preceding week usually pales in comparison. Another factor is that we all reminisce, which enhances old memories, and we may remember best those memories that we periodically recall.

A number of recent studies have highlighted problems older persons have in recalling old information. For instance, Bahrick, Bahrick, and Whittlinger (1975) found that the ability to remember the names of persons in one's high school class decreases over time. Older persons also experience more "tip of the tongue" responses for the names of well-known persons; that is, they feel they know the name but cannot recall it. One study found that, when given a multiple-choice question, older individuals almost always could pick out the correct name on items for which they had a tip of the tongue response, while on the items they initially stated they did not know, they would select an incorrect answer. Overall, they appeared to have a larger fund of information to draw upon than younger persons (Lachman, Lachman, & Thronesberry, 1979). In a variation on that experiment, Botwinick and Storandt (1974) asked questions on historical events that were grouped according to decades (e.g., the 1930s or the 1940s). Subjects tended to do best in recalling events that occurred when they were 15 to 25 years of age than events that occurred in earlier or later periods of their lives.

It has been speculated that the problems in learning new information are related to changes that occur in the brain in normal aging, especially those in the hippocampus, which is involved in memory. One hypothesis is that older people cannot encode new information as "deeply"; that is, they are unable to make as many associations to stimuli and therefore do not learn or remember as efficiently as younger people (Hartley, Harker, & Walsh, 1980). Another hypothesis is that older people simply do not use efficient learning strategies. For instance, they are less likely to try to remember by organizing the stimuli or by utilizing mnemonics; their performance improves if they adopt some strategy (Denny, 1974; Hulicka & Grossman, 1967; Whitbourne & Slevin, 1978).

These findings suggest a number of practical steps that may be helpful in improving memory. Recall is improved if the material to be remembered is presented slowly and the older person has sufficient time to study and respond to it. Older persons will also do better when there are fewer distractions. If there is vision or hearing loss, stimuli can be presented in ways that overcome these deficits to whatever extent is possible. The use of mental strategies will also improve performance. Finally, such practical steps as making notes or keeping an appointment book should not be overlooked in dealing with specific memory problems.

One clinically relevant dimension of memory is that older people's evaluations of their own abilities can be misleading. Complaints about failing memory are common but are not necessarily related to deficits in functioning. Patients with dementia, for instance, are less likely to complain about failing memory than older persons with no evidence of dementia, even though the dementia patients have significantly more memory problems (Kahn, Zarit, Hilbert, & Niederehe, 1975). Furthermore, complaints about failing memory have generally been found to be more strongly associated with depression than actual memory function (Kahn et al., 1975; Popkin, Gallagher, Thompson, & Moore, 1982; Zarit, 1980, 1982).

There are several reasons for these discrepancies between complaint and performance. Dementia patients may complain less than normal older persons because their memory becomes so poor that they cannot remember they cannot remember. Their refusal to acknowledge their problem may also be part of a protective denial. Trying to make dementia patients aware of their deficits is often upsetting, and they typically will not acknowledge the existence of any problem. In contrast to dementia patients, the normal older person will notice everyday instances of forgetting. If individuals are concerned about memory loss in aging or with becoming senile, they may be more upset when they forget ordinary things. They may not be forgetting much more than they ever did, but they worry that they are suffering from a major decline. This tendency to magnify the significance of complaints is especially pronounced in someone who is depressed. The reassurance that a certain amount of forgetting is normal is often sufficient to lessen older people's anxiety about failing memory (Zarit, Cole, & Guider, 1981; Zarit, Gallagher, & Kramer, 1980).

In summary, then, in the absence of dementia, changes in memory are relatively mild. Although older persons are at a disadvantage with respect to certain types of learning and memory (e.g., rapidly paced), these changes do not result in any loss of competence. Nonetheless, memory changes may be upsetting to some older persons because of their fear of senility. For the older person who wants to improve memory, there are strategies that can compensate for age-related changes. It is also important to recognize that complaints about memory loss do not necessarily reflect dementia.

SUMMARY

Overall, there is evidence of physiological and psychological changes with age, but these are not as severe or as universal as popular stereotypes of aging suggest. Some abilities are affected, while others are not, and there are considerable individual differences in the extent of change. Methodological refinements are still needed to separate normal age changes from such confounds as generational differences, increased interindividual variability, and disease. While it is possible to identify physiological changes with advancing age in all systems of the body, it is not possible to determine the relative contributions of genetics, nutrition, environment, and disease. Generally, there is a decrease in vital capacities and an increase in collagen and connective tissues with age, as well as declines in all five senses. Current research indicates that intelligence remains stable until age 67, and sometimes much later. Some research identifies a difference in the preservation of crystallized and fluid intelligence, although there are potential confounds in the method of testing. Memory capacity appears to be maintained, but retrieval time may be longer, and older subjects demonstrate fewer spontaneous strategies. Our knowledge of normal aging is still in its infancy, as indicated by the tentative nature of the research presented and the large number of confounds present. Perhaps the most relevant aspect of aging is the tremendous interindividual variability the implications of which have not yet been fully defined.

REFERENCES

Abbott, M., Murphy, E., Bolling, D., & Abbey, H. (1974). The familial component in longevity—A study of offspring of nonagenarians: 2. Preliminary analysis of the completed study. *Johns Hopkins Medical Journal, 134,* 1–16.

Arvidson, K. (1979). Location and variation in number of tastebuds in human fungiform papillae. *Scandinavian Journal of Dental Research, 87,* 435–442.

Auerbach, O., Garfinkel, L., & Hammond, E.C. (1974). Relation of smoking and age to findings in lung parenchyma: A microscopic study. *Chest, 65,* 29–35.

Bahrick. H. P., Bahrick, P. O., & Whittlinger, R. P. (1975). Fifty years of memory for names and faces: A cross-sectional approach. *Journal of Experimental Psychology: General, 104,* 54–75.

Baltes, P. B. (1984). Intelligenz im alter. *Spektrum der Wissenschaft, 5,* 46–60.

Baltes, P. B., Dittman-Kohli, F., & Dixon, R. A. (1984). New perspectives on the development of intelligence in adulthood: Toward a dual-process conception and a model of selective optimization with compensation. In P. B. Baltes & O. G. Brim, Jr. (Eds.), *Life span development and behavior* (vol. 6). New York: Academic.

Baltes, P. B., & Schaie, K. W. (1976). On the plasticity of intelligence in adulthood and old age: Where Horn and Donaldson fail. *American Psychologist, 31,* 720–725.

Baltes, P. B., & Schaie, K. W. (1976) On the plasticity of adult and gerontological intelligence: Where Horn and Donaldson fail. *American Psychologist, 31,* 720–725.

Bell, B., Wolf, E., & Bernholz, C. D. (1972). Depth perception as a function of aging. *Aging and Human Development, 3,* 77–81.

Bergman, M., Blumenfield, V. G., Cascardo, D., Dask, B., Levitt, H., & Margulies M. K. (1976). Age-related decrement in hearing for speech: Sampling and longitudinal studies. *Journal of Gerontology, 31,* 533–538.

Birren, J. E. (1959). Principles of research on aging. In J. E. Birren (Ed.), *Handbook of aging and the individual: Psychological and biological aspects* (pp. 3–12). Chicago: University of Chicago Press.

Birren J. E., Butler, R. N., Greenhouse, S. W., Sokoloff, L., & Yarrow, M. (1963). *Human aging: A biological and behavioral study.* Washington, D.C.: U.S. Dept. of Health, Education, and Welfare.

Birren, J. E., & Zarit, J. (1985). *Concepts of health, behavior and aging: Cognition, stress and aging* (pp. 1–18). Englewood Cliffs, Prentice-Hall.

Bjorksten, J. (1974). Crosslinkage and the aging process. In M. Rockstein, M. L. Sussman, & J. Chesky (Eds.), *Theoretical aspects of aging* (pp. 43–59). New York: Academic Press.

Botwinick, J. (1977). Intellectual abilities. In J. E. Birren & K. W. Schaie (Eds.), *Handbook of the psychology of aging* (pp. 580–605). New York: Van Nostrand Reinhold.

Botwinick, J. (1978). *Aging and behavior (2nd ed.).* New York: Springer.

Botwinick, J., & Storandt, M. (1974). *Memory, related functions and age.* Springfield, IL: Charles C. Thomas.

Broadbent, D. E., & Gregory, M. (1965). Some confirmatory results on age differences in memory for simultaneous stimulation. *British Journal of Psychology, 56,* 77–80.

Busse, E. W. (1969) Theories of aging. In E. W. Busse & E. Pfeiffer (Eds.), *Behavior and adaptation in late life.* Boston: Little, Brown.

Canestrari, R. E., Jr. (1963). Paced and self-paced learning in young and elderly adults. *Journal of Gerontology, 18,* 165–168.

Chalke, H. D., Dewhurst, J. R., & Ward, C. W. (1958). Loss of sense of smell in old people. *Public Health, 72,* 223–230.

Comalli, P. E. (1970). Life-span changes in visual perception. In L. R. Goulet & P. B. Baltes (Eds.), *Life-span developmental psychology: Research and theory.* New York: Academic Press.

Cooper, A. F., Kay, D. W. K., Curry, A. R., Garside, R. F., & Roth, M. (1974). Hearing loss in paranoid and affective psychoses of the elderly. *Lancet, ii,* 851–854.

Corso, J. F. (1977). Auditory perception and communication. In J. E. Birren & K. W. Schaie (Eds.), *Handbook of the psychology of aging.* New York: Van Nostrand Reinbold.

Craik, F. I. M. (1977). Age differences in human memory. In J. E. Birren & K. W. Schaie (Eds.), *Handbook of the psychology of aging* (pp. 384–420). New York: Van Nostrand Reinhold.

Crimmins, E. M. (1984). Life expectancy and the older population: Demographic implications of recent and prospective trends in old age mortality. *Research on Aging, 6,* 490–514.

Dalderup, L. M., & Fredericks, M. L. C. (1969). Colour sensitivity in old age. *Journal of the American Geriatrics Society, 17,* 388–390.

deVries, H. A. (1970). Physiological effects of an exercise training regimen upon men aged 52–88. *Journal of Gerontology, 25,* 325–336.

deVries, H. A. (1983). Physiology of exercise and aging. In D. S. Woodruff & J. E. Birren (Eds.), *Aging: Scientific perspectives and social issues (2nd ed.).* Monterey, CA: Brooks/Cole.

Denny, N. W. (1974). Evidence for development change in categorization criteria for children and adults. *Human Development, 17,* 41–53.

Fozard, J. L., & Popkin, S. J. (1978). Optimizing adult development: Ends and means of an applied psychology of aging. *American Psychologist, 33,* 975–989.

Fozard, J. L., Wolf, E., Bell, B., McFarland, R. A., & Podolsky, S. (1977). Visual perception and communication. In J. E. Birren & K. W. Schaie (Eds.), *Handbook of the psychology of aging.* New York: Van Nostrand Reinhold.

Genensky, S., & Zarit, S. H. (1986). Low vision care in a clinical setting: General and clinical perspectives. In A. A. Rosenbloom & M. M. Morgan (Eds.), *Vision and aging.* Chicago: Professional Press.

Gilbert, J. G. (1957). Age changes in color matching. *Journal of Gerontology, 12,* 210–215.

Harman, D. (1968). Free radical theory of aging: Effect of free radical reaction inhibitors on the mortality rate of male LAF mice. *Journal of Gerontology, 23,* 476–482.

Hartley, J. T., Harker, H. O., & Walsh, D. A. (1980). Contemporary issues and new directions in adult development of learning and memory. In L. W. Poon (Ed.), *Aging in the 1980's.* Washington, DC: American Psychological Association.

Horn, J. L., & Cattell, R. B. (1967). Age differences in fluid and crystallized intelligence. *Acta Psychologica, 26,* 107–129.

Horn, J. L., & Donaldson, G. (1976). On the myth of intellectual decline in adulthood. *American Psychologist, 31,* 701–719.

Hulicka, I. M. (1967). Age differences in retention as a function of interference. *Journal of Gerontology, 22,* 46–51.

Hulicka, I. M., & Grossman, J. L. (1967). Age-group comparisons for the use of mediators in paired-associate learning. *Journal of Gerontology, 22,* 46–51.

Hulicka, I. M., & Weiss, R. L. (1965). Age differences in retention as a function of learning. *Journal of Consulting Psychology, 29,* 125–129.

Hultson, D. F. (1969). Adult age differences in the organization of free recall. *Developmental Psychology, 1,* 673–678.

Hultson, D. F. (1975). Adult age differences in retrieval: Trace-dependent and cue-dependent forgetting. *Developmental Psychology, 11,* 197–201.

Jones, H. B. (1956). A special consideration of the aging process, disease and life expectancy. In J. H. Lawrence & J. G. Hamilton (Eds.), *Advances in biological and medical physics (Vol. 4).* New York: Academic Press.

Kahn, R. L., Zarit, S. H., Hilbert, N. M., & Niederehe, G. (1975). Memory complaint and impairment in the aged. *Archives of General Psychiatry, 32,* 1569–1573.

Kare, M. R. (1975). Changes in taste with age—infancy to senescence. *Food Technology, 78.*

Kausler, D. H. (1982). *Experimental psychology and human aging.* New York: Wiley.

Kenshalo, D. R. (1977). Age changes in touch, vioration, temperature, kinesthesis, and pain sensitivity. In J. E. Birren & K. W. Schaie (Eds.), *Handbook of the psychology of aging* (pp. 562–579). New York: Van Nostrand Reinhold.

Kliegl, R., Smith, J., & Baltes, P. B. (1986). Testing-the-limits, expertise, and memory in adulthood and old age. In F. Klix & H. Hagendorf (Eds.), *Human memory and cognitive capabilities.* North Holland: Elsevier.

Klocke, R. A. (1977). Influence of aging on the lung. In C. E. Finch & L. Hayflick (Eds.), *Handbook of the biology of aging* (pp. 432–444). New York: Van Nostrand Reinhold.

Kohn, R. R. (1977). Heart and cardiovascular system. In C. E. Finch & L. Hayflick (Eds.), *Handbook of the biology of aging* (pp. 281–317). New York: Van Nostrand Reinhold.

Lachman, J. L., Lachman, R., & Thronesberry, C. (1979). Metamemory through the adult life-span. *Developmental Psychology, 15,* 543–551.

Light, L. L., Zelinski, E. M., & Moore, M. (1982). Adult age differences in reasoning from new information. *Journal of Experimental Psychology: Learning, Memory, and Cognition, 8*(5), 435–447.

Lorden, R., Atkeson, B. M., & Pollack, R. H. (1979). Differences in the magnitude of the Belboeuf illusion and Usnadze effect during adulthood. *Journal of Gerontology, 34,* 229–233.

McFarland, R. A., & Fisher, M. B. (1955). Alterations in dark adaptation as a function of age. *Journal of Gerontology, 10,* 424–428.

McFarland, R. A., Domey, R. G., Warren, A. B., & Ward, D. C. (1960). Dark adaptation as a function of age: 1. A statistical analysis. *Journal of Gerontology, 15,* 149–154.

McKeown, T. (1978). Determinants of health. *Human Nature, 1,* 60–67.

Miller, E., & Lewis, P. (1977). Recognition memory in elderly patients with depression and dementia: A signal detection analysis. *Journal of Abnormal Psychology, 86,* 84–86.

Monge, R., & Hultsch, D. (1971). Paired associate learning as a function of adult age and the length of anticipation and inspection intervals. *Journal of Gerontology, 26,* 157–162.

Mortimer, J. A., Schuman, L. M., & French, L. R. (1981). Epidemiology of dementing illness. In J. A. Mortimer & L. M. Schuman (Eds.), *The epidemiology of dementia* (pp. 2–23). New York: Oxford University Press.

Norris, A., Mittmann, C., & Shock, N. W. (1964). Lung function in relation to age: Changes in ventilation with age. In L. Cander & J. H. Moyer (Eds.), *Aging of the lung* (p. 138). New York: Grune & Stratton.

Olsho, L. W., Harkins, S. W., & Lenhardt, M. L. (1985). Aging and the auditory system. In J. E. Birren & K. W. Schaie (Eds.), *Handbook of the psychology*

Chapter 3

Environment and the Need Satisfaction of the Aging

M. Powell Lawton

WHY BE CONCERNED ABOUT THE ENVIRONMENT?

It is necessary to be constantly aware of the two-way character of the transaction between a person and the environment. An objective environmental deficit is a deficit for anyone, but if the user is marginally independent, the impact of the deficit on behavior will be greater. This constitutes a statement of the environmental docility hypothesis (Lawton & Simon, 1968). Stated another way, an environmental feature that is not a defect for most users may constitute an impenetrable barrier for an impaired person. Thus, one can say that the elderly are, statistically speaking, more vulnerable to environmental pressures than the young. To the extent that they are solvent, healthy, and socially integrated, they will experience no differential impact from the environment.

The positive side of this vulnerability is that improvements in environmental quality may have a disproportionately favorable effect on impaired older people. Thus, our goal in seeking environmental interventions will be to find approaches to environmental design, conceptualization of theoretical models of person–environment transactions, and the administration of programs that take into account the kinds of deprivations and impairments

to which the older population is selectively vulnerable.

Vulnerable populations are much more likely to be impaired in significant ways than the aged population as a whole. Therefore, we must consider some of the basic dimensions of both person and environment that may help determine how well the patient will do in a particular health care setting. This chapter will discuss personal competences and needs and describe the environmental factors that will enhance the congruity of person and context.

PERSONAL COMPETENCES

One way of looking at people is to view them in terms of how well they perform the behaviors necessary for adequate everyday functioning. I have tried to classify these behaviors in terms of their complexity, as shown in Figure 3.1. I would argue that the most important aspects of the person are represented by these five domains of behavioral competence and that we cannot plan either a treatment or an environment adequately without having basic information about each domain. One example of an attempt to operationalize these domains in a standardized fashion is the Philadelphia Geriatric Center Multilevel Assess-

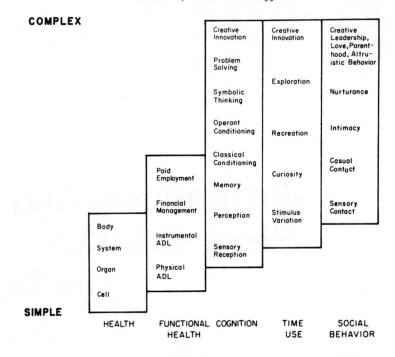

COMPLEX

SIMPLE

HEALTH   FUNCTIONAL COGNITION   TIME   SOCIAL
HEALTH   USE   BEHAVIOR

HIERARCHY OF BEHAVIORAL COMPETENCE

Figure 3.1. Hierarchy of behavioral competence. (From: "Assessment, Integration Environments for Older People" by M. P. Lawton, 1970, *The Gerontologist, 10*, p. 41. Copyright 1970 by The Gerontological Society of America. Reprinted by permission of *The Gerontologist*.)

ment Instrument (MAI), (Lawton, Moss, Fulcomer, & Kleban, 1982).

Standard assessment procedures do well by some of these functions and not by others. Clinical medical examinations and laboratory testing are carried out for every patient in most health care settings, and professional judgments about overall health are made. Thus, for the most part, biological health is adequately assessed. However, such evaluations are usually relatively unstructured, since we do not have good scales measuring the overall level of health.

Our assessment procedures do particularly well in what we might call "applied health," or functional health, that is, the activities of daily living (ADL). Almost everyone agrees on what the most important ADL are, and we have a variety of good scales to measure them: toileting, dressing, eating, ambulation, bathing, and grooming. A more complex set of behaviors is necessary if one is to live relatively independently: shopping, cooking, cleaning, laundering, telephoning, transporting, medicating, and managing money—the "instru-

mental activities of daily living" (Lawton & Brody, 1969).

Assessment of the next domain of behavioral competence, cognition, has also been well developed; there are many varieties of Mental Status Questionnaires (Kahn, Goldfarb, Pollack, & Peck, 1960), Mini-Mental State Examination (Folstein, Folstein, & McHugh, 1975), and other more sophisticated and complex measures of memory, information processing, and abstract thinking.

The more complex domains of time use and social behavior, by contrast, have been relatively neglected by many assessment efforts. In our preoccupation with psychopathology, diagnosis, and narrow medical treatment, it is easy to ignore the fact that a great deal of each person's day is spent in behaviors unrelated to the obligatory activities of health care and self-maintenance. The domain of time use attempts to account for discretionary activities other than social interaction. This domain, if the person is fortunate, includes hobbies, entertainment, and learning; sometimes the uses of time by the more vulnerable people are covered by such categories as "sitting and thinking," "looking out the window, " or "resting" (Lawton et al., 1982).

Finally, social behavior is something we are used to assessing when we ask for a list of relatives, the person's household composition, or the name of a confidant. It is important to recognize, however, that people's functioning social networks include friends (who are sometimes more important to the person's well-being than family), neighbors, health care staff, shopkeepers, and enemies, to name a few. In addition, the frequency of interaction, whether face-to-face or by phone, among many of these network members is an important class of information that we frequently omit.

The foregoing five domains constitute the bare minimum number of domains of behavioral competence that we need to assess. However, the kinds of behaviors one should assess vary somewhat according to the particular environment inhabited by the individual. The most widely used assessment instruments assume that the person is living in an ordinary community. Institutions, nursing homes, and many other residential types do not conform to the independent community model. Thus, in an institution it is possible that cooking or the use of public transportation may not be relevant, but constructs not included in most assessment instruments, such as "degree of observance of institutional schedules," might be important to measure. To an even greater extent, one may need to tailor the content of time use and social interaction to the environmental context. For example, the list of time-use activities obviously ought to reflect what is theoretically available; social behavior with a nursing-home roommate or with the foster-home owner might be explicitly inquired about. The fact that packaged instruments like the MAI do not exist for such environments means only that we ought to either add such content or, better yet, derive total instruments with the versatility to assess these special types of behavioral competence.

With respect to the environment, it is necessary to emphasize that there can be little useful characterization of the environment without simultaneously specifying the user. Therefore, the types of behavioral competences that I have described are an essential component of the way environment functions for any person. If we are to maximize the person's psychological well-being or adequacy of behavior, we shall need to know what

the person's behavioral strengths and weaknesses are before we attempt to specify a satisfying environment for the person. These competences may be thought of as having cognates in the environment; that is, the environment has characteristics that may act either as barriers or facilitators for the varieties of behavioral competence.

Two theoretical notions are relevant to the person-environment transaction: that of the press-competence model and that of person–environment congruence. The press-competence model, developed by Nahemow and myself (Lawton & Nahemow, 1973), suggests that for any given level of competence, no matter how low, there is a range of environmental press or demands within which the behavioral or effective outcome is favorable. Where demand is too great (or too low), maladaptive behavior or negative affect will ensue. Thus our task is to find environments that demand neither too little nor too much of a person.

The concept of person–environment congruence (French, Rodgers, & Cobb, 1974; Kahana, 1982) allows us to be more explicit in defining areas of match and nonmatch in a residential environment. Some examples will be cited of environmental attributes whose demands may be within or outside the range of optimal outcome. Table 3.1 shows some examples of limitations in competence. For each case, an environmental intervention that might enhance the outcome is given, as well as the environmental press that might be too strong or too weak.

One should note that what is called *environment* may be either a space, a physical structure, an object, an item of decor, another person, or the collective behavior of a number of people. Another useful general principle in discussing environmental issues is that the behavior of other individuals, the rules governing their behavior, and their organized activities may often provide alternative pathways to the same outcomes as those we attempt to facilitate by the design of the physical environment.

These examples are only illustrative. The abundant literature on the needs of older users (Hiatt, 1983; Koncelik, 1976, 1982; Lawton, 1975) provides in-depth analysis of ways in which the environments of the hospital, the nursing home, the foster home, the shared residence, congregate housing, and other types of long-term residential care may enhance the adaptive outcomes of older users. Another way of viewing the design task is to consider the following classes of environmental

Table 3.1. Examples of Optimal, Excessive, and Inadequate Environmental Demands

Domain	Behavioral Competence	ENVIRONMENTAL PRESS	
		Positive Outcome	Negative Outcome
Physical Health	Physical illness	Proximity to medical care	Medical care too distant The "sick milieu" is omnipresent because care is too near
	Susceptibility to infection	Aseptic housekeeping	Insufficient infection control Sterile social environment Segregation, isolation, and stigmatization of vulnerable
	Hearing problem	Hearing aid, with training in use	Sensory isolation Shouting, loud PA system
Activities of Daily Living	Ambulation in wheelchair only	Most resources located on one level of building	Barrier-laden environment So barrier-free that personal hands-on care is eliminated
Cognition	Can't remember own room	Multiple environmental markers for subject's room	Institutional sameness, lack of adornment Restriction of resident to limited area Staff anxiety, excessive surveillance
	Slow cognitive processing	Walks streets with companion or group; traffic signal installed	Traffic-hazard exposure Locked in house or yard—isolated
Time Use	Anergic, apathetic	Provide seating where action can be watched	Seat in bedroom Daily pressure to engage in group activities
	Stereotypical body rocking	Behavior therapy with sensory enhancement	Belted to chair Excessive staff attention
Social Interaction	Social withdrawal	Seating midway between active and private space	Bedroom at far end of hall Assigned to 4-bed room
	Moaning at night	Peripheral bedroom	Door closed Repeated scolding

attributes as attainable goals leading to person–environment congruence:

1. *Safety.* The ability of an environment to minimize accidents and hazards and to afford assistance should the need occur. Physical health is the most relevant of the several domains of behavioral competence.
2. *Security.* The ability of the environment to provide psychological reassurance that safety and other personal needs will be met. Security, thus, subsumes the psychological aspect of maintaining physical health but also includes non-health-related security needs.
3. *Accessibility.* The ability of the environment to afford entry, transport, and the use of its resources. Most of the functional health, time-

use, and social behaviors are facilitated by accessibility.

4. *Legibility.* The ability of the environment to be comprehended by the person, whether through signs, denotative objects, or patterned stimuli. While cognitive competence is specifically enhanced by increased legibility, many other types of competent behavior are amplified by making the environment understandable and predictable.

For the most part, safety, security, accessibility, and legibility serve the most basic varieties of competence. These attributes are related only indirectly to time use and social competence. My recent thinking about the difference between the basic and the more complex manifestations of

Table 3.2. Adaptive Maneuvers with Active or Passive Individual Roles and Individual or Environmental Points of Application

Point of Application	Passive responder	Active initiator
Environment	Social and environmental engineering	Environment redesigned by individual
Individual	Rehabilitation, prosthesis	Self-therapy, growth

competence has been directed by earlier theoretical work in gerontology (Anderson, 1959; Carp, 1984; Lieberman & Tobin, 1983), by the long tradition of theory in the psychology of stimulation (Berlyne, 1978; Wohlwill, 1966), and by the many demonstrations of the importance of personal control in the lives of people in general (deCharms, 1968; Rotter, 1966; Seligman, 1975) and older people in particular (Langer & Rodin, 1976; Schulz, 1976).

The major point of this turn of thought is that not all behavior is explained or controlled by environmental forces (see Lawton, in press, for a more complete discussion of this issue). Far from being pawns, older people engage in active behavior by choosing what is desirable or relevant from all that exists in the "environment out there." An even more active level is to create an environment of one's own choice. Table 3.2 illustrates four varieties of change, initiated by the individual himself or externally. This dimension forms a fourfold typology with the question of whether the change is applied to the person or to his/her environment. A great deal of the literature about environment and aging has dealt with cell A, where experts design environments that act upon the person. We need to give much more consideration to cell B, where the older person constructs his own environment.

The environmental docility hypothesis deals with cell A. The lower a person's competence, the greater the influence of the environment on outcome. Several years ago Carp (1984) called attention to the passivity inherent in the idea that one could enhance or diminish the adaptive quality of a person's behavior by the design of the environment; she suggested that a complementary statement was needed about enriching and active behaviors. She thus incorporated a series of active intrapersonal processes, preferences, and a conjunctive set of environmental facets which she called *resources* into the press-competence theoretical framework. Carp rightly suggested that an entire neglected aspect of person–environment congruence described processes by which personal

needs and preferences were met by resources in the environment, which were actively chosen and manipulated through behaviors more complex than those involved in life maintenance. At around the same time, Lieberman and Tobin (1983), in examining the extent to which characteristics of the receiving environment were associated with adaptation among relocated older mental hospital patients, found results diametrically opposed to the environmental docility hypothesis; that is, environmental characteristics were associated with later adaptation *only* among those who had originally shown themselves more competent. It is of interest that these significantly predictive dimensions were the extent to which the new environment fostered achievement and independence and provided warmth and cue richness. Each of these attributes is clearly in that resource category.

I should therefore like to suggest the environmental proactivity hypothesis as a way of stating this other side of person–environment transactions: As competence increases, the environment becomes a potential source of increasing diversity in the person's ability to satisfy needs. In the Lawton and Nahemow (1973) model, the environmental dimension may need to be renamed *environmental richness*, defined as a mixture of positive and negative press. This revision allows us to view higher values on the environment scale as implying both greater strength and greater diversity of press. It also implies that greater personal competence is in itself associated with the likelihood that the person's behavioral space is richer, more demanding, but also more potentially satisfying.

The docility and proactivity conceptions underline what I see as a basic dialectic in conceptualizing services for the elderly: support versus autonomy. Decline and deprivation demand support, but the human spirit demands autonomy. The view that either aspect of this duality tells the whole story is sheer fantasy. Protective environments, such as institutions, were not constructed to crush the human spirit but to attempt to adjust the average press level of vulnerable people to one consistent with their competences. Our errors have come in assuming that all forms of press are negative and that autonomy ends once competence is low enough to require a specialized environment.

My colleagues who have worked within the congruence framework—Carp (1984), Kahana (1982), and Kiyak (1978), for example—have specified analogous person and environmental attributes that extend the concepts of personal autonomy richness. On the person side these attributes extend upward from competence on two higher order dimensions: complexity, which is represented in my hierarchy of behavioral competence, and efficacy, the extent to which the behavior is initiated by the person. As complexity and efficacy increase, it becomes more difficult to characterize qualities of persons as competence. At lower levels of complexity, the norms for competent behavior in spheres of physical health, functional health, and cognition are relatively clear.

In the more complex areas, behavior is more discretionary and the norms are more ambiguous. Not everyone must use time efficiently or in an enriching way, nor must everyone display a high level of social interaction. People vary in the extent to which they wish to engage in such behavior. Thus the concepts of *need* (Carp, 1984) and *preference* (Kahana, 1982; Kiyak, 1978) recognize the discretionary nature of complex behavior and the fact that people in how salient to their well-being are opportunities to behave in these more complex ways. The set of needs and preferences may be thought of as presenting *enrichment*, as contrasted with the behaviors discussed as competence.

The more complex levels of competence merge into the sphere of enrichment. Cognition, for example, includes discretionary *learning* for its own sake or self-selected learning that enlarges one's competence beyond the point merely necessary for continued adaptive behavior. *Aesthetic experience* and other forms of stimulus variety have a strong cognitive component and are often actively sought by the person: aesthetic pursuits may also constitute an important time use. The cluster of social behaviors may be differentiated into discretionary elements, such as the need for *privacy*, for *solitude*, for affective *affiliation*, and *social contact*. Finally, although *autonomy* and *efficacy* are needs that may be ultimately served by the satisfaction of many of the other needs mentioned or by the successful exercise of competent behavior, the need for effi-

Table 3.3. Examples of Environmental Resources that Serve Four Needs/Preferences

Need/Preference Domain	Environmental Resource
Learning	Graphics, denoting room use Current events Bulletin board
Aesthetics/Stimulation	Textural variation Side lighting in halls
Social Interaction Regulation	Informal seating near natural traffic Space for two-person privacy Space for solitude
Control/Effectance	Space for personal displays Residents' decor committee

cacy (or control) may exist as a general overall need and thus is designated as a need/preference domain in its own right.

The needs thus mentioned constitute only a small number of those that appear in the need systems of Murray (1938) and others. The ones discussed here were chosen because they have logical environmental cognates and thus afford the possibility of assessing person–environment congruence.

Using the residential long-term care continuum as the focus of examples, Table 3.3 provides some example of specific preferences, along with examples of environmental resources that might satisfy them. In the case of preference, the barrier is most often the simple absence of the resource.

Comparing Tables 3.1 and 3.3 one can see that the boundary between environmental design features that compensate for losses and those that enrich is often uncertain. The ultimate effect of providing compensations is to broaden the range and complexity of stimuli that can be comfortably managed, and this is what is defined by enrichment. Proactivity is illustrated particularly in the last entries in Table 3.3 but it can be seen in every domain of personal competence and preference, regardless of the person's level of competence. Our institutional practices too often ignore this principle. In fact, through such practices as mandating or encouraging glossy surfaces, hospital beds, or pastel colors, the entire thrust of regulations in the service of cleanliness, order, and cost cutting has worked directly against affording opportunities for the exercise of personal efficacy. Beyond these physical limitations on design friendliness is an even more negatively influential set of restrictions on how the spaces and structures may be used. It is extremely difficult for a resident to have a sense of personal agency in how his environment is arranged in the face of tradition that assumes his incompetence. The excessive standardization and sanitization of the medical model persists in hundreds of ways that are disaffirming to the aging resident's feelings of personal competence.

One ought to begin with the simple task of attempting to determine preferences. This is not an easy task, given the inarticulateness of many residents, the long-accepted widespread assumption that it is imprudent to express personal opinions in a bureaucracy, and the actual impossibility of querying those who are grossly cognitively impaired. Direct-care staff need to be trained to elicit preferences from the resident, to learn to persist in such questioning, and to create a conversational milieu for such inquiry that minimizes any feeling of threat. It is probable that there is more to be discovered about how to determine the choices of impaired people as well, for example, by providing actual choices rather than merely asking for verbal expressions of hypothetical choices.

There are many more degrees of freedom for environmental choice within purpose-built long-term-care settings than are usually exercised. Sometimes it is possible to discern a generalized preference for some particular alternative and to build that alternative into a design. Sometimes one is surprised by the results of such an endeavor, however, as in a survey by Duffy, Bailey, and Beck (1982) of small groups of nursing-home residents, nursing-home administrators, and design students about preferences for design and furnishings. Administrators and designers generally agreed in their preferences for a social arrangement of lounge furniture, four-person dining-room tables, free seating in the dining room, rotating tablemates, and personal as well as institutional furniture. The residents in each of these cases preferred the private (or "sociofugal," Sommer, 1969) arrangement and the externally imposed control. The first conclusion is that it is risky to impose experts' choices across the board. These findings also illustrate quite well the dilemma of allowing preference to be satisfied, on the one hand, and on the other, imposing on a client an environment that we think will achieve therapeutic or prosthetic goals even if it is not satisfying to the client.

More often one needs to think of variations that can be managed on a one-to-one basis, such as the choice of room furniture, objects to keep in one's room, and wall hangings. It should be within the realm of possibility to extend such choices to the color of the room paint, the scheduling of some activities, or the staking out of personal territory in a common space, an outdoor location, or a garden patch.

In a recent study of impaired older people receiving services in their homes in the community, we identified a very strong compulsion to create what we called a *control center* (Saperstein, Lawton, Moleski, & Sharp, 1984). This behavior illustrates best what some of the priorities of such people are, as well as the ingenuity that is possible in shaping one's environment to meet personal needs, such as security, learning, stimulation, and social regulation. A control center consists of a favorite chair in the living room oriented towards the window and the door. Full surveillance of these security-relevant areas is thus easy, as is, frequently, the view of other people on the street. The television is near enough to operate. There are usually tables on both sides of the chair, containing telephone, medication, reading matter, and sometimes food and drink, photographs, or favorite objects.

We need to translate this compulsion to be environmentally proactive into the way we run our institutional care. Granted, it is more difficult to achieve proactivity in the nursing home than in a private home. We should view the task of promoting proactivity as a challenge, whether it be in a hospital ward, a nursing home, or a community residence. We need to be creative both in thinking of environmental features that can be shaped by the person and in devising ways of influencing the people who prescribe how the environment will be used, whether these people be the writers of regulations, medical-center directors, nurses, foster-home operators, or any of the many other figures involved in providing institutional care.

CONCLUSION

In summary, assessment is necessary in order to establish boundaries for what can be expected from the person. For the most part, assessment reflects the outcomes given a current environmental press-resource level and therefore may frequently represent the minimum boundary. In its present state, the art of assessment is not equal to the task of measuring the person's potential for autonomy, efficacy, and environmental proactivity. We should assume once more that these potentials are likely to be underestimated in the institutional environment. Our task is to develop our sensitivity to the ways in which opportunities for environmental proactivity may be increased by increasing both environmental variety and the human social milieus that support proactivity.

REFERENCES

Anderson, J. E. (1959). The use of time and energy. In J. E. Birren (Ed.), *Handbook of aging and the individual* (pp. 769–796). Chicago: University of Chicago Press.

Berlyne, D. E. (1978). Curiosity and learning. *Motivation and Emotion, 2,* 97–175.

Carp, F. (1984). A complementary/congruence model of well-being or mental health for the commuity elderly. In I. Altman, M. P. Lawton, & J. Wohlwill (Eds.), *Human behavior and the environment: The elderly and the physical environment.* New York: Plenum Press.

deCharms, R. (1968). *Personal causation.* New York: Academic Press.

Duffy, M., Bailey, S., & Beck, B. (1982, August). *Architectural design and preventive mental health in nursing homes.* Paper presented at the annual meeting of the American Psychological Association, Washington, DC.

Folstein, M. F., Folstein, S. E., & McHugh, P. R. (1975). Mini-Mental State: A practical method for grading the cognitive state of patients for the clinician. *Journal of Psychiatric Research, 12,* 189–198.

French, J. P. R., Rodgers, W., & Cobb, S. (1974). Adjustment as person-environment fit. In G. V. Coelho, D. A. Hamburg, & J. E. Adams (Eds.), *Coping and adaptation* (pp. 316–333). New York: Basic Books.

Hiatt, L. G. (1983). Environmental design and the frail older person at home. *Price Institute Journal of Long-Term Home Health Care, 2,* 13–22.

Kahana, E. (1982). A congruence model of person-environment interaction. In M. P. Lawton, P. G. Windley, & T. O. Byerts (Eds.), *Aging and the environment: Theoretical approaches* (pp. 97–121). New York: Springer.

Kahn, R. L. Goldfarb, A. I., Pollack, M., & Peck, A. (1960). Brief objective measures for the determination of mental status in the aged. *American Journal of Psychiatry, 117,* 326–328.

Kiyak, H. A. (1978). A multidimensional perspective on privacy preferences of institutionalized elderly. In W. E. Rogers & W. H. Ittlelson (Eds.), *New directions in environmental research.* Tempe: University of Arizona Press.

Koncelik, J. A. (1976). *Designing the open nursing home.* Stroudsburg, PA: Dowden, Hutchinson and Ross.

Koncelik, J. A. (1982). *Aging and the product environment.* Stroudsburg, PA: Hutchinson and Ross.

Langer, E., & Rodin, J. (1976). The effects of choice and enhanced personal responsibility for the aged. *Journal of Personality and Social Psychology, 34,* 191–198.

Lawton, M. P. (1970). Assessment, integration, and environments for older people. *Gerontologist, 10,* 38–46.

Lawton, M. P. (1975). *Planning and managing housing for the elderly.* New York: Wiley-Interscience.

Lawton, M. P. (in press). Metaphors of environmental influences on aging. In J. E. Thornton (Ed.), *Aging as metaphor.* Vancouver: University of British Columbia Press.

Lawton, M. P., & Brody, E. (1969). Assessment of older people: Self-maintaining and instrumental activities of daily living. *Gerontologist, 9,* 179–185.

Lawton, M. P., Moss, M., Fulcomer, M., & Kleban, M. H. (1982). A research and service-oriented Multilevel Assessment Instrument. *Journal of Gerontology, 37,* 91–99.

Lawton, M. P., & Nahemow, L. (1973). Ecology and the aging process. In C. Eisdorfer & M. P. Lawton (Eds.), *Psychology of adult development and aging* (pp. 619–674). Washington, DC: American Psychological Association.

Lawton, M. P., & Simon, B. (1968). The ecology of social relationships in housing for the elderly. *Gerontologist, 8,* 108–115.

Lieberman, M. A., & Tobin, S. S. (1983). *The experience of old age.* New York: Basic Books.

Murray, H. A. (1938). *Explorations in personality.* New York: Oxford University Press.

Rotter, J. B. (1966). Generalized expectancies for internal versus external control of reinforcement. *Psychological Monographs, 80* (1, Whole No. 609).

Saperstein, A., Lawton, M. P., Moleski, W. H., & Sharp, A. (1984). *A housing quality component for in-home services.* Philadelphia: Philadelphia Corporation for the Aging.

Schulz, R. (1976). Effects of control and predictability on the physical and psychological well-being of the institutionalized aged. *Journal of Personality and Social Psychology, 33,* 563–573.

Seligman, M. E. (1975). *Helplessness: On depression, development and death.* San Francisco: Freeman.

Sommer, R. (1969). *Personal space.* Englewood Cliffs, NJ: Prentice-Hall.

Wohlwill, J. F. (1966). The physical environment: A problem for a psychology of stimulation. *Journal of Social Issues, 22,* 29–38.

Part II

Psychiatric Disorders

The incidence of mental health problems increases with age. An understanding of the clinical picture of these problems and their prevalence and consequences will allow the practitioner to make informed decisions about treatment. This section covers the most common disorders of senescence—depression, paranoia, and dementia—as well as some less common but highly significant problems, such as alcohol abuse and sexual dysfunction. The disorders and their treatments are discussed.

Chapter 4

Paranoid and Schizophrenic Disorders Among the Aging

Felix Post

CURTAIN RAISER

Some workers are of the opinion that schizophrenic disorders always originate in early or middle adult life and that when they are encountered in older people they represent the end states of chronic or recurrent psychoses. Long-term follow-up of schizophrenics has shown that they have a much higher death rate, but with increasing age, the psychotic symptoms are much ameliorated in surviving patients. Increasing numbers of these survivors can now be found in the community, rather than in institutions. Although they may exhibit only a few and largely encapsulated symptoms, they tend to remain seriously impaired in terms of social status and interpersonal relationships (Ciompi, 1980; Post, 1980). By contrast, there is general agreement that paranoid disorders arise mostly in later adult life, sometimes in association with organic cerebral disease, but more often as a personality development or illness in cerebrally unimpaired persons. The schizophrenias are still an ill-defined group of mental disorders, and their relationship to paranoid conditions is under frequent and heated discussion.

In what follows I shall concentrate on paranoid disorders. Their symptomatology tends to be confined to overvalued ideas, delusions, and hallucinations. Clinical experience is almost entirely limited to the more severely ill patients, who are suffering either delusions, hallucinations, or both. In the past, late-life illnesses with persistent paranoid delusions and hallucinations were incurable. Both these symptoms have proved to be largely sensitive to suppression by major tranquilizing (ataractic) drugs. The results of treatment with elderly paranoid patients are now even better than those achieved in the case of most younger schizophrenics.

PARANOID DELUSIONS

Rather interestingly, the word *paranoia* is first encountered in Greek law, denoting the disturbed and deteriorated mental state of old men that entitled sons to take over the management of their fathers' affairs. *Paranoia* later came to be used in the different sense of craziness associated with fixed and clearly pathological beliefs, technically called *delusions*. Paranoiacs are very rarely encountered in psychiatric practice. They harbor a single delusion, usually supported by a few additional false beliefs, but they otherwise evidence neither psychiatric symptoms nor gross and obvious aberrations of conduct. The great majority of deluded patients are, however, more generally disordered than paranoics. Their delusions are varied, widespread, and similar to those of paranoiacs; hence the term *paranoid* (Lewis, 1970).

Delusions were originally conceptualized as unshakable false beliefs arising in the patient's mind as a sudden illumination, which the doctor could not explain in terms of the patient's life situation or psychological mechanisms. "True" delusions were thought to occur only in the setting of a schizophrenic process or of certain cerebral disorders, for example, in the course of some epilepsies. When delusions occurred in other mental illnesses, it seemed always possible to derive their origin and content from the patient's situation, psychological difficulties, or prevailing abnormal mood. False beliefs of this kind were distinguished from true delusions by employing the term *delusional ideas*. We shall not enter into the complex relationship between delusional ideas and overvalued ideas (McKenna, 1984), which are fixed and dominating convictions. They usually occur in abnormal personalities, but are sometimes encountered in normal people, whose lives are completely taken up by religious concepts, political ideas, or excessively idealistic beliefs. Being in love can also become an overvalued idea. Regardless of content, overvalued ideas are occasionally the precursors of delusional ideas, and in a given case psychopathological exploration may fail to achieve a clear differentiation. However, delusional ideas always occur in a setting of developing or established mental illness.

Let us now turn from these theoretical and somewhat conjectural matters to clinical reality. In doing so, the following points must be made. The false and unshakable beliefs of older people coming to psychiatric notice always take the form of delusional ideas rather than of true delusions. To avoid the charge of being pedantic, I shall in the remainder of this chapter always employ the term *delusions* in the general and imprecise sense. In content, the delusions of younger patients are highly varied, ranging from beliefs of being identical with a deity or a saint, being royal or of royal descent, or being loved or envied to the conviction of having been unjustly treated during litigations or in employment or of being interfered with in one's possessions, love relationships or marriage (morbid jealousy). By contrast to what is found in younger patients, in the psychopathology of the elderly, *paranoid* is synonymous with *deluded* in a persecutory fashion. Moreover, the content of the delusions is almost exclusively related to domestic surroundings, as we shall see from the discussion of the various paranoid syndromes.

HALLUCINATIONS

False sensory perceptions have been categorized as illusions, pseudohallucinations, and true hallucinations; in addition, there are true hallucinations that are thought to be pathognomonic for schizophrenia. Not only are these distinctions largely of academic interest, but more important, they cannot often be achieved in older mentally disordered patients with whom, for various reasons, verbal communication tends to be difficult. Precise descriptions of their symptoms are therefore often impossible to obtain.

In psychogeriatric practice, visual hallucinations are the most common form of false sensory perceptions. In a recent study (Berrios & Brook 1984), they were found in 29% of the cases and were not related in frequency to age, sex, or psychiatric diagnosis. They were, however, often associated with delusions and with eye pathology. Hallucinations of touch, smell, or taste are also sometimes encountered, but less frequently than auditory hallucinations (noises, voices). Auditory hallucinations are almost always associated, sooner or later, with delusions. Although they occur more frequently in deaf persons, they also appear in patients not afflicted with any demonstrable cerebral pathology. The false visual perceptions of old people with eye trouble, most often caused by cataracts, by blindfolding following the removal of cataracts, or by retinal degeneration, tend to occur when vision is impaired rather than during the stage of complete blindness. The patients either immediately or very soon realize that their visual hallucinations do not originate in objects or persons of the environment but are due to their eye condition. As in the case of recently bereaved persons, who not infrequently "see" their lost loved ones, the visual hallucinations of visually impaired old people hardly ever signal mental illness. Similarly, deaf persons are often merely amused or annoyed by the noises or music they hear in their ears, but in this case, delusional elaborations are probably more frequent. We shall see that deafness is a well-documented factor of paranoid illnesses, both in the young and in the old.

PARANOID SYMPTOMATOLOGY

Three separate kinds of paranoid clinical pictures were defined by me in a consecutive series of patients over 60 who had been under my care because of persistent persecutory states. In all instances, the onset of their illnesses had occurred a few months or years before their admission into this 1966 study (Post, 1980). The existence of these three patterns of paranoid symptomatology has since been confirmed by others (e.g., Grahame, 1984). Because nowadays paranoid symptomatology is suppressed or much modified by drug therapy, it is no longer possible to follow its natural course, but from retrospective accounts given by friends and relatives it seems likely that these three kinds of clinical pictures do not present stages in the development of the condition and that in each case the symptom pattern remains largely unchanged over time. It is important to note that all three are seen in a great variety of psychiatric illnesses, both with and without obvious brain pathology, and for this reason the three hallucinatory–delusional symptom complexes will be described first and the psychiatric conditions in which they occur later.

Simple Paranoid Symptom Patterns

The clinical pictures under this heading are called simple because they contain only one or two pathological features. Even more than in other paranoid disorders of old age, delusions and hallucinations are largely confined to the patient's domestic and family environment. For instance, a patient may complain that noises are created in neighboring apartments or that machinery has been installed to annoy her.[1] Children are encouraged to engage in noisy behavior underneath her windows. Food is being stolen from her store. During her absence her rooms are entered and her belongings are disarranged, sometimes stolen. Less often, relatives are accused of talking maliciously behind her back, of hatching some plot, of purloining sums of money, or of interfering with financial arrangements. Often, very dangerously, a husband may accuse his aged wife of being

unfaithful; suspicious stains are looked for and pointed out. Much more rarely, the old person believes her home and person to be infested (delusional parasitosis), scratches continuously, claims to see bugs on or under her skin, and alarms the sanitary authorities.

Some of these paranoid symptoms are never discovered during the patient's life, as she may think that to divulge her observations would prove too dangerous. For instance, the relatives of an old man in my wider acquaintance discovered after his death a meticulously kept diary concerning a man following him about, making signs, and implying threats. In most instances, the families try to deal with the accusations and complaints by humoring the patients. Quite often, the patient repeatedly complains to the police, who take a similar line and, like the relatives, regard the patient as a rather odd old person developing some strange ideas in his dotage. Doctors and psychiatrists are rarely consulted, and then only when the patience of the family, neighbors, and police has become exhausted.

By contrast, the other two types of paranoid pathology very soon lead to disturbed behavior and medical referral. First discussed will be paranoid schizophreniform psychoses, then conditions that are practically identical with the paranoid schizophrenias of younger subjects.

Schizophreniform Pictures

With schizophreniform symptomatology, patients suffer not just from a single delusional belief, possibly with a few ramifications and related hallucinations. Simple paranoid symptoms tend to be confined to certain situations, for example, when the patient is alone in her home. In schizophreniform illnesses, symptoms are widespread, and tend to disturb patients almost continuously during the day as they go about their activities and at night when they try to sleep. They become distressed, frightened, accusatory, and even aggressive. They may shout from their windows, and very soon, especially in industrial-urban societies, cases will be brought to medical attention.

At this stage, patients are likely to look disheveled, anxious, agitated, or perplexed. They will overwhelm the doctor with tirades concerning the persecutions to which they are being subjected.

---

[1] Here and later, in describing various symptoms, I shall refer mainly to female patients, not for sexist reasons, but because in old age paranoid conditions are far more common in women than in men.

However, sometimes they may be calm but hostile, denying the behavior and complaints that had been reported by their friends. Dissimulation of all symptoms may also occur in patients with more restricted, simple paranoid conditions, but in the case of both disorders, it is usually abandoned when prompting friends or relatives are asked to join the interview. The content of these psychoses is varied and multiform, and a full recital of the delusions and hallucinations along with related conduct disorders would be tedious. To render the flavor, a few examples will be given from the case histories of patients who have been under my care.

One patient claims there is a conspiracy in the house to get her out of her apartment: she is envied or disliked because of her aloofness. She is being observed through a hole bored into the wall or through a special optical apparatus in the ceiling. Gases or nasty smells are pumped into her room. The electricity supply is interfered with. Obscene names are shouted at her from next door, or even when she is walking along the street.

Another patient gathers from hints or from wrongly interpreted remarks that she is regarded as a former member of a gang of thieves. She is being followed; signs are made. Police cars are continuously passing her house. Headlights are made to shine into her room.

Not uncommonly, patients feel they are being accused of sexual misconduct; for example, she claims she is being called a tart, obscene pictures are projected onto her wall, or, in a more disguised fashion, phallic objects, like cigar-shaped balloons, appear illuminated in the night sky. To return to a more domestic setting, children are heard crying underneath the floorboards, even sometimes emerging to run around the room. Television sets speak, or involve the patient in the actions shown on the screen.

Here again the psychopathological content is banal, related to petit bourgeois chicaneries or quarrels; certainly it is understandable in terms of fantasies or superstitions of ordinary folk.

Paranoid Schizophrenic States

In addition to the phenomena just described, patients in this subgroup also exhibit symptoms that psychiatrists have recently come to regard as of first-rank importance in diagnosing schizophrenia for the purposes of research and epidemiological comparisons. In the elderly, not all first-rank symptoms are readily demonstrated. Prominent symptoms tend to be feelings of passivity (outside influences causing sensations, movements, speech), thought withdrawal, thought insertion, and thought reading. The easiest to ascertain is a form of auditory hallucinosis in which the patient hears herself referred to by name or, more commonly, as "she",—that is, in the third person singular. Typically, several voices discuss the patient or conduct a running commentary on her activities, which they seem to be able to observe from next door or even over long distances.

The content of these psychotic experiences is often more bizarre than that reported by old people with only schizophreniform symptomatology. A parson of the patient's acquaintance, now a bishop in South Africa, squeezes her leg and produces sexual sensations inside her. The archangel Michael touches another patient with a feather from his wings to signify to her that she is good. Legs are made to move by electricity or radio waves. Thoughts are believed to be read, as voices are heard repeating them or replying to them. More often the voices discuss the patient: "She is a dirty old woman." "No, she keeps herself very nicely." Or they engage in a running commentary: "Now she is heating up her soup." "It smells pretty good." "I am surprised she can eat that much."

I have given examples of paranoid symptomatology under three separate headings because of the convenience for the purposes of description. In clinical practice, however, simple paranoid, schizophreniform, and schizophrenic delusions and hallucinations are all equally suppressed by major tranquilizing drugs. Only one personal observation, which thus far has not been confirmed by other researchers, may be of practical importance. I have found that ongoing simple paranoid and schizophreniform symptoms quite often disappear as soon as patients are moved into protected surroundings, like a relative's home or a hospital. In addition, they may not reappear over long periods of time. On the other hand, paranoid schizophrenic symptoms never recede into the background, and the patient will describe here-and-now experiences in the doctor's office and after admission to a hospital. In the case of patients with only simple paranoid or schizophrenic clinical pictures, it may be difficult to decide whether drug treatment has any effect before the patient has been allowed to return to her own home.

A discussion of the various psychiatric illnesses

in which one of the three types of paranoid symptomatology may occur follows.

ORGANIC BRAIN SYNDROMES

Hallucinosis is usually a prominent feature of acute brain syndromes, that is, of delirious states. In a setting of impaired and fluctuating awareness, the patient is frightened or, more rarely, amused by sensory experiences, mainly visual, of a very simple and unstructured kind: for example, floating colored patterns, colored animals, or repetitive noises. In less acutely confused and disturbed mental states, the hallucinosis may be more complex, consisting of such dreamlike experiences as animals crawling on the body, barroom scenes (in alcoholics), or persecution by the police. It seems likely that these kinds of false sensory perceptions are due to cerebral-releasing mechanisms, rather than to anything that might operate in schizophrenia. On the other hand, the longer-lasting brain syndromes without marked alterations of awareness, as seen in some chronic alcoholics and amphetamine addicts, may carry a symptomatology clinically indistinguishable from that of paranoid schizophrenia; these are rarely seen in older persons, in whom acute brain syndromes are much more often caused by physical illness. Possibly, the brief paranoid states seen in healthy old people after they have been transferred to unfamiliar surroundings occur as a display of temporary confusion and thus are akin to the hallucinoses resulting from sensory deprivation.

Far more common and important are paranoid symptoms occurring in the course of chronic brain syndromes. In younger persons, apart from alcoholism, paranoid and schizophrenic symptoms are mainly encountered in the course of temporal lobe epilepsy. In the aged, paranoid phenomena of all kinds are often seen in dementia, especially with Alzheimer's cerebral pathology. The simplest but most commonly encountered paranoid symptoms occur where an old dement hides her belongings, cannot find them again, and then accuses others of having stolen them. More complex paranoid states may also be seen, such as delusions concerning the spouse's fidelity, as well as schizophreniform or paranoid schizophrenic symptoms. The presence of impaired memory and loss of intellectual abilities may be difficult to demonstrate at first, but in the course of a few months the dementia will progress, with increasing cognitive impairment causing a gradual fading of the paranoid admixtures.

AFFECTIVE PSYCHOSES

Severe depressive illnesses, especially when they affect rigid, shut-in, and suspicious people, are often complicated or heavily overlaid by paranoid or even schizophrenic symptoms. Delusions of theft or poisoning may occur. The patient may believe that she is shunned because of unpleasant body odour. There may be more elaborate delusions of persecution by the authorities for imagined transgressions, like tax frauds or, in the case of female patients, abortions induced many years before. As a rule, these delusions and sometimes associated hallucinations are clearly secondary to the pervasive depressive mood, and to its content of ideas of poverty and guilt. Sometimes, however, the depression may be difficult to detect. There is also a small number of elderly patients whose illness might be labeled as schizoaffective because both schizophreniform and schizophrenic features are seen concurrently with depression or because depressive breakdowns alternate with seemingly schizophrenic episodes (Post, 1971).

Aged manics are often not clearly elated and euphoric but more haughty, hostile, and resentful. Paranoid symptoms may then for a time overshadow flights of ideas and overactivity. Diagnosis may be difficult because both manic and depressive paranoid symptoms are suppressed by major tranquilizers. In the case of depression, any schizophrenia-like symptoms are only slightly modified by these drugs, and they disappear only after the basic condition has been successfully treated with antidepressant remedies.

SENILE SECLUSION

Senile seclusion, an interesting condition on the border of paranoid illnesses, is of some importance for geriatric services.

Earlier surveys of old people living in their own homes had found that some of them, possibly around 4%, were vigorous, apparently happy, but definitely eccentric. That the picture was not always such a rosy one was shown in a paper (Granick & Zeman, 1960) based on sensational and lurid newspaper stories reporting the discovery of over 100 senile recluses. By their nature, recluses are difficult to investigate, and I am aware of only a few studies. In a community search, MacMillan and Shaw (1966) found an annual incidence rate of only 0.5 case per 1,000 persons over 60. Only half survived after admission to a geriatric hospital long enough to undergo psychological and psychiatric investigation by Clark, Mankikar, and Gray (1975). These researchers suggested the eye-catching eponymous diagnostic label of Diogenes syndrome, which is, however, a misnomer. True enough, Diogenes lived in a dog kennel, but he was also the founder of the Cynic (doglike) school of philosophy and as such would walk around the crowded Athenian agora in broad daylight carrying a lighted lantern, saying that he was looking for honest men.

In stark contrast, senile recluses shun people. They had always been eccentric and withdrawn loners, but with the approach of old age, they virtually shut themselves up in their homes, seldom venturing out (dressed in rags when they do), possibly receiving occasional supplies from one relative, who is never allowed to cross the threshold. After some years, neighbors, concerned one day by peculiar smells or the cessation of signs of life, call the authorities, who force open the door. The recluse is found dead or very ill, often suffering from hypothermia in winter, and in a very dirty condition, in indescribably neglected and poverty-stricken surroundings. In fact, large sums of money are often found hidden away; the recluse is usually ascertained as having come from a comfortable middle-class background and, when able to be tested, having, at the very least, average intelligence. In some cases, the patients may be undiagnosed schizophrenics, or senile dementia with paranoid features may have supervened. In many cases, no formal psychiatric diagnosis seems appropriate. It seems likely that in these cases one is dealing with an extreme form of senile character development with long-standing overvalued ideas of wishing to live in isolation from other human beings. A relationship of this condition to paranoid disorders is suggested by the occasional occurrence of a folie à deux. Sometimes seclusion is shared with another submissive person, usually a sibling, who proves otherwise quite normal and able to resume an ordinary civilized existence once freed from the domination by the patient. The recluse herself (evidence as to sex distribution is conflicting), if still physically fit, may also prove rehabilitable.

SENILE PARAPHRENIA

In one of the early modern investigations into the mental illnesses of old people, Roth and Morrissey (1952) had noted that among 150 consecu-

tively admitted patients aged 60 and over, there were 12 with paranoid delusions and hallucinations, occurring in clear consciousness and not associated with organic dementia or with depression. They had also reported that the disorder was paraphrenic in type, and in a further study Roth (1955) suggested the term *late paraphrenia*. Patients with this condition were, unlike late-life depressives, rarely discharged from the hospital. In contrast to patients with chronic brain syndrome, they remained alive and healthy for many years. The dubious nature of the concept of paraphrenia, which I discussed again quite recently (Post, 1984), was well known to Roth. He had applied it only for descriptive purposes: an illness characterized by paranoid delusions and hallucinations without any schizophrenic deterioration of affect, formal thinking, or psychomotor functions. All the same, the condition was conceptualized as a late form of schizophrenia (Kay & Roth, 1961).

By careful cognitive assessment it is not difficult as a rule to differentiate between senile paraphrenia and organic mental condition with paranoid features. In one study (Post, 1966), the latter was initially diagnosed in 17 patients out of 61 followed over 3 years and confirmed in the case of 13. Only 1 patient later appeared to be a dement, unexpectedly. On the other hand, a follow-up study over a period of 10 to 25 years (Kay, 1962) had shown that, in contrast to what is generally reported for depressives, dementia had supervened in the course of late paraphrenia more frequently than "expected" (in 20% of the cases). These findings were obtained at a time when no effective treatment was available, and they are not now of any practical importance.

In my early study (Post, 1966), out of a total of 93 patients, 24% had exhibited only a simple paranoid psychopathology, 40% were classified as schizophreniform, and 36% were classified as paranoid schizophrenic. However, this group of patients was treated at a university clinic and not really representative: None had been compulsorily admitted, and, as previously mentioned, some had organic cerebral disorders. More recently, Grahame (1984) investigated a series of patients consecutively admitted to a mental hospital from its catchment areas. All paranoid patients were cerebrally intact and not suffering from a primary affective illness. Moreover, Grahame was able to make use of various methods standardized for eliciting and precisely defining psychopathology, which had been introduced since my more impressionistic clinical study. He ascertained a rather larger proportion of patients with first-rank symptoms of paranoid schizophrenia, 14 out of 25, but because of the different sizes of our two samples, the preponderance of true schizophrenics found by him failed to be statistically significant. In addition, Levy and Maguib (1985) reported that out of 43 patients forming a consecutive sample of late paraphrenics, only 16 exhibited first-rank symptoms, which was closer to my 1966 findings.

Figures provided by Grahame (personal communication, January 1985) permitted the computation of an annual incidence of late paraphrenia of 0.02% among persons over 60 years of age. Recent prevalence estimates have been provided by Christenson and Blazer (1984), who found, in a survey of a community sample of 997 elderly people, 40 with marked paranoid ideation using as their instrument a short version of the Minnesota Multiphasic Personality Inventory. The majority of the paranoid subjects (58%) also suffered from some cognitive impairment, but in the absence of any detailed clinical examination it is not clear whether the remaining persons would have been diagnosed as paraphrenics. Just under 20 patients with this condition would render a prevalence value of slightly less than 2%, rather higher than the values suggested by some earlier community studies and the value calculated by me (0.5%) from Grahame's study.

CAUSATION OF PARANOID DISORDERS

The causation of paranoid disorders remains largely unknown, but there are a number of factors that almost certainly play important roles. The most obvious is aging, chronological and, possibly, biological aging. Children and adolescents do develop ideas of reference (e.g., in relation to clandestine masturbation), but these rarely lead to lasting or systematized paranoid delusions. Even in the course of schizophrenic illness, persistent paranoid delusions rarely occur before the age of 30. Beyond the fourth decade of life paranoid conditions become increasingly common.

It is tempting to speculate why there should be this link between aging and paranoid psychopathology. It is common knowledge that paranoid ideation tends to take root where the soil of social cohesion has become loosened. This may occur for social, interpersonal reasons, as witnessed by the

paranoid problems of immigrants and minority groups and by paranoid jealousy in a marriage that has become unsatisfactory. Whereas the young tend to move in wide social settings, more mature persons, even before they experience the dispersal of their children and bereavements, tend to become restricted within smaller circles. In growing old, most people turn increasingly inward, and some may come to look upon their human environment suspiciously, to view it as largely hostile. In other words, intrapersonal factors, such as age-linked introversion or longstanding deafness, may be seen as additive to a process of equally age-conditioned social isolation. This is especially likely to be the case with shut-in schizoid personalities.

Disruption of the relationship between a person and the surrounding environment can also occur as a result of the disintegration of the functioning of the person's central nervous system. This is most clearly seen when consciousness is impaired in acute and subacute brain syndromes. This may also be complicated by transient paranoid symptoms, as described earlier. Thus far, the personality background of paranoid and schizophrenic features sometimes encountered in patients experiencing chronic cerebral disease or deterioration has been investigated only within the area of general psychiatry (Davison & Bagley, 1969), more specifically, for temporal lobe epilepsy in younger patients (Slater & Clithero, 1963). Schizophrenia-like symptomatology in chronic brain syndromes is not associated with previously abnormal personality or with schizophrenic heredity, as in paranoid depressions. One might speculate that cerebral lesions affecting certain circuits could lead to paranoid thinking and behavior, whose early evolutional strata had long remained buried in the civilized and healthy human psyche. By contrast, late paraphrenia is frequently characterized by abnormal prepsychotic personality, by deafness, and probably by some hereditary predisposition.

There exists a considerable international literature on the deviant personality types out of which late paraphrenia has been found to develop in 70% to 90% of the cases. Only the salient facts will be presented here (for a more detailed account, see Post, 1980). Late paraphrenics, for the most part, have been quite stable people in the past, rarely exhibiting neurotic problems, delinquency, alcoholism, or unsatisfactory work habits. However, such persons have manifested marked deviance in their belief system and in their relationship to others. Thus, they have often adhered to esoteric sects and cults, not just in youth but during maturity as well. They have rarely followed current fashions of dress, have often cultivated odd food habits, and have been generally regarded as eccentric. Over and above this, they are frequently described as having always been quarrelsome, aggressive, and hostile; egocentric, obstinate, and domineering; or shy, sensitive, and withdrawn. Most have, in addition, had a tendency to become easily jealous and suspicious, almost to the point of harboring persecutory beliefs. Many have remained unmarried or had married late in life. In any case, late paraphrenics have a low fertility rate. In only 33% of my series was there good evidence of past normal sexual activity.

The other well-documented factor in paraphrenia is deafness. This is an important etiological factor of paranoid illness at all ages, but has been studied in great detail in late paraphrenia by Kay and Roth (1961), Cooper (1976), and Cooper, Garside, and Kay (1976). Visual defects were less convincingly implicated in paraphrenia (Cooper & Porter, 1976). Against what might be expected, the deafness associated with senile paraphrenia is not the source of recent sensory deprivation produced by senile degeneration of the neurocerebral auditory system. It is quite different from the deafness of old people and of aged depressives. The great majority of deaf paraphrenics have been found to be afflicted with conduction deafness, the onset dating back many years as sequelae of chronic suppurative otitis media and, less often, of otosclerosis or tympanosclerosis. Deaf late paraphrenics tend to have had less deviant personalities, and this suggests that long-standing deafness may produce in its own right the psychological changes that ultimately lead to paranoid illness.

Much as in the case of late-onset depression, hereditary-genetic factors are relatively less important in late paraphrenia than in the cases of younger affective psychotics and schizophrenics. There have been a number of detailed studies of this (e.g., Post, 1980). The most complete study is that by Kay (1963), who discovered, in 57 late paraphrenic probands, 13 secondary cases among first-degree relatives. Later, he calculated the risk of developing schizophrenia in the siblings and children of paraphrenics as 3.4% (Kay, 1972). The risk for the relatives of younger schizophrenics is 5.8%, and for members of the general population, 0.8%. However, these calculations were based on a risk period for schizophrenia ending at age 50. Some siblings of late paraphrenics are known to develop the disorder after 50 or even after the proband had come under observation. It follows that the risk figure is almost certainly higher than 3.4%. Kay, although not other researchers, found that late paraphrenia bred true, and he confirmed the original suggestion (Kay & Roth, 1961) that the condition was a late member of the group of schizophrenias. The relatively low family incidence was in keeping with a polygenic heredity of schizophrenia, with the disorder emerging only in later life because of fewer genetic factors. A recent finding must, however, be considered (Maguib, McGuffin, Levy, Festonstein, & Alonso, 1987). The human leucocyte antigens (HLA) have been employed as genetic markers for functional psychoses, and several investigators (most recently Ivanyi, Droes, Schreuder, D'Amaro, & Van Rood, 1983) discovered that the HLA-A9 antigen is strongly associated with paranoid schizophrenia. Maguib and his colleagues found no A9 antigen in any of 31 late paraphrenics in their study (but did find it in some controls). On the other hand, they discovered that another antigen, HLA-CW9, is strongly associated with late paraphrenia, suggesting that the condition might not only be a late, but also a rather different member of the schizophrenia group. Its specific nature is confirmed by the considerable predominance of female patients, while in the case of younger schizophrenics, males outnumber females.

As so frequently in the psychoses, the psychodynamics of paranoid and schizophrenic disorders tend to be transparently obvious. The deaf as well as the schizoid suffer with rising age from increasing isolation, inability to perform tasks, and impairment of reality testing. It seems quite plausible to suggest (Berger & Zarit, 1978) that the resulting loss of control makes them vulnerable to paranoid thinking and to seek defenses by psychodynamic mechanisms, like projection and displacement. As noted earlier, the content of the delusions and hallucinations is in most cases very banal and closely related to the patient's domestic and family surroundings. It is also easy to understand how the patient's paranoid experiences pertaining to neighbors and relatives are simple projections of their own long-standing hostile feelings toward them. Sexual delusions and hallucinations also tend to be very coarse and undisguisedly genital, and they seem to occur largely in patients with earlier absent or unsatisfactory sex lives; the homosexual undercurrent, which is so frequently obvious in younger paranoid cases, is hardly ever noted.

In the case of elderly depressives, both the onset and the recurrences of the disorder are temporally and causally related to recent life stresses in up to 90% of the cases (most recently reported by Murphy, 1982). These include physical illness; the loss of loved ones through death, moving away, or quarrels; and the loss of home or work after retirement. In striking contrast, late paraphrenic illnesses develop very gradually out of the previous brittle personality, often compounded by deafness. The patient's social isolation is obviously a result of the faulty personality, like deafness antedating the onset of the psychosis by many years. Sometimes this is linked by the informants to a recent event, like the death of a spouse. However, closer inquiry almost always demonstrates that the patient had paranoid symptoms long before she had been widowed or had been left by a sharer of her home. The husband or relative had managed to cope with the patient's psychotic experiences without outside contact, sometimes even succumbing themselves to such episodes. A confirmed sudden onset of paranoid symptoms should always suggest strongly a causative organic cerebral disorder.

MANAGEMENT AND TREATMENT

Only one single patient out of my series of over 90 late paraphrenics reported a spontaneous remission—in a letter that was, however, written rather ominously in red ink! A year or so later she returned to the clinic, and her simple paranoid psychosis responded satisfactorily to drug therapy.

In patients without first-rank symptoms of schizophrenia, a lasting remission can sometimes be achieved by relocation. It is, in any case, sometimes quite difficult to decide to what extent the patient has psychotic symptoms or is only overreacting to objectively unpleasant neighbors or to a lonely and neglected existence. A move to the home of sympathetic relatives may be possible, or a new apartment in a more pleasant area may be allocated to underprivileged patients. In many of the cases referred to the doctor, the patient herself, the housing authorities, or her friends had already tried these common-sense measures without lasting success. The doctor should advise moving away from the sources of alleged persecution only when relocation seems advisable for other social reasons and when it can be easily achieved. However, the great majority of patients will be helped only by successfully initiated and maintained treatment with a major tranquilizing drug.

This is much easier said than done; the patient does not as a rule feel ill and in need of drug therapy, but demands action to stop the persecution to which she firmly believes herself subjected. Many patients are not first seen in the doctor's office but are admitted as an emergency case to a psychiatric facility. Even where the admission has followed a legal committal procedure, the patient's informed consent to any form of treatment is now required in most states and countries. In cases where patients are unable or unwilling to cooperate in drug therapy on account of their mental disorder, its authorization may be difficult to obtain. However, in the great majority of patients, consent is granted after the practitioner employs an approach to the patient similar to that for a mental hospital inmate, a psychiatric outpatient, or a paraphrenic attending the office of a primary-care or geriatric physician. Where the patient did have prior contact with a medical attendant in spite of her isolation and eccentric life-style, the family physician is in a far better position to initiate and conduct treatment than a specialist. Except in the case of emergency admissions, psychiatric referral is only indicated when there are diagnostic doubts. The patient will be accustomed to receiving drugs from her regular doctor and is much more likely to comply with him, rather than a psychiatrist's, advice and instructions.

The only special advice to the nonpsychiatrist is that he must not follow in the footsteps of the patient's friends and try to talk the patient out of her delusions or to ascribe her hallucinations to imagination. Even worse, he/she should not fall into the temptation of interpreting the patient's symptoms along psychodynamic lines. Like an experienced psychiatrist, the doctor should allow the patient to talk without interruption, except when necessary for clarification, and should listen with obvious interest and sympathy. However, if the tirade has not stopped after more than 10 minutes, he can gently interrupt her, telling her that he is rather baffled by all she has told him and feels powerless as to what action to take, but will think the problem over until the next appointment. In the meantime, the patient, understandably in a highly nervous state, would take some medication.

This or a similar approach is often surprisingly successful, largely because the patient, lacking insight but seeking help, has begun to form a rapport with the doctor. After all, the doctor was probably the first person to listen to her quietly, without interruption! Outpatient treatment, however, should only be attempted when a reliable person is available who will supervise the taking of at least one daily dose, preferably in the evening or at bedtime. Where tablet ingestion is a problem, many antipsychotic preparations can be made up in a fluid base. When medication cannot be supervised or when the patient adamantly refuses to take any, admission to a hospital, preferably not a psychiatric one, should be recommended for a rest. If this ploy also fails, psychiatric help will have to be sought. This will, in many cases, have to take the form of compulsory admission to a mental hospital. The committal procedure usually requires participation of nonmedical people, who may feel reluctant to be party to "locking up a poor old woman." It should be made clear to them that compulsory treatment will lead almost certainly to the removal or considerable amelioration of the mental disturbance within a few weeks and that the patient will be able to leave the hospital at an early date.

Whether the patient is being treated in or out of the hospital, general management should be conducted along the guidelines previously recommended for the first interview. Very excited or resistant patients may need an initial injection of haloperidol, 3 mg, repeated several times as required. The mainstay of treatment at this stage should, however, be oral medication with a phenothiazine preparation. To avoid unpleasant neurological reactions, therapy should begin with small doses; initially, the drug of preference is one that has a low potency and a larger dose, thus allowing for a finer dosage adjustment. Personally, I prescribe thioridazine, 25 mg three times daily (or in patients supervised by a visitor, 50 mg at night only). Every week or 10 days the daily dose should be increased by 50 mg to 75 mg until the patient no longer experiences hallucinations, voices, or delusions about ongoing occurrences at home or in the hospital. Retrospective insight cannot be expected at this stage. Not more than 300 mg of thioridazine should be prescribed daily, and some patients may still not become symptom-free on this highest safe dose. In their case, a more potent drug will have to be tried, such as trifluoperazine, beginning with 5 mg daily and increasing at 10-

day intervals to a maximum of 30 mg a day. If this, too, fails or if oral administration proves impossible, depot injections should be instituted. This form of treatment must be administered by a specialist, as old people may be rather sensitive and reactions will have to be dealt with speedily and expertly.

In the case of hospitalized patients, trial periods at the patient's own home or in her future surroundings have to be established. A recurrence of symptoms obviously will require an increase in medication. When the patient remains symptom-free or no further improvement seems possible, a maintenance dose will have to be determined. With a good response, it should be considerably below the amount of drug originally required, for example, thioridazine, 50–100 mg, or trifluoperazine, 2–5 mg, daily. The long-term neurological complication of tardive dyskinesia cannot always be avoided, but patients are often not aware of its presence (Metha, Metha, & Mathew, 1977). Many old people who had never received antipsychotic drugs exhibit orofacial dyskinesia.

After the removal of psychotic symptoms, psychological and social rehabilitation is very important for both theoretical and practical reasons. Deaf patients should whenever feasible be issued hearing aids; the lonely should be resettled in more suitable surroundings; family ties should be strengthened; club attendances should be encouraged; and so on. Unfortunately, even when symptoms are completely in abeyance, the elderly person remains aloof, suspicious, resentful, and prone to hostility, as well as obstinate. Those who need rehabilitation the most are also the most likely to resist it strenuously.

TREATMENT OUTCOME

As was indicated earlier, paranoid symptoms in acute cerebral organic (delirious) states usually disappear when the basic condition responds to treatment, and those associated with chronic brain syndromes gradually fade out as cognitive deterioration progresses. The symptoms may, however, remain troublesome for a long time. There is a general belief that the paranoid phenomena of brain syndrome patients are as equally effectively suppressed as those of late paraphrenics, usually by much smaller doses of major tranquilizers. I am not aware of any publication proving this, and rather oddly there has also not been any report on the effectiveness of the drug treatment of late paraphrenia since my monograph (Post, 1966), which has been out of print for some years. Some of my findings, which preceded the more general use of depot injections, may well be out of date. All I can do is summarize them in the remainder of this chapter.

The first part of my study concerned the immediate results of drug treatment. Some members of my consecutive series of 93 patients with persistent persecutory states were suspected of and later confirmed to be suffering basically from organic brain syndromes, but their number was too small for separate analysis. Their outcome was assessed together with that of the late paraphrenics. This may not seem logical, but it will be recalled that rather more than "expected" senile paraphrenics may develop organic dementias at a later date. It is, therefore, more realistic to review the results of treatment in all patients with paraphrenic conditions, regardless of present or future organic cerebral involvement. Of the 93 patients studied, 20 had been assessed before ataractic drugs had come to be used in elderly patients, and 2 of the remaining 73 patients had defaulted from treatment (as outpatients) at an early stage. The following analysis is based on 71 cases, all of whom received an initial course of adequate treatment with chlorpromazine, trifluoperazine, or thioridazine.

For reasons that could not be explained, there was complete failure to modify symptomatology in only 6 of the 71 patients. A further 22 patients continued exhibiting some hallucinations or delusions. However, it could be demonstrated that in spite of their residual symptoms they could live outside the hospital without causing frequent or unmanageable difficulties. Finally, 43 patients ceased to have any psychotic experiences or to harbor any persecutory ideas. Only 14 of the patients making complete symptomatic recoveries were ready to agree that their recent experiences had been imaginary. They might even have volunteered statements like, "It was like in a dream" or "I must have been mentally deranged." Most patients showed no retrospective insight, but merely rationalized the disappearance of their symptoms: Their persecutors must have gotten tired or had moved away. Eight had variable insight or apparently merely wished to remain polite to the doctor ("Imaginary? If you say so, doctor.").

The assessment of long-term results was methodologically less satisfactory. In view of the low incidence of persistent paranoid illnesses, it is very difficult to collect a consecutive sample of reasonable size within the time span of a single-center investigation. This is no doubt the reason why my 1966 study has not so far been replicated and extended by others, though an interesting-looking longitudinal investigation of 43 late paraphrenics is now in progress. Most of my patients were followed over at least three years. Most were personally followed up, and in most instances relatives were also interviewed by a social worker or myself. The results, which on some points were updated later (Post, 1980), will be presented in abbreviated and simplified form below.

Of the 71 patients who received adequate courses of drug therapy after admission into the study, 65 survived the first year of the follow-up. Those who had died will be excluded here also because most of them had underlying cerebral disease or deterioration. Of the remaining 65 cases, 34% had continued to be free of symptoms and any recently acquired mental disabilities; 38% had varying lengths of time when they suffered from intermittent mental disturbances; and 28% remained psychotic for most of the follow-up period, including those who had benefited initially from the treatment.

Two parameters of social outcome were also investigated. Originally, two thirds of the patients had been meaningfully occupied (in this age group primarily only in household activities); by the end of the follow-up period, this had declined to barely one half. Worse even, the proportion of patients who were completely unoccupied had risen from about 1% to approximately 15%. Only some 5% had improved in their social relationships, some 13% had declined further, and the remainder had shown little change. When occupational and interpersonal adjustment were combined, it emerged that only some 7% had shown improvement, 46.5% had not changed, and 46.5% had deteriorated socially. This was in marked contrast with a finding for elderly depressives, 24.3% of whom had improved with respect to social parameters over the course of 6 years (Post, 1962). In their case, both upward and downward social changes correlated with freedom from or the presence of depressive symptomatology as an effect and also as a cause (Murphy, 1983). In paraphrenics, however, there was not the slightest suggestion that amount and degree of persistent symptomatology were related to social outcome: Those few patients who had improved in the social area almost always had good clinical outcomes, but many others also doing well—as far as suppression of symptoms was concerned—deteriorated socially. This would seem unlikely to be due to aging over a 3-year span; possibly it is related to an age-linked increase of disabilities, deriving from the patients' prepsychotic personality impairment.

PROGNOSIS OF LATE PARAPHRENIA

During my 1966 study, numerous variables affected the long-term results of treatment. It emerged that there were no valid indicators of prognosis but only some trends, which in not a single instance were of statistical significance. Somewhat favorable indicators were age (below 70), a continuing marriage, a lower social class membership, the absence of marked previous paranoid personality traits (as against only shyness and inadequacy), satisfactory past sexual adjustment, the presence of some close and lasting relationships, and a short duration of symptoms (less than 1 year before the start of treatment). Of unfavorable import were the appearance of organic cerebral disorders, deafness of a degree to impair social contact, and the presence of depressive admixtures. Equally insignificant was a tendency for patients with schizophreniform pictures to do a little worse than simple paranoid and true schizophrenic cases.

Very strikingly, the long-term outlook related clearly to the success or failure of maintenance drug therapy. As pointed out earlier, all but one patient who had not received adequate treatment with phenothiazine drugs remained mentally ill. Although there were a few exceptions, there was a significant ($p < .001$) positive relationship between the success of maintenance therapy and better long-term course. Of the same degree of significance was the finding that full remission of current symptoms following the initial treatment predicted a favorable long-term outcome. Moreover, the gaining of at least a modicum of illness insight at some stage was an equally strong indicator of good longitudinal prognosis.

The most favorable prognostic features were those that were likely to promote compliance with treatment regimes. The only exception was the presence of depressive features, which in spite of better compliance with treatment was associated with an inferior outcome. (Later I found that schizoaffective psychoses generally carried a poor prognosis; Post, 1971.) The only significant association was found between successful maintenance therapy and the preservation of some close interpersonal relationships. This invites speculation regarding the reasons why certain background and clinical variables might be associated with better compliance in treatment and, secondarily to this, with a better outcome. Possibly, the doctor–patient relationship is more likely to be good where the patient still has some rewarding social and marital contacts and when she is relatively younger, has submissive rather than hostile-paranoid personality traits, is not deaf, and has in addition to paranoid also some depressive and thus help-seeking symptoms. A lower social class membership also seems to induce a more compliant attitude toward the physician.

To avoid persistent neurological side effects of all phenothiazine drugs, like chlorpromazine, trifluoperazine, and thioridazine, many clinicians recommend drug holidays. Attempting to stop medication also prevents unduly prolonged drug treatment of patients in whom for some reason symptoms have disappeared, at least for the time being. In the case of my 1966 series, only 33 of the 65 patients surviving the first year of observation had been successfully maintained, and the complete withdrawal of phenothiazine proved practicable in 29 of them. Over an average period of 20 months, only 7 patients remained well, and only two thirds of those who had relapsed responded satisfactorily to the resumption of treatment. Thus, it seems likely that the interruption of maintenance treatment might not be advisable in the case of older patients.

CONCLUSION

The appearance of paranoid symptoms is in some way associated with both biological and social aging. In the elderly they occur in patients exhibiting acute and chronic brain syndromes, disabling personality disorder, senile seclusion, and late-type schizophrenias in senile paraphrenia. The complete or partial suppression of simple paranoid, schizophreniform, or paranoid schizophrenic symptoms is now possible in the great majority of patients, and the discharge rate for late paraphrenia has become the same as that for late-life depression (Blessed & Wilson, 1982). However, most patients remain handicapped by their long-standing personality deviation.

Late paraphrenia is a rare illness, but as most

patients are physically fit and tend to survive for many years, the total sum of the suffering experienced by the patients and their family and friends is considerable. It is regrettable that the condition so often remains unrecognized or is related to the still largely untreatable organic dementias of old age. I vividly recall how one of the early exponents of psychogeriatrics in the United States, my friend Alvin Goldfarb, expressed surprise after reading my 1966 study, telling me that he had never seen a case of late paraphrenia. More recently, after reviewing various European studies, Bridge and Wyatt (1980a) noted the paucity of American work (Bridge & Wyatt, 1980b) and stressed the need for a more scientifically sophisticated approach.

Most of the treatment ideas presented in this chapter were derived from a personal but uncontrolled investigation of the effects of phenothiazine therapy on elderly patients with persistent paranoid illnesses. A rigidly controlled study of both the effect of depot medication and the many factors operating in late paraphrenia is long overdue: one conducted by groups of researchers pooling patients under their care, would be most desirable.

REFERENCES

Berger, K. S., & Zarit, S. H. (1978). Late life paranoid states: Assessment and treatment. *American Journal of Orthopsychiatry, 48,* 528–537.

Berrios, G. E., & Brook, P. (1984). Visual hallucinations and sensory delusions in the elderly. *British Journal of Psychiatry, 144,* 662–664.

Blessed, G., & Wilson, I. D. (1982). The contemporary natural history of mental disorders in old age. *British Journal of Psychiatry, 141,* 59–67.

Bridge, T. P., & Wyatt, R. J. (1980a). Paraphrenia: Paranoid states of late life: 1. European research. *Journal of the American Geriatrics Society, 28,* 195–200.

Bridge, T. P., & Wyatt, R. J. (1980b). Paraphrenia: Paranoid states of late life: 2. American research. *Journal of the American Geriatrics Society, 28,* 201–205.

Christenson, R., & Blazer, D. (1984). Epidemiology of persecutory ideation in an elderly population in the community. *American Journal of Psychiatry, 141,* 1088–1091.

Ciompi, L. (1980). The natural history of schizophrenia in the long term. *British Journal of Psychiatry, 136,* 413–420.

Clark, A. N. G., Mankikar, G. D., & Gray, I. (1975). Diogenes syndrome: A clinical study of gross neglect in old age. *Lancet, i,* 366–373.

Cooper, A. F. (1976). Deafness and psychiatric illness. *British Journal of Psychiatry, 129,* 216–226.

Cooper, A. F., Garside, F. F., & Kay, D. W. K. (1976). A comparison of deaf and non-deaf patients with paranoid and affective psychoses. *British Journal of Psychiatry, 129,* 532–538.

Cooper, A. F., & Porter, R. (1976). Visual acuity and ocular pathology in the paranoid and affective psychoses of later life. *Journal of Psychosomatic Research, 20,* 107–144.

Davison, D., & Bagley, C. R. (1969). Schizophrenia-like psychoses associated with organic disorders of the central nervous system. A review of the literature. In R. N. Herrington (Ed.), Current problems in neuropsychiatry (*British Journal of Psychiatry Special Publications No. 4*). Ashford, Kent, England: Headly Brothers.

Grahame, P. S. (1984). Schizophrenia in old age (late paraphrenia). *British Journal of Psychiatry, 145,* 493–495.

Granick, R., & Zeman, F. D. (1960). The aged recluse— An exploratory study with special reference to community responsibility. *Journal of Chronic Diseases, 12,* 639–643.

Ivanyi, P., Droes, J., Schreuder, U. M. T. H., d'Amaro, J., & Van Rood, J. J. (1983). A search for association of HLA antigens with paranoid schizophrenia. *Tissue Antigens, 22,* 186–193.

Kay, D. W. K. (1962). Outcome and cause of death in mental disorders of old age: A long-term follow-up of functional and organic psychoses. *Acta Psychiatrica Scandinavica, 32,* 249–276.

Kay, D. W. K. (1963). Late paraphrenia and its bearing on the aetiology of schizophrenia. *Acta Psychiatrica Scandinavica, 39,* 159–169.

Kay, D. W. K. (1972). Schizophrenia and schizophrenic-like states in the elderly. *British Journal of Hospital Medicine, 8,* 369–376.

Kay, D. W. K., & Roth, M. (1961). Environmental and hereditary factors in the schizophrenias of old age ("late paraphrenia") and their bearing on the general problem of causation in schizophrenia. *Journal of Mental Science, 107,* 649–686.

Levy, R., & Maguib, M. (1985, October). Late paraphrenia [letter to the editor]. *British Journal of Psychiatry, 146,* 451.

Lewis, A. J. (1970). Paranoia and paranoid. *Psychological Medicine, 1,* 2–12.

McKenna, P. J. (1984). Disorders with overvalued ideas. *British Journal of Psychiatry, 145,* 579–585.

MacMillan, D., & Shaw, P. (1966). Senile breakdown in standards of personal and environmental cleanliness. *British Medical Journal, II,* 1032–1037.

Maguib, M., McGuffin, P., Levy, R., Festenstein, H., & Alonso, A. (1987). Genetic markers in late paraphrenia. *British Journal of Psychiatry, 150,* 124–127.

Metha, D., Metha, S., & Mathew, D. (1977). Tardive dyskinesis in psychogeriatric patients: A five year follow-up. *Journal of the American Geriatrics Society, 21,* 226–228.

Murphy, E. (1982). Social origins of depression in old age. *British Journal of Psychiatry, 141,* 135–142.

Murphy, E. (1983). The prognosis of depression in old age. *British Journal of Psychiatry, 142,* 111–119.

Post, F. (1962). *The significance of affective symptoms in old age.* (Maudsley Monograph No. 10.) London: Oxford University Press.

Post, F. (1966). *Persistent persecutory states of the elderly.* Oxford: Pergamon Press.

Post. F. (1971). Schizo-affective symptomatology in late life. *British Journal of Psychiatry, 118,* 437–445.

Post, F. (1980). Paranoid, schizophrenia-like, and schizophrenic states in the aged. In J. E. Birren & R. B. Sloane (Eds.), *Handbook of mental health and aging* (pp. 591–615). Englewood Cliffs, NJ: Prentice-Hall.

Post. F. (1984). Schizophrenic and paranoid psychoses. In D. W. K. Kay & G. D. Burrows (Eds.), *Handbook*

of mental health and aging (pp. 291–302). Amsterdam: Elsevier.

Roth, M. (1955). The natural history of mental disorders in old age. *Journal of Mental Science, 98,* 66–75.

Roth, M., & Morrissey, J. O. (1952). Problems in the diagnosis and classification of mental disorders in old age: With a study of case material. *Journal of Mental Science, 98,* 66–75.

Slater, E., & Clitheroe, E. (1963). Schizophrenia-like psychoses of epilepsy: 3. Genetical aspects. *British Journal of Psychiatry, 109,* 130–150.

Chapter 5

Alcohol Abuse Among the Elderly

Sheldon Zimberg

There is an increasing awareness of the existence of alcohol problems among the aging, substantiated by a variety of sources. These include the clinical experiences of individual and institutional alcoholism treatment providers, hospital admission surveys, community-based prevalence studies, data from public intoxication surveys, and written reports on treatment experiences with elderly alcoholics. This new information has been in sharp contrast to a number of studies (e.g., Cahalan, Cisin, & Crossley, 1974) suggesting that alcoholism peaks between the ages of 35 and 50, then declines with increasing age. The following will be a discussion of the emerging literature that supports the observation that alcoholism in the elderly is an important problem.

PREVALENCE OF ALCOHOLISM IN THE ELDERLY

In a household alcoholism prevalence survey using probability sampling techniques conducted in the Washington Heights area of Manhattan, Bailey, Haberman, and Alksne (1965) noted that the peak prevalence of alcoholism occurred in the 45–54 age group, with 23 cases reported per 1,000 population aged 20 years and over. Although prevalence decreased to 17 per 1,000 population for the age group 55–65 years, there was a second peak prevalence of 22 per 1,000 in the 65–74 age group, followed by a drop to 12 per 1,000 for the 75

and over age group. The highest prevalence of alcoholism was found among elderly widowers, with 105 cases per 1,000, compared to 19 per 1,000 for the entire population.

A probability sample of members of the United Automobile Workers union aged 21 years and over was conducted in the Baltimore metropolitan area (Siassi, Crocetti, & Spiro, 1973). This study found that among men aged 60 and over, 65% of the drinkers were heavy drinkers and 10% were heavy-escape drinkers. The latter were considered alcoholics in this study. Among the women drinkers aged 60 and over, 40% were heavy drinkers and 20% were heavy-escape drinkers. These women had the highest alcoholism rate of any age group studied, male or female.

In addition to the prevalence studies, there is other evidence that alcoholism is a significant geriatric problem. In a study of 534 patients over age 60 admitted to a psychiatric observation ward in San Francisco General Hospital, Simon, Epstein, and Reynolds (1968) found that 28% had a "serious drinking problem." Of these, 5% were considered heavy drinkers, but their drinking had played little role in their hospitalization. The other 23% were classified as alcoholics, whose problem was directly responsible for or was implicated in their hospitalization. Also in San Francisco, Epstein, Mills, and Simon (1970) found that of 722 individuals aged 60 and over arrested for minor crimes by the San Francisco Police, 82.3% were charged with drunkenness, a much higher proportion that in any other age group. Therefore, at least in San Francisco, many elderly people were admitted for psychiatric treatment because of alcoholism, while many others were arrested by the police for public intoxication.

A prevalence study of patients newly admitted to the medical wards of Harlem Hospital Center in New York City was conducted by McCusker, Cherubin, and Zimberg (1971). This study found that 63% of the men and 35% of the women in the 50 to 69-year-old age group were alcoholics. In the age group 70 and over, 5 of the 9 male patients, but none of the women, were alcoholics. Schuckit and Miller (1976) conducted a survey of admissions of patients 65 years of age and over to the acute medical wards of a California Veterans Administration hospital and found that 18% of the patients were alcoholics. Thus, elderly alcoholics have come to the attention of both inpatient medical services and psychiatric programs.

An alcoholism problem was noted by the author in his work with the elderly in a geriatric psychiatry outpatient program in the Harlem community (Zimberg, 1969). Twelve per cent of the patients seen during the program's first year were found to have an alcoholism problem. As a consultant to a medical home care program in Harlem (Zimberg, 1971), the author observed that 13% of the patients visited at home had a drinking problem.

The problem of alcoholism among the elderly is not confined to urban areas. At a federally funded community mental health center in suburban Rockland County, New York, 1,636 patients were admitted during the first 6 months of 1972, 87 of which were 65 years of age and over. It was noted that 17% of these patients had an alcohol abuse problem upon admission (Zimberg, 1978).

Carruth, Williams, Mysaic, and Boudreaux (1975) interviewed staff members of health, social service, and criminal justice agencies in three communities, representing urban, rural, and urban-rural populations regarding the extent of problem drinking among their elderly clients. The researchers found that 95% of the respondents had seen an older problem drinker as a client in the preceding year. They also noted that the alcoholism information and referral services that they surveyed reported that all calls came from persons over the age of 55.

Mishara and Kastenbaum (1980) presented an excellent review of the literature on alcohol use and misuse in the elderly. They concluded that older individuals tend to drink less than younger people and the quantity of alcohol consumed decreases with age, but that there are significant numbers of elderly who have problems with alcohol.

The author has had experience with geriatric psychiatry programs, in urban and suburban community mental health services, and in private practice, where significant numbers of elderly alcoholics were observed and treated. The reasons for the delayed perception of this subpopulation of alcoholics include the more subtle manifestations of alcoholism in the elderly and a greater denial of its existence by health care professionals and family members because of a *philosophical* bias. Most health professionals and family members of elderly alcoholics dismiss the problem by rationalizing that *elderly persons have nothing left except their bottle, so why take that away*. This view reflects the rejection of the elderly by our youth-oriented culture, as well as the feeling of helplessness in dealing with the many other complex health and psychosocial problems that are obscured by the excessive use of alcohol. The following will describe an effective system of care and psychosocial orientation that will help with and solve many of these complex problems of the elderly, including alcohol abuse.

CLASSIFICATION OF ELDERLY ALCOHOLICS

A number of authors have noted that elderly alcoholics can be differentiated into several diagnostic groupings. Simon et al. (1968) and Gaitz and Baer (1971) distinguished between elderly alcoholics with and without an organic mental syndrome. Such a distinction would imply differing prognoses and treatment approaches. Simon et al. (1968) indicated that alcoholics with an organic mental syndrome had a poorer prognosis for a longer life than elderly alcoholics without an organic mental syndrome. They also noted that of the 23% elderly alcoholic admissions for psychiatric observation, 7% became alcoholic after age 60 and 16% became alcoholic before age 60 and had long histories of alcohol abuse, thus indicating that about one third of the patients developed a drinking problem in later life and two thirds were longstanding alcoholics.

In developing a classification of elderly alcoholics, it would appear that a distinction between *late-onset* problem drinking and *early-onset* problem drinking would be a more useful approach than one based on a distinction of psychiatric diagnosis, particularly the presence or absence of an organic mental syndrome. The late- and early-onset problem drinking classification can permit observations regarding the effects of the stresses of aging that contribute to the onset of alcoholism and other mental health problems in the aged in contrast to factors that existed in alcoholics long before old age and thus may be unrelated to the developmental problems associated with aging.

Rosin and Glatt (1971) reviewed 103 cases of patients age 65 and over who were seen in psychiatric home consultations or admitted to a regional alcoholism unit or a hospital geriatric unit. They also found two distinct groups of alcoholics and noted, as did Simon et al. (1968), that two thirds of the patients were long-standing alcoholics, with their alcoholism persisting as they grew older, and one third developed alcoholism late in life. The longstanding alcoholics had personality characteristics similar to those found among younger alcoholics, but the late-onset alcoholics seemed to have developed their drinking problem concomitant with depression, bereavement, retirement, loneliness, marital stress, and physical illness. Alcoholism in the late-onset alcoholics seemed related to the stresses of aging.

Based on their data, Carruth et al. (1975) reported three distinct types of alcoholics: those who developed the problem during old age (late-onset); those whose occasionally experienced problems with alcohol throughout their lives but developed a more severe and persistent problem in old age (late-onset exacerbation); and those who had a long history of alcoholism and continued drinking into old age (early-onset). The authors did not indicate relative percentages in the three groups. It seems reasonable to conclude, however, that the two latter groups could be considered long-standing alcoholics with different patterns in their younger years. (The terms *late-onset*, *late-onset exacerbation*, and *early-onset* are this author's designation.)

The concept of early-onset (two thirds) and late-onset (one third) alcoholism among the elderly appears to be a more useful classification. First, through the history of the use of alcohol, it is possible to determine in which group an elderly alcoholic might be classified. Second, longstanding alcoholics are more likely to develop the medical complications of alcoholism and therefore require medical care. Third, the recognition of factors contributing to the development of the problem may make intervention more effective.

Important questions arise, however, if we accept this classification of early- and late-onset alcoholism among the elderly. They deal with different treatment approaches for these two groups, based on the differing psychological and social characteristics found among the patients.

DIAGNOSIS OF ALCOHOL ABUSE

The author has developed an alcohol-abuse scale (Table 5.1) that has proved clinically useful in establishing the diagnosis of alcoholism, based on the level of severity, and that can measure changes in severity over time as a result of spontaneous remission or treatment.

There are generally less physical sequelae and less evidence of signs and symptoms of alcohol addiction in the elderly. Therefore, Level 3 of the scale is the most likely point of severity in elderly alcoholics in contrast to Levels 4–6 in younger alcoholics. This observation is based on the fact that elderly people tend to consume smaller quantities of alcohol, possibly because they cannot metabolize it as readily as younger people (Salzman, Vander Kolk, & Shader, 1975).

The problems elderly alcoholics encounter are primarily social ones rather than medical problems requiring detoxification and extensive medical care. Although some elderly alcoholics have drinking-related medical problems, in most the manifestations of alcoholism are more subtle than in younger people, and greater efforts are required to elicit social problems associated with alcohol consumption. Organic brain syndromes can be exacerbated even by the smaller quantities of alcohol consumed by the elderly; in addition, alcohol consumed with medications often taken by older persons can produce states of confusion out of proportion to the amount of alcohol ingested. These factors, therefore, make the diagnosis of alcoholism much more difficult in the elderly.

If alcohol problems in the elderly are more difficult to discern, what questions should be asked in order to establish the diagnosis? Questions about the amount and frequency of alcohol consumption will not elicit reliable and valid responses, because alcoholics in general and the elderly in particular tend to deny or minimize this information. Table 5.2, which includes key questions to ask, can be

Table 5.1. Scale of Alcohol Abuse

Severity Level	Characteristics
1. None	Drinks only on occasion, if at all
2. Minimal	Drinking is not conspicuous; occasional intoxications (up to four per year); no social, family, occupational, health, or legal problems related to drinking
3. Mild	Intoxications occurring up to once a month, although generally limited to evenings or weekends, and/or some impairment in social, family, or occupational functioning related to drinking; no physical or legal problems related to drinking
4. Moderate	Frequent intoxications, up to one or two times per week, and/or significant impairment in social, family, or occupational functioning; some evidence of physical impairment related to drinking, such as tremors, frequent accidents, epigastric distress, occasional loss of appetite; no history of delirium tremens, cirrhosis, nutritional deficiency, hospitalization related to drinking, or arrests related to drinking
5. Severe	Almost constant drinking (practically every day); history of delirium tremens, cirrhosis, chronic brain syndrome, neuritis, or nutritional deficiency; severe disruption in social or family relations; unable to hold steady job but able to manage on public assistance; one or more arrests related to drinking (drunk or disorderly conduct); one or more hospitalizations related to drinking; two or more citations for driving while intoxicated
6. Extreme	All of the characteristics of severe impairments plus homelessness and/or inability to manage on public assistance (or both)

Note. From "Principles of Alcoholism Psychotherapy" by S. Zimberg, in *Practical Approaches to Alcoholism Psychotherapy* edited by S. Zimberg, J. Wallace, and S. Blume, 1985, New York: Plenum. Copyright 1985 by Plenum Press. Reprinted by permission.

used as a guide by the interviewer. The information should be obtained from the patient and from relatives or friends who are in a position to observe the patient. If the patient or other source of information indicates that any of the problem areas seem to be associated with the use of alcohol, that patient probably has an alcohol problem.

PSYCHOSOCIAL FACTORS THAT CONTRIBUTE TO ALCOHOL ABUSE

Cahalan et al. (1974) discussed, in a monograph based on a national survey of drinking behavior and attitudes in the United States, some interesting observations concerning the natural history of drinking behavior and problem drinking in the population studied. They noted that about one-third more individuals experienced drinking problems in the period preceding the 3-year study than during the study period itself, suggesting a tendency toward spontaneous remission.

Malzberg (1947), Locke and Duvall (1960), and Gorwitz, Bahn, Warthen, and Cooper (1970) presented data that showed a decline in admissions of elderly alcoholics to psychiatric hospitals and clinics. These data, based on admissions for treatment, seem to confirm the epidemiological data obtained by Cahalan et al. (1974) and, in fact, have been the major basis for the assumption that alcoholism is not a significant problem among the elderly.

Drew (1968) observed that data on mortality related to alcoholism and its treatment outcome could not account for the observed decrease in alcoholics among the older age groups. He suggested that alcoholism is a self-limiting disease with a significant spontaneous remission with advancing age. Imber, Schultz, Funderburk, and Flammer (1976) described a follow-up of 58 alcoholics who received no treatment for alcoholism. It was noted that the rate of abstinence was 15% at the end of 1 year and 11% at the end of 3 years.

Vaillant (1983) found that a significant number of alcoholics give up drinking and experience recovery as they get older and that this course of ultimate remission is the natural history of alcoholism. Therefore, spontaneous remission does seem to occur in alcoholism.

The question arises as to what factors might contribute to a spontaneous remission with advancing age. It has been established (Salzman et al., 1975) that in an aged person, drugs, including alcohol, tend to stay in the body longer and to have more prolonged and more powerful clinical and toxic effects in the body. In addition, there is a functional loss of neuronal tissue in the aged, which may account for the observed increased sensitivity to drugs of the sedative-hypnotic class, which includes alcohol. It is therefore quite possible that the effects of alcohol on mood and behaviour become less pleasant and produce more unpleasant side effects in elderly people. Even long-standing alcoholics are likely to give up alcohol if it has become a noxious substance to them because of their diminished tolerance and its increased toxic effects.

If the previous explanation is correct, what are the factors that contribute to the continued drinking among some alcoholics into old age and the development of late-onset alcoholism among a significant number of elderly people? The author has noted in his experience with both late-onset and early-onset alcoholics a significant number of social and psychological factors associated with

Table 5.2. Key Questions for the Suspected Elderly Alcoholic

---

1. Has there been any recent marked changes in behavior or personality?
2. Are there recurring episodes of memory loss and confusion?
3. Has the person tended to become more socially isolated and stay at home most of the time?
4. Has the person become more argumentative and resistant to offers of help?
5. Has the person been neglecting to maintain personal hygiene, to eat regularly, or to keep appointments, especially doctor's appointments?
6. Has the individual been neglecting his or her medical treatment regimen?
7. Has the individual been unable to manage his or her income effectively?
8. Has the individual been in trouble with the law?
9. Has the individual caused problems with the neighbors?
10. Has drinking been associated with any of the above problems?

---

aging that affect these patients. Rosin and Glatt (1971) and Droller (1964) noted in their treatment of elderly alcoholics that depression, bereavement, retirement, loneliness, marital stress, and physical illness were major contributing factors to the drinking problem. Treatment efforts directed at eliminating these factors were found to be most beneficial among the elderly, in contrast to treatment efforts directed at eliminating the use of alcohol among younger alcoholics.

On the basis of these observations, it is possible to construct a hypothesis that could account for the tendency of spontaneous remission with advancing age, as well as for the fact that some long-standing alcoholics do continue to exhibit drinking problems into old age and that some elderly individuals develop alcohol problems in later life. Both groups are reacting to the stresses of aging, which, in generating a great deal of anxiety and depression, lead to the use of alcohol as a form of self-medication. Apparently the adverse effects of alcohol prove to be less disturbing than facing overwhelming problems, particularly object loss. Therefore, the sociopsychological stresses of aging can prolong problem drinking in longstanding alcoholics into old age and contribute to the development of problem drinking in some elderly individuals. If this hypothesis is correct, treatment approaches will have to focus on the sociopsychological stresses of aging.

TREATMENT TECHNIQUES

Although the awareness of the existence of alcoholism among the elderly has emerged only recently, there have been reports of the successful treatment of elderly alcoholics. Droller (1964) reported on 7 cases of elderly alcoholics whom he had visited at home. He found that in addition to medical and supportive treatment, socially oriented therapy proved to be the most beneficial. Rosin and Glatt (1971), in their treatment of 103 elderly alcoholics, noted that environmental manipulation and medical services, along with day hospital treatment (3–7 hours per day, 5 days per week) and home visits by staff or good neighbours, were the most beneficial.

The author, in his experience in an outpatient geriatric psychiatric program (Zimberg, 1969) and as a psychiatric consultant to a nursing home (Zimberg, 1978) has noted similar responses to social interventions. The use of group socialization techniques and occasional antidepressant medication proved effective in eliminating alcohol abuse among the patients in these programs. The use of disulfiram or referral to AA or other alcoholism programs required by younger alcoholics was not necessary for these patients. It is of even further interest to note that both early-onset and late-onset alcoholics responded equally well to psychosocial interventions, suggesting common etiological factors for these two groups of elderly alcoholics. These observations were supported by the work of Atkinson (1984).

The hypothesis that psychosocial factors are the major contributors to alcoholism among the aged has been supported by the successful use of psychosocial methods of treatment. In young-adult and middle-aged alcoholics, treatment is initially directed at the drinking behavior itself. Only with such intervention can the use of alcohol be eliminated and other coping mechanisms learned. This direct-intervention approach is designed for the primary alcoholic, that is, one in whom alcoholism develops as the major behavioral disorder in response to sociocultural, psychological, and physiological factors but remains as the overwhelmingly severe disorder of addiction.

In contrast, the elderly alcoholic drinks in response to severe social and psychological stresses associated with aging. If these stresses are eliminated or attenuated, the secondary use of alcohol is diminished, thus leading to sobriety.

The most effective treatment techniques for such patients, based on the author's experiences in geriatric psychiatry outpatient programs, involve group therapy. Prior to admission to a group, every patient should have a complete physical and psychiatric evaluation so that physical or psychiatric disorders can be diagnosed and appropriate treatments instituted.

Group therapy can involve up to 20 patients and should not be insight-oriented or directive as far as alcoholism is concerned. The patients should be elderly persons with a variety of social, psychological, organic mental, and physical disorders, not just alcoholism. Alcoholic patients should be told that they have a drinking problem and that it is probably related to the difficulties encountered in adjusting to their current life situation.

The group should meet at least once a week for $1\frac{1}{2}$ to 2 hours. Cookies, coffee, and tea should be made available. If meals can be provided, eating together as a group would be helpful. The approach utilized by the group leaders should be supportive and oriented toward problem solving.

Drinking problems should be one of the areas discussed, but not the only one. Members of the group should be encouraged to discuss other members' problems, as well as their own, and to give advice and suggestions.

Each group session could be divided into an informal social and/or eating period (at the beginning), a discussion and problem-solving period, and a socializing period (at the end). The socializing period could be expanded through the use of activities therapy involving occupational therapy and/or planning for trips and outings, the development of a patient government, and the establishment of a patient kitty or dues. Patients requiring medication or medical follow-up can be seen by the physician individually after the group activities are completed.

The staff responsible for group programs should ideally consist of a psychiatrist knowledgeable about the problems of aging and alcoholism, a nurse or social worker, and one or two paraprofessional workers. Paraprofessional workers can provide numerous services for the patients, who will have many areas of difficulty. Such services include visiting the homes of patients who miss clinic appointments; accompanying patients to other clinics and community agencies to act as liaison and patient advocates; observing and reporting patient behavior to the professional staff, contacting the Department of Social Services to help with patients; providing economic and housing assistance; interviewing patients, friends, relatives, and neighbours to help support the patients living at home; and participating in group sessions.

In the current geriatric psychiatric group run by the author and a social worker, paraprofessional workers are not available for these outreach and coordinating activities. However, most of the group members have home attendants, who are invited to participate in the group and to discuss any problems with the staff after the group sessions. Thus, they are trained to observe their patients and make reports; they are given management suggestions to carry out at home, and instructions to bring patients to various clinics for medical care and to social agencies for housing and welfare problems. This system has been quite successful in extending therapeutic services and influence beyond the group sessions.

Many of the patients treated in such groups are clinically depressed. The judicious use of antidepressant medication can be helpful.

With increasing interest in the treatment of

elderly alcoholics, some new clinical observations have been made by the author and others. Elderly alcoholics who are well off financially and have retired from previously prominent positions seem to experience fewer of the social and economic stresses of aging and respond to more alcoholism-specific approaches. They need counseling and support to help them deal with a changed way of life, but the treatment of alcoholism must take priority. Another observation is that elderly alcoholics who do find their way to alcoholism programs can also be treated in an alcoholism-specific way with the addition of psychosocial interventions for the stresses of aging. Most elderly alcoholics, however, still resist referral to alcoholism programs (Atkinson, 1984).

TREATMENT OF THE ELDERLY ALCOHOLIC IN THE PHYSICIAN'S OFFICE

Although the ideal approach may be psychosocial therapy, a physician can provide significant help to elderly alcoholics on an individual basis in the office. Once the diagnosis of alcoholism has been determined, as well as any associated depression, the physician can discuss the problem with the patient and his or her family as one related to coping with the aging process. The patient can be detoxified on an outpatient basis or in the hospital using benzodiazepines, but this is generally unnecessary. Treatment for clinically significant depression can be instituted with tricyclic antidepressants. The family should be encouraged to involve the elderly person in meaningful family activities and in activities at senior citizen centers, volunteer work, and the like in order to help the elderly patient feel useful. Attention to medical problems should be maintained, and any mental problems should be addressed. The patient should be seen by the physician at least once a week for a few months and then gradually less frequently.

The visit to the doctor's office is often the most important activity of the week for these patients, and having someone who will listen to their concerns can produce major improvements in their emotional state. The physician can become not only the one who diagnoses and treats medical problems but also someone who is interested in the emotional well-being of the patient. Many elderly patients use the doctor's visits for this very reason, and physicians can capitalize on this to help

reduce a variety of psychological problems in their elderly patients, including alcoholism, simply by being there and listening attentively for 10 to 15 minutes.

In the prosperous as well as the less affluent elderly alcoholic, treatment efforts based on the alcoholism-specific approach or the psychosocial individual or group model will produce high rates of recovery, which can be extremely gratifying.

PREVENTION OF ALCOHOLISM AMONG THE ELDERLY

Rosin and Glatt (1971) documented that such environmental stress factors as the loss of a loved one, retirement, loneliness, physical illness, and marital problems contributed to alcohol abuse among the elderly. They also suggested that "manipulation of the environment and improvement in the medical condition are often beneficial . . . [and] pre-retirement courses help to avoid a social vacuum after the person leaves work."

Many of the stresses of aging can be reduced or eliminated through the development of an effective network of services for the elderly, involving social services, economic and housing assistance, medical care, and psychological counseling. Although the development of senile dementia and other chronic brain syndromes cannot be reversed at the present stage of medical knowledge, the impact of such disorders on functional capacity can be reduced by effective and comprehensive services. If alcohol abuse develops in the elderly as a reaction to such problems or, in the case of longstanding alcoholics, does not spontaneously remit, reducing the impact of senile dementia or social and psychological problems may help to reduce alcoholism among the elderly as a manifestation of the social breakdown syndrome (Gruenberg, 1974).

It has been proposed that the well-known sociability effects of alcohol might be helpful for elderly individuals experiencing behavioral and mood problems. Becker and Cesar (1973) investigated the effects of beer by giving beer to one group of elderly psychiatric patients in a mental hospital and fruit juice to another. After 11 weeks they noted increased social interaction within the group given beer but no improvement in ward behavior outside group sessions for either group. Chien, Stotsky, and Cole (1973) reported positive results from the use of alcohol in a nursing home to improve ward sociability and manageability of patients: "Following a four-week control period 64 nursing home patients receiving doxepin, other psychoactive drugs, or no medication were placed on an alcohol regimen of beer or wine in the ward or in a simulated pub set-up. The alcohol produced significant improvement in all groups, especially the doxepin group. However, the pub milieu did not demonstrate a significant superiority over ward milieu."

The results in these two studies should be expected, since the sociability effects of alcohol are well known. It should be noted, however, that the two studies mentioned investigated the effects of alcohol on behavior for only 11 and 4 weeks, respectively, much too short a time to determine any possible detrimental effects that might ensue through the continued use of alcohol. Alcohol is a potentially addicting substance, and since older people are more susceptible to sedative-hypnotic drugs, it is possible that tolerance to alcohol develops more rapidly in an elderly person. With the continued use of alcohol, more might be required to produce the same euphoriant effects. Patients developing tolerance may ask for more beer and wine and may be denied it by the institutional staff, which may create serious management problems. Nursing homes in particular may be prone to this problem, and because there is evidence that more and more alcoholic patients are being placed in such settings (Linn, Linn, & Greenwald, 1972), the widespread use of alcohol within an institutional environment may result in iatrogenic alcoholism (Blume, 1973).

The use of alcohol as a beverage may have some value outside the institutional setting during picnics and outings as part of normal social and recreational activities organized by therapeutic community programs for institutionalized elderly. However, the principles of the therapeutic community approach (Jones, 1953), in which elderly patients participate with the staff in meaningful activities fostering self-help and concern for other patients, can produce far more significant changes in behavior and functional capacities than alcohol. It is easy to give a drug, including alcohol, in an effort to improve mood and behavior. In fact, many physicians prescribe alcohol for the elderly patients who complain of loss of appetite or insomnia, although often such symptoms are manifestations of depression. However, there are far more effective antidepressant drugs than alcohol, and sociability can be better fostered through effective staff–patient and patient–patient interactions without the danger of producing iatrogenic alcoholism. It is important for physicians to become more aware of the social, physical, and psychological stresses of aging and to be able to recognize depression in the elderly. Current psychosocial therapies, skillfully applied, provide more effective treatment than the palliative effects of alcohol.

A major problem in dealing with alcoholism in general, and especially among the elderly, has been the unwillingness of health care professionals to recognize and diagnose the problem and the general prevailing feeling of hopelessness about the treatment of alcoholics.

It is necessary for physicians and other health care professionals to become knowledgeable about alcohol use and abuse in the United States. With such knowledge, they will be better able to diagnose individuals with alcoholism, including the elderly, early in the course of the disease and to treat them directly or to refer them elsewhere for proper treatment.

REFERENCES

Atkinson, R. M. (1984) *Alcohol and drug abuse in old age.* Washington, DC: American Psychiatric Association.

Bailey, M. B., Haberman, P. W., & Alksne, H. (1965). The epidemiology of alcoholism in an urban residential area. *Quarterly Journal of Studies on Alcohol, 26,* 19–40.

Becker, P. W., & Cesar, J. A. (1973). Use of beer in geriatric patient groups. *Psychological Reports, 33,* 42–182.

Blume, S. B. (1973). Iatrogenic alcholism. *Quarterly Journal of Studies on Alcohol, 34,* 1348–1352.

Cahalan, D., Cisin, I. A., & Crossley, H. M. (1974). *Amercian drinking practices: A national survey of drinking behavior and attitudes.* New Brunswick, NJ: Rutgers Center of Alcohol Studies.

Carruth, B., Williams, E. P., Mysaic, P., & Boudreaux, L. (1975). Community care providers and the older problem drinker. *Grassroots* (July suppl.), 1–5.

Chien, C., Stotsky, B. A., & Cole, J. O. (1973). Psychiatric treatment for nursing home patients: Drugs, alcohol and milieu. *American Journal of Psychiatry. 130,* 534–548.

Drew, L. R. H. (1968). Alcohol as a self-limiting disease. *Quarterly Journal of Studies on Alcohol, 29,* 956–967

Droller, H. (1954). Some aspects of alcoholism in the elderly. *Lancet, ii,* 137–139.

Epstein, L. J., Mills, C., & Simon A. (1970). Antisocial behavior of the elderly. *Comprehensive Psychiatry, 11,* 36–42.

Gaitz, C. M., & Baer, P. E. (1971). Characteristics of elderly patients with alcoholism. *Archives of General Psychiatry, 24,* 327–378.

Gorwitz, K., Bahn, A., Warthen, F. J., & Cooper, M. (1970). Some epidemiological data on alcoholism in

Maryland based on admissions to psychiatric facilities. *Quarterly Journal of Studies on Alcohol, 31*, 423–443.

Gruenberg, E. M. (1974). The social breakdown syndrome and its prevention. In S. Aireti and G. Caplan (Eds.) *American Handbook of Psychiatry*. New York: Basic Books.

Imber, S., Schultz, E., Funderburk, A. R., & Flammer, R. (1976). The fate of the untreated alcoholic. *Journal of Nervous and Mental Disease, 612*, 238–247.

Jones, M. (1953). *The therapeutic community*. New York: Basic Books.

Linn, M. W., Linn, B. S., & Greenwald, S. R. (1972). The alcoholic patient in the nursing home. *Aging and Human Development, 3*, 273–277.

Locke, B. Z., & Duvall, H. J. (1960). Alcoholism among first admissions to Ohio Public Mental Hospital. *Quarterly Journal of Studies on Alcohol, 21*, 457–474.

Malzberg, B. A. (1947). A study of first admissions with alcoholic psychoses in New York State. *Quarterly Journal of Studies on Alcohol, 8*, 274–295.

McCusker, J., Cherubin, C. F., & Zimberg, S. (1971). Prevalence of alcoholism in general municipal hospital population. *New York State Journal of Medicine, 71*, 751–754.

Mishara, B. L., & Kastenbaum, R. (1980). *Alcohol and old age*. New York: Grune & Stratton.

Rosin, A. J., & Glatt, M. M. (1971). Alcohol excess in the elderly. *Quarterly Journal of Studies on Alcohol, 32*, 53–59.

Salzman, C., Vander Kolk, B., & Shader, R. I. (1975). Psychopharmacology and the geriatric patient. In R. I. Shader (Ed.), *Manual of psychiatric therapeutics*. Boston: Little, Brown.

Schuckit, M. M., & Miller, P. L. (1976). Alcoholism in elderly men: A survey of a general medical ward. *Annals of the New York Academy of Sciences, 273*, 558–571.

Siassi, I., Crocetti, G., & Spiro, H. R. (1973). Drinking patterns and alcoholism in a blue collar population. *Quarterly Journal of Studies on Alcohol, 34*, 917–926.

Simon, A., Epstein, L. J., & Reynolds, L. (1968). Alcoholism in the geriatric mentally ill. *Geriatrics, 23*, 125–131.

Vaillant, G. E. (1983). *The natural history of alcoholism: Causes, patterns and paths to recovery*. Cambridge, MA: Harvard University Press.

Zimberg, S. (1969). Outpatients geriatric psychiatry in an urban ghetto with non-professional workers. *American Journal of Psychiatry, 125*, 1697–1702.

Zimberg, S. (1971). The psychiatrist and medical home care: Geriatric psychiatry in the Harlem community. *American Journal of Psychiatry, 127*, 1062–1066.

Zimberg, S. (1978). Treatment of the elderly alcoholic in the community and in an institutional setting. *Addictive Diseases: An International Journal, 3*, 417–427.

Zimberg, S. (1985). Principles of alcoholism psychotherapy. In Zimberg, S., Wallace, J., & Blume, S. B. *Practical approaches to alcoholism psychotherapy*. New York: Plenum.

Chapter 6

The Sexual Behavior and Problems of the Elderly

William T. O'Donohue

This chapter will examine several myths regarding the sexuality of the elderly and the possible reasons for their existence. Studies of attitudes regarding the sexuality of the elderly will be reviewed, as well as studies investigating whether the elderly are sexually desirable, desirous, and capable. The effects of aging on sexual physiology will be discussed, as will the effects of various pathologies on the sexual behaviour of the elderly. Changes in the male and female sexual arousal cycle will be examined. A brief discussion of psychotherapy for the sexual problems of the elderly will also be presented. This discussion is necessarily brief due to the lack of assessment and treatment studies of the sexual problems of the elderly. This chapter will conclude with several suggestions for future investigation.

THE MYTHS OF GERIATRIC SEXUALITY

It has been suggested that there are a number of myths—widely held but nonetheless false beliefs — regarding the sexuality of elderly individuals. In this section the more important ones will be examined and hypotheses regarding why they exist will be discussed briefly.

Margaret Kuhn (1976), leader of the Gray Panthers, lists the following five myths:

Myth 1: "Sex doesn't matter in old age. The later years of life are supposed to be (and usually are) sexless" (p. 118).

Myth 2: "Interest in sex is abnormal for old people" (p. 120).

Myth 3: "Remarriage after loss of spouse should be discouraged" (p. 121).

Myth 4: "It is all right for old men to seek younger women as sex partners, but it is ridiculous for old women to be sexually involved with younger men" (p. 122).

Myth 5: "Old people should be separated by sex in institutions to avoid problems for the staff and criticism by families and the community" (p. 123).

Kuhn suggests that these myths exist in the West as a part of a general devaluation of the aged, because the elderly are thought not to be involved in "profits and productivity." It is interesting to note that these myths are value statements and, at least according to Kuhn, false ones.

However, not all myths regarding the sexuality of the elderly have to do with values. False beliefs regarding factual matters might also be involved. Thus for the purposes of our discussion, Hotvedt's (1983) characterization of the myths of geriatric sexuality will be more useful. According to Hotvedt, the major myths are as follows:

Myth I: In the later years, individuals are not sexually desirable.
Myth II: In the later years, individuals are not sexually desirous.
Myth III: In the later years, individuals are not sexually capable.

In order for these to be properly categorized as myths, these must be false beliefs. Therefore, in order to establish that these are actually myths, we will review evidence that these propositions are indeed believed to be true, and that in fact these beliefs are false. However, before doing so, an important point must be made: These myths may be interpreted as false beliefs regarding facts and/or false beliefs regarding values. For example, Myth II can be interpreted as stating the factual proposition "It is an empirical fact that elderly individuals are not sexually desirous." Alternatively, this sentence can be plausibly construed to mean "Elderly individuals morally ought not to be sexually desirous." The first interpretation seems to be predominant in the literature, and therefore for the purposes of this chapter, these myths will be construed as involving factual claims.

First, let us review evidence relevant to the question of whether these propositions are actually believed. With respect to Myth I, Kaas (1978) found that the majority of 85 elderly nursing-home residents indicated that they did not feel themselves to be sexually attractive. White (1975), in clinical interviews of eight female nursing-home residents, found that they all thought themselves to be unattractive to members of the opposite sex. Ludeman (1979) interviewed 15 formerly married females over the age of 60 and found that these women also considered themselves to be sexually unattractive. Finally, Susan Sontag (1972) has suggested that a double standard exists such that elderly women are judged to be less sexually attractive than elderly men:

> Women become sexually ineligible much earlier than men do. . . . Thus, for most women, aging means a humiliating process of gradual sexual disqualification. . . . Getting older tends to operate in men's favor, since their value as lovers and husbands is set more by what they do than how they look. (pp. 31–32)

Thus, it seems at this point that more research is needed regarding whether it is a common belief that elderly individuals are not sexually desirable. There appears to be some research suggesting that this is believed by the nursing-home elderly, but there is little or no evidence concerning whether this is believed by others. It seems reasonable that such future research should examine such attitudes at least as a function of the gender of the respondent (males and females may differ in the extent to which age influences their feelings about sexual attraction), the age of the respondent (middle-aged adults might react differently than younger ones), and the gender of the elderly individual (people, as Sontag suggests, may find elderly males to be, in general, more sexually attractive than elderly females). It is also interesting to note the following possibility: Myth I might precede and cause these negative evaluations.

With respect to Myth II, that is that elderly individuals are not sexually desirous, Golde and Kagan (1959) found that 93% of college students in their sample completed the phrase "Sex for most old people is . . . " with "negligible, or unimportant," while only 5% completed the phrase "Sex for most people is . . . " in this manner. Cameron (1970) found that the elderly (aged 65–79) considered themselves and were considered by others to be below average in desire for sexual activity.

Therefore, there seems to be some evidence that the elderly, as well as others, actually believe that older individuals are not sexually desirous. Again, however, the evidence is far from overwhelming and further research is needed, which, again, should be grouped by the age and gender of the respondent and by the gender of the elderly individual.

With respect to Myth III, that is, that the elderly are not sexually capable, Cameron (1970) found that the elderly and others believed that older individuals were below average in skill in performing, capacity for, frequency of attempts at, and frequency of sexual activity. LaTorre and Kear (1977) found that university students and nursing-home staff rated stories with aged characters having sex as less credible, *and* less moral, than stories with younger characters.

Thus, there appears to be some evidence that suggests each of the beliefs involved in the three myths is actually held by some individuals. More research is needed, especially because there also exists some evidence indicating that there might be more positive attitudes regarding related issues. For example, Roff and Klemmack (1979) found that 90% of nonelderly adults interviewed in a Southern city considered sexual intercourse between married couples in their 60s and 70s to be appropriate. Damrosch (1984) reported that graduate student nurses rated a sexually active elderly woman depicted in a vignette as significantly more mentally alert, cheerful, and well adjusted than an elderly female in a vignette in which sex was not mentioned; she was also seen as more popular with the staff, healthier, more attractive, having warmer family relations, and a better patient. White (1982) has developed an instrument, the Aging Sexuality Knowledge and Attitudes Scale, with promising psychometric properties that might be useful in future research.

The next step in determining whether these are actually myths is to establish whether or not these beliefs are false beliefs. In other words, do they describe the actual state of affairs or not? Let us first consider Myth I. What would be considered as disconfirming evidence for the proposition that elderly individuals are not sexually desirable? Evidence indicating that the elderly actually have sex is not sufficient, for people can have sex even when they find their partner and perhaps even themselves sexually undesirable. The finding that individuals actually rate elderly individuals as sexually attractive would, of course, count as evidence against the claim that the elderly are sexually unattractive. However, there does not seem to be any research that investigates this question. Evidence that elderly individuals actually engage in sex, though not sufficient to establish the falsity of the claim that the elderly are sexually unattractive, is not irrelevant either. As we shall soon see, elderly individuals are sexually active and we can view this as disconfirming evidence, though problematic, against the proposition that elderly individuals are not sexually desirable. Admittedly, this involves the assumption that sexual attraction underlies sexual activity. Taking sexual activity on the part of the elderly as disconfirming evidence is reasonable because we would require not only for individuals to simply rate the elderly as sexually attractive, but also to behave in a manner that is consistent with this rating, for example, become sexually aroused when exposed to these individuals, actually engage in sex with them, etc.

There seems to be a fair amount of evidence indicating that the proposition that elderly individuals are not sexually desirous is false. Baras (1961) found that 52 elderly males and females (aged 65–95) had frequent sexual themes in their dreams. Freeman (1961) found that in 74 elderly individuals (mean age, 71), 75% of the males and 60% of the females reported that they still experienced sexual desire. Friedfield (1961) reported that in a review of 100 geriatric clinical cases, sexual interest was present in most. Pfeiffer (1968), in cross-sectional data from 254 individuals, found a gradual decline in sexual interest with age. However, about 14% actually showed an increase in sexual interest with increasing age. Pfeiffer, Verwoerdt, and Davis (1974) reported that 94% of elderly males were sexually interested, with a decline in interest to age 60 and then a rise after 65. They found a similar pattern for females. Wasow and Loeb (1979), in an investigation of 63 nursing-home residents (minimum age, 60), found that 10% of the males and 28% of the females said they had no interest in sex. Finally, Winn and Newton (1982) reported in a cross-cultural study of 106 societies that in 70% of the societies examined older males had little if any loss of sexual interest and in 84% of the societies examined elderly females continued to maintain sexual interest.

Thus, there appears to be considerable evidence suggesting that the majority of elderly individuals are sexually desirous. Hence, it appears that Myth II does indeed involve a false proposition.

Myth III, that is, that elderly individuals are not sexually capable, would be shown to be false by evidence indicating that the elderly actually engage in sex. Such evidence is plentiful. Kinsey, Pomeroy, and Martin (1948) found that in 126 male respondents over the age of 60, 80% were sexually active at 60 years, 70% at 70 years, 40% at 75 years, and 25% at 80 years. Kinsey, Pomeroy, Martin, and Gebhard (1953), after interviewing 56 women over the age of 60, reported that 80% of the married women indicated having sexual intercourse at least once every 2 weeks. Tarail (1962), in a study of 302 males selected from *Who's Who in America*, found that in the age group 65–92, 70% still engaged in intercourse, and 50% in the age group 75–92. Bowens, Cross, and Lloyd (1963), in a study of 157 males from 60 to 74 years of age, found that 55% were still potent. Of these, those aged 60–64 had a frequency of sexual intercourse of 18 times per year;

those aged 65–69, 22 times per year; and those aged 70–74, 25 times per year. Pfeiffer (1968), in a longitudinal study involving 256 individuals over the age of 60, reported that in the 60–71 age bracket, 40% to 65% were still sexually active, and in the group of those older than 78, 10% to 20% were still sexually active. Pfeiffer et al. (1974), in a study of 502 elderly individuals, reported that in the 66–71 age group, 76% of the males were sexually active as well as 27% of the females. Finally, Nigola and Peruzza (1974), in a study of 53 males and 32 females between the ages of 62 and 81, found that 45 males and 17 females were still sexually active.

Hence, there is strong evidence indicating that the elderly are often sexually active and therefore sexually capable. It is important to note that in these studies, reported inactivity does not imply incapability, because these individuals might be capable but remain inactive for other reasons, for example, lack of an available partner.

It appears, therefore, that all the evidence indicates that the beliefs that the elderly are not sexually desirable, desirous, or capable are indeed false beliefs. At the present state of knowledge, then, these are properly regarded as myths. Research, however, is needed to study the effects of these false beliefs on the elderly. Even without such research, it seems reasonable to assume that these false beliefs may contrive to engender anxiety, guilt, confusion, diminished feelings of self-efficacy, and negative role expectations in the elderly—in short, sexual problems. The refutation of these myths can be a major contribution in helping the elderly have healthier sex lives.

Why do these myths exist? The denial or disparagement by younger individuals of the sexuality of elderly individuals is especially puzzling because, younger individuals owe their existence to their sexuality. Researchers have suggested a number of factors that may account for the perceived difference in sexuality between younger and older individuals. Some investigators believe that cohort effects, that is, effects not caused by the aging process per se but rather by the phenomena associated with a generation, may be responsible for the more conservative sexual behaviour and attitudes in the present generation of elderly. First, for example, the present elderly were brought up in a sexually repressive atmosphere, and according to Pfeiffer (1968), they are thus more likely to have been raised with, and currently influenced by, the view that reproduction is the sole or primary purpose of sex. Second, the great advances in the technology of contraception in the last few decades are probably responsible for the different sexual behavior of the current younger generation. The current elderly were raised when effective contraception was not yet developed, and this might have had some effect on their sexuality. Third, the current elderly had less sex education and therefore are more likely to believe various sexual myths, such as the myth that there is a fixed amount of masculine fluid which is used up in youth and the middle years. Finally, it has been suggested that current younger adults as children were forced to inhibit their own sexuality, because of their parents' restrictive values, and as a result—perhaps because of some sort of revenge motive—are now attempting to inhibit the sexuality of their elderly parents (Sviland, 1978).

There are also hypotheses that are not based on putative cohort effects. Some investigators have suggested that the oedipal child believes his parents are sexless. This belief is perhaps the basic for the humor in the story attributed to comedian Sam Levinson: "When I first found out how babies were born, I couldn't believe it. To think that my mother and father could do such a thing." Then, after a moment's reflection: "My father—maybe: but my mother—never!"

Another possible reason for the existence of these myths is that they are accurate characterizations of a social role defined for the elderly (Barker, 1968). As there are social roles for the elderly such as the sick role and the grandparent role, so there is an asexual social role. Asexual behavior is reinforced in the elderly, and individuals are also reinforced for holding these role expectations of the elderly.

Finally, some sociobiologists, such as Symons (in press) argue that evolution by natural selection has determined two absolute criteria of sexual attractiveness for humans: good health and age. Symons argues that individuals are designed by evolution to be attracted by the reproductive value of the opposite sex. Males have a small parental investment (limited to the contribution of the sperm) in each progeny and thus are simply designed to be attracted to females that are maximally reproductively viable. Females are maximally viable, hence maximally attractive, between the ages of 17 and 28. On the other hand, females have a higher parental investment (gestation, the lower number of possible progeny) and therefore are influenced more by the status and resources of the male. The female is designed to be attracted to a male that will be able and to be willing to, give resources to her offspring. Status and resources can increase with age. This account does serve to explain the observed sexual double standard mentioned earlier: elderly females are not reproductively viable and thus, on this account, not sexually desirable to males; however, older males can have high status and resources and thus be attractive to females.

THE SEXUAL PHYSIOLOGY OF AGING

The functioning and the structure of the human body changes as the individual ages. In this section, some of the major physical changes relevant to sexuality will be briefly reviewed. The reader is referred to the following sources for more information regarding the effects of aging on sexual physiology: Felstein (1983), Rossman (1978), Schneider (1978) and Weg (1983).

Age-Related Physical Changes in the Male

Males undergo physiological changes more gradually than females: for males, there is no sharp demarcation of sexual change as in menopause. A number of investigators have found that testosterone levels gradually diminish after the age of 50 (Baker, Burger, DeKretser, Hudson, O'Conner, Wang, Mirovics, Court, Dunlop, & Rennie, (1976); Hallberg, Wieland, Zoin, Furst, & Wieland, 1976; Kirschner & Coffman, 1968), but this finding is not universal. Some investigators failed to find a decrease in testosterone (Gandy & Peterson, 1968). Greenblatt, Witherington, and Sipahioglu (1976) reported a 50% success rate with testosterone replacement therapy. Felstein (1983) suggested that arteriosclerosis can result with decreased male sex hormone production. Decreases in testosterone can also result in problems in protein synthesis, salt and water balance, cardiovascular functioning, immune surveillance, and muscle tone and strength.

There also appears to be an increase in circulating gonadotropins (luteinizing hormone and follicle stimulating hormone) in men after the age of 50 (Harman, Tsitouras, Costa, & Blackman, 1982; Haug, Aakvaag, Sand, & Torjesen, 1974). In the male, luteinizing hormone stimulates the interstitial cells of the testes to manufacture and secrete testosterone. Follicle-stimulating hormone is a necessary stimulus for the production of mature sperm (Katchadourian & Lunde, 1972).

In the elderly male, the testes become smaller and more flaccid. Testicular tubules that store and carry sperm become increasingly narrowed (Talbert, 1977). Fewer sperm and fewer viable sperm are produced. However, Blum (1936) reported that 69% of males between the ages of 60 and 70, 60% between the ages of 70 and 80, and 48% between the ages of 80 and 90 showed spermatozoa in their ejaculate. However, some investigators have found increased chromosomal abnormalities in the sperm of the aging male.

In about 50% of males who reach the age of 80, the prostate gland enlarges (Katchadourian & Lunde, 1972). The prostate is a chestnut-shaped structure that encircles the urethra, and when it becomes enlarged, it can interfere with the flow of urine, cause problems in voluntarily initiating urination, or lead to enuresis. Aching testes and discomfort at the distal end of the penis are also experienced. Leutert and Jahn (1970) found a decrease in the amount of blood supplied to the prostate with increasing age. Treatment includes prostate massage, tetracycline antibiotic therapy, and surgery (Felstein, 1983). Herr (1979) found that sexual activity was retained in 40 of the 41 patients that were sexually active before prostate surgery. Masters and Johnson (1970) found a reduction in the viscosity and volume of seminal fluid and a decrease in the force of ejaculation. Moreover, Harbitz and Haugen (1972) reported an increase in carcinoma of the prostate with increasing age.

Age-Related Physical Changes in the Female

The average age for the onset of menopause in women is 50–51 years (Treloar, 1981). At this time, the ovary becomes devoid of oocytes, thus ensuring infertility. Corpora lutea cease to be formed after ovulatory function stops. However, some women experience an increase in sexual desire, because the fear of pregnancy is no longer an issue.

After menopause the uterus decreases in size to a small fraction of its premenopausal size (Lang & Aponte, 1967). This is believed to be due to the low levels of circulating estrogens and progestins. The cervix and ovaries also grow smaller and may reach prepubertal size in some women (Weg, 1983).

There are decreased amounts of ovarian estrogen and progesterone after menopause. Small amounts of estrogen are secreted by the adrenal glands. There is only a small drop in testosterone (Judd, 1976). Follicle-stimulating hormone and luteinizing hormone are from 8 to 14 times greater than in the premenopausal period (Greenblatt et al., 1976).

The vaginas of postmenopausal women not receiving estrogen treatment decrease in length and diameter (Harman & Talbert, 1985). There appears to be a loss of elasticity in the vaginal walls (Lang & Aponte, 1967). The labia majora shrink, thus constricting the opening of the vagina. The major clinical problems associated with the vagina in postmenopausal women are thinning of the epithelial wall and inadequate glandular secretions that are not due to intrinsic changes but rather to inadequate hormonal stimulation. The vaginal lining can become less sensitive to estrogen. When it becomes pale, thin, and dry, owing to inadequate levels of circulating estrogen, it can lead to an inability to retain moisture even when directly applied (Felstein, 1983). Thus, lubricating creams can be ineffective in relieving painful intercourse. However, Felstein recommends the use of local applications of estrogen creams to restore the health of the epithelium. It has also been suggested that indications for postmenopausal estrogen replacement therapy include hot flashes, atrophy of the reproductive organs, osteoporosis, and the possible risk of arteriosclerosis.

Masters and Johnson (1970) also found that the production of vaginal lubrication as a response to stimulation is delayed and decreased. Vaginitis, an infection caused by yeast organisms, can become more prevalent after menopause, which can result in painful intercourse (Weg, 1983).

There is also a modest reduction in the size of the clitoris, although Masters and Johnson (1970) reported no loss in its sensitivity. There is a decrease in pubic hair, and the mons often flattens. The breasts are dependent upon female sex hormones and consequently undergo changes when these are not prevalent. Connective tissue begins to disappear. Breast cancer seems to be associated with age and hormonal states. Pilnick and Leis (1978) studied 1,859 cases of breast cancer and found that 66% occurred in women over the age of

50, with a median age of 55 when the disease was detected.

CONSEQUENCES OF PATHOLOGY FOR THE SEXUALITY OF THE ELDERLY

Other physical changes and illnesses can also result in sexual problems for the elderly. For example, coronary heart disease can lead to sexual problems, although probably for psychogenic reasons. Rossman (1978) maintains that with the exception of individuals who are left with severe myocardial insufficiency or congestive heart failure, individuals should be encouraged to lead a normal life if they can:

> A number of studies have shown that the cardiac expenditure in intercourse is approximately that involved in climbing two flights of stairs. Hence if a post-coronary patient can climb two flights of stairs without significant or disabling symptomatology, there is no reason for forbidding sexual activity. Even patients who experience some angina in sexual circumstances find that prophylactic nitroglycerine may solve the problem. (p. 73)

Less than 1% of sudden coronary deaths occurs during or immediately after intercourse. Of course, one must consider the possibility that this might be underreported.

The treatment of hypertension can cause potency problems. The sedative effects of antihypertensive drugs can interfere with male potency and may adversely affect the female (Felstein, 1983). Diuretics can also cause problems.

Poorly regulated maturity-onset diabetes can interfere with the proper functioning of the cranial nerves and the autonomic nervous system and thus cause potency problems in males (Felstein, 1983). Retrograde or premature ejaculation can also be a problem associated with diabetes (Weg, 1983). In addition, diabetes can result in local genital infections that can make intercourse painful. With the elderly female diabetic, vaginal lubrication can become further delayed and decreased, even with adequate estrogen. Usually, when the diabetes is controlled, all these problems disappear.

Renshaw (1981) has suggested that damage to the autonomic nervous system in male stroke patients can lead to partial erections, impaired ejaculation, or total impotency, and in female patients, to a decreased lubrication. Felstein

(1983) points out that strokes can also interfere with sensory appreciation, motor activity, and verbalization, which can make sexual activity problematic.

Arthritis can, of course, make sexual activity painful. Mastectomy can, through psychological pathways, contrive to diminish libido. It is interesting to note that Schofield (1972) has estimated that 3% of males over 60 in developed countries are infected with gonorrhea and consequently may have ejaculation and erectile problems. Investigators have also found a 1.5% incidence of latent syphilis in older communities (Krishman & Lomax, 1970). Finally, the elderly may experience sexual problems caused by pathology they may share with younger individuals: obesity, alcoholism, drug abuse, poor nutrition, and the like.

CHANGES IN MALE AND FEMALE SEXUAL AROUSAL

Elderly males are in general more sexually active than elderly females. Interest in sexual activity usually exceeds actual activity for both males and females. However, the activity-interest discrepancy is greater for males than for females (Verwoerdt, Pfeiffer, & Wang, 1969).

Masters and Johnson (1966, 1970) found the following changes in the elderly male's sexual response:

1. Excitement phase: There is an increased length of time needed to obtain full erection. More direct stimulation is needed.
2. Plateau phase: There is a longer plateau phase, with diminished skin flush, nipple erection, testes enlargement and elevation, and pre-ejaculatory fluid.
3. Orgasm phase: Ejaculatory control is increased. Ejaculatory inevitability is shorter or absent. There are slower and less forceful ejaculatory contractions.
4. Resolution phase: There is a more rapid detumescence and a longer refractory period.

Solnick and Birren (1977) reported that the mean rate of maximum penile circumference increase was 6 times more rapid for younger males (19–30 years of age) than for older males (48–65 years of age). They also found that younger men tended to respond rapidly to an erotic stimulus, partially lost their erection after some time had elapsed, and then again responded rapidly to another erotic stimulus. Older males tended to obtain an erection in a more gradual manner, never reaching the maximum levels of the younger males.

For the female, Masters and Johnson reported the following changes:

1. Excitement phase: decreased vasocongestion of the genital tissues occurred, and the purplish hue of younger years changes to pink. Lubrication can take 5 to 15 minutes longer.
2. Plateau phase: Uterine contractions are decreased. The labia majora no longer elevate, although the clitoral response remains unchanged.
3. Orgasm phase: The duration of the orgasm is reduced. Uterine contractions may be spastic rather than rhythmic and may be reduced from three to five in youth to 1 or 2 in old age. Multiple orgasms are still possible.
4. Resolution phase: There is a rapid resolution, with labia minora color fading even before orgasm occurs.

PSYCHOTHERAPY AND THE SEXUAL PROBLEMS OF THE ELDERLY

Most regrettably, there appear to be few, if any, outcome or process studies of psychotherapy aimed at treating the sexual problems of the elderly. Thus, unfortunately, no studies can be reviewed here. However, the reader is referred to the studies by Annon (1976), Croft (1982), Fischer and Gochros (1977), and Masters and Johnson (1970) for information regarding the assessment and treatment of sexual problems in the general population.

It is reasonable to assume at this point that the treatments shown to be effective with younger individuals will also prove to be generally effective with the elderly. However, some modifications might be necessary. For example, Felstein (1983) warns that the use of the squeeze technique with the elderly male may cause a local petechial effect in the penile skin. Also, the time frames of certain therapeutic techniques may have to be increased in order to take into account the longer periods necessary for the elderly male to achieve an erection and the elderly female to obtain lubrication.

Sviland (1978) suggests that communication training and assertion training may often be more necessary with the elderly because of the Victorian influence of their early environment. The same is true of sex education, because she believes that the elderly are more often ignorant of the following facts:

1. The clitoris is an important component of orgasm.
2. Some postmenopausal women are multi-orgasmic.
3. Many females require some form of clitoral contact and stimulation for arousal or orgasm, and to this end, touching or oral-genital contact is socially acceptable.
4. The improved ejaculatory control found in aging males allows for longer intercourse before orgasm, which can enhance the female's pleasure.
5. The aging male requires increased direct genital contact for arousal or orgasm, and to this end, touching or oral-genital contact is socially acceptable.

Finally, Thomas (1982) has voiced concern that mental health professionals may have a tendency to project their middle-aged sexual values and agendas on the elderly and thus suggests that mental health professionals study the elderly in order to ascertain what sex means to them. Such a study of the individual's values and agendas might be valuable in every psychotherapy case in order to determine both treatment goals and acceptable treatment techniques.

FUTURE PROSPECTS

First and foremost, future studies need to be more methodologically and statistically sophisticated (Ludeman, 1981). Few of the studies cited used proper subject sampling techniques. Also, few used true experimental designs, and thus casual inference is problematic. Finally, data analysis was often quite primitive: Usually raw data in percentages was reported with no use of inferential statistics. These problems need to be overcome in order to gain more reliable information.

Second, there is a tendency to focus solely on genital sex. Ludeman (1981) suggested that the whole sexual relationship should be studied rather than only the genital aspects of the sexual experience. Butler and Lewis (1978) suggested that for older individuals: sex may serve as a means of expressing passion, affection, admiration, and loyalty; affirming one's body and its functioning;

asserting oneself, protecting oneself from anxiety; defying the stereotypes of the elderly; creating a sense of romance; affirming life; and experiencing pleasure through touch. Clearly, sex is more than genital contact, and it needs to be studied as such.

Third, little is known about the sexuality of the elderly homosexual. It has been suggested that male homosexuals are negatively influenced by age—there is a saying, "No one loves you when you are old and gay" (Gagnon, 1977). Comparative studies of relationship factors, genital sex, attraction, and physiology involving both male and female heterosexuals and homosexuals could result in much interesting information. Moreover, Caven (1973) has suggested that elderly females deal with the problem of the lack of elderly male partners by experimenting with homosexual relationships. If this line of reasoning is followed, then it seems reasonable that these relationships should be studied to assess their benefits and problems.

Fourth, more treatment studies are desperately needed. Although the sexual problems of the elderly are probably treatable by the same techniques as those used for the nonelderly, studies of the elderly are needed in order to be able to rule out the possibility that the sexual problems of older individuals are refractory to such treatments, as well as to determine if changes in these techniques need to be made because of factors unique to the elderly.

Fifth, epidemiological studies need to be conducted so that we can gain an understanding of the extent to which the elderly experience different types of sexual problems. This is particularly important because it appears that mental health services are underutilized by the elderly. Administrative policies regarding sexual practices in long-term-care institutions also need to be examined (Miller, 1978).

Finally, prevention studies would be useful in order to determine ways to avoid the development of sexual problems in the elderly.

REFERENCES

Annon, J. S. (1976). *Behavioral treatment of sexual problems: Brief therapy.* Hagerstown, MD: Harper & Row.
Baker, H. W., Burger, H. G., Dekretser, D. M., Hudson B., O'Conner, S., Wang, C., Mirovics, A., Court, J., Dunlop, M., & Rennie, G. C. (1976). Changes in the pituitary testicular system with age. *Clinical Endocrinology, 5,* 349–372.
Baras, M. (1961). A survey of dreams in aged persons. *Archives of General Psychiatry, 4,* 438–443.

Barker, R. (1968). *Ecological psychology.* Stanford CA: Stanford University Press.

Blum, V. (1936). Das problem des männlichen Climaceriums. *Wiener Klinische Wochenschrift, 49,* 1133–1139.

Bowens,, L. M., Cross, R. R., & Lloyd, R. A. (1963). Sexual function and urologic disease in the elderly male. *Journal of the American Geriatrics Society, 11,* 647–652.

Butler, R. N., & Lewis, M. I. (1978). The second language of sex. In R. Solnick (Ed.) *Sexuality and aging.* Los Angeles: University of Southern California Press.

Cameron, P. (1970). The generation gap: Beliefs about sexuality and self-reported sexuality. *Developmental Psychology, 3,* 272.

Caven, R. S. (1973). Speculation on innovations to conventional marriage in old age. *Gerontology, 13,* 408–411.

Croft, L. H. (1982). *Sexuality in later life.* Boston: John Wright.

Damrosch, S. P. (1984). Graduate nursing students' attitudes toward sexually active older persons. *Gerontologist, 24,* 299–302.

Felstein, I. (1983). Dysfunction: Origins and therapeutic approaches. In R. Weg (Ed.), *Sexuality in the later years.* New York: Academic Press.

Fischer, J., & Gochros, H. L. (1977). *Handbook of behavior therapy with sexual problems.* Elmsford NY: Pergamon.

Freeman, J. T. (1961). Sexual capacities in the aging male. *Geriatrics, 16,* 37–43.

Friedfield, L. (1961). Geriatrics, medicine, and rehabilitation. *Journal of the American Medical Association, 175,* 595–598.

Gandy, H. M., & Peterson, R. E. (1968). Measurement of testosterone and 17-KS in plasma by the double isotope dilution derivative technique. *Journal of Clinical Endocrinological Metabolism, 28,* 949–956.

Gagnon, J. (1977). *Human sexualities.* Glenview, IL: Scott, Foresman.

Golde, P., & Kagan, N. (1959). A sentence completion procedure for assessing attitudes toward old people. *Journal of Gerontology, 14,* 355–360.

Greenblatt, R. B., Witherington, R., & Sipahioglu, I. B. (1976). Estrogen–androgren levels in aging men and women. *Drug Therapy, 6,* 101–104.

Hallberg, M. C., Wieland, R. G., Zoin, E. M., Furst, B. H., & Wieland, J. M. (1976). Impaired Leydig cell reserve and altered serum androgen in the aging male. *Fertility and Sterility, 27,* 812–814.

Harbitz, T. B., & Haugen, C. A. (1972). Histology of the prostate in elderly men. *Acta Pathologica et Microbiologica Scandinavica,* 301–313.

Harman, S. M., Tsitouras, P. D., Costa, P. T., & Blackman, M. R. (1982). Reproductive hormones in aging men: 2. Basal pituitary gonadotropins and gonadotropin responses to luteinizing hormone releasing factor. *Journal of Clinical Endocrinology and Metabolism, 54,* 537–541.

Haug, E. A., Aakvaag, A., Sand, T., & Torjesen, P. A. (1974). The gonadotropin response to synthetic LHRH in males in relation to age, dose, and basal levels of testosterone, estradiol-17-beta, and gonadotropins. *Acta Endocrinologica, 77,* 625–635.

Herr, H. W. (1979). Preservation of sexual potency in prostatic cancer patients after implantation. *Journal of the Amercian Geriatrics Society, 27,* 17–22.

Hotvedt, M. (1983). The cross cultural and historical context. In R. B. Weg (Ed.), *Sexuality in the later years.* New York: Academic.

Judd, H. L. (1976). Harmonal dynamics associated with the menopause. *Clinical Obstetrics and Gynecology, 19* 775–778.

Kaas, M. J. (1978). Sexual expression of the elderly in nursing homes. *Gerontologist, 18,* 372-378.

Katchadourian, H. A., & Lunde, D. T. (1972). *Fundamentals of human sexuality.* New York: Holt, Rinehart Winston.

Kinsey, A. C., Pomeroy, W. B., & Martin, C. E. (1948). *Sexual behavior in the human male.* Philadelphia: Saunders.

Kinsey, A. C., Pomeroy, W. B., Martin, C. E., & Gebhard, P. H. (1953). *Sexual behavior in the human female.* Philadelphia: Saunders.

Kirschner, M. A., & Coffman, G. D. (1968). Measurement of plasma testosterone and delta-4-androstenedione using electron capture gas liquid chromatography. *Journal of Clinical Endocrinological Metabolism, 28,* 1347–1352.

Krishnan, M., & Lomax, W. (1970). Venereal infection in the elderly. *Gerontological Clinician, 12,* 2.

Kuhn, M. E. (1976). Sexual myths surrounding the aging. In W. W. Oaks, G. A. Melchiode, I. Ficher (Eds.), *Sex and the life cycle.* New York: Grune & Stratton.

Lang, W. R., & Aponte, G. E. (1967). Gross and microscopic anatomy of the aged female reproductive organs. *Clinical Obstetrics and Gynecology, 10,* 454–465.

LaTorre, R. A., & Kear, K. (1977). Attitudes toward sex in the aged. *Archives of Sexual Behavior, 6,* 203–213.

Leutert, G., & Jahn, K. (1970). Uber alersabhangige histologische und histochemische Befunde an der Prostata des Menschen. *Acta Histochemische, 37,* 136–147.

Ludeman, K. (1979). *The sexuality of the older postmarital woman: A phenomenological inquiry.* Unpublished manuscript.

Ludeman, K. (1981). The sexuality of the older person: Review of the literature. *Gerontologist, 21,* 203–208.

Masters, W. H., & Johnson, V. E. (1966). *Human sexual response.* Boston: Little Brown.

Masters, W. H., & Johnson, V. E. (1970). *Human sexual inadequacy.* Boston: Little, Brown.

Miller, B. B. (1978). Sexual practices and administrative policies in long term care institutions. In R. Solnick (Ed.), *Sexuality and aging.* Los Angeles: University of Southern California Press.

Nigola, P., & Peruzza, M. (1974). Sex in the aged. *Journal of the American Geriatics Society, 22,* 481–484.

Pfeiffer, E. (1968). Sexual behavior in aged men and women. *Archives of General Psychiatry, 19,* 753–758.

Pfeiffer, E., Verwoerdt, A., & Davis, B. C. (1974). Sexual behavior in middle life. In E. Palmore (Ed.), *Normal aging II.* Durham, NC: Duke University Press.

Pilnick, S., & Leis, H. (1978). Clinical diagnosis of breast lesions. In H. Gallagher, H. Leis, R. Snyderman, & J. Urban (Eds.), *The breast.* St. Louis: Mosby.

Renshaw, D. (1981). Pharmacotherapy and female sexuality. *British Journal of Sexual Medicine, 71,* 34–37.

Roff, L. L., & Klemmack, D. L. (1979). Sexual activity among older persons: A comparative analysis of appropriateness. *Research on Aging*, 389–399.

Rossman, I. (1978). Sexuality and aging: An internist's perspective. In R. Solnick (Ed.), *Sexuality and aging* Los Angeles: University of Southern California Press.

Schneider, E.C. (1978). *The aging reproductive system.* New York: Raven Press.

Schofield C. B. (1972). *Sexually transmitted diseases.* Edinburgh: Livingstone.

Sontag, S. (1972, September 23). *Saturday Review,* pp. 29–38.

Solnick, R. L., & Birren, J. E. (1977). Age and male erectile responsiveness. *Archives of Sexual Behavior, 6,* 1–9.

Sviland, M. A. (1978). A program of sexual liberation and growth in the elderly. In R. Solnick (Ed.), *Sexuality and aging.* Los Angeles: University of Southern California Press.

Symons, D. (in press). An evolutionary approach: Can Darwin's view of life shed light on human sexuality. In J. Geer & W. O'Donohue (Eds.), *Theories of human sexuality.* New York: Plenum.

Talbert, G. B. (1977). Aging of the reproductive system.

In C. Finch & L. Hayflick (Eds.), *Handbook of the biology of aging.* New York: Van Nostrand Reinhold.

Tarail, M. (1962). Sex over sixty-five. *Sexology,* 440–445.

Thomas, B. (1982). Sexuality and aging: Essential vitamin or popcorn. *Gerontologist, 22,* 240–243.

Treloar, A. E. (1981). Menstrual activity and the premenopause. *Maturitas, 3,* 249–264.

Verwoerdt, A., Pfeiffer, E., & Wang, H. (1969). Sexual behavior in senescence. *Geriatrics, 24,* 137–154.

Wasow, M., & Loeb, M. E. (1979). Sexuality in nursing homes. *Journal of the American Geriatrics Society, 27,* 73–79.

Weg, R. B. (1983). The physiological perspective. In R. B. Weg (ed.), *Sexuality in the later years.* New York: Academic Press.

White, C. B. (1975 June). *Sexuality in the institutionalized elderly.* Paper presented at the meeting of the New York State Public Health Association, Buffalo, NY.

White, C. B. (1982). A scale for the assessment of attitudes and knowledge regarding sexuality in the aged. *Archives of Sexual Behavior, 11,* 491–502.

Winn, R. L., & Newton, N. (1982). Sexuality and aging: A study of 106 cultures. *Archives of Sexual Behavior, 11,* 283–298.

Chapter 7

Affective Disorders Among the Aging

Susan A. Gaylord
and William W. K. Zung

Most human beings experience the ups and downs of their lives without succumbing to a prolonged, unhealthy state of elation or depression. The process of aging represents a special challenge in this respect, with increased potential for sudden, often irreversible, declines in physical health or for slow but inexorable progressions of chronic illness, compounded by the loss of friends, family, and autonomy. Yet even among the aged, the great majority adapt with grace, good humor, and equanimity. This chapter deals with the minority— either those who throughout large portions of their lives have suffered the miseries of affective disorders, which often increase in frequency and severity with age, or those for whom stresses associated with aging have triggered their first episode of an affective illness.

The authors of this chapter take the view that aging is a normal aspect of the developmental process, involving not only the inevitable physiological losses but also the potential for continued positive growth and adaptation. Human beings of all ages, including the elderly, possess the inherent capacity to face their lives honestly and cheerfully, without resorting to artificial strategies that deny the realities of fear, loss, death, and decay. Failure in this regard can increase the likelihood of depression, physical illness, and suicide.

Affective disorders—depression and mania—

are pervasive disturbances of both body and mind involving changes in mood, bodily functions, and thought processes. Clinical depression is the most common psychiatric disorder found among the elderly, with a prevalence estimated at from 5% to 15%. Mania is found much less frequently, with a prevalence of less than 1%.

Depressed persons exist in varying degrees of pain and desperation, often undiagnosed or misdiagnosed by health care professionals. Even the sufferer may not be aware of having the disorder, which can be masked by various body aches and pains. Thus, the depressed elderly are underrepresented in mental health clinics and in the offices of psychologists and psychiatrists.

This chapter is devoted primarily to a discussion of the causes, diagnosis, treatment, and prevention of depression in the aging. Mania is also discussed but in less detail.

DEFINITIONS, SYMPTOMS, AND CLASSIFICATION

The disorders of depression and mania have been recognized since ancient times, yet there is still disagreement as to concepts, definitions, and classification (Andreasen, 1982). In general, it is recognized that a depressive disorder is to be distinguished from simple unhappiness, which is a normal response to unpleasant events, just as mania is to be distinguished from elation, a normal response to a happy turn of events. The boundary between affective disorders and normality is still disputed, however.

Symptoms of Depression

The following is a summary of a more detailed description of symptoms of depression provided by Hamilton (1982). Common symptoms of depression are dysphoric mood, loss of interest, and anxiety. Physical symptoms may include difficulty in falling asleep, loss of appetite and libido, lack of energy, and fatigability. There is often a sense of helplessness and ineffectuality about the present, hopelessness about the future, and a sense of worthlessness and failure about the past. Reassurances by others give little comfort. Objectively, loss of interest can be seen as a lack of desire to participate in work and other normal activities.

Anxiety may manifest as a constant state of apprehension and as irritability in the face of even minor frustrations. The depressed person may be tense and unable to relax. Forgetfulness may occur through lack of attention and difficulty in concentration. Physical concomitants of anxiety in the depressed person may include heart palpitations, sweating of the extremities, dryness of the mouth, headaches, and indigestion. Both difficulty in falling asleep and early-morning awakening may occur. Sleep itself may seem unrefreshing and may be blamed for the previously mentioned symptoms. As the depression progresses, guilty and suicidal thoughts may increase—15% of depressives ultimately do kill themselves. Paranoid delusions are relatively rare.

Psychomotor agitation is found more commonly in women than in men and manifests itself as fidgeting, excessive talking, and possibly wringing of the hands and pacing. Agitation is most characteristic of late-onset (involutional) depressions. On the other hand, psychomotor retardation is also a common symptom. Walking may be slowed and the posture drooped. The facial expression may be blank or fixedly melancholic; the voice, quiet and monotonous; responses to questions, delayed and brief. Patients may complain of difficulty in thinking and of confused or slowed thoughts. Such symptoms are responsible, at least partly, for the misdiagnosis of organic brain syndrome in the elderly, the so-called *pseudodementias*.

Masked depression is a term for depression that is dominated by physical symptoms, such as lack of energy and fatigability, with less noticeable changes in mood. The patient may feel exhausted all the time, although a physical examination reveals no cause. Masked depression may also manifest itself as vague, persistent headaches or muscular discomfort. Hypochondriasis is present in about one third of these patients.

Differences in Depression Symptoms in the Elderly

Symptoms of severe depression in the elderly are similar to those in younger persons. Some have described the elderly depressed as being more apathetic than emotive (Grauer, 1977). Post (1972) found delusional, nihilistic ideas to be less typical of the elderly than was once thought. Those presenting with such symptoms were severely depressed and agitated, and had delusional ideas of disease, poverty, and guilt. Post (1982) found that less severe, nonpsychotic depressives outnumber psychotic depressives among the elderly, as in other age groups. For nonpsychotic depressives, anxiety is often expressed in repeated complaints about unpleasant, ill-defined physical sensations or memory impairment. Complaints of a depressed mood may be minimal or absent.

Symptoms of Mania

The following is a description of symptoms of mania taken from Tyrer and Shopsin (1982). Mania is a rare disorder, rarer still in the elderly. A first episode of mania may be difficult to detect, even in close friends. In the early stages, the person tends to be full of self-reliance and feel that his or her problems have been overcome. As the disorder progresses, the person appears increasingly happy and carefree, and is often in a playful, expansive mood that may be infectious. However, his or her actions often display a disregard for the feelings of others or for social protocol. Delusional notions of power and self-importance, often religious in content, may emerge. Commonly, the manic will become involved in risky, seemingly ill-founded enterprises and will spend money excessively. Euphoria can change quickly, replaced by explosive anger and irritability in the face of frustration. Psychomotor activity is accelerated, and libido is increased. The flow of thoughts is rapid and easily disrupted. Grooming and health care may be overlooked. Delusions not related to mood are seen in 20% to 50% of patients (Pope & Lipinski, 1978). The symptoms of mania in the elderly may differ little, if at all, from those in younger persons (Post, 1982).

Diagnostic Criteria and Classification of Affective Disorders

Diagnostic criteria for affective disorders have been developed in the course of attempts to create a working basis for research and clinical practice. Examples of such diagnostic systems are the Research Diagnostic Criteria (RDC), developed by Spitzer, Endicott, and Robins (1978), and the third and latest edition of the *Diagnostic and Statistical Manual of Mental Disorders* of the American Psychiatric Association (1980). Such systems, with their explicit, operational definitions, have increased the uniformity in descriptions of affective disorders.

The *DSM-III* classifies affective disorders according to severity, categorizing them as either major affective disorders or minor specific affective disorders. Major affective disorders are further subdivided into bipolar disorders and major depression. Bipolar disorders are characterized by distinct mood shifts, involving periods of mania and depression. Major depression is characterized by a dysphoric mood of at least 1 week's duration, as well as by such symptoms as sleep disturbances, decreased appetite, weight loss, lack of energy, loss of interest and pleasure in activities, and thoughts of death or suicide.

Minor depressive disorders, less severe but chronic in duration, are subdivided into cyclothymic disorders, characterized by mood swings from hypomania to low moods, and dysthymic disorders, characterized by recurrent and chronic depression. A mild depressive episode, presumably precipitated by recent life changes, is classified as an adjustment disorder with depressive features.

Classifications in terms of endogenous and reactive and primary and secondary depression are not used in the *DSM-III*, but are still found widely in the literature. The term *reactive* implies the presence of an environmental cause, whereas the term *endogenous* implies the absence of an external cause. Endogenous depression is typically a severe form of depression that is particularly responsive to somatic therapy. Primary depression is said to occur in an individual with no previous history of psychiatric illness, whereas secondary depression is said to occur in a person who has a prior history of such illness (Munro, 1966; Woodruff, Murphy, & Herjanic, 1967). Secondary depression is thought to be less homogeneous in its course and treatment, because it may accompany or be a result of such disorders as alcoholism, anxiety disorder, or hysteria.

Some researchers have criticized the *DSM-III* classification system as being sterile and atheoretical (e.g., Carroll, 1983) because of its disregard of such subgroupings as endogenous and reactive, as well as such features of clinical importance as family history, previous episodes and responses to treatment, and history of manic and hypomanic episodes. Such information is useful to researchers in maximizing the homogeneity of subgroupings so as to isolate the causes of the disorder and the responses to treatment. We will discuss findings in terms of some of these factors and subgroupings in later sections.

DIAGNOSIS

Clinical Evaluation and Diagnosis in the Elderly

A thorough clinical evaluation for depression or mania should include a physical examination and history taking to ascertain the date of onset of symptoms, number of past episodes of affective disorders, treatment given and its effectiveness, actual versus imagined physical problems, and medications being taken that might produce depression-like symptoms. Diagnostic tests may aid in differentiating real versus imagined memory impairment, thus helping to rule out senile dementia.

Depression in an elderly person may manifest itself differently than in a younger person, creating problems in diagnosis. For example, the elderly are more likely to mask their depression than younger individuals (Salzman & Shader, 1978). Depression, regardless of severity, involving a predominance of somatic complaints or even cognitive impairment (termed *pseudodementia*) may be overlooked or misdiagnosed in the elderly, when in fact, if the identical clinical features were to be found in a younger patient, a diagnosis of depression would be made (Epstein, 1976). Gurland, Copeland, Sharpe, and Kelleher (1976) reported a tendency of elderly depressed subjects to readily admit to memory problems, even though formal testing showed no impairment of memory function.

Another problem may be clinical bias on the part of professionals toward the diagnosis of organic disorder in the elderly. For example, a study by Perlick and Atkins (1984) found that clinicians hearing a taped interview of an older man of unknown age presenting with sad affect along with mild cognitive impairment viewed the man as senile when told that he was 70 years of age and viewed him correctly as depressed when told that he was 50.

On the other hand, there is also the danger that older people who are actually physically ill may be diagnosed inaccurately as depressed, because depression scales, described in the next section, weigh physical symptoms heavily in the diagnosis of depression.

Diagnostic Scales and Their Application to the Elderly

At the individual level, the diagnostic tools that measure affective disorders allow the physician or psychologist to assess the patient's or client's condition and determine a course of treatment; at the community level, they measure the prevalence of disorders in the population, providing further information as to cause and possible avenues of treatment and prevention. The validity, reliability, and appropriate use of various measurement tools become important issues, especially as they are applied to the elderly.

Salzman, Kochansky, Shader, and Cronin (1972) reviewed depression inventories suitable for the study of a geriatric population. Among those they found suitable are the Hamilton Rating for Depression (Hamilton, 1960, 1967), Zung Self-Rating Depression Scale (Zung, 1965), Beck Depression Inventory (Beck, Ward, Mendelson, Mock, & Erbaugh, 1961), Depressive Scale (Cutler & Kurland, 1961), Psychiatric Judgment of Depression Scale (Overall, Hollister, Pokorny, Casey, & Katz, 1962), Longitudinal Observation of Behavior (Bunney & Hamburg, 1963), Depression Rating Scale (Overall, Hollister, & Meyer, 1964), Depression Adjective Checklist (Lubin, 1965), NIMH Collaborative Depression Mood Scale (Raskin, 1965), Sad-Glad Scale (Simpson, Hackett, & Kline, 1966), and the Dynamic Depression Scale (Hunt, Singer, & Cobb, 1967).

Since that review, several diagnostic tests have been developed specifically for the elderly, including the Geriatric Mental Status Review (Gurland et al., 1976) and the Geriatric Depression Scale (Yesavage, Brink, Rose, & Adey, 1983), which is partially based on the Zung Self-Rating Depression Scale.

Some of the more popular assessment tools and, where possible, their application to an elderly population are described below.

In 1961, Beck et al. published an interviewer-rated Inventory for Measuring Depression consisting of 21 categories relating to symptoms and attitudes of depressed patients, based on patient observations and consistent with the psychoanalytic literature on depression. Each category described a specific behavioral manifestation of depression, including mood, pessimism, sense of failure, lack of satisfaction, guilty feelings, sense of punishment, self-hate, self-accusations, self-punitive wishes, crying spells, irritability, social withdrawal, indecisiveness, negative body image, work inhibition, sleep disturbances, fatigability, decreased appetite, weight loss, somatic preoccupation, and loss of libido. During the initial formulation of the inventory, each patient was seen by two psychiatrists, who rated the patient on the depth of depression using a four-point scale, in which a value of 0 signified no depression; 1, mild depression; 2, moderate depression; and 3, severe depression. Concurrent validity was reported through comparisons with other standardized measures of depression. Nussbaum, Wittig, Hanlon, and Kurland (1963) found initial and final correlations between the D scale of the Minnesota Multiphasic Personality Inventory (MMPI) and the depression inventory to be .75 and .69, respectively. In a comparison of the depression inventory and the Hamilton Rating for Depression, Schwab, Bialow, and Holzer (1967) showed a correlation coefficient of .75. Beck subsequently condensed the scale to 13 items (Beck & Beck, 1972) and used it as a self-rating scale.

The Hamilton Rating for Depression (HAMD) devised by Hamilton (1960, 1967), employs a skilled observer to evaluate a patient during a clinical interview. The test comprises 21 items that commonly occur in depression. Most of the items are scored on a continuum of 0 to 4, where 0 represents the absence of a symptom and 4 reflects the highest level of severity. The Hamilton scale is the most widely used observer-rated scale for depression. Almost every new antidepressant drug that has been studied for efficacy has depended upon the demonstrated positive change over time in results on this scale. Drawbacks are that it requires a trained observer, favors somatic complaints associated with depression, contains a number of items that measure anxiety as well as neurotic complaints, and is time-consuming to perform.

The Zung Self-Rating Depression Scale (SDS), one of the most widely used tools for measuring depression, is the most popular self-rating scale. Simple and easy to use, it consists of 20 items, framed as sentences, constructed on the basis of clinical diagnostic criteria commonly used to characterize depressive disorders. The contents of the items are comparable to the *DSM-III* diagnostic criteria for major affective disorders (Zung, 1982). The subject using the SDS is asked to rate each of the 20 items as to how it applies to him or her at the time of testing in four quantitative terms, having values of 1 to 4: none or a little of the time, some of the time, a good part of the time, most or all of the time. Ten of the items are worded symptomatically negative, and ten, symptomatically positive. An SDS index, which ranges from 25 to 100, is derived by dividing the sum of the raw score values obtained in the 20 items by the maximum possible score of 80, converted to a decimal and multiplied by 100. Results from previous studies have shown that normal control subjects under 65 years of age had scores of 25 to 43, while subjects with mild to moderate depression had scores of 50 to 59; those with moderate to severe depression, 60 to 69; and those with severe depression, 70 and above.

Correlations between SDS indices obtained from patients and global ratings made by clinicians showed a significantly high correlation ($r = .75$) for depressed patients (Schaefer et al., 1985). Likewise, the validity of the Zung scale has been tested and found to have a significant correlation with the Hamilton Rating for Depression (Brown & Zung, 1972), the Beck Depression Inventory (Zung, 1969), and the D scale in the MMPI (Zung, Richards, & Short, 1965). Additional data demonstrated no correlation between the Zung scale and age, educational level, annual income, or intelligence level (Zung, 1967a).

Zung (1967b) used the SDS to measure the amount of depressive symptomatology present in normal subjects 65 years of age and over. Subjects from two groups—a retirement home (mean age, 80) and a Golden Age Club (mean age, 73)—had mean SDS scores that were significantly higher than those of a normal population under 65. The aged population evaluated themselves as highest on predominantly biological questionnaire items and lowest on the affective items. The observation of higher SDS scores for older populations has been repeated many times since then by numerous investigators, raising the issue of diagnostic criteria for depression in the elderly (Zung & Zung, 1986).

Okimoto, Barnes, Veith, Raskind, Inui, and Carter (1982) compared the SDS ratings with the diagnosis made by a psychiatrist using the *DSM-III* criteria, who was unaware of the scale results of patients seen in a geriatric medical clinic of a Veterans Administration medical center. Based on their findings, the authors suggested that the choice of cutoff index score for morbidity be dependent upon the purpose for which the depression scales are applied. For screening purposes, one might accept a lower specificity (i.e., a higher false-positive rate) in the first phase of depression detection. On the other hand, for research purposes, one might choose a higher cutoff index score in order to ensure greater specificity.

Blumenthal (1975) interviewed 160 married couples differing in age, education, and economic characteristics using a structured questionnaire that included the SDS. Twelve questions on the SDS were then grouped into four subindices: the Well-Being Index ("I find it easy to do the things I used to do"; "I find it easy to make decisions"; "I feel I am useful and needed"; "My life is pretty full"; "I still enjoy doing the things I used to"), the Depressed Mood Index ("I feel down-hearted and blue"; "I have crying spells or feel like it"; "I feel that others would be better off if I were dead"), the Somatic Symptoms Index ("My heart beats faster than usual"; "I get tired for no reason"), and the Optimism Index ("My mind is as clear as it used to be"; "I feel hopeful about the future"). She found that whereas correlations among all four subindices were moderate to high for young people (aged 27 or below), for older people (aged 58 or more) they were uniformly lower. For example, the correlation between the Depressed Mood and the Somatic Symptoms indices was .72 for the younger group and .21 for the older, and the correlation between the Well-Being and the Optimism indices was .75 for the younger group and only .31 for the older group. These differences indicate that for older people the indices might be measuring something other than, or in addition to, depression symptoms. For example, "My mind is as clear as it used to be," when answered in the negative, might be indicative of common complaints of mild memory impairment in the elderly, and "I feel hopeful about the future" is less likely to be answered in the affirmative by someone whose life has already been lived than by someone for whom most of life is ahead.

When the subscales were correlated with selected demographic measures, it was found that while the Optimism, Well-Being, and Somatic Symptoms indices all correlated significantly ($p < .05$) with age, the Depressed Mood Index did not, giving further indication that the first three indices are measuring something other than depression and that the aged are in fact not significantly more depressed than their younger counterparts.

Yesavage et al. (1983) conducted a study using the Geriatric Depression Screening scale (GDS), which they had developed and which comprised 30 items. Results of this study generated relevant data with respect to the SDS and how it compared to the Hamilton scale; the correlation between the SDS and the HAMD was .80. In another study using the GDS scale, the data demonstrated that all of the scales studied (GDS, SDS, HAMD) were able to distinguish between the depressed aged and the control aged groups (Brink, Yesavage, Lum, Heersema, Adey, & Rose, 1982).

Zung and Zung (1986) reviewed a number of studies that had used the SDS in research on the elderly and concluded that overall, the SDS has proved to be a useful and valid tool in measuring depression in the elderly. Differentiation between normal aging and depression and the question of morbidity cutoffs remain important issues.

PREVALENCE

It is difficult to estimate the percentage of the population afflicted with affective disorders. Such estimates are dependent upon not only the methodology used to gather data but also upon the definitions, the criteria established, and the diagnostic tools employed (Gurland, 1976; Copeland, Kelleher, Kellett, Fountain-Gourlay, Cowan, Barrow, & DeGruchy [UK] with Gurland, Sharpe, Simon, Kuriansky, and Stiller [USA], 1974). A number of studies of the prevalence of affective disorders in the general population, including the elderly, have shown that prevalence tends to peak in the 40- to 60-year age group. However, prevalence still remains high in the elderly.

One striking example of how variation in diagnosis leads to differences in measures of prevalence is the results of the Cross-National Project for the Study of the Mental Disorders in the United States and the United Kingdom (Cooper, Kendell, Gurland, Sharpe, Copeland, & Simon, 1972; Gurland, Sharpe, Simon, Kuriansky, & Stiller, 1972). In one part of that study, clinical conditions of patients were held constant across both countries (e.g., psychiatrists were shown videotapes of the same patients). British psychiatrists diagnosed affective disorders more often than American psychiatrists; the Americans diagnosed schizophrenia more often in the younger age group than the British and organic disorders more often in the older age group. When the clinical conditions were held constant for both old and young patients, both British and American psychiatrists diagnosed affective disorders more often in the middle-age range (35 to 59), with a bias toward schizophrenia in the younger age group and toward organic disorders in the older age group (Fleiss, Gurland, Simon, & Sharpe, 1973).

Thus, owing more to differences in methodology and definitions than to differences in epidemiological factors, estimates of the prevalence of depression range from less than 5% to 44% (Blazer & Williams, 1980). For major affective disorders, however, the reported prevalence is lower and less variable: Studies give estimates of 1% to 3% (Eaton & Weil, 1955; Essen-Möller, Larson, Uddenberg, & White, 1956).

Blazer and Williams (1980) used the operational criteria established by the *DSM-III* to measure the prevalence of dysphoric symptoms and the symptoms of major depressive disorders in a community population comprising individuals 65 years of age and over. They found that 14.7% of the elderly population had significant dysphoric symptomatology: 4.5% suffered from dysphoric symptoms only, and 3.7%, from a major depressive disorder. Of those suffering from major depression, 1.8% were classified as having a primary depressive disorder and 1.9% as having a secondary depressive disorder. Six and a half percent had depressive symptoms associated with impaired physical health.

CAUSAL FACTORS

There is a natural law that things change: The sun rises and sets, summer becomes autumn, friends and lovers come and go, our abilities wax and wane. It is a basic tendency of humans and other living creatures to adapt to changing situations—whether they be pleasant or unpleasant—to the extent that the situations themselves cannot be altered. This tendency contributes toward survival and promotes a sense of internal and external harmony. Affective disorders represent a malfunction of this adaptive process. At one level, the malfunction is biological, manifesting as an imbalance in the monoamine and endocrine systems, resulting in disruption of sleeping, eating, and energy levels. At another level, the malfunction is psychological, manifesting in distorted thought processes and exaggerated emotional states. Whether the origin of the malfunction is biological or psychological is difficult to say: Both kinds of theories have been proposed. Accumulating evidence suggests that mental and physical factors often interact to produce these undesired states of being.

The role of genetic versus environmental factors has also been studied. Again, evidence points toward an interaction of both factors. There is an inheritable vulnerability for some types of affective disorders, a vulnerability that could be mediated by, for example, a propensity toward imbalances in the aforementioned biological systems, which in turn could lead to a tendency to ignore more positive events and enhance more negative events. Environmental factors have also been implicated, even in the so-called endogenous depressions. The role of early childhood losses has received special attention, as has the theory of learned helplessness.

The following is a brief description of various theories and the evidence supporting them, beginning with the more biologically oriented and ending with the more psychosocially oriented hypotheses.

Genetic Studies

Twin studies have shown that affective disorders are indeed inheritable. One review of the literature (Nurnberger & Gershon, 1982) states that while about 65% of monozygotic twins are concordant for affective disorders, only about 14% of dizygotic twins are concordant. Concordance tends to be higher for bipolar than for unipolar affective disorders (in monozygotic twins, .79 vs. .54), and is higher for those with more severe disorders. The morbidity risk of relatives of depressed individuals rises with the degree of concordance. When both twins have the disorder, the morbidity risk of relatives is greater than if only one twin has the disorder, which, in turn, is greater than if neither twin has the disorder (Bertelsen, Harvald, & Hauge, 1977). Genetic factors appear to play a greater role in depression if the onset is before age 50 (Mendlewicz, 1976).

Biochemical Perspectives

Evidence of the contribution of biological factors to depression comes from basic research on the central nervous and endocrine systems and from findings regarding the effects of drugs and other somatic therapies on depression.

Role of Neurotransmitters in Mediating Depressive Disorders

Certain naturally occurring amines have been found to relate to the pathogenesis of mood disorders. These are norepinephrine, dopamine, and serotonin (5-HT)—all biogenic amines intimately involved with the centers of the central nervous system, such as the limbic structures, that regulate drives and emotions. Based upon a knowledge of anatomical structure and sites of nerve tracts mediated by these biogenic amines, the effects of disturbances of these systems have been postulated or identified. Noradrenergic tracts are believed to play a major role in mood disorders. Dopaminergic tracts have been identified as being involved in the pathophysiology of Parkinson's disease. Serotonergic tracts play a major role in producing sleep disturbances. These observations have led to a catecholamine hypothesis of mood disorders. There appears to be a significant disturbance in the metabolism of norepinephrine in patients with affective disorders, with the evidence indicating either an absolute or a relative deficiency of norepinephrine in depressives and an excess of norepinephrine in manics (Schildkraut, 1965).

In general, biogenic amines, including 5-HT and the catecholamines norepinephrine and dopamine, are metabolized to biologically inactive compounds via oxidative deamination by the enzyme monamine oxidase. It has been reported that monoamine oxidase activity appears to increase with advancing age (Robinson, Davis, Niles, Ravaris, & Sylvester, 1971), with a peak rise starting at about 45 years of age and steadily increasing thereafter. The importance of this finding can be understood in the light of the biogenic amine theory of mood disorders and our understanding of the pharmacology of psychotropic drugs. Evidence from psychopharmacology points to the fact that many of the drugs used in the treatment of depressive disorders are known to increase the levels of available neurotransmitters, such as norepinephrine. It has been inferred that their antidepressant effect is related in some way to their ability to increase the amount of norepinephrine. For example, the tricyclic antidepressants inhibit the reuptake of norepinephrine released at the synapse, thus increasing its levels at receptor sites. The monoamine oxidase inhibitors increase the supply of available norepinephrine by inhibiting its degradation within the presynaptic nerve ending.

Many of these findings are based on animal studies, and most of the postulates have heuristic value, still lacking the necessary chain of evidence that could translate theories into clinical practice. We must therefore be cautious about interpreting these findings as causal effects and not assume that the primary defects in depression of middle and late life are the results of these changes in the monoamine oxidase mechanism. Thus far, no biogenic amine theory has been able to explain the etiology of mood disorders, and in fact, altered biogenic amine metabolism may be secondary to other biochemical events (Shopsin, 1974).

Psychological Perspectives

Psychological theories have focused on depression rather than mania. Most psychological theories relate depression to loss. It is not the loss itself but the reaction to the loss that characterizes depression. It is important to emphasize that the loss can be real, threatened, or imaginary.

Psychoanalytic Theories

Freud described the features of melancholia as a "profoundly painful dejection, cessation of interest in the outside world, loss of the capacity to love, inhibition of all activity, and a lowering of the self-regarding feelings to a degree that finds utterances in self-reproaches and self-revilings, and culmi-

nates in a delusional expectation of punishment" (Mendelson, 1982, p. 162). He acknowledged that his observations and theory were based on his own patients, for whom the melancholic episodes were psychogenic rather than somatic in origin and thus were not necessarily generalizable (Mendelson, 1982). He theorized that for melancholic sufferers, the lost object has become identified with the patient's ego and that the hostility felt for the rejecting object is thus directed against the ego, into which the object has been incorporated.

For Bibring (1953), depressive illness was characterized by a loss of self-esteem, which could occur through the frustration of narcissistic aspirations during either the oral, anal, or phallic phases. Jacobson (1953, 1954, 1971) agreed that the "central psychological problem of depression" was the loss of self-esteem (i.e., a sense of helplessness, weakness, or inferiority). For her, however, the determinants of self-esteem were broadened to include self-representation, the superego, the ego ideal, and self-critical ego functions (Mendelson, 1982).

Behavioral and Cognitive Theories

Behavioral theories of depression emphasize the role of the loss of positive reinforcement in instigating depressive episodes. Ferster (1965) theorized that the loss of a major reinforcer (due perhaps to death or separation) results in reduction in positive reinforcement of adaptive behavior, which leads to a decline in the total behavioral repertoire. He hypothesized that a deficit in social skills might prevent a depressed person from coping effectively with such reduced reinforcement.

Costello (1972) hypothesized that depression is caused by the loss of reinforcer effectiveness, perhaps owing to biochemical or neurological changes or to the disruption of a chain of behaviors.

Lewinsohn and his colleagues (Lewinsohn, Biglan, & Zeiss, 1976; Lewinsohn, Munoz, Youngren, & Zeiss, 1978) emphasized the importance of the loss of response-contingent positive reinforcement in the development of depression, rather than the loss of positive reinforcement per se. The reasoning is that unless reinforcement is contingent upon a response from the depressed person, it will not help in the maintenance of a behavioral repertoire. Thus, depression results from a person's taking part in only a small number of activities that are either intrinsically reinforcing or reinforced by others. The lack of positive reinforcement causes a reduction in the output of behavior, as well as an increase in dysphoric mood. Depressed persons have been found to participate in few activities that they perceive as pleasant and to improve when these activities are increased. They also experience many current life events that they perceive as negative and report a decrease in depression with the reduction of these events.

Another behavioral formulation of depression is based on an animal model called *learned helplessness* (Seligman, 1973; Seligman & Maier, 1967). The experimental paradigm involves first forcing an animal, such as a dog, to undergo unpleasant stimuli (e.g., repeated shocks) that it would otherwise avoid, then exposing the animal to the unpleasant stimuli but allowing it to avoid them by some action on its part. The result is that the animal's normal escape response is extinguished, and the animal submits passively to the unpleasant experience. This response can be generalized to other similar situations. Subsequently teaching the animal that it can avoid the unpleasant stimulus reinstates the normal avoidance response. Seligman (1973) hypothesized that depression is a belief in one's own helplessness, based on previous conditioning (punishment or lack of positive reinforcement) that does not allow for control of one's environment. Passiveness and hopelessness result from repeated failures to control, escape, or avoid events. He also suggested that non-contingent positive events can result in helplessness and depression.

In cognitive theories of depression, the patient's thoughts play an important role in determining both activity and mood. Beck (1967, 1976) found a "cognitive triad" of negative thoughts to be typical of depressed persons, which consists of a negative view of oneself, current experiences, and the future. One important aspect of this view is that thoughts generally represent distorted views of reality. In one study, for example, a card-sort task was administered to depressed and nondepressed persons. Depressed subjects rated their performance as being poor more often than did nondepressed subjects; however, there was no significant difference in performance between the two groups (Loeb, Beck, & Diggory, 1971). There is interesting evidence that depressed persons sometimes view themselves more realistically than nondepressed persons (Lewinsohn, Mischel, Chaplin, & Barton, 1980). A good review of this literature has been provided by Zarit and Zarit (1984a).

Eastern Thought

The Buddhist tradition, which has studied emotional disorders extensively, views depression and mania as problems of ego, where the process of *ego* is defined as a tendency toward belief in a continuous and solid "self" (Trungpa, 1973). In reality, one's identity or self is transitory and discontinuous, maintained by habitual patterns that are re-created constantly (every one-sixtieth of a second by some calculations). However, belief in ego leads to attempts to maintain and enhance it by three major strategies: attracting pleasurable experiences (passion), pushing away threatening experiences (aggression), and ignoring neutral experiences (ignorance). To the extent that these strategies are successful in maintaining ego, they produce a distorted, ego-centered view of the world.

Because it is impossible to maintain a completely fixed self for more than a moment, these strategies sooner or later meet with failure. Such failures threaten to reveal ego's transitoriness and are a source of continual anxiety. Anxiety itself is a signal of failure, and more extensive strategies, such as concepts and belief systems are developed to suppress the expression of anxiety as well. Constant attempts to patch up the facade of ego produce conflicting thoughts and emotions. To varying degrees, most human beings experience the suffering of ego.

How does depression develop within this framework? A healthy response to loss is sadness. However, the loss of a particular experience that has been incorporated into ego's maintenance structure is a threat to ego. The response of ego to perceived loss is anxiety, which sets in motion one of the strategies of passion, aggression, or ignorance. When none of these strategies works—when the loss is either a major one, over which ego has no control, or a minor one, which triggers an overgeneralizing process linking it to past losses (called minute-to-expansion logic)—ego experiences a partial breakdown in its operation and may give up some of the strategies it has developed to maintain and expand its version of reality. Thus, the hopelessness and helplessness of depression are experienced. From the Buddhist perspective, depression is not necessarily an entirely negative experience, because it can represent the achievement of some degree of insight into the inability to maintain ego-oriented strategies and the potential for a more sane approach to one's life.

The experience of mania, on the other hand,

shows no such potential for insight. Here, ego receives confirmation of its existence, albeit confirmation based on distorted perception and over-generalization, and ego's maintenance mechanism is accelerated to the point that cracks in ego's facade, and thus anxiety, are not experienced.

Environmental Factors

Aging is a continuous process punctuated in life by events and/or processes that often produce stress. Stress can result from any event or process, whether originating from within the person or from without, and leads to a situation requiring the person to resolve that event or process. Stress can and does occur at any age, but with aging, it can and does become a greater risk factor for disease since the elderly's vulnerability to the vicissitudes of life is increased.

Stress as a factor contributing to the development of mood disorders can result from the following types of object losses, many of which affect the elderly:

1. Loss of a loved person—family member, friend, or associate—through death or separation.

2. Loss of health through loss of or damage to the body or bodily functions. In addition to the loss of physical health, the loss of physical attractiveness is significant when it involves emotionally invested parts of the body, such as the face.

3. Loss of a job from which a person earned a livelihood and enjoyed status as a productive member of society. For the woman of certain cohorts, her life as she ages is affected largely through changes in the pattern of her husband's life and economic status. In addition, the woman who has devoted the largest part of her life and efforts to motherhood and homemaking may find herself relatively less occupied and less needed as the children leave home.

4. Loss of a valued personal possession — home, property, or memorabilia—that is vested with memories. Such a loss involves more than the material value of the object. Many elderly, especially, cling to the old, where familiarity provides comfort and security.

5. Changes in the way of life such that an established and comfortable mode of living no longer exists.

6. Failure of plans or ventures where investments of time and effort have been lost.

7. Loss of membership or status in a group (social, political, professional, ideological). This can imply the loss of personal acceptability by a group that shared common goals and activities.

8. Loss of a pet as a significant object that filled a unique role to which the owner may have ascribed many qualities. For the elderly, for whom a pet can be the most important living object, the loss of a pet is profoundly felt.

Loss as an etiological factor in producing stress can be of three kinds, all of which are equally important as stressors:

1. Real loss. The change in status here is irrevocable and the object lost no longer has real existence in the world.

2. Threatened loss (the loss has not occurred but there exists in reality a potential loss). The anticipation that such a loss will or might take place requires the person to deal with the loss before it actually takes place.

3. Imaginary or fantasized loss (the person experiences a sense of loss or anticipates a loss for which no basis in reality exists). Such a fantasy may originate from a misinterpretation or exaggeration of the environment to mean loss or separation when in actuality none was threatened.

Much research has been devoted to determining if and how preceding life events affect the onset of episodes of affective disorders, particularly depression. One problem with such studies has been the possibility of distortion of retrospective reporting of recent life events; studies have shown, for example, that depressed persons tend to emphasize negative events (e.g., Loeb, Beck, and Diggory, 1971). Another problem has been to eliminate those life events that are the result, rather than the cause, of a depressive episode. One solution has been to focus on life events for which the patient presumably has no responsibility, such as the death of a close family member. The results of a number of controlled retrospective studies point toward a greater number of negative life events preceding depression, including separations, threatening events, and stress (Paykel, 1982).

Prospective studies of persons having undergone a particular life event, to detect subsequent depression, avoid the pitfalls of retrospective studies. A study of 40 bereaved persons found increases in crying and sleep disturbances but little guilt or suicidal thoughts. Twenty-five percent saw a physician for symptoms related to grief, but few saw psychiatrists (Clayton, Desmarais, &

Winokur, 1968). Bornstein, Clayton, Halikas, Maurice, and Robins (1973), in a second study of 40 bereaved persons, found 35% with symptoms of depression after 1 month and 17% after 1 year.

It seems that life events, although possibly contributing factors in persons with a predisposition to affective disorders, are relatively low risk factors in the general population. One hypothetical calculation of the risk of clinical depression following stressful life events arrived at a figure of less than 10% (Paykel, 1974). Paykel (1978), using data he had collected, determined that there was a sixfold increase in the risk of developing depression within the first 6 months after a stressful life event, with the risk falling off rapidly with time. Such a risk is of similar magnitude to the risk of developing tuberculosis after contact with a person with an active case of the disease (Paykel, 1979). According to Paykel (1982), this suggests, "causative effects which are of importance but not overwhelming" (p. 152).

Other predisposing factors, aside from major life events, that might render the person vulnerable to depression have also been studied. Vulnerability factors found by Brown and Harris (1978) in a study of depressed females in the community included presence of young children in the home, lack of a confidant, lack of employment, and loss of mother before age 11.

Other studies have confirmed that social support has an ameliorating effect on the stress of life events and thus on depression (Miller & Ingham, 1976; Miller, Ingham, & Davidson, 1976). Chronic stress also seems to be a factor in precipitating depression (Brown & Harris, 1978).

The role of early loss, particularly the loss of one or both parents, has been studied extensively, perhaps because of the importance this theory has been given in the psychoanalytic literature. Results are equivocal, with Paykel (1982) reviewing seven studies that showed a correlation of early parent death with affective disorders and seven that did not. Based on the evidence, Paykel argues for a weak positive effect on later depressive episodes of such loss, but not enough to bolster the psychoanalytic theory. The importance of early loss in depression in the elderly is not known.

Animal models have been used to elucidate the role that parental or peer separation plays in depression. When rhesus monkeys are separated from their mothers at ages 5.5 to 7 months, they first undergo a "protest" stage of screeching, disoriented scampering, and general increased activity. Later they undergo a "despair" stage, involving decreased activity, vocalization, and food and water consumption. Withdrawal results, and sometimes even death (Seay, Hansen, & Harlow, 1962). Factors influencing this response include age at separation, nature of pre-separation relationship, length of separation, and species studied (McKinney & Moran, 1982). For example, species with broader social networks develop alternative relationships that ameliorate the above stages (Rosenblum & Kaufman, 1968). Such species would seem to bear more resemblance to humans in this regard.

PREVENTION AND TREATMENT

Physical Health and Mental Illness

Most aged patients, whatever their primary diagnosis, are most likely to have multiple health problems, both medical and psychiatric. This fact must be taken into account when discussing the prevention of depression in the elderly patient and its treatment. Physicians can help prevent mental illness in their elderly patients by improving the patients' general physical health and treating any existing illnesses. When the severity of physical illness is decreased, mental health is improved, thus decreasing the high risk of suicide in this population group. Suicide occurs with alarming frequency among the aged, particularly males, with the highest correlation of suicide among those with physical illnesses and depressive disorders.

Drug Therapies and Differences with Age

Detailed descriptions about the general use of pharmacological agents in the treatment of mood disorders can be found in standard textbooks on psychopharmacology; more specific information on treating the elderly can be found in various articles and books (e.g., Liptzin, 1984; Salzman & Kolk, 1984).

It would be helpful to keep in mind the following age-related changes when using psychotropic agents to treat the elderly—changes that have a direct bearing on the pharmacology of the drug being used.

First, the elderly have diminished physiological functions, including the following:

1. Decreased protein synthesis and binding.

Most drugs act by being protein-bound. When less plasma protein is available, the conjugation of a drug with the body protein will proceed at a slower rate, resulting in more active molecules of drugs available for action. The implications are that lower doses of drugs need to be administered in the elderly.

2. Decreased liver function. The majority of drugs prescribed today are metabolized and detoxified in the liver. When liver enzyme induction is diminished, more free drug is available, with the consequence that the usual dose of most drugs has a more intensive effect and longer duration of action in the system.

3. Decreased gastric-acid production. Certain drugs, such as the barbiturates, require an acidic substrate to dissolve. When there is decreased gastric secretion, there is decreased total absorption of acid-requiring drugs.

4. Decreased intestinal motility. The result is that more of a given drug will be available for a longer time since its transit time in the intestinal tract has increased.

Second, the elderly have a different fat-to-muscle ratio, with more fat and less muscle tissue, so that the absorption of any fat-soluble drug will be greater. In addition, when fat deposition increases, the amount of intracellular water is reduced, resulting in decreased excretion and increased duration of drug action.

In the decision process to determine the pharmacological treatment of a depressed patient, the patient's general health history and status, nutritional history and status, and drug history and status should be kept in mind, as well as the laboratory results of selective tests. In selecting the treatment drug, the following factors are of importance:

1. If there is a history of previous depression, what treatment was used and what was the efficacy of drug therapy?
2. If there is a history of a positive response to a particular drug, the same drug should be selected for treatment. If there is a history of a negative response, a review of the dose and duration of treatment is necessary before deciding that the patient was refractory to the particular medication used, since underdosage and inadequate duration of clinical trials are common.
3. The history of previous treatment responses to

psychotropic drugs by the patient's relatives should be determined.

Tricyclic Antidepressants and Amine Precursors

Of the tricyclic antidepressants, imipramine is often the drug of choice. In fact, it is often used as the standard against which new drugs are compared. A review of placebo-controlled experimental trials with imipramine (Rogers & Clay, 1975) found it to be effective in acute endogenous depression; its value in chronic atypical and neurotic depression is less clear. Other tricyclics, such as amitriptyline, desipramine, and clomipramine, although varying in their potency and side effects, are similar in their therapeutic properties. Anticholinergic effects of antidepressant drugs that are particularly important for the elderly, and their possible consequences, include dry mouth ulceration, parotitis; constipation, resulting in fecal impaction or paralytic ileus; blurred vision, impairing visual acuity; worsening of incipient glaucoma; urinary retention, possibly acute if the prostate is enlarged; and anticholinergic crisis producing a central delirium state (Mindham, 1982).

Amitriptyline or imipramine is used as follows. The patient is started on a low dose, which is progressively increased to the maximum therapeutic dose that is needed clinically and can be tolerated by the patient. The nonelderly adult maximum dose is 300 mg, but the elderly patient may not be able to tolerate a total daily dose higher than half of that. Thus it is important to start with low doses, especially if there is a history of sensitivity to drugs in general and the patient reports a number of side effects, and gradually reach the maximum by the end of the third week. A suggested program is to start with a total daily dose of 40–50 mg (divided dose or single dose at bedtime) for several days, increasing it to 75 mg by the end of the first week, to 100 mg by the end of the second week, and to 150 mg by the end of the third week. The doses are increased if therapeutic effects are not seen and if the previous dosage regimen has been adequately tolerated.

There are differences of opinion as to whether medication should be given in divided daily doses or in single bedtime doses. Those favoring divided doses believe it provides better control of side effects in the event of their occurrence, prevents peaking blood levels, and satisfies the need for pill taking, thus fostering the placebo effect in the elderly patient who is actively doing something to help his or her condition. Those favoring single bedtime doses believe it minimizes daytime side effects, such as orthostatic hypotension, maximizes sedative side effects, and facilitates drug compliance.

It is important that the patient and the family are informed that there may be no visible sign of improvement for 2 to 3 weeks; otherwise there is a great likelihood that the patient will refuse to continue with the medication. A 4-week trial period is necessary before it can be ascertained whether or not a tricyclic antidepressant is effective. After the patient has achieved a clinical remission of depression, the drug should be continued for an additional 6 months. Again, the patient and the family should be informed of the importance of the continuation of the drug therapy; otherwise there is a great likelihood that the patient will discontinue medication.

If the tricyclic antidepressant appears to be ineffective after a clinical trial of at least 4 weeks and if the patient clinically can tolerate being drug-free for a period of 1 week, then the use of another class of antidepressant drugs, such as the monamine oxidase inhibitors (MAOIs), should be considered.

Monoamine Oxidase Inhibitors

Phenelzine (Nardil) has been the most widely used and studied MAOI in clinical studies. In addition to exerting an antidepressant effect, this compound is probably the most likely MAOI to alleviate phobic and obsessive symptoms; it is clearly better in controlling agoraphobia than tricyclic antidepressants. Many depressed patients who do not respond to tricyclic compounds will exhibit considerable mood improvement with this drug (Bernstein, 1983). Other MAOIs available to the physician are isocarboxazid (Marplan) and tranylcypromine (Parnate). The nonelderly adult maximum total daily dose is 75 mg, and as with tricyclics, the elderly depressed patient may not be able to tolerate the same maximum dose. The same principles used in prescribing tricyclic antidepressants are used in prescribing MAOIs: Treatment is started with low doses, gradually increasing and titrating for maximum clinical effect with minimum side effects; maintenance therapy after clinical remission of depression is continued for 6 months.

The use of MAOIs may be contraindicated in the elderly because of the likelihood of drug-drug interaction, because the elderly are more likely to be taking a number of other medications for other conditions. Rabin (1972), in a review of prescribed and nonprescribed medication use, found that the elderly (65 years of age and over), although constituting only 9% of the population, received 22% of all prescribed drugs. In addition to the problem of polypharmacy, there is also the problem of maintaining the restrictions of a necessary tyramine-free diet. Patients on MAOIs need to be instructed about dietary restrictions, and they can be provided with a sample instruction sheet.

Lithium

The use of lithium for the treatment of manic states is well documented (Bernstein, 1983) whereas its use for the treatment of depression is not. Thus, lithium is indicated for the treatment of bipolar manic attack and for the prevention of recurrence of bipolar mania and depression. It does not seem to be useful in unipolar depressive disorders.

As with tricyclic antidepressants and MAOIs, the elderly are more vulnerable to lithium's pharmacological effects, and toxicity may occur at a serum level that is lower (e.g., 1.0 meq/L) than the recommended level for nonelderly depressed patients (1.2 to 1.5 meq/L). Again, treatment is started with low doses, gradually increasing and titrating for maximal clinical effect with minimal side effects and therapeutic serum blood levels. The half-life of lithium is longer in the aged, and a patient may often achieve an adequate blood level on smaller doses than suggested for nonelderly adults. For example, to achieve the recommended therapeutic serum level of 1.2 to 1.5 meq/L, a younger patient might receive a daily total dose of 1,500 mg of lithium, but an elderly patient might need only 600 to 900 mg to achieve the same blood level.

Because there is a lag time of several weeks before the therapeutic effects of lithium are apparent, the immediate and concomitant use of antipsychotic drugs, such as haloperidol or phenothiazines, may help gain a more rapid control of the manic episode.

As with the use of MAOI and tricyclic antidepressants, the dangers of polypharmacy must be kept in mind, as the concomitant use of diuretics and low-salt diets increases the possibility of toxic side effects. Therefore, when lithium is used in the elderly, lithium and electrolyte levels should be monitored frequently. Increased confusion is one of the predominant signs of lithium toxicity; the patient and the family need to be instructed to watch for this change in behavior.

Electroconvulsive Therapy

Detailed descriptions of the use of electroconvulsive therapy (ECT), such as examinations prior to ECT, preparation of the patient, use of muscle-relaxant drugs, present ECT techniques, the spacing of treatments, prognostic tests for ECT, complications, contraindications, indications, and results, may be found in standard textbooks on somatic treatment (e.g., Kalinowsky & Hippius, 1969).

The clinical effectiveness of ECT has been summarized in a number of studies (Greenblatt, Grosser, & Wechsler, 1964; Lehmann, 1965; Medical Council, 1965; Wechsler, Grosser, & Greenblatt, 1965; Zung, 1968). ECT has been shown to be more effective in producing significant improvement than antidepressant drugs (tricyclic antidepressants and MAOIs). Improvement is also more rapid over time, and follow-up studies show that 85% of the improved patients have remained well without further symptoms (Abrams, 1972; Lippincott, 1968; Tait & Burns, 1951). The differences in efficacy between ECT and antidepressant drugs may be the result of inadequate drug doses and insufficient duration of the drug treatment.

Several investigators have attempted to identify the clinical signs and symptoms that would predict response to ECT (Carney, Roth, & Garside, 1965; Hamilton & White, 1960; Zung & Wonnacott, 1970). The results of their studies indicate that depressives who respond best are those with characteristics most often ascribed to patients with endogenous depressions. However, such results may reflect the circular thinking involved in selecting patients for ECT treatment to begin with (Zung & Wonnacott, 1970). Data from Greenblatt, et al. (1964) indicate relative effectiveness of ECT of 77%, 78%, and 85% for psychoneurotic depressive reaction, manic-depressive psychosis, depression, and involutional melancholia, respectively. The main criteria for selecting ECT as the treatment of choice are the severity of the depression and the necessity for an immediate response; the type of depression is not a factor.

There are no lower or upper age limits with ECT. Kalinowsky and Hippius (1969) consider depression in the elderly to respond well to ECT. They recognize that pre-ECT and preexisting pronounced intellectual impairment, disorientation, and other clinical expressions of arteriosclerotic changes make the elderly desirable candidates for ECT in view of their posttreatment organic-like changes. They support the view that except when there is a questionable psychiatric diagnosis, one should never exclude a patient in definite need of ECT because of any concomitant disease. They report treating patients with ECT who were in their eighth and ninth decades of life, even in the presence of marked neurological pathology secondary to cerebral arteriosclerosis.

A number of studies have reported less memory impairment when using unilateral ECT with depressed patients. These studies have been reviewed and summarized by D'Elia and Raotma (1975). The finding that patients experience less confusion and less memory impairment is an important factor when considering the use of ECT in the elderly, for whom the least amount of organic impairment is desirable.

The effectiveness of ECT in the treatment of mania and hypomania is not as well investigated or documented as its use in the treatment of depression. One recent retrospective study compared groups of manic patients in the same institution before and after the introduction of ECT and reported that the patients who had received ECT were significantly better on discharge than those who had not (Langley, 1975). Kalinowsky stated that the manic phase of the manic-depressive psychosis differs from the depressive phase in its response to ECT. Treatments given twice or three times a week are frequently ineffective; however, treatments given at closer intervals, such as two or three times per day, have produced better results (Kalinowsky & Hippius, 1969).

The conclusion of the NIMH consensus development conference with respect to ECT is that ECT has been found to be demonstrably effective for a narrow range of severe psychiatric disorders in a limited number of diagnostic categories, including delusional and severe endogenous depression and mania (National Institute of Mental Health, 1985).

Individual and Group Psychotherapy

An excellent description of psychotherapy and sociotherapy with older adults is provided by Verwoerdt (1976). Both insight and supportive forms of psychotherapy have been used successfully with depressed older adults. Successful therapy requires empathy on the part of the therapist and confidence in the therapist on the part of the client or patient. Age differences can be, but are not necessarily, a barrier. The phenomena of transference and countertransference occur equally often with younger and older clients. For example, an elderly woman client may regard the therapist as a son or daughter she never had; the therapist, in turn, may unconsciously regard the client in terms of the relationship with his or her own mother.

The goal of insight-oriented psychotherapy is to alter the personality structure so that it may function more adaptively, and involves conscious recognition and dissolution of maladaptive defenses and character rigidities. Reactivation of early memories mobilizes feelings associated with them. The role of these feelings in the present may then be explored. In the elderly depressed, although insight may be achieved, a practical solution to problems based on insight may not be possible due to the fact that the patients have already lived most of their lives. Guilt about a deceased spouse or demoralization over missed opportunities for fame and fortune must be resolved without the patients actually being able to make reparations.

In supportive therapy, the goal is the support of existing coping mechanisms to better face and resolve current difficulties. The goal is not insight, although it may occur, but the strengthening of adaptive defenses and the replacement of maladaptive defenses. A group context has often proved successful for supportive therapy with older adults (Verwoerdt, 1976).

Behavioral and Cognitive Therapy

Both behavior therapy and cognitive therapy have been used successfully with older adults (Gallagher & Thompson, 1982; Gallagher, Thompson, Baffa, Piatt, Ringering, & Stone, 1981). At the start of behavioral treatment, which is time-limited, there is typically a diagnostic phase, in which the client monitors his or her mood and activities and lists activities that are perceived as pleasant (Zarit & Zarit, 1984b). Home observations may be made at this time. The therapist then presents the client with a behavioral diagnosis and discusses treatment goals and procedures. Specific therapy techniques are used to reach two major goals: an increase in the client's activity level, particularly pleasant activities, and an enhancement of social skills. Since depressed persons may find it difficult to increase pleasant activities, it is helpful first to illustrate to clients

the relationship between pleasant activities and depression, by gathering baseline data on mood and activities. Clients are asked to keep a log of daily activities and to rate daily mood. Contingencies may be used to increase the client's activity level, such as linking undesirable high-frequency behaviors to desired low-frequency behaviors and promoting social reinforcement for non-depressive behaviors. One aspect of the behavioral approach that is helpful with depressed clients is to set attainable goals, develop specific plans for reaching those goals, and break up assignments into small, manageable steps (Zarit & Zarit, 1984b). Clients are often asked to reward themselves for accomplishments. Training in relaxation techniques is often used as an adjunct therapy (Lewinsohn et al., 1978). Group therapy sessions have proved quite successful.

Cognitive therapy emphasizes the role of negative thought processes in producing depression and assists clients in substituting negative and depressive thought patterns for more positive and adaptive ones. Clients are first instructed to keep a daily log of activities and moods in order to provide a baseline for later intervention. Treatment often begins by instructing the client to increase pleasant activities (Beck, Rush, Shaw, & Emery, 1979) in a manner similar to behavior therapy. Discussion of such activities provides the therapist with a chance to point out to the client how negative thoughts and emotions deter him or her from involvement in positive activities. A second stage involves the introduction of thought records. These are used to make a clearer connection between the feeling of depression and the accompanying thought. Eventually, clients are able to identify the dysfunctional thought and to generate another, more rational thought. This self-monitoring process is a crucial aspect of cognitive therapy. Results with both younger and older clients have been successful (Beck et al., 1979; Emery, Gallagher, Thompson, Bisno, Kahn, & Zarit, in press; Rush, Beck, Kovacs, & Hollon, 1977).

Contemplative Approaches

Through the ages, meditative disciplines have been prescribed as remedies for troubled minds. There are many popular approaches, from movement forms (e.g., T'ai Chi) to Yoga to Zen, all of which are helpful in producing an alert but relaxed state. All can be adapted for use with the elderly.

The technique of mindfulness practice will be described here in a general way. For more specific techniques, such references as Goldstein (1976), Tendzin (1982), and Trungpa (1984) should be consulted. In most Eastern meditative disciplines, it is recognized that erect posture is an important first step toward a cheerful state of mind. Slumping posture is indicative of depression or drowsiness. Most meditative techniques use the breath as a reference point, although the amount of attention to the breath varies. In mindfulness practice, the breath is not manipulated in any way; rather, one breathes normally. The object is to be fully in the present; thoughts, feelings, sights, and sounds may come and go without being either blocked out or indulged in excessively. The practitioner becomes the interested observer of his own state of mind and the immediate world in which he exists. Some practices suggest labeling thoughts and feelings to highlight their presence.

With practice, thoughts are no longer seen as either "good" or "bad", but just as "thoughts." Thus they lose some of the overwhelming potency that they had when the person identified himself or herself with them. When the contents of mental life are less overwhelming, one begins to see the simplicity, and even humor, of what is actually occurring rather than the seeming complexity of conflicting emotions and fantasies of past and future. One's world becomes more spacious, since there is less a sense of a "big deal" quality to the self. As a Zen master might put it, "One can now make a simple cup of tea, properly and fully."

Contemplative techniques have some points in common with cognitive techniques. Both recognize that thoughts are often distortive of reality, and that indulgence in particular thought patterns leads to unwholesome states of mind, such as depression. Contemplative techniques, such as mindfulness training, go a step further in advocating the non-pursuit of any particular state of mind, thus boycotting ego altogether. Such a technique ultimately can be quite powerful. However, for those suffering from acute and crippling phases of depression, it is recommended that such techniques be practiced only in conjunction with other prescribed courses of action, such as drug treatment or psychotherapy, as advised by a professional.

CONCLUSION

This chapter has focused on the causes, diagnosis, treatment, and prevention of depression and mania in the elderly. The affective disorders of mania and depression are malfunctions of the normal human biological systems, as well as of the adaptive and coping mechanisms in response to life changes and stress. The elderly are more susceptible to depression since they experience biological aging as well as negative life circumstances, which are often greater in number and irreparable.

The symptomatology of depression encompasses changes in mood, bodily functions, and thought processes. Specific diagnostic considerations are necessary to identify depressions in the elderly, because it may sometimes be masked by numerous physical symptoms and may be easily confused with pseudodementia or senility. Although the symptoms of depression in the elderly differ little from those in younger persons, elderly depressed patients are more often misdiagnosed. Diagnostic criteria have been listed in the *DSM-III* classification system, which provides operational definitions for these disorders. In the clinical practice of psychiatry, the operational definitions of depression have been used to develop rating scales, such as the Hamilton Rating for Depression, the Zung Self-Rating Depression Scale, and the Beck Depression Inventory. Studies show that such scales continue to be useful diagnostic tools, although confusion of depression with normal aging remains a problem for the clinician.

Attempts to identify the causes of depression have given rise to various theories, both psychological and biological. In all probability, most depressions originate through a combination of factors, both psychological and biological, with homeostatic imbalances in both the internal milieu and the external milieu. Biological theories have focused on the observed deficiencies of neurotransmitters in depressed patients and on changes in the levels of biogenic amines as a result of pharmacotherapy. Psychological theories emphasize the role of loss, whether real, threatened, or imaginary, in the origin of depression. Behavioral theories attribute depression to the loss or weakening of positive reinforcement, with the result that the person no longer finds his adaptive behavior affirmed and so aborts it. Cognitive theories hold that the source of depression is the patient's negative thought patterns and distorted views of reality. In the Far Eastern approach, the person has successfully maintained an egocentric view of the world before depression, whereas depression begins with a loss that disrupts that scheme of the ego.

Theories concerning the prevention and treatment of depression are also manifold. Since the elderly depressed patients are often afflicted with several physical ailments, the initial treatment of the elderly depression patient should be directed at those physical malfunctions. At times, progression toward physical health enhances the remission of the depression.

Special pharmacological techniques must be employed in treating the elderly patient, taking into account their diminished physiological functions and higher fat-to-muscle ratio. In general, lower doses of drugs must be used. The prescribing doctor should also consider the patient's health, nutritional needs, and drug history, both of psychotropic and nonpsychotropic drugs. Drugs that have proven most useful in treating depression are tricyclic antidepressants and monoamine oxidase inhibitors. Lithium has proven most effective in treating mania.

Electroconvulsive therapy has been shown to be more effective than pharmacological treatments and to have a more rapid effect and higher rate of permanent remission. It is to be selected particularly in cases of severe depression and where an immediate response is required. Psychotherapy, both individual and group, has also proved successful. Supportive therapy focuses on strengthening adaptive defenses, while insight therapy seeks to make patients recognize and thwart their maladaptive defenses and character rigidities. Other approaches to treatment include behavioral therapy, cognitive therapy, and contemplative techniques that use self-monitoring to help patients identify and change negative patterns of thought or response.

REFERENCES

Abrams, R. (1972). Recent clinical studies of ECT. *Seminar in Psychiatry, 4*, 3–12.

American Psychiatric Association. (1980). *Diagnostic and statistical manual of mental disorders* (3rd ed.). Washington, DC: Author.

Andreasen, N. C. (1982). Concepts, diagnosis, and classification. In E. S. Paykel (Ed.), *Handbook of affective disorders* (pp. 24–44). New York: Guilford.

Beck, A. T. (1967). *Depression: Clinical, experimental, and theoretical aspects.* New York: Harper & Row.

Beck, A. T. (1976). *Cognitive therapy and the emotional disorders.* New York: International Universities Press.

Beck, A. T., & Beck, R. W. (1972). Screening depressed patients in family practice: A rapid technique. *Postgraduate Medicine, 52*, 81–85.

Beck, A. T., Rush, A. J., Shaw, B. F., & Emery, C. (1979). *Cognitive therapy of depression.* New York: Guilford.

Beck, A. T., Ward, C. H., Mendelson, M., Mock, J., & Erbaugh, J. (1961). An inventory for measuring depression. *Archives of General Psychiatry, 4*, 561–571.

Bernstein, J. G. (1983). *Handbook of drug therapy in psychiatry.* Boston: John Wright.

Bertelsen, A., Harvald, B., & Hauge, M. (1977). Danish twin study of manic-depressive disorders. *British Journal of Psychiatry, 130*, 330–351.

Bibring, E. (1953). The mechanism of depression. In P. Greenacre (Ed.), *Affective disorders* (pp. 14–47). New York: International Universities Press.

Blazer, D., & Williams, C. D. (1980). Epidemiology of dysphoria and depression in an elderly population. *American Journal of Psychiatry, 137*, 439–444.

Blumenthal, M. D. (1975). Measuring depressive symptomatology in a general population. *Archives of General Psychiatry, 32*, 971–978.

Bornstein, P. E., Clayton, P. J., Halikas, J. A., Maurice, W. L., & Robins, E. (1973). The depression of widowhood after thirteen months. *British Journal of Psychiatry, 122*, 561–566.

Brink, T. L., Yesavage, J., Lum, O., Heersema, P., Adey, M., & Rose, T. (1982). Screening tests for geriatric depression. *Clinical Gerontologist, 1*, 37–43.

Brown, G. L., & Zung, W. (1972). Depression scales: Self- or physician-rating. *Comparative Psychiatry, 13*, 361–367.

Brown, G. W., & Harris, T. (1978). *Social origins of depression.* London: Tavistock.

Bunney, W. E., & Hamburg, D. A. (1963). Methods for reliable longitudinal observation of behavior. *Archives of General Psychiatry, 9*, 280–294.

Carney, M., Roth, M., & Garside, R. (1965). The diagnosis of depressive syndromes and the prediction of ECT response. *British Journal of Psychiatry, 111*, 659–674.

Carroll, B. J. (1983). Neurobiologic dimensions of depression and mania. In J. Angst (Ed.), *The origins of depression: Current concepts and approaches* (pp. 163–186). New York: Springer-Verlag.

Clayton, P., Desmarais, L., & Winokur, G. (1968). A study of normal bereavement. *American Journal of Psychiatry, 125*, 168–178.

Cooper, J. E., Kendell, R. E., Gurland, B. J., Sharpe, L., Copeland, J., & Simon, R. J. (1972). *Psychiatric diagnosis in New York and London: A comparative study of mental hospital admissions* (Maudsley Monograph No. 20). London: Oxford University Press.

Copeland, J., Kelleher, M., Kellett, J., Fountain-Gourlay, A., Cowan, D., Barrow, G., & DeGruchy, J. (UK) with Gurland, B., Sharpe, L., Simon, R., Kuriansky, J., & Stiller, P. (USA) (1974). Diagnostic differences in psychogeriatric patients in New York and London. *Canadian Psychiatric Association, 19*, 267–271.

Costello, C. G. (1972). Depression: Loss of reinforcers or loss of reinforcer effectiveness? *Behavior Therapy, 3*, 240–247.

Cutler, R. P., & Kurland, H. D. (1961). Clinical quantification of depressive reactions. *Archives of General Psychiatry, 5*, 280–285.

D'Elia, G., & Raotma, H. (1975). Is unilateral ECT less effective than bilateral ECT? *British Journal of Psychiatry, 126*, 83–89.

Eaton, J. W., & Weil, R. J. (1955). *Culture and mental dis-*

order: A comparative study of Hutterites and other popula-tions. Glencoe, IL: The Free Press.

Emery, G., Gallagher, D. E., Thompson, L. W., Bisno, B., Kahn, J., & Zarit, J. M. (in press). *Cognitive ther-apy of depression in older adults*. New York: Guilford.

Epstein, L. J. (1976). Symposium of age differentiation in depressive illness: Depression in the elderly. *Journal of Gerontology, 31*, 278–282.

Essen-Möller, E., Larson, H., Uddenberg, C. E., & White, G. (1956). Individual traits and morbidity in a Swedish rural population. *Acta Psychiatrica et Neuro-logica Scandinavica, 100* (Suppl.) 1–160.

Ferster, C. B. (1965). Classification of behavioral patho-logy. In L. Krasner & L. P. Ullmann (Eds.), *Research in behavior modification*. New York: Holt, Rinehart & Winston.

Fleiss, J. L., Gurland, B. J., Simon, R. J., & Sharpe, L. (1973). Cross-national study of diagnosis of mental disorders: Some demographic correlates of hospital diagnosis in New York and London. *International Jour-nal of Social Psychiatry, 19*, 180–186.

Gallagher, D., & Thompson, L. W. (1982). Treatment of major depressive disorders in older adult outpatients with brief psychotherapies. *Psychology: Theory, Research, and Practice, 19*, 482–490.

Gallagher, D., & Thompson, L. W., Baffa, G., Piatt, C., Ringering, L., & Stone, V. (1981). *Depression in the elderly: A behavioral treatment manual*. Los Angeles: University of Southern California Press.

Goldstein, J. (1976). *The experience of insight*. Santa Cruz: Unity Press.

Greenblatt, M., Grosser, G., & Wechsler, H. (1964). Dif-ferential response of hospitalized depressed patients to somatic therapy. *American Journal of Psychiatry, 120*, 935–943.

Grauer, H. (1977). Depression in the aged: Theoretical concepts. *Journal of the American Geriatrics Society, 25*, 447–449.

Gurland, B. J. (1976). The comparative frequency of depression in various adult age groups. *Journal of Ger-ontology, 31*, 283–292.

Gurland, B. J., Copeland, J., Sharpe, L., & Kelleher, M. (1976). The Geriatric Mental Status Interview (GMS). *International Journal of Aging and Human Devel-opment, 7*, 303–311.

Gurland, B. J., Sharpe, L., Simon, R. J., Kuriansky, J. B., & Stiller, P. (1972). On the use of psychiatric diagnosis for comparing psychiatric populations. *Psy-chiatric Quarterly, 46*, 461–473.

Hamilton, M. (1960). A rating scale for depression. *Jour-nal of Neurological and Neurosurgical Psychiatry, 23*, 56–62.

Hamilton, M. (1967). Development of a rating scale for primary depressive illness. *British Journal of Social and Clinical Psychology, 6*, 278–296.

Hamilton, M. (1982). Symptoms and assessment of depression. In E. S. Paykel (Ed.), *Handbook of affective disorders* (pp. 3–11). New York: Guilford.

Hamilton, M., & White, J. (1960). Factors related to the outcome of depression treatment with ECT. *Journal of Mental Sciences, 106*, 1031–1041.

Hunt, S. M., Jr., Singer, K., & Cobb, S. (1967). Compo-nents of depression. *Archives of General Psychiatry, 16*, 441–447.

Jacobson, E. (1953). Contribution to the metapsycho-logy of cyclothymic depression. In P. Greenacre (Ed.), *Affective disorders* (pp. 49–83). New York: Inter-national Universities Press.

Jacobson, E. (1954). The self and the object world: Vicissitudes of their infantile cathexes and their influence on ideational and affective development. *Psychoanalytic Study of the Child, 9*, 75–127.

Jacobson, E. (1971). *Depression*. New York: International Universities Press.

Kalinowsky, L., & Hippius, H. (1969). *Pharmacological, convulsive, and other somatic treatments in psychiatry*. New York: Grune & Stratton.

Langley, G. E. (1975). Functional psychoses. In J. G. Howells (Ed.), *Modern perspectives in the psychiatry of old age* (pp. 326–355). New York: Brunner/Mazel.

Lehmann, H. (1965). The pharmacotherapy of the depressive syndrome. *Canadian Medical Journal, 92*, 821–828.

Lewinsohn, P. M., Biglan, A., & Zeiss, A. M. (1976). Behavioral treatment of depression. In P. O. David-son (Ed.), *The behavioral management of anxiety, depression, and pain*. New York: Brunner/Mazel.

Lewinsohn, P. M., Mischel, W., Chaplin, W., & Barton, R. (1980). Social competence and depression: The role of illusory self-perceptions. *Journal of Abnormal Psychology, 89*, 203–212.

Lewinsohn, P. M., Munoz, R. F., Youngren, M. A., & Zeiss, A. M. (1978). *Control your depression*. Englewood Cliffs, NJ: Prentice-Hall.

Lippincott, R. (1968). Depressive illness: Identification and treatment in the elderly. *Geriatrics, 23*, 149–152.

Liptzin, B. (1984). Treatment of mania. In C. Salzman (Ed.), *Clinical geriatric psychopharmacology* (pp. 116–131). New York: McGraw-Hill.

Loeb, A., Beck, A. T., & Diggory, J. (1971). Differential effects of success and failure on depressed and non-depressed patients. *Journal of Nervous and Mental Dis-ease, 152*, 106–114.

Lubin, B. (1965). Adjective checklists for measurement of depression. *Archives of General Psychiatry, 12*, 57–62.

McKinney, W. T., & Moran, E. C. (1982). Animal models. In E. S. Paykel (Ed.), *Handbook of affective dis-orders* (pp. 202–211). New York: Guilford.

Medical Council Report: Report by Clinical Psychiatry Committee. (1965). Clinical trial of the treatment of depressive illness. *British Medical Journal, 1*, 881–886.

Mendelson, M. (1982). Psychodynamics of depression. In E. S. Paykel (Ed.), *Handbook of affective disorders* (pp. 162–174). New York: Guilford.

Mendlewicz, J. (1976). The age factor in depressive ill-ness: Some genetic considerations. *Journal of Geronto-logy, 31*, 300–303.

Miller, P. M., & Ingham, J. G. (1976). Friends, confi-dants, and symptoms. *Social Psychiatry, 11*, 51–58.

Miller, P. M., Ingham, J. G., & Davidson, S. (1976). Life events, symptoms, and social support. *Journal of Psychosomatic Research, 20*, 515–522.

Mindham, R. (1982). Tricyclic antidepressants and amine precursors. In E. S. Paykel (Ed.), *Handbook of affective disorders* (pp. 231–245). New York: Guilford.

Munro, A. (1966). Some familial and social factors in depressive illness. *British Journal of Psychiatry, 122*, 429–441.

National Institute of Mental Health. (1985). Electroconvulsive therapy. *Consensus Development Conference Statement, 5.*

Nurnberger, J. I., & Gershon, E. S. (1982). Genetics. In
E. S. Paykel (Ed.), *Handbook of affective disorders*
(pp. 126–145). New York: Guilford.

Nussbaum, K., Wittig, B. A., Hanlon, T. E., & Kurland,
A. A. (1963). Intravenous nialamide in the treatment
of depressed female patients. *Comprehensive Psychiatry,
4,* 105–116.

Okimoto, J., Barnes, R., Veith, R., Raskind, M., Inui,
T., & Carter, W. (1982). Screening for depression in
geriatric medical patients. *American Journal of Psychiatry, 139,* 799–802.

Overall, J. E., Hollister, L. E., & Meyer, F. (1964).
Imipramine and thioridazine in depressed and schizophrenic patients. Are these specific antidepressant
drugs? *Journal of the American Medical Association, 189,*
605–608.

Overall, J. E., Hollister, L. E., Pokorny, A. D., Casey, J.
F., & Katz, G. (1962). Drug therapy in depressions:
Controlled evaluation of imipramine, isocarboxazid,
dextroamphetamine-amobarbital and placebo. *Clinical Pharmacological Therapy, 3,* 16–22.

Paykel, E. S. (1974). Recent life events and clinical
depression. In E. K. Gunderson & R. H. Rahe
(Eds.), *Life stress and illness.* Springfield, IL: Charles C
Thomas.

Paykel, E. S. (1978). Contribution of life events to causation of psychiatric illness. *Psychological Medicine, 8,*
245–253.

Paykel, E. S. (1979). Causal relationships between clini-
cal depression and life events. In J. E. Barret (Ed.),
Stress and mental disorder (pp. 71–86). New York:
Raven.

Paykel, E. S. (1982). Life events and early environment.
In E. S. Paykel (Ed.), *Handbook of affective disorders*
(pp. 146–161). New York: Guilford.

Perlick, D., & Atkins, A. (1984). Variations in the
reported age of a patient: A source of bias in the diagnosis of depression and dementia. *Journal of Consulting
and Clinical Psychology, 52,* 812–820.

Pope, H., & Lipinski, J. (1978). Differential diagnosis of
schizophrenia and manic depressive illness: A
reassessment of the specificity of "schizophrenia"
symptoms in the light of current research. *Archives of
General Psychiatry, 35,* 811–828.

Post, F. (1972). The management and nature of depressive illnesses in late life: A follow-through study.
British Journal of Psychiatry, 121, 393–402.

Post, F. (1982). Affective disorders in old age. In E. S.
Paykel (Ed.), *Handbook of affective disorders*
(pp. 393–402). New York: Guilford.

Rabin, D. L. (1972). Use of medicine: A review of prescribed and non-prescribed medicine use. Department of Health, Education and Welfare,
Washington, DC: U.S. Government Printing Office.

Raskin, A. (1965). *N.I.M.H. Collaborative Depression Mood
Scale.* Washington, DC: National Institute of Mental
Health.

Robinson, D., Davis, J., Niles, A., Ravaris, C., & Sylvester, D. (1971). Relation of sex and aging to monoamine oxidase activity of human brain, plasma, and
platelets. *Archives of General Psychiatry, 24,* 536–539.

Rogers, S. C., & Clay, P. M. (1975). A statistical review
of controlled trials of imipramine and placebo in the
treatment of depressive illness. *British Journal of Psychiatry, 127,* 599–603.

Rosenblum, L. A., & Kaufman, I. C. (1968). Variations
in infant development and response to maternal loss
in monkeys. *American Journal of Orthopsychiatry, 38*
418–426.

Rush, A. J., Beck, A. T., Kovacs, M., & Hollon, S.
(1977). Comparative efficacy of cognitive therapy
and imipramine in the treatment of depressed outpatients. *Cognitive Therapy and Research, 1,* 17–37.

Salzman, C., Kochansky, G., Shader, R., & Cronin, D.
(1972). Rating scales for psychotropic drug research
with geriatric patients: 2. Mood ratings. *Journal of the
American Geriatrics Society, 20,* 215–221.

Salzman, C., & Kolk, B. (1984). Treatment of
depression. In C. Salzman (Ed.), *Clinical geriatric
psychopharmacology* (pp. 77–115). New York: McGraw-
Hill.

Salzman, C., & Shader, R. I. (1978). Depression in the
elderly: 1. Relationships between depression, psycho-
logic defense mechanisms, and physical illness. *Journal of the American Geriatrics Society, 36,* 253–260.

Schaefer, A., Brown, J., Watson, C., Plemel, D.,
DeMotts, J., Howard, M., Petrik, N., & Balleweg, B.
(1985). Comparison of the validities of the Beck,
Zung, and MMPI depression scales. *Journal of Consulting and Clinical Psychology, 53,* 415–418.

Schildkraut, J. (1965). The catecholamine hypothesis of
affective disorders: A review of supporting evidence.
American Journal of Psychiatry, 122, 509–522.

Schwab, J. J., Bialow, M. R., & Holzer, C. E. (1967). A
comparison of two rating scales for depression. *Journal of Clinical Psychology, 23,* 94–96.

Seay, B. M., Hansen, E., & Harlow, H. F. (1962).
Mother-infant separation in monkeys. *Journal of Child
Psychology and Psychiatry, 3,* 123–132.

Seligman, M. (1973). Fall into helplessness. *Psychology
Today, 7,* 43–48.

Seligman, M., & Maier, S. (1967). Failure to escape
traumatic shock. *Journal of Experimental Psychology, 74,*
1–9.

Shopsin, B. (1974). Catecholamines and affective
disorders revisited: A critical assessment. *Journal of
Nervous and Mental Disease, 158,* 368–383.

Simpson, G. M., Hackett, E., & Kline, N. S. (1966). Difficulties in systematic rating of depression during outpatient drug treatment. *Canadian Psychiatric Association
Journal, 11,* 116–122.

Spitzer, R. L., Endicott, J., & Robins, E. (1978).
Research diagnostic criteria: Rationale and reliability. *Archives of General Psychiatry, 35,* 773–782.

Tait, C., Jr., & Burns, G. (1951). Involutional illnesses:
A survey of 379 patients, including follow-up of 114.
American Journal of Psychiatry, 108, 27–36.

Tendzin, O. (1982). *Buddha in the palm of your hand.* Boston: Shambhala Publications.

Trungpa, C. (1973). *Cutting through spiritual materialism.*
Boston: Shambhala Publications.

Trungpa, C. (1984). *Shambhala: The sacred path of the war-
rior.* Boston: Shambhala Publications.

Tyrer, S., & Shopsin, B. (1982). Symptoms and assessment of mania. In E. S. Paykel (Ed.), *Handbook of affective disorders* (pp. 12–23). New York: Guilford.

Verwoerdt, A. (1976). *Clinical geropsychiatry.* Baltimore, MD: Williams & Wilkins.

Wechsler, H., Grosser, G., & Greenblatt, M. (1965). Research evaluating antidepressant medications on hospitalized mental patients: A survey of published reports during a five-year period. *Journal of Nervous and Mental Disease, 141,* 231–239.

Woodruff, R. A., Murphy, G. E., & Herjanic, M. (1967). The natural history of affective disorders: 1. Symptoms of 72 patients at the time of initial hospital admission. *Journal of Psychiatric Research, 5,* 255–263.

Yesavage, J. A., Brink, T. L., Rose, T. L., & Adey, M. (1983). The Geriatric Depression Rating Scale: Comparison with other self-report and psychiatric rating scales. In T. Crook, S. Ferris, & R. Bartus (Eds.), *Assessment in geriatric psychopharmacology* (pp. 153–167). New Canaan, CT: Mark Powley Associates.

Zarit, S. H., & Zarit, J. M. (1984a). Depression in later life: Theory and assessment. In J. P. Abrahams & V. Crooks (Eds.), *Geriatric mental health* (pp. 21–39). New York: Grune & Stratton.

Zarit, S. H., & Zarit, J. M. (1984b). Depression in later life: Treatment. In J. P. Abrahams & V. Crooks (Eds.), *Geriatric mental health* (pp. 41–53). New York: Grune & Stratton.

Zung, E. M., & Zung, W. (1986). Use of the Zung self-rating depression scale in the elderly. In T. Brink (Ed.), *Clinical gerontology: A guide to assessment and intervention* (pp. 137–148). New York: Haworth Press.

Zung, W. (1965). A self-rating depression scale. *Archives of General Psychiatry, 12,* 63–70.

Zung, W. (1967a). Factors influencing the Self-rating Depression Scale. *Archives of General Psychiatry, 16,* 543–546.

Zung, W. (1967b). Depression in the normal aged. *Psychosomatics, 8,* 287–295.

Zung, W. (1968). Evaluating treatment methods for depressive disorders. *American Journal of Psychiatry, 124* (Suppl.), 40–48.

Zung, W. (1969). A cross-cultural survey of symptoms in depression. *American Journal of Psychiatry, 126,* 116–121.

Zung, W. (1982). The puzzle of depression diagnoses: A binomial solution. In J. O. Cavenar & H. Brodie (Eds.), *Critical problems in psychiatry* (pp. 157–179). Philadelphia: Lippincott.

Zung, W., Richards, C. B., & Short, M. J. (1965). Self-rating depression scale in an outpatient clinic. *Archives of General Psychiatry, 13,* 508–515.

Zung, W., & Wonnacott, T. (1970). Treatment prediction in depression using a self-rating scale. *Biological Psychiatry, 2,* 321–329.

Chapter 8

Dementia

Thomas Crook

Few conditions associated with old age are more feared than dementia. In dementia, one may literally "lose one's mind," being reduced from the unique product of decades of personal experience to a drifting, vegetative state in which the children and spouse to whom a lifetime was devoted become unrecognizable and, eventually, even the abilities to move about and utter interpretable sounds are lost. More than 1.5 million older Americans are now incapacitated as a result of dementing disorders, and that number may double within the next 50 years as the rapid and unprecedented growth of the elderly population continues. Indeed, within the very rapidly expanding population of persons over 85 years of age, dementing disorders may now afflict more than one of every five individuals.

Although there is clearly a very real basis for the fear of dementing disorders among older persons and members of their families, it is important for clinicians to recognize that the *fear* of dementia may itself be a significant problem. It is not an unusual occurrence in many clinical settings to have older patients appear in a state of heightened anxiety, having made a self-diagnosis of Alzheimer's disease because of problems in misplacing objects, remembering names after introduction, or forgetting which item they intended to buy upon arrival at the pharmacy or grocery store. It is difficult to know how many other older persons have unstated doubts about dementia because they believe they are no longer able to remember certain information as well as was once the case. It is important for clini-

cians to reassure older individuals that it is normal for certain types of memory ability to decline with age and that such changes are not generally predictive of dementia. The term Age-Associated Memory Impairment (AAMI) (Crook, Bartus, Whitehouse, Gershon, & Cohen, 1986) has been used to describe normal, age-related memory decrements. Although the personal and social problems associated with dementing disorders are extraordinary, it must be emphasized to older patients that nearly 95% of persons over 65 *do not* suffer from dementing disorders.

HISTORICAL PERSPECTIVE

Formal recognition that mental abilities may decline in old age can be traced as far back as the Grecian laws of Solon in 500 B.C. (Torack, 1983). The term *dementia* first appeared in the first and second centuries A.D. in the writings of the Romans Aurelius Cornelius Celsus and Galen (Alexander & Selesick, 1966). Galen is also generally credited with the first clinical description of the memory loss and other cognitive changes that characterize dementia.

Between the second century and late eighteenth century, little progress was made in characterizing dementia. However, during the early 19th century in France, Philippe Pinel and his outstanding student Jean Esquirol distinguished three types of dementia—acute, chronic, and senile—and defined senile dementia in terms much like those in current use. The description provided by Esquirol in 1838 is as follows: "Senile dementia is

established slowly. It commences with enfeeble-
ment of memory, particularly the memory of
recent impressions. The sensations are feeble; the
attention, at first fatiguing, at length becomes
impossible; the will is uncertain and without
impulsion; the movements are slow and impractical" (Esquirol, 1976, p. 261).

Knowledge also evolved slowly concerning the
organic pathology underlying the clinical picture
of dementia. In fact, not until the present century
was the term *dementia* generally restricted to mental disturbances arising from organic rather than
functional etiologies. Of particular importance in
uncovering the organic pathology associated with
dementia was the work of Alois Alzheimer, who in
1907 described the classic histopathological
changes now associated with the disease that bears
his name. However, the patient in whom these
changes were described was only 51 years of age,
and, until very recently, the term *Alzheimer's disease*
was used to describe a dementing disorder with
"presenile" onset. Not until the work of Tomlinson, Blessed, and Roth (1970) were the same histopathological changes reported in persons with
early- and late-life onset of dementia, and only in
recent years has the diagnostic term *Alzheimer's disease* been used without regard to the age of the
individual at the onset of dementia.

CURRENT DIAGNOSTIC CONCEPTS

The term *dementia* is used to describe not a specific disease but a constellation of cognitive symptoms that may arise from a number of organic
disorders. Table 8.1 provides the criteria specified
by the American Psychiatric Association (1980) in
the third edition of the *Diagnostic and Statistical
Manual of Mental Disorders (DSM-III)*. As described
in the table, the essential features of dementia are
memory and other cognitive deficits, of probable
organic origin, without delirium. Of course, this is
quite a broad definition, incorporating both reversible and irreversible conditions, without regard to
age or clinical course.

DEMENTING DISORDERS OF LATE LIFE

The factors that may produce dementia are
given in Table 8.2. It is important to recognize
that many possible causes of dementia are subsumed under each of the 11 categories listed.
Table 8.3 for example, provides a partial listing of

Table 8.1. *DSM-III* Criteria for Dementia

A. Loss of intellectual abilities of sufficient severity to interfere with social or occupational functioning
B. Memory impairment
C. At least one of the following:
(1) impairment of abstract thinking
(2) impaired judgment
(3) other disturbances of higher cortical function
(4) personality change
D. State of consciousness not clouded
E. Either (1) or (2)
(1) evidence of specific organic factor of etiologic significance
(2) in the absence of such evidence, non-organic etiological factors must be reasonably excluded and the behavioral change must represent cognitive impairment in a variety of areas

Note. Adapted from *Diagnostic and Statistical Manual of Mental Disorders* (3rd ed.) by American Psychiatric Association, 1980, Washington, DC. Copyright 1980 by American Psychiatric Association.

the disorders included under the "Degenerative
Diseases" heading in Table 8.2.

This chapter will focus on the major degenerative diseases of late life listed in Table 8.3:
Alzheimer's disease, Multi-infarct dementia, Parkinson's disease, Pick's disease, Creutzfeldt–Jakob
disease and other infectious disorders, and normal-pressure hydrocephalus. Pseudodementia, a
not infrequent concomitant of serious depression,
will also be discussed. Because Alzheimer's disease
is the leading cause of dementia in the elderly, it
will be described first and in greatest detail.

Alzheimer's Disease

Alzheimer's disease (AD), a disorder of unknown
etiology is now recognized as the major cause of
dementia among the elderly. Approximately 65%
of elderly persons with dementia may have AD
(Mortimer, 1983). Thus, possibly more than 1 million persons now suffer from the disorder in the
United States alone.

Neuropathology
At present time, AD can be diagnosed defini-
tively only by direct microscopic examination of
brain tissue. Thus, because of the obvious risks
associated with brain biopsy, the diagnosis is, with
rare exception, confirmed only at autopsy. The
microscopic brain changes described by Alzheimer
(1907) that are characteristic of AD are senile
plaques and neurofibrillary tangles distributed

throughout the cortex and elsewhere, including the amygdala and hippocampus. Senile plaques are spherical lesions consisting of a core of amyloid, a homogeneous protein material, surrounded by degenerated cellular fragments. The number of senile plaques in the cortex is related to the severity of dementia in AD (Blessed, Tomlinson, & Roth, 1968). Neurofibrillary tangles are accumulations of pairs of neuronal filaments wrapped around each other in a helical fashion. As in the case of senile plaques, the density of neurofibrillary tangles appears to be related to the severity of dementia in AD (Farmer, Peck, & Terry, 1976). Other structural brain changes seen in AD include degeneration of cells in the hippocampus resulting in the formation of intracellular "vacuoles" filled with fluid and granular materials. In addition to these three characteristic microscopic changes— senile plaques, neurofibrillary tangles, and granulovacuolar degeneration—macroscopic brain changes, including atrophy in certain regions, may also occur. However, macroscopic changes are generally not considered pathognomonic of AD and may vary considerably among patients with the disorder.

Neurochemical Abnormalities

In addition to structural brain changes, postmortem studies have also revealed specific neurochemical abnormalities in the brains of AD patients. Most notable is a decrease in the enzyme choline acetyltransferase (Davies & Maloney, 1976; Perry, Perry, Blessed, & Tomlinson, 1977), a marker for acetylcholine, a neurotransmitter clearly involved in learning and memory (Drachman & Leavitt, 1974). A deficiency of other cholinergic markers has also been found, leading to convincing evidence of a

Table 8.2. Causes of Chronic Organic Reactions

1. Degenerative diseases
2. Space-occupying lesions
3. Trauma
4. Infection
5. Vascular
6. Epileptic
7. Metabolic
8. Endocrine
9. Toxic
10. Anoxia
11. Vitamin lack

Note. Adapted from *Organic Psychiatry: The Psychological Consequences of Cerebral Disorder* by W. A. Lishman, 1978, Oxford, England. Blackwell Scientific Publications. Copyright 1978 by Blackwell Scientific Publications.

Table 8.3. Adult-Onset Degenerative Diseases Marked by Cognitive Impairments

Alzheimer's disease
Pick's disease
Creutzfeldt–Jakob disease
Kuru
Progressive multifocal leucoencephalopathy
Normal-pressure hydrocephalus
Huntington's chorea
Parkinson's disease
Progressive supranuclear palsy
Wilson's disease
Progressive myoclonic epilepsy

Note. Adapted from *Organic Psychiatry: The Psychological Consequences of Cerebral Disorder* by W. A. Lishman, 1978, Oxford, England. Blackwell Scientific Publications. Copyright 1978 by Blackwell Scientific Publications.

cholinergic deficit in AD. Although this deficit is found generally throughout the cortex, amygdala and hippocampus, there is convincing evidence that it is due in large part to neuronal degeneration in discrete areas of the basal forebrain, notably the nucleus basalis of Meynert and adjacent structures (Whitehouse, Price, Struble, Clark, Coyle, & De Long, 1982). In addition to the cholinergic deficit observed in AD, postmortem studies have demonstrated neuronal loss in the locus coeruleus with a consequent depletion in the noradrenergic neurotransmitter system (Bondareff, Mountjoy, & Roth, 1982); they have also shown reductions in both the serotonergic system (Gottfries, Roos, & Winblad, 1976) and the dopaminergic system (Gottfries, Gottfries, & Roos, 1969). At least two biologically active peptides that function as neurotransmitters—somatostatin and substance P (Davies, Katz, & Crystal, 1982)—are also depleted in the brains of AD patients as compared with those of normal persons of the same age.

Studies of neurotransmitter metabolites in the blood and the cerebrospinal fluid (Gottfries, 1983) have yielded findings consistent with those obtained at autopsy. Also, beyond studies of specific neurotransmitter systems, *in vivo* studies using positron emission tomographic techniques (Ferris et al., 1980) and glucose tracers have demonstrated decreased cerebral metabolism in different brain areas of AD patients. It is noteworthy that these metabolic changes affect cerebral blood flow, and thus group differences in regional cerebral blood flow have been reported (albeit inconsistently) between AD patients and age-matched controls (Ingvar, 1983). However, these changes are probably secondary and, in general, vascular differences

Table 8.4. *DSM-III* Criteria for Primary Degenerative
Dementia

A. Dementia
B. Insidious onset with progressive deteriorating course
C. Exclusion of all other specific causes of dementia by
   the history, physical examination, and laboratory
   tests.

Note. Adapted from *Diagnostic and Statistical Manual of Mental
Disorders* (3rd ed.) by American Psychiatric Association, 1980,
Washington, DC. Copyright 1980 by American Psychiatric
Association.

between AD and non-AD elderly patients are
minimal.

Although various neurochemical deficits have
been found in AD, it is important to bear in mind
that most of these same deficits, including the cholinergic deficit, also characterize normal brain
aging (Gottfries, 1985). Although these changes
are exaggerated in AD so that significant differences emerge in comparisons with age-matched
controls, significant differences also emerge on
most measures when the age-matched controls are
compared with young normal subjects. Thus, the
neurochemical deficits seen in AD may, in most
cases, be exaggerations of those seen in normal
aging. As will be illustrated later in this chapter,
cognitive deficits associated with these neurochemical abnormalities may also be seen, for the
most part, as exaggerations of those seen in normal
aging.

Clinical Diagnosis

Clinically, AD remains essentially a diagnosis of
exclusion, although behavioral, neuroradiological
and biochemical markers are aggressively being
sought (Crook & Miller, 1985). Table 8.4 provides
the criteria from the *DSM-III* for primary degenerative dementia, the psychiatric term used at present to describe the clinical symptoms of AD.
Somewhat more specific are the criteria for clinical
diagnosis developed by a work group convened by
the National Institute of Neurological and Communicative Disorders and Stroke (NINCDS)
(McKhann, Drachman, Folstein, Katzman, Price,
& Stadlam, 1984). These criteria are provided in
Table 8.5.

It is apparent from Tables 8.3 and 8.4 that
before reaching a clinical diagnosis of AD, a great
deal of attention must be paid to the exclusion of
medical, neurological, and psychiatric factors that
may produce symptoms that are similar or identical to those seen in AD. This is particularly

important because dementia may result from
reversible conditions. Many factors may produce
dementia as shown in Table 8.2 and each must be
considered carefully before accepting a diagnosis
of AD.

Clinical Course

The clinical course of AD is variable, but, as
outlined in Table 8.6, different stages of the disorder may be identified. It is important for clinicians to recognize that among individuals such as
those described as Stage 2 on Reisberg's scale in
Table 8.6, very few (less than 10%) will be
expected to develop more serious cognitive impairments within several years of the interview (Kral,
1978; Reisberg, Ferris, Anand, de Leon, Schneck,
& Crook, 1985). By contrast, cognitive deficits
such as those described by Reisberg as Stage 3
symptomatology often signal the presence of a
malignant cognitive decline characteristic of AD
(Reisberg et al., 1985). The course of decline
varies, however, with some individuals reaching
plateaus where they remain for years, while other
deteriorate strikingly and tragically from month to
month. Although there are many individual exceptions, the course of AD is generally more rapid
when onset occurs relatively early in life (Bondareff, 1983).

Genetics

A topic that is obviously of great significance to
the families of AD patients is the genetic basis of
the disorder. It appears on the basis of a classic
study conducted in Sweden more than 20 years
ago (Larsson, Sjogren, & Jacobsen, 1963), that the
risk of developing AD may be more than 4 times
greater among first-degree relatives of patients
who had the disorder than among others. The
genetic component in AD appears substantially
greater with early-life onset than with late-life
onset, and both autosomal dominant and polygenic models of transmission are possible (Heston,
1976; Heston & Mastri, 1977). Folstein and
Breitner (1981) have argued that a familial form of
AD marked by autosomal dominant transmission
is more common than has been apparent because
individuals in earlier generations died before the
symptoms of the disease were apparent.

Of relevance to the question of a genetic component is the relationship between AD and Down's
syndrome. Of course, Down's syndrome is a condition marked by profound mental retardation and
early death resulting from an extra chromosome

Table 8.5. Criteria for Clinical Diagnosis of Alzheimer's Disease

I.   Criteria for clinical diagnosis of *probable* Alzheimer's disease include:
     Dementia established by clinical examination and documented by Mini-
         Mental State Test (Folstein, Folstein, & McHugh, 1975), Blessed
         Dementia Scale (Blessed, Tomlinson, Roth, 1968), or some similar
         examination and confirmed by neuropsychological tests
     Deficits in two or more areas of cognition
     Progressive worsening of memory and other cognitive functions
     No disturbance of consciousness
     Onset between ages 40 and 90, most often after age 65
     Absence of systemic disorders or other brain diseases that in and of
         themselves could account for progressive deficits in memory and
         cognition.

II. Diagnosis of *probable* Alzheimer's disease is supported by:
     Progressive deterioration of specific cognitive functions, such as language
         (aphasia), motor skills (apraxia), and perception (agnosia)
     Impaired activities of daily living and altered patterns of behavior
     Family history of similar disorders, particularly if confirmed
         neuropathologically
     Laboratory results of normal lumbar puncture as evaluated by standard
         techniques, normal pattern or nonspecific changes in EEG, such as
         increased slow-wave activity, and evidence of cerebral atrophy on CT
         with progression documented by serial observation.

III. Other clinical features consistent with diagnosis of *probable* Alzheimer's
         disease, after exclusion of causes of dementia other than Alzheimer's
         disease, include:
     Plateaus in course of progression of illness
     Associated symptoms of depression, insomnia, incontinence, delusions,
         illusions, hallucinations, catastrophic verbal, emotional, or physical
         outbursts, sexual disorders, and weight loss
     Other neurological abnormalities in some patients, especially with more
         advance disease and including motor signs, such as increased muscle
         tone, myoclonus, or gait disorder
     Seizures in advance disease
     CT normal for age.

IV. Features that make diagnosis of *probable* Alzheimer's disease uncertain or
         unlikely include:
     Sudden, apoplectic onset
     Focal neurological findings such as hemiparesis, sensory loss, visual field
         deficits, and uncoordination early in the course of the illness
     Seizures or gait disturbance at onset or very early in course of illness.

V.   Clinical diagnosis of *possible* Alzheimer's disease:
     May be made on basis of dementia syndrome, in absence of other
         neurological, psychiatric, or systemic disorders sufficient to cause
         dementia and in the presence of variations in onset, in presentation, or
         in clinical course
     May be made in presence of second systemic or brain disorder sufficient to
         produce dementia, which is not considered to be cause of dementia
     Should be used in research studies when single, gradually progressive severe
         cognitive deficit is identified in absence of other identifiable cause.

VI. Criteria for diagnosis of *definite* Alzheimer's disease are:
     Clinical criteria for probable Alzheimer's disease
     Histopathological evidence obtained from biopsy or at autopsy

VII. Classification of Alzheimer's disease for research purposes should specify
         features that may differentiate subtypes of the disorder, such as:
     Familial occurrence
     Onset before age of 65
     Presence of trisomy-21
     Coexistence of other relevant conditions, such as Parkinson's disease.

Table 8.6. Global Deterioration Scale (GDS)

GDS Stage	Clinical Phase	Clinical Characteristics
1. No cognitive decline	Normal	No subjective complaints of memory deficit. No memory deficit evident on clinical interview.
2. Very mild cognitive decline	Forgetfulness	Subjective complaints of memory deficit, most frequently in following areas: (a) forgetting where one has placed familiar objects; (b) forgetting names one formerly knew well. No objective evidence of memory deficit on clinical interview. No objective deficits in employment or social situations. Appropriate concern with respect to symptomatology.
3. Mild cognitive decline	Early confusional	Earliest clear-cut deficits. Manifestations in more than one of the following areas: (a) patient may have gotten lost when traveling to an unfamiliar location; (b) co-workers become aware of patient's relatively poor performance; (c) word and name finding deficit become evident to intimates; (d) patient may read a passage or a book and retain relatively little material; (e) patient may demonstrate decreased facility in remembering names upon introduction to new people; (f) patient may have lost or misplaced an object of value; (g) concentration deficit may be evident on clinical testing. Objective evidence of memory deficit obtained only with an intensive interview conducted by a trained geriatric psychiatrist. Decreased performance in demanding employment and social settings. Denial begins to become manifest in patient. Mild to moderate anxiety accompanies symptoms.
4. Moderate cognitive decline	Late confusional	Clear-cut deficit on careful interview. Deficit manifest in following areas: (a) decreased knowledge of current and recent events; (b) may exhibit some deficit in memory of one's personal history; (c) concentration deficit elicited on serial subtractions; (d) decreased ability to travel, handle finances, etc. Frequently no deficit in following areas: (a) orientation to time and person; (b) recognition of familiar persons and faces; (c) ability to travel to familiar locations. Inability to perform complex tasks. Denial is dominant defense mechanism. Flattening of affect and withdrawal from challenging situations occur.
5. Moderately severe cognitive decline	Early dementia	Patient can no longer survive without some assistance. Patients are unable during interview to recall a major relevant aspect of current lives: e.g., their address or telephone number of many years, the names of close members of their family (such as grandchildren), the name of the high school or college from which they graduated. Frequently some disorientation to time (date, day of week, season, etc.) or to place. An educated person may have difficulty counting back from 40 by 4s or from 20 by 2s. Persons at this stage retain knowledge of many major facts regarding themselves and others. They invariably know their own names and generally know their spouses and children's

GDS Stage	Clinical Phase	Clinical Characteristics
		names. They require no assistance with toileting or eating, but may have some difficulty choosing the proper clothing to wear and may occasionally clothe themselves improperly (e.g., put shoes on the wrong feet, etc.).
6. Severe cognitive decline	Middle dementia	May occasionally forget the name of the spouse upon whom they are entirely dependent for survival. Will be largely unaware of all recent events and experiences in their lives. Retain some knowledge of their past lives but this is very sketchy. Generally unaware of their surroundings, the year, the season, etc. May have difficulty counting from 10, both backward and, sometimes, forward. Will require some assistance with activities of daily living, e.g., may become incontinent, will require travel assistance but occasionally will display ability to travel to familiar locations. Diurnal rhythm frequently disturbed. Almost always recall their own name. Frequently continue to be able to distinguish familiar from unfamiliar persons in their environment.
		Personality and emotional changes occur. These are quite variable and include: (a) delusional behavior (e.g., patients may accuse their spouse of being an imposter; may talk to imaginary figures in the environment, or to their own reflection in the mirror); (b) obsessive symptoms (e.g., person may continually repeat simple cleaning activities); (c) anxiety symptoms, agitation, and even previously nonexistent violent behavior may occur; (d) cognitive abulia (i.e., loss of willpower because an individual cannot carry a thought long enough to determine a purposeful course of action).
7. Very severe cognitive decline	Late dementia	All verbal abilities are lost. Frequently there is no speech at all—only grunting. Incontinent of urine; requires assistance toileting and feeding. Lose basic psychomotor skills (e.g., ability to walk). The brain appears to no longer be able to tell the body what to do. Generalized and cortical neurological signs and symptoms are frequently present.

Note. Adapted from "The Global Deterioration Scale for Assessment of Primary Degenerative Dementia" by B. Reisberg, S. H. Ferris, M. J. de Leon, and T. Crook, 1982, *American Journal of Psychiatry, 139,* pp. 1136–1139. Copyright 1982 by *American Journal of Psychiatry.*

attached to the 21st chromosomal pair. It is remarkable that Down's syndrome patients who survive to age 35 or beyond develop severe dementia superimposed on the existing cognitive deficit and also the histopathological changes, senile plaques, and neurofibrillary tangles characteristic of AD (Wisniewski, Wisniewski, & Wen, 1983). Also, the incidence of Down's syndrome has been found to be substantially higher in the families of patients with AD than in the general population (Heston & Mastri, 1977).

It is important for clinicians dealing with the families of AD patients to bear in mind the importance of questions concerning genetics and to provide straightforward information on both absolute and relative risks.

Pharmacologic Treatment

Drugs currently on the market in the United States to treat the primary symptoms of AD are listed in Table 8.7. By far the most widely used drug is dihydroergotoxine, a combination of three ergot alkaloids in their dihydrogenated forms. The drug was approved for marketing nearly 15 years ago on the basis of studies conducted in heterogeneous patient populations. Some patients included in these trials would meet present-day diagnostic criteria for AD and others clearly would not. In general, the drug is unlikely to improve the principal cognitive symptoms of the disease but may have a mild activating or mood-elevating effect that may be beneficial in some patients (Crook, 1985). In view of the absence of reason-

Table 8.7. Drugs Currently Prescribed in the United States to Treat Cognitive Symptoms of Alzheimer's Disease

Dihydroergotoxine

Vasodilators
  Papaverine
  Isoxsuprine
  Cyclandelate

Stimulants
  Methylphenidate
  Pentylenetetrazole

Procain GH3 (in Nevada)

able alternatives, a trial of the drug may be worthwhile. It has been argued (Hollister & Yesavage, 1984) that if such a trial is undertaken, a dose of 6 mg rather than the standard 3 mg and an extended treatment period of 6 months should be considered. Aside from dihydroergotoxine, the drugs listed in Table 8.7 do not appear to merit serious consideration in AD (Crook, 1985).

It is important to emphasize that, although the drugs currently available for treating the primary cognitive symptoms of AD are of quite limited utility, established psychotropic drugs may play quite an important role in treating secondary symptoms that typically arise in the course of the disease. Neuroleptic drugs, such as thioridazine and haloperidol, for example, which are used primarily in younger patients for the treatment of schizophrenia, are also effective in treating a broad range of psychotic and dysocial symptoms that may develop as AD progresses (Salzman, 1984). Similarly, antidepressants, such as the tricyclics nortriptyline and desipramine, may be effective in treating the affective symptoms that may accompany and even mimic AD (Crook & Cohen, 1983), and sedative-hypnotic medication, if used prudently, may be of considerable value in treating the sleep disorders that predictably occur in AD (Kupfer & Crook, 1984). An extremely important caveat in the use of all such medications, however, is that dosage requirements for many psychotropic drugs may be far lower in older than younger patients, and side effects that are tolerable in younger patients may be extremely problematic in the elderly (Salzman, 1984).

Aside from drugs currently marketed in the United States, a number of compounds are being studied as possible treatments for AD. Many of these compounds are listed in Table 8.8. As noted previously, the neurochemical deficit most firmly established in AD is in the cholinergic system, and consequently many of the experimental compounds studied are compounds designed to facilitate cholinergic function (Bartus, Dean, & Fisher, in press). The most thoroughly studied are the acetylcholine precursors choline and lecithin. More than 20 controlled clinical trials have been conducted with these compounds in patients with presumed AD. As a result of these trials, it now appears reasonable to conclude that precursor therapy is not an effective treatment in AD (Rosenberg, Greenwald, & Davies, 1983). One study (Little, Chauqui-Kidd, & Levy, 1984) argues that long-term lecithin administration exerts a therapeutic effect in a subgroup of AD patients, but this study is clearly open to methodological criticism.

Studies have also been conducted with drugs that inhibit acetylcholinesterase, the enzyme responsible for the degradation of acetylcholine. Acetylcholinesterase inhibitors studied include

Table 8.8. Investigational Drugs for Alzheimer's Disease

Cholinomimetics

Acetylcholine precursors
  Choline chloride
  Lecithin (phosphatidylcholine)
  Phosphatidylserine
Acetylcholinesterase inhibitors
  Physostigmine
  Tetrahydroaminoacridine (THA)
  Oxotremorine
Agonists
  Arecoline
  Bethanechol
  RS-86

Neuropeptides

Adrenocorticotrophic hormone (ACTH) 4–10
ORG 2766 (ACTH 4–9 analog)
Vasopressin
Lysine vasopressin (LVP)
1-desamino-8-D-arginine vasopressin (DDAVP)
Desglycinamide-arginine vasopressin (DGAVP)
Naloxone, naltrexone

Other Investigational drugs of Interest

Piracetam and analogs (aniracetam, oxiracetam, pramiracetam) CI-911
4-Aminopyridine; 3,4-diaminopyradine
Active Lipid
Pentoxifylline
Nimodipine
Vincamine and apovincamine

physostigmine, oxotremorine, and tetrahydroaminoacridine (THA). Studies with physostigmine, used both alone (Mohs, Rosen, Greenwold, Levy, & Horvath, 1983) and in combination with lecithin (Thal, Fuld, Masur, & Sharpless, 1983; Thal, Masur, Sharpless, Fuld, & Davies, 1984), and with THA (Summers, Viesselman, & Marsh, 1981), have been somewhat more encouraging from an academic perspective than from an immediate clinical one. These drugs have been shown to produce measurable effects in some AD patients on certain carefully selected cognitive measures. However, the clinical significance of these changes is unknown at present and probably quite limited.

Another strategy for cholinergic intervention has been to focus on the "receiving" rather than the "sending" cholinergic neuron by stimulating the postsynaptic receptor. In the cholinergic system there are at least two types of receptors, muscarinic and nicotinic, and several subtypes of each (Mash, Flynn, & Potter, 1985). Trials have been conducted with the relatively nonselective muscarinic agonists arecoline (Christie, Shering, Ferguson, & Glen, 1981), given orally, and bethanechol (Harbaugh, Roberts, & Coombs, 1984), delivered directly into the ventricles through a surgically implanted infusion pump and catheter. In the arecoline study, improvement comparable to that reported with acetylcholinesterase inhibitors was reported, and in the bethanechol study, patients reported clinical improvement but objective test data were limited. Another study with bethanechol, including such objective outcome measures, is now under way. In general, cholinergic agents studied to date have not been clearly established as being clinically effective therapeutic agents in AD. However, studies with cholinesterase inhibitors and muscarinic agonists demonstrate that small but reliable changes can be produced in a disease previously thought to be marked by inexorable deterioration.

Future studies are likely to focus on cholinergic drugs with more specific receptor effects than those used to date. This is also true for interventions involving other neurotransmitter systems as well. For example, a reduction in specific serotonergic receptors appears to occur in AD (Cross, Crow, Ferris, & Johnson, 1986).

Another class of drugs studied in AD is neuropeptides—short chains of amino acids that affect the central nervous system. The rationale for these drugs comes not, as in the case of cholinergic drugs, from empirical findings of neurochemical deficits in the brains or body fluids of AD patients but from demonstrations in rats that depletions in two neuropeptides. ACTH (adrenocorticotropic hormone) and vasopressin, produce learning and memory deficits that are reversed when the compounds or their synthetic analogs are replaced. Based on these findings, the ACTH and vasopressin compounds listed in Table 8.8 have been studied in AD patients as well as in normal persons and those suffering from other types of cognitive impairment. In general, these studies have been disappointing, although clinical effects of these compounds have been reported and the search continues for more effective compounds (Berger & Tinklenberg, 1981; Tinklenberg & Thornton, 1983). It appears that the principal effects of the ACTH and vasopressin peptides are quite subtle and are related to mood and attention rather than learning and memory. The other compound list in Table 8.8 as a neuropeptide is the opiate antagonist naloxone, together with its oral analog naltrexone. As in the case of the other neuropeptides, these drugs may exert subtle clinical effects in AD (Reisberg, Ferris, & Roberts, 1983) but the effects probably involve attentional processes rather than learning and memory (Arnstein, 1984).

Many other compounds have also been studied or are currently under study in AD, and some are listed in Table 8.8. Of these, the drug piracetam and its various analogs have received the most attention. They have clear behavioral effects in animal learning paradigms and do not produce the side effects seen with other psychoactive drugs. Piracetam is an analog of gamma aminobutyric acid (GABA), which has clear effects on brain metabolism, facilities performance on measures of learning and retention in rats, and protects against hypoxia-induced memory impairment in animals (Giurgea, 1976). Controlled clinical studies in AD have been equivocal, suggesting that any cognitive improvement in AD may be quite subtle (Ferris et al., 1982). Treatment with piracetam in combination with the acetylcholine precursor lecithin has been found to be more effective than treatment with either drug alone in facilitating retention in aged rats (Bartus, Dean, Sherman, Friedman, & Baer, 1981), and recent studies (Smith, Vroulis, Johnson, & Morgan, 1984) suggest that some patients with AD may also show response to this treatment. However, as in the case of piracetam alone, any effects of this combination treatment are likely to be quite subtle. As in the case of the neuropeptides, nootropics may be most appropriate for treating cognitive deficits more subtle than those seen in AD.

In view of the emerging neurochemical evidence that AD involves multiple neurotransmitter systems (Gottfries, 1985) as well as metabolic deficits, it may be necessary to develop therapeutic strategies involving combination treatments or even the individualized "cocktail" approach (Carlson, 1981) for the management of this tragic and dehumanizing disorder.

Non-somatic treatment

It is extremely important for clinicians to recognize that, even though a cure of AD is not yet at hand, a great deal can be done to minimize disability and help the patient's family cope with the disorder. Early in the disease the primary cognitive symptoms can be minimized by simple behavioral strategies, ranging from note taking to creation of a "prosthetic environment" (Skinner & Vaughan, 1983). Creative and effective strategies can also be employed for dealing with the tasks of everyday life involving memory (Yesavage, 1985; West, 1985). As the disease progresses and the individual loses the ability to employ strategies for remembering information, he or she may still benefit considerably from behavioural techniques to assist memory such as those described by Mace and Rabins (1981) in their outstanding book *The 36-Hour Day*.

Aside from the cognitive symptoms, secondary symptoms, such as depression, irritability, nighttime wandering, dysocial behavior, delusions, paranoid ideation, and incontinence, can be extremely difficult for family members. As noted previously, many of these symptoms may respond to pharmacotherapy. Many such problems may also respond to relatively simple behavioral interventions, which do not carry with them the risks associated with drug therapy. Night-time sleep, for example, may be greatly improved through attention to such straightforward issues as appropriate scheduling of meals, medications, exercise, and daytime napping; control of lighting, noise, and temperature in the sleeping environment; and appropriate treatment of medical conditions that may complicate sleep (Hauri, 1984; Reynolds, 1984).

Above all else it is critical that clinicians understand that AD is a disorder that effects not only the individual but also members of his or her family. A supportive, caring family is the most valuable resource available to the AD patient, but the stress of dealing with the disorder may compromise this resource and even threaten the integrity of the family itself. Interventions should be considered to assist family members in dealing with the disorder and in facing difficult decisions, such as those relating to institutionalization. In this regard, an extremely valuable resource is the Alzheimer's Disease and Related Disorders Association (ADRDA), with headquarters in Chicago and chapters in many communities throughout the United States. Beyond directing families to appropriate community resources, clinicians should emphasize that much can be done by family members to minimize disability and to assure that skilled and humane care is provided.

Multi-Infarct Dementia

It was long believed that most cases of dementia resulted from cerebral atherosclerosis and consequent reductions in brain-tissue oxygenation. Thus, such diagnostic terms as *dementia due to cerebrovascular insufficiency* were commonly used until recent years. As noted earlier, it is now believed that AD is responsible for the majority of dementia cases and that AD is not a vascular disorder.

Of course, serious cognitive impairment often results from vascular accidents, such as large strokes, but focal deficits are seen most often rather than the generalized cognitive impairment characteristic of dementia. It is believed, however, that multiple small strokes may produce this characteristic pattern, and the diagnostic term most frequently applied to describe the condition is Multi-infarct dementia (MID) (Hachinski, Lassen, & Marshall, 1974). MID may account for 10% to 15% of all cases of dementia in the elderly, and characteristic MID vascular pathology may coexist with AD in one quarter of all cases (Tomlinson et al., 1970). Table 8.9 provides the *DSM-III* diagnostic criteria for the disorder, and Table 8.10 presents a set of criteria frequently used in practice to distinguish MID from AD (Rosen, Terry, Fuld, Katzman, & Peck, 1980). A score of 6 or higher on this scale in a demented patient is generally considered indicative of MID (Blass & Barclay, 1985).

It is apparent from both sets of criteria that the clinical course in MID is generally described as stepwise or stuttering following sudden onset. This is in contrast to AD, where insidious onset and a generally gradual, progressive course is held to be characteristic.

Table 8.9. *DSM-III* Criteria for Multi-Infarct Dementia

A. Dementia
B. Stepwise deteriorating course with "patchy" distribution of deficits early in the course
C. Focal neurologic signs and symptoms
D. Evidence of significant cerebrovascular disease that is judged to be etiologically related to the disturbance

---

Note. Adapted from *Diagnostic and Statistical Manual of Mental Disorders* (3rd ed.) by American Psychiatric Association, 1980, Washington, DC. Copyright 1980 by American Psychiatric Association.

Table 8.10. Hachinski Ischemia Score

Feature	Score if present
a) Abrupt Onset	(2)
b) Stepwise Deterioration	(1)
c) Somatic Complaints	(1)
d) Emotional Incontinence	(1)
e) History of Hypertension	(1)
f) History of Stroke	(2)
g) Focal Neurological Symptoms	(2)
h) Focal Neurological Signs	(2)
Total Ischemia Score	———

Note. Adapted from "Pathological Verification of Ischemic Score in Differentiation of Dementias," by W. G. Rosen, R. D. Terry, P. A. Fuld, R. Katzman, and A. Peck, 1980, *Annals of Neurology,* 7, pp. 486–488.

Blass and Barclay (1985) have argued that, in their series of MID patients, the median survival of patients from the time of diagnosis is only 2 to 3 years and that the diagnosis should be reconsidered if the patient survives for 2 years without a major vascular event. Thus, the prognosis in MID is often grave. This is particularly tragic because the incidence of MID may parallel that of stroke, peaking between the ages of 40 and 60 about three decades earlier than in the case of AD.

Recommended treatments for MID are the standard measures employed with poststroke patients and may include aspirin and agents that decrease platelet aggregation and clotting; antihypertensives; and possibly anticoagulants. Among the experimental drugs listed in Table 8.8 several, including pentoxifylline and nimodipine, are currently being evaluated in MID, as well as in AD.

In general, although MID may affect fewer older individuals, the clinical consequences of the disorder may well be as tragic as those of AD. Unlike AD, however, there are known risk factors associated with MID that may be controlled. These, of course, are hypertension and other well-

known risk factors associated with cardiovascular disease. It is certainly hoped that, because of the increased public attention regarding these factors in recent years and the resultant decline in morbidity associated with cardiovascular disease, we will witness a decline in the incidence of MID in coming years.

Parkinson's Disease

Parkinson's disease (PD) is a neurological disorder characterized by rigidity, a resting tremor, bradykinesia, and gait disorder. The disease may affect over 250,000 Americans, most of whom are elderly (Lieberman, 1974). Neuropathologically, the disease is characterized by the degeneration of the neurons in the upper midbrain, mainly in the substantia nigra, that produce the neurotransmitter dopamine. The replacement of dopamine through the administration of its immediate precursor, L-Dopa, has been repeatedly shown to alter the course of the disorder (Lieberman, 1974).

Until recent years, an association between PD and dementia was not generally recognized. However, it is now believed that 30% to 50% of PD patients develop dementia (Boller, 1980). Not only are the clinical symptoms and course of dementia seen in PD generally indistinguishable from those seen in AD but, in fact, the brains of demented PD patients show the same neuropathological changes—primarily senile plaques and neurofibrillary tangles—as those in AD patients (Boller, Mizutani, & Roessmann, 1980; Hakim & Mathieson, 1979).

It has been argued (Boller et al., 1980; Lieberman et al., 1979) that PD marked by AD symptomatology and histopathology is a disorder distinct from other forms of PD, but it remains unclear why the two disorders are apparently so closely related. Of relevance to this question is a specific parkinsonian-dementia complex that is confined to the Chamorro people on the island of Guam (Chen, 1981). Further study of this disorder may help clarify the interrelationships between AD, PD, and other degenerative neurological disorders.

The picture with regard to treatment is no more promising in PD dementia than in AD. L-Dopa does not appear to improve cognitive symptoms in such patients, and, in fact, Lieberman and his colleagues (1979) have argued that PD patients with dementia tolerate all antiparkinsonian drugs poorly in comparison to other PD patients and are at greatly increased risk of developing a toxic confusional syndrome.

Pick's Disease

Pick's disease is a very rare dementing disorder, first described in 1892, that is neuropathologically distinct from AD but clinically difficult to differentiate. A description of classic Pick's pathology includes atrophy in the frontal and temporal lobes, the absence of both senile plaques and neurofibrillary tangles, and the presence of characteristic Pick bodies in neurons. It is, of course, academically interesting that dementia indistinguishable from that seen in AD occurs without senile plaques and neurofibrillary tangles. Clinically, it is characterized by inappropriate mood (facile hilarity and aspontaneity) and social behavior prior to the onset of memory impairment (Lishman, 1978), but this is not well established.

Pick's disease appears to be determined by a single autosomal dominant gene, possibly with other genes that modify its manifestations (Sjogren, Sjogren, & Lindren, 1952), and there appears to be profound cell loss in the nucleus basalis of Meynert, suggesting a cortical cholinergic deficit such as that seen in AD (Price et al., 1982). It is not surprising in view of the rarity of the disorder that studies on the treatment of Pick's disease have not been reported. In view of the cholinergic lesion, however, drugs found effective in AD may also be beneficial in Pick's disease.

Creutzfeldt–Jakob Disease

As in the case of Pick's disease, Creutzfeldt–Jakob disease (CJD) is a rare dementing disorder that is of considerable academic interest. The disease was first described in 1920 and is marked clinically by early onset, a rapid course, and severe neurological signs and symptoms (Siedler & Malamud, 1963). It received attention in the popular press not too long ago when it was revealed that George Balanchine, the famed artistic director of the New York City Ballet, died of the disorder. Neuropathology in CJD is marked by neuronal degeneration, very marked proliferation of astrocytes, and a highly characteristic spongy appearance of the gray matter; there are no senile plaques or neurofibrillary tangles as in AD, no massive atrophy as in Pick's disease and no evidence of vascular disease as in MID (Lisham, 1978).

A striking feature of CJD is that it is a transmissible dementing disorder of probable viral etiology. It is transmissible to chimpanzees (Gibbs et al., 1968) and a wide variety of other laboratory animals. There are also at least three confirmed cases of accidental CJD transmission to humans—through a corneal transplant in one case (Duffy, Wolf, Collins, De Voe, Strecten, & Cowen, 1974) and through contaminated implanted electrodes in two others. CJD is pathologically and clinically related to the transmissible dementing disorder *kuru*, described by Gajdusek (1977) among the Fore linguistic group in New Guinea. The Nobel Prize-winning work on *kuru* by Gajdusek, Gibbs, and their colleagues established that a dementing disorder may be transmitted (in this case through endocannibalism) by an infectious agent with an incubation period of many years—in other words, by a slow virus. Although the disease is transmissible, a familial pattern of occurrence has been demonstrated that is similar to that reported in AD (Masters, Gajdusek, & Gibbs, 1981). Both diseases occur in a pattern consistent with autosomal dominant inheritance. The clinical and genetic similarities between CJD and AD, particularly familial AD, have led to speculation that there might be a possible etiological relationship between the two diseases and thus AD may be a disorder of viral etiology (Salazar, Brown, Gajdusek, & Gibbs, 1983). However, attempts to test this hypothesis through transmission of the disease to experimental animals have been inconclusive.

Normal-Pressure Hydrocephalus

Normal-pressure hydrocephalus (NPH) is characterized pathologically by enlarged cerebral ventricles with normal cerebrospinal fluid pressure. Such a condition can arise following a head injury or subarachnoid hemorrhage, but it is sometimes seen in patients who present with otherwise uncomplicated dementia (Hakim & Adams, 1965). Even though intraventricular pressure is normal, nearly half of these idiopathic NPH patients respond to shunting, which reduces pressure still further.

Clinically, NPH is characterized by global dementia that is generally indistinguishable from that seen in AD, together with a gait disturbance and often urinary incontinence as the condition advances (Ojemann, 1971). The gait disturbance may precede symptoms of dementia and may evolve from a slow stiff-legged, shuffling gait to severe difficulties in walking, standing, or even turning in bed (Lishman, 1978). Such signs of gait disturbance in dementia patients should alert the clinician to the possibility of NPH and the necessity for CT scanning and other appropriate diagnostic procedures.

Pseudodementia

The term *pseudodementia* is applied to conditions marked by apparent dementia without primary organic etiology. Depression is the most common cause of pseudodementia in the elderly and a source of concern to the clinician. Its prevalence among elderly persons in the community may be approximately 13% (Gurland, Golden, & Dean, 1980), and among elderly persons in medical settings it may exceed 30% (Cheah & Beard, 1980).

Depression may exist independently of dementia, may accompany dementia, or may mimic dementia. It is, of course, this last case to which the term *pseudodementia* is applied.

In general, among young adults the pattern of cognitive decline that accompanies depression is subtle and reflects little more than a motivational deficit (Crook, 1979). However, among elderly persons, complaints of memory impairment are frequently symptoms of depression rather than dementia (Kahn, Zarit, Hilbert, & Niederehe, 1975). The same self-denigrating thoughts are seen in young and old depressed patients, but among the elderly the thoughts may focus on mental processes rather than on physical appearance, social acceptance, or other factors that are the subjects of complaints among young adults. These complaints, together with such classic symptoms of depression as psychomotor retardation and social withdrawal, may lead clinicians to misdiagnose depression as dementia in the elderly (Wells, 1983).

In general, clues to *depressive pseudodementia* include a history of depression, the abrupt onset and rapid progression of dementia, and the selective impairment of cognitive function (Wells, 1983). Clinicians today are far more aware of the problem of pseudodementia than was the case as recently as several years ago, and, indeed, it has been suggested (Reifler, Larson, & Hanley, 1982) that the term is no longer useful.

CONCLUSION

The dementing disorders of late life clearly represent major challenges to the individual clinician and to the scientific and medical communities in general. However, the magnitude of the problem is gradually being recognized. During the past several years, genuine, even dramatic, progress has been made in describing the clinical symptomatology and course of these disorders and in discovering their structural and neurochemical bases. Clear progress is also being made toward developing effective treatments. This progress is extremely encouraging and gives us reason to believe that dementia will one day be described by old men and women to their grandchildren as a terrible problem that once existed.

REFERENCES

Alexander, F. G., & Selesnick, S. T. (1966). *The history of psychiatry.* New York: Harper & Row.

American Psychiatric Association. (1980). *Diagnostic and statistical manual of mental disorders* (3rd ed.). Washington, DC: Author.

Arnstein, A. F. T. (1984). Behavioral effects of naloxone in animals and humans: Potential for treatment of aging disorders. In R. J. Wurtman, S. H. Corkin, & J. H. Growdon (Eds.), *Alzheimer's disease: Advances in basic research and therapies* (pp. 407–426). Zürich: Center for Brain Sciences and Metabolism Charitable Trust.

Bartus, R., Dean, R. L., & Fisher, S. K. (1986). Cholinergic treatment for age-related memory disturbances: Dead or barely coming of age. In T. Crook, R. Bartus, S. Ferris, & S. Gershon (Eds.), *Treatment development strategies for Alzheimer's disease.* New Canaan, CT: Mark Powley Associates.

Bartus, R. T., Dean, R. L., Sherman, K. A., Friedman, E., & Baer, B. (1981). Profound effects of combining choline and piracetam on memory. *Neurobiology of Aging, 2,* 105–111.

Berger, P. A., & Tinklenberg, J. R. (1981). Neuropeptides and senile dementia. In T. Crook & S. Gershon (Eds.), *Strategies for the development of an effective treatment for senile dementia* (pp. 155–171). New Canaan, CT: Mark Powley Associates.

Blass, J. P., & Barclay, L. L. (1985). New developments in the diagnosis of dementia. *Drug Development Research, 5,* 39–58.

Blessed, G., Tomlinson, B. E., & Roth, M. (1968). The association between quantitative measures of dementia and of senile change in the cerebral grey matter of elderly subjects. *British Journal of Psychiatry, 114,* 797–811.

Boller, F. (1980). Mental status of patients with Parkinson disease. *Journal of Clinical Neuropsychology, 2,* 157–172.

Boller, F., Mizutani, T., & Roessmann, V. (1980). Parkinson's disease, dementia and Alzheimer's disease:

Clinicopathological correlations. *Annals of Neurology, I*, 329–335.

Bondareff, W. (1983). Age and Alzheimer's disease. *Lancet, i*, 1447.

Bondareff, W., Mountjoy, C. Q., & Roth, M. (1982). Loss of neurons or origin of the adrenergic projection to celebral cortex (nucleus locus ceruleus) in senile dementia. *Neurology, 32*, 164–168.

Carlson, A. (1981). Aging and brain neurotransmitters. In T. Crook & S. Gershon (Eds.), *Strategies for the development of an effective treatment for senile dementia* (pp. 93–104). New Canaan, CT: Mark Powley Associates.

Cheah, K. C., & Beard, O. W. (1980). Psychiatric findings in the population of a geriatric evaluation unit: Implications. *Journal of the American Geriatrics Society, 28*, 153–156.

Chen, L. (1981). Neurofibrillary changes on Guam. *Archives of Neurology, 38*, 16–18.

Christie, J. E., Shering, A., Ferguson, J., & Glen, A. I. M. (1981). Physostigmine and arecoline: Effects of intravenous infusions in Alzheimer presenile dementia. *British Journal of Psychiatry, 138*, 46–50.

Crook, T. (1979). Psychometric assessment in the elderly. In A. Raskin & L. F. Jarvik (Eds.), *Psychiatric symptoms and cognitive loss in the elderly* (pp. 207–220). New York: Hemisphere.

Crook, T. (1985). Geriatric psychopathology: An overview of the ailments and current therapies. *Drug Development Research, 5*, 5–23.

Crook, T., Bartus, R., Ferris, S., Whitehouse, P., Cohen, S., & Gershon, S. (1986). Age-associated memory impairment: Proposed diagnostic criteria and measures of change. *Developmental Neuropsychology, 2*, 261–276.

Crook, T., & Cohen, G. (1983). *Physicians' guide to the diagnosis and treatment of depression in the elderly.* New Canaan, CT: Mark Powley Associates.

Crook, T., & Miller, N. (1985). The challenge of Alzheimer's disease. *American Psychologist, 40*, 1245–1250.

Cross, A. J., Crow, T. J., Ferris, I. N., & Johnson, J. A. (1986). The selectivity of the reduction of serotonin S2 receptors in Alzheimer-type dementia. *Neurobiology of Aging, 7*, 3–7.

Davies, P., Katz, D. A., & Crystal, H. A. (1982). Choline acetyltransferase, somatostatin, and substance P in selected cases of Alzheimer's disease. In S. Corkin, K. L. Davis, J. H. Growdon, E. Usdin, & R. J. Wurtman (Eds.), *Aging: Vol. 19. Alzheimer's disease: A report of progress in research* (pp. 9–14). New York: Raven.

Davies, P., & Maloney, A. J. F. (1976). Selective loss of central cholinergic neurons in Alzheimer's disease. *Lancet, 2*, 1403.

Davis, K. L., Mohs, R. C., Rosen, W. G., Greenwald, B. S., Levy, M. I., & Horvath, T. B. (1983). Memory enhancement with oral physostigmine in Alzheimer's disease. *New England Journal of Medicine, 308*, 721–723.

Drachman, D. A., & Leavitt, J. L. (1974). Human memory and the cholinergic system. A relationship to aging? *Archives of Neurology, 30*, 113–121.

Duffy, P., Wolf, J., Collins, G., DeVoe, A. G., Strecten, B., & Cowen, D. (1974). Possible person-to-person transmission of Creutzfeld-Jakob disease. *New England Journal of Medicine, 299*, 692–693.

Esquirol, J. E. D. (1976). *Des maladies mentales* [Mental diseases] (Vol. 2). New York: Arno.

Farmer, P. M., Peck, A., & Terry, R. D. (1976). Correlations among neuritic plaques, neurofibrillary tangles, and the severity of senile dementia. *Journal of Neuropathology and Experimental Neurology, 35*, 367–376.

Ferris, S. H., de Leon, M. J., Wolf, A. P., Farkas, T., Christman, D. R., Reisberg, B., Fauler, J. S., MacGregor, R., Goldman, A., George, A. E., & Rampal, S. (1980). Positron emission tomography in the study of aging and senile dementia. *Neurobiology of Aging, 1*, 127–131.

Ferris, S. H., Reisberg, B., Crook, T., Friedman, E., Schneck, M., Mir, P., Sherman, K. A., Corwin, J., Gershon, S., & Bartus, R. T. (1982). Pharmacologic treatment of senile dementia: Choline, L-Dopa, piracetam, and choline plus piracetam. In S. Corkin, K. L. Davis, J. H. Growdon, E. Usdin, & R. J. Wurtman (Eds.), *Alzheimer's disease: A report of progress in research* (pp. 475–481). New York: Raven.

Folstein, M. F., & Breitner, J. C. S. (1981). Language disorder predicts familial Alzheimer's disease. *Johns Hopkins Medical Journal, 149*, 145–147.

Folstein, M. F., Folstein, S. E., & McHugh, P. R. (1975). "Many-mental state": A practical method for grading the cognitive state of patients for the clinician. *Journal of Psychiatric Research, 12*, 189–198.

Gajdusek, D. C. (1977). Unconventional viruses and the origin and disappearance of kuru. *Science, 197*, 943–960.

Gibbs, C. J., Gajdusek, D. C., Asher, D. M., Alpers, M. P., Beck, E., Daniel, P. M., & Matthews, W. B. (1968). Creutzfeldt–Jakob disease (spongiform encephalopathy): Transmission to the chimpanzee. *Science, 161*, 388–389.

Giurgea, C. (1976). Piracetam: Nootropic pharmacology of neurointegrative activity. *Current Developments in Psychopharmacology, 3*, 221–276.

Gottfries, C. G. (1983). Biochemical changes in blood and cerebrospinal fluid. In B. Reisberg (Ed.), *Alzheimer's disease: The standard reference* (pp. 122–130). New York: Free Press.

Gottfries, C. G. (1985). Alzheimer's disease and senile dementia: Biochemical characteristics and aspects of treatment. *Psychopharmacology, 86*, 245–252.

Gottfries, C. G., Gottfries, I., & Roos, B. E. (1969). The investigation of homovanillic acid in the human brain and its correlation to senile dementia. *British Journal of Psychiatry, 115*, 563–574.

Gottfries, C. G., Roos, B. E., & Winblad, B. (1976). Monoamine and monoamine metabolites in the human brain post mortem in senile dementia. *Aktuelle Gerontologie, 6*, 429–435.

Gurland, B. J., Golden, R., & Dean, L. (1980). Depression and dementia in the elderly of New York City. In *Planning for the elderly in New York City.* New York: Community Council of Greater New York.

Hachinski, V. C., Lassen, N. A., & Marshall, J. (1974). Multi-infarct dementia—A cause of mental deterioration in the elderly. *Lancet, 2*, 207–210.

Hakim, A. M., & Mathieson, G. (1979). Dementia in Parkinson's disease: Neuropathologic study. *Neurology, 29*, 1209–1214.

Hakim, S., & Adams, R. D. (1965). The special clinical

problem of symptomatic hydrocephalus with normal cerebrospinal fluid pressure: Observations on cerebrospinal fluid hydrodynamics. *Journal of the Neurological Sciences, 2,* 307–327.

Harbaugh, R. E., Roberts, D. W., & Coombs, D. W. (1984). Preliminary report: Intracranial cholinergic drug infusion in patients with Alzheimer's disease: *Neurosurgery, 15,* 514–518.

Hauri, P. J. (1984). Nonpharmacologic treatment of sleep-wake disorders in the elderly. In D. J. Kupfer & T. Crook (Eds.), *Physician's guide to the recognition and treatment of sleep disorders in the elderly* (pp. 23–31). New Canaan, CT: Mark Powley Associates.

Heston, L. L. (1976). Alzheimer's disease, trisomy 21, and myeloproliferative disorders: Associations suggesting a genetic diathesis. *Science, 196,* 322–323.

Heston, L. L., & Mastri, A. R. (1977). The genetics of Alzheimer's disease: Associations with hematologic malignancy and Down's syndrome. *Archives of General Psychiatry, 34,* 976–981.

Hollister, L. E., & Yesavage, J. (1984). Co-Dergocrine for senile dementias: After thirty years many unanswered questions. *Annals of Internal Medicine, 100,* 894–898.

Ingvar, D. H. (1983). Cerebral blood flow and cerebral metabolism in Alzheimer's disease: Technical considerations. In B. Reisberg (Ed.), *Alzheimer's disease: The standard reference* (pp. 278–285). New York: Free Press.

Kahn, R. L., Zarit, S. H., Hilbert, N. M., & Niederehe, G. M. (1975). Memory complaint and impairment in the aged. *Archives of General Psychiatry, 32,* 1569–1573.

Kral, V. A. (1978). Benign senescent forgetfulness. *Aging NY, 7,* 47–51.

Kupfer, D. J., & Crook, T. (1984). *Physicians' guide to the recognition and treatment of sleep disorders in the elderly.* New Canaan, CT: Mark Powley Associates.

Larsson, T., Sjogren, T., & Jacobsen, G. (1963). Senile dementia: A clinical, sociomedical and genetic study. *Acta Psychiatrica Scandinavica, 39* (Suppl. 167), 1–259.

Lieberman, A. (1974). Parkinson's disease: A clinical review. *American Journal of Medical Science, 267,* 66–80.

Lieberman, A., Dzietolowski, M., Kupersmith, M., Serby, M., Goodgold, A., Korein, J., & Goldstein, M. (1979). Dementia in Parkinson's disease. *Annals of Neurology, 6,* 255–259.

Lishman, W. A. (1978). *Organic psychiatry: The psychological consequences of cerebral disorder.* Oxford: Blackwell Scientific.

Little, A., Chauqui-Kidd, P., & Levy, R. (1984). Early results from a double-blind, placebo-controlled trial of high dose lecithin in Alzheimer's disease: Psychometric test performance, plasma choline levels and the effects of drug compliance. In R. J. Wurtman, S. H. Corkin, & J. H. Growdon (Eds.), *Alzheimer's disease: Advances in basic research and therapies* (pp. 313–331). Zürich: Center for Brain Sciences and Metabolism Charitable Trust.

Mace, N. L., & Rabins, P. V. (1981). *The 36-hour day: A family guide to caring for persons with Alzheimer's disease, related dementing illness, and memory loss in later life.* Baltimore, MD: Johns Hopkins University Press.

Mash, D. C., Flynn, D. D., & Potter, L. T. (1985). Loss of M_2 muscarinic receptors in the cerebral cortex in Alzheimer's disease and experimental cholinergic denervation. *Science, 228,* 1115–1117.

Masters, C. L., Gajdusek, D. C., & Gibbs, C. J., Jr. (1981). The familial occurrence of Creutzfeldt–Jakob disease and Alzheimer's disease. *Brain, 104,* 535–558.

McKhann, G., Drachman, D., Folstein, M., Katzman, R., Price, D., & Stadlam, E. M. (1984). Clinical diagnosis of Alzheimer's disease: Report of the NINCDS-ADRDA Work Group under the auspices of the Department of Health and Human Services Task Force on Alzheimer's Disease. *Neurology, 34,* 939–944.

Mortimer, J. A. (1983). Alzheimer's disease and senile dementia: Prevalence and incidence. In B. Reisburg (Ed.), *Alzheimer's disease: The standard reference* (pp. 141–148). New York: Free Press.

Ojemann, R. G. (1971). Normal pressure hydrocephalus. In *Clinical neurosurgery* (Chap. 16). *Proceedings of the Congress of Neurological Surgeons* (Vol. 18). Baltimore, Williams & Wilkins.

Perry, E. K., Perry, R. H., Blessed, G., & Tomlinson, B. E. (1977). Necropsy evidence of central cholinergic deficits in senile dementia. *Lancet, i,* 189.

Price, D. L., Whitehouse, P. J., Struble, R. G., Clark, A. W., Coyle, J. T., De Long, M. R., & Hedreen, J. C. (1982). Basal forebrain cholinergic systems in Alzheimer's disease and related dementias. *Neuroscience Commentaries, 1,* 84–92.

Reifler, B. V., Larson, E., & Hanley, R. (1982). Coexistence of cognitive impairment and depression in geriatric outpatients. *American Journal of Psychiatry, 139,* 623–626.

Reisberg, B., Ferris, S. H., Anand, R., de Leon, J. M., Schneck, M. K., & Crook, T. (1985). Clinical assessment of cognitive decline in normal aging and primary degenerative dementia: Concordant ordinal measures. In P. Pinchot, P. Berner, R. Wolf, & K. Thau (Eds.), *Psychiatry* (Vol. 5, pp. 333–338). New York: Plenum.

Reisberg, B., Ferris, S. H., de Leon, M. J., & Crook, T. (1982). The global deterioration scale for assessment of primary degenerative dementia. *American Journal of Psychiatry, 139,* 1136–1139.

Reisberg, B., Ferris, S., & Roberts, G. (1983). Effects of naloxone in senile dementia: A doubleblind study. *New England Journal of Medicine, 308,* 721–722.

Reynolds, C. F. (1984). Managing sleep disorders in institutionalized aged patients. In D. J. Kupfer & T. Crook (Eds.), *Physicians' guide to the recognition and treatment of sleep disorders in the elderly* (pp. 45–49). New Canaan, CT: Mark Powley Associates.

Rosen, W. G., Terry, R. D., Fuld, P. A., Katzman, R., & Peck, A. (1980). Pathological verification of ischemic score in differentation of dementias. *Annuals of Neurology, 7,* 486–488.

Rosenberg, G. S., Greenwald, B., & Davis, K. (1983). Pharmacologic treatment of Alzheimer's disease: An overview. In B. Reisberg (Ed.), *Alzheimer's disease: The standard reference* (pp. 329–339). New York: Free Press.

Salazar, A. M., Brown, P., Gajdusek, D. C., & Gibbs, C. J., Jr. (1983). Relation to Creutzfeldt–Jakob disease and other unconventional virus diseases. In B. Reisberg (Ed.), *Alzheimer's disease: The standard reference* (pp. 311–318). New York: Free Press.

Salzman, C. (1984). *Clinical geriatric psychopharmacology.* New York: McGraw-Hill.

Siedler, H., & Malamud, N. (1963). Creutzfeldt–Jakob's disease: Clinicopathologic report of 15 cases and review of the literature. *Journal of Neuropathology and Experimental Neurology, 22,* 381–402.

Sjogren, T., Sjogren, H., & Lindgren, A. G. H. (1952). Morbus Alzheimer and morbus Pick. *Acta Psychiatrica Scandinavica, 82* (Suppl.), 68–108.

Skinner, B. F., & Vaughan, M. (1983). *Enjoy old age.* New York: Warner Books.

Smith, R. C., Vroulis, G., Johnson, R., & Morgan, R. (1984). Comparison of therapeutic response to long-term treatment with lecithin versus piracetam plus lechithin in patients with Alzheimer's disease. *Psychopharmacology Bulletin, 20,* 542–545.

Summers, W. K., Viesselman, J. O., & Marsh, G. M. (1981). Use of THA in treatment of Alzheimer-like dementia: Pilot study in twelve patients. *Biological Psychiatry, 16,* 145–153.

Thal, L. J., Fuld, P. A., Masur, D. M., & Sharpless, N. S. (1983). Oral physostigmine and lecithin improve memory in Alzheimer's disease. *Annals of Neurology, 13,* 491–496.

Thal, L. J., Masur, D. M., Sharpless, N. S., Fuld, P. A., & Davies, P. (1984). Acute and chronic effects of oral physostigmine and lecithin in Alzheimer's disease. In R. J. Wurtman, S. H. Corkin, & J. H. Growdon (Eds.), *Alzheimer's disease: Advances in basic research and therapies* (pp. 333–347). Zürich: Center for Brain Sciences and Metabolism Charitable Trust.

Tinklenberg, J. R., & Thornton, J. E. (1983). Neuropeptides in geriatric psychopharmacology. *Psychopharmacology Bulletin, 19,* 198–211.

Tomlinson, B. E., Blessed, G., & Roth, M. (1970). Observations on the brains of demented old people. *Journal of the Neurological Sciences, 11,* 205–242.

Torack, R. M. (1983). The early history of senile dementia. In B. Reisberg (Ed.), *Alzheimer's disease: The standard reference* (pp. 23–28). New York: Free Press.

Wells, C. E. (1983). Differential diagnosis of Alzheimer's dementia: Affective disorder. In B. Reisberg (Ed.), *Alzheimer's disease: The standard reference* (pp. 193–197). New York: Free Press.

West, R. (1985). *Memory fitness over 40.* Gainesville, FL: Triad Publishing.

Whitehouse, P. J., Price, D. L., Struble, R. G., Clark, W. W., Coyle, J. T., & De Long, M. R. (1982). Alzheimer's disease and senile dementia: Loss of neurons in the basal forebrain. *Science, 215,* 1237–1239.

Wisniewski, K., Wisniewski, H., & Wen, G. Y. (1983). Plaques, tangles and dementia in Down's syndrome. *Journal of Neuropathology and Experimental Neurology, 42,* 340–346.

Yesavage, J. A. (1985). Nonpharmacologic treatments for memory losses with normal aging. *American Journal of Psychiatry, 142,* 600–605.

Chapter 9

Depression and Dementia

Linda Teri and Burton V. Reifler

This chapter will review the literature on depression and dementia in older adults. As discussed earlier in this volume, depression and dementia are common disorders of aging and represent a significant diagnostic dilemma to clinicians working with older adults. Often the differential diagnosis of these two conditions is complicated because severely depressed patients can exhibit cognitive impairment extensive enough to resemble dementia. The term *pseudodementia* has been used to describe the cases in which impaired cognitive states resemble dementia but, when the underlying depression improves, the cognitive impairment also improves.

Although it is commonly thought that depression and dementia are mutually exclusive categories (i.e., patients are *either* demented *or* depressed, and pseudodementia is a subset of depression), data are accumulating to suggest that this is not so. Patients can be both demented and depressed. Further, the depression seen in such patients can be effectively treated. This conceptualization of coexistent depression and dementia will be presented and elaborated upon in this chapter. The clinical literature most relevant to the discussion of coexistence will be summarized, and then the empirical studies that have investigated the question of coexistence will be reviewed. The chapter will conclude with a discussion of inci-

dence and prevalence estimates and a summary of findings.

CLINICAL LITERATURE: DIFFERENTIAL DIAGNOSIS OR COEXISTENT DISORDER?

A number of authors have addressed the difficulty of differentially diagnosing dementia and depression in older adults (see chapters 7 and 8 in this volume, as well as Gallagher & Thompson, 1983; Post, 1976; Wells, 1977; Zarit & Zarit, 1983). The main concern stems from the presence of cognitive impairments in both depression and dementia. When cognitive impairment in depression is severe, it is thought to resemble dementia and so has given rise to such terms and phrases as *pseudodementia* (Libow, 1973), *depressive pseudodementia* (Raskin & Rae, 1980), *dementia syndrome of depression* (Folstein & McHugh, 1973), and *reversible dementia caused by depression* (Rabins, 1981). These have been offered to provide a description of the theorized gray zone of severe cognitive impairments that are probably psychiatric in origin, not organic.

To determine the cause of cognitive impairments, practitioners must be able to identify the full syndromes of depression and dementia and understand the degree to which these different disorders are related to each other. To this end, Table 9.1 lists diagnostic criteria for dementia and major

Table 9.1. *DSM-III* Criteria for Dementia and Depressive Disorders

Dementia	Major Depressive Disorder (MDD)
1. Loss of intellectual ability of sufficient severity to impair social/occupational functioning.	1. Dysphoric mood
2. Memory loss	2. At least 4 for at least two weeks:
3. At least 1:	a) appetite disturbance
a) impairment of abstract thinking	b) sleep disturbance
b) impaired judgment	c) psychomotor agitation or retardation
c) disturbances of higher cortical dysfunction (e.g., aphasia, apraxia or agnosia).	d) loss of interest or pleasure
d) personality change	e) fatigue
4. No clouding of consciousness	f) feeling of worthlessness, guilt or self-reproach
5. Presence or absence of organic factor (Note: This criteria will effect type of dementia diagnosed, e.g., Dementia of the Alzheimer Type vs. Multi-infarct Dementia).	g) concentrational difficulties
	h) suicidal thoughts or actions
	3. No preoccupation with mood—incongruent delusion, hallucination or bizarre behavior
	4. Not superimposed on schizophrenia, Schizophreniform disorder or a paranoid disorder
	5. Not due to any organic mental disorder or uncomplicated bereavement

Dysthmic Disorder (or Depressive Neurosis)
1. Dysphoria
2. For at least two years, problems with most or all symptoms of MDD
3. No more than a few months of normal mood during episode
4. At least 3 of the following during episode:
a–h) See MDD, above
i) tearfulness or crying
j) pessimism
k) decreased activity
l) irritability or excessive anger
5. Does not meet full criteria for MDD
6. No psychotic features

Note. Adapted from *Diagnostic and Statistical Manual of Mental Disorders* (3rd ed.) by American Psychiatric Association, 1980, Washington, DC. Copyright 1980 by American Psychiatric Association.

depressive disorder that appear in the *Diagnostic and Statistical Manual of Mental Disorders (DSM-III)* published by the American Psychiatric Association (1980). As can be seen, complaints of impaired concentration and memory are symptoms of both depression and dementia. However, according to the *DSM-III*, a diagnosis of major depressive disorder cannot be given if symptoms are "due to" organic mental disorder. In that event, a subclassification of "with depression" is given, with a primary diagnosis of dementia. Thus, the *DSM-III* standards identify criteria but do not help clarify the overlap of symptoms in a diagnosis of depression or dementia.

The *DSM-III* offers no diagnostic criteria for pseudodementia. However, enough researchers (Busse, 1975; Kiloh 1961; Post, 1975; Wells, 1979) have published discussions of it to enable a description here. Caine (1981) provides four criteria

for pseudodementia that are consistent with these writings: (a) intellectual impairment *with a primary psychiatric disorder*, (b) features of neuropsychological abnormality that in part resemble neuropathologically induced cognitive deficits, (c) reversible intellectual disorder, and (d) no apparent neuropathological process accounting for the genesis of the disorder. Pseudodementia, therefore, describes the occurrence of severe cognitive impairments, such as memory loss and impaired judgment, that are refractory: Upon the cure of the primary psychiatric disorder, the cognitive deficits remit.

As can be seen from the above description, pseudodementia is not confined to depression. It can be utilized with any number of psychiatric causes of cognitive impairment. The label of pseudodementia is meant to distinguish reversible cognitive complaints from irreversible ones.

In a recent review of depression in older adults,

Gallagher and Thompson (1983) offered the following advice to assist in identifying reversible and irreversible causes of cognitive complaints:

> On a practical level, it is helpful to remember that clinical depression is primarily a disturbance of mood. Although truly depressed persons often complain about memory impairment and difficulty in thinking and concentrating, they usually perform adequately when their abilities are tested under standard conditions. Dementia, on the other hand, is primarily a disturbance of intellectual functioning. . . . On formal testing, demented persons are, in contrast to depressives, apt to perform poorly although they tend to complain less about their functioning. . . . Studies investigating the relationship between memory functioning, complaints about memory, and affective status in older adults generally support the notion that depressed individuals complain of greater deficits than are actually the case when memory performance is objectively evaluated. (p. 13).

Therefore, a potential solution for the difficult differential diagnosis of dementia versus depression is a more thorough objective evaluation of cognitive impairments (see chapter 8, this volume; Fuld, 1982; Jarvik, 1980).

Thus far, we have addressed the literature that attempts to distinguish dementia from depression. This, of course, still assumes that the two are mutually exclusive. (Figure 9.1 presents a graphic representation of the argument that depression and dementia are mutually exclusive.) The *DSM-III* classification scheme and the clinical writings on dementia and depression were probably influenced by the same school of thought that argues for differential diagnosis between functional and organic disorders. Clinicians are challenged to decide between the two rather than to examine the possibility of coexistence. (For a more detailed discussion of this general issue, the interested reader is referred to Lezak, 1983).

It is not difficult to conceptualize the coexistence of the two disorders. (Figure 9.2 illustrates this concept of coexistent depression and dementia.) For example, psychiatric patients can be in motor-vehicle accidents and suffer brain trauma; cancer patients can become depressed; and depressed patients can succumb to heart disease. Following this logic, patients can have an irreversible dementia and an affective disorder. It is not difficult to envisage a depressed patient growing older and developing Alzheimer's disease or a patient with multi-infarct dementia becoming

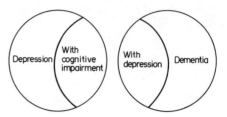

Figure 9.1. Illustration of diagnostic categorization of depression and dementia as mutually exclusive disorders.

painfully aware of his or her new limitations and becoming clinically depressed. Adults may certainly have organic and functional disorders simultaneously. To suggest otherwise would be to imply that one protects against the other or vice versa. Indeed, quite to the contrary, a number of researchers have suggested that depression commonly presents early in a dementing illness and may perhaps be a precursor to organic involvement (e.g., Busse, 1975; Goldstein, 1975; Pearce & Miller, 1973; Wells, 1977).

As early as 1976, Post argued, "I don't like the term [pseudo] 'dementia' at all. Intellectual and cognitive impairment are more acceptable" (p. 229). Reifler (1982) has also argued to "abandon" the term *pseudodementia* and has posed two arguments: (a) The concept of pseudodementia implies that organic cognitive impairment and functionally derived cognitive impairment are mutually exclusive and thereby interferes with the recognition of cognitive impairment resulting from multiple causes, and (b) the term is often mistakenly used diagnostically rather than descriptively (as it was intended) and thereby sometimes obfuscates correct diagnosis and treatment.

The term pseudodementia also raises the specter of masked depression: depression that is somehow manifestly different from other depressions. In this case, the depression would have as its chief manifestation cognitive impairment rather than dysphoric mood. For childhood and adolescence, the concept of masked depression has also been posed, and has been refuted by empirical documentation that the dysphoric mood can be observed and remains the predominant symptom in depression (Lewinsohn, Teri, & Hoberman, 1983; Teri, 1985). Such data are available with older adults as well. Dysphoria can be identified as the predominant symptom in depression in older adults; in addition, the syndrome of depression has been identified in older adults and resembles that found in younger adults

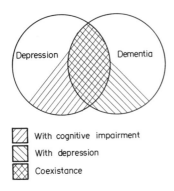

With cognitive impairment

With depression

Coexistance

Figure 9.2. Illustration of diagnostic categorization of depression with coexistence.

(Gallagher & Thompson, 1983; Gaylord & Zung, Chapter 7, this volume; Rad' off & Teri, 1985; Teri & Lewinsohm, 1982). Thus, if probed, older adults with depression may well identify or exhibit the dysphoric mood, vegetative signs, and symptomatic complaints of a depressive disorder. In addition, as will be discussed next, depression can also be identified among dementia patients. Thus the concept of a masked depression, a pseudodementia, is questionable and is likely of limited, if not detrimental, utility.

EMPIRICAL EVIDENCE

In the last fifteen years or so, only a handful of studies have investigated the presence of identifiable depression in dementia patients. These studies have varied in their method of assessment, methodological design, and sample characteristics. Despite this variability, however, they have yielded surprisingly consistent support for the hypothesis that both disorders can coexist.

In one of the first studies on depression in dementia patients, Tourney (1970) examined 1,317 consecutive admissions to an acute treatment center. Depression symptoms were defined as depression secondary to another psychiatric or physical disorder. Seventy-one percent of all patients with "organic brain syndrome" had such symptoms. Of these, 22% were rated severely depressed, 24% were rated moderately depressed, and 31% were rated mildly depressed. The criteria for diagnosis and severity were unspecified. Another retrospective study yielded similarly high proportions. Liston (1978) reviewed the charts of 50 "presenile" patients and rated the presence of depressive symptoms such as disturbed mood, abnormal psychomotor activity, rumination or

preoccupation, somatic symptoms, disordered cognition or concentration, and impaired reality testing or perception. A depressive syndrome was defined as having at least 3 of the above mentioned symptoms. Depressive symptoms were evident in 57% of this sample, a depressive syndrome was evident in 28%.

Two studies reported depression in dementia patients on the basis of results obtained upon administration of the Zung Self-Rating Depression Scale. Heidell and Kidd (1975) obtained Zung scores on 120 "older adults." Subjects residing in the community were "assumed to be non-senile," and subjects residing in convalescent and nursing homes were "rated by nurses and attendants as non-senile or moderately senile." Subjects classified as severely senile were excluded. The diagnostic criteria were unspecified. Although mean Zung scores were not reported, the authors indicated that the "senile" subjects scored significantly higher than the "non-senile" subjects. In a more controlled study, Knesevich, Martin, Berg, and Danziger (1983) investigated 30 patients identified with senile dementia of the Alzheimer type and 30 "healthy controls matched for age, sex, race and social position." Those with a history of depression were excluded, as were those with "evidence of another etiology" for their dementia. Among other measures, subjects completed the Hamilton Rating Scale for Depression and the Zung Self-Rating Depression Scale. Patients with senile dementia of the Alzheimer type scored significantly higher than normals both on the Hamilton scale ($x = 5.50$ [s.d. = 4.69] vs. $x = 3.07$ [s.d. = 2.75]) and on the Zung scale ($x = 47.23$ [s.d. = 9.93] vs. $x = 44.93$ [s.d. = 7.57]), although the difference on the Zung scale was not significant. All scores were within normal limits (not surprising given the exclusion criteria).

Using a more diverse sample, Raskin and Rae (1980) identified depression in dementia patients by employing the *DSM-III* criteria. Ratings were obtained for 35 inpatients, 21 outpatients, and 150 normal older adults. Subjects were classified as demented if they met the *DSM-III* criteria for dementia. All dementia subjects were diagnosed as having progressive idiopathic dementia, senile onset. Subjects were classified as depressed if they obtained a total score of 7 or more on the Raskin Three-Area Severity of Depression Scale and met the *DSM-III* criteria for any depressive disorder, such as adjustment reaction with depression, depressive personality, or episodic or recurrent depression. Subjects were classified as normal if they obtained 21 or more on the Folstein Mini-Mental State Exam and met the *DSM-III* criteria for "not currently or never mentally ill." All subjects were rated on the Inventory of Psychic and Somatic Complaints—Elderly, and on the Global Assessments of Psychopathology, by psychologists and psychiatrists. Depression was evident among those subjects classified as demented, although percentages were not reported. In addition, patients with both depression and dementia were rated as the most severely ill, although they did not exhibit more overall cognitive impairment than nondepressed demented patients.

Approaching the question of depression and dementia via cluster analysis, Ballinger, Reid, and Heather (1982) analyzed the symptoms of 100 dementia patients. Dementia was restricted to "progressive dementing syndromes," but the criteria for the diagnoses were not reported. The symptoms were rated by psychiatrists and ward nursing staff according to various scales, including the Stockton Rating Scale, The Clifton Assessment Schedule, the Manifest Abnormalities Scale of the Clinical Interview Schedule, and a 5-point "overall rating for psychiatric disorder." Four of the eight identified clusters contained depressive symptoms.

Reifler, Larson, and Hanley (1982) examined patients who had sought help at or were referred to the Geriatric and Family Services Clinic at the University of Washington in Seattle. (This clinic has been described in detail by Reifler and Eisdorfer, 1980.) Dementia was determined via the Mental Status Questionnaire and *DSM-III* criteria. Depression was determined with the Research Diagnostic Criteria. Of the 88 cognitively impaired patients in this study, 20 (23%) also met the Research Diagnostic Criteria for depression. When the level of severity was examined, 9 out of 27 (33%) mildly impaired patients were depressed, compared to 8 out of 35 (23%) moderately impaired patients and 3 out of 26 (12%) severely impaired. This difference in depression according to severity was statistically significant, indicating that the worse the cognitive impairment, the less likely the patient would meet *DSM-III* criteria for depression. In addition, the investigators attempted to determine the proportion of patients with cognitive impairment caused by depression, versus those with depression superimposed on a dementing illness. Of the 20 depressed patients with cognitive impairment, 17

(85%) had the depression superimposed on an underlying dementia, usually dementia of the Alzheimer's type.

Consistent with this finding, Rabins, Merchant, and Nestadt (1984) reported on 36 patients who had been hospitalized over a 1 year period at a psychiatric clinic: 18 who met the *DSM-III* criteria for depression *and* dementia and 18 who met the *DSM-III* criteria for dementia only. Subjects with dementia and depression were more likely to have prior histories of depression problems, more likely to report delusions, and less likely to be cognitively impaired, as indicated by the Folstein Mini-Mental State Examination (MMSE) ($x = 17.2$ vs. 11.2). At the 2-year follow-up, those with both depression and dementia were more likely to have recovered cognitive functioning while those with dementia only had not (MMSE $x = 25.7$ vs. 4.2).

Investigating a larger clinical sample, Reifler, Larson, Teri, and Poulsen (1985) studied 131 patients diagnosed according to the *DSM-III* criteria for primary degenerative dementia. Of these, 41 (31%) also met the *DSM-III* criteria for a major depressive disorder. In this case, the mean MMSE scores for depressed and non depressed demented patients were not statistically different ($x = 18.2$ vs. 17.8). This lack of differences was also found at the 18-month follow-up: Depressed patients with primary degenerative dementia had a mean follow-up MMSE of 15.6, compared to 15.4 for the non depressed patients with primary degenerative dementia.

These last two studies provide apparently contradictory data. Rabins et al. (1984) reported differences in cognitive status between depressed and nondepressed patients that became more pronounced over time. Reifler et al. (1985) found no such differences. This discrepancy may be explained by the differences in the two samples. The former study included patients with both chronic and acute cognitive impairment (P. V. Rabins, personal communication, 1985); the latter study included only patients with chronic (and progressive) memory loss. Thus, differences in follow-up may be a function of different etiologies for the cognitive impairment. Despite this, their results and those of earlier studies are consistent in support of the hypotheses that depression symptoms are evident in dementia patients and that depression and dementia can coexist. Although the variations across studies make conclusions difficult, it may be estimated that between 20% and 30% of demented patients are also depressed.

With this documented presence of depression in a subset of dementia patients, additional questions arise regarding the impact of depression on dementia patients and the potential role of treatment.

Reifler et al. (1985) investigated the impact that treatment of depression may have on patients with both depression and dementia. Treatment for depression was determined retrospectively by chart review. Twenty patients had received anti-depressant pharmacotherapy; of these 17 (85%) had reported improvement in mood, vegetative signs, and/or activities of daily living. This suggested that depression may contribute to excess disability in patients with dementia of the Alzheimer's type (DAT) by causing these symptoms and that treatment of the depression may alleviate these difficulties.

INCIDENCE AND PREVALENCE

Estimates of the incidence and prevalence of depression in dementia patients stem primarily from studies of clinical samples just reviewed. Consequently, while we can estimate the rate of coexistence in a sample seeking help, we can only extrapolate the rate of coexistence in community-based samples. In a study discussed earlier (Reifler et al., 1982), the researchers investigated the prevalence of coexistence in 88 specifically "cognitively impaired" geriatric outpatients. Twenty patients (23%) were diagnosed per Research Diagnostic Criteria as depressed (including probable and definite, primary and secondary). Of these, 17 (85%) were also evaluated as being demented using criteria proposed by Wells (1979). The researchers concluded that dementia and depression coexisted in 20% to 25% of all patients seen in the geriatric outpatient clinic.

Estimates of the number of patients with cognitive impairments that were originally diagnosed as presenile dementia but at follow-up were found no longer to meet the criteria vary between 8% and 57% (Caine, 1981; Haward, 1977; Marsden & Harrison, 1972; Nott & Fleminger, 1975; Ron, Toone, & Garralda, 1979) and estimates of the presence of "clinically significant cognitive impairment" among depressed patients average around 1. % (Klerman, 1983). Extrapolating from these percentages to prevalence figures of dementia (i.e., 10% of those over 65 years of age are thought to be demented, Zarit & Zarit, 1983) and prevalence figures of depression (i.e., 9% of those over 65

years of age are thought to be depressed, Gallagher & Thompson, 1983), it can be estimated that between 1% and 4% of those over 65 are both demented and depressed. It is likely that a number of factors contribute to this difference in findings, including the degree of cognitive impairment considered sufficient to warrant a diagnosis of dementia; the method of evaluation; the concomitant medical, psychiatric, and historic factors that complicate an individual patient's diagnostic picture; the skill and expertise of those making the diagnosis; and the setting in which the patient is evaluated. Thus, these estimates must be read cautiously until more consistent large-scale data are available.

CONCLUSION

The investigation of coexistent dementia and depression is clearly a new area, and as such has a number of methodological shortcomings. Paramount among these is the lack of standard methods of assessment. For example, five of the eight studies reviewed did not report their criteria for dementia, and thus, it is unclear whether patients with mixed dementias were grouped together or what diagnostic criteria were used. Similarly, studies differed in their definition of depression, ranging from self-ratings (such as the Zung Self-Rating Depression Scale) to clinical ratings (such as the Hamilton Depression Scale) to diagnostic criteria (such as the Research Diagnostic Criteria and the *DSM-III* criteria). Often, it is unclear who conducted the diagnostic evaluations or how they were performed. Certainly, with cognitively impaired adults, self-ratings must be suspect. In most of these studies, structured clinical interviews were not reported, and therefore the liability of the ratings is unknown.

Despite these limitations, however, consistent evidence has accumulated suggesting that depression symptoms do exist in dementia patients, and that depression and dementia are not mutually exclusive syndromes. In addition, preliminary data suggest that depression does impact on the affective and functional status of the dementia patient but is less likely to impact on cognition. As such, depression may well be considered a cause of excess disability and increased problems for effective care. Practitioners working with depressed and/or demented older adults would do well to investigate the existence of each disorder and consider treating the depression when present. Support for the efficacy of pharmacological and nonpharmacological treatment of depression in older adults is accumulating (Breslau & Haug, 1983; Gallagher & Thompson, 1983), and preliminary results suggest tricyclic antidepressants can alleviate depression in dementia patients as well (Reifler et al., 1985). Further clinical and empirical work is clearly needed.

REFERENCES

American Psychiatric Association. (1980). *Diagnostic and statistical manual of mental disorders* (3rd ed.). Washington, DC: Author.

Ballinger B. R., Reid A. H., & Heather B. B. (1982). Cluster analysis of symptoms in elderly demented patients. *British Journal of Psychiatry, 140*, 257–262.

Breslau, L. D., & Haug, M. R. (Eds.). (1983). *Depression and aging: Causes, care and consequences*. New York: Springer.

Busse, E. W. (1975). Aging and psychiatric diseases of late life. In S. Ariete (Ed.), *American handbook of psychiatry* (pp. 67–89). New York: Basic Books.

Caine, E. D. (1981). Pseudodementia: Current concepts and future directions. *Archives of General Psychiatry, 38*, 1359–1364.

Folstein, M. F., & McHugh P. R. (1973). Dementia syndrome of depression. In R. Katzman, R. D. Terry, & K. L. Bick (Eds.), *Alzheimer's disease*: Senile dementia and related disorders. New York: Raven.

Fuld, P. A. (1982). Psychological testing in the differential dementias. In R. Katzman, R. D. Terry, & K. L. Bick (Eds.), *Alzheimer's disease: Senile dementia and related disorders* (pp. 185–193). New York: Raven Press.

Gallagher, D., & Thompson, L. (1983). Depression. In P. Lewinsohn & L. Teri (Eds.), *Clinical geropsychology*. Elmsford, NY: Pergamon Press.

Goldstein, K. (1975). Functional disturbances in brain damage. In S. Arieti (Ed.), *American handbook of psychiatry* (pp. 182–206). New York: Basic Books.

Heidell, E. D., & Kidd, A. H. (1975). Depression and senility. *Journal of Clinical Psychology, 31*, 643–645.

Haward, L. R. C. (1977). Cognition in dementia presinilis. In W. L. Smith & M. Kinsbourne (Eds.), *Aging and dementia* (pp. 189–202). New York: Spectrum.

Jarvik, L. (1980). Diagnosis of dementia in the elderly. In C. Eisdorfer (Ed.), *Annual Review of Geriatrics and Gerontology, 2*, 180–203.

Kiloh, L. G. (1961). Pseudodementia. *Acta Psychiatrica Scandinavica, 37*, 336–351.

Klerman, G. (1983). Problems in the definition and diagnosis of depression in the elderly. In L. D. Breslau & M. R. Haug (Eds.), *Depression and aging: Causes, care and consequences* (pp. 3–19). New York: Springer.

Knesevich, J. M., Martin, R. L., Berg, L., & Danziger, W. (1983). Preliminary report on affective symptoms in the early stages of senile dementia of the Alzheimer type. *American Journal of Psychiatry, 140*, 233–235.

Lewinsohn, P. M., Teri, L., & Hoberman H. (1983). Depression: A perspective on etiology, treatment, and life span issues. In M. E. Rosenbaum, C. Franks,

& Y. Jaffe (Eds.), *Perspectives on behaviour therapy in the 80's* (pp. 155–183). New York: Springer.

Lezak, M. (1983). *Neuropsychological assessment*. New York: Oxford University Press.

Libow, L. S. (1973). Pseudo-senility: Acute and reversible organic brain syndromes. *Journal of the American Geriatrics Society, 21*, 112–120.

Liston, E. H. (1978). Diagnostic delay in presenile dementia. *Journal of Clinical Psychiatry, 39*, 599–603.

Marsden, L. D., & Harrison M. J. G. (1972). Outcome of investigation of patients with presenile dementia. *British Medical Journal, 2*, 249–52.

Nott, P. M., & Fleminger J. J. (1975). Presenile dementia: The difficulties of early diagnosis. *Acta Psychiatrica Scandinavica, 51*, 210–217.

Pearce J., & Miller E. (1973). *Clinical aspects of dementia*. Baltimore, MD: Williams & Wilkins.

Post, F. (1975). Dementia, depression and pseudodementia. In D. F. Benson & D. Blumer (Eds.), *Psychiatric aspects of neurological disease* (pp. 99–120). New York: Grune & Stratton.

Post, F. (1976). Diagnosis of depression in geriatric patients and treatment modalities appropriate for the population. In D. M. Gallant (Ed.), *Depression* (pp. 205–231). New York, Spectrum.

Rabins, P. V. (1981). The prevalence of reversible dementia in a psychiatric hospital. *Hospital and Community Psychiatry, 32*, 249–52.

Rabins, P. V., Merchant, A., & Nestadt, G. (1984). Criteria for diagnosing reversible dementia caused by depression: Validation by 2 year follow-up. *British Journal of Psychiatry, 144*, 488–492.

Radloff, L. S., & Teri, L. (1986). Use of Center for Epidemiological Studies: Depression scale with older adults. *Clinical Gerontologist., 5*, 119–137.

Raskin A., & Rae, D. (1980). Distinguishing depressive pseudodementia from true dementia. *Psychopharmacology Bulletin, 16*, 23–25.

Reifler, B. V. (1982). Arguments for abandoning the term pseudodementia, *Journal of the American Geriatrics Society, 30*, 665–668.

Reifler, B. V., & Eisdorfer, C. (1980). A clinic for the impaired elderly and their families. *American Journal of Psychiatry, 137*, 1399–1403.

Reifler, B. V., Larson, E., & Hanley, R. (1982). Co-existence of cognitive impairment and depression in geriatric outpatients. *American Journal of Psychiatry, 139*, 623–626.

Reifler, B. V., Larson, E., Teri, L., & Poulsen, M. (1985, August). *Alzheimer's disease and depression*. Paper presented at the meeting of the Second International Congress and Psychogeriatric Medicine, Umeå, Sweden.

Ron, M. A., Toone, B. K., & Garralda, M. E. (1979). Diagnostic accuracy in presenile dementia. *British Journal of Psychiatry, 134*, 161–168.

Teri, L. (1986). Severe cognitive impairment in older adults. *The Behavior Therapist, 9*, 51–54.

Teri, L., & Lewinsohn, P. (1982, August). *Assessing depression in the elderly: Physical and psychological symptomatology*. Paper presented at the meeting of the American Psychological Association, Washington, DC.

Tourney, G. (1970). The severely depressed patient in medical practice. In A. J. Enelow (Ed.), *Depression in medical practice* (pp. 171–192). P. A.: Merck Sharp & Dohme.

Wells, C. E. (1977). Dementia: Definition and description. In C. E. Wells (Ed.), *Dementia* (pp. 1–14). Philadelphia, PA: F. A. Davis.

Wells, C. E. (1979). Pseudodementia. *American Journal of Psychiatry, 136,* 895–900.

Zarit, S., & Zarit, J. (1983). Cognitive impairment. In P. Lewinsohn & L. Teri (Ed.), *Clinical geropsychology,* (pp. 38–80). Elmsford, NY: Pergamon Press.

Part III

Common Medical Problems

The expression "Nobody ever died of old age" alludes to the extensive incidence of physical impairment and disease among the elderly population. This section provides a review of the most common medical problems that the elderly face and their treatment. Treatment for most of these disorders involves drug therapy. At the conclusion of the section is a chapter on drug use in the geriatric patient.

Chapter 10

Cancer Management Issues

Jerome W. Yates and Rosemary Yancik

The elderly, faced with an accumulation of health, social, and economic problems, constitute a group of Americans whose well-being is of growing national concern. Of particular importance is the complexity of medical care required by older persons, who, as the years accrue, acquire a multiplicity of diseases that can be severely debilitating. Diminished physical capacity and physiological reserve are common; cancer treatment is often long-term and not curative. Continuing care and rehabilitation needs associated with the condition and with the dependencies of advanced age exceed those required in younger patients.

With demographic shifts and concurrent greater increases in proportions of the elderly in the U.S. population, the importance of cancer as a major future medical problem for the elderly is apparent. This chapter focuses on some of the more common cancers that afflict the older population and provides an overview on the salient epidemiological, diagnostic, and treatment issues relevant to persons 65 years or older. Until recently, little attention has been paid to characterizing the management of cancer in the elderly, although age is the greatest single risk factor for cancer. Even descriptive information is still needed to define optimum approaches to the management of cancer in the elderly.

Cancer management in the elderly provides a series of challenges throughout its course from the time the disease is first suspected to the time it is cured or death occurs (Yancik, Carbone, Patterson, Steel, & Terry, 1983). Because cancer is a disease that affects older individuals disproportionately, it occurs in persons who usually have other medical problems or disabilities.

The demographic changes under way in the United States indicate that by the year 2030, almost 10% of the country's population will be 75 years or older (U.S. Senate Special Committee on Aging and American Association of Retired Persons, 1984). This compares with the less than 5% of our population in the same group in 1982 (U.S. Bureau of the Census, 1984). This expanding age group is also the population segment at greatest risk of developing cancer.

In considering the management of cancer in the elderly, at least five questions may be raised about the factors unique to older persons:

1. How does the risk of developing cancer change as one ages?
2. What cancers occur commonly in older persons?
3. Could early detection decrease morbidity and mortality in the elderly?
4. How does old age influence selection and implementation of cancer therapies?
5. What basic principles of management for cancer in the elderly should be followed?

These questions provide a framework for the discussion that follows. In medical practice and the assessment of clinical research involving aged cancer patients, the key issue professionals must address is a three-way relationship involving the aging process, the disease, and the treatment.

CANCER RISKS AND THE ELDERLY

According to data from the Surveillance, Epidemiology, and End Results (SEER) Program of the National Cancer Institute, covering the 5-year period 1973–1977, age is a significant risk factor for most cancers (Young, Percy, & Asire, 1981). The median age of cancer patients, obtained from data representing almost 11% of the U.S. population, is 65.4 years. Figure 10.1 depicts the SEER incidence rates of cancer in age groups according to 5-year increments. Each bar represents the proportion of patients in each age group. As can be seen in the figure, the largest number of cases occur in the 60–70 age group. After age 40, with each 20-year interval of life, the incidence rate increases rapidly. Thus at age 60, it is approximately 1,000 cases per 100,000 population, but by age 80, it is twice as high—about 2,200 per 100,000. Of the 327,627 malignant primary-site cases in the SEER data, more than 50% occurred in individuals 65 years or older. The SEER mortality figures indicate that almost 60% of all cancer deaths occurred in the 65 and over age group. The median age for cancer deaths is 67.9 years, reflecting poorer survival for the elderly with cancer.

Special Considerations for Elderly Cancer Patients

Health professionals should be able to distinguish between the changes that occur as a result of aging and those that may be attributed to cancer and other comorbid processes. In addition to having a sound clinical information base and a variety of skills in cancer care and treatment, oncology professionals must be aware of the special surveillance and monitoring needed to consider the concomitant effects of aging.

In the normal process of aging, significant changes occur in body structure, composition, and function. The skin and mucosa grow thinner, stature decreases as the skeleton changes in size, bone density decreases, functional capacities and resilience of organs decline, muscle size and strength diminish, and sensory loss occurs over

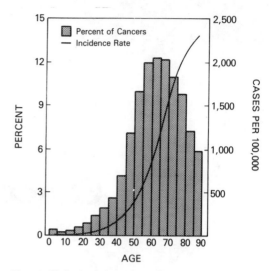

Figure 10.1. Age-related proportions of cancers and their incidence rates for 1973–1977. (*Note.* From *Aging: Vol. 24. Perspectives on Prevention and Treatment of Cancer in the Elderly* (p. 7) by R. Yancik, P. P. Carbone, W. B. Patterson, K. Steel, and W. D. Terry (Eds.), 1983, New York: Raven Press. Copyright 1983 by Raven Press. Reprinted by permission.)

time. These changes are gradual, and most persons accommodate readily. But the altered levels of functioning and decreased sensitivities, when accompanied by an illness such as cancer, can intensify treatment and care problems for providers.

It is not unreasonable to think that surgical, radiotherapeutic, and chemotherapeutic treatments, used alone or in combination, require special considerations for the elderly, just as they do for the very young. Anatomical development and degeneration, as well as physiological factors, influence treatment selection. The choice of surgical procedure, conservative or aggressive in approach, curative or palliative in intent, is influenced by age. In addition, the incidence of postoperative complications increases with age. Unfortunately, descriptive data outlining the basis for the choice of surgical treatment for the elderly are not available.

Although administration of radiotherapy to the aged cancer patient is a common practice, little attention is given to the incidence and type of complications that may occur with advancing age. It is known that tolerance to irradiation varies with the radiation fields, dose, and type of cancer (Fletcher, 1980).

Age-dependent differences in drug absorption, distribution, metabolism, and excretion must be

Table 10.1. Average Annual Age-Specific Incidence Rates per 100,000 Population (All Races, Males and Females, 1978–1981)

Cancer	Sex	AGES				
		65–69	70–74	75–79	80–84	85+
Lung & bronchus	M	429.9	512.8	538.4	505.8	394.1
	F	133.6	134.5	117.1	96.3	80.8
Prostate	M	358.0	584.6	825.0	1035.4	1130.3
Breast	F	292.0	319.6	338.7	340.6	378.4
Corpus uteri	F	109.7	100.2	92.7	74.9	59.4
Colon	M	169.2	248.1	324.4	421.7	487.2
	F	131.7	192.9	260.4	334.4	367.1
Urinary bladder	M	113.2	166.4	213.4	255.1	282.6
	F	29.1	37.8	49.9	62.0	79.9
Rectum	M	88.7	122.7	140.8	164.4	181.8
	F	49.2	67.7	86.1	98.5	107.1
Buccal cavity & pharynx	M	78.4	77.6	83.3	84.6	89.9
	F	27.4	28.0	27.8	28.2	29.2
Stomach	M	57.0	76.0	105.3	133.2	157.9
	F	21.7	32.5	48.0	65.8	80.1
Pancreas	M	52.1	70.4	87.3	87.7	106.7
	F	35.9	45.2	55.9	72.8	84.4
Larynx	M	46.9	42.4	36.9	35.4	28.8
	F	6.5	5.0	5.5	3.6	2.6
Ovary	F	46.1	46.7	54.8	47.4	42.4
Non-Hodgkin's lymphomas	M	42.3	54.5	73.4	83.5	84.3
	F	35.8	45.0	57.3	59.7	55.2
Leukemias	M	40.5	63.6	81.7	115.8	147.5
	F	21.2	33.4	40.5	62.8	70.9
Kidney & renal pelvis	M	40.6	49.3	55.6	65.2	59.2
	F	18.0	19.6	24.2	23.1	22.1
Cervix uteri	F	24.7	25.0	23.9	24.1	27.6
Melanoma of skin	M	23.2	26.9	30.9	26.1	32.8
	F	14.4	14.6	13.8	17.1	21.2

Data from the SEER program of the National Cancer Institute.

recognized. Drug-drug interactions receive less attention than pharmacokinetics and pharmacodynamics, but they represent a significant hazard in the multiply medicated elderly. Relatively mild chemotherapy reactions (e.g., the stomatitis from Adriamycin or 5-fluorouracil) in the elderly may be life-threatening. Underlying heart disease may increase the risk of exposure to such cytotoxic drugs as Adriamycin. Changes in physiology (e.g., decreased renal function), anatomy (e.g., intracavitary fluid retention acting as a drug reservoir), and weight (where drug-to-weight ratios are significantly altered) can all be potentially hazardous for older patients.

COMMON CANCERS IN THE ELDERLY

Table 10.1 presents SEER data for the period 1978–1981, giving the average annual age-specific incidence rates of cancers that occur most fre-

quently in persons 65 years of age and older. Cancers that exceed an incidence rate of 25 per 100,000 population for either sex are included in the table.

The incidence rates of the cancers common to both sexes are generally higher for men. For example, cancers of the lung and bronchus, colon, rectum, pancreas, urinary bladder, and stomach all occur more frequently in men of all age groups. Even the incidence of leukemias and non-Hodgkin's lymphomas is higher in men. Both older men and women have high incidence rates of colon cancer. It is the single most common malignancy in both sexes.

The most common malignancies in aged men are cancer of the lung and bronchus and cancer of the prostrate. Breast cancer is the most common malignancy in aged women. The highest cancer mortality rates for the period 1978–1981 for older males and females are presented in Tables 10.2 and 10.3, using SEER data combined with data

Table 10.2. Average Annual Age-Specific Mortality Rates per 100,000
Population (All Races, Males, 1978–1981)

Cancers with Highest Rates	AGES				
	65–69	70–74	75–79	80–84	85+
Lung & bronchus	325.6	421.6	465.3	459.7	366.5
Colon	85.4	131.4	178.3	252.0	295.8
Prostate	76.7	153.8	261.9	417.5	600.3
Pancreas	48.6	65.9	83.8	86.3	115.1
Stomach	38.3	52.7	79.0	105.6	129.9

Data from the SEER program of the National Cancer Institute.

Table 10.3. Average Annual Age-Specific Mortality Rates per 100,000
Population (All Races, Females, 1978–1981)

Cancers with Highest Rates	AGES				
	65–69	70–74	75–79	80–84	85+
Breast	97.9	110.0	112.1	144.7	170.4
Lung & bronchus	96.3	100.6	92.3	84.1	79.5
Colon	64.1	91.1	133.3	175.8	235.5
Pancreas	32.1	42.0	55.9	71.8	82.0
Ovary	33.3	36.1	45.2	43.1	37.5

Data from the SEER program of the National Cancer Institute.

from the National Center for Health Statistics (Holm, Asire, Young, & Pollack, 1984). For men, cancers of the lung and bronchus, prostate, and colon are the most frequent causes of cancer deaths in the 65 years or older age group. Cancer deaths of older women are most frequently attributed to breast, lung and bronchus, and colon cancers.

THE PROMISE OF EARLY DETECTION

The point in time when the older person enters the medical care system is critical to the cure of malignant lesions. Unless detected early and treated properly, most of the common cancers occurring in the elderly are incurable. Early cancer detection programs specifically targeted for older persons have been minimal. Little or no information is available on what actions older persons take when they become aware of the signs of cancer, or on the factors affecting promptness in the decision to seek medical advice. Excretory function changes, pain, masses, or bleeding may be overlooked because the sensory experience of a lifetime blunts individual sensitivity. The importance of early detection in maximizing potential for cure cannot be stressed enough.

The relevance of signal symptoms (e.g., blood in the stool) may be minimized by either the patient or physician. With advancing age, the ability to tolerate a variety of symptoms, which when experienced earlier in life have generally led to the diagnosis of benign conditions, promotes subsequent disregard. Pain, bleeding, and vague abdominal and thoracic manifestations may be readily ignored by the elderly. Health professionals may not approach these problems with vigor because explanations other than cancer are often available (e.g., arthritis, haemorrhoids, constipation, bronchitis). Similarly, many cancer survivors could develop second cancers, and thus their follow-up should be carried out scrupulously. For example, surveillance for specific combinations that tend to occur (e.g., breast and colon cancer in women, prostate and colon cancer in men) could assure the earliest possible detection of the second primary cancer.

Staging

After diagnosis, the selection of appropriate therapy is determined by the extent of disease. Staging is a descriptive categorization that indicates the extent of disease, provides information for appropriate treatment selection, and indicates prognosis. Cancers may be localized in the organ of origin, or they may spread to adjacent regions or to distant sites in the body. Other important factors that affect outcome are (a) the biology of the tumor (how rapidly it grows), (b) patient accessibility to good treatment, and (c) the ability of the patient to withstand the treatment. Obviously, the last is of the greatest concern when managing cancer in an elderly population, with therapeutic intent being guided by the maxim *primum non nocere*. Do no harm—particularly if you can do no good.

Common Cancers

Three cancers—colorectal, prostate, and breast—are common in the elderly. All are treatable if detected early.

Colorectal Cancer

Colorectal cancer is a neoplasm in which the symptomatology varies with the location of the lesion. Anemia from chronic blood loss in right-sided disease and obstructive symptoms with left-sided lesions are often described. Early diagnosis, when the disease is still localized, is dependent on early symptom recognition by the patient and the skill of the primary physician.

SEER data demonstrate an age-related shift in colon cancer with an increase in the number of lesions to the right side of the hepatic flexure in the elderly. This difference is more marked in females than in males. Changes in bowel habits often seen with left-sided lesions are less common with right-sided lesions, making screening a necessity for early detection. Air contrast barium enemas, colonoscopy, and testing for occult blood could be applied with greater vigor in the high-risk elderly persons who do not have serious comorbid conditions. Again, it should be noted that patients with a history of breast cancer are at increased risk for colon cancer.

Prostate Cancer

The incidental discovery of prostatic carcinoma increases with age (Hradac, Jarolim, & Motlik, 1980). Patients operated on for benign prostatic hypertrophy or cases that come to autopsy have what appears to be localized carcinoma of the prostate with a likelihood of occurrence increasing to about 40% at 85+ years of age (Beckner, Berg, & Fray, 1985). This finding could represent early localized cancer, but it appears to be more consistent with a biologically less aggressive cancer. A better understanding of this histological phenomenon is important in developing state-of-the-art screening and treatment guidelines for the elderly.

Breast Cancer

Women over the age of 60 with breast cancer are more likely to have estrogen and progesterone receptors. This has important treatment implications that should not be overlooked. Excessive dietary fat has been implicated as a potential cause of breast cancer in postmenopausal women (De Waard & Baanders-van Halewijn, 1974). Hormonal treatment with tamoxifen as an adjuvant to surgery is appropriate for women demonstrating positive hormone receptors. Similar treatment has little or no beneficial effect in women under the age of 50. Understanding that there are etiological, histological, biological, and hormonal variations in cancer in the elderly is important for good management.

THERAPY CONSIDERATIONS

Both curative and palliative therapies create logistic stresses and physiological threats in addition to those already imposed by the cancer and other comorbidities in the elderly. Once cancer is diagnosed, the inability of many older persons to negotiate the somewhat fragmented U.S. medical care system may adversely affect critical decisions. This could lead to inadequate, inappropriate, and/or untimely advice resulting in suboptimal management. Although treatment-imposed disturbances may be only temporary in upsetting the normal homeostasis, they could lead to long-term ill effects on physical and social activity, sleep, and nutrition. Selection of treatment for elderly cancer patients requires consideration of a variety of factors: physiological functioning; comorbid conditions; cognition; level of activity; tolerance to stress; home environment; support systems (personal care, nutritional, financial, spiritual, and legal); and treatment and rehabilitation expertise in the available facilities.

Although all of the aforementioned factors are also important to younger cancer patients, the frailty of older individuals makes them more vulnerable to the ravages of cancer and aggressive treatment.

Age-associated biological differences in histologically similar cancers are poorly understood. Because of histological differences, age-related differences in prognosis may be seen with cancers emanating from the same organ (brain, thyroid), with the poor prognosis histologies occurring more commonly in the elderly (Cady, Sedgwick, Meissner, Wool, Salzman, & Werber, 1979).

Age is an important prognostic variable in Hodgkin's disease. Persons over the age of 40 demonstrate a poorer survival rate in spite of treatment that would be curative in a younger patient (Coltman, 1980; Peterson et al., 1982). Thus judgments on treatment for elderly patients based on extrapolation from the treatment results of young adults can be erroneous.

BASIC PRINCIPLES OF CANCER MANAGEMENT

Health professionals who work in oncology settings are often required to apply unusual skills and techniques, in order to manage the various adverse social, economic, and environmental influences that may override routine management decisions for the aged cancer patient. The health of the elderly, perhaps to a greater degree than that of younger patients, is affected by certain social factors. Together with the stresses of daily living, such age-related life crises as reduced income, loss of loved ones and family support, and change in living arrangements are all interrelated with the older person's physical condition. A thorough understanding of the elderly cancer patient's life situation in conjunction with his or her medical symptoms and probable course of illness may provide for more successful treatment planning for the patient, family, and physicians.

In managing the elderly cancer patient, the physician must consider the treatment risks and benefits along with the realistic probability of success. Each patient is a unique member of a heterogeneous group. Individualizing therapy without compromising opportunities for favorable results should be the primary consideration. Each patient should have a complete understanding of his or her situation. If the patient's mental abilities are impaired, responsible family members should participate in the decision-making process.

Localized Cancer

For the elderly patient with a localized malignancy, surgical treatment alone or in combination with radiotherapy is appropriate if comorbid conditions do not preclude aggressive treatment. When one considers that the average life expectancy for a 70-year-old is approximately another decade or so and for an 80-year-old about 8 years, timid approaches are certainly not in the best interests of the patient. This is not to minimize the problems encountered in effecting a total cure in these patients, but rather to indicate that selected curative treatment approaches are appropriate. The palliative treatment of the elderly requires individualization and a thorough understanding of the expectations of the patient and family.

Regional and Metastatic Cancer

For the treatment of regional and metastatic malignancies, an understanding of the biology of the tumor (including time to progression and metastatic predilection) is important for preventing complications and anticipating individual needs. Local circulatory changes creating marginal tissue oxygenation may decrease the effectiveness of palliative radiotherapy. Changes in pharmacokinetics (drug distribution, metabolism, and excretion) and pharmacodynamics (cardiac output, vascular changes, and altered anatomy) could play a role in altering the expected response to all medications. The margin for therapeutic error is reduced when managing the elderly cancer patient; an understanding of the complexities and an anticipation of potential problems are key factors in assuring better patient survival.

Advanced Cancer

For some patients with advanced disease, symptomatic management may be the only appropriate decision. For example, the use of electrocautery for the management of localized rectal carcinoma in the older patient unable to undergo a successful resection may actually improve the quality and quantity of survival. Scheduling radiotherapy to accommodate the work schedule of the individual transporting the patient minimizes disruption and facilitates outpatient treatment and independence. The use of placebos or therapeutic techniques with questionable efficacy is seldom justified.

Supportive Care

Anticipation of treatment complications and employment of optimal supportive care techniques are critical to successful patient management. An increase in the number of infections secondary to poor circulation can result from either cancer or surgery, as well as local tissue necrosis and mechanical and physiological obstructions preventing the movement of secretions and excretions. Decreased pulmonary function, followed by infection, may occur after general anesthesia with tracheal incubation. The relative inefficiency in moving pulmonary secretions, diminished pulmonary function, and decreased patient mobility all contribute to the possibility of postoperative pulmonary infection. Surgery-related blood loss, compromised circulation, and diminished cardiac output often affect mental status or renal function. Maintenance of blood pressure, monitoring blood loss, and assuring adequate but not excessive hydration are all safeguards the anesthesiologist must follow during the course of the surgical procedure.

Because most patients will be taking other medications, the possibility of adverse drug interactions requires attention before selection of surgical medications. The elderly cannot tolerate long periods of deranged physiology as well as their younger counterparts.

An adequate assessment of the patient's medical status, support systems, and anticipated needs can do much to prevent these complications. As with all cancer patients, but particularly in the elderly, success can be assured with greater consistency when health care professionals are able to avoid crises rather than react to them.

Cautious Interpretation of Available Treatment Results

There is a wide divergence in physiological age with advancing years. Thus, it is not difficult to generate a sample of highly selected physiologically young patients from the available elderly population. Figure 10.2 demonstrates the increasing possibility of selection bias that can occur as populations of older patients are chosen for studies.

Such a systematic bias is not amenable to statistical correction; it is not possible to generalize results from such studies to all elderly persons. Overly aggressive or appropriate but inadequate treatment may result from optimistic interpretations of treatment results. Whereas the therapeutic nihilist fails to appreciate the potential benefit from curative or even palliative efforts, the treatment enthusiast uses results from poorly analyzed

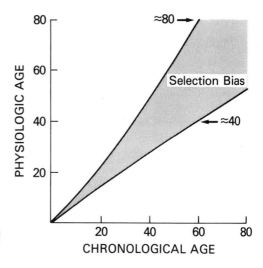

Figure 10.2. Age-related selection bias. As age advances, there is an increasing variation in physiologic age, providing the potential for significant selection bias in clinical trials research in the elderly.

studies to push harmful treatments. Each contributes to the increased morbidity and/or mortality in the elderly when physiological age is ignored. With the number of outpatient management situations increasing dramatically in cancer patients, ad hoc diagnostic and treatment decisions made by physicians without consultation may lead to an increase in suboptimal patient management.

The management of the elderly cancer patient requires good clinical judgment: a thorough understanding of the applicable treatment literature, an anticipation of the avoidable complications, and a healthy exchange of information between the patient's family and the responsible health professionals. Attention to these factors should lead to optimal management.

Systematic studies of cancer management in the elderly in the literature are rare. Some clinical trials in the past have explicitly excluded patients over the age of 65 years. Data on older persons have largely been extracted from multi-institutional clinical trials that happened to have included a large number of elderly patients. Indeed, most clinical research studies include only those patients who appear physiologically younger than their chronological age. Cautious interpretation of such studies is important. For example, in a retrospective study of elderly patients treated according to six different protocols by the Eastern Cooperative

Oncology Group*, no increase in either the frequency or severity of drug toxicity in the elderly patients was noted (Begg, Cohen, & Ellerton, 1980). The patients had cancers of the lung, breast, or colon and rectum. Protocol eligibility criteria included normal renal hepatic and cardiovascular function and allowed no other significant comorbidity. Indeed, underreporting of all but the most severe toxicities commonly occurs in multi-institutional clinical trials. Inaccurate reporting or nonreporting of information promotes a bias toward the null hypothesis or an underestimation of treatment-related toxicity. Differences may exist but often will not be discovered.

As another example, a protocol study of acute myelocytic leukemia was conducted by the Cancer and Acute Leukemia Group B* in which only life-threatening comorbid conditions were excluded. A distinct age-response relationship was noted, with the elderly not responding as well as younger patients (Yates et al., 1982). In this study there was a monotonic decrease in the frequency of complete remission with increasing age and a dramatic increase in death as an early outcome for patients 60 years of age and over. Because of the large number of patients studied, there was an opportunity to realistically assess treatment effects on a large group of elderly patients.

A number of single-institution studies suggest that the treatment of leukemia in the elderly can be beneficial (Foon, Zighelboim, Yates, & Gale, 1981; Grann, Erichson, Flannery, Finch, & Clarkson, 1974; Keating et al., 1981; Peterson & Bloomfield, 1977). These pilot studies report complete remission rates of 50% to 76%, which are higher than those generally achieved in large controlled studies. Even though these investigators claim to have treated all available elderly patients, the tertiary referral status of the institutions where the studies were conducted must be considered. Physicians generally decline to refer patients who appear too frail to withstand the rigors of aggressive treatment. This results in the selection of only the best candidates.

One should be cautious in interpreting pilot studies with small numbers of patients that report inordinate success in the management of the elderly patient with acute leukemia. With the relocation of oncologists to smaller communities and

their ability to successfully treat younger patients with acute leukemia even in the smallest of hospitals, unrealistic expectations in the management of this disease in the elderly are understandable, but should be avoided. Lack of experience, due to the relatively rare occurrence of cancer in most general practices and the complexity of assessing what is best for the elderly patient, should lead the conscientious physician to secure appropriate consultation.

SUMMARY

It is important to increase the awareness of physicians and health professionals of the rising incidence of cancer with advancing age, as well as problems that arise in those cured of a previous cancer. The continuing decline in deaths from heart disease can only increase the proportion of those who will succumb to cancer. Earlier detection, resulting in a lower stage of disease at diagnosis, leads to a greater potential for cure.

Health professionals have to interpret signs and symptoms in the elderly with care because of the broad spectrum of patient presentations they will encounter. Illness is an important topic of conversation among the elderly. Excessive information sharing, sometimes inaccurate, may influence older individuals' interpretations of their illnesses. Some minimize their symptoms to avoid being labeled ill, while others may exaggerate their symptoms. Health professionals must sort out the differences and initiate appropriate diagnostic action.

Physicians and other health professionals should be aware of the importance of determining the extent of disease (staging), understand the treatment options that are applicable to the elderly, and anticipate a greater number of treatment complications. Plans for rehabilitation and future continuing care should be outlined at the initiation of treatment.

Some situations warrant administering only comfort measures to the patient. Implicit judgments about the potential for a good quality of life in the future are commonly made by those caring for elderly patients with cancer. Just as the novice may not recognize the possible benefit from appropriate treatment, he or she may also err on the side of excessive treatment. Explicit statements, such as the living will, represent one

---

* Both the Eastern Cooperative Oncology Group and the Cancer and Acute Leukemia Group B are multi-institutional bodies that conduct clinical trials research and are supported by the National Cancer Institute's Division of Cancer Treatment.

approach to avoiding this unacceptable situation. Using good medical judgment based on discussions with the patient and family to assess probable outcomes represents a better approach.

With the expansion of the elderly segment of the population, demands on the health care system will rise, and health policy decisions will be made with an emphasis on containing costs. An appreciation of the extent of these future demands gained through research and efforts to prioritize the most effective supportive techniques can enhance the efficiency of the existing system.

REFERENCES

Beckner, M., Berg, J. W., & Fray, L. W. (1985). The contribution of subclinical cancer to Denver's high prostate cancer incidence rate. *Journal of Chronic Diseases, 38*, 225–231.

Begg, C. B., Cohen, J. L., & Ellerton, J. (1980). Are the elderly predisposed to toxicity from cancer chemotherapy? *Cancer Clinical Trials, 3*, 369–374.

Cady, B., Sedgwick, C. E., Meissner, W. A., Wool, M. S., Salzman, F. A., & Werber, J. (1979). Risk factor analysis in differentiated thyroid cancer. *Cancer, 43*, 810–820.

Coltman, C. A., Jr. (1980). Chemotherapy of advanced Hodgkin's disease. *Seminars in Oncology, 7*, 155–173.

De Waard, F., & Baanders-van Halewijn, E. A. (1974). A prospective study in general practice on breast-cancer risk in postmenopausal women. *International Journal of Cancer, 14*, 153–160.

Fletcher, G. H. (1980). *Textbook of radiotherapy* (3rd ed.). Philadelphia: Lea & Febiger.

Foon, K. A., Zighelboim, J., Yate, C., & Gale, R. B. (1981). Intensive chemotherapy is the treatment of choice for elderly patients with acute myelogenous leukemia. *Blood, 58*, 467–470.

Grann, V., Erichson, R., Flannery, J., Finch, S., & Clarkson, B. (1974). The therapy of acute granulocytic leukemia in patients more than fifty years old. *Annals of Internal Medicine, 80*, 15–20.

Holm, J. W., Asire, A. J., Young, J. L. Jr., Pollack, E. S. (Eds.) (1984). *SEER Program: Cancer incidence and mortality in the United States, 1973–1981* (NIH Publication 85–1837). Bethesda, MD: U.S. Department of Health and Human Services.

Hradac, E., Jarolim, L., & Motlik, K. (1980). Carcinoma of the prostate in specimens removed for benign hyperplasia. *Scandinavian Journal of Urology Nephrology, 55* (Suppl.), 193–196.

Keating, M. J., McCredie, K. B., Benjamin, R. S., Brodey, G. P., Zander, A., Smith, T. L., & Freireich, E. J. (1981). Treatment of patients over 50 years of age with acute myelogenous leukemia with a combination of rubidazone and cytosine arabinoside, vincristine, and prednisone (ROAP). *Blood, 58*, 584–591.

Peterson, B. A., & Bloomfield, C. D. (1977). Treatment of acute nonlymphocytic leukemia in elderly patients: A prospective study of intensive chemotherapy. *Cancer, 40*, 647–652.

Peterson, B. A., Pajak, T. F., Cooper, M. R., Nissen, N. I., Glidewell, O. J., Holland, J. F., Bloomfield, C. D., & Gottlieb, A. J. (1982). Effect of age on therapeutic response and survival in advanced Hodgkin's disease. *Cancer Treatment Reports, 66*, 889–898.

U.S. Bureau of the Census. (1984). *Current population reports: Americans in transition: An aging society* (Special Studies, Series P–23, No. 128). Washington, DC: U.S. Government Printing Office.

U.S. Senate Special Committee on Aging & American Association of Retired Persons. (1984). *Aging America: Trends and projections*. Washington, DC: American Association of Retired Persons.

Yancik, R., Carbone, P. P., Patterson, W. B., Steel, K., & Terry, W. D. (Eds.). (1983). *Perspectives on prevention and treatment of cancer in the elderly*. New York: Raven Press.

Yates, J. W., Glidewell, O., Wiernik P., Cooper, M. R., Steinberg, D., Dosik, H., Levy, R., Hoagland, C., Henry, P., Gottlieb, A., Cornell, C., Berenberg, J., Hutchinson, J. L., Raich, P., Nissen, N., Ellison, R. R., Frelick, R., James, G. W., Falkson, G., Silver, R. T., Haurani, F., Green M., Henderson, E., Leone, L., & Holland, J. F. (1982). Cytosine arabinoside with daunorubicin or Adriamycin for therapy of acute myelocytic leukemia: A Cancer and Acute Leukemia Group B study. *Blood, 60*, 454–462.

Young, J. L., Percy, C. L., & Asire, A. J. (Eds.). (1981). *Incidence and mortality data: 1973–1977* (National Cancer Institute Monograph 57, DHHS No. [NIH] 81–2330). Washington, DC: U.S. Government Printing Office.

Chapter 11

Cardiovascular Disease

John T. Santinga

This chapter will review the major cardiac illnesses found in the elderly, including coronary disease, valvular disease, hypertension, and arrhythmias. The management of cardiovascular disease is more complicated in the elderly than in the younger age group. Cardiac medications may have increased side effects, and the indications for invasive and surgical management are less clear-cut because of other associated illnesses and the effect of age itself on other organ systems.

CORONARY DISEASE

Coronary artery disease is a common medical problem in the elderly. The pathology of the arterial obstruction is similar to that observed in younger patients, and the narrowings are proximal with reasonably patent vessels in the distal segments. There may be increased calcium in the coronary vessel wall in older patients.

When coronary blood flow is decreased, anoxia develops in the heart muscle, which leads to chest pain. The coronary flow may be decreased slowly by progressive narrowing of the vessel or acutely by a thrombus at the site of the obstruction. In addition, the coronary arteries may exhibit spasm, which can increase the obstruction acutely and lead to chest pain.

The symptoms of typical angina are most often present with fixed coronary obstruction. This discomfort is described by some patients as a chest pressure, burning pain, or squeezing. These complaints will radiate from the chest to the back,

neck, and arms. The pain in typical angina will be brought on by physical exertion. It is relieved within 5–10 minutes by rest. If spasm of the artery is a factor, the pain may come on at rest. Spasm may be related to cold exposure, mental stress, and isometric physical exercise. Atypical location of the pain, which occurs in some patients, may delay the diagnosis. Such unusual areas would be aching in the arms, back, or jaw; upper abdominal distress may also occur and, early in the evaluation, may be confused with gastrointestinal disease.

The physical examination may be normal in patients with coronary disease. In some patients there may be evidence elsewhere of vascular disease, such as blockage of the vessels to the legs or carotid vessels in the neck. Hypertension is commonly present. The cardiac exam will usually show a regular rhythm. The heart will be normal in size. The sounds are normal. A presystolic atrial contraction sound (S4) is often heard, which suggests scarring of the heart muscle. Heart murmurs are not common in patients with coronary disease.

Diagnosis

The diagnosis can usually be made after receiving the patient's medical history. The resting electrocardiogram is often normal in the early stages of the disease. Exercise electrocardiography is helpful in determining the diagnosis and severity of the illness. The electrocardiogram may be normal at rest but will develop ischemic changes with exercise. The sensitivity and specificity of this test is not affected by age. Nuclear diagnostic tests, such as thallium scanning, may also help in the diagnosis. Thallium is absorbed by the heart muscle; any scar in the heart would absorb less isotope, and so a "hole' or "defect' will be evident. Exercise may bring out this defect by having less isotope absorbed in the area of the narrowed coronary artery. The blood flow through the normal arteries will be increased by exercise, bringing more isotope to that portion of the myocardium; this will leave a defect in the area supplied by the narrowed blood vessel. Another nuclear test is the gated blood pool study, in which a radioactive isotope (technetium) is labeled to the patient's red cells. Counts from the blood within the heart are measured for certain time intervals of the cardiac cycle, providing the number of counts in the heart chamber when the heart is at rest and at the end of the cardiac systole. The difference will give the percentage of the ejection fraction. A drop in the ejection fraction with exercise may indicate coronary obstruction, and thus, less oxygen delivery, resulting in decreased heart muscle contraction. The resting ejection fraction does not decrease with age. However, in the elderly the exercise wall motion may become abnormal, sometimes mimicking coronary disease (Port, Cobb, Coleman, & Jones, 1980).

Treatment

Catheterization, Bypass Surgery, and Balloon Angioplasty

Cardiac catheterization of the elderly is performed when medical treatment has not proved satisfactory and surgery is being considered. Catheterization has proven to be a safe procedure in the older age group; according to the Coronary Artery Surgery Study, only 4 deaths were reported out of 2,144 catheterizations in patients over the age of 65 (Gersh et al., 1983).

Coronary artery bypass surgery is being done with increasing frequency (Knapp et al., 1981). Because there is an increased chance of mortality from this surgery in the elderly, the effect of coronary bypass on the prolongation of life is not as well documented as catheterization. It is, however, usually indicated for relief of symptoms. According to the Coronary Artery Surgery Study, mortality from the surgery is 4.6% for the 65–69 age

group, 6.6% for the 70–74 age group, and 9.5% for the over 75 age group (Gersh et al., 1983). Over the years there has been a steady decline in the mortality rate; for example, Elayda reported a drop in mortality from 13.9% for the period 1970–1975 to 4.7% for the period 1976–1980 (Elayda, Hall, Gray, Mathur, & Cooley, 1984). In addition, large numbers of patients in the older age groups are receiving the surgery. Indications for surgery include the continued presence of disabling symptoms in spite of medical management. Patients with critical narrowing of the left main artery and those with three vessel disease with decreased left ventricular function should also be considered for surgery.

Another useful technique in treating coronary disease is balloon angioplasty. A balloon is inserted through the obstruction; with repeated inflations of the balloon, the degree of obstruction may be reduced. Initially, this technique was not done in older patients for fear of arterial rupture. However, with more experience, a success rate of 50% has been reported in patients over age 65 (Mock et al., 1984). Balloon angioplasty is restricted to lower risk patients (such as those with obstruction of only one or two vessels). However, death (in 2.2% of cases), emergent coronary bypass surgery (6.8%), and infarction (5.6%) have been known to occur. Eventually, 25.4% of the patients required additional elective bypass surgery. The advantage of using balloon angioplasty in the elderly is the avoidance of a thoracotomy and bypass surgery.

Drug Treatments

Medical management of the elderly patient with angina pectoris is similar to that of younger patients. Nitrate therapy remains the mainstay of treatment. Sublingual nitrates are effective within 1–2 minutes and offer protection for up to 1 hour. Long-acting nitrate preparations include tablets or time-release capsules, which should be taken every 6 hours. The dosage should be increased to maximum tolerable levels, which are signaled by the onset of headaches or orthostatic hypotension. The cutaneous application of a nitroglycerin ointment or time-release patches is another method of administering long-acting nitrates. The ointment may be preferable, because the patches are expensive and may not provide 24 hour protection (Parker & Fung, 1984). Which of these approaches is best has not been reported in the literature. There are no data on the absorption rates for the nitroglycerin ointment in different age groups. Neither are there data on whether the time-release capsules are absorbed better than the tablets. There is evidence, however, that continuous exposure to a constant blood level of nitroglycerin may produce tolerance, which may make the medication ineffective.

Beta-blocking agents, such as propranolol, timolol, or tenormin, are effective for exertional angina. They inhibit the action of adrenaline on the heart, thus decreasing the resting and exercise heart rate, and lowering the resting and exercise blood pressure. The combination of the slower heart rate and lower blood pressure results in the heart doing less work and therefore requiring less oxygen. Consequently, anoxia-related pain will be present less frequently. However, beta blockers' side effects are increased in the older age group. This may occur partly because of the decreased drug excretion rate in the elderly, resulting in higher blood levels. Common side effects are fatigue, nightmares, symptomatic bradycardia and hypotension. Syncopal episodes also increase (Hale, Stewart, & Marks, 1984). Therefore, the elderly may require lower doses.

Calcium-blocking agents, such as nifedipine, diltiazem, and verapamil, may also be used to treat angina pectoris in the elderly. These agents act on the membrane of the muscle cell to prevent calcium entry, relaxing the smooth muscles of the walls of the coronary arteries. Nifedipine has the most vasodilatory action of the three agents. It also has an effect on the pacemaker muscle in the heart, resulting in a slowing of the heart rate. Verapamil has the most pronounced effect on the cardiac pacemaker and conduction system. Calcium blockers may suppress heart muscle contraction, which could reduce the heart's oxygen requirements. Finally, these agents lower the blood pressure because of their vasodilatory action. These agents will be useful in the treatment of exercise angina from fixed coronary obstruction, by lowering the blood pressure and the heart rate. They will also be effective if there is an element of coronary spasm, and can therefore benefit patients with rest or emotion-related angina. Side effects include headache, orthostatic symptoms, and gastrointestinal nausea. Bradycardia accompanied by dizziness may also occur, especially with verapamil and diltiazem. A drop in blood pressure upon standing up may cause dizziness, especially with nifedipine.

Diet and Life-Style

There has been a 36% decrease in the mortality rate from cardiovascular disease in the past 20 years (Kannel & Thom, 1984). Much of this can be attributed to a decline in smoking and to better control of hypertension. There has been increasing evidence that lowering the serum cholesterol level is important in slowing the progression of artery blockage both in the natural vessels and in the vein grafts following bypass surgery (Bourassa, Enjalbert, Campeau, & Lesperance, 1983). These factors may delay the onset of coronary disease until a later age.

In the past, a link between hyperlipidemia and coronary disease has not been observed in the elderly. A diet low in fats or cholesterol may be optional in this age group, depending on the nutritional status of the patient. However, with the population living longer, vascular events may develop in patients with high cholesterol, and cholesterol-restricted diets may be indicated. This area of research should be examined more thoroughly. It is the experience of the author that elderly patients with high cholesterol have a greater incidence of vascular complications.

The degree to which current diagnostic and therapeutic techniques should be used in the disabled elderly patient with coronary disease is a complex issue. With this population, therapy is directed primarily at relieving symptoms, with life prolongation being less important. When the patient is in a medical facility that has cardiac resuscitation capacity, the level of care agreed upon by the patient, family, and attending physician should be clearly stated in the medical record. Cardiopulmonary resuscitation can be carried out with a 10% success rate in the elderly (Hurowitz & Gordon, 1984). However, in the disabled elderly this may be inappropriate.

Myocardial Infarction

Another major complication of coronary disease is a myocardial infarction, which occurs when coronary flow drops below the level needed to sustain viable myocardium and results in a core of necrosis surrounded by ischemic and poorly functioning myocardium. Infarction may result from coronary spasm, progression of the atheromatous plaque, or, most commonly, a thrombotic occlusion. In the elderly, a thrombus superimposed on an atheromatus narrowing is almost always present in the patient with infarction.

The symptoms of myocardial infarction are identical to those of angina pectoris, but are more severe and prolonged. The character and radiation of the pain is the same as in patients with angina. The pain is often more severe and unremitting and narcotics are usually needed to control it. There are also general symptoms of nausea, vomiting, sweating and profound weakness. In up to 25% of patients, chest pain may be absent and the patient may not recognize the presence of infarction. "Silent" myocardial infarction has been reported to be more common in the elderly, especially if longstanding diabetes mellitus with neuropathy is present.

The usual treatment for acute myocardial infarction is admission to a coronary care unit for detection of any serious heart arrhythmias and pain control. The patient is kept on bed rest the first several days. If no complications occur, such as congestive heart failure or low blood pressure (shock), the patient will begin sitting and walking around the room. Transfer out of the coronary care unit to a general or monitored bed occurs after the third or fourth day, and a patient with no further complications can be discharged on the eighth or ninth day, post infarction. Beta blocking agents, such as propranolol, are commonly used during this time because recent studies have shown a decrease in mortality with their use (Frishman, Furberg, & Friedewald, 1984). The elderly patient is apt to have increased complications—such as heart failure, persistent angina, or arrhythmias—after myocardial infarction, as well as increased risk of mortality. There is a 7.8% death rate in the age group 50–59, whereas the death rate is 31.8% over the age of 70 (Latting and Silverman, 1980). Shock and cardiac rupture may also be increased in the older age group.

Currently, there is considerable interest in attempting to open the closed artery causing the heart attack. This is most effective if done within a few hours of onset of the infarction. One approach is to infuse intravenous streptokinase, the thrombolytic agent, which may dissolve the clot; another is to take the patient immediately to the cardiac catheterization laboratory and place a catheter in the involved artery to infuse the streptokinase directly against the clot (Hartzler, Rutherford, & McConahay, 1984). Another approach is to push a catheter through the clot, dilating the narrowed segment. What place these acute interventions play in treatment is uncertain; the elderly patient may have increased bleeding complications from the streptokinase, or kidney failure caused by the contrast media used to visualize the arteries. However, as with most other cardiac procedures, these techniques will be more commonly used in the older age group as they are increasingly used in the general population.

In the patient with no complications, an exercise test should be done prior to discharge. This may detect residual narrowing of additional coronary arteries or serious ventricular arrhythmias and will give an objective measurement of the patient's ability to exercise (Haskell & DeBusk, 1979). If angina occurs postinfarction and/or the exercise test is abnormal, coronary angiograms should be considered to determine if the patient is a surgical candidate. Some patients may benefit from a rehabilitation program that would include electrocardiographic monitoring during exercise sessions, education on coronary risk factors, and a supportive environment to prevent postinfarction depression (DeBusk, Houston, Haskell, Fry, & Parker, 1979). Elderly patients with infarction should benefit equally as the younger patients from these programs (Williams, Maresh, Esterbrooks, Harbrecht, & Sketch, 1985).

VALVULAR HEART DISEASE

Valvular heart disease is not uncommon in the older patient; it is most commonly a result of degenerative disease. Involvement of the aortic and/or mitral valve is the most common: the aortic valve leaflets, which may have been normal at birth, develop calcium deposits and scarring with age. There may be increased stiffness of the leaflets as well. As a result, the valve will not open properly during the ejection of blood, possibly obstructing outflow of the blood from that chamber. This stenosis can lead to exertional fainting, chest pain, and shortness of breath. With exercise, the arterioles in the exercising muscles of the arms and legs may dilate, and, if the valve narrowing is severe, blood pressure may drop significantly. In addition, the blood delivered to the heart muscle may decrease with the low pressure, leading to ischemia and a weakened heart muscle contraction. This combination may explain the exertional syncope or chest pain. The chronic inability of the left ventricular muscle to empty the chamber across the narrowed aortic valve will lead to failure, with backing up of the blood into the lungs and the development of shortness of breath. The physical examination usually will show a slow upstroke of the carotid artery pulsations in the neck and signs of left ventricular hypertrophy, such as a forceful outthrust and an atrial sound (S4). The major finding is a harsh systolic ejection murmur heard over the upper chest that may radiate into the neck.

Diagnosis

Diagnosis in younger patients is not difficult, but this diagnosis is often missed in older patients. Heart murmurs are present in at least 30% of elderly patients; the murmur of aortic stenosis is often overlooked as a normal murmur in the elderly (Perez, Jacob, Bhat, Rao, & Luisada, 1976). The chest will expand, which may move the heart away from the stethoscope and make the murmur inaudible. Another important point is the lowered physical activity of the older person; symptoms are either absent or accepted as part of the aging process. Therefore, unexplained symptoms of syncope, angina, or congestive failure in the elderly should lead to a careful search for aortic stenosis. The best screening test for this condition is the echocardiogram—a diagnostic technique in which sound waves sent out from a transmitter will bounce back from any liquid–solid interface, such as blood to heart muscle. The returning waves are then recorded on a moving paper to give a visual record and the practitioner can see the valve opening, thickness of the valve leaflets, size of the heart chambers, and thickness of the heart muscle. In patients with aortic stenosis, there will be aortic valve thickening and lack of opening, as well as left atrial enlargement with thickening of the ventricular muscle (DeMaira, Bommer, Joye, Garrett, Bouteller, & Mason, 1980).

Treatment

If the patient has symptoms and findings of aortic valve disease, cardiac catheterization should be carried out to measure the pressure difference gradient over the valve. If there is a gradient excess of 50 mm Hg or if calculations of a valve area are below 1.0 cm_2, valve replacement should be considered. Associated coronary artery narrowing is not uncommon in these patients and aortic valve surgery has in the past had a high mortality in the elderly patient (Copeland, Griepp, Stinson, & Shumway, 1977). However, with the use of potassium cardioplegia and hypothermia to protect the heart muscle during surgery, operative results have improved in this age group (Berger et al., 1981). The operative mortality should be below 5% in the patient with no complications. The addition of coronary bypass to the operative procedure will increase the risk of mortality. The surgeon will usually choose an animal tissue valve for implantation, thus eliminating the use of anticoagulants, which are hazardous for the older patients because of bleeding complications.

It is important that the patient with an artificial heart valve should be instructed in endocarditis prevention, especially for dental procedures. Dental procedures such as cleaning, extractions, and gum surgery require antibiotic coverage. Antibiotics, usually penicillin, should be given 2 hours prior to the procedure and then repeated for one dose 4 hours following the procedure. In the elderly, poorly fitting false teeth can lead to ulcers beneath the plates and become a source for endocarditis.

Operations on the urinary system are common in the elderly and procedures such as cystoscopy (looking into the bladder) or prostate surgery require antibiotics such as ampicillin and gentamycin. The American Heart Association's recommendations give more complete information on the indications for and type of antibiotics recommended (Shulman, Amren, Bisno, Dajani, Durack, Gerber, Kaplan, Millard, Sanders, Schwartz, & Watanakunakorn, 1984).

MITRAL HEART DISEASE

Mitral Insufficiency: Diagnosis and Treatment

Mitral disease is less common that aortic disease in the elderly, while non-rheumatic mitral insufficiency is more common in this age group (Roberts, 1983). A common cause of mitral insufficiency in the elderly is a defect in the supporting structures of the valve, such as the papillary muscles and chordae tendineae, which fix the valves' position during contraction. Scarring of the papillary muscle or elongation or breaking of the chordae tendineae will leave the valve unsupported during contraction and can cause leakage during systole. In addition, the elderly, especially women, may develop a ring of calcified tissue in the annulus of the mitral valve (Nestico, Depace, Morganroth, Kotler, & Ross, 1984), leading to a closure defect and insufficiency. In mitral insufficiency, the left ventricle unloads into a low pressure chamber, allowing the left ventricle to empty without excessive work. Therefore, the chamber may not develop much hypertrophy, and symptoms of congestive failure—such as shortness of breath—frequently occur many years after the onset of the lesion. Atrial fibrillation, a rapid disorganized activity of the atrium, may occur, and the chordae tendineae may rupture, leading to sudden massive leakage and severe pulmonary edema. The diagnosis usually is obvious on physical examination. There is a loud apical systolic regurgitation murmur. A decrease in the first heart sound associated with a third heart sound implies major mitral regurgitation.

If the patient has symptoms of congestive failure, usually valve replacement is indicated. Symptoms may, however, not be present even though the muscle is being damaged (Schuler, Peterson, Johnson, Francis, Dennish, Utley, Daily, Ashburn, & Ross Jr., 1979). The patient should be followed by studies such as echocardiography to detect lack of contractility of the left ventricle. Gated blood pool ejection fractions of 40% or below, although suggesting poor contractility, may also predict a poor outcome after mitral valve replacement.

As in aortic valve surgery, a porcine tissue valve is commonly used for replacement in the elderly patient, avoiding the use of anticoagulants if atrial fibrillation is not present. If bleeding does occur, these patients can be managed more safely without anticoagulants than if another type of mechanical device was present. Endocarditis prophylaxis is indicated in patients with mitral insufficiency and, of course, after valve replacement.

Mitral obstruction or stenosis is usually a result of rheumatic valvular disease. In this condition, the leaflets become adherent from the inflammation, which reduces the valve opening. Submitral calcification may occasionally develop in the elderly patient, leading to symptoms of congestive failure from obstruction and/or valve leakage. The obstruction to left atrial emptying causes an increase in pressure in this chamber, which, if transmitted back into the lungs, may cause acute pulmonary edema and an inability to breathe. With exercise or other stress, this may be dramatic in onset and produce severe symptoms. Increased pressure in the left chamber can also lead to enlargement and atrial fibrillation, reducing cardiac efficiency and possibly resulting in congestive heart failure. In addition, atrial fibrillation will lead to stasis and increase the chances of clot formation, increasing the risk of major stroke or ischemic damage to other organs. Treatment of atrial fibrillation, therefore, must include anticoagulation with Coumadin to prevent this catastrophic complication.

Mitral Stenosis: Diagnosis and Treatment

The diagnosis of this condition can usually be made on physical examination. There will be enlargement of the right ventricle, with a lift of the chest wall along the left side of the sternum. If the valve is flexible, there will be a snapping first sound and an opening snap of the narrowed valve. When the blood forces its way through the narrowed valve, the result is a diastolic murmur, which is best heard at the apex of the heart. If the valve is scarred and nonmobile there will not be a first sound or opening snap. There may be a systolic murmur at the apex, as well as the diastolic murmur, and the heart rhythm is often irregular from the atrial fibrillation. The echocardiogram has proved to be a powerful diagnostic tool in this condition: mitral stenosis can be seen in left atrial enlargement and abnormal movement of the mitral valve. The valve may also be scarred and thickened.

If the patient is young and has a flexible noncalcified valve, mitral repair (commissurotomy) can be carried out to relieve symptoms. If the valve is calcified, it is not amenable to repair, and replacement with an artificial valve is indicated. Again, in the elderly this would be a porcine or tissue valve. The anticoagulant and endocarditis management are the same as in the previous discussion of mitral insufficiency. Valve replacement is based upon the development of symptoms in mitral stenosis. The left ventricle should not have any damage from this type of valve obstruction.

HYPERTENSION

Hypertension is present in 30% of patients over the age of 65 (Stamler, Stamier, Riedlinger, Algera, & Roberts, 1976). Hypertension is defined in this age group as a blood pressure in excess of 160 systolic and 90 diastolic. If only the systolic value is elevated, this condition is called systolic hypertension, whereas if both values are increased, combined systolic and diastolic hypertension results.

Isolated Systolic Hypertension

Isolated systolic hypertension is found mainly in the older age group (Adamopoulos, Chrysanthakopoulos, & Frohlich, 1975). This abnormality is caused by increasing stiffness of the aorta and arterial system. Dehydration then makes the patient prone to develop hypotension, because a loss of blood volume cannot be compensated for by adequate constriction. These patients are prone to syncope in hot weather, with diuretic use, or with diarrhea.

In longitudinal community studies isolated systolic hypertension has been found to be associated with an increased incidence of stroke and myocardial infarction. There is, however, debate about whether or not to treat this condition. Those against treatment believe that the underlying vascular disease leads to increased complications and would not be prevented by control of the systolic blood pressure. On the other hand, those who favor treatment believe that control of the systolic blood pressure may prevent additional vascular disease. Presently there is an ongoing multicenter study, through the National Institutes of Health, which should answer this question.

Treatment for systolic hypertension is often not as effective as in combined hypertension. Treatment is started when the blood pressure is above 160 mm Hg and begins with salt restriction. Patients need to be educated as to what foods contain sodium, especially as many of the foods most commonly eaten by the elderly are prepared foods high in salt content, such as frozen dinners. Weight loss is advised for the obese patient. Regular, dynamic exercise can be safely advised in this condition, preferably walking, biking, or swimming. This should not be high intensity, because the increase in cardiac output may increase the systolic pressure.

Diuretic therapy, usually a long-acting agent such as a thiazide, is most often the first choice in beginning drug treatment in these patients. This may lead to low potassium levels. Many clinicians will use a potassium-sparing agent such as a triamterene or amiolioride in combination with a thiazide, thus avoiding the need for the patient to take supplemental potassium. These combinations may elevate potassium levels in the elderly; therefore it is important to monitor bloods levels carefully in patients taking these agents. Other complications of thiazides include an increase in blood sugar levels and uric acid, causing difficulties in control of diabetes.

If the blood pressure is not well-controlled by the previous regimen, methyldopa (Aldomet) or clonidine are often selected and added to the program. These agents act by cutting down on sympathetic outflow from the brain to the arteriolar system. Side effects of these medications are sedation and, rarely, toxic effects on the liver and blood. Another medication that could be added to the thiazides is propranolol, which lowers the cardiac output and may have other actions not well understood that lower the blood pressure. These agents cause fatigue in some patients and may be associated with increased syncopal episodes, especially if the patient is also on a diuretic (Hale, Stewart, & Marks 1984). Newer agents, mainly arterial dilators, are receiving more attention for treating systolic hypertension. One of these agents is nifedipine, a calcium blocking agent, the side effects of which are orthostatic symptoms and ankle edema. Another arterial dilator, furazosin (Prazosin), also has been used for treating systolic hypertension, either with diuretics or as a first-line agent. It is important to decrease the diuretic dosage in some patients during the warm summer months, when they may be losing salt and fluids from sweating, because such loss may result in fainting episodes from low blood pressure. The combination of propranolol and a diuretic is most likely to produce such episodes.

Essential Hypertension

The usual form of hypertension, with elevations of the systolic and diastolic components of the blood pressure, may persist into the older age group. This type of blood pressure, which often has no known etiology, usually begins in the 40–60 age range. This condition is associated with a family history of hypertension, obesity, and diabetes mellitus, as well as, in certain populations, the ingestion of excess amounts of salt. This type of blood pressure will be found, in rare instances, in patients with endocrine disorders, such as Cushing's syndrome or pheochromocytomas. The kidneys may also be a source of hypertension, due to renal artery narrowing or chronic infection. Atheromatous narrowing of the renal arteries may develop late in life and cause severe hypertension that responds poorly to treatment. A renal artery arteriogram would be needed to make the correct diagnosis of this etiology.

Usually, the laboratory evaluation should include a serum creatinine, potassium, calcium, and urine analyses; chest x-ray; and electrocardiogram. In severe cases kidney studies such as pyelogram and angiogram are indicated. Control of blood pressure will decrease the risk of stroke, congestive heart failure, and renal failure. However, the incidence of myocardial infarction has not been reduced by controlling the blood pressure. The reason for this lack of preventive effect could be the other risk factors for coronary artery disease such as obesity, cholesterol levels, and smoking.

Treatment of this form of hypertension will lower the frequency of complications such as stroke, renal failure, and congestive failure. Treatment also will prolong life (Hale et al., 1984; Hypertension Detection and Follow-Up Cooperative Group, 1979 I, 1979 II; Veterans Administration Cooperative Study Group on Antihypertensive Agents, 1967, 1970, 1972). Treatment for these patients should start with weight loss, salt restriction, and a moderate exercise program. If this is not successful in controlling blood pressure, a diuretic would be the first agent of choice. Doses of hydrochlorothiazide would be in the range of 25 to 50 mg a day. Additional agents, such as Aldomet, calcium blocking agents, and propanolol, may be added to control the blood pressure. If control is not satisfactory and renal artery stenosis is present, surgical revascularization may be useful in selected patients.

There is presently active discussion as to what constitutes good control of the blood pressure. Increasing evidence exists that the working or active blood pressures are more important than the resting values in the effect on the heart. The heart muscle may become thickened from the extra work of pumping blood at an elevated pressure. This thickness or hypertrophy may lead to heart failure and enlargement of the atrium, which could lead to atrial fibrillation. These side effects of hypertension are even more important in the older patient.

Prevention of hypertension has not received the attention that coronary disease has in our society. However there is a general consensus that weight control and salt restriction are useful in preventing essential hypertension. Which factors lead to isolated systolic hypertension is not known.

ARRHYTHMIAS

Arrhythmias become increasingly common with age. There may be atrial arrhythmias, such as atrial fibrillation, flutter, or tachycardia, or ventricular arrhythmias, such as premature beats or ventricular tachycardia. Conduction defects, such as atrial ventricular block, also are common in the elderly.

The pathophysiology of these arrhythmias is complex. Increased ventricular stiffness will lead to an increased filling pressure in the ventricle, which will elevate the atrial pressure and dilate the chamber. This may cause a disorganized rhythm, such as atrial fibrillation, where the atria may contract several hundred times a minute. Other problems may include areas of scarred atrial muscle, which can also lead to disordered depolarization with subsequent fibrillation; degenerative changes of the atrial pacemaker (sinus node), which may lead to lower heart rates and escape rhythms; and increased sensitivity to the effects of caffeine, theophylline, and adrenalin, which are used in the treatment of obstructive pulmonary disease. Agents such as beta blocker and calcium blocking drugs may cause excessive slowing of the heart rate in the elderly.

Atrial Fibrillation

In the older patient the most common significant atrial arrhythmia, which may be either chronic or paroxysmal, is atrial fibrillation. This arrhythmia is characterized by disordered atrial depolarization, with rapid atrial depolarization waves in excess of 350 per minute, and a slower irregular ventricular response. The ventricular rate can vary from normal to 160 per minute, depending on the conduction rate through the atrial ventricular node. The patient may perceive the arrhythmias as a palpitation of the heart, with dizziness due to an associated drop in blood pressure. These symptoms may occur with the onset of the arrhythmia or at its cessation with a sinus pause.

Treatment involves control of the ventricular rate by agents that slow conduction through the atrial ventricular node. Digitalis preparations are a time-honored therapy with digoxin and digitoxin the two most commonly used forms of this drug. In patients over the age of 65, doses should generally be one-half the usual recommended dose (digoxin: 0.125 mg/day). Toxic symptoms are nausea, visual symptoms, and an irregular or slow pulse. The calcium blocking agent verapamil also has been effective in slowing the ventricular rate in atrial fibrillation. Side effects include ankle swelling, constipation, hypotension, and a decrease in left ventricular function. Beta blocker therapy, with agents such as propranolol, is also useful in slowing the ventricular response. Often small doses are adequate, such as 10 to 20 mg three times a day.

In some patients who have had recent onset of the atrial fibrillation and do not tolerate the arrhythmia well, cardioversion to a normal sinus rhythm can be attempted. This may be chemical, using such medications as quinidine or procaine amide, or involve electrical cardioversion. In the latter, an electrical shock which will cross the heart and depolarize the atrium, is put over the chest, allowing a regular rhythm to return. Conversion to regular rhythm is done infrequently in the elderly patient, because it may be difficult to maintain a regular rhythm.

There is a major debate about the need for anticoagulants in patients with chronic atrial fibrillation. Anticoagulants are recommended to prevent stasis and clots from forming in the atrium, and there is an increase in the frequency of strokes in patients with atrial fibrillation (Wolfe, Dawber, Thomas Jr., & Kannel, 1978). Therefore, it has been recommended that all patients with atrial fibrillation be anticoagulated. However, chronic anticoagulant therapy in the elderly is associated with a high rate of bleeding complications; most clinicians do not use such therapy unless the patient has indications of an embolus. If there is no other source for embolism, Coumadin therapy is indicated.

Atrial premature beats, common in the elderly, are perceived by the patient as palpitations or skipped beats. These are benign and no treatment is indicated, although the physician should check for caffeine excess and limit regular coffee to two cups a day.

Rapid regular heart rates, possibly associated with light headed episodes may indicate the presence of atrial tachycardia, which should not be treated if they are found in brief runs on electrocardiographic monitoring and are not associated with symptoms. Treatment is indicated if tachycardia are sustained or symptomatic. Drugs used may include a digitalis preparation such a digoxin, which may disrupt the timing of the reentry wave to prevent the arrhythmia, or the use of verapamil and propranolol, which also may change conduction through the atrial ventricular node or the reentrant pathway, thus preventing the initiation of the arrhythmia. Quinidine may be useful in suppressing the arrhythmias.

Ventricular Arrhythmias

Ventricular arrhythmias are abnormal beats that originate in the muscle of the ventricle and are associated with dilatation, increased mass of the myocardium, and areas of scarring with disruption of the normal depolarization patterns. In these conditions, there will be areas of myocardium that are depolarized at the same time. These areas may then spontaneously depolarize at different times, resulting in premature ventricular beats, or, if the area develops a reentry cycle, ventricular tachycardia can result. Patients with advanced heart disease often have the more serious ventricular arrhythmias. Prognosis is directly related to the functioning state of the heart muscle.

Ventricular arrhythmias are graded by their frequency and complexity. They may be of one configuration and are called "unifocal" beats. Two different configurations are labeled multifocal premature beats. When the beats are consecutive, this is called "pairing." When there are three or more consecutive beats in a row, ventricular tachycardia is present. Ventricular tachycardia may be sustained or non-sustained.

It has been shown that isolated and multifocal premature ventricular beats are best left untreated. Nonsustained ventricular tachycardia in the presence of good ventricular function does not require antiarrhythmic treatment (Kennedy, Whitlock, Sprague, Kennedy, Buckingham, & Goldberg, 1985). Whether treating nonsustained ventricular tachycardia in patients with decreased left ventricular function will prevent sudden deaths is still not known. Certainly, patients with sustained tachycardia require pharmacologic or electrical treatment. Patients with near sudden death episodes and symptomatic ventricular tachycardia will require specialized studies, known as electrical physiologic study. During this procedure, repetitive premature beats are placed behind the normal QRS complex, in an attempt to induce the ventricular arrhythmia. If the arrhythmia is inducible, intravenous introduction of drugs useful in the managements of these arrhythmias can be performed rapidly, and the patient rechallenged to see if the patient is now protected against the arrhythmia.

For the acute treatment of these arrhythmias, intravenous drugs are used. Lidocaine has been the first drug of choice for many years. Side effects in the elderly result from high blood levels, and include confusion and occasional seizures. For chronic treatment, procaine amide is the first agent of choice. This can be given either intravenously or orally. Blood levels of the drug can be measured to assist in determining the proper dosage. This agent lowers blood pressure significantly and may also cause nausea and abdominal pain. In addition, some patients will develop an arthritic-type disease resembling lupus erythematosis. Very high blood levels can lead to myocardial suppression and cardiac failure. In addition, some patients will develop a rapid ventricular tachycardia with cyclic variation in complex size, which is called twisting about a point or torsade de pointe (Bauman, Bauernfeind, Hoff, Strasberg, Swiryn, & Rosen, 1984). Quinidine and disopyramine are similar to procaine amide and can be used in place of that agent.

In some patients with refractory ventricular tachycardia that is nonresponsive to drugs, surgery may be necessary. In this procedure, the origin of the abnormal heart beat is localized within the heart muscle and the endocardium of that area removed. This may ablate the focus of the abnormal heart rhythm.

Slowed Heart Rate

A slow heart rate requiring a pacemaker is a common problem in the elderly. The conducting system begins in the sinus node near the superior vena cava in the right atrium. This tissue spontaneously depolarizes itself and initiates the heart beat. The sinus node becomes scarred with age and becomes defective. This can lead to sinus pauses with no heart beat for several seconds or the presence of escape rhythms leading to atrial tachycardia or fibrillation. The cardiac impulse from the sinus node is carried through the atrial muscle and then captured in the specialized myocardium called the atrioventricular node. This tissue allows the depolarization wave to go through slowly, so that the mechanical events of the heart contraction can catch up to the electrical depolarization wave. The impulse then travels down the HIS bundle and the right bundle (to the right ventricle) and the left bundle (to the left ventricle). The atrioventricular node may have disease and not allow conduction to occur, leading to heart block, which slows the ventricle. The degree of block can vary from slow but completed impulse conduction (1st degree AV block), to intermittent failure to conduct (second degree AV block), to no conduction and a slow escape rhythm (complete

atrioventricular block). Certain medications may prolong conduction time and could lead to first or second degree AV block, usually at the level of the AV node. These medications are digitalis, beta blockers, and calcium blockers, and should be stopped before a final decision can be made on the need for a pacemaker.

Complete atrioventricular block in the elderly is usually associated with symptoms of faintness, syncope, and, at times, heart failure. In these patients, a permanent pacemaker should be implanted. This involves placing an electrode through a vein into the right ventricle, attaching a power source (battery), and burying the unit beneath the skin. These units may function for several years before a replacement is needed. In cases where there has been failure of conduction at a level below the atrial ventricular node, where the escape rhythms in this circumstance are less reliable, a pacemaker may be life-saving. It is possible to place an electrode in the atrium as well as the ventricle in order to mimic atrial ventricular conduction, which may lead to better cardiac output. However, the elderly may commonly have slow or irregular sinus node activity without symptoms and without requiring pacemaker therapy.

SUMMARY

Heart disease is a common problem in the elderly, although symptoms present in younger patient groups may be absent because of decreased functional needs of the elderly. Common conditions such as hypertension and coronary artery disease persist into the later years of life. In addition, degenerative changes also present themselves, such as aortic valve stenosis and conducting tissue disease. Medications must be given in appropriate (lower) doses, and judicious use of surgery and pacemakers can relieve symptoms and prolong life. Research is needed in many areas, including the pathogenesis of disease and the development and validation of effective therapy. This should provide an area of fruitful study for cardiologists and geriatricians in the future.

REFERENCES

Adamopoulos, P. N., Chrysanthakopoulos, S. G., & Frohlich, E. D. (1975). Systolic hypertension: Non-homogeneous diseases. *American Journal of Cardiology,* 36, 697–701.

Bauman, J. L., Bauernfeind, R. A., Hoff, J. V., Strasberg, B., Swiryn, S., & Rosen, K. M. (1984). Torsade de pointes due to quinidine: Observations in 31 patients. *American Heart Journal, 107*, 425–430.

Berger, R. K., Davis, K. B., Kaiser, G. C., Foster, E. D., Hammond, G. L., Tong, T. G., Kennedy, J. W., Sheffield, T., Ringqvist, I., Wines, R. D., Chaitman, B. R., & Mock, M. (1981). Preservation of the myocardium during coronary artery bypass grafting. *Circulation, 64*, 61–66.

Bourassa, M. G., Enjalbert, M., Campeau, L., & Lesperance, J. (1983). Progression of atherosclerosis in coronary arteries and bypass grafts: Ten years later. *American Journal of Cardiology, 53*, 102C–107C.

Copeland, J. G., Griepp, R. B., Stinson, E. B., & Shumway, N. E. (1977). Isolated aortic valve replacement in patients older than 65 years. *Journal of the American Medical Association, 237*, 1578.

DeBusk, R. F., Houston, N., Haskell, W., Fry, G., & Parker, M. (1979). Exercise training soon after myocardial infarction. *American Journal of Cardiology, 44*, 1223–1240.

DeMaira, A. N., Bommer, W., Joye, J., Garrett, L., Bouteller, J., & Mason, D. T. (1980). Valve and limitations of cross-sectional echocardiography of aortic valve in the diagnosis and quantification of valvular aortic stenosis. *Circulation, 62*, 304–312.

Elayda, M. A., Hall, R. J., Gray, A. G., Mathur, V. S., & Cooley, D. A. (1984). Coronary revascularization in the elderly patient. *Journal of the American College of Cardiology, 3*, 1398–1402.

Frishman, W. H., Furberg, C. D., & Friedewald, W. T. (1984). B-adrenergic blockade for survivors of acute myocardial infarction. *New England Journal of Medicine, 310*, 830–836.

Gersh, B. J., Kronmal, R. A., Frye, R. L., Schaff, H. V., Ryan, T. J., Gosselin, A. J., Kaiser, G. C., Killip T., III & participants in the Coronary Artery Surgery Study. (1983). Coronary arteriography and coronary artery bypass surgery: Morbidity and mortality in patients 65 years and older. A report from the Coronary Artery Surgery Study. *Circulation, 67*, 482–490.

Hale, W. E., Stewart, R. B., & Marks, R. G. (1984). Central nervous system symptoms of elderly subjects using antihypertensive drugs. *Journal of the American Geratric Society, 32*, 5–10.

Hartzler, G. O., Rutherford, B. D., & McConahay, D. R. (1984). Percutaneous transluminal coronary angioplasty: Application for acute myocardial infarction. *American Journal of Cardiology, 53*, 117C–121C.

Haskell, W. L., & DeBusk, R. (1979). Cardiovascular responses to repeated treadmill exercise testing soon after myocardial infarction. *Circulation, 60*, 1247–1252.

Hurowitz, E., & Gordon M. (1984). Cardiopulmonary resuscitation of the elderly. *Journal of the American Geriatric Society, 32*, 930–934.

Hypertension Detection and Follow-Up Cooperative Group. (1979). Five-year findings of the hypertension detection and follow-up program. 1. Reduction in mortality of persons with HBP, including mild hypertension. *Journal of the American Medical Association, 242*, 2562–2571.

Hypertension Detection and Follow-up Cooperative Group (1979). Five-year findings of the hypertension

detection and follow-up program. II. Mortality by race, sex, and age. *Journal of the American Medical Association, 242*, 2572–2577.

Kannel, W. B., & Thom, T. J. (1984). Declining cardiovascular mortality. *Circulation, 70*, 331–336.

Kennedy, H. L., Whitlock, J. A., Sprague, M. K., Kennedy, L. J., Buckingham, T. A., & Goldberg, R. J. (1985). Long-term follow-up of asymptomatic healthy subjects with frequent and complex ventricular ectopy. *New England Journal of Medicine, 312*, 193–197.

Knapp, W. S., Douglas, J. S., Jr., Craver, J. M., Jones, E. L., King, S. B. III., Bone, D. K., Bradford, J. M., & Hatcher, C. R., Jr. (1981). Efficacy of coronary artery bypass grafting in elderly patients with coronary artery disease. *American Journal of Cardiology, 47*, 923–930.

Latting, C. A., & Silverman, M. E. (1980). Acute myocardial infarction in hospitalized patients over age 70. *American Heart Journal, 100*, 311–318.

Mock, M. B., Holmes, D. R., Jr., Vlietstra, R. E., Gersh, B. J., Detre, K. M., Kelsey, S. F., Orszulak, T. A., Schaff, H. V., Piehler, J. M., Van Raden, M. J., Passamani, E. R., Kent, K. M., & Gruentzig, A. R. (1984). Percutaneous transluminal coronary angioplasty (PTCA) in the elderly patient: Experience in the National Heart, Lung and Blood Institute PTCA Registry. *American Journal of Cardiology, 53*, 89C–91C.

Nestico, P. F., Depace, N. L., Morganroth, J., Kotler, M. N., & Ross, J. (1984). Mitral annular calcification: Clinical pathophysiology, and echocardiographic review. *American Heart Journal, 100*, 989–996.

Parker, J. O., & Fung, H. (1984). Transdermal nitroglycerin in angina pectoris. *Amercian Journal of Cardiology, 54*, 471–476.

Perez, G. L., Jacob, M., Bhat, P., Rao, D. B., & Luisada, A. A. (1976). Incidence of murmurs in the aging heart. *Journal of the American Geratric Society, 24*, 29–31.

Port, S., Cobb, F. R., Coleman, R. E., & Jones, R. H. (1980). Effect of age on the response of the left ventricular ejection fraction to exercise. *New England Journal of Medicine, 303*, 1133–1137.

Roberts, W. C. (1983). Morphologic features of the normal and abnormal mitral valve. *American Journal of Cardiology, 51*, 1005–1028.

Schuler, G., Peterson, K. L., Johnson, A., Francis, G. Dennish, G., Utley, J., Daily, P. O., Ashburn, W., & Ross, J., Jr. (1979). Temporal response of left ventricular performance to mitral valve surgery. *Circulation, 59*, 1218–1231.

Shulman, S. T., Amren, D. P., Bisno, A. L., Dajani, A. S., Durack, D. T., Gerber, M. A., Kaplan, E. L., Millard, H. D., Sanders, W. E., Schwartz, R. H., & Wantanakunakorn, C. (1984). Prevention of bacterial endocarditis: A statement for health professionals by the Committee on Rheumatic Fever and Infective Endocarditis of the Council on Cardiovascular Disease in the Young. *Circulation, 70*, 1123A–1127A.

Stamler, J., Stamier, R., Ridlingher, W. F., Algera, G., & Roberts, R. H. (1976). Hypertension screening of 1 million Americans: Community Hypertension Evaluation Clinic (CHEC) Program, 1973 through 1975. *Journal of American Medical Association, 235*, 2299–2036.

Veterans Administration Cooperative Study Group on

Antihypertensive Agents. (1967). Effects of treatment on morbidity: Results in patients with diastolic blood pressures averaging 115 through 129 mm Hg, *Journal of the American Medical Association, 202,* 1028.

Veterans Administration Cooperative Study Group on Antihypertensive Agents. (1970). Effects of treatment on morbidity in hypertension, II: Results in patients with diastolic blood pressure averaging 90 through 114 mm Hg. *Journal of the American Medical Association, 213,* 1143.

Veterans Administration Cooperative Study Group on Antihypertensive Agents. (1972). Effects of Treatment on morbidity in hypertension, III: Influences of age, diastolic pressures, and prior cardiovascular disease: Further analysis of side effects. *Circulation, 45,* 991.

Williams, M. A., Maresh, C. M., Esterbrooks, D. J., Harbrecht, J. J., & Sketch, M. H. (1985). Early exercise training in patients older than 65 years compared with that in younger patients after acute myocardial infarction or coronary artery bypass grafting. *American Journal of Cardiology, 55,* 263.

Wolfe, P. A., Dawber, T. R., Thomas, H. E., Jr., & Krannel, W. B. (1978). Epidemiologic assessment of chronic atrial fibrillation and risk of stroke: The Framingham Study. *Neurology, 18,* 973–977.

Chapter 12

Orthopedic Issues in the Elderly

Robert R. Karpman

Musculoskeletal problems are among the most common complaints among the elderly. In several studies (E. Brody, 1985; Verbrugge, 1986) conducted both in independent environments and in institutions, pain and decreased function secondary to musculoskeletal disorders were the most frequent complaints. The manner in which the complaints were managed varied significantly, from denial to over-the-counter medications, to prescription medications, to medical advice. Although musculoskeletal problems usually do not affect longevity per se, they can lead to severe disability, which can significantly affect the quality of life. Several questions on the subject will be addressed in this chapter:

1. How frequently do musculoskeletal complaints lead to severe disability?
2. If the disability results in decreased function and mobility, how can one minimize the disability?
3. What are the psychosocial influences on musculoskeletal disability?
4. How can medications and/or surgery improve mobility and independence in an elderly population?
5. Are there methods to prevent disability resulting from musculoskeletal disease?

In order to answer these questions, one must have a basic knowledge of the musculoskeletal diseases that affect primarily the elderly population, as well as some knowledge of the changes that occur normally in the musculoskeletal system with age.

MUSCLE

Several changes occur with age in muscle tissue on various levels: anatomical, molecular, and biochemical. This is manifested clinically by decreased strength, especially in the lower extremities. In a recent study (Steinberg & Schuessler, 1986) it was noted that although muscle strength and speed of contraction, as measured by CYBEX testing, was markedly decreased in the lower extremities of elderly patients as compared to younger controls, the overall muscle endurance was minimally affected. This is probably related to changes in the type of muscle fiber that occur with the aging process, which leads to increased muscle endurance. In addition, it has been found that athletic training can indeed improve muscle strength in elderly individuals. This is of particular clinical importance in those patients who experience increased falls because of lower extremity weakness. Through proper rehabilitation and training techniques, strength can be improved ultimately preventing further falls. Of the three tissues in the musculoskeletal system, it is apparent that muscle, indeed, has the ability to regenerate in a normal fashion and that strength can be increased through proper training.

BONE

It is extremely important to recognize that bone is not a static tissue but one that is in a constant state of flux, with bone formation and bone resorption occurring continuously. Besides the mineral content of bone, consisting primarily of hydroxyapatite crystals, there are bone-forming cells (osteoblasts), bone-resorbing cells (osteoclasts), and collagen, which serves as a scaffolding for the laying down of hydroxyapatite. Although bone turnover rate and cell function may decrease slightly with age, bone healing continues to occur at essentially the same rate, unless there are extenuating circumstances, such as metastatic disease, poor nutrition, infection, or immunosuppression.

Why, then, are fractures so common in the elderly? The answer is related essentially to one important factor—*bone mass*—which changes significantly with age.

Bone mass can be defined as the total amount of bone present in the body at any one point in time. There are constant changes in bone mass related to the bone turnover rate. Bone mass increases at a steady rate until one essentially reaches his or her maximum bone mass (approx. age 30). In the following years, it declines slowly by approximately 0.5% to 1% per year. In the female, there is significant change after menopause, when there is a greater reduction in bone mass, leading to osteoporosis and fractures. It is estimated that in the postmenopausal period, perhaps 2% to 5% of bone mass is lost each year. By about age 80, however, the male population has caught up to the female population, and bone mass in both males and females is essentially the same. When bone mass reaches a critically low level, there is a 75% to 80% risk of fracture secondary to a significant decrease in structural strength. Minimal or even no trauma can lead to fracture. The loss in bone mass is referred to as *osteopenia*.

When fractures have developed secondary to osteopenia, the clinical syndrome of osteoporosis is present. Approximately 40% to 50% of women over age 50 in the United States will develop osteoporosis, leading to more than 150,000 hip fractures per year and a greater number of fractures in the vertebral bodies of the spine, wrist, and shoulder (Avioli, 1983: Owen et al., 1980). These fractures entail major health expenditures; for example it is estimated that approximately $3 billion is spent each year managing patients with hip fractures alone. There are several risk factors for osteoporosis, including the long-term use of steroids, parathyroid and thyroid disorders, poor nutrition, high intake of caffeine, alcohol abuse and smoking. The most common form is *senile*, or *postmenopausal osteoporosis*, the exact causal mechanism of which remains unknown. It is believed that the rapid decrease in estrogen levels following menopause has a somewhat destabilizing effect on bones leading to increased bone resorption. This effect may be related to calcitonin, a naturally occurring hormone produced in the thyroid. To date, there are few ways of actually increasing bone mass once osteoporosis has developed; however, there are several methods to either stabilize bone mass or certainly prevent bone mass loss prior to menopause. The structural strength of the bone can be decreased as a result of vitamin D deficiency, leading to a condition known as *osteomalacia*. Elderly patients whose exposure to sunlight is limited, particularly those who are institutionalized, are at greatest risk for osteomalacia.

The diagnosis of osteopenia is made when a fracture actually occurs or during a routine chest Xray, in which thinning of the vertebral bodies is noted. This often leads to the so-called *codfish vertebra* described in radiology texts; however, 40% of the bone mass is lost before any radiographic changes are noted. Methods of diagnosing osteopenia include single and dual photon densitometry and quantitative CAT scanning, which measure bone mass. The accuracy of dual photon densitometry and CAT scanning is about the same with a 2% to 3% variance in measurements. One or the other of these techniques is available in most cities. It should be noted that Medicare does not reimburse the cost of dual photon densitometry, but does reimburse the cost of single photon and CAT scanning, providing the correct indications are present. Bone mass measurements should be made approximately every 6 months to 1 year to determine the overall rate of bone loss. A single measurement will not enable the physician to determine the exact rate of bone loss, and it is the *rate* of bone loss that is important in determining treatment.

Bone Disorders and Their Treatment

The best treatment of osteopenia is prevention, and it should be stressed that women in their 30s and 40s should already be on some type of calcium-replacement therapy in order to maintain adequate bone mass. In addition, physical exercise, which helps strengthen bones and thus makes them less susceptible to stress, is equally important. Other treatments still remain controversial. However, most clinicians agree that significant bone loss and subsequent fractures can be prevented by a calcium intake of approximately 1,200 to 1,500 mg per day, a vitamin D intake of 400 units per day, and the initiation of estrogen use immediately after onset of menopause (Paganini-Hill et al., 1981; Weiss et al., 1980). Following these recommendations, however, does not increase bone mass—it only prevents significant loss. Other treatment recommendations include the use of sodium fluoride, calcitonin, and, most recently, electrical stimulation (Brighton, 1985); however, definitive changes and increases in bone mass have not yet been observed with these treatments.

With respect to what form of calcium is most beneficial, it appears that calcium gluconate is the most desirable, followed by calcium carbonate and other calcium preparations. One of the simplest ways of obtaining the mineral is the use of the antacid Tums, one tablet of which provides approximately 200 mg of calcium. Tums is certainly less expensive than the other preparations, and will also treat gastric irritation.

Orthopedic surgeons are faced with the task of treating the complications of osteopenia and osteoporosis, primarily fractures. In most cases, vertebral body fractures can be managed with a *short* period of bed rest (1 or 2 days) and the use of analgesics followed by gradual mobilization. A back corset is often helpful in relieving pain initially, but should be discarded as soon as the pain has subsided in order to prevent further diffuse osteopenia. Elderly patients often have difficulty in using the standard hyperextension braces, which often exert undue pressure over the sternum. Therefore, corsets should always be tried on for fit and comfort. Other types of braces that provide similar support should also be considered, perhaps those with a shoulder strap for greater comfort and ease of application. In addition, I have found that the use of a transcutaneous nerve stimulator (TENS) unit with surface electrodes around the thoracic muscles seems to decrease the pain, and thus the necessity for oral analgesics during the initial period is significantly decreased and often allows for early mobilization. Most patients should be free of pain approximately 4 to 6 weeks follow-

ing the fracture. It is also important to note that other causes of vertebral body fractures must be ruled out, such as malignancies and infection, before accepting a diagnosis of osteoporosis.

Other fractures directly related to osteopenia include fractures of the wrist and hip. Most fractures of the distal radius (Colles' fractures) are treated by closed reduction, utilizing a local or regional anesthetic followed by immobilization in a plastic or fiberglass cast for approximately 4 to 6 weeks. Again, early mobilization of the joints following the cast immobilization is encouraged in order to obtain the best possible functional result. Occasionally, complex injuries require an open reduction and fixation, or the application of pins and external fixation. Therapy to maximize the range of motion of the fingers is begun almost immediately after the fracture, in order to decrease swelling and prevent stiffness. Because of the osteopenia, there is frequently a settling of the fracture, which makes accurate anatomical alignment difficult to maintain. In this instance, early rehabilitation is again stressed in order to decrease functional impairment. There may, however, remain a cosmetic deformity, although it is of little functional significance.

Hip Fractures

Each year, approximately 150,000 elderly in the United States, primarily women, suffer a hip fracture. It is estimated that in the United States approximately $3 billion is spent annually on the management of these patients, both in an acute- and chronic-care setting. Although advanced technology in both the surgical and medical management of patients with hip fractures has markedly decreased the perioperative and mortality to less than 10%, there remains a 40% to 50% chance of 1-year mortality. This appears to be due to several factors, including advanced age, concomitant medical problems, and, most recently, a significant psychosocial component, which plays an equal if not more important role in overall survival (Nickens, 1983). In several studies carried out in Europe (Ceder et al., 1980), the ability to shop on one's own and to have a family or friend living with the patient following surgery seems to be the most important factor in long-term survival. In a study of patients 90 years of age and greater (Karpman, 1983), with hip fractures, the ability to return home was the single most important factor in long-term survival. The survival rate of these patients differed little from that studied in patients aged 65 to 90. In some patients, a severe phobia of falling developed after a fracture, often leading to complete immobility and death within 6 months after the fracture. The cause of this phobia and the type of patient susceptible to it have not been elucidated. In addition, very few studies have been performed to determine what psychosocial factors play a role in overall survival in patients following hip fractures. It is, therefore, imperative that a multidisciplinary team approach be utilized in managing the patient with a fractured hip—*not* at the time of discharge but immediately after admission in an attempt to deal with not only the medical but also the psychosocial factors. In Europe and Canada, geriatric orthopedic inpatients units have been designed in an attempt to prevent long-term care and to enable the patient to return to a more independent functional level at the time of discharge. This appears to be quite successful, not only in returning the patient to the premorbid environment but also in cost savings.

There are certain technical factors that must be considered as well. In severely osteopenic patients, fixation of the bone is often difficult and may require supplementation with bone cement in order to assure stability during early mobilization. Again, early mobilization is the most important factor in managing hip-fracture patients. In fractures of the femoral neck, a metal prosthesis is utilized, again, to allow for early ambulation. With internal fixation of such fracture, there is a high incidence of loss of blood supply to the femoral head. This results in the necessity for surgery, usually hemiarthroplasty. In some cases, primary total hip replacement, although more difficult, may provide earlier mobilization and earlier independence than the more traditional surgical approaches. Aggressive surgical intervention should be considered in most cases, again in order to provide early mobilization and pain relief and to prevent problems arising from prolonged bed rest, including pneumonias, urinary incontinence, and thrombophlebitis. In addition to technical failures, including failure of the prosthesis or hardware, complications can include thrombophlebitis and pulmonary embolism, as well as a significantly high incidence of incontinence, both bowel and bladder. In a recent study by S. Brody (1983), 15% of patients discharged from the hospital following a hip fracture experienced some type of bowel incontinence, and an even higher number, urinary incontinence. The exact etiology of this

also remains unknown. An indwelling catheter, however, should be avoided if at all possible to prevent urinary tract infections. If that is not possible, extra nursing care may be required because of the high incidence of shock and sepsis following indwelling catheterization.

Recently, some physicians have advocated the nonsurgical treatment of hip-fracture patients with severe organic brain syndrome, noting that the overall morbidity and mortality with such treatment was significantly lower than with surgical intervention. It should be mentioned, however, that the nonsurgical management of hip fractures is labor-intensive, requiring constant care to prevent decubitus formation and other problems of prolonged bed rest. Such treatment therefore should be reserved only for those facilities that are able to provide such care; their numbers are very limited. In the majority of cases, surgical treatment provides more rapid pain relief and earlier mobilization and entails less care.

In summary, elderly patients with a fractured hip should be treated aggressively, not only by the surgeon and medical practitioner but through a multidisciplinary approach, in order to prevent some of the psychosocial problems that may indeed have a stronger influence than medically related factors in the overall outcome following the fracture.

CARTILAGE DISEASES AND THEIR TREATMENT

Cartilage is connective tissue. Consisting of chonodrocytes, fibers, and chondromucoid. It is characterized by its nonvascularity and firm consistency. Diseases of the cartilage, including arthritis and rheumatism, are the most common musculoskeletal complaints among the elderly. One study found that 20% of patients seen in an outpatient clinic presented with some type of arthritic manifestation (Reynolds, 1978). Arthritis can be divided into several groups, some of which are more prevalent in the elderly population.

The most common type of arthritis in the elderly is *osteoarthritis*. More prevalent in females than in males, it usually involves the joints of the lower extremities, particularly those of the knees and hips. The exact cause of osteoarthritis is not known. However, certain biological and chemical changes are noted in arthritic cartilage, including decreased water content, changes in the glucosaminoglycan content, and direct cellular changes in the cartilage cells (chondrocytes). Other causes of arthritis in the elderly that should be considered in differential diagnosis include gout, pseudogout, and infection.

Gout is a disease characterized by the deposition of uric-acid salts in the joints. It usually affects the big toe, but can also involve the smaller toes, knees, and upper extremities. Recently, a high incidence of gout has been noted, particularly in elderly women, although in general there is a higher male-to-female ratio.

Pseudogout, or chondrocalcinosis, is similar to gout but with calcium crystals rather than uric-acid crystals deposited in the joints.

Diagnosis of both gout and pseudogout can be made easily by aspiration of the involved joint and microscopic examination of the crystals.

Infection, particularly slow-growing fungal infections or granulomatous infections, such as tuberculosis, often go undiagnosed for as long as a year prior to onset. Again, diagnosis can be made by aspiration of the joint fluid or perhaps a biopsy of the lining of the joint to check for the presence of bacteria or fungal agents.

The most common type of inflammatory arthritis in the elderly is *rheumatoid* arthritis. Approximately 15% of new cases of rheumatoid arthritis were found in the age group of 60 and above age group (Brown & Sones, 1967; Ehrlich & Katz, 1970; Moesmann, 1969). Diagnosis is usually easily made by clinical examination and laboratory tests. Symptoms include symmetrical pain and swelling in the joints, morning stiffness, and loss of motion.

Among the other rheumatic diseases that occur in the elderly is *polymalgia rheumatica,* which affects primarily the muscles around the shoulder and pelvic girdle. It is marked by severe stiffness in the morning and is often confused with other types of arthritic and rheumatic syndromes. However, patients suffering from polymalgia rheumatica have an abnormal sedimentation rate, which usually serves as the basis of diagnosis. If not treated, other complications can occur, including inflammation of the great vessels around the heart and in the temporal artery, the latter leading to irreversible blindness. It is extremely important that the diagnosis of polymalgia rheumatica, and/or temporal arteritis, be made quickly, so that treatment can be instituted and blindness prevented. Treatment usually involves oral steroids, which can rapidly decrease the symptoms and prevent further complications.

Other soft tissues problems include bursitis, involving primarily the shoulder, hip, and knee; tendinitis, particularly in the rotator cuff muscles around the shoulder; and fibrositis, which effects the muscles in the neck and back. Certain trigger points are noted in the patient suffering from fibrositis. Patients with fibrositis are often depressed, have difficulty sleeping, and exhibit little change in their symptoms with a variety of medications. In a recent study by Baum (1986) it was noted that patients suffering from fibrositis in addition to bursitis or tendinitis seemed to show improvement in the fibrositis following treatment of the bursitis. A correlation between poor sleeping habits and the development of fibrositis has been observed. Antidepressants have been somewhat helpful in the treatment, as well as the use of physical therapy, trigger-point injections, and other procedures all with only moderate results.

Arthritis and Rheumatism and Their Treatment

The treatment of most arthritic rheumatic complaints usually begins with the use of oral anti-inflammatory agents, primarily aspirin. Like most other drug therapy in the elderly, doses must be modified, depending on pre-existing medical problems, which may impede absorption of the drug, causing increased sensitivity or decreased excretion. Enteric-coated aspirin, usually two tablets taken 3 times a day, seems to be the most well tolerated by the older patient, causing no gastric upset. However, there should be careful monitoring of clotting factors if the patient is on any type of anticoagulant medication, such as Coumadin. Should oral anti-inflammatory medication prove ineffective, non-steroidal anti-inflammatory agents could be used. These, however, frequently cause gastric irritation, as well as some fluid retention and occasionally renal changes. The once a day or twice-a-day doses seem to allow for better patient compliance, and if one nonsteroidal agent is unsuccessful, that does not preclude the clinician from trying others. Overall, one nonsteroidal agent does not seem to work better than another or prevent the complications associated with the use of nonsteroidal drugs. Other medications tend to be more specific for the disease involved, such as remittive agents (gold, penicillamine, and cytotoxic agents) in the treatment of rheumatoid arthritis; colchicine and allopurinol in the treatment of gout; and oral steroids in rheumatoid arthritis and connective tissue disorders. Again, the patient must be carefully monitored, including serial blood testing to evaluate changes in liver function, bleeding time, and renal function.

An important adjunct to medications in the treatment of arthritis and rheumatism is physical therapy, which can help decrease muscle spasm, maintain a normal range of mobility and aid the patient in the normal activities of daily living, considered the ultimate goal of treatment. Assistive devices, such as walkers, canes, reachers, and utensil modifications, are also helpful in maintaining normal or near-normal activities.

When medications and other conservative forms of treatment have failed and severe degeneration of the joint is evident from clinical examination and radiographic evaluation, surgery should be considered as an alternative. Approximately 200,000 total-joint replacements are performed annually in the United States, primarily in elderly patients. Morbidity or mortality among geriatric patients undergoing total-joint replacement is not significantly higher than in younger patients (Karpman, 1980). The joints most commonly replaced are those of the hip, knee, fingers, and toes, followed by the shoulder, elbow, and ankle. The most common complications following joint replacement include loosening; infection, which may require removal and reinsertion of the prosthesis; or an inability to replace the prosthesis, leading to a flail joint. Thrombophlebitis is also a particular problem in patients undergoing hip- and knee-joint surgery. To date, no specific anticoagulant regimen seems to be the definitive technique for preventing thrombophlebitis prior to total-joint replacement surgery.

Although the expense is significant, joint replacement can be shown to be cost-effective if it allows the patient to function more independently, eliminating the need for further care and reducing reliance on social support systems. Most patients find the procedure extremely gratifying, because it affords them greater independence and mobility. Again, age should *not* be a factor in the decision for joint replacement surgery.

Another surgical technique that may be of some value in arthritis and other inflammatory problems is arthroscopy, in which a small scope is inserted into the knee and loose bony fragments, a torn meniscus, or other debris is removed on an outpatient basis.

It should also be mentioned that local steroid injections, particularly in the treatment of bursitis, tendinitis, or acute inflammation of a joint, is extremely effective and does not produce the long-term side effects related to oral steroid medication, including gastric ulcers, increased bleeding, fluid retention, and subcutaneous tissue loss. One should never, however, inject the Achilles tendon for fear of potential rupture.

BACK PROBLEMS

In younger patients, back pain is usually secondary to mechanical problems, such as low back strains, sprains, and congenital anomalies, which normally respond to bed rest and medications. Other disease entities include neurological impairment secondary to a herniated disc. The elderly patient with back problems often is more difficult to diagnose and treat. As mentioned previously, an elderly patient may present with vertebral body fractures, most often caused by osteoporosis. However, it is extremely important that malignancy be ruled out, a primary responsibility of the clinician treating an elderly patient with a back problem. The most common malignancy is multiple myeloma, followed by metastatic disease from the prostate, breast, and lung. Diagnosis is often obscured by preexisting diseases, such as arthritis or osteoporosis. A bone scan is often helpful in detecting malignancy, because bones other than the spine may be involved. Treatment of the spinal problem essentially depends upon the treatment of the primary malignancy. Once malignancy has been ruled out, other disease processes should be considered, including osteoporosis and arthritis which have already been discussed, and particularly spinal stenosis.

Spinal stenosis is a rather recently recognized disease in which one or more segments of the spinal canal can be narrowed either by excessive bone spurs related to arthritis or by hypertrophy of the tissues, particularly the ligamenta flavum. Patients presenting with spinal stenosis often complain of back pain, particularly after short periods of ambulation, usually relieved by rest. The term angina lumboris seems to be quite descriptive regarding spinal stenosis, just as angina pectoris is descriptive in the diagnosis of heart disease. The back pain frequently does not have a specific radicular component and is often missed because there does not appear to be any evidence of neurological impairment. Progressive spinal stenosis, however, can present with neurological impairment, including loss of bowel and bladder continence. On clinical examination, the most common finding is pain upon straightening of the back. In most other nerve compressions, pain is usually elicited on flexion. Pain on extension is pathognomonic of spinal stenosis. Radiographs of the spine may help the physician identify spinal stenosis; however, other diagnostic techniques may be necessary, including CAT scanning and myelography, to make the definitive diagnosis. Often complete blockage of the spinal canal at one or several points can be seen on a myelogram. If the symptoms are persistent, surgical decompression is utilized, often with excellent results, including the complete relief of symptoms and return of neurological function, which is often not the case following most back operations.

Degenerative disk disease, although common radiographically, rarely causes significant neurological impairment in the elderly patient; however, if neurological findings are noted, then a similar workup and decompression, if necessary, should be carried out. Other back problems that should be considered include disk space infection, particularly in males who had recently undergone some type of urological procedure, because bacterial infection can easily reach the disk spaces through a series of veins surrounding the spinal area.

For the most part, elderly patients suffering from other lower back problems can be managed with physical therapy, anti-inflammatory agents, and corsets. Again, supports are advised only for severe cases, because osteoporosis and muscle atrophy can occur quite rapidly with prolonged use of a corset. Again, any elderly patient with recent onset of acute back pain should be evaluated carefully to rule out malignancy.

FOOT PROBLEMS

A physical examination, particularly in an elderly patient, should not be considered complete without a careful evaluation of the foot. Frequently, the first signs of a systemic illness can be recognized in the foot, particularly diabetes, thyroid disorders, and rheumatic diseases. A frequent faller may simply have improper footwear, which can be easily corrected to prevent further injury.

A proper evaluation of the foot should begin with examination of the footwear for correct size and abnormal wear on the heel or sole, followed by examination of the socks for texture and wear, because abnormal thickness leads to excessive

sweating and possible fungal infections. Next a careful gait analysis should be performed, with and without shoes, to detect such abnormalities as pain secondary to arthritis, painful callosities, wide-based gait secondary to neurological disturbance, and antalgic gait secondary to hip, knee, or back disease. Then, the skin should be carefully examined to detect corns or calluses secondary to poor footwear, as well as bony prominences, nail deformities, ingrown toenails, fungal infections, and discoloration and/or cool temperature suggesting vascular disease. A sensory examination should be done to rule out peripheral neuropathy. Any joint swelling should also be noted.

Common foot disorders in the elderly include peripheral neuropathies secondary to diabetes, as well as other neurological disorders leading to insensitive feet and potential unrecognized infections. A missed ingrown toenail in an insensitive foot or a first- or second-degree burn could lead to serious infection. Diabetic feet should be carefully monitored to rule out skin problems. Most soft-tissue problems, including corns, calluses, and bunions, can be managed with modified footwear and/or pads placed in appropriate areas. If significant bony deformities are present, surgical correction can be performed with minimal complications, provided a proper vascular workup has been performed to avoid healing problems. Small modifications in the shoe or insertion of pads can often lead to significant pain relief and improved function. Again, it should be noted that careful monitoring of the foot, particularly in elderly patients with diabetes, is mandatory.

CONCLUSION

In summary, musculoskeletal problems in the elderly patient, although not life-threatening, can often lead to severe disability and loss of independence. This is particularly true in patients with fractured hips or severe arthritis. Careful evaluation for the elderly patient with musculoskeletal disease is mandatory in order to rule out the possibility of malignancies. Various treatments are extremely successful in improving mobilization and independence, including medications, physical therapy, and surgery if necessary. It cannot be stressed enough that a multidisciplinary approach should be utilized in the management of the elderly patient with musculosketal disease in order to manage not only the specific medical problems, but also the psychosocial problems that are associated with the disease process. Finally, increased function, whether independently or with the use of certain assistive devices, should be the primary goal not only of the orthopedist but also of any clinician involved in the care of the geriatric patient with musculoskeletal disease.

REFERENCES

Avioli, L. (1983). *The osteoporotic syndrome: Detection, prevention, treatment.* New York: Grune & Stratton.

Baum, J. (1986, March). *Effect of shoulder bursitis on the fibrocytic syndrome.* Paper presented at Them Ol' Bones III: A National Multidisciplinary Conference on Musculoskeletal Diseases in the Aged, Scottsdale, AZ.

Brighton, C. (1985, March). *The use of electrical stimulation in the treatment of osteoporosis.* Paper presented at Them Ol' Bones II: A National Multidisciplinary Conference on Musculoskeletal Disease in the Aged, Phoenix, AZ.

Brody, E. (1985). *Mental and physical health practices of older people.* New York: Springer.

Brody, S. S. (1983, November). *The fractured hip: A multidisciplinary problem.* Symposium presented at the meetings of the Gerontological Society of America, San Francisco, CA.

Brown, J. W., & Sones, D. A. (1967). The onset of rheumatoid arthritis in the aged. *Journal of the American Geriatric Society, 15,* 873–881.

Ceder, L., Thorngren, K., et al. (1980). Prognostic indicators and early home rehabilitation in elderly patients with hip fractures. *Clinical Orthopaedics, 152,* 173.

Ehrlich, G. E., & Katz, W. A., (1970). Rheumatoid arthritis in the aged. *Geriatrics, 25,* 103–113.

Karpman, R. R. (1983, November). *Fractures of the hip in the elderly: A multidisciplinary approach.* Symposium presented at the meetings of the Gerontological Society of America, San Francisco, CA.

Karpman, R. R. (1980, November). *Total joint replacement: A comparison of morbidity between elderly and younger patients.* Paper presented at the meetings of the Gerontological Society of America, San Diego, CA.

Moesmann, G. (1969). Malignancy and mortality in subacute rheumatoid arthritis in old age. *Acta Rheumatica Scandinavica, 15,* 193–199.

Nickens, H. (1983). A review of factors affecting occurrence and outcome of hip fracture with special reference to psychosocial issues. *Journal of the American Geriatrics Society, 31,* 166–170.

Owen, R. R., Melton, L. J., Gallagher, J. C., et al. (1980). The national cost of the acute care of hip fractures associated with osteoporosis. *Clinical Orthopaedics and Related Research, 150,* 172.

Paganini-Hill, A., Ross, R. K., et al. (1981). Menopausal estrogen therapy and hip fractures. *Annuals of Internal Medicine, 95,* 28.

Reynolds, M. D. (1978). Prevalence of rheumatoid diseases as cause of disability and complaints by ambulatory patients. *Arthritis and Rheumatism, 21,* 377–382.

Steinberg, F., & Schuessler, P. (1986, March). *Decline of muscle strength and speed of contraction in aging women.* Paper presented at Them Ol' Bones III: A National Multidisciplinary Conference on Musculoskeletal Disease in the Aged, Phoenix, AZ.

Verbrugge, L. (1986, March). *Treatment of musculoskeletal symptoms on a day by day basis.* Paper presented at Them Ol' Bones III: A Multidisciplinary Conference on Musculoskeletal Diseases in the Aged, Phoenix, AZ.

Weiss, N. S., Nu, C. L., et al. (1980). Decreased risk of fractures of the hip and lower forearm with postmenopausal use of estrogen. *New England Journal of Medicine, 303,* 1195.

Chapter 13

Drug Use in the Geriatric Patient

Rubin Bressler

Elderly subjects have a higher incidence of medical and psychiatric disorders than the general adult population and, in response to signs and symptoms that are complex and confusing, are often treated with drugs (Fottrell, Sheikh, Kathari, & Sayed, 1976; Gibson, Mueeler, & Fisher, 1977; O'Malley, Judge, & Crooks, 1980; Vestal, 1978; Wilson, Lawson, & Braws, 1962).

The geriatric population has increased in recent years because of the medical factors that favor prolonged life. This increased lifespan, combined with decreasing birth rates, has resulted in an increased proportion of elderly people. In most economically developed countries, approximately 12% of the population is more than 65 years of age, and the percentage is increasing. A consequence of an increased geriatric population is the increased cost of health care. Studies have found that the elderly constitute 12% of the population, but incur 30% of the drug prescription costs (Achong, Bayne, Gerson, & Golshani, 1978; Fottrell et al., 1976; Gibson et al., 1977; O'Malley et al., 1980; Vestal, 1978; Wilson et al., 1962). The elderly population uses more drugs because of the greater incidence of chronic illness (Bender, 1974; Reichel, 1965; Seidl, Thornton, Smith, & Cluff, 1966). Moreover, a number of these illnesses are treated with multiple-drug therapy, which results in a potential for drug-drug interactions (Hurwitz, 1969; May, Stewart, & Cluff, 1977; Melmon, 1971; Morrelli & Melmon, 1978; Smith, Seidl, & Cluff, 1966). The

elderly experience considerably more adverse drug reactions (Hurwitz, 1969; Smith et al., 1966). A study of hospitalized patients showed that the 40- to 50-year-old age group experienced less than half the adverse drug reactions of the 70- to 80-year-old age group (7% to 12% vs. 12% to 25%) (Vestal, 1978).

In recent years, considerable attention has been focused on the factors influencing drug therapy in elderly patients. The increased frequency of adverse drug reactions in the elderly has resulted in a substantial literature on the effects of aging on pharmacokinetics (the time course of drug absorption, distribution, metabolism, and excretion), pharmacodynamics (the clinical aspects of response to a drug), and drug sensitivity, which has been studied less extensively (Crooks, O'Malley, & Stevenson, 1976; Richev & Bender, 1977; Triggs & Nation, 1975; Vestal, 1984).

The factors influencing adverse drug reactions include (a) impairment of pharmacokinetic systems resulting in higher blood and tissue levels of active drug; (b) decreases in homeostatic mechanisms, such as capacity to respond to postural changes, and changes in blood pressure, blood glucose, temperature, and cardiac output, which create difficulty in compensating for drug effects; and (c) changes in sensitivity, defined as diminished or augmented responses to a drug in the absence of changes in blood or tissue concentrations of the drug. These alterations may result

Table 13.1. Chronic Diseases at Different Ages

Chronic disease	INCIDENCE OF DISEASE			Significance of finding (p)
	67 patients 17–44 years (%)	68 patients 45–64 years (%)	62 patients 65 years and over (%)	
Hypertension	16.4	42.6	43.5	<0.001
Ischemic heart disease	1.5	10.3	24.2	<0.0005
Chronic lung disease	6.0	13.2	24.4	<0.01
Dementia	1.5	1.5	9.7	<0.05
Congestive heart failure	1.5	16.2	29.0	<0.001
Obesity	11.9	20.6	6.5	<0.05

Note. Adapted from *Current Concepts* (p. 13) by J. R. Bianchine et al., 1981, Kalamazoo, MI: Upjohn Co. Copyright 1981 by *Upjohn Co.*

from changes in drug binding at receptor sites or structural and/or functional alterations of the responsive tissue (Roberts & Goldberg, 1979; Roth, G. S., 1979; Shepherd, Hewick, Moreland, & Stevenson, 1977; Triggs & Nation, 1975).

Table 13.1 shows the incidence of a number of chronic diseases in various age categories (Bianchine, Gerber, & Andresen, 1981). It is obvious that there is a significant rise in the incidence of hypertension, ischemic heart disease, and congestive heart failure with increasing age (Bender, 1965; Harris, 1971, 1975; Lakatta, 1979). Cardiac hypertrophy in elderly people may be enhanced by increased peripheral vascular resistance (Bender, 1965; "Five-Year Findings," 1979; Port, Cobb, Coleman, & Jones, 1980). The heart of the elderly subject may have a limited response to exercise because of a decreased response to adrenergic stimulation, baroreceptor and sinus node inadequacies, and consequent inadequate compensatory reserve (Kendall, Woods, Wilkins, & Worthington, 1982; Lakatta, 1979).

In the industrialized nations of the West, the incidence of hypertension is high. The beneficial value of lowering elevated diastolic blood pressure in the elderly has been proven ("Five-Year Findings," 1979). The lowering of both diastolic and systolic blood pressures affords protection from the probability of death or disability from myocardial infarction, congestive heart failure, and cerebrovascular disease.

Cardiac diseases are frequent in the elderly. They include calcific aortic stenosis, mitral regurgitation, and disease of the sinus node. These problems are often dealt with by means of valve replacements, pacemaker placement, and drugs.

Cardiovascular diseases are a paramount threat to the elderly, possibly resulting in disability and premature death. These include congestive heart failure deriving from hypertension, coronary artery disease, or valvular dysfunction; angina pectoris caused by coronary artery disease and cardiac arrhythmias; and hypertension.

A number of pharmacological agents have brought symptomatic benefit and, in some instances, such as hypertension and the postmyocardial infarction period, have changed the natural history of the diseases ("Beta-Blocker," 1981).

Most adverse drug reactions in the elderly are not idiosyncratic. They are an extension of the expected effects of the drug. In order to understand the pathogenesis of the problem, the effects of aging on drug pharmacokinetics and pharmacodynamics are reviewed briefly in the following.

DRUG HANDLING IN THE ELDERLY

Drug Absorption

There are no substantial data to support a diminished or increased capacity for drug absorption from the gastrointestinal tract in the elderly (Crooks et al., 1976; O'Malley et al., 1980; Triggs & Nation, 1975; Vestal, 1978). Despite decreased intestinal blood flow, increased gastric pH, and decreased intestinal motility, drug absorption appears to be undiminished in the elderly. Although there is evidence of a decrease in active transport in the gastrointestinal tract of the elderly (galactose, 3-methylglucose, calcium, iron, thiamine), most drugs are absorbed by passive diffusion. Studies on the gastrointestinal absorption of sulfamethizole, acetaminophen, and phenylbutazone have not shown any significant age-related changes (Crooks et al., 1976; Richev & Bender, 1977; Triggs & Nation, 1975).

Alterations in drug absorption solely as a consequence of aging do not seem to be clinically significant. However, concomitant disease states and pharmacologic therapy of these states may result in disturbances in drug absorption. A number of drugs, such as anticholinergic agents and metoclopramide, influence gastrointestinal motility and possibly alter drug absorption quantitatively or temporally.

Drug Distribution

A number of age-related physiological changes may influence drug distribution. These changes include a decrease in lean body mass and water content and an increase in adipose tissue. The percentage of adipose tissue increases in elderly males (from 18% to 36%) and elderly females (from 33% to 48%) (Bender, 1965; Bianchine et al., 1981; Ouslander, 1981).

The increase in adipose tissue favors deposition of lipophilic drugs, such as diazepam and other long-acting benzodiazepines, as well as of digitoxin and synthetic steroids. Water-soluble drugs reach higher plasma levels in elderly patients because of the lesser quantity of body water into which the compound can distribute. A number of the commonly used drugs are water-soluble, including procainamide, quinidine, propranolol, theophylline, warfarin, and a number of sedative-hypnotics (O'Malley et al., 1980; Vestal, 1978, 1979, 1981).

Cardiac output may decrease in the elderly because of organic heart disease deriving from arteriosclerotic heart disease, hypertension or diabetes mellitus. This can result in a redistribution of a particular drug resulting from decreased visceral blood flow.

Drug distribution is quantified by relating the plasma concentration of a drug that results from a known total amount of drug in the body (Levy, 1978; Schmucker, 1979). The term to describe this relationship between the amount of drug in the body and that in the plasma is the *apparent volume of distribution* (V_D). It is not a true physiological space, but rather a value that indicates the magnitude of drug distribution out of the plasma. The apparent volume of distribution provides an estimate of the drug dose required to achieve a given plasma drug concentration at steady state. The distribution of a drug in the body is a function of the drug's distribution into tissues and the affinity of the tissues for the drug. At therapeutic drug doses, tissue and plasma drug binding sites are not saturated, and therefore the volume and the drug affinity of each tissue are effectively independent of drug concentration.

At steady state the following equation holds:

$$LD = C_{SS} = V_D$$

Where LD is the loading dose (amount of drug in the body), C_{SS} represents the plasma drug concentration at a steady state, and V_D is the volume of distribution.

If the V_D of a drug is known (from pharmacology textbooks) then the loading dose (LD) needed to achieve a desired steady-state plasma concentration of the drug can be readily ascertained: Examples follow.

1. *Oral procainamide:* $\quad C_{SS} = 4\ mg/L$
$\qquad\qquad\qquad\quad V_D = 150\ L/70\ kg\ man$
$\qquad\qquad\qquad\quad$ Oral availability, 0.85
$\quad LD = C_{SS} \times V_D$
$\qquad\quad = 4\ mg/L \times 150\ L \times \dfrac{1}{0.85}$
$\qquad\quad = 660\ mg\ orally$

2. *Intravenous digoxin:* $\quad C_{SS} = 1\ \mu g/L$
$\qquad\qquad\qquad\quad V_D = 700\ L/70\ kg\ man$
$\qquad\qquad\qquad\quad$ IV availability, 1.0
$\quad LD = C_{SS} \times V_D$
$\qquad\quad = 1\ \mu g/L \times 700\ L$
$\qquad\quad = 700\ \mu g, or\ 0.70\ mg,\ IV$

3. *Oral thephylline:* $\quad C_{SS} = 15\ mg/L$
$\qquad\qquad\qquad\quad V_D = 40\ L/70\ kg\ man$
$\qquad\qquad\qquad\quad$ Oral availability, 1.0
$\quad LD = C_{SS} \times V_D$
$\qquad\quad = 15\ mg/L \times 40\ L$
$\qquad\quad = 600\ mg\ orally$

Attainment of a steady-state plasma level of a drug given repeatedly at a fixed dose requires around five half-lives of drug dosing. If the time required to reach steady state is not long relative to the efficacy requirements of the disease state being treated, then a loading dose is not necessary. This is generally the situation in the treatment of hypertension and diabetes mellitus. However, when drug effect is needed rapidly, as in cardiac arrhythmias or asthmatic episodes, then waiting five drug half-lives is not optimal therapy. For example, the oral administration of procainamide without a loading dose would take 15 hours to reach a steady state plasma level, whereas digoxin would take 5 days. In the case of both drugs, a parenteral or oral loading dose would rapidly produce a steady-state plasma drug level and more immediate efficacy.

Congestive heart failure is associated with significant decreases in the volume of distribution and the clearance rates of drugs (Halkin, Meffin, Melmon, & Rowland, 1975; Thomson, 1974; Thomson,

Melmon, Richardson, Cohn, Steinbrunn, & Cudihee, 1973). Recent studies have established that loading doses of lidocaine, procainamide, quinidine, and theophylline should be decreased by at least one-third in patients with significant congestive heart failure (Halkin et al., 1975; Stenson, Constantino, & Harrison, 1971; Thomson et al., 1973). Furthermore, maintenance doses of these drugs (as well as other drugs eliminated by the liver) need to be reduced in the presence of congestive heart failure, because of decreased biotransformation and resultant prolonged half-life caused by decreased blood flow to the liver and impairment of hepatic function (Thomson, 1974; Thomson et al., 1973).

Protein Binding of Drugs

Plasma protein-bound drugs are inactive. They are mainly bound to serum albumin. Drug binding is a function of plasma albumin concentrations and the acidic nature of the drug. Free drug concentration is an important determinant of drug distribution and elimination. Alterations in the bindings of drugs to plasma proteins, red blood cells, and other body tissues may be important causes of altered pharmacokinetics in elderly patients. Serum albumin is slightly reduced in old age. One study compared serum protein concentrations in 50 young normal adults (average age 27 years) with those in 90 elderly subjects (aged 65 to 103 years). There was essentially no difference in total serum protein. However, the younger subjects had a 20% greater plasma albumin concentration than the older subjects (Cammarata, Rodnan, & Fennell, 1967).

Alterations in the binding of drugs to plasma proteins are responsible for some adverse effects in the elderly. It is a common clinical finding, for example, that a narcotic dose needs to be reduced in the elderly patient because of increased sensitivity to respiratory depressant effects. In a time study of meperidine plasma concentration following intravenous injection in surgical patients and normals (Mather, Tucker, Pflug, Lindop, & Wilkerson, 1975), the older patients had higher unbound (free) drug fractions. It was found that the diminished warfarin-binding capacity in the elderly was proportional to lower plasma albumin levels (Hayes, Langman, & Short, 1975). Several studies have documented a significant reduction in serum albumin in healthy subjects over 50 years of age (Bender, Post, Meirer, Higson, & Reichard, 1975). Chronic illness can further lower plasma protein levels. The resultant reduced drug binding allows more unbound (free) drug to be available for distribution to body tissues, causing enhanced drug effects. Drugs that are highly protein-bound include warfarin, phenytoin, furosemide, and antidiabetic sulfonylureas.

Because elderly patients have reduced concentrations of serum albumin, they are more susceptible to the effects of multiple drug therapy on drug binding.

In the elderly patient a decrease in serum albumin may not result in lower concentrations of unbound active drug. A number of drugs are extensively bound to plasma proteins (80% or more), and although decreased levels of serum albumin may result in depressed total plasma levels of drugs like warfarin, propranolol, quinidine, phenytoin, and tolbutamide, their unbound concentrations may be in the therapeutically active range (Levy & Moreland, 1984). Because most laboratories report total plasma drug levels, one can be misled by a slightly depressed, but therapeutically effective plasma drug concentration. Renal disease, with its decreased serum albumin and its frequent acidosis, is a clinical state where drug binding is characteristically decreased.

REGIONAL BLOOD FLOW

Changes in regional blood flow can significantly alter the way drugs affect patients, affecting distribution, metabolism, and excretion. It is known that, in general, peripheral circulation decreases with advancing age, whereas coronary and cerebral flows are better maintained. Certain diseases are known to be associated with increased or decreased regional blood flow, as evidenced by the decreased hepatic and renal flow in patients with congestive heart failure and the increased joint flow in patients with arthritis.

In addition to disease states, age itself is associated with changes in regional blood flows, and this may be related to some of the age-related changes in pharmacologic response. This aspect of age-dependent pharmacology deserves further investigation, because little information exists. Local blood flow is controlled by a multitude of local and remote elements, including vasoconstrictor and vasodilator nerves, blood flow, excitatory and inhibitory factors, local tissue metabolites, and positive feedback from blood pressure stretch receptors (Bender, 1974; Crooks et al., 1976; Ouslander, 1981; Triggs & Nation, 1975; Vestal, 1978).

Cardiac output decreases in the aged because of a number of disease states affecting the heart (Bianchine et al., 1981); a preferential distribution of blood flow to the brain, heart, and muscle occurs at the expense of the blood flow to the liver and kidneys. Reduced hepatic blood flow may limit active drug clearance and metabolism (Lakatta, 1979; Nies, Shand, & Wilkinson, 1976). Reduced renal blood flow decreases the removal of active pharmacological agents via glomerular filtration and tubular secretion (McLachlan, 1978; Weiner, 1971). Tissue permeation and storage of drugs may increase with age. It has been shown that less local anesthetic is required to block a given area in the elderly than in the young. One could speculate that distribution is altered with increasing age, but in precisely what manner is not known (Bender, 1974; Crooks et al., 1976; Triggs & Nation, 1975; Vestal, 1978).

DECREASED HOMEOSTATIC MECHANISMS

Age decrements are more marked in physiological adjustments that require the integrated activity of several organ systems than in those that involve a single system (Gillette, 1979; Sellers, Frecher, & Romach, 1983; Vestal, 1978, 1979). The impairments of renal, hepatic, cardiac, respiratory, neuromuscular, and endocrine vitality with aging result in a slower rate of recovery following a variety of physiological displacements (Finch, 1979; Roberts & Goldberg, 1979; Roth, G. S., 1979). Aging is characterized by a diminution of the adaptive capacity to a variety of inputs. The reduced homeostatic responses of the elderly result in adverse drug reactions that may be compensated for in the younger patient. Decreased cardiac outputs, lowered plasma volumes, diminished vasomotor controls, and decreased glucose tolerance all give rise to a greater frequency of adverse reactions in response to a variety of drugs. Moreover, the elderly are frequently afflicted with several chronic diseases that may necessitate multiple-drug therapy (Bressler, 1982a; Reichel, 1965; Vestal, 1982).

The impaired homeostatic capacity, multiple chronic illnesses, and multiple-drug therapy afford greater opportunity for adverse drug reactions. Because of decreased capacity for cardiovascular homeostasis, elderly patients are more prone to postural hypotension secondary to the use of diuretics, sympatholytics, nitrates, phenothiazines, tricyclic antidepressants, quinidine, procainamide,

and antihypertensive drugs (Bressler, 1982b; Vestal, 1982). Adverse drug reactions are also more common in the elderly because of the multiplicity of drugs required, their long-term use, and the occurrence of drug-drug interactions.

The inability to respond normally to postural changes, changes in blood pressure, blood glucose, temperature, or augmentation of cardiac output with exercise may create difficulty in compensating for drug effects (Rodeheffer, Gerstenblith, Becker, Fleg, Weisfeldt, & Lakatta, 1984). It has long been recognized that plasma norepinephrine levels are increased with age. In contrast, plasma epinephrine levels are unchanged (Pfeifer, Weinberg, Cook, Best, Reenan, & Halter, 1983). Recently, it was shown that both the sympathetic response and the parasympathetic response of the iris are reduced with age. These findings, coupled with observations of diet-associated hypotension, suggest that baroreceptor function is reduced in the elderly (Gerstenblith, Lakatta, & Weisfeldt, 1976; Learoyd, 1972; Pfeifer et al., 1983).

Elderly patients experience adverse drug reactions even with the most careful medical care. Sedative-hypnotics depress mentation and cerebral circulation, resulting in manifold mental and physical changes. The combination of alcohol, barbiturates, and tranquilizers is poorly tolerated by elderly subjects (Learoyd, 1972; Sellers et al., 1983; Vestal, McGuire, Tobin, Andres, Norris, & Mezey, 1977).

Hallucinations and other forms of disturbed cerebral function, as well as glaucoma or urinary retention, may follow the administration of antiparkinsonian, sympathomimetic, or anticholinergic drugs (Conrad & Bressler, 1984; Hollister, 1973; Learoyd, 1972; Saltzman Shader & Van der Kolk 1976; Thompson, Moran, & Nies, 1983). An apparent suicide may be, in fact, an accidental death, when sedatives have been prescribed injudiciously or if they are taken repeatedly by an increasingly confused aged person.

A general rule of therapeutics is that the correct dose for every patient should be empirically determined. In the elderly, it is especially important to individualize therapy. When one deals with such patients, unusual responses, including tolerance, hypersensitivity, and toxicity, should all be suspected and carefully evaluated.

DRUG ELIMINATION

Drug elimination by any means is quantitatively described in terms of the clearance of the drug from the body. Elimination routes are primarily via the kidney and liver. The removal of a drug by these organs can be described by the product of the blood flow to the organ and the extraction ration of the drug by the organ (Nies et al., 1976; Rowland, 1984; Rowland 1978; Weiner, 1971) as follows:

Organ Clearance = Blood flow to the organ × Extraction ratio of drug

In general, the kidneys and liver have sufficient capacity to eliminate therapeutic plasma levels of drugs presented to them. Thus, clearance is independent of plasma drug concentration. This would of course not be true with parenchymal organ damage or drug overdoses.

The extraction ratio is independent of plasma drug concentration. Quantitative drug elimination is a function of blood flow through the liver and/or kidney and the overall metabolic (liver) or transport (kidney) systems that effect drug elimination (intrinsic organ clearance).

If the intrinsic clearance of a drug is large, then its clearance by the liver or kidney is a function of blood flow to the organ. Such drugs are said to have blood flow limited clearance. If the intrinsic clearance is small, then drug clearance is independent of blood flow. These drugs are said to have capacity limited clearance (Nies et al., 1976; Roland, 1984; Vestal Wood, Branch, Shand, & Wilkinson, 1979; Wood, Vestal, Wilkinson, Branch, & Shand, 1979).

Linearity in pharmacokinetics is generally found with drug use in the therapeutic dose range. However, with increasing doses of drugs, simultaneous use of multiple drugs, and/or decreased concentrations of serum albumin nonlinearity may occur. This can cause non predictable changes in the dose-response characteristics of a drug resulting in increased drug plasma levels and/or drug effects.

RENAL EXCRETION OF DRUGS

Compounds of low lipid solubility are readily excreted by the kidneys, and their rate of elimination is primarily dependent on the glomerular filtration rate (Davies & Shock, 1950; McLachlan, 1978; Moholm-Hansen, Kampmann & Larsen, 1970; Rowe, Andres, Tobin, Norris, & Shock, 1976; Weiner, 1971). Highly lipid-soluble drugs are reabsorbed by the renal tubule, and their elimination is effected by conversion to a more water-soluble derivative via oxidative metabolism cata-

lyzed by the microsomal drug-metabolizing enzymes of the liver and then renal excretion of the metabolite (Roland, 1984). The kidney plays an important role in the elimination of active drugs from the body and is a determinant of blood and tissue levels of drugs. Renal excretion of drugs can be altered by changes in renal blood flow, glomerular filtration rate, tubular secretion, or reabsorption.

A number of studies have demonstrated a decline in renal function with aging (Davies & Shock, 1950; Moholm-Hansen et al., 1970; Rowe et al., 1976). Because of the diminished muscle mass and decreased creatinine production, serum creatinine is not an accurate measure of glomerular filtration rate in the elderly. Creatinine clearance may be estimated using the following formula:

$$\text{Creatinine clearance} = \frac{(140 - \text{Age})}{72} \times \frac{\text{Weight in kg}}{\text{Serum creatinine mg/dL}}$$

This equation applies to males only, the product should be multiplied by 0.85 for women (Cockroft & Gault, 1976).

It has been shown that renal blood flow and tubular secretion also decline with age proportionately to creatinine clearance. A linear relationship obtains in the elderly between creatinine clearance and the renal clearance of drugs, whether the medications are filtered (procainamide) or secreted (digoxin).

A progressive reduction in the number of functioning nephrons and the decrease in plasma flow to the kidneys with increasing age have been demonstrated to produce a significant decrease in renal function. Between the ages 20 and 90, renal plasma flow decrease by about 53% and the glomerular filtration rate (as measured by inulin clearance) decreases by about 46% (Davies & Shock, 1950; Moholm-Hansen et al., 1970; Rowe et al., 1976). The maximum capacity of the renal tubules for both reabsorption and secretion shows approximately the same percentage change with age, probably reflecting the reduction in absorbing and secreting surfaces. The general reduction in renal function with age is reflected by a decrease in creatinine clearance; however, it is not reflected by a change in serum creatinine. This latter observation is probably a consequence of decreased creatinine production with age (Cockroft & Gault, 1976; Rowe et al., 1976).

One study of 249 patients found that 24-hour

Table 13.2. The Excretion of Digoxin in Young and
Elderly Subjects

Group	Number	Age (years)	Digoxin clearance (ml/min per 1.73 m^2)	Blood half-life (hr)
Young	9	27 ± 4	83 ± 17	51
Old	5	77 ± 4	53 ± 9	73

Note. Adapted from "Digoxin Metabolism in the Elderly" by
Ewy et al., 1960, *Circulation, 39*, pp. 449–453. Copyright 1969 by
American Heart Association, Inc.

creatinine excretion decreases by 50% from the
third to the ninth decade of life (Vartia & Leikola,
1960). Thus, a "normal" serum creatinine of 1 mg
may correspond to a creatinine clearance of 120
mL/min at age 20 but only 60 mL/min at age 80
(Rowe et al., 1976). For drugs with both a narrow
therapeutic index and primarily renal elimination
(digoxin, procainamide, gentamicin), downward
dose adjustment should be considered. The effects
of a decreased secretory capacity on plasma drug
concentration are shown by the pronounced effects
of probenecid (a drug that blocks the tubular secretion of certain drugs) in raising the plasma levels
of penicillin. Studies in man have shown that the
plasma levels of a number of antibiotics that are
renally excreted are higher in elderly patients. The
decrement in renal function in older persons may
range from 20% to 59% (Davies & Shock 1950;
Rowe et al., 1976).

It has long been known that elderly patients
may develop toxic effects when given the usual
therapeutic doses of drugs. Increased tissue sensitivity in the aged was previously proposed but
recent evidence favors impaired renal, hepatic and
homeostatic functions as the cause of adverse
responses to drugs in the elderly (Ouslander, 1981;
Vestal, 1982). Decreased renal functions result in
inordinately high blood levels of drugs when administered to elderly patients in the usual therapeutic
doses. Typical studies are shown in Tables 13.2
and 13.3, in which drugs eliminated by the kidneys
were studied in control and geriatric groups.

Generally renal dysfunction secondary to age
and disease brings about proportional decreases in
the three processes that constitute renal clearance:
glomerular filtration, tubular secretion, and passive reabsorption. Renal dysfunction impairs the
excretion of drugs handled in different ways by the
kidney (Crooks et al., 1976). These include gentamicin (filtered unbound drug), penicillin (tubular
secretion of bound drug), and furosemide (combination of both).

Digoxin Dosing in a Patient with Renal Disease

Usually, digoxin clearance is 70% renal and
30% non-renal. A patient whose creatinine clearance is 10% of normal would need digoxin dose
adjustment. Total body digoxin clearance would
be the sum of the non-renal and renal clearances:
30% nonrenal + 10% of 70% renal clearance. The
patient's digoxin clearance is only 37% of normal.
The patient's dose could either be cut to one third
of the usual daily dose, or the usual adult dose
could be given every third day.

A number of disease states further impair renal
function in the elderly and the renal clearance of
drugs. These include hypertension, the nephropathies of diabetes mellitus, and the glomerulo-
nephropathies. Congestive heart failure commonly
reduces renal blood flow, and diuretic therapy can
decrease intravascular volume and impair renal
function.

HEPATIC DRUG METABOLISM IN THE ELDERLY

Drugs and other xenobiotics are metabolized by
the enzyme systems of the liver and, to a lesser
extent, of the kidney, lung, and gastrointestinal
tract. These enzyme systems convert lipid-soluble
(nonpolar) compounds to more water-soluble ones
(polar compounds that may be pharmacologically
more or less active but are usually more readily
excreted by the kidney) (Bressler, 1982a; Gillette,
1979; Wood et al., 1979).

Animal data and some indirect studies in
humans have suggested that aging is associated
with a reduced capacity to metabolize certain
drugs. There is little firm evidence for many clinically significant reductions in drug metabolizing
activity in healthy elderly subjects. The liver is
about 2.5% of the body weight until middle age;
then it decreases to around 1.6% with aging
(Geokas & Haverback, 1979; Rasmussen, Hansen,
Kampmann, Skovstad, & Bach, 1976). This represents a 36% decrement in size, with an anticipated decrease in the liver's capacity to metabolize
drugs.

The reduction of liver size and the accompanying decrease in hepatic blood flow are superimposed on the genetically based large variations in
drug metabolism found in the elderly population.
A decline in hepatic blood flow of 40% to 45%
occurs between the ages of 25 and 65. This may be

Table 13.3 Renal Excretion of Penicillin in the Elderly According to Sex and Age Groups

	Men (age 50–70)		Women (age 30–65)	
Number of patients	9	18	7	8
Creatinine clearance (ml/min)	93.2	40.3	112.0	61.4
Penicillin half-life (min)	23.7	55.5	20.7	39.1

Note. Adapted from "Renal Excretion of Drugs in the Elderly" by Moholm-Hansen et al., 1970, *Lancet, i*, p. 1170. Copyright 1970 by *Lancet.*

due in part to decreases in cardiac output (Brandfonbrener, Landowne, & Shock, 1955; Harris, 1975; Nies et al., 1976; Stenson et al., 1971). Individualization of dosing schedules is important in the elderly because of these considerations.

The results of routine measurements of liver function, that is, serum bilirubin, liver enzymes, and alkaline phosphates, do not change with age alone. Nor are the hepatic enzyme systems that are responsible for drug oxidation, reduction, hydrolysis, and conjugation reactions altered predictably. On the one hand, studies of antipyrine and propranolol suggest that the ability of cigarette smoke to stimulate or induce the enzymes responsible for the metabolism of these drugs is reduced in the elderly. On the other hand, cigarette smoking reportedly continues to induce hepatic metabolism of theophylline in the elderly (Kornhauser, Wood, Vestal, Wilkinson, Branch, & Shand, 1978; Vestal, 1984; Vestal, Wood, & Shand, 1979; Vestal, Norris, Tobin, Cohen, Shock, & Andres, 1975; Wood et al., 1979).

Important changes in the hepatic clearance of diazepam, chlordiazepoxide, desmethyldiazepam, desalkylflurazepam, alprazolam, quinidine, propranolol, and nortriptyline have been described in the elderly (Table 13.4). More significant reductions in the clearance of diazepam, desmethyldiazepam, desalkyflurazepam, and alprazolam occur in men than in women, although data have been conflicting (Greenblatt, Sellers, & Shader, 1982; Thompson et al., 1983). No significant changes are found in the clearance of oxazepam, lorazepam, temazepam, warfarin, lidocaine, isoniazid, ethanol, metoprolol, or digitoxin. Conflicting data are reported for acetaminophen, imipramine, phenytoin, theophylline, and amobarbital (Bianchine, 1981).

Congestive heart failure may produce important alterations in both hepatic and renal drug elimination. It has been shown that hepatic drug metabolizing activity may be impaired in patients with congestive heart failure (Hepner, Vessel & Tantum,

1978; Kessler, Lowenthal, Warner, Gibson, Briggs, & Reidenberg, 1974; Thomson, 1974; Thomson et al., 1973). A 75% reduction in the metabolic clearance rate of aminopyrine has also been shown, attributed to reduced enzyme

Table 13.4. Relation of Age to Drug clearance by Hepatic Biotransformation

Drug or Metabolite	Initial Pathway of Biotransformation
Evidence suggesting age-related reduction in clearance	
Antipyrine	Oxidation (OH, DA)
Diazepam	Oxidation (DA)
Chlordiazepoxide	Oxidation (DA)
Desmethyldiazepam	Oxidation (OH)
Desalkylflurazepam	Oxidation (OH)
Alprazolam	Oxidation (OH)
Quinidine	Oxidation (OH)
Propranolol	Oxidation (OH)
Nortriptyline	Oxidation (OH)
Small or negligible age-related change in clearance	
Oxazepam	Glucuronidation
Lorazepam	Glucuronidation
Temazepam	Glucuronidation
Warfarin	Oxidation (OH)
Lidocaine	Oxidation (DA)
Isoniazid	Acetylation
Ethanol	Oxidation (alcohol dehydrogenase)
Metoprolol	Oxidation
Digitoxin	Oxidation
Prazosin	Oxidation
Data conflicting or not definitive	
Meperidine	Oxidation (DA)
Phenylbutazone	Oxidation (OH)
Phenytoin	Oxidation (OH)
Imipramine	Oxidation (OH, DA)
Amitriptyline	Oxidation (OH, DA)
Acetaminophen	Glucuronidation, sulfation
Amobarbital	Oxidation (OH)
Theophylline	Oxidation

Note. From "Drug Disposition in Old Age" by D. J. Greenblatt, E. M. Sellers, and R. I. Shader, 1983, in J. Koch-Weser (Ed.), "Drug Therapy" (special issue), *New England Journal of Medicine, 306*, p. 1088. Copyright 1983 by the *New England Journal of Medicine.*

activity. Congestive heart failure is associated with a reduction in lidocaine clearance, probably because of both reduced hepatic blood flow and reduced hepatic enzyme activity (Hepner et al., 1978). Reductions in quinidine and theophylline clearance occur in heart failure (Kessler et al., 1974; Thomson, 1974; Thomson et al., 1973). Both quinidine and theophylline have low hepatic clearances; for such drugs, changes in hepatic blood flow per se would not be expected to alter hepatic drug clearance unless enzyme activity was affected as well.

Although the disposition of several hepatically metabolized drugs has been determined, interindividual variability in hepatic metabolism is great in elderly patients. For that reason, when one is prescribing a drug with a narrow therapeutic index, the best approach is to make use of pharmacokinetic information from the literature to estimate the initial dose and to confirm this estimate by checking plasma drug concentrations at steady state, or sooner if toxicity or inadequate responses demands it.

PHARMACODYNAMIC CHANGES IN THE ELDERLY

The literature on drug responses in the elderly has focused on pharmacokinetics because of the greater ease of quantifying these changes. However, changes in pharmacodynamics also occur in the elderly and may be an important factor in drug-drug interactions and drug responses.

Increased Sensitivity with Age

Increased sensitivity to the benzodiazepines has been reported in the elderly. For example, lower dose and lower plasma concentration of diazepam are required to produce central nervous system depression prior to cardioversion and endoscopy (Figure 13.1). Increased sensitivity to nitrazepam has been described (Castleden, George, Marcer, & Hallet, 1977). Both diazepam and chlordiazepoxide reportedly produce a greater *degree* of sedation in elderly patients than in younger ones (Learoyd, 1972; Ouslander, 1981; Reidenberg et al., 1978; Thompson et al., 1983). Cigarette smoking appears to reduce the incidence of central nervous system activity, even though it does not alter benzodiazepine kinetics. The increased incidence of central nervous system toxicity in elderly patients who receive flurazepam in doses of 30 mg or more daily is well documented (Greenblatt, Allen, & Shader, 1977).

Studies indicate a greater anticoagulant response in elderly patients to warfarin at any given dose or plasma concentration (O'Malley, Stevenson, Ward, Wood, & Crookes, 1977).

Decreased Sensitivity with Age

Elderly patients are less sensitive to the effects of infused isoproterenol (Figure 13.2). Almost 5 times the amount of isoproterenol is required to produce a 25-beat increase in the resting heart rate in patients aged 70 years as opposed to those aged 20. Similarly, the effectiveness of propranolol also diminishes with age (Figure 13.3). Because most investigators report normal β-receptor numbers with age, it is presumed that these results reflect a possible reduced receptor sensitivity.

A reduced renal response to furosemide has been observed in the elderly despite an increase in the plasma levels of this drug (Kerremans, Tan, Van Baars, Van Ginneken, & Gribnau, 1983). This occurs because of a decrease in the glomerular filtration of electrolytes and water in the elderly, as well as a reduction in renal furosemide secretion. If renal disease is also present, an even greater reduction of furosemide effects would be expected.

DRUG USE IN THE ELDERLY PATIENT

The optimal therapy of the geriatric patient with cardiovascular disease requires that drugs be used only when specifically indicated, only when the benefit-to-risk ratio is favorable, and only after the pharmacokinetic and pharmacodynamic factors altered by age and disease have been considered.

Elderly patients requiring specific therapy may be afflicted with multiple diseases—arteriosclerotic heart diseases, cardiac arrhythmias, hypertension, diabetes mellitus, and cerebrovascular disease—necessitating multiple treatment, which can engender drug interactions. Adverse drug reactions in the elderly may occur because of decreased compensatory responses to drug actions, which may magnify minor excesses of drug actions.

Specific examples of drug use in the elderly are presented below.

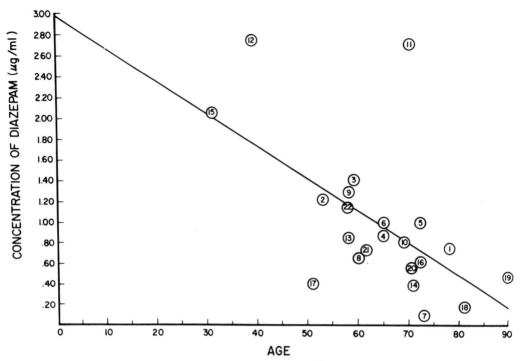

Figure 13.1. Relationship between age of patient and plasma concentration of diazepam that causes failure to respond to vocal but not to painful stimuli. (From: "Relationship Between Diazepam Dose, Plasma Level, Age, and Central Nervous Depression" by M. M. Reidenberg et al., 1978, *Clinical Pharmacology and Therapeutics*, 23, p. 374. Copyright 1978 by C. V. Mosby. Reprinted by permission.)

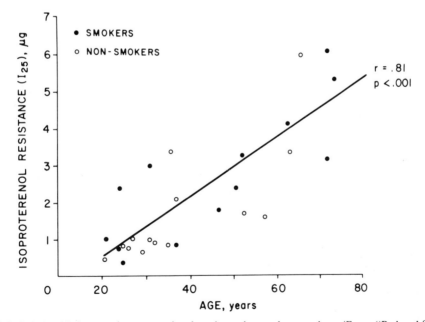

Figure 13.2. Relationship between isoproterenol and age in smokers and nonsmokers. (From: "Reduced β-Adrenoreceptor Sensitivity in the Elderly" by R. E. Vestal, A. J. J. Wood, and D. G. Shand, 1979, *Clinical Pharmacology and Therapeutics*, 26, p. 183. Copyright 1979 by C. M. Mosby. Reprinted by permission.)

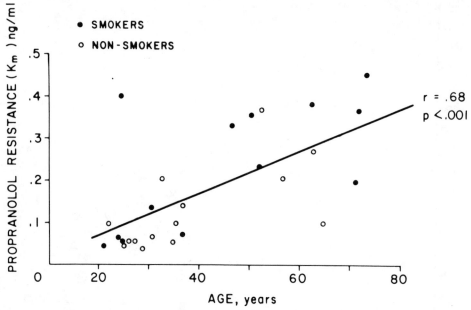

Figure 13.3. Relationship between propranolol resistance and age in smokers and nonsmokers. (From: "Reduced β-Adrenoreceptor Sensitivity in the Elderly" by R. E. Vestal, A. J. J. Wood, and D. G. Shand, 1979, *Clinical Pharmacology and Therapeutics, 26,* p. 184. Copyright 1979 by C. V. Mosby. Reprinted by permission.)

Digitalis Glycosides

Ten to 15% of hospitalized and nursing home patients receive a cardiac glycoside (Carter, Small, & Garnett, 1981). The incidence of adverse effects from chronic digitalis therapy is 15 to 20% (Merry, Lowe, Larson, & Writing, 1981). The risk of digitalis toxicity in the elderly can be reduced by carefully selecting patients before prescribing digitalis; by being aware of altered dosing requirements, drug interactions, and concomitant illness; and by recognizing the multiple manifestations of digitalis intoxication.

Altered Pharmacokinetics and Dosing Requirements in the Elderly

Oral digoxin is distributed extensively to body tissues at a relatively slow rate, over a period of 6 hours. Kidney, cardiac muscle, and liver avidly bind digoxin, but the largest depot is skeletal muscle. One cause of increased digoxin serum concentration is the decrease in muscle mass with age (Ewy, Kapadia, Yao, Lullin, & Marcus, 1969). It has been shown that serum digoxin concentration in elderly patients is nearly twice that in younger subjects given the same dose intravenously. It has also been shown that the digoxin volume of distribution is reduced by 40% in the elderly, suggest-

ing the use of smaller doses (Cusack, Morgan, Kelly, Lavan, Noel, & O'Malley, 1978).

The decline in the glomerular filtration rate with advanced age results in a decrease in digoxin clearance (Table 13.2) (Cusack et al., 1978; Ewy et al., 1969). Since muscle mass is also reduced, lower doses of digoxin should be used in geriatric patients even if the serum creatinine is normal.

The reduction in the glomerular filtration rate does not significantly alter the half-life of digitoxin. Digitoxin is eliminated primarily by hepatic metabolism, a process that is not significantly altered in the elderly (Donovan, Castleden, Pohl, & Kraft, 1981).

A loading dose of digoxin should be avoided if possible. It is needed only in the recent onset of atrial fibrillation with a rapid ventricular response and in acute heart failure states.

Drugs Affecting Digitalis Pharmacokinetics

Because certain drug interactions cause digoxin toxicity, it is important to be aware of these. Quinidine reduces digoxin total body clearance, renal clearance, and volume of distribution, producing a two fold rise in serum digoxin concentration (Fenster, Powell, Graves, Hager, Wandell, & Conrad, 1980; Fichtl & Doering, 1983; Hager et al., 1979). Although it is difficult to determine which drug is the culprit, toxicity may be avoided by halving the digoxin dose prior to adding quinidine. If necessary, the digoxin dose may be increased later.

In addition, the reduction of total body clearance of digitoxin by quinidine prolongs the half-life, of the former even at relatively low serum quinidine concentrations (Fenster et al., 1980). Therefore, the digitoxin dose should be lowered prior to the addition of quinidine.

The calcium channel blocker verapamil reduces both the renal clearance and the non renal clearance of digoxin and prolongs the digoxin elimination half-life with a rise in serum digoxin. The resulting depression of atrioventricular nodal conduction may be clinically useful for treating atrioventricular nodal reentrant rhythms or in slowing the ventricular response to atrial fibrillation. However, there exists the risk of atrioventricular nodal block.

Spironolactone blocks the renal tubular secretion of digoxin, decreases digoxin non renal clearance, and reduces the volume of distribution of digoxin. The magnitude of these effects is comparable to that of quinidine.

Beta Blockers

Beta-adrenergic blocking agents are useful in the management of hypertension, angina pectoris, arrhythmias, migraine, and benign tremors. They reduce mortality during 1 to 3 years following myocardial infarction. In the Beta Blocker Heart Attack Trials (a multi-hospital study), the 2-year post infarction mortality among patients 60 to 70 years of age was 9.6% in those receiving propranolol, significantly less than the 14.4% mortality in the matched placebo-treated group ("Beta-Blocker," 1981). Thus, in the absence of contraindications, beta blockers should be prescribed to patients soon after myocardial infarction.

Cardiac responsiveness to beta-receptor stimulation is diminished in elderly individuals, as is the chronotropic response to isoproterenol (Yin, Spurgeon, Raizes, Greene, Weisfeldt, & Shock, 1976). The cardiac response to peripheral vasodilation is also blunted (Kendall et al., 1982), so that compensatory mechanisms to maintain blood pressure in response to postural changes or drug administration are less effective. A consequence of this diminished beta-adrenergic sensitivity is a reduction in the cardiac effects of a given plasma concentration of propranolol. One study showed that

increased doses of isoproterenol were required to raise the pulse rate after intravenous propranolol (Vestal, 1979), and the effectiveness of any given free plasma concentration of propranolol diminished variably but progressively with age.

This suggests that larger doses of beta-blocking agents are required in the elderly than in younger patients, but this is not necessarily the case. Greater plasma levels of propranolol are found in elderly subjects, compared to younger individuals, after a single oral dose (Castleden, Kay, & Parsons, 1975). This appears to be due to an increased bioavailability secondary to decreased intrinsic clearance by hepatic metabolism and to slower distribution to the tissues. Beta blockers should therefore be prescribed cautiously in elderly patients. Doses should be low initially, then slowly increased as needed. However, elderly subjects are less sensitive to the effects of beta-blocking agents, thereby lessening overdose problems.

Differences in pharmacokinetic properties may help in choosing the most appropriate beta blocker. Propranolol, metoprolol, and timolol are extensively metabolized in the liver. Their dose should be substantially reduced in patients with cirrhosis or other intrinsic liver disease and in patients with decreased liver blood flow because of reduced cardiac output. In contrast, atenolol and nadolol are eliminated primarily by renal excretion. They may be preferred in the presence of liver disease but should be used cautiously when renal impairment is present. These two beta blockers have long elimination half-lifes and are effective when given only once daily.

Atenolol and metoprolol are relatively cardioselective beta blockers. They should be used with caution, in low doses, in patients with reactive airways disease if blockade of cardiac beta receptors is of importance. However, at higher doses the cardioselective effect is lost and bronchospasm may occur.

Lidocaine

Acute myocardial infarction accompanied by ectopy often requires the use of lidocaine, but most studies demonstrating its beneficial effect have excluded patients over 70 years of age. In fact, elderly patients may have a lower incidence of ventricular fibrillation in acute myocardial infarction (DeSilva, Lown, Hennekens, & Casscells, 1981). The elderly are sensitive to the adverse central nervous system effects of lidocaine, including drowsiness, confusion, and seizures. Therefore, the risk-to-benefit ratio should be considered prior to administering lidocaine routinely to elderly patients with acute myocardial infarction. In patients with normal liver function, approximately 70% of the drug is metabolized during a single portal circulation (Pond & Tozer, 1984; Rowland, Blaschke, Meffin, & Williams, 1976; Williams, 1983). Therefore, the kinetics are sensitive to changes in either hepatic blood flow or function.

In one study, the volume of distribution of lidocaine was shown to be significantly greater in elderly patients than in young males (1.59 L/Kg vs. 0.90 L/Kg) (Nation, Triggs, & Selig, 1977). The half-life was 140 minutes in the elderly, significantly longer than the 80 minutes in the younger subjects. However, the plasma clearance of lidocaine was not significantly different in the two groups, suggesting that lidocaine doses need not be altered in the elderly. This rule applies to patients with normal cardiac and hepatic function.

Because congestive heart failure is associated with reduced hepatic blood flow and increased lidocaine blood levels (Collinsworth, Strong, Atkinson, Winkle, Perlroth, & Harrison, 1975; Halkin et al., 1975; Stenson et al., 1971), the dose should be lowered. Beta blockers may decrease cardiac output and hepatic blood flow and thereby decrease lidocaine clearance. In renal failure, lidocaine metabolism is unaltered, but the metabolites of lidocaine are excreted in the urine and accumulate in the blood of renal failure patients (Collinsworth et al., 1975). These compounds are pharmacologically active and may contribute to lidocaine toxicity. The dose of lidocaine should be reduced in elderly subjects with decreased renal function.

Quinidine

Quinidine is the most frequently used antiarrhythmic agent in the United States, and side effects are common. Toxicity may be associated with life-threatening arrhythmias (Ochs, Greenblatt, Woo, & Smith, 1978; Federman & Vlietstra, 1979).

One study found that in the elderly, the total body clearance of quinidine is 2.64 mL/min/kg, significantly less than the 4.04 mL/min/kg in younger subjects (Ochs et al., 1978). Elimination half-life was prolonged from 7.3 hours in the young to 9.7 hours in the elderly. Renal clearance of quinidine and creatinine clearance were also reduced,

but the volume of distribution and the percentage of protein bound were the same in the two groups. These age-related decreases in hepatic biotransformation and renal excretion of quinidine indicate that doses should be reduced in the elderly in order to avoid excessive drug accumulation and possible toxicity.

Higher plasma levels are found after the intravenous administration in cases of heart failure; this is due to a decrease in the volume of distribution (Ueda & Dzindzio, 1978). However, quinidine absorption may be decreased by reduced intestinal blood flow, although the net effect is difficult to predict; plasma quinidine levels should be measured if the clinical response is unsatisfactory of if toxicity is suspected at low doses (Kessler et al., 1974).

Procainamide

Procainamide is effective in the treatment of a variety of supraventricular and ventricular arrhythmias and may be given by the oral or intravenous route (Federman & Vlietstra, 1979; Reidenberg, Camacho, Kluger, & Drayer, 1980).

Procainamide is well absorbed from the gastrointestinal tract, and 40% to 70% is excreted unchanged in the urine. The remainder is metabolized in the liver to N-acetylprocainamide. The metabolite has antiarrhythmic effects and is excreted by the kidneys.

The reduction in renal function in the elderly decreases the renal clearance of procainamide prolonging its half-life, and a greater proportion is metabolized to N-acetylprocainamide (Federman & Vlietstra, 1979; Galeazzi, Omar-Amberg, & Karlaganis, 1981). Since N-acetylprocainamide has a longer half-life than procainamide, the duration of effect from the procainamide dose is considerably longer (Galeazzi et al., 1981). Similar changes occur in the presence of congestive heart failure or intrinsic renal disease.

The reduced dose of procainamide in older patients may be conveniently accomplished by administering the drug two or three times daily, rather than every 4 to 6 hours.

Diuretics

Compared with young healthy patients, the elderly have a reduced total body and renal clearance and a prolonged half-life of elimination of furosemide (Kerremans et al., 1983). These kinetic changes are associated with higher blood levels of the drug. However, the higher levels of furosemide are not associated with a greater diuretic effect. In fact, the effect of the drug is diminished. Furosemide exerts its effect by tubular secretion after entry into the renal tubule. Because renal tubular secretion is diminished in the elderly (Davies & Shock, 1950; Moholm-Hansen et al., 1970; Rowe et al., 1976), a smaller concentration reaches the active site. A given dose of furosemide produces higher blood levels of the drug in the elderly but exerts a weaker diuretic effect than in younger individuals.

Congestive heart failure is associated with a diminished renal blood flow and a reduced glomerular filtration rate, which enhances proximal tubular reabsorption of water and electrolytes. This results in reduced solute at the ascending limb of Henle's loop upon which the furosemide in the tubule can act, reducing the effect of the diuretic.

The usual adult doses of furosemide are given to elderly patients with congestive heart failure, and the responses determine subsequent dose changes. Smaller doses of furosemide reduce the risk of hypovolemia in patients with normal cardiac and renal function.

Thiazides are commonly employed in the treatment of hypertension, heart failure, and edema due to cirrhosis or renal failure. Hypokalemia of some degree occurs in up to 70% of the treated patients (Healy, McKenna, Canning, Brien, Duffy, & Muldowney, 1970; Wilkinson, Hesp, Issler, & Raftery, 1975). This is usually mild, with a serum potassium between 3.0 and 3.5 mEq/l and potassium supplementation is not required unless the serum potassium falls below 3.0 mEq/l. Exceptions include patients with hypokalemic symptoms such as muscle weakness, cramps, malaise, or fatigue (Barruther, 1981).

Benzodiazepines

Long-acting benzodiazepines are frequently prescribed for the treatment of anxiety in the elderly (Cohen, 1981; Harvey, 1980; Kaplan et al., 1973). The long-acting benzodiazepines— chlordiazepoxide, diazepam, flurazepam, chlorazepate, and prazepam—produce more intense and longer-lasting effects in elderly subjects (Castleden et al., 1977; Crooks et al., 1976; Greenblatt et al., 1977; Klotz, Avant, Hoyumpa, Schenker, & Wilkinson, 1975; Reidenberg et al., 1978). These

effects derive from impairment of drug elimination and increased end-organ sensitivity. The half-life of diazepam increases from 20 hours in 20-year-old subjects to 90 hours in 80- year-old subjects (Klotz et al., 1975). This delay in the elimination of diazepam and chlordiazepoxide results in drug accumulation in the elderly producing excessive sedation, chronic fatigue, and diminution of mental alertness (Reidenberg et al., 1978; Thompson et al., 1983). These unwanted effects may be attributed to dementia in the elderly subject (Conrad & Bressler, 1984; Thompson et al., 1983). The incidence of depression is high in the elderly, as is the use of long-acting benzodiazepines (RB Drub Rx, NEJM). The use of these drugs in depression may aggravate the patient's condition. The benzodiazepines with shorter half-lives—oxazepam, lorazepam, temazepam, and alprazolam—should also be used in reduced doses because of potential sensitivity changes (Thompson et al., 1983).

The use of cimetidine has been found to impair the clearance of plasma diazepam and chlordiazepoxide (Desmond, Patwardhan, Schenker, & Speeg, 1980; Klotz & Reimann, 1980; MacLeod et al., 1978).

Among the benzodiazepines, which are frequently prescribed as sedative-hypnotics, is the widely used drug flurazepam (Solomon, White, Parron, & Mendelson, 1979). This long-acting benzodiazepine must be used in reduced doses in the elderly to avoid adverse effects. Excessive sedation and other side effects were found in 39% of elderly subjects treated with 30 mg or more of flurazepam per day. This is the usual adult dose but around twice the recommended geriatric dose (Greenblatt et al., 1977). The adverse effects of excessive drug doses in the elderly include impaired mentation and mechanical function, which can lead to injuries due to falls, driving accidents, and pseudodementia.

Drug interactions with benzodiazepines can result in excessive response of elderly patients to these drugs. These interactions may be simply pharmacokinetic as in the case of cimetidine, or pharmacodynamic as well as with ethanol.

Antidepressants (Tricyclic Antidepressants)

Depression is a significant medical problem in the elderly population (Fassler & Gaviria, 1978; Roth, M., 1976; Salzman & Shader, 1979; Thompson et al., 1983), affecting between 7% and 11% of people over 65 years of age (Bressler, 1982b; Gurland, 1976). More than half of these patients experience their first episode of depression after the age of 60.

When a cross section of elderly people was tested for depression in a North Carolina study, 3.7% were found to have a major depressive illness requiring treatment, 4.5% exhibited a dysphoric mood without vegetative signs, and 6.5% manifested a dysphoric mood in a setting of serious organic health problems (Blazer & Williams, 1980; Weissman & Myers, 1978). Reportedly, almost 50% of patients between the ages of 60 and 70 who are hospitalized for psychiatric treatment have a depressive illness (Hollister, 1978a; Pfeiffer & Busse, 1973). These levels of major depression explain in part the increasing rate of suicide with advancing age.

Depression is probably more amenable to therapy than any other emotional disorder in the elderly. Drug therapy significantly improves behavior, cognition, and other aspects. However, depression in the elderly is often undiagnosed or inadequately treated (Hollister, 1978a; Schmidt, 1974).

The signs and symptoms of depression in an elderly person may represent a normal response to adverse life events, such as loss of friends, health, mobility, and finances. Such reverses cause a kind of sadness that is of brief duration and appropriate intensity. Major depression, however, is not only more severe but also longer lasting and more resistant to therapy (Bressler, 1982b).

The diagnosis of major depression in the elderly is based on diagnostic criteria of the American Psychiatric Association (Secunda, Katz, Friedman, & Schuyler, 1973; Spitzer, Endicott, & Robins, 1975). The self-rating inventories, such as the Beck Depression Inventory (Beck, 1967) and the Zung and Hamilton depression scales (Zung, 1965; Hamilton, 1967), are useful as screening tests.

The signs and symptoms of major depression usually allow the physician to make the diagnosis readily. Major depression is more than a mood disorder. In the elderly person, it is often associated with physical symptoms (such as sleep disturbances), confusion, impaired intellectual function and memory, apathy (anhedonia equivalent), and agitation, as well as diminished self-esteem (Bressler, 1982b).

Major depressive illness is also characterized by diurnal variation of symptoms (i.e. symptoms are worse in the morning than during the day) and by a lack of significant reactivity to the enviroment.

Although the molecular basis of depression is as yet not known, research on central nervous system (CNS) neurotransmitters has given rise to the biogenic amine theory of depression (Beckmann & Goodwin, 1975; Garver & Davis, 1979; Goodwin, 1977; Goodwin & Post, 1977; Maas, 1975; Maas, Fawcett, & Dekimenjian, 1972; Schildkraut, 1973). The theory is attractive because of its simplicity and implications for therapy (Beckman & Goodwin, 1975; Maas et al., 1972; Richelson, 1982). It is, however, subject to criticism. The theory holds that unipolar depressions derive from a deficit of CNS neurotransmitters (Maas, 1975). Such deficits in the synaptic clefts of CNS neurons utilizing either norepinephrine or 5-hydroxytryptamine result in a depressive syndrome characterized by either psychomotor retardation and hypersomnia (norepinephrine deficit) or by extreme anxiety, excessive agitation, and severe sleep disturbances (5-hydroxtryptamine deficit) (Garver & Davis, 1979).

The tricyclic antidepressants (TCAs) are the most extensively used drugs in the treatment of depression in the elderly. Although the mechanisms of TCA action are not completely understood, their capacity to increase the availability of synaptic norepinephrine or 5-hydroxtryptamine is a necessary part of their clinical efficacy. The mechanism of this effect is thought to be two fold (Bressler, 1982b, Goodwin et al., 1977):

1. TCAs diminish the reuptake of norepinephrine and 5-hydroxytryptamine by CNS neurons, which normally recapture 85% of the neurotransmitter released. The tertiary amine TCAs—amitriptyline and doxepin—inhibit predominantly 5-hydroxytryptamine reuptake, whereas the secondary amines—nortriptyline, desipramine, and protriptyline—inhibit primarily norepinephrine reuptake (Goodwin et al., 1977; Hollister, L., 1982; Maas, 1978).

2. TCAs augment the CNS neuronal release of neurotransmitters. This effect is slower in onset and may not be maximal for weeks.

Although the TCA-induced elevation of neurotransmitters in the synaptic cleft can be explained by these two TCA actions, the neurobiology of the CNS and depression is obviously more complex. The information presently available serves primarily as a basis for therapeutic choices.

Moreover, the time course of clinical response is

different from the time course of TCA effects on neurotransmitter increase in the synapse: Reuptake blockade by TCAs (as well as the reduction of biogenic amine catabolism by monoamine oxidase inhibitors occurs in minutes to hours, whereas clinical efficacy may not be apparent for 3 to 4 weeks (Hollister, 1978b).

Absorption and Distribution

TCAs are absorbed rapidly and well from the gastrointestinal tract. They undergo extensive first-pass extraction by the liver, where they are metabolized.

TCAs and some of their active metabolites have large apparent volumes of distribution, and this extensive distribution in the tissues results in long plasma elimination half-lives. The extensive tissue distribution of TCAs leaves only 1% to 2% of the total body content of drug in the blood. This property precludes significant drug removal in over dose cases by either hemoperfusion or dialysis (Hollister, 1978b; Byck, 1975; Jackson, 1982).

Antidepressant Therapy

Depression is generally a self-limited disease with a natural history of spontaneous recovery in 6 to 9 months. However, the risk of suicide, the social disruptions caused by depression, and the lessened life expectancy of elderly patients are good reasons to prescribe drug therapy.

The efficacy of TCAs in the treatment of geriatric depression is well established (Bressler, 1982b; Byck, 1975; Thompson et al., 1983). Although electroconvulsive therapy has been found to be more effective in some cases than antidepressant drugs, it is possible that patients who had not responded to antidepressant drug therapy had not received adequate doses.

Predictors of Patient Responses

Elderly patients in whom TCA therapy is likely to be successful tend to have the following characteristics: (a) onset of depressive symptoms before age 70, (b) positive family history of affective disorders, (c) predepression outgoing personality and multiple interests, (d) severe symptoms, including confusion and agitation, (e) preservation of emotional responsivity, and (f) good recovery from previous depression. Features associated with a poorer response to TCA therapy include serious physical illness, dependence, obsessiveness, and schizoaffective states (Hollister, 1978b).

Selection of Antidepressant

Geriatric depression is usually treated with TCAs (Fann, 1976; Hollister, 1978b; Post, 1978). The selection of a TCA can be based on what symptoms are more prominent: anxiety and agitation, or psychomotor retardation. The tertiary amine TCAs—amitriptyline and doxepin—as well as the non-TCA trazodone, are more effective for agitated depressions than for psychomotor retardation. The secondary amines—desipramine, protriptyline, and nortriptyline, as well as maprotiline and amoxapine—are more useful in patients with psychomotor retardation (Bressler, 1982b; Goodwin, 1977; Maas, 1975). The effects of the currently available antidepressants on neurotransmitter levels are shown in Table 13.5.

The physician should keep in mind that these recommendations are only guidelines and therapy must be individualized. If a past episode of depression has responded successfully to a particular TCA, this drug should be tried again, since similar responses usually occur. (Hollister, 1978b).

Determination of Dose

Elderly patients are treated with lower doses because they experience a higher incidence of adverse effects at the usual adult dose (Bressler, 1984; Kessler, 1978). Doses range from one half to one third of the usual adult dose (Table 13.6). The drug can be given once a day, although divided doses help minimize unwanted anticholinergic effects. A bedtime dose enhances sleep, except in the case of protriptyline.

Doses are started low and gradually increased over weeks until symptoms improve or disappear. Doses used in the elderly are shown in Table 13.6 (Bressler, 1982b; Hollister, 1978b).

Because all TCAs have long half-lives, it may take around 2 weeks to reach a steady-state plasma level of any dose in elderly patients with depressed drug clearances. Raising the antidepressant dose before a steady state is reached may result in a drug overdose.

All antidepressant agents have a characteristic latent period of up to several weeks, except for beneficial effects on sleep disturbances, which occur early in therapy (Hollister, 1978b). The antidepressant efficacy takes time, even at therapeutic dose levels. In addition, a gradual increase in drug dose allows the patient to develop some tolerance to the sedative, hypotensive, and anticholinergic effects of these drugs. It is therefore

Table 13.5. Pharmacology of Antidepressant Drugs

Drug	Predominant CNS Level Elevated	Anticholinergic Effect[a]	Sedation	α-Adrenergic Blockade
Tertiary amines				
Amitriptyline	5-HT	3+	3+	4+
Doxepin	5-HT	3+	3+	4+
Trazodone[b]	5-HT	1+	1+	3+
Secondary amines				
Desipramine	NE	1+	1+	1+
Nortriptyline	NE	2+	2+	2+
Protriptyline	NE	2+	0	2+
Amoxapine*	NE	2+	2+	2+
Maprotiline[c]	NE	2+	2+	1+

Note. Adapted from "Second-Generation Antidepressants" by L. E. Hollister, 1982, *Rational Drug Therapy, 16*, p. 2.
Data from Richelson, 1982.
[a] 0 = no effect; 4+ = considerable effect.
[b] Chemically trazodone is not a tricyclic compound; however, its pharmacologic effects are those of a tertiary amine tricyclic, such as amitriptyline or doxepin.
[c] From Hollister, 1982.

Table 13.6. Dose Range of Antidepressants

Drug	DOSE, mg/day	
	Averaged Adult	Elderly
Amitriptyline	75–300	20–75
Doxepin	75–250	30–150
Imipramine	75–300	20–75
Trazodone	150–400	25–200
Desipramine	75–300	25–75
Nortriptyline	50–150	10–50
Protriptyline	20–40	20–30
Amoxapine	150–300	50–150
Maprotiline	75–250	25–150

necessary to wait for the maximum drug effect and blood level before advancing the dose.

Patient Response

Drug efficacy is assessed by physician interview of the patient and family and by means of self-report inventories, such as the Beck Depression Inventory or the Zung depression scale (Zung, 1965).

The usual sequence of events in response to TCA therapy given in adequate doses is as follows (Hollister, 1978a):

1. The patient's sleep disturbance improves within the first few days or first week of therapy.
2. Within 2 to 3 weeks, the patient becomes more aware of and interested in his or her surround-ings and responds more appropriately to people and activities.
3. The physician, nurses, family, and friends note this improvement, and feel substantially better.
4. The patient feels better.

Adverse Effects

TCAs are fairly safe when given in the usual doses appropriate for elderly patients (Bressler, 1982b; Thompson et al., 1983). However, the adverse effects of TCAs are more frequent and more severe in the elderly because of the higher incidence of cardiovascular, renal, and cerebrovascular disease in this age group, which results in impaired compensatory responses to TCA overdose, and because of age-related decreases in TCA clearance from the body.

The adverse effects of TCAs include sedation, antihistaminic (H_1) activity, anticholinergic activity, and α-adrenergic blocking activity (see Table 13.7). In general, these effects are more prominent with the drugs that increase the levels of 5-hydroxytryptamine in the brain.

The anticholinergic effects are usually the most troublesome and may be especially distressing to elderly subjects. These include constipation, urinary hesitancy or retention, excessive sedation, and precipitation of narrow-angle glaucoma. Dry mouth and impaired visual accommodation are frequent and annoying (Bressler, 1984; Richelson, 1982). Weight gain is a potentially serious adverse

Table 13.7. Adverse Effects of Tricyclic Antidepressants

Effects	Frequent	Infrequent
Anticholinergic	Blurred vision Constipation Urinary hesitancy Fuzzy thinking	Aggravation of glaucoma Paralytic ileus Urinary retention Delirium
Cardiovascular/ Sympathomimetic	Tachycardia Tremor Sweating Orthostatic hypotension Electrocardiogram abnormalities	Agitation Insomnia Aggravation of psychosis Delayed cardiac conduction Arrhythmias Cardiomyopathy Sudden death
Neurologic	Paresthesias Electroencephalogram alterations	Seizures
Allergic/Toxic	—	Cholestatic jaundice Agranulocytosis
Metabolic/Endocrine	Weight gain Sexual disturbances	Gynecomastia Amenorrhea

Note. Adapted from "Treatment of Depression with Drugs" by L. E. Hollister, 1978, *Annals of Internal Medicine, 89,* p. 78.

drug effect (Hollister, 1978b). Also, α-adrenergic blockade can produce orthostatic hypotension, another serious danger in elderly subjects. Elderly patients are especially vulnerable to the TCA-induced central anticholinergic syndrome, characterized by visual and auditory hallucinations, agitation, hyperthermia, confusion, memory loss, and disorientation, as well as by the usual peripheral anticholinergic signs—tachycardia, dry mouth, and bowel and bladder atony. The syndrome is precipitated at lower doses of TCAs when used in conjunction with antipsychotic drugs (phenothiazines) or antiparkinsonian drugs (anticholinergics). Patients with central anticholinergic syndrome may be confused with patients with senile psychoses and cerebrovascular thrombosis because of a number of common features.

TCAs and phenothiazines are used in geriatric populations with a high incidence of hypertension. The α-adrenergic blocking effects of these drugs make them potential blood-pressure-lowering agents. However, both have been found to block the blood-pressure-lowering effects of the potent antihypertensive agent guanethidine. This has been attributed to the blocking of guanethidine uptake into adrenergic neurons by both TCAs and phenothiazines (Marco, Randels, & Sexauer, 1979).

Anticholinergic agents, such as benztropine mesylate, trihexyphenidyl, and atropine, are used to treat Parkinson's disease. All these drugs can induce the central anticholinergic syndrome. Drugs with a propensity for causing agitated or confusional states in elderly patients can have their toxic manifestations confused with functional changes or physical illness in the patient. Although it has not been documented in a satisfactory manner, it is likely that the anticholinergic drugs may also have toxic effects at lower doses in the elderly.

DRUG DOSING IN THE ELDERLY

A loading dose is employed if the time required to attain steady state is long relative to the need for drug action. In general, a loading dose is not affected by impaired renal function. It is affected by changes in the volume of distribution, which may be decreased in the elderly due to diminished drug distribution, changes in body composition and decreased serum albumin. This entails a lower loading dose (LD) which is a function of volume of distribution: $LD = V_D \times C_{SS}$, where V_D is the volume of distribution and C_{SS} is the plasma drug concentration at steady state. The loading dose would thus be reduced in a healthy elderly subject and more so in the elderly patient with congestive heart failure (Thomson, 1974; Thomson et al., 1973; Rowland et al., 1976; Ueda & Dzindzio, 1978).

The maintenance dose (MD) is described by the following equation:

$$MD = \frac{C_{SS} \times Cl}{F}$$

Where C_{SS} is the plasma drug concentration at steady state, F is the fraction of drug absorbed (obtained from pharmacology tables), and Cl is the Clearance (also obtained from pharmacology tables).

Dosing intervals are chosen to minimize wide fluctuations in plasma drug concentrations. Generally, the dosing interval is such that it is equal to or less than the half-life of the drug. Plasma levels of the drug are ascertained at four to five drug half-lives.

Drugs eliminated by renal excretion—digoxin, phenobarbital, procainamide, acetylsalicylic acid, chlorpropamide, gentamicin, lithium, and atenolol—have prolonged half-lives in elderly patients with renal disease (Epstein, 1979; Reidenberg, 1971). This results in greater plasma drug concentrations per drug dose and entails either the reduction of the usual drug maintenance dose of ingestion of the usual drug dose at less frequent intervals. The use of digoxin in elderly patients with impaired renal function may be dealt with by both a reduction of dose and drug administration every second or third day.

SUMMARY

The elderly population is afflicted with a greater incidence of diseases requiring drug therapy. Because of relative pharmacodynamic and pharmcokinetic inadequacies, this population experiences more adverse drug reactions. Moreover, elderly patients often have multiple diseases that are treated with multiple drugs, which increases the potential for adverse drug interactions.

Homeostatic mechanisms are decreased in the elderly. The diminished capacity to alter cardiac output, heart rate, blood pressure, peripheral vascular tone, autonomic functions, and metabolism limits the body's ability to compensate for even slight excesses of drug action. This is a major cause of adverse drug reactions in the elderly.

The liver and kidney are the primary organs of drug inactivation and elimination. The functions of these organs significantly decrease with age. This pharmacokinetic deficiency engenders adverse drug reactions. Drugs are more slowly cleared and inactivated, which results in higher (toxic) plasma levels of drugs used in standard therapeutic doses. These pharmacodynamic and pharmacokinetic inadequacies in the elderly are of even greater concern because of the frequency of multiple drug use.

The avoidance of adverse drug reactions in the elderly is a worthwhile goal. Careful attention to the special jeopardy of the elderly patient can minimize adverse drug reactions. Adverse reactions can be avoided by minimizing the use of drugs, which should be reserved for major problems, where the gain–risk balance is clear. Elderly patients should be treated with smaller doses of drugs because they achieve steady-state blood levels of drugs at lower doses.

REFERENCES

Achong, M. R., Bayne, J. R. D., Gerson, L. W., & Golshani, S. (1978). Prescribing of psychoactive drugs for chronically ill elderly patients. *Canadian Medical Association Journal, 118*, 1503–1508.

Barruther, A. (1981). Potassium replacement: Therapeutic alternatives. *Drug Therapy, 11*, 146–149.

Beck, A. T. (1967). *Depression*. New York: Harper & Row.

Beckmann, H., & Goodwin, F. K. (1975). Antidepressant response tricyclics and urinary MHPG in unipolar patients. *Archives of General Psychiatry, 32*, 17–21.

Bender, A. D. (1965). The effect of increasing age on the distribution of peripheral blood flow in man. *Journal of the Amercian Geriatrics Society, 13*, 192–198.

Bender, A. D. (1974). Pharmacodynamic principles of drug therapy in the aged. *Journal of the American Geriatrics Society, 22*, 296–303.

Bender, A. D., Post, A., Meirer, J. P., Higson, J. E., & Reichard, G. (1975). Plasma protein binding as a function of age in adult human subjects. *Journal of Pharmaceutical Sciences, 64*, 1711–1713.

Beta-blocker heart attack study group, (1981). The β-Blocker heart attack trial. *Journal of the American Medical Association, 246*, 2073–2074.

Bianchine, J. R., Gerber, N., & Andresen, B. D. (1981). Geriatric medicine. *Current Concepts* (pp. 1–42). Kalamazoo, MI: Upjohn Co.

Blazer, D., & Williams, C. D. (1980). Epidemiology of dysphoria and depression in an elderly population. *American Journal of Psychiatry, 137*, 439–444.

Brandfonbrener, M., Landowne, M., & Shock, N. W. (1955). Changes in cardiac output with age. *Circulation, 12*, 557–566.

Bressler, R. (1982a). Adverse drug reactions. In K. A. Conrad & R. Bressler (Eds.), *Drug therapy for the elderly* (pp. 277–294). St. Louis, MO: Mosby.

Bressler, R. (1982b). Antidepressant agents. In K. A.

Conrad & R. Bressler (Eds.), *Drug therapy for the elderly* (pp. 295–315). St. Louis, MO: Mosby.

Bressler, R. (1984). Treating geriatric depression. *Drug Therapy, 14*, 129–144.

Byck, R. (1975). Drugs used in the treatment of psychoses. In L. S. Goodman & A. Gilman (Eds.), *Pharmacological basis of therapeutics* (pp. 156–157). New York: Macmillan.

Cammarata, R. J., Rodnan, G. P., & Fennell, R. H. (1967). Serum antigamma-globulin and anti-nuclear factors in the aged. *Journal of the American Medical Association, 199*, 445–448.

Carter, B. C., Small, R. E., & Garnett, W. R. (1981). Monitoring digoxin therapy in two long term facilities. *Journal of the American Geriatrics Society, 29*, 263–268.   •

Castleden, C. M., George, C. F., Marcer, D., & Hallet, C. (1977). Increased sensitivity to nitrazepam in old age. *British Medical Journal, 1*, 10–12.

Castleden, C. M., Kay, C. M., & Parsons, R. L. (1975). The effect of age on plasma levels of propranolol the practolol in man. *British Journal of Clinical Pharmacology, 2*, 303–306.

Cockroft, D. W., & Gault, M. H. (1976). Prediction of creatinine clearance from serum creatinine. *Nephron, 16*, 31–41.

Cohen, S. (1981). A clinical appraisal of diazepam. *Psychosomatics, 22*, 761–769.

Collinsworth, K. A., Strong, J. M., Atkinson, A. J., Winkle, R. A., Perlroth, F., & Harrison, D. (1975). Pharmacokinetics and metabolism of lidocaine in patients with renal failure. *Clinical Pharmacology & Theraputics, 18*, 59–64.

Conrad, K. A., & Bressler, R. (1984). Drugs and advanced age. In W. Modell (Ed.), *Drugs of choice* (pp. 21–40). St. Louis, MO: Mosby.

Crooks, J., O'Malley, K., & Stevenson, I. H. (1976). Pharmacokinetics in the elderly. *Clinical Pharmacokinetics, 1*, 280–296.

Cusak, B., Morgan, J., Kelly, J. G., Lavan, J., Noel, J., & O'Malley, K. (1978). Pharmacokinetics of digoxin in the elderly. *Proceedings of the British Pharamaceutical Society, 15*, 439–440.

Davies, D. F., & Shock, N. W. (1950). Age changes in glomerular filtration rate, effective renal plasma flow, and tubular excretory capacity in adult males. *Journal of Clinical Investigations, 29*, 496–507.

DeSilva, R. A., Lown, B., Hennekens, C. H., & Casscells, W. (1981). Linocaine prophylaxis in acute myocardial infarction: an evaluation of randomised trials. *Lancet, ii*, 855–858.

Desmond, P. V., Patwardhan, R. V., Schenker, S., & Speeg, K. V., Jr. (1980). Cimetidine impairs elimination of chlordiazepoxide (Librium) in man. *Annals of Internal Medicine, 93*, 266–268.

Donovan, M. A., Castleden, C. N. M., Polh, J. G., & Kraft, C. A. (1981). The effects of age on digoxin pharmacokinetics. *British Journal of Clinical Pharmacology, 11*, 401–402.

Epstein, M. (1979). Effects of aging on the kidney. *Federal Proceedings, 38*, 168–172.

Ewy, G. A., Kapadia, C. G., Yao, L., Lullin, L., & Marcus, P. I. (1969). Digoxin metabolism in the elderly. *Circulation, 39*, 449–453.

Fann, W. F. (1976). Pharmacotherapy in older depressed patients. *Journal of Gerontology, 31*, 304–310.

Fassler, L. B., & Gaviria, M. (1978). Depression in old age. *Journal of the American Geriatrics Society, 26*, 471–475.

Federman, J., & Vlietstra, R. E. (1979). Antiarrhythmic drug therapy. *Mayo Clinic Proceedings, 54*, 531–542.

Fenster, P. E., Powell, J. R., Graves, P. E., Hager, W. D., Wandell, M., & Conrad, K. (1980). Digitoxin–quinidine interaction: pharmacokinetic evaluation. *Annuals of Internal Medicine, 93*, 698–701.

Fichtl, B., & Doering, W. (1983). The quinidine–digoxin interactions in perspective. *Clinical Pharacokinetics, 8*, 137–154.

Finch, C. E. (1979). Neuroendocrine mechanisms and aging. *Federal Proceedings, 38*, 178–183.

Fottrell, E., Sheikh, M., Kothari, R., & Saved, I. (1976). Long-stay patients with long-stay drugs. A case for review: a cause for concern. *Lancet, i*, 81–82.

Galeazzi, R. L., Omar-Amberg, C., & Karlaganis, G. (1981). N-acetylprocainamide kinetics in the elderly. *Clinical Pharmacology and Therapeutics, 29*, 440–446.

Garver, D. L., & Davis, J. M. (1979). Biogenic amine hypothesis of affective disorders. *Life Sciences, 24*, 383–394.

Geokas, M. C., & Haverback, B. J. (1979). The aging gastrointestinal tract. *American Journal of Surgeons, 117*, 881–886.

Gerstenblith, G., Lakatta, E. G., & Weisfeldt, M. L. (1976). Age changes in myocardial function and exercise response. *Progress in Cardiovascular Diseases, 19*, 1–21.

Gibson, R. M., Mueeler, M. S., & Fisher, C. R. (1977). Age differences in health care spending, fiscal year 1976. *Social Security Bulletin, 40*, 3–14.

Gillette, J. R. (1979). Biotransformation of drugs during aging. *Federal Proceedings, 38*, 1900–1909.

Goodwin, F. K. (1977). Drug treatment of affective disorders: general principles. In M. E. Jarvik (Ed.), *Psychopharmacology in the practice of medicine* (pp. 241–253). New York: Appleton–Century–Crofts.

Goodwin, F. K., & Post, R. M. (1977). Serotonin and norepinephrine subgroups in depression. *Scientific Proceedings of the American Psychiatric Association, 130*, 108.

Greenblatt, D. J., Allen, M. D., & Shader, R. I. (1977). Toxicity of high-dose flurazepam in the elderly. *Clinical Pharmacology and therapeutics, 21*, 355–361.

Greenblatt, D. J., Sellers, E. M., & Shader, R. I. (1982). Drug disposition in old age. In J. Koch-Weser (Ed.), "*Drug Therapy*". *New England Journal of Medicine* (special issue) *306*, 1081–1088.

Gurland, B. J. (1976). The comparative frequency of depression in various adult age groups. *Journal of Genontology, 31*, 283–292.

Hager, W. D., Fenster, P. E., Mayersohn, M., Perrier, D., Grazes, P., Marcos, F. I., & Goldman, S. (1979). Digoxin–quinidine interaction: pharmacokinetic evaluation. *New England Journal of Medicine, 300*, 1238–1241.

Halkin, H., Meffin, P., Melmon, K. L., & Rowland, M. (1975). Influence of congestive heart failure on blood vessels of lidocaine and its active monodeethylated metabolite. *Clinical Pharmacology and Therapeutics, 17*, 669–676.

Hamilton, M. (1967). Development of a rating scale for primary depressive illness. *British Journal for the Society of Clinical Psychologists*, 6, 278–296.

Harris, R. (1971). Special features of heart disease in the elderly patients. In A. B. Chinn (Ed.), *Clinical aspects of aging: Workling with older people—A guide to practice* Vol. 4, No. 1459, (pp. 81–88). Washington, DC: U.S. Department of Health, Education and Welfare, Public Health Service.

Harris, R. (1975). Cardiac changes with age. In R. Goldman & M. Rockstein (Eds.), *The physiology and pathology of human aging* (pp. 109–232). New York: Academic Press.

Harvey, S. C. (1980). Hypotics and sedatives. In A. G. Gilman, L. S. Goodman, & A. Gilman (Eds.), *The pharmacological basis of therapeutics* (6th Ed.) (pp. 342–375). New York: Macmillan.

Hayes, M. J., Langman, M. J. S., & Short, A. H. (1975). Changes in drug metabolism with increasing age. I. Warfarin binding and plasma proteins. *British Journal of Clinical Pharmacology*, 2, 69–72.

Healy, J. J., McKenna, T. J., Canning, B. S., Brien, T. G., Duffy, G. J., & Muldowney, F. P. (1970). Body composition in hypertensive subjects on long-term oral diuretic therapy. *British Medical Journal*, 1, 716–719.

Hepner, G. W., Vessel, E. S., & Tantum, K. R. (1978). Reduced drug elimination in congestive heart failure: studies using aminopyrine as a model drug. *American Journal of Medicine*, 65, 271–276.

Hollister, L. E. (1978a). *Clinical pharmacology of psychotherapeutic drugs.* New York: Churchill-Livingstone.

Hollister, L. E. (1978b). Tricyclic antidepressants. *New England Journal of Medicine*, 299, 1106–1168.

Hollister, L. E. (1978c). Treatment of depression with drugs. *Annals of Internal Medicine*, 89, 78–81.

Hollister, L. E. (1982). Second-generation antidepressants. *Rational Drug Therapy*, 16, 1–7.

Hollister, L. E. (1973). Clinical use of psychotherapeutic drugs. Springfield, IL: Charles C. Thomas.

Hypertension Detection and Follow-up Program Cooperative Group. Five-year findings of the hypertension detection and follow-up program: 1979, I; Reduction in mortality of persons with high blood pressure, including mild hypertension. (1979). *Journal of the American Medical Association*, 242, 2562–2571.

Hurwitz, N. (1969). Predisposing factors in adverse reactions to drugs. *British Medical Journal*, 1, 536–539.

Jackson, J. E. (1982). Cardiovascular effects of tricyclic antidepressants. In G. A. Ewy & R. Bressler (Eds.), *Cardiovascular drugs and the management of heart disease* (pp. 285–309). New York: Raven

Kaplan, S. A., de Silva, J. A. F., Jack, M. L., Alexander, K., Strojny, N., Weinfeld, R. E., Puglisi, C. Z., & Weisfman, L. (1973). Blood level profile in man following chronic oral administration of flurazepam hydrochloride. *Journal of Pharmaceutical Sciences*, 62, 1932–1935.

Kendall, M. J., Woods, K. L., Wilkins, M. R., & Worthington, D. J. (1982). Responsiveness to β-adrenergic receptor stimulation: the effects of age are cardioselective. *British Journal of Clinical Pharmacology*, 14, 821–826.

Kerremans, A. L. M., Tan, Y., Van Baars, H., Van Ginneken, C. A., & Gribnau, F. W. (1983). Furosemide kinetics and dynamics in aged patients. *Clinical Pharmacology and Therapeutics*, 34, 181–189.

Kessler, K. A. (1978). Tricylic antidepressants: Mode of action and clinical use. In M. A. Lipton, A. DiMascio, & K. F. Killam (Eds.), *Psychopharmacology: A generation of progress* (pp. 917–922). New York: Raven.

Kessler, K. M., Lowenthal, D. T., Warner, H., Gibson, T., Briggs, W., & Reidenberg, M. (1974). Quinidine elimination in patients with congestive heart failure or poor renal function. *New England Journal of Medicine*, 290, 706–709.

Klotz, U., Avant, G. R., Hoyumpa, A., Schenker, S., & Wilkinson, G. R. (1975). The effects of age and liver disease on the disposition and elimination of diazepam in adult man. *Journal of Clinical Investigations*, 55, 347–359.

Klotz, U., & Reimann, I. (1980). Influence of cimetidine on the pharmacokinetics of desmethyldiazepam and oxazepam. *European Journal of Clinical Pharmacology*, 18, 517–520.

Kornhauser, D., Wood, A. J. J., Vestal, R. E., Wilkinson, G. R., Branch, R. A., & Shand, D. G. (1978). Biological determinates of propranolol disposition in man. *Clinical Pharmacology and Therapeutics*, 23, 165–174.

Lakatta, E. G. (1970). Alterations in the cardiovascular system that occur in advanced aged. *Federal Proceedings*, 38, 163–167.

Learoyd, B. M. (1972). Psychotropic drugs and the elderly patient. *Medical Journal of Australia*, 1, 1131–1133.

Levy, G. (1978). Pharmacokinetic assessment of the effect of age on the disposition and pharmacologic activity of drugs. *Advances in Experimental Medicine and Biology*, 97, 47–53.

Levy, R. H., & Moreland, T. A. (1984). Rationale for monitoring free drug levels. *Clinical Pharmacokinetics*, 9 (Suppl. 1), 1–9.

Maas, J. W. (1975). Biogenic amines and depression: biochemical and pharmacological separation of two types of depression. *Archives of General Psychiatry*, 32, 1357–1361.

Maas, J. W. (1978). Clinical implications of pharmacological differences among antidepressants. In M. A. Lipton, A. DiMascio, & K. F. Killam (Eds.), *Psychopharmacology: A generation of progress* (pp. 955–960). New York: Raven.

Maas, J. W., Fawcett, J. A., & Dekimenjian, H. (1972). Catecholamine metabolism, depressive illness and drug response. *Archives of General Psychiatry*, 26, 252–262.

MacLeod, S. M., Sellers, E. M., Giles, H. G., Billings, B. J., Martin, P. R., Greenblatt, D. J., & Marshman, J. A. (1978). Interaction of disulfiram with benzodiazepines. *Clinical Pharmacology and Therapeutics*, 24, 583–589.

Marco, L. A., Randels, P. M., & Sexauer, J. (1979). A guide to drug interactions with psychotropic agents. *Drug Therapy*, 9, 45–56.

Mather, L. E., Tucker, G. T., Pflug, A. E., Lindop, M. J., & Wilkerson, C. (1975). Meperidine kinetics in man: intravenous injection in surgical patients and volunteers. *Clinical Pharmacology and Therapeutics*, 17, 21–30.

May, F. E., Stewart, R. B., & Cluff, L. E. (1977). Drug interactions and multiple drug administration. *Clinical Pharmacology and Therapeutics, 22*, 322–328.

McLachlan, M. S. F. (1978). The aging kidney. *Lancet, ii*, 143–145.

Melmon, L. L. (1971). Preventable drug reactions—causes and cures. *New England Journal of Medicine, 284*, 1361–1368.

Merry, D. A., Lowe, J. M., Larson, D. A., & Writing, B. (1981). The changing pattern of toxicity of digoxin. *Postgraduate Medical Journal, 57*, 358–362.

Moholm-Hansen, J., Kampmann, J., & Larsen, H. (1970). Renal excretion of drugs in the elderly. *Lancet, i*, 1170.

Morrelli, H. F., & Melmon, K. L. (1978). Drug interactions. In H. F. Morrelli & K. L. Melmon (Eds.), *Clinical pharmacology* (pp. 982–1007). New York: Macmillan.

Nation, R. L., Triggs, E. J., & Selig, M. (1977). Lignocaine kinetics in cardiac patients and aged subjects. *British Journal of Clinical Pharmacology, 4*, 439–448.

Nies, A. S., Shand, D. B., & Wilkinson, G. R. (1976). Altered hepatic blood flow and drug disposition. *Clinical Pharmacokinetics, 1*, 125–155.

O'Malley, K., Judge, T. G., & Crooks, J. (1980). Geriatric clinic pharmacology and therapeutics. In G. S. Avery (Ed.), *Avery drug treatment* (pp. 158–179). Philadelphia: Adis Press.

O'Malley, K., Stevenson, I. H., Ward, C. A., Wood, A. J. J., & Crooks, J. (1977). Determinants of anticoagulant control in patients receiving warfarin. *British Journal of Clinical Pharmacology, 4*, 309–314.

Ochs, H. R., Greenblatt, D. J., Woo, E., & Smith, T. W. (1978). Reduced quinidine clearance in elderly persons. *American Journal of Cardiologists, 42*, 481–485.

Ouslander, J. G. (1981). Drug therapy in the elderly. *Annals of Internal Medicine, 95*, 711–722.

Pfeifer, M. A., Weinberg, C. R., Cook, D., Best, J. D., Reenan, A., & Halter, J. B. (1983). Differential changes of autonomic nervous system function with age in man. *American Journal of Medicine, 75*, 249–258.

Pfeiffer, E., & Busse, E. (1973). Mental disorders in later life: affective disorders, paranoid, neurotic, and situational reactions. In E. Busse & E. Pfeiffer (Eds.), *Mental illness in later life* (pp. 107–144). Washington, DC: American Psychiatric Association.

Pond, S. M., & Tozer, T. N. (1984). First-pass elimination: Basic concepts and clinical consequences. *Clinical Pharmacokinetics, 9*, 1–25.

Port, S., Cobb, F. R., Coleman, R. E., & Jones, R. H. (1980). Effect of age on the response of the left ventricular ejection fraction to exercise. *New England Journal of Medicine, 303*, 1133–1137.

Post, F. (1978). Psychiatric disorders. In *Textbook of geriatric medicine and gerontology* (2nd ed., pp. 185–200). New York: Churchill-Livingstone.

Rasmussen, S. N., Hansen, J. M., Kampmann, J. P., Skovstad, L., & Bach, B. (1976). Drug metabolism in relationship to liver volume and age. *Scandinavian Journal of Gastroenterology, II* (Suppl. 36), 82.

Reichel, W. (1965). Complications in the care of 500 elderly hospitalized patients. *Journal of the American Geriatrics Society, 13*, 973–981.

Reidenberg, M. (1971). *Renal function and drugs action.* (pp. 5–18, 33). Philadelphia: Saunders.

Reidenberg, M. M., Camacho, M., Kluger, J., & Drayer, D. E. (1980). Aging and renal clearance of procainamide and acetylprocainamide. *Clinical Pharmacology and Therapeutics, 28*, 732–735.

Reidenberg, M. M., Levy, M., Warner, H., Coutinho, C. B., Schwartz, M. A., Yu, G., & Cheripko, J. (1978). Relationship between diazepam dose, plasma level, age, and central nervous system depression. *Clinical Pharmacology and Therapeutics, 23*, 371–374.

Richelson, E. (1982). Pharmacology of antidepressants in use in the United States. *Journal of Clinical Psychiatry, 43*, 4–11.

Richev, D. P., & Bender, A. D. (1977). Pharmacokinetic consequences of aging. *Annual Review of Pharmacology and Toxicology, 17*, 49–65.

Roberts, J., & Goldberg, P. B. (1979). Changes in responsiveness of the heart to drugs during aging. *Federal Proceedings, 38*, 1927–1932.

Rodeheffer, R. J., Gerstenblith, G. M. D., Becker, L. G., Fleg, J. L., Weisfeldt, M. L., & Lakatta, E. G. (1984). Exercise cardiac output is maintained with advancing age in healthy human subjects: cardiac dilatation and increased stroke volume compensation for a diminished heart rate. *Circulation, 69*, 203–213.

Roland, M. (1984). Protein binding and drug clearance. *Clinical Pharmacokinetics, 9* (Suppl.), 10–17.

Roth, G. S. (1979). Hormone receptor changes during adulthood and senescence: Significance for aging research. *Federation Proceedings, 38*, 1910–1914.

Roth, M. (1976). The psychiatric disorders of later life. *Psychiatric Annals, 6*, 417–445.

Rowe, J. W., Andres, R., Tobin, J. D., Norris, A. H., & Shock, N. W. (1976). The effect of age on creatinine clearance in man. *Journal of Gerontology, 31*, 155–163.

Rowland, M. (1978). Drug administration and regimens: absorption, distribution, excretion, pharmacokinetics. In K. L. Melmon & H. F. Morrelli, *Clinical pharmacology* (pp. 25–70). New York: Macmillan.

Rowland, M., Blaschke, T. F., Meffin, P. J., & Williams, R. L. (1976). Pharmacokinetics in disease states modifying hepatic and metabolic function. In Benet, L. Z. (Ed.), *The effect of disease state on drug pharmacokinetics* (pp. 53–75). Washington DC: Public American Pharmaceutical Association, Academy of Pharmaceutical Sciences.

Salzman, C., Shader, R. I., & Van der Kolk, B. A. (1976). Clinical psychopharmacology and the elderly patient. *New York State Journal of Medicine, 76*, 716–777.

Salzman, C., & Shader, R. I. (1979). Clinical evaluation of depression in the elderly. In A. Raskin & L. F. Jarvik (Eds.), *Psychiatric symptoms and cognitive loss in the elderly* (pp. 39–72). New York: Holstead.

Schildkraut, J. J. (1973). Catecholamine metabolism and affective disorders. Studies of MHPG excretion. In E. Usdin & S. Snyder (Eds.), *Frontiers in catecholamine research* (pp. 1165–1171). Elmsford, NY: Pergamon.

Schmidt, C. W. (1974). Psychiatric problems of the aged. *Journal of the American Geriatric Society, 22*, 355–359.

Schmucker, D. L. (1979). Age-related changes in drug disposition. *Pharmacological Reviews, 30*, 445–456.

Secunda, S. K., Katz, M., Friedman, R. J., & Schuyler,

D. (1973). *The depressive disorders.* Washington, DC., U.S. Department of Health, Education, and Welfare.

Seidl, L. G., Thornton, G. F., Smith, J. W., & Cluff, L. E. (1966). Studies on the epidemiology of adverse drug reactions. III. Reactions in patients on a general medical service. *Bulletin of Johns Hopkins Hospital, 119,* 299–330.

Sellers, E. M., Frecher, R. C., & Romach, M. K. (1983). Drug metabolism in the elderly: confounding of age, smoking and ethanol effects. *Drug Metabolism Reviews, 14,* 225–250.

Shepherd, A. M., Hewick, D. S., Moreland, T. A., & Stevenson, I. H. (1977). Age as a determinant of sensitivity to warfarin. *British Journal of Clinical Pharmacology, 4,* 315–320.

Smith, J. W., Seidl, L. G., & Cluff, L. E. (1966). Studies on the epidemiology of adverse drug reactions: V. Clinical factors influencing susceptibility. *Annuals of Internal Medicine, 65,* 629–640.

Solomon, F., White, C. C., Parron, D. L., & Mendelson, W. B. (1979). Sleeping pills, insomnia and medical practice. *New England Journal of Medicine, 300,* 803–808.

Spitzer, R. L., Endicott, J., & Robins, E. (1975). Research diagnostic criteria. *Psychopharmacology Bulletin, 11,* 22–25.

Stenson, R. E., Constantino, R. T., & Harrison, D. C. (1971). Interrelationships of hepatic blood flow, cardiac output, and blood levels of lidocaine in man. *Circulation, 43,* 205–211.

Thompson, T. L., Moran, M. G., & Nies, A. S. (1938). Psychotropic drug use in the elderly. *New England Journal of Medicine, 308,* 134–138, 194–199.

Thomson, P. D. (1974). Alterations in pharmacologic response induced by cardiovascular disease. In K. L. Melmon (Ed.), *Cardiovascular drug therapy* (pp. 55–61). Philadelphia: F. A. Davis.

Thomson, P. D., Melmon, K. L., Richardson, J. A., Cohn, K., Steinbrunn, W., & Cudihee, R. (1973). Lidocaine pharmacokinetics in advanced heart failure, liver disease and renal failure in humans. *Annual of Internal Medicine, 78,* 499–508.

Triggs, E. J., & Nation, R. L. (1975). Pharmacokinetics in the aged: A review. *Journal of Pharmacokinetics and Biopharmaceutics, 3,* 387–418.

Ueda, C. T. & Dzindzio, B. S. (1978). Quinidine kinetics in congestive heart failure. *Clinical Pharmacology and Therapeutics, 23,* 158–164.

Vartia, K. L., & Leikola, E. (1960). Serum levels of antibiotics in young and old subjects following administration of dihydrostreptomycin and tetracycline. *Journal of Gerontology, 15,* 392–394.

Vestal, R. E. (1978). Drug use in the elderly: A review of problems and special considerations. *Drugs, 16,* 358–382.

Vestal, R. E. (1979). Aging and pharmacokinetics:

Impact of altered physiology in the elderly. In A. Cherkin, C. E. Finch, N. Karash, T. Makinodan, F. L. Scott, & B. Strehler (Eds.), *Physiology and cell biology of aging* (Vol. 8, pp. 185–201). New York: Raven.

Vestal, R. E. (1981). Drug metabolism and therapeutics in the elderly. In K. Steel (Ed.), *Geriatric education,* (pp. 129–142). Lexington, KY: Collamore Press.

Vestal, R. E. (1982). Pharmacology and aging. *Journal of the American Geriatrics Society, 30,* 191–200.

Vestal, R. E. (1984). Geriatric clinical pharmacology: An overview. In R. E. Vestal (Ed.), *Drug treatment in the elderly* (pp. 12–28). Sydney, Australia: ADIS Health Science Press.

Vestal, R. E., Norris, A. H., Tobin, J. D., Cohen, B. H., Shock, N. W., & Andres, R. (1975). Antipyrine metabolism in man: influence of age, alcohol, caffeine, and smoking. *Clinical Pharmacology and Therapeutics, 18,* 425–432.

Vestal, R. E., McGuire, E. A., Tobin, J. D., Andres, R., Norris, A. H., & Mezey, E. (1977). Aging and ethanol metabolism. *Clinical Pharmacology and Therapeutics, 21,* 343–354.

Vestal, R. E., Wood, A. J. J., Branch, R. A., Shand, D. G., & Wilkinson, G. R. (1979). The effects of age and cigarette smoking on propranolol disposition. *Clinical Pharmacology and Therapeutics, 26,* 8–15.

Weiner, I. M. (1971). Excretion of drugs by the kidney. In B. B. Brodie & J. R. Gillette (Eds.), *Concepts in biochemical pharmacology* (Part I, Vol. 28, pp. 328–353). New York: Springer-Verlag.

Weissman, M. M., & Myers, J. K. (1978). Affective disorders in a U.S. community: the use of research diagnostic criteria in an epidemiologic survey. *Archives of General Psychiatry, 35,* 1304–1311.

Wilkinson, P. R., Hesp, R., Issler, H., & Raftery, E. B. (1975). Total body and serum potassium during prolonged thiazide therapy for essential hypertension. *Lancet, i,* 759–762.

Williams, R. L. (1938). Drug administration in hepatic disease. *New England Journal of Medicine, 309,* 1616–1622.

Wilson, L. A., Lawson, I. R., & Braws, W. (1962). Multiple disorders in the elderly: A clinical and statistical study. *Lancet, ii,* 841–843.

Wood, A. J. J., Vestal, R. E., Wilkinson, G. R., Branch, R. A., & Shand, D. G. (1979). The effects of aging and cigarette smoking antipyrine and indocyanine green elimination. *Clinical Pharmacology and Therapeutics, 26,* 16–20.

Yin, F. C. P., Spurgeon, H. A., Raizes, G. S., Greene, H. L., Weisfeld, T. M. L., & Shock, N. W. (1976). Age associated decrease in chronotropic response to isoproterenol. *Circulation, 54* (Supp. 2), 167.

Zung, W. W. K. (1965). A self-rating depression scale. *Archives of General Psychiatry, 12,* 63–70.

Part IV

Behavior Problems and Their Management

Many elderly people say that the inevitability of death does not trouble them: rather it is the likelihood of experiencing the problems of old age that they fear. This section contains chapters on problems common among the aged. Included are chapters dealing with functional disabilities that stem from physical insult, as well as with problems that are very likely grounded in the social structure of our society.

Part IV

Behavior Problems and Their Management

Chapter 14

Wandering and Disorientation

Richard A. Hussian

Mental health professionals are beginning to turn their attention to problem behaviors exhibited by elderly persons, which, if left untreated, are highly likely to cause institutionalization or continued treatment in fairly restrictive settings (e.g., Haley, 1983; Mace & Rabins, 1981). Within these facilities such behavior is likely to lead to further restrictions, sedation, restraint, confinement, avoidance by others, seclusion, and limited access.

Most geriatricians view many of these behaviors as either operant behavior occasioned by the environment (e.g., Baltes & Barton, 1977; Hoyer, 1973) or the result of ill-defined aging processes. The former view, which lends itself to functional analysis and successful rehabilitation, has been applied to a variety of behavioral problems in the aged. Most of the research concerning these problems has focused on the remediation of skills or activity deficits. There is also a sizable collection of response reduction techniques garnered from research with younger populations that may be applied to the elderly. Some of these techniques are correction, differential reinforcement of alternative behavior, and time out from reinforcement.

Reviews of such techniques used with psychological/behavioral problems among the elderly generally show positive results (Hussian, 1984a, 1984b; Patterson et al., 1982; Pinkston & Linsk, 1984, Wisocki, 1984). However, there are certain maladaptive responses that are extremely difficult

to manage and this may lead to institutionalization, as well as maladaptive responses that do not fit neatly into a behavioral analysis and therefore are not often the targets for behavioral change techniques. These behaviors include wandering, trespassing, self-stimulation or stereotypies, bowel evacuation away from appropriate receptacles, sexual behavior in inappropriate areas, and disorientation as to time and location. Typically these behaviors, or a subset thereof, are exhibited by clients with severe cognitive and/or perceptual impairment. The cause may be either of an acute nature, as is the case in delirium, or of a chronic nature, as is the case with dementia or sensory loss. The impairment, regardless of etiology, results in what appears to be *stimulus-free responding*, that is, behavior that appears unrelated to environmental controls.

Two of these frequently occurring responses, thought to be due to insufficient stimulus discrimination, are wandering and disorientation as to location and time. They are chosen for further discussion because they represent the classic and most heavily researched areas that exemplify the overall problem of poor stimulus control. They represent an impaired ability to locate relevant stimulus markers in the environment that are important to successfully locomote, exhibit independent self-care responses such as toileting and feeding, avoid potential hazards, and remain generally alert and responsive.

DISORIENTATION

Disorientation is a general term usually referring to a person's inability to (a) respond verbally to questions concerning current location, current day or date or month or year or season, and/or the names of significant others or (b) locate specific areas in the environment and utilize these areas as intended. Standard mental status examinations are used to measure verbal ability, although responses are influenced by other variables, such as communication disorders, level of arousal, depression, recent relocations, and lack of discriminative stimuli. Orientation in the environment is usually less readily assessed but can be ascertained through careful observation and specialized environment-orientation scales.

A wide variety of orientation measures have been used in practice and in research (see a summary by Holden & Woods, 1982). These include the Stockton Geriatric Rating Scale, the Geriatric Rating Scale, the Philadelphia Geriatric Center Mental State Questionnaire, and the Short Portable Mental Status Questionnaire (Raskin & Jarvik, 1979). Most of these cover similar areas, such as knowledge of the current time, place, and personal data; the main differences between them are in the length of administration.

Although these examinations are useful in the establishment of global assessment of verbal orientation and memory, a functional approach may yield more useful information about significantly impaired individuals. A more accurate measure of orientation, for example, might be through direct observations of one's ability to navigate through space from one "landmark" to another. Certainly, the person's ability to function within his or her environment is a more useful statement about orientation than his or her ability to respond to questions concerning current events.

Disorientation may be a result of a variety of causes, including abnormal central nervous system arousal, impaired peripheral functioning, low level of motivation, absence of discriminable stimuli, the presence of competing stimuli, impaired memory, and/or lack of familiarity with available stimuli. Therefore, a careful functional analysis of the behavior is required to determine which cause is contributing to the incorrect verbal or physical response.

Disorientation as to location, important environmental cues, and time are important targets for management, particularly if the results of such disorientation cause significant problems for the client and/or caregivers. For example, the inability to discriminate between entrances to hazardous and nonhazardous areas may lead to a variety of unfortunate consequences, such as burns, falls, trespassing incidents, traffic accidents, overexposure, hypothermia, heat stroke, physical aggression by others, and unauthorized departure. Time disorientation can lead to missed medication ingestion, irregular medication spacing, and missed meals or activities. An inability to discriminate between persons and their functions can lead to physical aggression and missed detection of illness, if the person cannot recognize medical personnel or describe physical symptoms. Certainly, all types of disorientation may prohibit independent functioning in the community, and may lead to continued institutionalization, unemployment, and limited access to active treatment.

WANDERING

We shall define *wandering* as apparent non-goal-directed ambulation or locomotion, although, as we shall discuss later, this behavior is not, in fact, random or purposeless. However, the client who is exhibiting true wandering behavior is ambulating independently of the traditional cues and stimuli that shape ambulation for most people. In other words, exit signs, identification plates, and the like are not being attended to and the behavior appears to be occurring simply because some aspect of the ambulation is reinforcing. Wandering may be viewed as a special instance of disorientation, a physical representation of the failure to identify salient cues.

Researchers have found that wandering is associated with decreased mental status and non-social behavior (Snyder, 1978), increased range of motion (Cornbleth, 1977), and a high premorbid level of activity and a high stress level (Monsour & Robb, 1982). It is a behavior or set of behaviors that may not be solely associated with the elderly but tends to be more frequently exhibited by elderly institutionalized individuals than by younger institutionalized populations.

The importance of analyzing and treating wandering, or non-stimulus-controlled ambulation, is fairly obvious. Besides serving as an aid to differential diagnosis, the presence of wandering can lead to serious consequences. In noninstitutionalized settings, wandering can lead to exposure to hazardous materials or sites, traffic incidents, crime, dangerous weather, sedation, restraint of mobility, and/or loss of access to open areas. Within more restrictive settings, wandering is a bit less problematic; outside privileges may be severely curtailed as a result of wandering and/or mobility may be limited if the behavior results in falls, incidents of trespassing, and/or aggression directed against the wanderer.

Wandering, like disorientation, is a fairly broad term, encompassing a variety of behaviors and etiologies. A careful functional analysis of an individual's wandering behavior may reveal that the client is actually not having difficulty discriminating stimuli in the environment but may be ambulating because of medication effects or a desire to exit. A recent study by Hussian and Davis (1983) reported that wandering might be more accurately viewed as four distinct types of ambulation. In their study, 13 institutionalized geriatric clients were observed closely due to their high frequency and duration of ambulation. The amount of time spent exhibiting ambulation behavior, as well as a variety of other responses, was measured.

The four classes of ambulators included akathisiacs—neuroleptic-induced pacing and restlessness; exit seekers—newly admitted clients who tried to open locked exit doors; self-stimulators—clients who spent a good deal of time engaging in other self-stimulatory activity in addition to the continuous pacing; and modelers—clients who tagged onto or "shadowed" ambulators from one or more of the other categories. The last would not wander unless they were in close physical contact with another ambulator.

In Hussian and Davis's view, clients who ambulated in the absence of the traditional cues fell into either the self-stimulatory category (since it was sensory feedback from doorknob turning that appeared to have maintained the ambulation) or the modeler category (since the wandering was related to another ambulator, who served as the stimulus regardless of the route taken). These two patterns could most likely be due to inappropriate or insufficient stimulus control.

Of course, other causes of topographically similar behavior might be at work with a particular person. Often, excessive ambulation may be due to a need to exercise or to gain access or privilege by attempting to get in front of lines, going through other person's belongings, looking for cigarette butts, and the like. These ambulators would, of course, not fit into the category of insufficient sti-

mulus control even though the consequences may be just as problematic.

Problems of insufficient stimulus-controlled behavior and especially disorientation and wandering can develop from two psychiatric causes: delirium and dementia. Although insufficient or confusing environmental cues may play a significant or contributing role as well (Spivack, 1984), we will concentrate on delirium and dementia. The manipulation of environmental cues is one of the crucial components of effective management of these two behaviors.

ACUTE CAUSES OF DEFICIENT STIMULUS CONTROL

A variety of physical illnesses and imbalances can lead to inappropriate behavior that appears to the observer to be free from stimulus control. In the psychiatric literature such a condition is referred to as *delirium*, although the *DSM-III* diagnosis (diagnosis according to the 3rd ed. of the American Psychiatric Association's *Diagnostic and Statistical Manual of Mental Disorders*) would be subsumed under the *organic brain sydrome* label as amnestic syndrome, organic delusional syndrome, and the like. Synonyms often encountered in the literature include *acute confusional state* and *reversible dementia* (Liston, 1982). These acute conditions are quite common in the aged population (Eisdorfer & Cohen, 1978; Fox, Topel, & Huckman, 1975; Hughes, Myers, Smith, & Libow, 1973). In general, they are distinguished from chronic problems only by the onset (Lipowski, 1982), although Rabins and Folstein (1982) also found that persons with delirium had a higher mortality rate than those with dementia.

Overt signs of delirium can include perceptual distortions, babbling speech, increased psychomotor activity, reduced attention span, agitation, sleep pattern disruption (Janowsky, 1982), incontinence, ataxia (Mueller, Hotson, & Langston, 1983), disorientation, lack of recognition of acquaintances (Stoudemire, Baker, & Thompson, 1981), tachycardia, hypotension, hyperthermia (Rabins & Folstein, 1982), and changes in the auditory evoked potential (Goodin, Starr, Chippendale, & Squires, 1983). Therefore, three response classes can be affected: First, there may be physical indicants, such as tachycardia and abnormal laboratory values; second, there may be motor signs, such as agitation and ataxia; and third, there may be perceptual–cognitive symptoms, as reflected by tangential speech and shortened attention span.

This third response class most clearly appears to affect a person's ability to utilize environmental information in order to achieve a response in the appropriate context.

Since the causes of acute behavioral disturbances are treatable, thus restoring appropriate stimulus-response associations, it is important to identify the etiology promptly. Many of the causes are presented in Table 14.1.

McAllister, Scowden, and Stone (1978) reported that clients with chronic renal failure who received between 100 and 1,000 mg of chlorpromazine for 2 to 7 days exhibited motor restlessness and hallucinations. DePaulo, Folstein, and Correa (1982) studied 9 clients (age range, 19–82 years) with lithium intoxication using the Mini-Mental State Examination. The clients showed confusion and disorientation when serum lithium levels were above the therapeutic window. Even when the serum lithium levels fell to within normal limits, cognitive impairment did not improve appreciably for 1 to 2 weeks thereafter.

A 39-year-old male exhibited agitation and confusion after receiving the antifungal antibiotic amphotericin B for disseminated histoplasmosis (Weddington, 1982). Tollefson (1981) cited a case of a 31-year-old male receiving phenytoin and dipropylacetate for a seizure disorder who abruptly began showing disorientation, impaired cognitive ability and memory functioning, and euphoria. When the phenytoin was reduced, the behavioral manifestations cleared.

Plasma levels of the tricyclic antidepressant amitriptyline predicted the incidence of delirium in a study of 14 subjects (age range, 29–73 years) by Preskorn and Simpson (1982). Six of the seven clients with plasma amitriptyline levels above 450 mg/mL showed delirium, whereas none of the 7 subjects with plasma levels below 450 mg/mL showed signs of delirium.

Mondimore, Damlouji, Folstein, and Tune (1983) compared 10 depressed clients who received one or two treatments of electroconvulsive therapy (ECT) with 10 depressed clients who received three to ten treatments (age range, 17–76 years). Using the Mini-Mental State Examination, they reported that subjects with higher anticholinergic drug levels at 1 hour post-ECT showed significantly more confusion than those with lower serum anticholinergic levels. This difference did not hold at 5 hours post-ECT. This relationship is supported by other studies. Tune, Damlouji, Holland, Gardner, Folstein, and Coyle (1981) showed a strong relationship ($p < .001$) between high serum anticholinergic levels and confusion in 29 postcardiotomy patients (age range, 29–75 years). Tune, Strauss, Lew, Breitlinger, and Coyle (1982) found an inverse correlation between levels of serum anticholinergics in chronic schizophrenics and the results of a verbal recall test. No correlation was found, however, between serum levels and the WAIS verbal score.

These findings suggest that elevated anticholinergic levels may cause or at least coincide with confusion. Other physical abnormalities may also precipitate disorientation.

Freely, O'Hare, Veale, and Callaghan (1982) reported that eight of nine family members across four generations diagnosed as having familial hemiplegic migraine also showed acute confusion at times, even when headache or other neurological signs were absent.

Silverfarb and Bates (1983) reported that of eight multiple myeloma patients (age range, 51–85 years), five showed psychiatric illness, and four of these five showed symptoms of delirium. The authors listed as possible causes of this delirium radiotherapy, renal failure, electrolyte imbalance, anemia, chemotherapy, or the illness itself. In a study by Massie, Holland, and Glass (1983) of 19 cancer patients (age range, 29–77 years), 11 of the 13 who died showed symptoms of delirium. The authors attributed these symptoms to metabolic encephalopathy or brain metastasis.

Mueller et al. (1983) reported that a 66-year-old male with increased serum viscosity secondary to multiple myeloma showed signs of acute onset of dementia, including ataxia, grasp and snout release signs, dysarthria, and bowel and bladder incontinence.

Other conditions related to the exhibition of disorientation include hyponatremia, hypernatremia, hypoglycemia, ketoacidosis, infection, hypothyroidism, hyperthyroidism, hypovitaminosis, myocardial infarction, congestive heart failure, trauma, vascular insufficiency, drug withdrawal, impaction, fracture, sensory deprivation, alcohol intoxication, and the use of antihistamines, decongestants, and nitrates (Liston, 1982).

The mechanism(s) behind delirium have not yet been elucidated. It is likely that multiple causal foci are present, including insufficient vascular flow to the brain, disturbed nerve conduction, insufficient neurotransmitter substance avail-

Table 14.1. Causes of Acute Behavioral Disturbances

Cause	Potential for Correction	Behavioral Signs
Medial thalamic hemorrhage (Choi, Sudarsky, Schacter, Biber, & Burke, 1983)	Low	Wandering, memory disturbance, disorientation, amnesia
Dehydration/volume depletion (Seymour, Henschke, Cape, & Campbell, 1980)	High	Confusion
Serum hyperviscosity with multiple myeloma (Mueller et al., 1983)	Moderate	Dysarthria, ataxia, incontinence, soft neurological signs
Familial hemiplegic migraine (Freely, O'Hare, Veale, & Callaghan, 1982)	Unknown	Confusion
Multiple myeloma (or its treatment) (Silverfarb & Bates, 1983)	Unknown	Delirium
Terminal cancer (Massie, Holland, & Glass, 1983)	Low	Delirium
Cardiac surgery (Owens & Hutelmyer, 1982)	Partial	Hallucinations, time disorientation
Heavy metal toxicity (Janowsky, 1982)	Unknown	Clouded consciousness
Electroconvulsive therapy (Daniel & Crovitz, 1982)	High	Disorientation
Amphotericin B (Weddington, 1982)	High	Agitation, confusion
Podophyllin (Stoudemire et al. 1981)	Unknown	Hallucinations, ataxia, disorientation
Phenytoin and dipropylacetate (Tollefson, 1981)	High	Disorientation, impaired memory, euphoria
Elevated tricyclic level (Preskorn & Simpson, 1982)	Unknown	Delirium
Lithium intoxication (DePaulo, Folstein, & Correa, 1982)	High	Cognitive impairment
Chlorpromazine and chronic renal failure (McAllister, Scowden, & Stone, 1978)	High	Restlessness, hallucinations
Elevated anticholinergic level (Mondimore, Damlouji, Folstein, & Tune, 1983; Tune, Damlouji, Holland, Gardner, Folsteim, & Coyle, 1981; Tune, Strauss, Lew, Breitlinger, & Coyle, 1982)	High	Confusion, poor recall
Hyponatremia and hypernatremia	High	Hyperactivity
Hypoglycemia	High	Confusion
Ketoacidosis	High	Hyperactivity, disorientation
Hypothyroidism and hyperthyroidism	High	Confusion, mania
Drug withdrawal	High	Hallucinations, agitation
Sensory deprivation	High	Hallucinations, disorientation
Congestive heart failure	Moderate	Confusion
Impaction	High	Confusion
Vascular insufficiency	Moderate	Fluctuating orientation
Fracture	High	Agitation, confusion

ability, poor metabolism, waste accumulation, cell volume changes, sedation, cerebral tissue loss, and/or changes in cerebral pressure. Any or all of these changes may affect stimulus-response accuracy, thus making disorientation, wandering, and similar behaviors highly likely to occur.

CHRONIC CAUSES OF DEFICIENT STIMULUS CONTROL

Inappropriate stimulus control may also result from chronic, permanent, and usually progressive changes in the brain. Although these changes may, of course, result from many of the causes of delirium described earlier if left unchecked, they typically have entirely different etiologies. The mechanisms, however, are likely to be the same.

Most dementias are a result of Alzheimer's disease or multi-infarcts, although neoplasms, long-term alcohol consumption, nutritional deficiencies, head trauma, normal-pressure hydrocephalus, Pick's disease, and Creutzfeldt–Jakob disease may also lead to dementia. Generally, the more global the effect on brain tissue, the more stimulus-free responding is observed. Therefore, it is likely that persons with Alzheimer's disease will show more apparent stimulus-free responding, including disorientation and wandering, than persons with more focal damage.

The typical course of dementia is progressive, beginning with mild memory loss, word search difficulty, depression, and personality changes. With time, more blatant aphasia, agitation, and bizarre behavior become evident, for example, genital exposure, wandering, getting lost, dyscalculia, misplacement of items, loss of abstract ability, and sleep–wake cycle disturbance. With further progression of the dementia, more stimulus-free responding occurs, such as hallucinatory behavior, apraxia, disintegrating speech, neologisms, stereotyped motor movements, incontinence, and loss of self-care ability.

Differential diagnosis among dementia types has met with equivocal results. This is due, in large part, to a lack of sound behavioral indices in studies of dementia, even though sophisticated structural measures have been developed (for an example of such a measure, see Tachibana, Meyer, Okaysasu, Shaw, Kandula, & Rogers, 1984). The lack of diagnostic specificity is of little concern in treatment of wandering and disorientation, however, since the behaviors of consequence are functionally similar.

Once a functional analysis has shown that disorientation and wandering are due to insufficient stimulus control, the underlying chronic cause may have little relevance. Once delirium, depression, and reinforcement seeking have been excluded, techniques to strengthen stimulus control can be implemented.

INSUFFICIENT ENVIRONMENTAL STIMULI AS A CAUSE

It should be noted briefly that the exhibition of disorientation and wandering may result from an interaction between limited processing (acutely or chronically caused) and limited sources of available information. The relative influence of each factor, internal versus external, varies. On the one hand, in severe, late-stage Alzheimer's disease, for example, it is doubtful that a stimulus- and reinforcement-rich environment would compensate for the cerebral damage enough to shape appropriate behavior for any length of time.

On the other hand, even mildly impaired individuals, particularly when recently relocated, may exhibit a variety of responses out of context if there are no cues to indicate rest rooms, individual beds or rooms, time of day, staff function, pills, and the like.

It is also true that extremely limited sensory information could, *alone*, cause observed behavior to appear irrational in the absence of any intrapersonal abnormalities (Cluff & Campbell, 1975; Koncelik, 1982). This rather obvious point is included only to alert clinicians to temper their conclusions regarding the appropriateness of a given behavior, and thus their zeal to intervene, when the behavior may well be inappropriate due to deficient cues. When this is the case, medical or psychotherapeutic interventions may be unwarranted and counterproductive.

FUNCTIONAL ANALYSIS OF POOR STIMULUS CONTROL

As we have noted, the behavior of interest that is due to insufficient stimulus or context control can appear exactly like that due to other causes. Since the choice of treatment is likely to depend on the hypothesized cause, it is extremely important to determine accurately the controlling variable(s).

If one has eliminated severe sensory loss and severely deprived environment as the primary causes for disorientation and wandering, he or she should proceed as follows:

A. Specify to what the person is or is not oriented. This can be done via observation in a natural setting, with mental status examination, or using ward/environment orientation scales.

B. See if the person is consistently disoriented across time. Fluctuations in orientation may reflect a process of delirium as opposed to a progressive dementia.

C. Conduct observations to assess the correlations between orientation and laboratory values or clinical signs. Such temporal correlations may suggest the nature of the acute etiology.

D. Identify types of stimuli or components of stimuli that tend to elicit maladaptive responses. Answers to the following questions will provide very useful information in this regard:

1. Does the client spend a great amount of time relocating furniture, moving cushions, and carrying about other articles? This behavior has been identified, at least as shown by male geriatric inpatients, as being positively correlated with dementia (Hussian & Davis, 1983). Are these items hoarded in a personal area or are they left in what appears to be random areas? The difference may suggest a problem of stealing versus a problem of insufficient stimulus control.

2. Does the elderly individual respond inappropriately more in some areas of his or her residence that in other areas? For example, does the person continually enter areas designated for others or is the behavior less selective? The answer might distinguish between purposeful trespassing and true wandering.

3. What components of a stimulus field appear to attract the individual? In the author's experience, certain colors, mirrors, and areas containing a lot of visual information seem to attract attention and trigger inappropriate behavior. Lines separating tiles on floors, raised areas on walls, such as electrical outlets and switches, and places where carpet meets uncarpeted floor are also attractions. These areas involve contrast between surfaces and provide more perceptual information.

4. Are exit doors more selectively approached during ambulation than other doors?

5. Is there much self-stimulation being exhibited during ambulation, such as knob twirling, hand clapping, vent rubbing, or door shaking?

E. Determine the onset and course of the problem behavior from reliable sources. A gradual onset generally suggests a dementing process, while a sudden onset suggests the possibility of a reversible cause.

F. Determine if the behavior is, indeed, resulting in consequences that require modification. Is the behavior actually placing the exhibitor in jeopardy, or is it simply annoying or inconvenient to those around the person? In some cases, intervention will be required even when only significant others and not the exhibitor are receiving the unfortunate consequences. However, functional analysis should reveal whether intervention would be solely to soothe others at great expense to the freedom of the exhibitor. If response reduction techniques are being considered, such concern should be foremost.

There are several cases when intervention is *not* recommended. These include the following:

1. Extreme disorientation as to time, place, and person when the effects of retraining are not only unlikely to be realized but may also exacerbate depression and/or agitation.

2. When inappropriate sexual behavior involves no helpless or incompetent victim. If no alternatives are made available to the exhibitor, response reduction could be considered unethical.

3. When the behavior, even when extremely bizarre (e.g., "sowing seeds" in hallways, "fishing" in lobbies, "changing tires" on sofas), results in only minor environmental change. Such behavior, frequently observed in the late stages of Alzheimer's disease, usually results in little disruption and requires little corrective measures on the part of others.

4. When free and safe ambulation does not result in problematic consequences to the exhibitor or to those around the exhibitor *and* the likelihood of placement to a setting where such behavior might be problematic is doubtful. This may be true in highly restrictive settings, where entry into hazardous areas is impossible.

Once it has been determined that intervention is warranted, there are several approaches that may be used. Most of these are designed to reorient the elderly individual. Attempts to modify wandering are less frequently reported. Treatment of acute problems are as numerous as the causes.

MANAGEMENT

Acute Causes of Disorientation and Wandering

The treatments for delirium symptoms are primarily medical and therefore beyond the scope of this chapter. However, support, education, and environmental modifications might be appropriate adjunctive interventions. For example, to reduce the intensity of the symptoms and the consequences of delirium, Liston (1982) suggests several courses to take, such as improving the physiological status of the exhibitor, increasing nighttime illumination, providing verbal orientation and moderate amounts of sensory stimulation, and protecting the client.

One of the few attempts to intervene *prior* to anticipated delirium shows promising results. Owens and Hutelmyer (1982) studied 64 cardiac surgery patients (age range, 21–74 years; mean age, 54.1 years) and found that 44 (68%) showed hallucinations and time disorientation after the surgery. However, patients who had received preoperative intervention that provided coping skills for postoperative problems reported being able to control the nature and duration of the delirium better than controls. An equal number of unusual experiences were reported by the two groups.

It should be noted that the management techniques described in the next section for chronic problems could be utilized for behaviors associated with acute confusional states as well. However, physiological stabilization is the top priority in dealing with delirium, and successful educational, rehabilitation, psychotherapeutic, and environmental techniques usually result in improvements well after the acute etiology has been adequately resolved.

Chronic Disorientation and Wandering

A variety of techniques have been suggested to shape appropriate orienting responses, including reality orientation training, remotivation, resocialization, attitude therapy, reinforcement therapy, sensory stimulation, sensory retraining, memory retraining, and milieu therapy (Barns, Sack, & Shore, 1973). The most widely applied and evaluated technique is reality orientation, a loose collection of strategies usually involving the repetition of factual data, the continual presence of current information, and socialization components (Drummond, Kirchhoff, & Scarbrough, 1978; Folsom, 1968; Merchant & Saxby, 1981).

Research provides at least minimal support for reality orientation efforts, particularly in the area of verbal reorientation (Brook, Degun, & Mather, 1975; Cornbleth & Cornbleth, 1979; Drummond et al., 1978; Holden & Woods, 1982; Woods, 1979). For example, Brook et al. (1975) provided nine psychogeriatric patients (mean age, 73.3 years), most with diagnoses of dementia, with 16 weeks of daily active reality orientation training; another nine merely had stimulus items available. The patients receiving the active training showed improvements in nursing ratings of orientation and social functioning. The authors noted that encouragement and reinforcement are important elements in retraining orientation.

Woods (1979) compared reality orientation to no treatment and "social therapy" groups (mean age, 76.6 years) on several tests, including the Wechsler Memory Scale and a test of concentration. It should be noted that social therapy was basically a conversation group, not a social learning technique. Reality orientation classes were held 5 days a week for 5 months. Woods found that the subjects receiving reality orientation performed better than those in the conversation group or the controls on the Wechsler Memory Scale, the concentration test, and an orientation device. Cornbleth and Cornbleth (1979) studied 22 nursing-home patients with diagnoses of organic brain syndrome (mean age, 75 years). Subjects attended reality orientation classes 5 days a week for 3 months. No control group was included. Verbal orientation and independent functioning were said to have increased.

Citrin and Dixon (1977) utilized both 24-hour reality orientation (continuously available information regarding day, date, etc.) and reality orientation classes. Twelve "moderately disoriented" clients (mean age, 84 years) received the combined reality orientation training, and 13 subjects (mean age, 83 years) served as controls. Clients were assessed on the Geriatric Rating Scale (GRS) and the Reality Orientation Information Sheet

(ROIS), an index consisting of training stimuli. The group receiving the reality orientation training did better on the ROIS but not on the GRS.

Many other studies show results similar to the Citrin and Dixon (1977) study—namely that verbal orientation tends to improve after reality orientation training—but broader measures and behavioral indices are either not evaluated or show little improvement after treatment. For example, Hanley, McGuire, and Boyd (1981) compared classroom reality orientation with ward behavior orientation with psychogeriatric patients ($N = 58$). Classroom reality orientation training resulted in increases in cognitive functioning but not in appropriate behavior on the ward. The clients receiving ward orientation training showed improvements in their ability to locate key areas of the ward. This training involved giving clients prompts during guided ambulation.

Zepelin, Wolfe, and Kleinplatz (1981) compared combined 24-hour and classroom reality orientation training with a no-treatment control group. At 6 months, clients who received the combined reality orientation training showed slight improvements on a mental status questionnaire relative to the controls, who worsened. There were no differences on an Activities of Daily Living measure or in interpersonal behaviors.

A study of 14 confused male Veterans Administration inpatients (mean age, 59.1 years) by Goldstein, Turner, Holzman, Kanagy, Elmore, and Barry (1982) suggested that reality orientation training improved scores on a reality orientation questionnaire. However, there was no generalization to novel items or to activity level.

A 68-year-old female with Korsakoff's syndrome who received reality orientation training successfully learned three lists of items, but her responses did not generalize outside of the experimental setting (Woods, 1983). Powell-Proctor and Miller (1982) reported some benefits with reality orientation but also noted the sparse evidence for generalization in the relevant literature.

A number of published studies have failed to show any significant benefits of reality orientation training. For example, Barnes (1974) found no change on an orientation questionnaire for six geriatric patients with confusion and disorientation after 6 days of classroom reality orientation training that lasted 6 weeks. Hogstel (1979) compared 20 nursing-home clients (mean age, 80 years) who received reality orientation training with 20 in a no-treatment control group (mean age, 84 years). All were described as confused. There were no significant differences on an 18-item reality orientation questionnaire, which included such items as "What is your name?"

Several investigators (e.g., Voelkel, 1978) have found, like Hanley et al. (1981), that other approaches or components may be more effective than reality orientation. One such study, by MacDonald and Settin (1978), compared reality orientation training with participation in a sheltered workshop on a life satisfaction rating, nursing ratings, and behavioral observation. The reality orientation training covered 15 sessions of 50 minutes each in groups of five elderly individuals. The training involved the use of news articles and a reality orientation board. The sheltered workshop involved reinforcement for production. The mean age of the 30 institutionalized subjects was 64.4 years. No benefits of reality orientation were observed, and, in fact, some decrease in life satisfaction was noted. The sheltered workshop, however, as rated by nurses, resulted in improved life satisfaction and greater social interest.

Although a substantial body of research supports the efficacy of reality orientation training, mainly for verbal orientation, there are problems with the supportive literature. These problems include an abundance of alternative explanations for success (Letcher, Peterson, & Scarbrough, 1974); methodological problems (Schwenk, 1979), such as the use of training stimuli alone as post-treatment measures; inappropriate statistics; and the lack of ecological validity (i.e., generalization).

An alternative approach is to consider disorientation as a memory problem. This view leads to alternative treatment methods. If disorientation and wandering are viewed simply as a problem with short-term memory, memory retraining should help decrease the disorientation. Most memory retraining involves either the use of visual imagery, the loci method, motor coding, and verbal strategy training or the use of external cues (see Kurlychek, 1983, for a description of the use of an alarm chronograph to improve memory functioning).

Furthermore, memory loss can be seen, at least partially, within a learning framework. According to an operant conditioning model of memory problems (Moffat, 1984), forgetting is due to a reduction of repetition of crucial information via extinction and/or differential reinforcement of other behavior. This suggests that retraining programs should include prompts and positive reinforcement for accurate orientation or cue identification.

Wilson (1984) has presented the advantages of a behavioral approach to memory retraining. These advantages include adaptability to a variety of problems of settings, encouragement of specificity of treatment goals, concomitance of assessment and treatment, the continual monitoring of treatment effects, and proven effectiveness. Wilson suggests that memory training include shaping, chaining, prompting, modeling, and fading procedures.

Wood (1984) supports this approach for the remediation of attention disorders secondary to brain trauma. He contends that the use of cues to improve the duration of attention alone is not sufficient. Rather, positive reinforcement, shaping, and feedback are necessary components of successful treatment. He states: "Possibly the most effective, least technological and therefore easiest attentional training procedure is that offered by behavior learning" (p. 167).

For example, Langer, Rodin, Beck, Weinman, and Spitzer (1979) provided positive reinforcement in the form of tokens to a group of memory-impaired elderly. Tokens, earned for producing correct information, were exchanged for gift items. This group not only produced significantly more correct information than the no-treatment control group but could generalize to new material in both immediate and remote memory areas.

Memory retraining is designed to teach *strategies* rather than *material*, as is the case with reality orientation training. A third method involves the use of cues, signs, or symbols in the environment, usually paired with prompts to attend to these cues and reinforcement for accurate performance. This approach does not involve the teaching of strategies or factual information per se but seeks to control certain behaviors by associating the symbols-cues-signs with appropriate response and with positive reinforcement. This approach may appear to be more passive and to demand little "self-control" on the part of the disoriented individual or wanderer. However, it may be the only approach in cases of extremely deficient stimulus control. Both orientation and safe ambulation may be enhanced via this approach, known as *stimulus enhancement/control*.

Stimulus Enhancement/Control

The pairing of a stimulus (color, noise, flash of light) that is typically noninformative in its own right with differential consequences for the observer in order to shape a concurrent behavior is referred to as *stimulus control*. The intensification of existing stimuli in order to increase the rate of a particular response is referred to as *stimulus enhancement*.

The provision of an enriched or enhanced environment alone has been shown to shape certain behaviors in elderly clients other than orientation or ambulation. For example, Mishara and Kastenbaum (1973) reduced self-injurious behavior in institutionalized elderly by enriching the environment and by providing a token economy. Quattrochi-Tubin and Jason (1980) increased activity attendance and social interactions by providing announcements before the activity and access to refreshments during the activity. Likewise, Pollock and Liberman (1974) placed colored tape on the floor to guide a demented patient to the toilet, thus reducing inappropriate urination. Even something as simple as different seating arrangements can differentially affect the rate of social interactions (Peterson, Knapp, Rosen, & Pither, 1977) and eating behaviors (Melin & Gotestam, 1981).

If disorientation and wandering (as a special case of spatial disorientation) are viewed as responses to poor stimulus control, both should be amenable to stimulus enhancement/control techniques. For example, Ejd and Olsson (1979) trained an 82-year-old male diagnosed as having senile dementia to navigate through his living area without errors. The client was taught via prompts, instructions, and symbols, to locomote from one "landmark" to another (e.g., bed to toilet, table to bed, dayroom to table).

Hanley (1981) used verbal orientation prompts and signposts to improve ward orientation scores of demented elderly inpatients. He found that the use of signposts alone was not sufficient to improve orientation and that some sort of instructions were needed.

Hussian (1982) successfully modified wandering behavior by the placement of two different colored symbols in a nursing home. One color had been associated with positive consequences, while the other color was paired with a noxious noise. Three clients with diagnoses of senile dementia (mean age, 73.4 years) were then allowed to ambulate freely after these cues were placed in the environment: the cue associated with positive consequences where ambulation was safe and the cue associated with aversive consequences where continued ambulation could be hazardous. The number of potentially dangerous entries was reduced significantly. These three studies suggest that environmental manipulations, along with instructions or training to utilize these environmental guideposts, may remove the unfortunate consequences of disorientation and wandering among the demented elderly. The major benefit of such an approach is that the behavior itself is not being drastically reduced. Certainly, ambulation is not a behavior that should be reduced. Rather, the ambulation is being shaped to occur in safe environs and without error.

Wandering and the Differential Reinforcement of Other Behavior

One final and promising report, by Fatis, Surdy, Shawchuck, and Ulrich (1984), suggests another method designed to reduce wandering while at the same time increasing positive, appropriate behavior. These authors utilized verbal prompts and differential reinforcement of other behavior to reduce the wandering of a 76-year-old institutionalized female with Alzheimer's disease. When the client began to exhibit wandering and trespass behaviors, these behaviors were interrupted and she was prompted to engage in either household activities or social interaction. Positive reinforcement, in the form of primaries (food rewards) or praise, then followed. A reversal design clearly demonstrated that, during intervention, the wandering decreased and social interactions increased in frequency.

Disorientation and wandering, then, can be viewed as special cases of responses to inappropriate stimulus control. Although the literature is small, the use of stimulus enhancement and stimulus control techniques appears promising. Certainly, a considerate use of verbal orientation procedures, strategy training, differential reinforcement of other behavior, and external cues can be effective in dealing with these serious problems.

REFERENCES

American Psychological Association. 1982. *Diagnostic and statistical manual, 3rd edition* Washington, DC: Author.

Baltes, M. M., & Barton, E. M. (1977). New approaches toward aging: A case for the operant model. *Educational Gerontology, 2,* 383–405.

Barnes, J. A. (1974). Effects of reality orientation classroom on memory loss, confusion, and disorientation in geriatric patients. *Gerontologist, 14,* 138–142.

Barns, E. K., Sack, A., & Shore, H. (1973). Guidelines to treatment approaches. *Gerontologist, 13,* 513–527.

Brook, P., Degun, G., & Mather, M. (1975). Reality orientation, a therapy for psychogeriatric patients: A controlled study. *British Journal of Psychiatry, 127,* 42–45.

Choi, D., Sudarsky, L., Schacter, S., Biber, M., & Burke, P. (1983). Medial thalamic hemorrhage with amnesia. *Archives of Neurology, 40,* 611–613.

Citrin, R. S., & Dixon, D. N. (1977). Reality orientation: A milieu therapy used in an institution for the aged. *Gerontologist, 17,* 39–43.

Cluff, P. S., & Campbell, W. H. (1975). The social corridor: An environmental and behavioral evaluation. *Gerontologist, 15,* 516–523.

Cornbleth, T. (1977). Effects of a protected hospital ward area on wandering and non-wandering geriatric patients. *Journal of Gerontology, 32,* 573–577.

Cornbleth, T., & Cornbleth, C. (1979). Evaluation of the effectiveness of reality orientation in a nursing home unit. *Journal of the American Geriatrics Society, 27,* 522–524.

Daniel, W. F., & Crovitz, H. F. (1982). Recovery of orientation after electroconvulsive therapy. *Acta Psychiatrica Scandinavica, 66,* 421–428.

DePaulo, J. R., Folstein, M. F., & Correa, E. I. (1982). The course of delirium due to lithium intoxication. *Journal of Clinical Psychiatry, 43,* 447–449.

Drummond, L., Kirchhoff, L., & Scarbrough, D. R. (1978). A practical guide to reality orientation: A treatment approach for confusion and disorientation. *Gerontologist, 18,* 568–573.

Eisdorfer, C., & Cohen, D. (1978). The cognitively impaired elderly: Differential diagnosis. In M. Storandt, I. C. Sigler, & M. F. Elias (Eds.), *The clinical psychology of aging* (pp. 7–42). New York: Plenum.

Ejd, A., & Olsson, B. (1979). Training of spatial orientation with a senile demented patient: An experimental case study. *Scandinavian Journal of Social Medicine, 7,* 173–180.

Fatis, M., Surdy, T. M., Shawchuck, C., & Ulrich, T. (1984). *Prompting prosocial behavior in an "Alzheimer's" patient who exhibited wandering and combative behavior.* Paper presented at the meeting of the *Association for the Advancement of Behavior Therapy,* Philadelphia.

Folsom, J. C. (1968). Reality orientation for the elderly mental patient. *Journal of Geriatric Psychiatry, 1,* 291–307.

Fox, J. H., Topel, J. L., & Huckman, M. S. (1975). Dementia in the elderly: A search for treatable illnesses. *Journal of Gerontology, 30,* 557–564.

Freely, M. P., O'Hare, J., Veale, D., & Callaghan, N. (1982). Episodes of acute confusion or psychosis in familial hemiplegic migraine. *Acta Neurologica Scandinavica, 65,* 369–375.

Goldstein, G., Turner, S. M., Holzman, A., Kanagy, M., Elmore, S., & Barry, K. (1982). An evaluation of reality orientation theory. *Journal of Behavioural Assessment, 4,* 165–178.

Goodin, D. S., Starr, A., Chippendale, T., & Squires, K. C. (1983). Sequential changes in the P3 component of the auditory evoked potentials in confusional states and dementing illnesses. *Neurology, 33,* 1215–1218.

Haley, W. E. (1983). A family-behavioral approach to the treatment of the cognitively impaired elderly. *Gerontologist, 23,* 18–20.

Hanley, I. G. (1981). The use of signposts and active training to modify ward disorientation in elderly patients. *Journal of Behavior Therapy and Experimental Psychiatry, 12,* 241–247.

Hanley, I. G., McGuire, R. J., & Boyd, W. D. (1981). Reality orientation and dementia: A controlled trial of 2 approaches. *British Journal of Psychiatry, 138,* 10–14.

Hogstel, M. O. (1979). Use of reality orientation with aging confused patients. *Nursing Research, 28,* 161–165.

Holden, V. P., & Woods, R. T. (1982). *Reality orientation: Psychological approaches to the confused elderly.* Edinburgh: Churchill–Livingstone.

Hoyer, W. J. (1973). Applications of operant techniques to the modification of elderly behavior. *Gerontologist, 13,* 18–22.

Hughes, C. P., Myers, F. K., Smith, K., & Libow, L. S. (1973). Pseudosenility: Acute and reversible organic brain syndromes. *Journal of the American Geriatrics Society, 21,* 112–120.

Hussian, R. A. (1982). Stimulus control in the modification of problematic behavior in elderly institutionalized patients. *International Journal of Behavioral Geriatrics, 1,* 33–46.

Hussian, R. A. (1984a). Behavioral geriatrics. In M. Hersen, R. M. Eisler, & P. M. Miller (Eds.), *Progress in behavior modification* (Vol. 16, pp. 159–183). Orlando, FL: Academic.

Hussian, R. A. (1984b). Geriatric behavior therapy. In J. P. Abrahams & V. Crooks (Eds.), *Geriatric mental health* (pp. 109–122). Orlando, FL: Grune & Stratton.

Hussian, R. A., & Davis, R. L. (1983 May). *Analysis of wandering in institutionalized geriatric patients.* Paper presented at the meeting of the *Association for Behavior Analysis,* Milwaukee, WI.

Janowsky, D. S. (1982). Pseudodementia in the elderly: Differential diagnosis and treatment. *Journal of Clinical Psychiatry, 43,* 19–25.

Koncelik, J. A. (1982). *Aging and the product environment.* Stroudsburg, PA: Hutchinson Ross.

Kurlychek, R. T. (1983). Use of a digital alarm chronograph as a memory aid in early dementia. *Clinical Gerontologist, 1,* 93–94.

Langer, E. J., Rodin, J., Beck, P., Weinman, C., & Spitzer, L. (1979). Environmental determinants of memory improvement in late adulthood. *Journal of Personality and Social Psychology, 37,* 2003–2013.

Letcher, P. B., Peterson, L. P., & Scarbrough, D. (1974). Reality orientation: A historical study of patient progress. *Hospital and Community Psychiatry, 25,* 801–803.

Lipowski, Z. J. (1982). Differentiating delirium from dementia in the elderly. *Clinical Gerontologist, 1,* 3–10.

Liston, E. H. (1982). Delirium in the aged. In L. F. Jarvik & G. W. Small (Eds.), *The psychiatric clinics of North America* (Vol. 5, pp. 49–66). Philadelphia: Saunders.

MacDonald, M. L., & Settin, J. M. (1978). Reality orientation versus sheltered workshops as treatment for the institutionalized aging. *Journal of Gerontology, 33,* 416–421.

Mace, N. L., & Rabins, P. V. (1981). *The 36-hour day: A family guide to caring with Alzheimer's disease, related dementing illnesses, and memory loss in later life.* Baltimore, MD: Johns Hopkins University Press.

Massie, M. J., Holland, J., & Glass, E. (1983). Delirium in terminally ill cancer patients. *American Journal of Psychiatry, 140,* 1048–1050.

McAllister, C. J., Scowden, E. B., & Stone, W. J. (1978). Toxic psychosis induced by phenothiazine administration in patients with chronic renal failure. *Clinical Nephrology, 10,* 191–195.

Melin, L., & Gotestam, K. G. (1981). The effects of rearranging ward routines on communication and eating behaviors of psychogeriatric patients. *Journal of Applied Behavior Analysis, 14,* 47–51.

Merchant, M., & Saxby, P. (1981). Reality orientation: A way forward. *Nursing Times, 77,* 1442–1445.

Mishara, B. L., & Kastenbaum, R. (1973). Self-injurious behavior and environmental change in the institutionalized elderly. *International Journal of Aging and Human Development, 4,* 133–145.

Moffat, N. (1984). Strategies of memory therapy. In B. Wilson & N. Moffat (Eds.), *Clinical management of memory problems* (pp. 63–88). Rockville, MD: Aspen.

Mondimore, F. M., Damlouji, M. N., Folstein, M. F. & Tune, L. (1983). Post-ECT confusional states associated with elevated serum anticholinergic levels. *American Journal of Psychiatry, 140,* 930–931.

Monsour, N., & Robb, S. S. (1982). Wandering behavior in old age: A psychosocial study. *Social Work, 27,* 411–416.

Mueller, J., Hotson, J. R., & Langston, J. W. (1983). Hyperviscosity-induced dementia. *Neurology, 33,* 101–103.

Owens, J. F. & Hutelmyer, C. M. (1982). The effect of preoperative intervention on delirium in cardiac surgical patients. *Nursing Research, 31,* 60–62.

Patterson, R. L., Dupree, L. W., Eberly, D. A., Jackson, G. M., O'Sullivan, M. J., Penner, L. A., & Kelly, C. D. (1982). *Overcoming deficits of aging: A behavioral approach.* New York: Plenum.

Peterson, R. G., Knapp, T. J., Rosen, J. O., & Pither, B. F. (1977). The effects of furniture arrangement. *Behavior Therapy, 8,* 464–467.

Pinkston, E. M., & Linsk, N. L. (1984). *Care of the elderly: A family approach.* Elmsford, NY: Pergamon.

Pollock, D. D., & Liberman, R. P. (1974). Behavior therapy of incontinence in demented inpatients. *Gerontologist, 14,* 488–491.

Powell-Proctor, L., & Miller, E. (1982). Reality orientation: A critical appraisal. *British Journal of Psychiatry, 140,* 457–463.

Preskorn, S. H., & Simpson, S. (1982). Tricyclic antidepressant-induced delirium and plasma drug concentration. *American Journal of Psychiatry, 139,* 822–823.

Quattrochi-Tubin, S., & Jason, L. A. (1980). Enhancing social interactions and activity among the elderly through stimulus control. *Journal of Applied Behavior Analysis, 13,* 159–163.

Rabins, P. V., & Folstein, M. F. (1982). Delirium and

dementia: Diagnostic criteria and fatality rates. *British Journal of Psychiatry, 140,* 149–153.

Raskin, A., & Jarvik, L. F. (1979). *Psychiatric symptoms and cognitive loss in the elderly.* Washington, DC: Hemisphere Publishing.

Schwenk, M. A. (1979). Reality orientation for the institutionalized aged: Does it help? *Gerontologist, 19,* 373–377.

Seymour, D. G., Henschke, P. J., Cape, R. D. T., & Campbell, A. J. (1980). Acute confusional states and dementia in the elderly: The role of dehydration/volume depletion, physical illness and age. *Age and Ageing, 9,* 137–146.

Silverfarb, P. M., & Bates, G. M. (1983). Psychiatric complications of multiple myeloma. *American Journal of Psychiatry, 140,* 788–789.

Snyder, L. H. (1978). Wandering. *Gerontologist, 18,* 272–280.

Spivack, M. (1984). *Institutional settings.* New York: Human Sciences Press.

Stoudemire, A., Baker, N., & Thompson, T. L. (1981). Delirium induced by topical application of podophyllin: A case report. *American Journal of Psychiatry, 138,* 1505.

Tachibana, H., Meyer, J. S., Okaysasu, H., Shaw, T. G., Kandula, P., & Rogers, R. L. (1984). Xenon contrast CT-CBF scanning of the brain differentiates normal age-related changes from multi-infarct dementia and senile dementia of Alzheimer type. *Journal of Gerontology, 39,* 415–423.

Tollefson, G. D. (1981). Delirium induced by the competitive interaction between phenytoin and dipropylacetate. *Journal of Clinical Psychopharmacology, 1,* 154–158.

Tune, L. E., Damlouji, N., Holland, A., Gardner, T. J.,

Folstein, M. F., & Coyle, J. T. (1981). Association of postoperative delirium with raised serum levels of anticholinergic drugs. *Lancet, ii,* 651–652.

Tune, L. E., Strauss, M. E., Lew, M. F., Breitlinger, E., & Coyle, J. T. (1982). Serum levels of anticholinergic drugs and impaired recent memory in chronic schizophrenic patients. *American Journal of Psychiatry, 139,* 1460.

Voelkel, D. (1978). A study of reality orientation and resocialization groups with confused elderly. *Journal of Gerontological Nursing, 4,* 13–18.

Weddington, W. W. (1982). Delirium and depression associated with amphotericin B. *Psychosomatics, 23,* 1076–1078.

Wilson, B. (1984). Memory therapy in practice. In B. Wilson & N. Moffat (Eds.), *Clinical management of memory problems* (pp. 89–111). Rockville, MD: Aspen.

Wisocki, P. A. (1984). Behavioral approaches to gerontology. In M. Hersen., R. M. Eisler., & P. M. Miller (Eds.), *Progress in behavior modification* (Vol. 16, pp. 121–158). Orlando FL: Academic.

Wood, R. L. (1984). Management of attention disorders following brain injury. In B. Wilson & N. Moffat (Eds.), *Clinical management of memory problems* (pp. 148–170). Rockville, MD: Aspen.

Woods, R. T. (1979). Reality orientation and staff attention: A controlled study. *British Journal of Psychiatry, 134,* 502–507.

Woods, R. T. (1983). Specificity of learning in reality orientation sessions: A single case study. *Behaviour Research and Therapy, 21,* 173–175.

Zepelin, H., Wolfe, C. S., & Kleinplatz, F. (1981). Evaluation of a yearlong reality orientation program. *Journal of Gerontology, 36,* 70–77.

Chapter 15

Pain Management in the Elderly

Ellie T. Sturgis, Jeffrey J. Dolce, and Patricia C. Dickerson

One current challenge in the field of behavioral medicine is the assessment and treatment of chronic pain in the rapidly growing geriatric population. Until recently, it was commonly believed that pain was inevitable in the aging process. This view has been challenged, and the quality of life for the geriatric patient is becoming an increasingly important area of interest for behavioral medicine researchers and practitioners.

In 1900, those aged 65 and over made up only 4.17% of the population. Today the number is about 11% and is growing (Steinburg, 1984). It is estimated that 75% to 80% of this group is suffering from one or more chronic illnesses with accompanying discomforts (Bonica, 1980; Lewis, 1984). Pain is often a significant component of those discomforts.

THEORIES OF PAIN

Through the centuries, physicians and philosophers have developed and discarded a number of theoretical models as they have attempted to explain the phenomenon of pain. Several of the most common theories of pain are the specificity, gate control, learning, and interactive models. Each of these theories has made a significant contribution to the approaches clinicians have used in the mangement of pain.

The first dominant theory of pain control was the specificity model, which can be traced to the writings of Descartes in 1644 (Melzack, 1973). In this model pain is considered to be a sensory event arising from damage to a specific body tissue. It is regarded as a neuroanatomical phenomenon resulting from the stimulation of peripheral receptors (see Figure 15.1). Impulses from these receptors enter the spinal cord by way of the sensory nerves that synapse in the substantia gelatinosa of the dorsal horn (Barr, 1979; Carpenter, 1978). Connections from the dorsal horn and laminae 6, 7, and 8 then cross to the other side of the cord through the white commissure and ascend to higher brain centers through the lateral spinothalamic tract, which projects to the ventral posterior thalamic nucleus. The tract synapses in the thalamus and then projects through the internal capsule to the sensory cortex, where pain is supposedly represented on a one-to-one basis with fibers from specific areas of the body. Pain, in the specificity model, is regarded as a sensation resulting from a neuroanatomical process that is related to peripheral tissue damage.

Treatment modeled on the specificity theory involves the interruption of the transmission of signals along the pathway. Clinicians have tried to disrupt the pathway using surgical and pharmacological methods (Halpern, 1984; Schurmann, 1975). These efforts have provided quick, effective relief for many forms of pain, but have been of limited utility with chronic benign pain conditions (Black, 1975; Long, 1980; Sternbach, 1974). Such

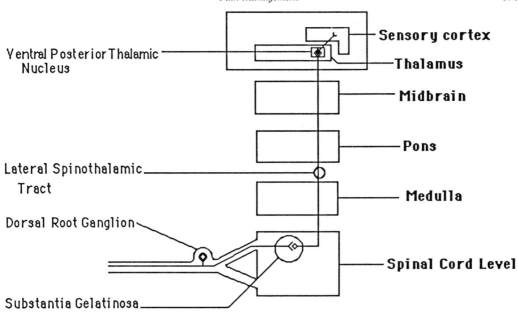

Figure 15.1 Specificity model. Impulses enter the nervous system through the spinal cord and travel centrally to the sensory cortex where pain is represented on a one to one basis with fibers from specific areas of the body.

treatment failures point out the limited utility of a simple model in which one considers pain as directly related to tissue damage.

The complexity of clinical pain and the limitations of the specificity model are further highlighted when considering the impact of psychological factors on pain. Beliefs, expectancies, anxiety, depression, and the personal interpretation of pain all affect the perception of pain (Weisenberg, 1977). Environmental factors, such as positive and negative reinforcement, also contribute to the experience of pain (Fordyce, 1976). The fact that pain is influenced by other factors suggests that it is more than a physical response to tissue damage—it is also a psychological experience, affected by a variety of cognitive and environmental variables. Such observations led the Subcommittee on Taxonomy (1979) of the International Association for the Study of Pain to define *pain* as "an unpleasant experience which we primarily associate with tissue damage *or* describe in terms of tissue damage or both" (p. 250). This definition acknowledges the role of physical stimuli, as well as the roles of behavior and subjective distress in the experience of pain.

The limitations of the specificity model spurred advances in the conceptualization of pain, one of which was the development of the gate control theory by Melzack and Wall (1965). The gate control model recognizes that a one-to-one correspon-

dence between perceived pain and peripheral stimulation is insufficient to explain the complex phenomenon of pain. It is an interactive neuroanatomical model that proposes that sensory perception is modified at the level of the spinal cord, subcortex, and cortex. It hypothesizes the existence of a gating mechanism in the dorsal horns of the spinal cord (see Figure 15.2). This mechanism is influenced by the various types of ascending sensory information entering the spinal cord, as well as by central brain centers. Sensory information from large-diameter myelinated nerve fibers entering the gating mechanism inhibit the transmission of nociception at the spinal cord level, while activation of small-diameter unmyelinated sensory fibers facilitates nociception. Centers at various levels of the brain are also activated by cognitive processes and ascending information from other parts of the body. These brain centers exert a mediating effect on the spinal cord gating mechanism through descending pathways (Melzack, 1973; Melzack & Wall, 1983). Attention, affective states, and cognition affect the perception of pain through the brain centers. The gate control theory therefore is a much broader theory of pain perception.

Although the gate control model has received criticism (Nathan, 1976), it provides a useful alternative to the specificity model. It has stimulated much research, extending the knowledge of the specific pathways involved in pain and anal-

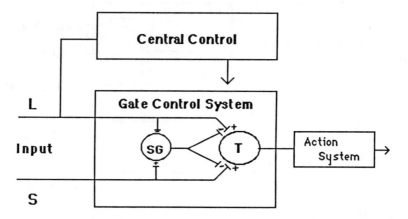

Figure 15.2 Gate control theory. The large (L) and small (S) fibers project to the substantia gelatinosa (SG) and first central transmission (T) cells. The central control trigger is represented by a line running from the large fiber system to central control mechanisms, which in turn project back to the gate control system. The T cells project to the entry cells of the action system. +=excitation; −+inhibition. From "Pain Mechanisms: A New Theory" by R. Melzack and P. D. Wall, 1965, *Science, 150*, p. 972. Reprinted by permission of Dr. Ronald Melzack, McGill University.

gesia (Fields & Basbaum, 1979; Mayer, 1979; Mayer & Price, 1976; Terman, Lewis, & Liebeskind, 1984; Wall, 1984). The role of neurochemical factors, such as endorphins (Mayer & Watkins, 1981; Millan, 1981; Terinius, 1979; Watkins & Mayer, 1982) and serotonin (Messing & Lytle, 1977), has similarly been delineated. Such research has confirmed the importance of cortical and subcortical processes in the perception of pain.

The application of learning theory to pain has also advanced the understanding of the phenomenon. This theory differentiates between *nociception* and the resulting pain behaviors. Nociception refers to the neurophysiological process associated with tissue damage that is experienced as pain. Nociception typically leads to variety of observable pain behaviors, actions emitted by an individual that signal to others that a person is hurting and that communicate the occurrence of the process (Fordyce, 1976). Examples include facial expression, gait, medication intake, and verbal complaints. Such pain behaviors termed *respondent pain behaviors* are controlled by specific antecedent stimuli (i.e., nociception). Respondent pain behaviors convey the need to determine and treat the underlying physical pathology presumed to be antecedent to the pain behaviors.

Fordyce (1976) postulated the existence of "operant pain behaviors" which are actions influenced by events that follow, not precede, their occurrence. The likelihood of recurrence of an operant behavior can be increased or decreased by reward or punishment, respectively. This principle implies that if respondent pain behaviors persist long enough to be affected by reinforcement contingencies, learning can occur and pain behaviors will, to some extent, come under the control of environmental stimuli. The fact that pain behaviors can be affected and maintained by environmental factors explains the fact that complaints of pain often persist despite adequate healing of the original damage. The concepts of operant and respondent pain behaviors are increasingly being used to explain pain problems (Brena & Chapman, 1983).

Still another theory of pain, developed by Loeser (1980), offers an interactive model, which incorporates the behavioral, nociceptive, affective, and cognitive aspects of pain. In this model, pain is viewed as a complex composite of nociception, perception, suffering, and pain behaviors (Haley & Dolce, in press; Urban, 1982). The presence, nature, and intensity of a noxious stimulus all influence pain perception through the nociceptive process (the neurophysiological process of signaling pain). The actual perception of pain, however, is also influenced by cognitive and affective factors, such as suffering, which can include not only distress from pain but also distress from other stressful life events. In this model, pain behavior serves as a means of communicating the presence of both nociception and suffering to others.

Numerous factors influence an individual's perception of and response to pain. The models reviewed here are but a few of the many proposed through the years. Unfortunately, the understanding and management of pain disorders is further complicated by the fact that pain problems are diverse and may differ with respect to a number of dimensions. The critical issue in the successful management of pain is that the clinician utilize a model appropriate to the specific type of pain. The theoretical model of pain adopted interacts with the classification category to direct the treatment process.

Basic conceptual distinctions between classes of pain that are useful to the clinician include acute, recurrent acute, chronic benign, and chronic malignant pain. Attempts to clarify the role of nociception in persistent pain have resulted in a distinction between acute and chronic pain (Black, 1975; Crue, 1983a; Fordyce, 1976; Sternbach, 1974). *Acute pain* is pain of recent onset (usually less than 6 months) that is associated with nociceptive stimulation and its resulting respondent pain behaviors. It functions as a warning signal for the detection and treatment of tissue damage or a disease process. Traditional medical management based on a nociceptive model has been the most effective in the treatment of acute pain problems, although psychological factors remain relevant (Turk, Meichenbaum, & Genest, 1983).

Chronic benign pain is pain that has persisted for at least 6 months despite adequate healing and in the absence of physical findings sufficient to explain the severity of the problem. Crue (1983a, 1983b) postulates that chronic benign pain is not produced by peripheral sensory imput resulting from tissue damage but is centrally generated within the brain. Chronic pain is a form of operant pain behavior. Models of pain emphasizing environmental and affective factors are extremely important for understanding and managing chronic pain. Anxiety, depression, and suffering (Loeser, 1980), as well as reinforcement contingencies (Fordyce, 1976), can exacerbate pain complaints and pain behaviors. Thus, successful treatment of chronic benign pain is best accomplished by a shift from a disease model that stresses nociception to a rehabilitation model that focuses on the management of pain, suffering, and disability.

Chronic malignant pain and *recurrent acute* pain are hybrids of acute and chronic benign pain (Crue, 1983a, 1983b). Chronic malignant pain is associated with an active metastatic disease process, whereas recurrent acute pain is associated with disorders in which the patient experiences recurrent flare-ups related to peripheral tissue patho-

logy (e.g. rheumatoid arthritis, migraine headaches). In both cases, pain is associated in part with organic pathology and must utilize a theoretical model of pain that adequately distinguishes nociception from peripheral tissue damage. In addition, however, both chronic malignant and recurrent acute pain may persist over long periods of time and may be influenced by affective and environmental variables. For example, Redd (1982) has demonstrated the role of learning in the distress experienced by cancer patients. The successful management of chronic malignant and recurrent acute pain should include a careful assessment of the relevant factors impacting on the suffering and disability of the patient.

In summary, the theoretical model of pain adopted by the clinician influences the treatment process. In working with the elderly, the clinician will encounter a number of different types of pain. The effective caretaker must be prepared to use a model of pain that recognizes the biopsychosocial factors that contribute to pain. It is not uncommon for elderly patients to have multiple chronic diseases, each of which can be related to pain complaints. For example, an individual may simultaneously experience acute pain secondary to a fall, recurrent acute pain secondary to arthritis, and chronic benign pain related to poor body mechanics, depression, and lack of exercise. Treatment of the pain problems of any patient, therefore, should start with a complete assessment of all relevant factors including medical, environmental, and psychological variables.

COMMON CAUSES OF PAIN IN THE ELDERLY

Headache

Tension, or muscle-contraction, headaches are the most frequent causes of head pain. In the elderly patient, contributing factors include cervical osteoarthritis, psychological stress, and depression. In addition, these factors can interact, so that a tension headache precipitated by stress may be worsened by the presence of an arthritic condition (Poser, 1976).

Migraine headaches are relatively rare in this population but can occur alone or in combination with muscle-contraction headaches. The more common vascular headaches are related to congestive heart failure, transient ischemia, increased intracranial pressure, and various metabolic disturbances. Giant cell arteritis, an inflammation of the temporal artery, is the most prevalent type of vascular headache in the elderly and is particularly resistant to treatment with analgesic medication (Butler & Gastel, 1980; Freemoon, 1978; Poser, 1976).

Accurate diagnosis of headaches in the elderly patient is extremely important, particularly for chronic headaches with onset after the age of 50. Such headaches are not common and may be symptomatic of a more serious problem. A comprehensive medical examination which includes a thorough and accurate history, is the most critical element in treating the elderly patient with headaches.

Degenerative Diseases

Chronic joint diseases are seen so often among the elderly that most people expect to experience some type of joint pain some time after middle age. Two of the most frequently occurring arthritic pain disorders are osteoarthritis and rheumatoid arthritis (see also chapter 12, this volume).

Osteoarthritis is the more common and milder of the two (Brooks, Kean, Kassam, & Buchanan, 1984; Ehrlich, 1982; Wigley, 1984). Osteoarthritis, or degenerative joint disease, is characterized by a loss of joint cartilage and by hypertrophy of the bone. The exact mechanisms have not been defined, but abnormal stress and injuries to subchondral bone are contributory factors. More than 90% of patients over the age of 40 show radiological evidence of osteoarthritis, particularly in the weight-bearing joints—the knees and ankles (Wigley, 1984). However, many persons with such abnormalities have no musculoskeletal or pain complaints.

Rheumatoid arthritis is a chronic systemic disease of unknown etiology that is manifested primarily by inflammatory arthritis of the peripheral joints, usually in a symmetrical distribution. It occurs in approximately 0.5% to 3.8% of the population typically between the third and the seventh decade of life (Gilliland & Mannick, 1973). Rheumatoid arthritis is more disabling than osteoarthritis and has a greater impact on the quality of life of the geriatic patient. It is not uncommon, however, for the two diseases to coexist and to accompany other diseases of the musculoskeletal system. Unfortunately, the diagnosis of arthritis in any form conveys the prospect of diminished function or disability for the patient;

however, treatment that emphasizes activity balanced with period of rest will increase the probability of continued mobility.

Other inflammatory arthropathies that are common in the elderly include polymyalgia rheumatica, psoriatic arthritis, ankylosing spondylitis, adhesive capsulitis, and systemic lupus. In any of these diseases, pain is the primary source of disability, resulting in confinement, reduced activity, and isolation of the patient.

Osteoporosis is another cause of chronic pain in the elderly patient. It may develop because of a variety of diseases of diverse etiology, all of which are characterized by a reduction in the mass of bone per unit volume to a level below that required for adequate mechanical support. Because the bone mass is decreased and the rate of bone resorption exceeds that of bone formation, eventually the bone can no longer resist the mechanical forces to which it is subjected, resulting in fractures (Krane & Holick, 1973; Lane, Vigorita, & Falls, 1984). Fractures of the thoracic and lumbar spine, long bones, hip, humerus, and wrists are frequently seen in individuals with osteoporosis. Women are at greater risk for osteoporosis, with 50% of the women over the age of 65 showing evidence of sufficient bone loss to increase their chances of suffering a fracture (Lukert, 1982). The exact etiology of this process is unknown; however, osteoporosis occurs more frequently in post-menopausal Caucasian females, individuals who show excessive acid intake, patients treated with heparin, and individuals with rheumatoid arthritis who have been treated with glucocorticosteroid therapy (Krane & Holick, 1983; Lukert, 1982).

Cancer

As the proportion of the population over the age of 65 increases, so does the risk of cancer. Data show that 25% of the population will contract some form of neoplastic disease during their lifetime. Approximately 50% of all cancers occur in the 11% of the population aged 65 and older (Rimer, Jones, Wilson, Bennett, & Engstrom, 1983). Although the exact incidence of pain associated with cancer is unknown, malignant disease is the most common cause of intractable pain seen in patients with terminal illness (Swerdlow, 1973; Turk & Rennert, 1981). The progression of metastatic disease accounts for 78% of the pain complaints in cancer cases, while pain resulting from treatment accounts for approximately 20%, with only 3% resulting from pain syndromes unrelated to the cancer (McGivney & Crooks, 1984).

Differences in Older and Younger Individuals

The aging process is associated with changes in physiology, such as decreases in the muscle-to-fat ratio of the musculoskeletal system, the density and thickness of the bone, and maximal cardiac output (Shock, 1977; Timiras, 1972). Visual acuity and handgrip strength also decrease, factors that can interfere with the ability of the elderly patient to live independently or to engage in a satisfying life-style.

Researchers have used a variety of methods to examine the pain responsivity in older and younger individuals. Harkins, Kwentus, and Price (1984) concluded that the two populations show no difference in pain threshold; however, the elderly were less likely to label faint noxious stimuli as painful and were less able to discriminate between different levels of shock. They hypothesized that age-related changes in the central nervous system cause a deficit in the processing of sensory information. Further examination of the laboratory response of the elderly to painful stimuli should lead to a better understanding of the clinical differences between the pain reports of younger and older populations.

Often the perception and recognition of pain in the elderly patient differs from that observed in other patients. Diseases usually associated with severe pain (e.g., myocardial infarction, appendicitis) may evoke minimal discomfort, while relatively painless procedures may produce much complaining (MacDonald, 1984). Behavioral changes, such as noisiness or agitation in an otherwise quiet patient, may indicate the onset of a new painful process (Hunt, 1980). The differences in laboratory studies and clinical reports of pain in elderly patients indicate a need for further research to better understand the pain experience in this population.

Hunt (1980) suggests that referred pain—discomfort originating at a site other than the one where it is experienced—occurs more frequently in the elderly. The mechanisms by which pain perception is altered in the aged patient, relative to the younger patient, are not clear, but the physiological changes that accompany aging are likely contributors. These findings have direct impli-

cations for the treatment of the elderly patient complaining of pain, thus emphasizing the importance of a detailed history and careful evaluation.

SPECIAL PROBLEMS OF THE ELDERLY

Complexities of Assessment

Assessment and diagnosis of pain are frequently more complicated in elderly patients than in younger patients. An accurate and detailed history is important in diagnosing a chronic pain condition; however, the failing memory of an elderly patient may interfere with the ability to obtain an accurate historical account of the onset of pain and the precipitating events (Hunt, 1980; Rubenstein & Robbins, 1984). Neuropsychological difficulties can also complicate assessment in other ways. Patients with a functional impairment secondary to a minor stroke or arteriosclerosis may rationalize their problem as a pain problem. In this instance, the patient may experience difficulties in short-term memory or in the ability to carry out complex perceptual-motor functions, or may have problems with sensory perception, such as hearing loss. By attributing the problem to pain, the patient can avoid activities in which the impairment would be witnessed by others (Butler & Gastell, 1980), thereby avoiding possible confrontation or embarrassment. Since this is a frequent problem, assessment of cortical and memory functioning in an elderly pain patient is important.

In addition to the problems in assessment posed by neurological difficulties, Fordyce (1978) has identified depression as a second confounding variable in the evaluation of geriatric pain patients. Patients, family, and physicians may mistakenly label a depressed individual as suffering from a debilitating pain problem. Depression is often associated with chronic pain, and this is especially true of the elderly population in which there is a high prevalence of depression (Fordyce, 1978; Romano & Turner, 1985). The two may coexist and interact, so that the depression increases the misery of the pain, and the pain in turn exacerbates the depression (Haley & Dolce, in press). Evaluation of the relative contribution of the two is an important factor in treatment.

Boredom and loneliness, occasionally associated with the aging process, can have a significant impact on the perception and report of pain. Frequently elderly patients have decreased activity levels. In addition, the societal norm of retirement by age 65 and the death of a spouse may leave the elderly patient with too much time alone. Such environmental deficits provide little stimulation to distract attention from the pain and can foster a preoccupation with symptoms of pain. Family and friends who may not attend to the patient when he or she is well may also inadvertently reinforce pain complaints and behaviors by giving attention and sympathy when the patient is complaining of pain (Fordyce, 1978; Miller & LeLieuvre, 1982).

The stress of bereavement in elderly patients may contribute significantly to their perception of pain and illness. It has been found that recently bereaved elderly patients are more likely to report newly developed illnesses and that these illnesses are slightly more severe than those reported by a comparison group. They also rate themselves as generally less healthy; although they do not visit their physicians any more frequently (Thompson, Breckenridge, Gallagher, & Peterson, 1984). This is not inconsistent with research indicating that, although the elderly experience more chronic diseases that cause pain, they are underrepresented among the patients who utilize pain clinics. Further complicating the situation of the geriatric patient, often living on a reduced, fixed income, is the financial strain associated with the increased number of medical problems. This may explain why the elderly have such a high occurrence of painful chronic illnesses but are seldom seen in pain clinics (Harkins et al., 1984).

Because of the many diseases that arise as part of the aging process, polypharmacy—the prescription of multiple medications—is a frequent occurrence in this patient group. The use of multiple drugs increases the possibility of drug interactions, including neutralization of the effects, enhancement of the desired effects, or exaggeration of the toxic or undesired side effects of one or more of the drugs (Gryfe & Gryfe, 1984). When two or more medications are taken, drug-induced changes may occur in the elderly patient which account for as much as 16% of the cases of changed mental status requiring hospitalization (Berlinger & Spector, 1984).

Many of the drugs used in the treatment of pain have adverse side effects. Older patients generally experience increased side effects from medications, probably from age-related changes in drug pharmacokinetics (Berlinger & Spector, 1984; see also chapter 13, this volume). The physiological changes that result from aging alter the effects of the drugs. For example, both hepatic metabolism and renal clearance of drugs decrease with age. This increases the concentration of the free drug in the blood supply, necessitating closer monitoring of drug levels in order to maintain therapeutic concentrations and to avoid toxic side effects (Berlinger & Spector, 1984; Hall & Beresford, 1984).

Aspirin the most commonly used drug for pain and the treatment of arthritis, is responsible for the greatest number of adverse drug reactions resulting in hospitalization (Pfeiffer, 1982). Seventy per cent of the people taking aspirin at dose levels used to treat arthritis experience a daily blood loss of about 5 ML as a consequence of gastric bleeding. Tinnitus, bronchospasm, and coagulation difficulties are also common. Steroids, effective in the treatment of inflammatory diseases can also produce serious side effects in some elderly patients. In an attempt to avoid the use of aspirin and steroids, the use of nonsteroidal anti-inflammatory drugs has increased, but even with brief, well-supervised periods of treatment, the incidence of adverse reactions in the general population ranges from 10% to 40%, with an even higher percentage in the elderly population. In addition to gastric irritation and bleeding, blood dycrasias, confusion, hepatitis, and nephritis may occur (Pfeiffer, 1982).

Antidepressants may have significant effects on the perception of pain (Butler, 1981). They can also be effective in treating problems with sleep continuity and early awakening that often occur in pain patients. However, the elderly patient is at greater risk of developing the side effects produced by these drugs, such as tremor, postural hypotension, cardiotoxicity, and anticholinergic effects, for example, urinary retention and constipation. This is most likely related to changes in drug pharmacokinetics in the elderly (Berlinger & Spector, 1984; chapter 13 of this volume).

The elderly have also been found to be more sensitive to narcotics, Morphine administered to the elderly may produce an effect similar to that produced by 4 times that dose when administered to younger adults (Kaiko, Wallenstein, Rogers, Brabinski, & Houda, 1982). The use of codeine and propoxyphene (Darvon compounds) can cause confusion, hallucinations, respiratory depression, dependence, and addiction. Other narcotics, such as Talwin and Percodan, can produce a toxic psychosis, while morphine and Demerol can interfere with the ability to cough and also can cause urinary retention (Pfeiffer, 1982). In addition, all of the narcotics, as well as the non-narcotic benzodiazepines, can cause depression, drug dependence, and addiction, all of which can exacerbate chronic pain problems.

TREATMENT

The intervention strategies needed in the successful treatment of the elderly pain patient are determined by the nature of the pain complaint and the results of the medical evaluation. The primary variables dictating the choice of intervention include the type of pain experiencd and the source of the pain problem. As is the case with younger pain patients, acute pain is treated more easily than chronic pain.

Acute Pain

Acute pain is primarily associated with nociception and serves as a warning that something is functioning inappropriately and needs attention. Although psychological factors such as anxiety and depression, may affect the perception of pain, physical stimuli are more important in the generation of this type of pain. As healing of the causative factors of the pain occurs, the pain is resolved. Treatment is focused on altering the disease process responsible for the pain and on making the patient as comfortable as possible while healing occurs. The administration of antibiotics, narcotic analgesics, hypnotics, anti-inflammatory agents, and sedatives and the use of general medical and surgical procedures are often appropriate in the treatment of acute pain problems, increasing the patient's ability to cope with and endure the discomfort. The patient understands why he or she is hurting and understands that the pain is time-limited.

Although the management of acute pain is simpler than that of chronic pain, there are still some issues that need to be remembered. Because of the differences in the physiology of the elderly and their effects upon drug pharmacokinetics, the use of medications must be monitored carefully. As noted earlier, the elderly are more sensitive to narcotic medications; thus the doses should initially be lower than that usually prescribed for younger patients and should be increased gradually if needed. In addition the health care professional must monitor both therapeutic drug effects and side effects, such as respiratory

depression, cough suppression, and changes in mental function. Oral agents are generally preferable to parenteral administration (Fordyce, 1976). Anti-inflammatory drugs also need to be monitored carefully since the safety margin between toxicity and therapeutic levels is reduced; furthermore, signs of gastric irritation need to be carefully watched (Harkins et al., 1984). A pharmacist's guidance can help reduce the likelihood of drug interactions caused by the use of numerous medications. Finally, because the elderly often live alone and frequently make errors in medication administration, some supervision of drug intake is recommended. This is especially true if memory deficits are seen on evaluation. The elderly may also need supervision to ensure that they receive adequate nutrition, rest, exercise, and hygienic care during acute illnesses.

Chronic and Recurrent Acute Pain

Treatment of chronic pain and recurrent acute pain is most effective if a multimodal approach is followed. As discussed earlier, chronic pain is more complex than acute pain and typically involves factors other than or in addition to nociception. The choice of which disciplines to include in treatment depends upon the assessment of the problem. However, treatment most frequently focuses on the physical, functional, and psychological components of the pain complaint. It is usually designed to help patients manage their pain rather than eliminate it and therefore it concentrates on increasing the level of functioning, and independence, improving self-control of the pain, and decreasing disability secondary to the pain (Haley & Dolce, in press). If patients understand the nature of a chronic pain problem and the rationale for multimodal treatment, they are more likely to adhere to the treatment strategy, less likely to "doctor-shop" for a magical or simple cure, and more likely to actively participate in their rehabilitation.

Physical

Physical treatment may be medical or surgical in nature, designed, when possible, to eliminate or modify the ongoing nociceptive process. While the elimination of nociception is frequently impossible for the chronic and recurrent acute pain patient, physical treatment can assist in its reduction. Recent advances in such treatment include the use of medications, physical modalities, and selective surgery.

The pharmacological treatment of persistent pain has several functions, including appropriate management of concurrent medical problems (e.g., diabetes, cardiovascular diseases and the use of non-narcotic analgesics, antidepressants, anti-inflammatory medications, and anticonvulsants).

Narcotic analgesics and hypnotics are contraindicated in the management of the chronic benign pain patient, due to their potential for abuse and dependence, the likelihood of producing psychological problems such as depression and sleep disturbance, and their ineffectiveness in managing the chronic pain syndrome. If used at all, these drugs should be administered only to manage acute flare-ups related to actual nociception, and then only with marked caution, on a time-contingent basis, and with careful monitoring.

Analgesics and anti-inflammatory drugs are most effective when administered regularly rather than at the first sign of increased distress. This increases the likelihood of their effectiveness and reduces the patient's anxiety about pain. Antidepressants are often valuable adjuncts to the treatment of chronic pain, particularly in patients who show signs of depressed mood, sleep disturbance, or neuropathy (Butler, 1984). Anticonvulsants may be helpful in controlling trigeminal neuralgias and thalamic pain. Phenothiazines may enhance the effectiveness of antidepressants and can assist in the management of postherpetic neuralgia (Butler & Gastel, 1980). Patients should be monitored carefully for side effects including gastric bleeding, respiratory depression, cardiac arrhythmias, and disturbances in mental functioning, and if they occur, alternatives to pharmacological management may be necessary. Again, as noted before, the elderly are likely to respond positively to small drug doses.

If the patient is dependent upon narcotic or anxiolytic medications, the use of a pain cocktail to detoxify the patient may be indicated (Fordyce, 1976). This procedure involves determination of the patient's daily medication intake, followed by staff-administered reduction of the active medication over time. The active ingredients are placed in a masking liquid and their concentration is faded over the course of treatment. In cases where alterations are made in drug doses, careful monitoring for side effects is needed (Haley & Dolce, in press).

Pain associated with progressive terminal illness presents different requirements to the health care team. For these patients, medical addiction is not a primary concern and the relief of pain is an appropriate goal. However because narcotic analgesics can interfere with cognitive functioning, the patient should be included in the determination of the most appropriate balance of pain relief and mental acuity. Again, the use of a time-contingent, rather than a pain-contingent, schedule is recommended (Carron, 1984; Dolce, Doleys, Raczynski, & Crocker, 1985).

The use of various physical modalities in the control of chronic and recurrent acute pain has increased markedly in recent years (Urban, 1982). They are most successful in the elimination or reduction of nociception, with treatment of symptomatology most common with the chronic pain patient. Pain perception may be changed by decreasing or augmenting afferent nerve impulses. Nerve blocks and epidural injections of corticosteroids are designed to reduce nerve impulses and can be of value in cases of back pain, causalgia, reflex sympathetic dystrophy, and myofascial pain. Various types of stimulation, such as transcutaneous electrical nerve stimulation (TENS), dorsal column, peripheral nerve, and thalamic stimulation, are examples of treatments designed to augment neural stimulation. These methods, which cause paresthesia, have been successful in the modulation of low back pain, myofascial pain, peripheral neuropathy, and central pain. Although response to the nerve blocks and stimulation varies, these techniques are at times useful adjuncts to treatment (Urban, 1982). Other physical modalities that have been shown to be beneficial in the modification of pain include hot and cold packs, paraffin baths, whirlpool baths, Hubbard tanks, acupuncture, acupressure, and massage (Wigley, 1984). As always, a comprehensive evaluation is necessary to determine which of these modalities or combinations would be the most effective. The disciplines of physical and occupational therapy are the ones best qualified to determine the appropriate physical modalities.

Surgery is typically contraindicated in the treatment of benign chronic pain because of poor long-term results, particularly if there is no demonstrable lesion or condition causing the problem (Long, 1980). Neurodestructive techniques and neuroaugmentation implants should only be used in patients who have exhausted other forms of therapy because these procedures have a low overall success rate (Urban, 1982). However, there are some instances of malignant and recurrent acute pain in which surgery is indicated. For these cases, the surgical removal of tumors, the use of chymopapaine injections, manipulation or surgical release of adhesive capsulitis, synovectomy, facet joint denervation, or prosthetic joint replacement may be appropriate. Because these procedures are invasive, a comprehensive assessment is recommended prior to surgical intervention. In addition, the long-term effectiveness of many of these procedures is dependent upon aggressive postsurgical rehabilitation, so close follow-up is needed.

Functional

The physical modalities discussed above are designed to improve the ability of the patient to carry out daily activities and to live independently with as little pain as possible. They may assist in the rehabilitation process by decreasing the nociception experienced by the acute and recurrent pain patient. In addition to these techniques, the physical and occupational therapy disciplines are involved in other aspects of rehabilitation, such as the use of exercise and assistive devices. Optimal results are achieved if principles of learning are integrated in the therapy and training process.

Exercise programs for pain patients have four functions: (a) to increase the range of motion, (b) to strengthen musculature, (c) to improve endurance, and (d) to decondition activity avoidance. When the programs are successful, increased physical conditioning is accompanied by a reduced fear of being active and more behavioral options incompatible with pain behavior. The exercises prescribed vary according to the presenting problem.

The patient's compliance to a given protocol is increased if the exercises are introduced in a graded fashion, so that initially the protocol is relatively easy to carry out and activity is increased gradually as the patient gains proficiency. Exercise quota systems in which increasingly difficult exercise goals are set for the patient have been effective in increasing exercise tolerance and physical conditioning among chronic pain patients (Doleys, Crocker, & Patton, 1982; Fordyce, 1976). Because quotas are increased gradually, therapeutically safe increases in activity are achieved that inhibit overexertions on "good days" and facilitate performance on "bad days". In addition to the quotas, praise is provided for the exercise success (Doleys et al., 1982; Haley & Dolce, in press). It is important that all exercise programs be designed for the particular patient to avoid accidental injury by overstressing unconditioned bodies. A realistic selection of exercises is also important so that the patient can engage in them daily and can see progress. The program should be reevaluated periodically and adjusted to the needs of the patient so that boredom is minimized and the selection of exercises remains appropriate for the patient (Ditunno & Ehrlich, 1970; Schaefer & Sturgis, 1982).

In addition to the use of exercise to increase the functional capabilities of the patient, the way in which exercise and normal movements are performed has been found to be important in the rehabilitation of patients with chronic pain. Chronic pain sufferers typically make many adaptations to help cope with the problem. However, these can cause excessive stress to the joints and surrounding musculature and therefore need to be altered (Ditunno & Ehrlich, 1970).

The breathing pattern of the subject, general posture, gait, and other normal activities may also need to be altered for the patient to return to optimal functioning (Schaefer, 1983). Again, shaping gradual improvements, feedback, and reinforcement for response acquisition will facilitate the acquisition of appropriate response patterns.

Assistive devices can also be useful in helping the patient remain as active and independent as possible. Splints on the hands, wrists, and knees may help reduce inflammation and maintain function in patients with arthritic problems. Crutches, braces, special shoes, and other devices may also reduce weight-bearing effects. Assistive devices can be useful in helping to reduce pain, restore alignment of joints, and prevent further deformity (Ditunno & Ehrlich, 1970). Other self-help devices and environmental adaptations may be of value in the functional rehabilitation of the patient. Such devices as long-handled shoehorns, raised toilet seats, built-up handles, and reaching devices may be effective ways to prevent unnecessary physical stress and improve functional ability. Although the use of such devices signals pain and potential disability, they are appropriate for some patients, since they allow the individual to remain more active and to engage in more adaptive behavior patterns.

Psychological

The goals of psychological approaches to pain management are to increase independence and the level of functioning and to maximize the patient's self-control abilities. Like other treatment approaches for chronic pain, the psychological approaches are designed to reduce the impact of the pain rather than to eliminate it. The psychological techniques commonly fall into several categories: (a) alteration of physiological functioning, (b) contingency management of pain behavior and well behavior, (c) management of affective factors contributing to the pain, (d) appropriate pacing of adaptive behavior, and (e) development of adaptive cognitive coping skills. In addition, as has been mentioned previously, the principles of reinforcement can be applied to the medical and functional treatments to increase their efficacy.

Some of the behavioral techniques, such as relaxation training, are directed at altering physiological functioning in the pain patient. Relaxation training has been shown to be beneficial in the management of anxiety, excessive muscular tension, and sleep problems related to pain (Haley & Dolce, in press; Sanders, 1983). It can also be used to help control the intensity of pain. Relaxation and controlled breathing strengthen the patient's belief that he or she can exert some control during periods of pain and stress (Turk & Rennert, 1981). Autogenic relaxation has been shown to be effective in reducing the autonomic arousal accompanying chronic pain. Biofeedback training has been shown to be effective in reducing tension, improving posture, and retraining musculature involved in the pain process (Dolce & Raczynski, 1985; Wolf, Nacht, & Kelly, 1982). Feuerstein, Adams, and Beiman (1976) reported that an elderly subject could be trained to alter vascular blood flow and cephalic electromyographic activity to effect a reduction in chronic headaches. Biofeedback and relaxation training can alter the aspects of physiology that are hypothesized to be involved in the production and maintenance of chronic pain syndromes, and may be used as adjuncts to other treatment.

Systematic contingency management procedures have been demonstrated to be effective in reducing pain behaviors in both young and elderly pain patients (Fordyce, 1978; Miller & LeLieuvre, 1982). These procedures employ principles of operant conditioning to reinforce the exhibition of appropriate behavior and reduce the frequency of pain behaviors. The operant procedures are designed to increase the likelihood that the patient will experience positive consequences for adaptive behavior patterns. New patterns may involve the development of new leisure outlets, changes in vocation or patterns of familial interaction, and

the establishment of a pleasurable life-style during retirement (Fordyce, 1976, 1978). As was discussed earlier, operant principles can also be used to shape appropriate functional activities and manage analgesic medication.

Affective states can influence the perception of pain, as we have mentioned earlier. Negative affective states such as depression, anxiety, frustration, anger, and irritation, appear to "open the gate" and increase the discomfort the patient experiences. Psychological treatments can be useful in reducing the impact of these emotional states on the patient. The elderly are at higher risk for problems of loneliness and depression caused by the loss of significant others and the reduction in the opportunities for social interaction. Psychological treatments for depression, including increasing pleasurable activities, altering depression-inducing thoughts through cognitive behavioral techniques, and providing support and the opportunity to express feelings and concerns, can be useful in the management of chronic pain. Furthermore, any techniques that provide the patient with more adaptive thought patterns will be helpful. Education about and imaginal and actual exposure to safe increases in activity can reduce the anxiety component of the pain problem. Improved problem-solving skills, particularly those related to the pain, can also be useful in the psychological management of the pain patient. If pain increases, patients should be able to understand why the discomfort has increased in this situation and plan alternative strategies to prevent its recurrence.

Behavioral techniques can be used to teach the patient to pace activities appropriately. Pacing helps the individual to maintain a satisfactory activity level and reduces the likelihood of bad days. Patients are taught to monitor their activities so they do not overexert themselves, thus avoiding a recovery time characterized by low activity levels. Appropriate pacing makes it easier for the patient to plan activities and carry out plans. It also helps foster a sense of self-control, as the individual learns a relationship between activity and pain and how to avoid setbacks by a steady activity schedule. The inclusion of pacing also enhances the patient's perceived role in the treatment and rehabilitative process as he or she becomes responsible for modulating activity level.

Finally, psychological treatments can be used to enhance the patient's ability to cope with pain. The patient can be taught ways to divert attention from the pain and discomfort. This can be accomplished by having the patient participate in activities that increase involvement with the environment and decrease attention to internal cues and by having the patient learn cognitive coping strategies, such as focusing on different aspects of the environment, on non-painful sensations, and on positive thoughts and imagining oneself engaged in pleasant pursuits. The use of guided imagery and hypnosis can be useful in teaching cognitive coping strategies (Turk & Rennert, 1981). These techniques can enhance the patient's perceived ability to cope with the pain.

There have been no studies with an older population that examine the differential effectiveness of the psychological approaches to pain management. It is likely that the procedures differ in effectiveness across individuals, and that older patients respond differently from younger patients to the varied strategies. Gerontological pain management is only beginning to receive attention from clinicians and researchers; however, given the increasing number of the elderly and the increased longevity for all, further research on the pain response, the effective coping strategies available, and the development of additional techniques for pain management remains a high-priority task in the field of behavioral medicine.

Acknowledgements— We gratefully acknowledge the assistance of Stephen C. Moore for comments on drafts of this article. Requests for reprints should be sent to Ellie T. Sturgis, Ph.D., VA Medical Center, 109 Bee Street, Charleston, SC, 29403.

REFERENCES

Barr, M. L. (1979). *The human nervous system* (3rd ed.). New York: Harper & Row.

Berlinger, W. G., & Spector, R. (1984). Adverse drug reactions in the elderly. *Geriatrics, 39,* 45–58.

Black, R. G. (1975). The chronic pain syndrome. *Surgical Clinics of North America, 55,* 999–1011.

Bonica, J. J. (1980). Pain research and therapy: Past and current status and future needs. In L. Ng & J. J. Bonica (Eds.), *Pain, discomfort, and humanitarian care* (pp. 1–46). New York: Elsevier.

Brena, S. F., & Chapman, S. L. (Eds.). (1983). *Management of patients with chronic pain.* New York: Spectrum.

Brooks, P. M., Kean, W. F., Kassam, Y., & Buchanan, W. W. (1984). Problems of antiarthritic therapy in the elderly. *Journal of the American Geriatrics Society, 32* 229–234.

Butler, R. N., & Gastel, B. (1980). Care of the aged. In L. Ng & J. J. Bonica (Eds.), *Pain, discomfort, and humanitarian care* (pp. 297–311). New York: Elsevier.

Butler, S. (1981) Present status of tricyclic antidepressants in chronic pain therapy. In C. Benedetti, C. R.

Chapman, & G. Moricca (Eds.), *Advances in pain research and therapy* (Vol. 1, (pp. 173–197). New York: Raven.

Carpenter, M. B. (1978). *Core text of neuroanatomy* (2nd ed.). Baltimore, MD: Williams & Wilkins.

Carron, H. (1984). Rational management of cancer pain. *Urban Health, 5,* 36–38.

Crue, B. L. (1983a). The peripheralist and centralist views of chronic pain. *Seminars in Neurology, 3,* 331–339.

Crue, B. L. (1983b). The neurophysiology and taxonomy of pain. In S. F. Brena & S. L. Chapman (Eds.), *Management of patients with chronic pain* (pp. 21–31). New York: Spectrum.

Ditunno, J., & Ehrlich, G. E. (1970). Care and training of elderly patients with rheumatoid arthritis. *Geriatrics, 25,* 164–172.

Dolce, J. J., Doleys, D. M., Raczynski, J. M., & Crocker, M. F. (1985). Narcotic utilization for back pain patients housed in private and semi-private rooms. *Addictive Behaviors, 10,* 91–95.

Dolce, J. J., & Raczynski, J. M. (1985). Neuromuscular activity and electromyography in painful backs: Psychological and biomechanical models in assessment and treatment. *Psychological Bulletin, 97,* 502–520.

Doleys, D. M., Crocker, M. F., & Patton, D. (1982). Response of patients with chronic pain to exercise quotas. *Physical Therapy, 62,* 1111–1114.

Ehrlich, G. E. (1982). Diagnosis and management of rheumatic diseases in older patients. *Journal of the American Geriatrics Society, 30* (Suppl. 11), S45–S51.

Feurstein, M., Adams, H. E., & Beiman, I. (1976). Cephalic vasomotor and electromyographic feedback in the treatment of combined muscle contraction and migraine headaches. *Headache, 16,* 232–237.

Fields, H. L., & Basbaum, A. I. (1979). Anatomy and physiology of a descending pain control system. In J. J. Bonica, J. C. Liebeskind, & D. G. Albe-Fessard (Eds.), *Advances in pain research and therapy* (Vol. 3, pp. 427–440). New York: Raven.

Fordyce, W. E. (1976). *Behavioral methods for chronic pain and illness.* St. Louis, MO: Mosby.

Fordyce, W. E. (1978). Evaluating and managing chronic pain. *Geriatrics, 33,* 59–62.

Freemoon, F. R. (1978). Evaluation and treatment of headache. *Geriatrics, 33,* 82–85.

Gilliland, B. C., & Mannick, M. (1973). Rheumatoid arthritis. In R. G. Petersdorf, R. D. Adams, E. Braunwald, K. J. Isselbacher, J. B. Martin, & J. D. Wilson (Eds.), *Harrison's principles of internal medicine* (pp. 1977–1984). New York: McGraw-Hill.

Gryfe, C. I., & Gryfe, B. M. (1984). Drug therapy of the aged: The problem of compliance and the roles of physicians and pharmacists. *Journal of the American Geriatrics Society, 32,* 301–307.

Haley, W. E., & Dolce, J. J. (in press). Assessment and management of chronic pain in the elderly. *Clinical Gerontologist.*

Hall, R. C., & Beresford, T. P. (1984). Tricyclic antidepressants. *Geriatrics, 39,* 81–93.

Halpern, L. M. (1981). Drugs in the management of pain: Pharmacology and appropriate strategies for clinical utilization. In C. Benedetti, C. R. Chapman,

& G. Moricca (Eds.), *Advances in pain research and therapy* (pp. 147–172). New York: Raven.

Harkins, S. W., Kwentus, J., & Price, D. D. (1981). Pain and the elderly. In C. Benedetti, C. R. Chapman, & G. Moricca (Eds.), *Advances in pain research and therapy* (pp. 147–172). New York: Raven.

Hunt, T. E. (1980). Pain and the aged patient. In W. L. Smith, H. Mersky, & S. C. Gross (Eds.), *Pain: Meaning and management* (pp. 143–157). New York: SP Medical & Scientific.

Kaiko, R. F., Wallenstein, S. L., Rogers, A. G., Brabinski, P.Y., & Houda, R. W. (1982). Narcotics in the elderly. *Medical Clinics of North America, 66,* 1079–1089.

Krane, S. M., & Holick, M. F. (1973). Metabolic bone disease. In R. G. Petersdorf, R. D. Adams, E. Braunwald, K. J. Isselbacher, J. B. Martin, & J. D. Wilson (Eds.), *Harrison's principles of internal medicine* (pp. 1949–1954). New York: McGraw-Hill.

Lane, J. M., Vigorita, V. J., & Falls, M. (1984). Osteoporosis: Current diagnosis and treatment. *Geriatrics, 39,* 40–47.

Lewis, C. B. (1984). Rehabilitation of the older person: A psychosocial focus. *Physical Therapy, 64,* 517–521.

Loeser, J. D. (1980). Perspectives on pain. *Proceedings of the First World Conference on Clinical Pharmacology and Therapeutics* (pp. 313–316). London: Macmillan.

Long, D. M. (1980). Surgical therapy of chronic pain. *Neurosurgery, 6,* 317–328.

Lukert, B. P. (1982). Osteoporosis—A review and update. *Archives of Physical Medicine and Rehabilitation, 63,* 480–487.

MacDonald, J. B. (1984). Presentation of acute myocardial infarction in the elderly—A review. *Age and Ageing, 13,* 196–200.

Mayer, D. J. (1979). Endogenous analgesia systems: Neural and behavioral mechanisms. In J. J. Bonica, J. C. Liebeskind, & D. G. Albe-Fessard (Eds.), *Advances in pain research and therapy* (Vol. 3, pp. 385–410). New York: Raven.

Mayer, D. J., & Price, D. D. (1976). Central nervous system mechanisms of analgesia. *Pain, 2,* 379–404.

Mayer, D. J., & Watkins, L. R. (1981). Role of endorphins in endogenous pain control systems. In T. A. Ban (Ed.), *Modern problems of pharmacopsychiatry* (pp. 68–96). Nashville, TN: Karger Basel.

McGivney, W. T., & Crooks G. M. (1984). The care of patients with severe chronic pain in terminal illness. *Journal of the American Medical Association, 251,* 1182–1188.

Melzack, R. (1973). *The puzzle of pain.* New York: Basic Books.

Melzack, R., & Wall, P. D. (1965). Pain mechanisms. A new theory. *Science, 150,* 971–979.

Melzack, R., & Wall, P. D. (1983). *The challenge of pain.* New York: Basic Books.

Messing, R. B., & Lytle, L. D. (1977). Serotonin containing neurons: Their possible role in pain and analgesia. *Pain, 4,* 1–21.

Millan, M. J. (1981). Stress and endogenous opioid peptides. A review. In T. A. Ban (Ed.), *Modern problems of pharmacopsychiatry* (pp. 49–67). Nashville, TN: Karger Basel.

Miller, C., & LeLieuvre, R. B. (1982). A method to reduce chronic pain in elderly nursing home residents. *Gerontologist, 22,* 314–317.

Nathan, P. W. (1976). The gate control theory of pain: A critical review. *Brain, 99,* 123–158.

Pfeiffer, R. F. (1982). Drugs for pain in the elderly. *Geriatrics, 37,* 67–76.

Poser, C. M. (1976). The types of headache that affect the elderly. *Geriatrics, 31,* 103–106.

Redd, W. H. (1982). Behavioral analysis and control of psychosomatic symptoms of patients receiving intensive cancer treatment. *British Journal of Clinical Psychology, 21,* 351–358.

Rimer, B., Jones, W., Wilson, C., Bennett, D., & Engstrom, P. (1983). Planning a cancer control program for older citizens. *Gerontologist, 23,* 384–389.

Romano, J. M., & Turner, J. A. (1985). Chronic pain and depression: Does the evidence support a relationship? *Psychological Bulletin, 97,* 18–34.

Rubenstein, L. Z., & Robbins, A. S. (1984). Falls in the elderly: A clinical perspective. *Geriatrics, 39,* 67–78.

Sanders, S. H. (1983). Component analysis of a behavioral treatment program for chronic low back pain. *Behavior Therapy, 14,* 697–705.

Schaefer, C. A. (1983). It only hurts when I breathe. *Aches and Pains, 4,* 51–53.

Schaefer, C. A., & Sturgis, E. T. (1982). Physical therapy: A prominent compenent of a pain clinic. *Proceedings of the 9th International Congress of the World Confederation for Physical Therapy* (pp. 506–509). Stockholm, Sweden: AB Grafiska Gruppen.

Schurmann, K. (1975). Surgical treatment: Fundamental principles of the surgical treatment of pain. In M. Weisenburg (Ed.), *Pain* (pp. 261–274). St. Louis, Mo: Mosby.

Shock, N. (1977). Systems integration. In L. Hayflick & C. E. Finch (Eds.), *Handbook of the biology of aging.* New York: Van Nostrand Reinhold.

Steinberg, F. U. (1984). Education in geriatrics in physical medicine residency training problems. *Archives of Physical Medicine and Rehabilitation, 65,* 8–10.

Sternbach, R. A. (1974). *Pain patients: Traits and treatment.* New York: Academic Press.

Subcommittee on Taxonomy. (1979). Pain terms: Recommended by the International Association for the Study of Pain. *Pain, 6,* 249–252.

Swerdlow, M. (1973). Relieving pain in the terminally-ill. *Geriatrics, 28,* 100–103.

Terinius, L. (1979). Endorphins and chronic pain. In J. J. Bonica (Ed.), *Advances in pain research and therapy* (pp. 103–121). New York: Raven.

Terman, G. W., Lewis, J. W., & Liebeskind, J. C. (1981). Endogenous pain inhibitory substrates and mechanisms. In C. Benedetti, C. R. Chapman, & G. Moricca (Eds.), *Advances in pain research and therapy* (pp. 43–56). New York: Raven.

Thompson, L. W., Breckenridge, J. N., Gallagher, D., & Peterson, L. (1984). Effects of bereavement on self-perceptions of physical health in elderly widows and widowers. *Journal of Gerontology, 39,* 309–314.

Timiras, P. S. (1972). *Developmental physiology and aging.* New York: Macmillan.

Turk, D. C., Meichenbaum, D., & Genest, J. (1983). *Pain and behavioral medicine: A cognitive behavioral perspective*. New York: Guilford.

Turk, D. C., & Rennert, K. (1981). Pain and the terminally ill cancer patient: A cognitive-social learning perspective. In H. J. Sobel (Ed.), *Behavior therapy in terminal care: A humanistic approach*. Cambridge, MA: Ballinger.

Urban, B. J. (1982). Therapeutic aspects in chronic pain: Modulation of nociception, alleviation of suffering, and behavioral analysis. *Behavior Therapy, 13*, 430–437.

Wall, P. D. (1981). Neurophysiology of acute and chronic pain. In C. Benedetti, C. R., Chapman, & G. Moricca (Eds.), *Advances in pain research and therapy* (Vol. 7, pp. 13–25). New York: Raven.

Watkins, L. R., & Mayer, D. J. (1982). Organization of endogenous opiate and nonopiate pain control systems. *Science, 216*, 1185–1192.

Weisenberg, M. (1977). Pain and pain control. *Psychological Bulletin, 84*, 1008–1044.

Wigley, F. M. (1984). Osteoarthritis: Practical management in older patients. *Geriatrics, 39*, 101–120.

Wolf, S. L., Nacht, M., & Kelly, J. L. (1982). EMG feedback training during dynamic movement for low back pain patients. *Behavior Therapy, 13*, 395–406.

Chapter 16

Dependence in Aging

Margret M. Baltes* and Hans Werner-Wahl

It is commonplace knowledge that in our Western societies the cultural imperative is on self-reliance and independence. A cultural belief system declaring dependency as something aversive and not to be sanctioned must exert a strong negative impact on any person exhibiting dependent behaviors. Such a cultural belief system is confirmed but at the same time qualified by the following three statements: one by the anthropologist Margaret Clark, and two by psychiatrists, Sigmund Freud and Alvin Goldfarb.

> Only by being independent can an American be truly a person, self-respecting, worthy of concern and the esteem of others. (Clark, 1969, p. 59)
>
> It should be emphasized that whether a class of people are believed to have "something of value" to exchange in social relationships is largely a matter of cultural definition. . . . If an individual arbitrarily is defined as having "nothing of value" to exchange, then any claim he makes on others is evidence of dependency. (p. 67)
>
> In jeder Beziehung liegt eine Abhängigkeit, selbst mit einem Hund. (There is an element of dependence in every relationship, even with a dog.) (Freud, cited by Wortis, 1954, p. 23)
>
> Dependent relationships are not "regressed" to, they persist throughout the life of most people. They are more troublesome in old age, primarily because they are less elaborately disguised, and are expressed in ways that are less acceptable socially than before. (Goldfarb, 1969, p. 3)

From these statements—and we could enumerate many more—we can deduce three major issues confronting research on dependence in aging: multicausality, multidimensionality, and multifunctionality.

The first issue is multicausality. Dependence is not only a phenomenon of old age but of all life stages. Thus, it is not only associated with biological status but is strongly influenced by social-environmental conditions as well. Many factors—such as social, cultural, economic, and psychological—play a role in the development and maintenance of dependence. Because of the nature of Western society, with its differential economic and social structure, certain groups (e.g., the elderly, women, the unemployed) are more readily labeled *dependent* than others. In societal systems where different values, expectations, and goals prevail, the elderly often retain their former importance because of economic or psychosocial reasons (experience, wisdom) and are not labeled as readily, despite similar declines in biological features. In this vein, Clark (1969) speaks of the arbitrariness of the cultural definition of who is dependent, when, and where.

Second, dependence is a highly multifaceted, or multidimensional, construct, much like other concepts, such as depression, self-control, or agression. Thus, it is not surprising to find in the

---

* Dedicated by Margret M. Baltes to Dr. Helmut Coper, Professor of Neuropsychopharmacology, on the occasion of his 60th birthday, December 30, 1985. Professor Coper's work in and commitment to gerontology was most influential in my returning to Germany and joining the faculty of the Free University of Berlin.

literature a whole array of dependencies, including mental, physical, economic, social, emotional, cognitive, real, pseudo, normal, crisis, and neurotic dependencies. Dependence is also analyzed at many different levels, such as behavioral, personal, situational, and interpersonal, depending on the theoretical and methodological approach. Thus, any approach will most likely concentrate on specific aspects of dependence and rarely perhaps never on dependence in its total complexity. It also follows that dependencies may affect one another or may occur independently of one another. For example, a person may be physically dependent with or without exhibiting psychological dependencies.

A third issue pertains to the multifunctionality of dependence. In general, dependence appears to be undesirable in Western societies. However, there are variations on this theme not only in different cultures but also within Western cultures. Certain dependencies are not only tolerated but accepted by society for certain individuals at certain times, during illness or mourning, or in young children, where the expectation is toward increasing competence and thus independence. In this vein. it is argued by some authors (e.g., Clark, 1969) that there are some forms and/or occasions during one's life in which dependent behaviors are judged to be necessary either as a state of transition toward health or as a typical expectation of a stage in life. Goldfarb (1969) underlines this notion when maintaining that a successful therapist–client relationship is only possible on the basis of the client's dependence (see also Dollard & Miller, 1950). Freud, in the statement above, as well as other scholars (Munnichs & van den Heuvel, 1976) broaden this view of dependence even further and speak about interdependence necessary for social relationships in general. Thus, we need to examine under which conditions certain aspects of dependence in old age are to be judged functional and desirable.

This chapter will first provide an idea of the magnitude of the phenomenon of dependence in old age. We start out with a consideration of the term *dependency ratio* and examine some epidemiological research findings. At the same time, we will discuss the limitations of such data for a full understanding of dependence. Next, we will present an overview of theoretical perspectives that lend themselves to the empirical analysis of dependence beyond a mere quantitative account. Then we will summarize our own research program on

dependence as a demonstration of an empirical realization of one such theoretical perspective. Finally, we will discuss the theoretical and practical implications.

ESTIMATES OF THE MAGNITUDE OF DEPENDENCE IN THE ELDERLY

Dependency Ratio

In the search for an estimate of the magnitude of dependency in old age, one will most likely encounter the term *dependency ratio*. This term has been coined by demographers to represent the relative productivity of persons forming the age structure of a society and its implications for societal functioning (for a full discussion, see Hauser, 1976). The dependency ratio reflects the proportion of the working population that is available to support those who are out of the labor force. Commonly, it relates the number of people who are under 15 and over 65 years of age to those between 15 and 65. This ratio—admittedly very rough and only a crude estimate of the needs of the dependents—plays a crucial role in social planning because it provides information about the locations along the age stratum at which there are more dependents than work-related producers. Social planning and policies will take different directions depending on whether the dependents are mostly young or old people.

Statistics show that dependency ratios are increasing in Western cultures due to an increase of elderly in the population. It is interesting to note that this, in turn, is due to general improvements in the standard of living, resulting in higher life expectancies for the population. A comparison of dependency ratios in the United States, for instance, shows an increase from .09 in 1930 to .18 in 1980; it is estimated to increase to .29 by the year 2030 (U.S. Bureau of the Census, 1978).

It is obvious that in the context of dependency ratios, dependence is defined solely as being out of the labor force. No information is yet provided about the specific needs or dependencies that might be characteristic of elderly out of the labor force and might require environmental change to yield the resources for prolonged autonomy. Nevertheless, information about such dependency ratios should alert researchers, practitioners, and politicians to the necessity for inquiry into the needs and dependencies of the elderly population. In light of large interindividual variations among the elderly (P. B. Baltes & M. M. Baltes, 1980; M. M. Baltes & Kindermann, 1985), such information also needs to be especially attentive to subgroup differences.

In keeping with the international trend toward a relative increase in the elderly population, as well as toward improvement of health of the population as a whole, it is not surprising to find attempts to improve medical, social, and psychological services for the elderly. In this context, epidemiological studies play an important role in providing information about the needs of the elderly.

Epidemiological Research Findings

An estimated 4% of older individuals live in long-term care institutions. This rather low estimate is based on simple cross-sectional and one-shot studies. The likelihood that a given individual in his/her lifetime will be institutionalized is judged to be much higher, but any given estimate is less clear, as it requires good cohort-longitudinal studies (P. B. Baltes, Reese, & Nesselroade, 1977). In any case, it is generally assumed that institutionalization is preceded by increasing dependency and need for support and help. This is not to negate Maddox's (1984) argument that about 40% of the institutionalized elderly could manage at home given adequate resources for independent living. Let us turn to what we know about the dependencies in the elderly living at home, a group representing by far the largest proportion of the elderly population.

Definition and Measurement of Dependency in Epidemiological Studies

In epidemiological studies the term *dependence* is defined pragmatically as "functional incapacity" (Akhtar, Broe, Crombie, McLean, & Andrews, 1973; Shanas, Townsend, Wederburn, Friis, Miløj, & Stehouwer, 1968; Wan, Odell, & Lewis, 1982) or as "practical helplessness" (van den Heuvel, 1976). The basic position of epidemiological research on dependence is perhaps best characterized by the following statement: "Another extremely important factor related to adjustment is the individual's capacity to carry out the essential activities of daily living" (Gallagher, Thompson, & Levy, 1980, p. 30). Similarly, Garrad and Bennet (1971), in a well-known epidemiological study used the following definition of dependency: "We define disability as limitations in perfor-

mance in one or more activities which are generally accepted as essential basic components of daily living, such that inability to perform them necessitates dependence on another person. The severity of disability is then proportional to the degree of dependence" (p. 97). In some epidemiological studies we find an attempt to differentiate between dependency and disability. In this sense, Akhtar et al. (1973), for instance, restrict dependence to problems related to personal maintenance activities.

In addition to such differentiations, there is the International Classification of Impairments, Disabilities, and Handicaps (ICIDH), published by the World Health Organization (WHO) in 1980. This classification scheme is characterized by a strong association between disease, impairment, and disability on the one hand, and *handicap* as the role-impairing result of disability, on the other. In addition to activities of daily living, the list of dependencies accompanying this classification scheme includes dysfunctions in communication, orientation, and cognitive performances.

Despite the existing differences in the definition of dependence, there is a general consensus regarding dependent-relevant activities that most epidemiological studies attempt to assess, namely the areas of self-maintenance, home maintenance, mobility, and, frequently, impairment in hearing and vision.

There remain, however, differences in the rating procedure of independence/dependence. The ratings in the compared studies in Table 16.1 range from a global estimate (covering three areas—self-care, mobility, incontinence—as used by Silberstein, Kossowsky, & Lilus, 1977) to a scoring system differentiating between domains of daily activities both in self-care and instrumental activities, such as using the telephone, shopping, and managing medications. There is also an attempt toward a more qualitative measurement. Thus, Isaacs and Neville (1976) assess dependency via rating the help needed in terms of duration and predictability, regardless of the area in which assistance is needed.

In most assessment instruments, dependency is rated as follows: activities can be executed without help and/or special efforts; activities can only be executed when special efforts are made by the individual; and activities are executed with the help of others. In this rating, either a global estimate for one entire domain, for example, self-care, is made, or each subarea within one domain—for example,

Table 16.1. Disability and Dependency in the Elderly: Empirical Findings from Different Countries

Country	Author(s)	N	Age	Type of Rating	Result
USA	Shanas et al., 1968	2430[1]	65+	Not disabled (Index of incapacity = 0–2)	84.9[2]
				Disabled (Index of 3 and more)	15.1
USA	Wan et al., 1982	1182	60+	Self-care:	
				Not disabled	92.0
				Disabled in at least one function	8.0
				Instrumental activity:	
				Not disabled	72.9
				Disabled in at least one activity	27.1
UK	Shanas et al., 1968	2436[1]	65+	Not disabled (Index of incapacity = 0–2)	78.7[2]
				Disabled (Index of 3 and more)	21.3
UK	Akhtar et al., 1973	808	65+	Not disabled	72.0
				Disabled in at least one ADL-area	28.0
				Dependent (no self-care)	3.0
UK	Isaacs & Neville, 1976	1035	65+	No potential need	64.5
				Potential needs in long or short intervals	35.5
				Critical interval needs	6.1
FRG	Cooper, 1984; Wahl, in press	343	65+	Self-care:	
				Not disabled	88.0
				Disabled (difficulties or help needed in at least one function)	22.0
				Household tasks:	
				Not disabled	49.5
				Disabled (difficulties or help needed in at least one function)	50.5
DK	Shanas et al., 1968	2415[1]	65+	Not disabled (Index of incapacity = 0–2)	79.0[2]
				Disabled (Index of 3 and more)	21.0
Israel	Silberstein et al., 1977	249	65+	Funct. independent	88.8[3]
				Funct. dependent	11.2
Swiss	Wieltschnig, 1982	4454	60+	Independent	88.9
				Dependent in one ADL function	4.9
				Dependent in at least two functions	4.7
				Dependent in all functions	1.4

[1] Bedridden persons excluded.
[2] New calculation from Table III-4, Shanas et al., 1968, p. 56.
[3] Data from the first measurement point.

grooming and bathing—is rated and the results added to obtain the overall score. An arbitrary cut-off point is often used to differentiate between independence and dependence. Recently efforts have been directed toward the development of Guttman-like scales (Sandholzer, 1982; Williams, 1979). Such scales will—provided certain prerequisites, such as satisfactory coefficients of reproducibility and scalability, are met (Torgerson, 1958)—improve the precision of measurement and predictability of degree of dependency in, as well as comparability of, both future large-scale studies and diagnostic procedures in applied settings.

Empirical Findings

In Table 16.1 we have summarized the findings of some well-known epidemiological studies carried out in different countries. All are aimed at the measurement of the prevalence rate of dependence in old age. Given the different definitions and criteria for assessment of dependencies previously discussed, it is not surprising that the findings are equivocal and thus should be taken only as rough guidelines.

On examining the different percentages listed for dependence, one notes the wide range in prevalence rates, varying between 3% and 35.5% with one estimate as high as 50%. Upon closer inspection, one realizes that the percentages vary depending on the definition of dependence used. If one considers only those old people who need actual and regular help in self-care tasks, the percentages are indeed very low. For instance, Akhtar et al. (1973) report a prevalence rate of 3%, and Isaacs and Neville (1976), one of 6.1%. These findings seem to support Maddox's (1984) statement that "the risk of impairment and dependency in later life should not be exaggerated" (p. 22).

When expanding the definition of dependence to include those elderly who need actual and regular help in both self-care and instrumental daily activities, such as household tasks, the percentages increase dramatically. For instance, Cooper (1984) reports that every second woman over 65 to be somewhat dependent. Similarly, Wan et al. (1982) identify 27.1% of old people over 60 who need some help in at least one instrumental daily activity. One needs to keep in mind that most percentages reported in the literature do include old people needing "potential" as well as "actual" help, thus referring to both the already-dependent and those who run the risk of becoming dependent in the near future. Accordingly, epidemiological findings on dependence need careful scrutiny, because prevalence rates differ widely. We desperately need more precise knowledge so as to be able to specify dependent-related needs of the elderly and to design optimal environmental conditions for the elderly.

Epidemiological work on dependence in aging largely has been limited to the presentation of frequencies of dependencies and the report of correlational relationships between dependency and other variables, such as age (Svanborg, Landahl, & Mehlström, 1984), sex, social class (Sosna & Wahl, 1983; Wan et al., 1982), and psychiatric impairment (Wahl, in press). When evaluated within the framework of the behavioral sciences, such epidemiological work would be considered by many researchers as rather atheoretical and less concerned with the processes underlying dependencies. Let us turn, therefore, to some theoretical efforts.

THEORETICAL CONSIDERATIONS OF DEPENDENCE

Historical Beginnings

Theoretical discussions about the "why" and "how" of dependency in old age are associated with two classical publications. The first, *The*

Dependencies of Old People was edited by Kalish and published in 1969. This volume represents an interdisciplinary collection of contributions by scientists presenting different theoretical views about the concept of dependence. With the exception of Kalish's paper presenting interview findings from a sample of mostly three-generation families, all papers are purely theoretical elaborations on dependence from a psychiatric, anthropological, medical, sociological, or social-work perspective. The second book, *Dependency and Interdependency in Old Age*, edited by Munnichs and van den Heuvel, was published in 1976. Again, we find an interdisciplinary collection of studies. This volume focuses on the need for both theoretical and empirical clarification of the term *dependency*.

Already in these early conceptual writings on dependence we find an emphasis on the multidimensional nature of the concept. There is no agreement on a general definition, and every author outlines alternative theoretical underpinnings of the concept. Nevertheless, there is some consensus. A multitude of potential alternative causes, beyond biological ones, are invoked. We find dependence being categorized along different domains such as mental, physical, economic, social, etc. (Blenkner, 1969; Clark, 1969; van den Heuvel, 1976).

There are, in addition, classification schemes that underline differences in the more functional properties of dependence. The classical example is the differentiation between instrumental and emotional dependence heralded in child psychology (Hartup, 1963; Heathers, 1955). This function-oriented approach is also used, for instance, by van den Heuvel (1976) when he organizes the different types of dependencies along three dimensions—practical helplessness, powerlessness in a relationship, and psychological need—or by Osgood and Mizruchi (1979) and Gordon and Vinacke (1971) when they propose the differentiation between instrumental and expressive dependence.

A function-orientated approach reminds us of the multifunctionality of dependence as well as that it is not necessarily a static condition imposed on the individual. Expressions of dependence can also create a rather instrumental role. For example, in Goldfarb's (1969) typology of dependencies, the person who seeks control over another person via passive, dependent behaviors figures quite prominently.

Among the early theoretical elaborations on

dependence, we find not only elaborations on the biological as well as societal and cultural conditions fostering dependence, but also those that stress dependence as personality characteristics that are acquired early in life and maintained through one's entire life span. This latter view is very much in accordance with the thinking on dependence in child psychology during the 1950s and 1960s, even though there apparently has been no mutual exchange on the topic between child psychology and gerontology (see M. M. Baltes & Reisenzein, 1986). In these personality- or "trait"-oriented approaches, it is assumed that dependence as a trait affects the structure of social relationships. This notion of the structural quality of dependence, either on a personal or interpersonal level, has been entertained most often by sociologists and psychiatrists in the field of gerontology (Emerson, 1969; Goldfarb, 1969).

From this early literature on dependence, it seems rather obvious to conclude that the different disciplines concerned with dependence will continue to concentrate on different types and levels of dependence; thus, one definition will never be agreed upon by everyone. Therefore, it seems worthwhile to turn one's attention away from the question of "what is dependence", toward "how does dependence come about" and "how is it maintained"—to the processes underlying dependence. In this vein, we understand the more recent theoretical developments that lend themselves to a process analysis of dependence.

Modern Theoretical Developments

The last decade has witnessed a growing interest among psychologists in the importance of autonomy and control for human development across the life span. Examples are the models of self-efficacy (Bandura, 1977, 1982), control (Lefcourt 1976; Schulz 1976) or illusion of control (Langer, 1979, 1983), learned helplessness (Seligman, 1975) or agency (Kuhl, 1981, 1986; Skinner, 1985). Despite the differences in the theoretical focus of these models ranging from a cognitive to an action-theoretical orientation, the major link between dependence and control or efficacy is assumed to be based on two major expectations or beliefs on the part of the individual: (1) "The world in which I live is a contingent one and I am dealing with a responsive environment", and (2) "I am in command of behaviors or skills pro-

ducing specific outcomes and consequences that are required by the situation at hand." Consequently, lack or loss of control in a specific situation will result from either not expecting a contingent and responsive environment or not expecting to be competent, that is, to have the skills to cope with the situation in question. According to these theoretical approaches, dependent behaviors are considered the product of experiences with either lack of contingency or lack of competence. Most of these theoretical models differentiate environmental contingencies in, for instance, outcome and consequence (Bandura, 1977) and competencies in, for instance, skills to manage or cope with an aversive event that has already occurred and skills to prevent the occurrence of the event altogether (Gatz, Siegler, George, & Tyler, 1986). Such differentiations might be helpful in gaining a more detailed understanding of dependence and its modifiability, but do not change the basic two expectations assumed to link dependence with lack of control.

There is a body of empirical work demonstrating dependence or dependent behaviors as the result of *the presence of specific contingencies rather than the presence of noncontingency*. This work is based on the operant learning model within which dependent behaviors in the elderly are described and explained as instrumental behaviors, that is, as the product of existing contingencies either in the form of direct reinforcement or in the form of avoidance of punishment (e.g., pain). The following section will summarize the rationale and findings of this research on dependence.

DEPENDENCE FROM AN OPERANT-LEARNING PERSPECTIVE

Rationale and Objective

In the early 1970s, frustrations with a long-standing but disappointing body of research on dependence in children led both Cairns (1972) and Gewirtz (1972) to argue for the necessity to study dependence at a level of analysis that was more molecular and closer to the events or phenomena to which the global construct "dependence" referred. The operant learning approach advocated by Gewirtz and Cairns was geared toward the demonstration of precise antecedent–consequent relationships; it permits one to treat the dyadic social phenomena subsumed under dependence as processes that are worth studying in their own right. In other words, such molecular analyses shift our interest away from global constructs to concrete behaviors and their interrelationships, traditionally considered indices of the higher order constructs. It is this approach that we have adopted in our own research on dependence with the elderly (see also Willems, 1972).

The operant learning model stresses the following: (a) reciprocity and mutual influence in the interaction between organism and environment, an aspect of the interrelationship that seems so important in the development and maintenance of social behaviors; (b) discriminative and reinforcing (and punishing) stimuli in the environment, and (c) the voluntary, overt responses or behaviors (the operant). The unit of analysis is the stimulus–response unit, the behavioral sequence rather than the single behavioral event. Such a framework, focusing on the conditions under which behaviors do or do not occur, requires the specification of both the actor's behavior (in our case, that of the elderly person), as well as its cueing and reinforcing determinants (in our case, the behaviors of the social partners or interactants of the elderly).

Systematic use of the operant paradigm, as of any other methodological or theoretical paradigm, influences the definition of the phenomenon under study. Dependence, in the present case, is defined and therefore limited to observable and overt behaviors in the context of self-care and social accuracy at the cost of complexity in defining the term dependence. We do not, for instance, include emotional dependence, unless exhibited in overt concrete behaviors by the actor. We also do not consider the structure of relationships as sociologists do when using the term dependence (e.g., Emerson, 1969). However, we will be able to describe the social environmental conditions surrounding dependent behaviors of the elderly and explain the behavioral sequences between actor and environment in terms of operant principles. The use of the operant learning approach for the analysis of dependence favors, in addition to the observation and measurement of concrete behaviors of the actor, a microanalytic treatment of the environengagement. It may be said that we thereby gain ment as well. Thus, the role of the staff, the goals of the institution, and the philosophy of the administration, for instance, are not assessed; instead we record the overt observable acts of each social partner—staff member, teacher, mother, fellow resident, or visitor—interacting with the actor.

In summary, the use of the operant–social learning approach in the study of dependence in aging emphasizes (a) the importance of the role of the environment, thereby, establishing a codetermining force to any biological decline model of aging; (b) the importance of behavioral phenomena and the plasticity of behaviors rather than traits with their inherent notion of stability; and (c) a multimethod approach to the study of dependence, because the operant model provides three convergent phases of research (an operant-experimental, operant-observational, and operant-ecological strategy according to Baer, 1973).

Empirical Findings

Since 1975, Margret Baltes, along with a number of colleagues, has conducted a program of research on dependence in the aged. The basic goal has been to investigate the possibility of dependent behaviors not as a necessary concomitant of aging but as a product of environmental factors. The focus of our research has been on the potential influence of social environmental conditions on the occurrence of dependent and independent behaviors.

The research program has addressed four issues:

1. The degree of plasticity of behavior in the elderly. How modifiable are existing dependent behaviors of the elderly as a function of manipulations in social contingencies?
2. The descriptive analysis of the extant social ecology of old people and its relevance for the development and/or maintenance of dependent and independent behaviors.
3. The problem of setting specificity. Are the observed interaction patterns the effect of the institution in general, or is the age of the inhabitants the essential factor affecting the dynamics of the interaction?
4. The functional validity of the temporal behavior sequences observed in real life.

From a methodological perspective, these four issues are approached by three distinct research tactics provided by the operant model: operant-experimental, operant-observational, and operant-ecological (Baer, 1973; M. M. Baltes & Lerner, 1980). To address the first issue, that of modifiability, an operant-experimental research strategy aimed at examining changes in dependent behavior is employed. To address the second issue — the identification of existing behavior-consequent relationships—observations of naturally occurring behavioral sequences (antecedent-consequent relationships) between the actors (elderly) and their social partners are conducted. The third issue—setting specificity—is addressed with the same operant-observational strategy using comparative samples, such as institutionalized children, toddlers interacting with their mothers at home, or elderly at home. The fourth issue, the functional validity of the behavioral sequences, is addressed using an operant-ecological intervention strategy. Here interventions into natural settings are designed—based on evidence from operant-experimental and operant-observational work—such that either the behaviors of the actor or those of the social partners observed in the interactions are changed.

Behavioral Plasticity

Operant-experimental work, including our studies as well as those by other operant researchers, reveal substantial behavioral plasticity in the elderly (for review see M. M. Baltes & P. B. Baltes, 1982; M. M. Baltes & Barton, 1977, 1979; Hoyer, 1974; Hussian, 1981; Patterson & Jackson, 1980, 1981). Such operant-experimental findings support the possibility of behavioral optimization and corrective compensation in old age and the importance of the influence of both social and physical environmental factors on the level of functioning of the elderly. The very fact that dependent behaviors are reversible suggests that environmental conditions codetermine the acquisition and maintenance of dependence in elderly nursing home residents. Operant-experimental research thus has demonstrated that environmental conditions are sufficient (although not necessary) conditions involved in the acquisition, maintenance, and modification of dependence-related behaviors in the elderly.

Furthermore, the modifiability of even long-standing dependent behaviors negates the assumption concerning lack of competence, propagated by the above cognitively oriented theories as linking dependence and control. Obviously, the elderly in many cases are still competent, that is, still possess the basic skills to perform the task at hand when prompted or reinforced for doing so. The importance of the role of environmental conditions, particularly in a biologically vulnerable elderly subject, is obvious.

Description of Existing Contingencies

Technical data of the studies. For the identification and analysis of naturally existing environmental conditions in the ecology of the elderly, operant-observational strategies—observations of naturally occurring behavior sequences—are warranted. So far, we have restricted the sampling for the observational studies to elderly persons living in institutions. The selection of institutional environments was guided, aside from practical reasons and the interest in institutions per se, by the notion that such environments represent extreme conditions of the social ecology of aging in general. In this vein, we consider them as simulations (P. B. Baltes & Goulet, 1971), or research analogues, for the socialization into old age.

Six studies exist to date (M. M. Baltes, Burgess, & Stewart, 1980; M. M. Baltes, Honn, Barton, Orzech, & Lago, 1983; M. M. Baltes, Kindermann, & Reisenzein, 1986; M. M. Baltes, Kindermann, Reisenzein, & Schmid, 1988; Barton, Baltes, & Orzech, 1980; Lester & M. M. Baltes, 1978). Even though each successive study builds upon the former ones, all have certain design characteristics in common:

1. Samples were randomly selected with the exclusion of highly confused, acutely ill, completely bedfast residents.
2. Subjects were over 65 years of age and came from a lower- to middle-social class stratum.
3. The observational coding system, validated via a behavior mapping study (M. M. Baltes, Barton, Orzech, & Lago, 1983) focused on overt and concrete acts related to independence and dependence.
4. Repeated sequential observations of interactions between target residents and their social partners were employed.
5. For data collection, an apparatus (Datamyte and Datapad) that performs data collection, storage, and computer transference functions was used.
6. Inter-observer reliabilities were computed using different statistics ranging from rank correlations to Kappa.
7. Data analyses on the interaction level were performed via Sackett's (1979; Sackett, Holm, Crowley, & Henkins, 1979) method of sequential lag analysis. Sackett's method provides not only a representation of the probabilities of behavior sequences but also a statistical test

indexing significant departures of observations from baseline expectation.

In Table 16.2 the coding system is presented. A total of 12 categories for type of behavior comprised the final observation code. Six of these involved behaviors of the target residents and six referred to the behavior of their social partners. The behaviors of target residents included two categories of dependent behaviors: dependent self-care behaviors (needing or asking for help when dressing, eating, etc. or refusing to do it) and passive, non-engaged behaviors (staring at the wall). Also included were three categories related to independent behaviors: independent self-care behaviors (bathing, combing oneself etc. or refusing help in carrying out these activities), prosocial or constructively engaged (reading newspaper, playing cards), and obstructively engaged behaviors (screaming, hitting).

The six behavior categories for social partners were differentiated as supportive of independent self-care behaviors (any encouragement of independent or discouragement of dependent behaviors); supportive of dependent self-care behaviors (any encouragement of dependent or discouragement of independent self-care behaviors); supportive of engaged behaviors; supportive of non-engaged behaviors; no response; and leaving. All behavior categories are defined such that they are independent of one another.

A further refinement of the coding system used so far only in the most recent studies (M. M. Baltes et al., 1985, 1988; Kindermann, 1986; Neumann, 1986) permits the differentiation of each type of behavior according to its "form." This was done to allow a first glimpse at the functional nature of the temporal behavior sequences. Six form categories were used: suggestion/request/command, intention, compliance/cooperation, refusal/resistance, conversation (small talk), and miscellaneous other. Thus, each behavioral act was simultaneously characterized in terms of both type and form.

Summary of operant-observational findings. The findings of all studies, both in American and German long-term care institutions, support and complement each other. The transcultural replication was highly consistent, especially as to the patterns of social interactions obtained.

Two characterizations are dominant when comparing the social consequences of dependent versus independent self-care behaviors of elderly persons in long-term care institutions. First, generally dependent self-care behaviors are followed by a high amount of social action; independent self-care behaviors are not. More specifically, we can talk about only one complementary relationship between elderly residents and social partners regarding dependent self-care; the social environment responds, in the case of dependent self-care behaviors, in a task-congruent manner. As to independent self-care, the dominant response of social partners is no response, which may be adequate according to general social norms, but nonetheless does not generate an interaction sequence. Consequently, dependent behaviors in the context of self-care have the highest probability of being followed by not only attentive but supportive acts from social partners. In a world where social contact is rare, such a behavior sequence should have strong implications.

There are, however, other independent behaviors of the elderly resident, namely constructively engaged behaviors such as writing a letter or playing a game with a fellow resident, for which supportive consequences are forthcoming from the social environment. Yet, when compared to the social ecology of dependent self-care behaviors, one perceives that such supportive behaviors of social partners are exhibited in an inconsistent and irregular manner. We interpret this response pattern of the social partners as being similar to an intermittent reinforcement schedule for the institutionalized person. Thus, in these instances the naturally occurring social contingencies do not have the same continuity and immediacy as do dependent self-care behaviors. Finally, it should be mentioned that the second category of dependent behaviors, namely passive or nonengaged behaviors—similar to the social consequences for independent self-care behavior—seem to occur unnoticed.

In contrast, when looking at an elderly person's behaviors as contingencies to the behaviors of social partners, we find a high degree of complementarity. Dependence-supportive behaviors of social partners are followed by dependent behaviors of residents, independence-supportive ones by independent behaviors, and so on. It seems that the elderly discriminate very well between the different behaviors of social partners.

In sum, the least amount of social connectedness is associated with nonengaged and with independent self-care behaviors. The highest degree of

Table 16.2. Observation Coding Scheme

Source of Behavior	1*	Resident with others
	2	Resident alone
	3	Social partner
Person Identification	10 –XX	Target resident ID
	01	Staff
	02	Fellow resident
	03	Visitor
	04	Volunteer helper
	05	Group
Type of Behavior		Behaviors of Target Residents
	00	Sleeping
	01	Constructively engaged
	02	Destructively engaged
	03	Nonengaged
	04	Independently self-caring
	05	Dependently self-caring
		Behaviors of Social Partners
	06	Supportive of engagement
	-07	Supportive of nonengagement
	08	Supportive of independent self-care
	09	Supportive of dependent self-care
	10	No response
	11	Leaving
Form Category	1	Suggestion, command, request
	2	Intention
	3	Compliance, cooperation
	4	Refusal, resistance
	5	Conversation
	6	Miscellaneous other
Behavior Flow	1	Change in behavior category
	2	Same behavior of same category
	3	New behavior of same category

* The numbers represent the code number.

social connectedness is accompanied with dependent self-care behavior; the second highest with independent constructively-engaged behavior. These results are supported by the findings about the dyadic form of the interaction patterns between residents and social partners. There are few interactions in which acts on the part of the resident are aimed at producing a change in the social partners' behavior. Most of the behaviors of the elderly are expressed in the form of compliance or cooperation. In contrast, most of the behaviors of social partners take the form of a request/command/suggestion or cooperation. Rarely did we observe refusal, either on the part of residents or social partners. This additional information about the form of interactional patterns is particularly interesting, because it seems to support the notions of dominance and directionality running from the social partner to the elderly resident and not vice versa. The elderly individual seems to comply with what is requested by the social environment, whether in direct form, as in request from a social partner, or indirect form as in institutional rules.

This basic picture, showing distinctly different interaction patterns related to independent and dependent functioning between elderly residents and their social ecology, is quite robust. Factors such as length of institutionalization, care status, sex of the elderly, or type of institution yield some differences in the quantitative level of behaviors; however, they do not alter, the pattern of the observed behavior sequences.

Discussion of findings. At first glance these results seem to be at odds with operant principles. On the basis of the contingencies observed, one would expect dependent behaviors to show the highest frequency among the behaviors of the elderly, independent self-care as well as nonengaged behaviors to show the lowest frequencies, and constructively engaged behaviors to range in between. In fact, the frequency distribution of the behaviors of the elderly observed in our studies show a picture quite different from expectations. Dependent self-care behavior is less frequent than independent behavior, and both constructively engaged and nonengaged behaviors are the most frequent.

Careful consideration shows the above expectations to be rather naive, and can give insight into the findings. Operant psychologists have always noted (see Patterson, 1982) that acquisition and maintenance of behaviors can be, and most often are, governed by different contingencies. Individuals have acquired independent self-care acts long before they enter a nursing home. They have become automatic habits or mindless behaviors, according to Langer (1983). It is in line with social norms and expectations not to expect external reinforcers for their maintenance. Most of these acts are so well embedded in chains of behaviors, and so self-regulated, that external reinforcers become only necessary when difficulties in the execution of such acts become blatantly obvious.

Second, dependent self-care acts, despite being followed by social reinforcers, cannot increase freely. There is a ceiling effect due to the naturally existing occasions on which dependent self-care acts can occur. In addition, the frequency of dependent self-care acts is lowered because we have excluded from our studies those elderly who are completely bedfast, highly confused, or acutely ill. Furthermore, our behavior coding system is biased positively towards independent self-care acts. For example, in a situation in which the elderly person is dressed by a staff member, any behavioral act, even the most minute one demonstrating any independence (for example, lifting the foot or the arm when the shoe or a shirt is put on) would be coded as an instance of independent self-care behavior.

Third, the findings with regard to the high frequency of nonengaged behaviors demonstrate that these behaviors are maintained by a lack of discriminative stimuli, setting the occasion for engaged behaviors.

Considering now the patterns identified, we would like to argue that these observed interaction patterns demonstrate a highly structured and differentiated social world in the nursing home. There is evidence for systematic and differential contingencies. In a recent series of discussions (M. M. Baltes & Skinner, 1983; Peterson & Raps, 1984; Raps, Peterson, Jonas, & Seligman, 1982) the question was raised whether institutionalized settings produce learned helplessness. In line with the present findings, one of us contended (M. M. Baltes & Skinner, 1983) that one would have to demonstrate noncontingency in the institution in order for dependent or passive behavior to be labeled "helpless" behavior. If, however, behavior is followed consistently and differentially by specific consequences, a condition different from learned helplessness is responsible for dependent behavior.

The institutional environment, thus, is not one of prevailing helplessness, but a world in which different behaviors, albeit dependent rather than independent ones, are instrumental in securing contingencies, for example, social contact.

Identifying the presence of social contingencies for dependent self-care behaviors questions, thus, the assumption linking dependency and lack of control, namely the existence of noncontingency. The present findings, on the basis of the analysis of social contingencies, support a differentiation between dependence and lack of control as well as a differentiation within dependent and independent behaviors.

Setting Specificity

The interaction patterns previously reported are based on cross-sectional or, at best, short-term longitudinal studies of institutionalized aged. We know that the interaction patterns are robust and are not disturbed by variables such as care status, length of institutionalization, sex, or type of institution. We do not know, however, whether the interaction patterns found are typical for institutions at large, regardless of the age of inhabitants or whether the age of the inhabitants plays a decisive role in the dynamics of the interaction. In an attempt to answer this question, there are basically two research avenues: (a) varying age and keeping institution constant and (b) varying setting and keeping age constant. For this reason we have conducted comparative studies with institutionalized (M. M. Baltes et al., 1985) and noninstitutionalized children (Kindermann, 1986) and are in the process of observing noninstitutionalized elderly.

Interaction patterns, from sequential lag analyses linking children's behaviors to their social partners, evince the following picture. To begin with, there is far more behavioral reciprocity in the homes for children than in the homes for the elderly. Behaviors of the target children are usually followed by "complementary" behaviors of their social partners and vice versa. It should be remembered that in the homes for the aged, high complementarity for the elderly person's behavior is found only in the case of dependent self-care behaviors where social partners are most likely to react with dependence-supportive behaviors. Only when the antecedent–consequent sequence is reversed—when the behaviors of social partners are considered as antecedents—is complementarity equally high in the homes for elderly. Behaviors of social partners are most likely followed by the respective complementary behaviors of elderly residents. In other words, children's behaviors as well as those of their social partners have similar discriminative control (stimulus control) for the behaviors of the respective partner. For the elderly resident, this is true only in the case of dependent behaviors. The behavior of elderly individuals seems to be less productive of complementarity than is true for the behavior of institutionalized children.

Furthermore, as with elderly persons, we find with the institutionalized children that many independent self-care and constructively engaged behaviors are occurring in chains. That is, when independent behavior occurs, it is not regularly interrupted by behaviors of social partners. The argument is that independent self-care behaviors seem to be maintained by "chaining" as well as by self-regulatory processes (see Kanfer, 1971; Kanfer & Hagerman, 1981). This is not the case when the independent behavior is still being acquired. The interaction patterns between toddlers and their mothers demonstrate that when the child is learning an independent behavior (for instance, to eat independently) this is followed most likely by independence-supportive behavior of the mother. In contrast, when the child has not yet entered the learning or acquisition phase, dependent self-care behaviors of the child are met with dependence-supportive behavior of the mother (Kindermann, 1986).

Finally, the complementary relationship between dependent and dependence-supportive behaviors exists in all children's data, too. This typical pattern found with elderly individuals shows up in the case of the toddlers with high fre-

quency, prior to the learning phase of a specific self-care task. In the case of institutionalized children, it is a rather infrequent interaction pattern. Two points need special attention in this context.

First, the findings on the interaction patterns between mothers and their toddlers at home (Kindermann, 1986), as well as casual observations of children in the institutional setting, suggest that the context in which dependent and dependence-supportive behaviors are occurring, is one of true "incompetence" in the children. This is to say that children are unable, because of age, developmental status, height, weight, or similar factors, to perform certain tasks by themselves. Kindermann (1986) has demonstrated that the interaction patterns between toddler and mother change with the developmental status of the child in specific developmental tasks (for example, learning to eat independently). That is, the mother tailors her own dependence- or independence-supportive behavior to the developmental stage or the competence of the child.

In contrast, observations in the intervention study by Neumann (1986), as well as the operant-experimental findings with the elderly, suggest that in a number of dependence-related situations the elderly are able, in principle, to perform the required behavior. However, they are prevented from doing so by the immediate help from staff, regardless of whether the older person shows many or few dependent behaviors. Individual sequential analyses performed on randomly selected subjects, who by the mere frequency of behaviors are ranked the most dependent and the most independent of the sample, show no differences in the interaction patterns (M. M. Baltes, 1979). Dependence-supportive behavior is the usual response to dependent self-care behavior, regardless of whether it is exhibited by an elderly person ranked as most independent or a person ranked as most dependent.

This age difference in social interactions can be interpreted as evidence for the relative dominance of children in the interactional relations observed in the present studies. Children and their social partners in the institution interact more on even terms in the sense of codetermining the terms of the interaction. This is illustrated, for instance, when independent self-care behaviors in institutionalized children are more frequently followed by independence-supportive behaviors than in the homes for the elderly.

Institutionalized children and toddlers at home

seem to have a higher degree of input into the nature of the social exchange; more of their behavioral repertoire is responded to in a fashion conducive to a development-enhancing, socially supportive environment than is true for the institutionalized elderly. Furthermore, for institutionalized children, dependent self-care behaviors are *not* the principal instrumental acts by which social contact is most likely, and most consistently, gained. Other behaviors, such as constructively engaged and independent self-care acts exhibit similar control.

In addition to considering control as defined by the presence of contingency, Patterson (1982) also calculates a "power" index to explain the variance of the contingency accounted for by the antecedent event. This type of usage of the term is not to be confused with that of many sociologists (Emerson, 1969). Patterson believes that control and power indices together yield a more complete understanding of the behavioral sequences at hand. To illustrate: there are 100 dependent behaviors and all of them are followed by dependence-supportive behaviors, of which there are, however, 200 instances. In this case, half of the dependence-supportive behaviors are preceded by behaviors other than dependent behavior. If one compares control and power, one finds that dependent behavior has significant control but little power, because half of dependence-supportive behaviors are attached to other antecedent behaviors and not prompted exclusively (even half of the time) by dependent behaviors.

The findings demonstrate that in the case of the elderly, the most significant control as well as power is exhibited by dependent self-care behavior. Dependent behaviors are usually followed by dependence-supportive behaviors, and the latter are usually preceded by dependent behaviors. Constructively engaged behaviors exhibit more power than control. The occurrence of engagement-supportive behaviors is almost always preceded by engaged behaviors of the elderly, but the latter often occur without being followed by engagement-supportive behaviors. For the elderly, there seems to be only *one* behavior—dependent self-care behavior—with the highest probability of securing supportive or attentive behaviors from social partners. (However, it should still be noted that this behavior occurs relatively infrequently compared to the total number of residents' behaviors.) Moreover, dependent self-care situations demonstrate the only truly reciprocal situation in

the world of the institutionalized elderly, where social partners react in a task-congruent fashion. The meaning for the elderly appears to be: If I want to have social contact, there is one sure way to get it, with respect to both the behavioral act (dependent behavior) and the situation (self-care).

In the case of institutionalized children, in contrast, constructively engaged behavior has the most significant power and control. In addition, we see destructively engaged behaviors showing significant control but little power, and conversely, independent self-care behaviors possessing significant power but little control. That is, independence-supportive behaviors are usually preceded by independent behaviors, but often the latter are exhibited without being followed by support.

What are the conclusions to be drawn from these age-comparative findings for the interpretation of our gerontological data? What are the conclusions pertaining to the question of an institution versus an age explanation? We take the position that an orientation toward dependence has incompetence as its basic feature. Institutionalization is a factor in dependence when incompetence is perceived as an essential characteristic of the inhabitants of the institution. Thus, we maintain that the social interaction patterns related to independent and dependent functioning identified in the homes for the elderly seem to be primarily the result of old age and not of institutionalization. We draw this conclusion from findings that (a) other clusters of behavior (e.g., independent and constructively engaged behaviors) of the elderly receive less complementarity and social equity in defining the nature of the social exchange than is true for institutionalized and noninstitutionalized children, and (b) elderly persons are treated as dependent-prone, even in situations where they are able to perform. Thus, despite similarities in the interaction patterns involving dependence, we believe that the social interaction patterns are primarily the product of old age and secondarily the product of institutionalization.

Functional Validity of the Temporal Behavior Sequences

Time is only one criterion, among others, necessary for the influence of a cause-effect or functional relationship. In operant psychology, the final proof of a functional relationship is experimental manipulation. If the manipulation of a consequent leads to the predicted change in behavior, then we can infer a functional relationship between antecedent and consequent. For this reason, an operant-ecological intervention study was designed and completed in which the behavior of the staff was modifed. Specifically, a training program for staff aimed at minimizing dependence-supportive and increasing independence-supportive behaviors of staff was implemented by Neumann (1986) in a pre- and posttest-control-group design. The results show that the behavior of staff was modified effectively and that as a consequence, the behaviors of the elderly changed in the predicted direction (less dependent behaviors). Thus, it seems valid to interpret the temporal behavior sequences as causal or functional behavior sequences as well.

Summary

In sum, the findings of operant-experimental, operant-observational, and operant-ecological work seem to converge on the following picture:

1. Dependent behaviors are codetermined by environmental conditions with a change in the latter reversing dependent behaviors in the elderly.
2. Dependent and independent self-care behaviors experience different social ecologies—whereas the latter is mostly ignored, the former is followed by immediate social consequences in a highly continuous and regular fashion.
3. When considering the environmental contingencies, there is further differentiation within the two behavior classes of dependent and independent behaviors. People who exhibit passive, nonengaged behaviors of the dependent behavior class are likely to experience no reactions from the social environment; this also holds true for destructively engaged behavior from the independent behavior class. Constructively engaged behavior, a third one in the independent behavior class, is supported by an intermediate social contingency schedule.
4. Reconstructing these findings within the operant learning framework, we have to conclude that dependent behavior has the most control and power with regard to social contingencies.
5. Describing dependence as a function of the presence of social contingencies, and as reversible following a change in those contingencies, questions the relationship between dependence, helplessness, and lack or loss of control or self-efficacy.

DISCUSSION AND IMPLICATIONS

On the basis of the presented empirical work on dependence we have shown that a molecular, process-oriented analysis provides us—despite its possible restriction in scope—with a precise description and explanation of the relationships between dependent and independent behavior and their respective environmental conditions. As a consequence, the findings underline the three issues presented in the beginning of this chapter: multicausality, multidimensionality, and multifunctionality. The present findings add confirmation to the idea of multicausality of dependence, arguing for an interplay between biological vulnerability and environmental conditions. On the level of environmental contingencies, dependence has to be regarded also as a multidimensional concept. The demand for a differential use of such terms as helplessness, loss of control or self-efficacy, and dependence is warranted. In addition, dependent behaviors seem to serve different functions. They can represent, on the one hand, instrumental acts gaining and securing control, albeit passive control. On the other hand, they can represent passive behaviors that seem to have no external social consequences. Dependent behaviors, thus, may be regarded as an adaptive process to both environmental and biological conditions in aging, but may also be the result of lack of stimulation to do otherwise. We are in need, therefore, of a comprehensive framework in which to interpret dependence. This is particularly urgent in light of questions concerning intervention.

One key principle of adaptation to old age has been proposed by one of us under the label "compensation with selective optimization" (P. B. Baltes & M. M. Baltes, 1980) and since then has been elaborated on (M. M. Baltes, 1987; P. B. Baltes, 1984; P. B. Baltes, Dittmann-Kohli, & Dixon, 1984; Dixon & P. B. Baltes, 1986). This model or strategy describes and explains the dynamic between gains and losses, independence and dependence in development. The assumption of the model is that given the normative and nonnormative events occurring in one's life, individuals experience increased biological vulnerability as they reach old age. In order to maintain or even increase performance in one class of behavior, other behaviors have to be abandoned. A general level of high productivity can no longer be maintained. Thus, the kind of dependent behaviors an individual would exhibit, to what degree, and in what situations would depend largely upon his or her own life or learning history, his or her present physical and psychological status and present environmental conditions. All factors together would define the amount and degree of compensatory efforts necessary to stay independent and productive and would decide when and where dependent behaviors are exhibited.

Compensation with selective optimization, therefore, implies added investment in one domain and, at the same time, reduction of investment in others to keep one's level of performance in the chosen domain. The adaptive task, then, for the aging individual is to select and concentrate on those domains which are of high priority and involve a convergence of environmental demands, individual motivations, skills, and biological capacity. Thus, dependent behaviors could be highly adaptive behaviors, by which the individual uses elements of his or her environment as prosthetic devices in order to maintain certain competencies. Skinner (1983) described a whole array of environmental prostheses that can be used to maintain intellectual performance in old age. At the same time, other domains would have to be abandoned, resulting possibly in dependent behaviors. In this vein, dependent behaviors could play an integral part in successful aging.

The presence of increased vulnerability and age-related reduction in maximum biological functioning strengthens the idea that proactive and reactive selection in the direction of less demanding ecologies and tasks becomes increasingly important. Dependent behaviors in an ecology with low demands (such as a long-term care institution), would ideally allow the elderly to maintain autonomy and selective optimization in other domains as long as possible.

Skinner stated once that the goal of therapy is not to do away with institutions: some people, in order to exist in a more autonomous fashion, need prosthetic environments always and all the time. The only problem with the existing institutions for the elderly is that they do not foster compensation with selective optimization but instead tend towards "overcare" (Ransen, 1978, 1981). Accordingly, the question arises: When is dependence-supportive behavior of social partners a necessary ingredient to allow successful aging, and when is it detrimental? Should one intervene, both on an individual and group level, to change or prevent dependent behaviors of the elderly? Do our

findings suggest that institutions are doing wrong in supporting dependent behaviors?

According to the adaptive principle of compensation with selective optimization, any affirmative answer as to interventions would have to depend upon the analysis of the conditions that surround dependent behaviors. There are at least two conditions under which dependent behaviors are not to be changed and there is at least one condition in which changing dependent behavior is desirable.

We would not want to intervene to change or reverse dependent behaviors in cases where they are the product of true biological decline, and/or in cases where they are the result of a choice or selection by the elderly person in order to maintain optimal functioning in other domains.

In the first case, any intervention to change the social environmental conditions so as not to support dependent behavior would be to the detriment of the elderly person, increasing the individual's sense of inefficacy and loss of control. In the second case, in which the individual's choice to be dependent in domains x, y, and z is due to individual motivation and skills, it also would not be desirable to change dependent behaviors, unless one can provide additional new resources that allow successful avoidance of existing dependent behaviors without special efforts on the part of the elderly person.

In contrast, intervention is warranted when dependent behaviors are the result of conformity with social stereotypes and prejudices, or of an underestimation of one's resources and of the environmental responsiveness. Social pressure towards passivity, inactivity, calmness, stability, even "wisdom" in the elderly, as well as the elderly person's underestimation of his/her still existing skills, abilities, and resources, lead to a restriction of and reduction in physical and psychological activity. We know from research, even with young people (Bortz, 1982), that disuse of functions will, in turn, have ill effects. Today, we have a wealth of data showing the negative effects of physical inactivity on a wide variety of health variables in all age groups (deVries, 1970; Pace, 1977). Of particular importance to old age are data on the effect of physical and mental activity on brain functions (for a summary see Bortz, 1982).

If dependent behaviors are not the result of true biological decline and selective optimization, but the result of social pressure and/or underestimation of resources, they are the beginning of a vicious cycle. Dependent behavior increases the disuse of functions, hereby accelerating their decline and, in turn, increasing dependence. In these instances, corrective, preventive, and optimizing interventions are called for in order to restore, maintain, and optimize internal as well as external resources aimed at optimal functioning of the elderly.

Acknowledgment— This chapter was written during the time the research program described was supported by the Volkswagen Foundation, and Hans-Werner Wahl was research associate on that project.

REFERENCES

Akhtar, A. J., Broe, G. A., Crombie, A., McLean, W. M. R., & Andrews, G. R. (1973). Disability and dependence in the elderly at home. *Age and Ageing, 2,* 102–111.

Baer, D. J. (1973). The control of developmental processes: Why wait? In J. R. Nesselroade & H. W. Reese (Eds.), *Life-span developmental psychology: Methodological issues* (pp. 187–193). New York: Academic.

Baltes, M. M. (1979). *Comparison of interaction patterns of the most dependent vs. the most independent nursing home residents.* Unpublished raw data.

Baltes, M. M. (1982). Environmental factors in dependency among nursing home residents: A social ecology analysis. In T. A. Wills (Ed.), *Basic processes in helping relationships.* New York: Academic.

Baltes, M. M. (1987). Erfolgreiches Altern als Ausdruck von Verhaltenskompetenz und Umweltqualität (Successful aging as a product of behavioral and environmental competence). In C. Niemitz (Ed.), *Erbe und Umwelt* (pp. 353–376). Frankfurt: Suhrkamp.

Baltes, M. M., & Baltes, P. B. (1982). Micro-analytic research on environmental factors and processes in psychological aging. In T. Field, A. Huston, H. C. Quay, L. Troll, & G. E. Finley (Eds.), *Review of human development* (pp. 524–539). New York: Wiley.

Baltes, M. M., & Barton, E. M. (1977). New approaches toward aging: A case for the the operant model. *Educational Gerontology: An International Quarterly, 2,* 383–405.

Baltes, M. M., & Barton, E. M. (1979). Behavioral analysis of aging: A review of the operant model and research. *International Journal of Behavioral Development, 2,* 297–320.

Baltes, M. M., Barton, E. M., Orzech, M. J., & Lago, D. (1983). Die Mikroökologie von Bewohnern und Personal: Eine Behavior–Mapping Studie im Altenheim. *Zeitschrift für Gerontologie, 16,* 18–26.

Baltes, M. M., Burgess, R. L., & Stewart, R. (1980). Independence and dependence in self-care behaviors in nursing home residents: An operant-observational study. *International Journal of Behavioral Development, 3,* 489–500.

Baltes, M. M. Honn, S., Barton, E. M., Orzech, M. J., & Largo, D. (1983). Dependence and independence in elderly nursing home residents: A replication and extension. *Journal of Gerontology, 38,* 556–564.

Baltes, M. M. Kindermann, Th., & Reisenzein, R. (1986). Unselbständiges und selbständiges Verhalten im Alter: Die soziale Umwelt als Einflussgrosse. *Zeitschrift für Gerontologie, 79,* 14–24.

Baltes, M. M., Kindermann, Th., Reisenzein, R., & Schmid, U. (1988). Further observational data on the behavioral and social world of institutions for the aged. *Psychology and Aging, 3,* in press.

Baltes, M. M., & Lerner, R. M. (1980). Roles of the operant model and its methods in the life-span view of human development. *Human Development, 23,* 362–367.

Baltes, M. M., & Reisenzein, R. (1986). The social world in long-term care institutions: Psychosocial control towards dependency? In M. M. Baltes & P. B. Baltes (Eds.), *The psychology of control and aging* (pp. 315–343). Hillsdale, NJ: Erlbaum.

Baltes, M. M., Reisenzein, R., & Kindermann, Th. (1985) *Dependence in institutionalized children: A comparative analysis.* Unpublished raw data.

Baltes, M. M., & Skinner, E. A. (1983). Cognitive performance deficits and hospitalization: Learned helplessness, instrumental passivity or what? *Journal of Personality and Social Psychology, 45,* 1013–1016.

Baltes, P. B. 1984. Intelligenz im Alter. *Spektrum der Wissenschaften, 5,* 46–60.

Baltes, P. B., & Baltes, M. M. (1980). Plasticity and variability in psychological aging: Methodological and theoretical issues. In G. E. Gurski (Ed.), *Determining the effects of aging on the central nervous system* (pp. 41–60). Berlin: Schering.

Baltes, P. B., Dittman-Kohli, F., & Dixon, R. (1984). New perspectives on the development of intelligence in adulthood: Toward a dual-process conception and a model of selective optimization with compensation. In P. B. Baltes & O. G. Brim, Jr. (Eds.), *Life-span development and behavior* (Vol. 6, pp. 33–76). New York: Academic.

Baltes, P. B., & Goulet, R. R. (1971). Exploration of developmental variables by manipulation and simulation of age differences in behavior. *Human Development, 14,* 149–170.

Baltes, P. B., Reese, H. W., & Nesselroade, J. R. (1977). *Life-span developmental psychology: Introduction to research methods.* Monterey, CA: Brooks/Cole.

Bandura, A. (1977). Self-efficacy: Toward a unifying theory of behavioral change. *Psychological Review, 84,* 191–215.

Bandura, A. (1982). Self-efficacy mechanism in human agency. *American Psychologist, 37,* 122–147.

Barton, E. M., Baltes, M. M., & Orzech, M. J. (1980). On the etiology of dependence in nursing home residents during morning care: The role of staff behavior. *Journal of Personality and Social Psychology, 38,* 423–431.

Blenkner, R. (1969). The normal dependencies of aging, In R. A. Kalish (Ed.), *The dependencies of old people* (pp. 27–37). Ann Arbor, MI: Institute of Gerontology, The University of Michigan.

Bortz, W. M. (1982). Disuse and aging. *Journal of the American Medical Association, 248,* 1203–1208.

Cairns, R. S. (1972). Attachment and dependency. A psychological and social learning synthesis. In J. L. Gewirtz (Ed.), *Attachment and dependency* (pp. 29–95). New York: Wiley.

Clark, M. (1969). Cultural values and dependency in later life. In R. A Kalish (Ed.), *The dependencies of old people* (pp. 59–72). Ann Arbor, MI: Institute of Gerontology, University of Michigan.

Cooper, B. (1984). Home and away: The disposition of mentally ill old people in an urban population. *Social Psychiatry, 19,* 187–196.

deVries, H. (1970). Physiological effects of an exercise training regimen upon men aged 52–88. *Journal of Gerontology, 25,* 325–336.

Dixon, R. A., & Baltes, P. B. (1986). Towards life-span research on the functions and pragmatics of intelligence. In R. J. Sternberg & R. K. Wagner (Eds.), *Origins of competence in the everyday world* (pp. 203–235). New York: Cambridge University Press.

Dollard, J., & Miller, N. E. (1950). *Personality and psychotherapy: An analysis in terms of learning, thinking, and culture.* New York: McGraw-Hill.

Emerson, R. M. (1969). Operant psychology and exchange theory. In R. L. Burgess & D. Bushell, Jr. (Eds.), *Behavioral sociology* (pp. 379–405). New York: Columbia University Press.

Gallagher, D., Thompson, L. W., & Levy, S. M. (1980). Clinical psychological assessment of older adults. In L. W. Poon (Ed.), *Aging in the 1980s* (pp. 19–40). New York: American Psychological Association.

Garrad, J., & Benett, A. E. (1971). A validated interview schedule for use in population surveys of chronic disease and disability. *British Journal of Preventive and Social Medicine, 25,* 97–104.

Gatz, M., Siegler, I. C., George, L. K., & Tyler, F. (1986). Attributional components of locus of control: Cross-sectional and longitudinal analysis. In M. M. Baltes & P. B. Baltes (Eds.), *The psychology of control and aging* (pp. 237–264). Hillsdale, NJ: Erlbaum.

Gewirtz, J. L. (Ed.). (1972). *Attachment and dependence.* New York: Wiley.

Goldfarb. A. I. (1969). The psychodynamics of dependency and the search for aid. In R. A. Kalish (Ed.), *The dependencies of old people* (pp. 1–15). Ann Arbor, MI: Institute of Gerontology, University of Michigan.

Gordon, S. K., & Vinacke, W. E. (1971). Self and ideal self-concepts and dependency in aged persons residing in institutions. *Journal of Gerontology, 26,* 337–343.

Hartup, W. W. (1963). Dependency and independence. In H. W. Stevenson (Ed.), *Child psychology: The 62nd Yearbook of the National society for the Study of Education* (Part 1, pp. 333–363). Chicago: University of Chicago Press.

Hauser, P. M. (1976). Aging and world-wide population change. In R. H. Binstock & E. Shanas (Eds.), *Handbook of aging and the social sciences* (pp. 58–86). New York: Van Nostrand Reinhold.

Heathers, C. (1955). Acquiring dependence and independence: A theoretical orientation. *The Journal of Genetic Psychology, 87,* 277–291.

Van den Heuvel, W. (1976). The meaning of dependency. In J. M. A. Munnichs & W. van den Heuvel (Eds.), *Dependency or interdependency in old age* (pp. 162–173). The Hague, Netherlands: Martinus Nijhoff.

Hoyer, W. J. (1974). Aging as intra-individual change. *Developmental Psychology, 10,* 821–826.

Hussian, R. A. (1981). *Geriatric psychology: A behavioral perspective.* New York: Van Nostrand Reinhold.

Isaacs, B., & Neville, Y. (1976). The needs of old people. The "interval" as a method of measurement. *British Journal of Preventive and Social Medicine, 30,* 79–85.

Kalish, R. A. (Ed.) (1969). *The dependencies of old people.* Ann Arbor, MI: Institute of Gerontology, The University of Michigan.

Kanfer, F. H. (1971). The maintenance of behavior by self-generated stimuli and reinforcement. In J. A. Jacobs & L. B. Sachs (Eds.), *Psychology of private events.* New York: Academic.

Kanfer, F. H., & Hagerman, S. (1981). The role of self-regulation. In L. P. Rehm (Ed.), *Behavior therapy for depression: Present status and future direction.* New York: Academic.

Kindermann, Th. (1986). *Entwicklungsbedingungen von selbständigem und unselbständigem Verhalten in der frühen Kindheit: Mikroökologische Analyse von Mutter-Kind-Interaktionen.* Unpublished doctoral dissertation. Free University, Berlin, Germany.

Kuhl, J. (1981). Motivational and functional helplessness: The moderating effect of state versus action orientation. *Journal of Personality and Social Psychology, 40,* 155–170.

Kuhl, J. (1986). Aging and models of control: The hidden costs of wisdom. In M. M. Baltes & P. B. Baltes (Eds.), *The psychology of control and aging* (pp. 1–34). Hillsdale, NJ: Erlbaum.

Langer, E. J. (1979). The illusion of incompetence. In L. C. Perlmuter & R. A. Monty (Eds.), *Choice and perceived control* (pp. 301–313). Hillsdale, NJ: Erlbaum.

Langer, E. J. (1983). *The psychology of control.* New York: Sage.

Lefcourt, M. M. (1976). *Locus of control: Current trends in theory and research.* Hillsdale, NJ: Erlbaum.

Lester, P. B., & Baltes, M. M. (1978). Functional interdependence of the social environment and the behavior of the institutionalized aged. *Journal of Gerontological Nursing, 4,* 23–27.

Maddox, G. L. (1984). Aging people and aging population: A framework for decision making. In II. Thomae & G. Maddox (Eds.), *New perspectives on old age—A message to decision-makers* (pp. 19–30). New York: Springer.

Munnichs, J. M. A., & van den Heuvel, W. J. A. (Eds.). (1976). *Dependency or interdependency in old age.* The Hague, Netherlands: Martinus Nijhoff.

Neumann, E. M. (1986). *Personaltraining zur Modifizierung passiven und unselbständigen Verhaltens alter Menschen in der Institution: eine Interventionsstudie.* Unpublished doctoral dissertation, Free University, Berlin, Germany.

Osgood, N., & Mizruchi, E. H. (1979 November). *Aspects of independence: A conceptualization.* Paper presented at the Annual Meetings of the Gerontological Society, Washington, D. C.

Pace, N. (1977). Weightlessness: A matter of gravity. *New England Journal of Medicine, 297,* 32–37.

Patterson, G. R. (1982). *Coercive family processes.* Eugene, OR: Castalia Publishing Co.

Patterson, R. L., & Jackson, G. M. (1981). Behavioral approaches to gerontology. In L. Michelson, M. Hersen, & S. Turner (Eds.), *Future perspectives in behavior therapy* (pp. 293–313). New York: Plenum.

Patterson, R. L., & Jackson, G. M. (1980). Behavior modification with the elderly. In M. Hersen, R. M. Eisler, & P. Miller (Eds.), *Progress in behavior modification.* (Vol. 9, pp. 205–239). New York: Academic.

Peterson, L. C., & Raps, C. S. (1984). Helplessness and hospitalization: More remarks. *Journal of Personality and Social Psychology, 46*, 82–83.

Ransen, D. L. (1978). Some determinants of decline among the institutionalized aged: Overcare. *Cornell Journal of Social Relations, 13*, 61–74.

Ransen, D. L. (1981). Long-term effects of two interventions with the aged: An ecological analysis. *Journal of Applied Development Psychology, 2*, 13–27.

Raps, C. S., Peterson, C., Jonas, M., & Seligman, M. E. P. (1982). Patient behavior in hospitals: Helplessness, reactance, or both? *Journal of Personality and Social Psychology, 42*, 1036–1041.

Sackett, G. P. (1979). The lag sequential analysis of contingency and cyclicity in behavioral interaction research. In J. Osofsky (Ed.), *Handbook of infant development* (pp. 623–649). New York: Wiley.

Sackett, G. P., Holm, R., Crowley, C., & Henkins, A. (1979). Computer technology: A Fortran program for lag sequential analysis of contingency and cyclicity in behavioral interaction data. *Behavior Research Methods and Instrumentation, 11*, 366–378.

Sandholzer, H. (1982). Measuring impairment and disability in the elderly: A study in general practice. *Social Psychiatry, 17*, 189–198.

Schulz, R. (1976). The effects of control and predictability on the psychological and physical well-being of the institutionalized aged. *Journal of Personality and Social Psychology, 33*, 563–573.

Seligman, M. E. P. (1975). *Helplessness. On depression, development, and death.* San Francisco: Freeman.

Shanas, E. P., Townsend, P., Wederburn, D., Friis, H., Miløj, J., & Stehouwer, J. (Eds.) (1968). *Old people in three industrial societies.* New York: Atherton Press.

Silberstein, J., Kossowsky, R., Lilus, P. (1977). Functional dependency in the aged. *Journal of Gerontology, 32*, 222–226.

Skinner, B. F. (1983). Intellectual self-management in old age. *American Psychologist, 38*, 239–244.

Skinner, E. A. (1985). Action, control judgments, and the structure of control experience. *Psychological Review, 92*, 39–58.

Sosna, U., & Wahl, H. W. (1983). Soziale Belastung, psychische Erkrankung und körperliche Beeinträchtigung: Ergebnisse einer Feldstudie. *Zeitschrift für Gerontologie, 16*, 107–114.

Svanborg, A., Landahl, S., & Mellström, D. (1984). Basic issues of health care. In H. Thomae & G. Maddox (Eds.), *New perspectives on old age—a message to decision-makers* (pp. 31–52). New York: Springer.

Torgerson, W. S. (1958). *Theory and methods of scaling.* New York: Wiley.

U.S. Bureau of the Census (1978). *Demographic aspects and the older population in the United States.* Washington, DC: Government Printing Office.

Wahl, H. W. (in press). Behinderung in der Altersbevölkerung: Ergebnisse einer Feldstudie. *Zeitschrift für Gerontologie.*

Wan, T. T. H., Odell, B. G., & Lewis, D. T. (1982). *Promoting the well-being of the elderly: A community diagnosis.* New York: Haworth Press.

Wieltschnig, E. 1982. *Unabhängigkeit im Alter. Ein theoretisch-empirisches Konzept.* Bern: Paul Haupt.

Willems, E. P. (1972). The interface of the hospital environment and patient behavior. *Physical Medicine and Rehabilitation, 53*, 115–122.

Williams, R. G. A. (1979). Theories and measurement in disability. *Epidemiology and Community Health, 33*, 32–47.

World Health Organization. (1980). *International classification of impairments, disabilities, and handicaps.* Geneva: WHO.

Wortis, J. (1954). *Fragments of an analysis with Sigmund Freud.* New York: Simon & Schuster.

Chapter 17

Age-related Changes in Social Activity*

Laura L. Carstensen

As people age, they begin to slow, both biologically and psychologically. Organ systems function at reduced capacity, slowed response speed is observed, and, at a social level, the rate of activity declines. Although certainly there are very active old people, intraindividual reductions in social interactions appear to be the modal response to old age.

The nature of the change in social activity with age is intriguing. Some hold that social withdrawal is normal and adaptive; others contend that it is solely the result of social and physical barriers and that optimal aging involves the maintenance of social activity levels into old age. Although there currently exists a relatively large literature on social activity among the aged, including numerous reports of interventions designed to increase the rates of social interaction, there is little consensus about the significance of social interaction for the elderly.

This chapter presents a discussion of theoretical issues related to social inactivity, an overview of psychological and physical health implications, and a selective review of the intervention literature on social inactivity. At the close of the chapter, a life span theory of social activity is proposed, and clinical recommendations based on this theoretical view are made.

THEORETICAL ISSUES

To date, the most hotly disputed issues in social gerontology have been those surrounding the meaning of decreased social activity for the elderly. During the early 1960s, two directly contrasting views of changes in social behavior in late life were proposed: disengagement theory and activity theory. The *disengagement theory*, developed by Cumming and Henry (1961), was based on the empirical observation that the rates of social interaction decrease with age. Rooted in the functional theory of sociology, disengagement is seen as a preparatory response to the impending death of the elder member of society: Society releases the individual from social responsibilities and the aged person simultaneously imposes psychological distance in social relationships. Central to the theory is the belief that withdrawal is mutual, natural, and adaptive. The elderly person is not abandoned by society. On the contrary, the individual voluntarily lessens his or her emotional involvement in social relationships. Disengage-

---

* This chapter is dedicated to the memory of Julia Berlove, who very generously shared her time and knowledge with me and with my students. Her insights and wisdom contributed much to the development of the ideas expressed herein.

ment is seen as inevitable because death is inevitable, and thus it represents the gradual disassociation from life.

Geropsychiatric views of social inactivity are quite similar. Dibner (1980) suggests that "lessened relatedness" in old age is the result of a progression of losses (e.g., loss of spouse, friends, and health) representing a symbolic progression toward death. Freud (1946) considered social isolation a defense mechanism, serving the same function as amnesia. According to Berezin (1980), the isolation of the elderly may represent normal mental functioning and "has to be respected as a self-preservative style" (p. 17).

The disengagement theory enjoyed great popularity during the 1960s and 1970s, but it was also met with sharp criticism. Proponents of what has come to be called *activity theory* strongly asserted that in order for elderly individuals to be well-adjusted in old age, they must remain active and involved. It should be noted that the activity theory is not a formal theory. Rather, it is a view of aging that is in direct opposition to the disengagement theory, holding instead that optimal psychological adjustment involves continued social engagement into late life. The activity theory was supported by the finding that people reporting the highest morale were also the most active (Maddox, 1963, 1968). Activity theorists did not deny that overall rates of activity decline with age. They asserted that the decrease in social interaction is not mutually initiated but is imposed externally. It is seen as the unfortunate result of declining health, a reduction in the number of social roles, and the deaths of friends and relatives. Psychologically healthy elderly, according to activity theory, are the elderly who stay active in spite of their losses, who replace lost roles and supports with new ones, and who maintain activity in old roles as long as possible (Maddox, 1970).

Revisions of the disengagement theory also appeared in the literature in the two decades following its introduction. Neugarten, Havighurst, and Tobin (1968) claimed that psychological disengagement did not coincide with the societal expression of withdrawal, namely retirement, but preceded it by approximately 10 years. Havighurst, Neugarten, and Tobin (1968) also claimed that disengagement described the aging process for only certain personality types. Troll and Smith (1976) suggested that the elderly disengage from circumscribed areas in their lives but become more involved in other aspects—specifically, they disengage from work-related contacts but become more involved in family relationships. And even Cumming (1963) herself acknowledged that the process may begin at different times for different people and that it may be mitigated by a host of societal factors.

An alternative view to the activity and disengagement theories was proposed by Kalish and Knudtson (1976), who suggested that the term *disengagement* be dispensed with and the focus be shifted to the study of *attachment*. According to Kalish and Knudtson, attachments are affective involvements with objects or people, and in the course of a lifetime, they are developed by mutual caregiving and self-produced feedback; i.e., the initiated action leads to a sensory, affective, or cognitive stimulus from the object of attachment. Throughout life, attachments provide the individual with a sense of mastery over the world. In later life, one faces not only diminished control over the social environment but also the loss of early objects of attachment, for example, parents. In old age, newly formed relationships are often based on caregiving rather than on mutual assistance, and are thus inherently weaker. In response, the older person shifts attention away from the social world to personal inner resources. Kalish and Knudtson liken this shift in attention to the shift described by Gutmann (1969), wherein aging people move from the active mastery of youth to the magical mastery of old age. Both of these views suggest that the shift toward a reliance on inner resources results in the older individual's behavior being less controlled by the immediate social environment and more controlled by his or her personal history.

In part, resolution of the debates sparked by the disengagement and activity theories was hampered by the methodological problems inherent in the empirical research designed to test the theories. The basic research paradigm used in empirical demonstrations in support of the activity theory was to recruit elderly individuals to participate in some form of an activity program and then to measure life satisfaction before and after participation (e.g., Harris & Bodden, 1978). If satisfaction improved, which it always did in the published reports, results were seen as supportive of the activity theory. Counterarguments were that subjects who volunteered were not representative of the population at large and/or that self-reporting was seriously contaminated by demand characteristics, such as the desire to please the experimenter.

Cross-sectional findings derived from group research are difficult to interpret: On the average, activity declines with age; on the average, active people are the happiest; and, on the average, physically healthy people are more active and happier than less healthy people. Averaged findings, however, do not answer questions about *intraindividual* change across the life span; rather, they document that some behavioral patterns of groups are associated with higher morale at a particular point in time.

A basic misinterpretation of the disengagement theory has permeated the field, one that is reflected in the methodology of subsequent theory testing. The specific aim of developmental theory is to identify intraindividual ontogenetic change (Goulet & Baltes, 1970). Yet the methods used to assess the disengagement theory have been methods that compare *groups* of individuals at a particular point in time. For the most part, investigators have either compared active and inactive individuals or experimentally manipulated the activity level of groups of individuals. Although not without merit, such methods do not allow one to draw conclusions about individual change over the life course. Disengagement, as proposed by Cumming and Henry (1961) is an intrapsychic process, in which relatively low rates of activity are one observable manifestation. The theory does not posit that social contacts are unimportant to the aged; it simply suggests that the psychological investment in social relationships is lessened relative to earlier periods in that individual's life. It is important to recognize that the change is intraindividual, and therefore the finding that the happiest old people are also the most active is irrelevant. Further, the fact that a person engages in social intercourse more frequently or less frequently in old age than in earlier years is also irrelevant. Of critical importance is the meaning of the interaction. Thus, disengagement theory is not limited to an explanation of observed activity level. Rather, it proposes a developmental change in the psychological/emotional function of social relationships. In this view, a person may remain relatively active in late life, but the interaction will have different meaning than it did, or would have had, in earlier years.

In addition to the problems just discussed, the activity/disengagement debate was fueled by an emotional reaction marked by trepidation: If, as a society, we accepted disengagement as adaptive, steps to remedy the austere social environments of some elderly may cease. The obvious relevance of the issues in question to social policy may have tainted the ability to maintain the objective view intrinsic to scientific inquiry. It appeared that over the years, most gerontologists grew tired of the highly polemical debates that raged during the 1960s and 1970s and instead tacitly agreed that the issue would not be resolved. Reference to activity theory continues to be made when it supports a particular point and to disengagement theory when it is congruent with a particular research finding. But the amount of systematic research aimed at the resolution of theoretical discrepancies has declined sharply.

The psychological issues related to the disengagement and activity theories are not only interesting, however, they are also central to our conceptualization of psychological and emotional development in late life. The idea that the aged begin to reduce the psychological investment afforded to social relationships earlier in life is consistent with a great deal of anecdotal and interview data. Although it would, indeed, be a mistake to accept a theory that dismisses the poverty of the social environment for some elderly as "adaptive," it would be just as serious a mistake to project our needs, wishes, and dreams on the elderly as if they face the same life tasks as younger people. The assumption that 80-year-olds desire the same social worlds as 40-year-olds is probably as erroneous as the assumption that 10-year-olds have the same social goals as 30-year-olds. For clinicians, knowledge about normal development is critical in order to proceed with effective treatments of abnormal behavior. What does one do with the older client who remains alone in his or her room, saying, "Look, I am old and I am too tired to do the things that I used to do. Please, just leave me alone?" Should we consider that response indicative of depression or, within the age context, normal?

PSYCHOLOGICAL IMPLICATIONS OF SOCIAL INACTIVITY

Thus far, the focus of this chapter has been on theoretical explanations of the psychological *precursors* to declining social activity level in old age. As one can surmise from the above discussion, the literature is largely speculative. It is clear, however, that the rate of social activity declines in old age. Also of interest are the *consequences* of this decline. Not only are the consequences of changes in activity patterns interesting in themselves, they may also help clarify antecedent processes. Many important questions remain: Are older persons satisfied with lower rates of social interaction? Are they depressed and lonely? Do older people feel abandoned or do they quickly accept the social concomitants of senescence?

It should be stated at the outset that *social activity* is not synonymous with *social support*, nor is either term synonymous with the term *social network*. In fact, much confusion has resulted from the interchangeable use of these terms. Social activity simply refers to the frequency of social contact. Social networks are social relationships and their characteristics surrounding a person, whereas social support refers to the emotional, instrumental, or financial aid that is derived from a particular network (Berkman, 1983). As will become clear from the following discussion, the implications of social inactivity may be quite different from the implications of poor social support (for an excellent discussion of social support, see chapter 22, this volume).

In recent years, social support has been implicated in a broad spectrum of outcomes, including significant influence on physical and mental health (Blazer, 1982; Berkman & Syme, 1979). These findings have had a marked impact on gerontological application and research. Yet as research in this area burgeoned, the distinction between social activity and social support became increasingly blurred. Ironically, the major epidemiological studies in this area have emphasized the distinctions between social support and social activity level. In the studies by Blazer (1982) and Berkman and Syme (1979), social contacts alone were not predictive of deleterious outcomes. Blazer found that social support and social contacts were not redundant to one another in statistical analyses of the data. Berkman and Syme pointed out that they used three questions to assess perceived social support:

1. How many close friends do you have?
2. How many relatives do you have that you feel close to?
3. How often do you see these people each month?

None of the items alone predicted negative outcomes; only when all three questions were combined were health outcomes predicted. Again, this suggested that the level of social activity and *perceived* social support predict different physical and psychological outcomes.

There is no definitive information about the factors that contribute to the individual's feeling of being socially supported. Berkman (1983) suggested that social networks be studied in an effort to identify the social conditions under which social support is most likely to be obtained. Although one logical avenue to explore is the level of social activity, the available research does not suggest a linear relationship between social activity and perceived social support.

A number of studies, however, support the claim that socially active elderly people are better adjusted psychologically than inactive elderly individuals. These include the findings from the Duke Longitudinal Study that active elderly report the highest morale (Maddox, 1968), as well as numerous reports from independent investigators. For example, Graney (1975), who followed a sample of 60 female subjects over a 4-year period, found that the women who increased their activity level reported, on subsequent testing, that they were happier, while those who decreased their activity level were less happy. Luke, Norton, and Denbigh (1981) interviewed 200 elderly persons. Of the 21% who exhibited some degree of psychological distress, level of social interaction was the best predictor, although mobility and health impairment also played a role. Studies such as these bolster the contention that social activity is an important factor in the lives of many elderly persons.

However, findings about the importance of social activity have been inconsistent. Conner, Powers, and Bultena (1979) reported, on the basis of interviews with 218 persons over the age of 70 years, that the number of social interactions in which the subjects engaged had little effect on adjustment. Instead, it was the quality of the interaction that determined successful adaptation to old age. Heltsley and Powers (1975) reported that feelings of isolation and the perceived inadequacy of interaction were more salient factors in adjustment than the actual frequency of interaction.

Duckitt (1982) reported an investigation in which multiple aspects of interactions were explored. The subjects completed a social interaction inventory, life-satisfaction indices, and the Affect Balance Scale. The results indicated that only intimate friendships and age-grading were of significant importance to well-being. Other aspects of interaction were not. Duckitt's findings about intimate friendships are consistent with the work by Lowenthal and Haven (1968) in which the presence of a confidant mediated the relationship between the level of social interaction and depression. In their research, if a target individual had a confidant, then the level of social interaction was relatively unimportant in predicting concomitant depression; that is, high or low interaction levels were not related to depressed mood. But if the target individual did not have a confidant, then the rate of social interaction was an important predictor of depression. In a second study, Duckitt (1983) assessed social resources, social activity, decremental life changes, and personality. He found that the best predictor of subjective well-being was level of neuroticism. Social activity with intimate friends again accounted for additional variance in the prediction, and physical health made an independent contribution to the prediction equation. Once again, however, there was no obvious relationship between overall frequency of interaction and subjective well-being.

In several studies of adjustment to institutional settings, Bennett and her associates (Bennett, 1968; Tec & Granick [Bennett], 1959; Weinstock & Bennett, 1971) found that people who were isolated prior to placement in a nursing home had greater difficulty interacting with peers and staff than those who had not been socially isolated prior to entering, and further found that this sometimes led to subsequent transfer to a mental hospital. Bennett (1973) put forth a theoretical explanation for the deleterious effects of social isolation, termed the *isolation-desocialization syndrome,* as illustrated by the following example:

> An old person in the community becomes isolated, then desocialized; he enters a home for the aged or some other setting, misperceives the norms and blunders socially soon after entry; others single him out, perhaps as a "troublemaker" and avoid him; he then becomes resentful and alienated; finally, he deviates further from the norms by becoming involved in overt conflict with staff members and/or other residents. (p. 186)

Bennett (1980) suggested that social isolation leads to problems that stem from desocialization. In this view, social skills are learned and maintained as a function of their social consequences. When social consequences are not present, such as in the case of an isolated individual, social skills are not maintained. Subsequently, inactive, isolated elderly become less socially able and are

placed at increased risk for interpersonal problems. Carstensen and Fremouw (1981) found that in nursing homes the socially isolated were less socially competent and more socially anxious than residents who were socially active.

Another potential implication of social inactivity is loneliness. Although it is clear that the elderly are less socially active, it is not clear whether they are lonelier than younger persons. In a cross-sectional study of loneliness across the life span, respondents 65 years of age and older were found to be the least lonely (Revenson, 1984). Elderly respondents also reported greater satisfaction with their relationships. The loss of an intimate attachment, not relative isolation per se, was the strongest correlate of loneliness. Creecy, Wright, and Berg (1983), however, found that loneliness was related to participation in some social activities but not in others. In their work with noninstitutionalized black elderly, integration into friendship groups and contact with friends and relatives were inversely correlated with loneliness. Participation in organizational activities, however, was not related to loneliness.

It is possible that inconsistent results in the literature are due to discrepancies in the measures used to assess social activity. Inherent in some measures of social activity is a subjective assessment of satisfaction with the activity. In Heltsley and Power's (1975) research, for example, inquiry into the *perceived inadequacy* of social interactions is made. In contrast, in the work by Bennett (1980), the assessment of social isolation is limited to the frequency of interaction with persons in predetermined categories of types of contacts (e.g., church-related, children). Obviously, different scales have tapped quite different aspects of social activity.

The range of activity level within samples may also contribute to discrepant findings in the literature. The investigator who recruits volunteer subjects from the community very likely obtains a different range of social activity than the investigator who recruits subjects from a nursing home. Similarly, a different range would be expected in a sample consisting of community elderly who attend meetings at a senior center than one consisting of individuals in the community who receive home health care services. Moreover, the rates of social activity among nursing-homes residents tend to be very low even among the most active residents (Carstensen & Fremouw, 1981). Comparisons of subjective perceptions of individuals who are extremely isolated to individuals who are extremely active may reveal differences, whereas comparisons of moderately active to extremely active individuals may reveal fewer differences.

Even though the measures of activity level show no relationship to well-being and perceived support in some samples, logic dictates that there must be a point at which a relationship emerges. If a person had no social contacts for an extended period of time, for example, it would be quite surprising to hear that the individual felt a great deal of social support. Thus, there may be a basal level of social contact below which inactivity has deleterious effects but above which it has less impact on well-being. We do not know the optimal base rates for activity levels for any age group.

Nearly all of the research reports on social activity have utilized correlational analysis. The implicit assumption, therefore, has been that the relationship between activity level and well-being is linear. A curvilinear relationship between social contacts and well-being is also plausible, however. In a study of the relationship between physical health and social interaction, Miller and Ingham (1976) found that people claiming to have "few acquaintances" exhibited the highest number of physical symptoms of all the people interviewed, but those claiming to have "some acquaintances" had fewer physical symptoms than those claiming to have "many acquaintances." The negative side of social interaction has been documented by Rook (1984). She found that negative social interactions had more influence on well-being than positive social interactions in a sample of elderly women, indicating that social interactions are not always beneficial.

Although obvious ethical considerations prohibit experimental manipulation of extreme social activity levels with humans, some intriguing case studies can be found in the early literature. Several cases of human children abandoned and raised by animals in the wilderness have been reported (Zingg, 1940). These children experienced extreme social deprivation. Even though details of the cases are of questionable veridicality, they suggest consistently that the age of the child when abandoned and the length of time without human contact were both factors directly related to adjustment upon return to society; that is, the younger the child and the longer the child was without human contact, the more severe the disturbance when found (Brownfield, 1965). Bowlby (1969) and Spitz (1954) wrote of the devastating

consequences minimal human contact had for institutionalized infants. Both observed higher rates of mortality among infants with little human contact. Although these studies have been faulted for their lack of methodological rigor, controlled studies of extreme social isolation in laboratory research with animals have been consistent with these reports. Most notable among these are the classic studies by Harlow and Harlow (1966) in which monkeys reared in social isolation exhibited bizarre sexual and social behaviors as adults.

PHYSICAL IMPLICATIONS OF INACTIVITY

Regardless of the psychological consequences of social inactivity among the aged, there are indisputable physical *benefits* to activity. Social activity often comes in the same package as physical activity. Sitting in a chair by a window and reminiscing may hold psychological benefits comparable to talking to another person, but few physical benefits. It has been shown, for example, that the changes in cardiovascular functioning, the circulatory system, and capacity for physical work that are seen in old age are mimicked in young adults who experience prolonged physical inactivity (Blumenthal & Williams, 1982). Exercise programs have been demonstrated not only to improve cardiovascular functioning but psychological well-being as well (Blumenthal & Williams, 1982).

In animals, social deprivation has been associated with changes at the brain level. Greenough, Volkmar, and Juraska (1973) found that rats reared in isolation had fewer higher-order cortical dendritic branches than rats raised in enriched environments. Juraska, Greenough, Elliott, Mack, and Berkowitz (1980) noted a similar effect in animals after they were isolated in early adulthood. And later, Green, Greenough, and Schlumpf (1983) replicated the effect in middle-aged rats. Their findings suggest that negative effects in animals occur not only during early critical periods, but histological changes continue to be manifested even when isolation occurs in later adulthood.

Levi (1972) posits that understimulation associated with inactivity is as potent a stressor as overstimulation. In a test of this theoretical model, Arnetz, Theorell, Levi, Kallner, and Eneroth (1983) examined psychoendocrine and metabolic effects of social isolation and understimulation in a sample of 60 elderly persons. A social activation program was implemented using half of the sample, while the other half served as the control group. Activity levels were successfully increased. Blood samples taken throughout the duration of the program indicated that the plasma levels of testosterone, dehydroepiandosterone, and estradiol increased significantly and hemoglobin AlC-decreased significantly in the experimental group. Furthermore, experimental subjects showed increases in height following the program. Arnetz and Theorell (1983) noted that although there were no changes in the indices of psychosomatic complaints in this sample, "feelings of restlessness" decreased over time (p. 454). It should be kept in mind that physical activity was confounded by social activity in this investigation, so results cannot be attributed exclusively to psychosocial variables. One could argue, however, that such a distinction is largely academic, since social activity and physical activity are confounded in daily life.

Interestingly, physical mobility, which is intimately tied to social activity, is considered to be one of the top three problems encountered by elderly patients (Burgio, Burgio, Engell, & Tice, 1985). In fact, lowered rates of social activity and restricted mobility could be seen as two aspects of the same basic problem. Hogue (1985) offers a conceptual model in which she links mobility to psychosocial variables, such as availability of social support, cognitive capacity, and ego strength, as well as to biological health. Little systematic research has been conducted on mobility among the elderly, but it appears that verbal praise and prompts can be used to increase rates of mobility (Burgio et al., 1985; MacDonald & Butler, 1974). The effects of improved mobility on the generalized rates of social interaction are, as yet, unclear. Thus, although a link between social interaction and physical health status has been clearly established, the extensiveness and directionality of the relationship remain unknown.

INTERVENTION LITERATURE ON SOCIAL ACTIVITY

The bulk of the research on social activity among the elderly consists of reports of interventions. Intervention studies designed to increase the rates of social interactions have been diverse, ranging from resocialization programs to operant reinforcement strategies.

Mulligan and Bennett (1978) reported an evaluation of the Teachers College Friendly Visiting Program (TC-FVP) in New York City, a resocialization program based on the desocialization view of social isolation proposed by Bennett (1973). In this investigation experimental subjects were visited every 2 weeks for a total of 12 visits, while members of the control group were visited only twice, once before and once after assessment. Apartment upkeep and personal appearance, as rated by graduate student visitors, improved in the experimental group only. Although changes on an isolation index were not found, the authors attributed other observed changes to the visitation program.

Rathbone-McCuan and Levenson (1975) conducted what they called "socialization therapy" with participants of a geriatric day-care service. Socially withdrawn persons were reportedly better adjusted following this procedure. Socialization referred to encouragement to create new roles and reestablish old ones, adjustment to changes in heterosexual peer relationships, increases in verbal and physical interaction with peers and staff, and the development of group identity. Berger and Rose (1977) and Lopez (1980) have reported successful interventions utilizing skills-training approaches based on role playing.

Most of the intervention research aimed at increasing social interactions has been conducted with institutionalized populations—populations that display notoriously low rates of interaction. Sommer and Ross (1958) and Peterson, Knapp, Rosen, and Pither (1977) demonstrated that simple rearrangement of furniture could facilitate verbal exchanges, and Cluff and Campbell (1975) reported that a resident's room position on the corridor was associated with frequency of activity as well as satisfaction with the home.

Early work by McClannahan and Risley (1973) demonstrated that alterations in the physical design of a nursing home could effect changes in the rates of social interactions among residents. In one study, these authors opened a resident-run store in the nursing home. Observations of social interactions outside the store were made. The hours that the store was open constituted the experimental condition, and the hours that the store was closed constituted the withdrawal condition. Interactions increased when the store was open and returned to baseline when the store was closed.

A year later McClannahan and Risley (1974) reported a study of the factors that influence residents' attendance at structured activities in nursing homes. In this manipulation, different types of prompts (e.g., written vs. spoken) were compared to assess their relative effectiveness in increasing attendance as compared to a no-prompt baseline condition. Although no differences among prompts were found, each was effective in increasing attendance as compared to a no prompt baseline condition. In a third investigation, McClannahan and Risley (1975) examined the rate of participation—in this case appropriate engagement with recreational equipment, materials, or another person—under both prompt and no prompt conditions. In one situation, only materials and equipment were provided. In another, materials and equipment were provided plus verbal prompts to engage in the use of the activity. Prompts were defined as such statements as "Let me show you" or "Now you try it." Again, prompts successfully increased the rates of activity among residents.

Hoyer, Kafer, Simpson, and Hoyer (1974) utilized an operant procedure to reinstate verbal behavior with four elderly mental patients. Within-session increases were observed, but generalization data were not reported. Mueller and Atlas (1972), also hypothesizing that the social withdrawal observed in nursing home residents was due to environmental conditions on the ward rather than to an intractable cognitive state, implemented a resocialization program designed to improve the social skills necessary for interaction. These authors reported that operant principles could be successfully applied to increase the initially low rates of social behaviors among the institutionalized elderly. The authors also noted that it appeared that the regressive, withdrawn behaviors of residents were reinforced, a finding later documented by Baltes and her colleagues (Baltes & Skinner, 1983; Barton, Baltes, & Orzech, 1980; chapter 16, this volume).

MacDonald (1978) reported an intervention with three elderly men described as chronically socially isolated by nursing-home staff. MacDonald utilized an operant procedure in which the investigator sat with and verbally reinforced the vocal behavior of residents during mealtimes. Over a 2-month period, verbalizations of each of the three subjects increased significantly over the baseline. Moreover, MacDonald stated, "Ward staff noted that prior to the study, each of the three men awaited dinner silently. In contrast, during days of the latter sessions, and after the

project was completed, the men frequently sat together and with no prompting spontaneously conversed among themselves" (p. 353). In this investigation, it appeared that once conversation had been initiated, the men continued to interact in the absence of external prompts.

Other investigators have demonstrated that social behavior can be modified through the use of stimulus control procedures. Blackman, Howe, and Pinkston (1976) implemented a program designed to increase the availability of social contact to elderly women residents of a nursing home. Prior to breakfast, residents typically lined up quietly outside the solarium. Blackman et al. provided coffee and juice during this period and found that the "social hour" resulted not only in increased attendance but also in increased social interactions among residents.

Quattrochi-Tubin and Jason (1980) also examined the stimulus control function of access to free coffee and other refreshments among elderly nursing home residents. Provision of refreshments was reported to result in increased attendance, generalized participation in a subsequent activity session, and decreased television-watching behavior.

Another notable study was conducted by Wisocki and Mosher (1980), who reported increasing the nonvocal behavior of psychiatric, aphasic, brain-damaged elderly patients through sign language training using modeling and positive practice. The involvement of peers was used to facilitate generalization of the use of signing to other ward residents. Increases in the mean frequency of interactions with peers were observed during generalization probes and were maintained 4 months later.

Goldstein and Baer (1976) conducted an intervention designed to increase the rates of social interactions of nursing-home residents with family members by improving letter-writing skills. Three subjects were selected by staff as persons who would be interested in receiving more personal mail. Using a multiple baseline design, each subject was trained in letter-writing strategies that would be likely to generate a reply. For example, participants were taught to ask questions in their letters and to include stamped, self-addressed envelopes; they were prompted to reply quickly to all correspondence received. This approach was demonstrated to be effective in increasing the amount of mail received. Moreover, the intervention was unique in that it increased social exchange with people with whom the subject had a prior relationship, as opposed to other residents, thereby expanding their social environments outside the nursing home.

Konarski, Johnson, and Whitman (1980) reported an intervention designed to increase the rates of participation of an institutionalized population. Effects of a treatment package and separate components of the package were systematically assessed. The treatment package consisted of verbal and nonverbal prompts plus positive reinforcement in the form of refreshments. Verbal prompts consisted of a general announcement that activities were available and individual prompts delivered to all subjects. The researchers found that each component of the treatment package led to increased social activity over the baseline, but that the treatment package was more effective than either component taken alone. In addition, a 10-week follow-up and probe sessions for generalization were conducted. Residents continued participation 10 weeks after the treatment had been terminated. Generalization probes, however, revealed no change in activity outside the experimental setting.

The primary significance of the study by Konarski et al. is found in the absence of generalization effects, because the program otherwise had demonstrable results. These researchers also noted that self-reports of satisfaction did not change with the intervention and further pointed out that, aside from the report by Blackman, Howe, and Pinkston of a subsequent increase in social interaction with increased activity participation, no one had demonstrated collateral benefits derived from participation in scheduled social events. Moreover, Konarski et al., to date the only investigators who have included a measure of satisfaction in their assessment, found no change in life satisfaction as a result of the intervention. A similar study by Simpson, Woods, and Britton (1981) suggests that it is the subjective enjoyment of events rather than the rate of participation that determines psychological well-being.

Carstensen and Erickson (1986) implemented a stimulus control procedure in which food was served during a prescribed social hour. Increased rates of interactions among residents during this time were consistent with earlier findings, but a content analysis of the verbal behavior that accompanied the increase was also conducted. These data suggested that the increase in interactive behavior of residents was largely accounted for by an increase in incoherent and unreciprocated vocal behavior.

In summary, intervention studies on social inactivity among the elderly have been diverse, imaginative, and effective at increasing the rates of social interactions. In addition, they attest to the malleability of the social behavior of the elderly. Few studies have reported generalization of effects outside of the experimental setting, however, and none have obtained changes in self-reported well-being. Thus, although it is clear that rates of social interactions can be manipulated, the value of such manipulations is much less clear.

A LIFE-SPAN THEORY OF SOCIAL ACTIVITY

A review of the existing literature reveals some consistent findings. First, there is no evidence that the elderly are more psychologically impervious to losses of confidants and significant others than younger people, nor do they withdraw from areas involving family and close friends. Second, although overall rates of interaction are reduced, this is not necessarily accompanied by higher rates of subjective distress, such as loneliness. Third, interventions aimed at increasing the rates of interaction appear to be effective on a short-term basis. Curiously, however, higher rates are not maintained after external contingencies for interaction are removed, nor do they appear to improve life satisfaction. What can one conclude? I propose below a theoretical view of age-related change in social behavior based on a synthesis of current findings. It is a view that requires a life span context.

During infancy, social interaction is determined primarily by forces outside the control of the organism, namely by the family. This is not to say that the infant is not an active participant in social interaction; rather, there is little opportunity for the infant to "negotiate' with whom he or she interacts (Corsaro, 1985; Hartup, 1984). As soon as social participation is under the control of the child, rates of interaction are very high. Corsaro observed that during the preschool years, children rarely engage in solitary play and, when alone, make consistent attempts to enter ongoing peer episodes. Moreover, there appears to be minimal selectivity in the choice of playmates. With age, children begin to become more selective in their choice of friends. A sociological study by Eder (1985) of the development of social stratification among middle school students suggests that by the seventh grade two main subgroups emerge in school activities. Children affiliate with one or the other. By early adolescence, stable cliques have formed, that is, small subsets of close friends accompanied by the simultaneous disdain of members of other subgroups. Young adults tend even more to narrow the range of persons with whom they interact, especially during the period when child bearing and child rearing are common. The intimate conversations of adolescence are then held only with one's mate or a few select confidants. In old age, the number of persons with whom one interacts on a regular basis is further reduced. Contacts through work or through one's children are lost, and the deaths of friends and relatives considerably alter the opportunity to interact.

Thus, there appears to be a continual reduction in the rate of interactions over the life span. This reduction does not appear suddenly in old age; rather, it is very gradual, with its origins traceable to early childhood. From the beginning of life, we begin to conserve our social energy, retaining it more and more throughout the life span. As we interact less frequently, however, the reinforcing value of the relationships we maintain may increase. That is, we may become more selective about the people with whom we interact, devoting more time to our most rewarding relationships and less time to aversive or less rewarding relationships. The social activity literature suggests that, in normal aged populations, overall rates of interaction are unrelated to well-being but *qualitative* aspects of social interaction are clearly related.

With the exception of activity theory, all of the traditional theoretical formulations about the psychological/emotional changes that parallel changes in social behavior during late life suggest that the elderly are less attached to their social worlds and that this lessened involvement leads to lower rates of social interaction. Part of the problem with such an interpretation is that it assumes social interaction with all persons to be equivalent. An examination of the overall rates of interaction obscures information about the person with whom one interacts and the content of that interaction. It is possible that the dimension with respect to which individuals change with age is sociability. Buss and Plomin (1984) define *sociability* as "the tendency to prefer the presence of others to being alone" (p. 63). Its characteristic feature is that the process rewards of interaction are reinforced independently of the content rewards of the inter-

action. *Process rewards* are components of interaction, like responsivity, attention, and arousal, that can be found in virtually any social interaction. *Content rewards*, however, refer to the reinforcing aspects of social interaction, such as sympathy, respect, and affection, that are clearly not obtainable from arbitrary social interaction. According to Buss and Plomin (1984), a person could be highly unsociable but still have strong attachments and affiliations with others; that is, content rewards of social interaction may be quite salient. With age, and a concomitant increase in the response cost necessary for social interaction, the reinforcing value of the process rewards of social interaction may decrease. This would result in the overall rate of interaction decreasing, but the rates of social interaction from which content rewards are derived would not decrease. If such is the case, the emotional intensity of social interaction, that is, the content rewards, would not decrease over the life span. In fact, a case could be made for the hypothesis that content rewards of social interaction increase over the life span, because an extended history of a friendship or family relationship provides a broader basis for understanding and respecting another individual.

For many years, the predominant view of emotional experiences in old age has been inconsistent with such a claim. Rather, old age has been viewed as a time of rigidity, flattened affect, egocentricity, and reduced intensity of emotional experience (for a review, see Malatesta, 1981; Malatesta & Izard, 1984). Recent empirical findings do not support these traditional views. In an effort to assess age differences in emotional experience, Malatesta and Kalnok (1984) interviewed 240 adults aged 17–88. They reported that the older subjects did not differ from middle-aged subjects in the degree of importance placed on emotions. Neither did they find an increase in the experience of negative emotions in the older age group, as compared to younger groups. Elicitors of emotion, however, did vary with age.

Schulz (1985) holds that identical events elicit different emotions over the life span. He cites as support for this position both cognitive and physiological changes that occur with age. At the cognitive level, the increasingly larger store of emotional experiences in long-term memory that accrues over the life span serves as the context within which to evaluate new emotion-related events. This reduces the probability that future events will be interpreted as highly emotional.

After one has experienced a number of highly emotional events, such as the deaths of loved ones, other losses may seem small by comparison. Moreover, emotional responses to events appear to become more mixed with age. In old age, it may be difficult to identify an event that is purely happy, for example. Instead, in late life an event previously experienced as happy may become poignant. An elderly woman's description of the happy event of a visit from her 90-year-old sister may be accompanied by sadness because she knows that this may be the last time she will see her. At the physiological level, reduction in regulatory effectiveness in the central nervous systems results in decreased homeostatic adaptation to environmental elicitors. The result is that the organism requires more time to return to baseline levels of arousal once high levels are instigated. This being the case, older individuals may learn to avoid emotionally laden interactions that carry little reward. In fact, the "process-rewards" described by Buss and Plomin (1984) may become "process-punishers" in late life.

To recapitulate, a view of emotional constriction is not supported by empirical findings. But a view that older people do not differ from younger people in their social and emotional behaviors is equally untenable. Instead, it appears that with age one learns to better conserve (direct) one's emotions and subsequently limits social interaction to interaction with those persons or situations most rewarding to the individual. As one ages, a lessened physical reserve demands that energy be expended judiciously. Thus, selective expenditure of one's social/emotional energy can be seen as an adaptive response to the reduction in physical stamina that accompanies old age. In illustration, consider the following life span example: Children strongly react to criticism and praise from almost any adult. With age, they afford fewer persons the power to affect them so profoundly. By old age, there may be few who can elicit positive or negative emotional responses. This is not to say that, once elicited, intensity of emotion is lessened in old age; rather, fewer emotion-eliciting stimuli exist. What has been termed *disengagement* may instead reflect increased conservation of emotions.

In old age there may be few relationships that provide enough rewards to justify the expended effort. Talking to another nursing-home resident or a college student assigned as part of a project may do little for the elderly individual. At the same time, those relationships that possess the characteristics essential to reciprocally reinforcing relationships may become more important than ever before. Again, consider the finding that the loss of confidantes predicts mental health in the elderly. Lowered rates of activity alone do not. In old age, the reinforcing value of an interaction may become more important than ever before, while the quantity of interactions simultaneously becomes less important.

The literature on social activity in old age consistently reveals the importance of qualitative aspects of social relationships. This is consistent with an "energy conservation" view of aging. Because one has limited physical energy in old age, efforts expended in social interactions may be best retained for the most significant individuals in one's life. Lowered rates of social interaction may be highly adaptive and represent the culmination of social development throughout the life span. What differentiates this view from a disengagement view is that rather than withdrawing from social and emotional contacts, the elderly individual becomes expert at directing social interactions and channeling emotions to the people most important to him or her.

In this proposed life span view, it is hypothesized that emotional development (i. e., learning the skill of controlling one's emotional reactivity) parallels changes in social interaction. In a pilot study at Indiana University, we have begun interviews about emotion control with individuals ranging in age from 12 to 80 years. Emotion control refers to the ability to direct and limit the experience of negative emotions and the ability to access positive emotions. Although we are in rudimentary stages of the research, a highly consistent finding is that subjects report that they can control their emotions better with age, particularly anger and sadness. Moreover, they see this increased control as a gradual adaptation throughout life. The following was taken from an interview with a 79-year-old subject:

(Q): *Looking back over your life, do you see changes in the way that you react emotionally?*

Indeed, I do. I have learned that one can control one's physical feelings, the various small illnesses to a great extent. . . . I have learned that one had better take all of the happiness one can whenever it is available because there are going to be times when things are not going to be good and it is going to help one through the difficult times. In the question of pain, sorrow, loss, [I have learned that] what can't be cured must be endured. And I have also learned to take a tremendous amount of happiness in small things that perhaps when I was younger I took for granted. These small emotions of happiness, these transient pleasures, assume the importance which they deserve, but which in a very, very, full life, one tends not to notice.

(Q): *Do you find that you direct social and emotional energy more prudently with age?*

Yes. Largely because of physical reasons. I am physically unable to do the things which I was accustomed to doing. I can't say that I have accepted this with the proper amount of resignation. I haven't. It is one of those things for which I shall have to school myself. But I realize that I cannot do the things which I formerly did and therefore must conserve even to the point of conserving nonessential emotions — those emotions that are not connected to my family or my closest friends.

Replies such as these suggest that the emotional lives of the elderly are qualitatively different from those of the young. The woman quoted above articulated a realization that she must reduce her participation in some areas in which she was previously involved. The result is not a flattening of affect, however, as the disengagement theory would suggest. Rather, she states that she has learned to direct her emotional energies to the people that she most values. The majority of older subjects we have interviewed affirm an experience of greater control over their emotions and related physical sensations with age.

Perhaps the reason why recognition of disengagement theory has persisted so long, in spite of the lack of strong empirical evidence, is that certain elements central to the theory ring true. Most older people becomes less active and, for whatever reasons, the majority seem to reduce their level of social involvement in some areas of life. Unfortunately, the theory consistently fails to explain and predict the lives of many elderly who remain passionately involved in their social worlds. The terms *disengagement* and *emotion conservation* both could be used to describe the same behavior, and both could be seen as adaptive processes by which

the impact of losses and problems of late life are reduced. But there is an important distinction. Emotion conservation suggests that emotional experience remains a vital part of life. Emotions are not flattened; rather, they are more judiciously expended. Moreover, emotion conservation can be seen as a lifelong process, not an exclusive stage of late life.

In summary, there is evidence that emotional and social development continue into late life. In disengagement theory, the behavior of older adults has been used to infer an internal state of detachment. Activity theory suggests that detachment does not occur in healthy aging, but rather that rates of social activity do decline. It is unlikely that there are no psychological consequences or precursors to this reduction. On the contrary, social/emotional development could be viewed as the one area in which refinement and maturation continue into very late life. With age one may become more selective about the people with whom one interacts in an effort to control physiological and psychological reactivity. A life span developmental approach to the study of social and emotional development will be necessary in order to understand the *progression* of change. Rates of activity may not be an appropriate dependent variable in empirical tests of these issues. Rather, focus on qualitative aspects of interaction style may yield more useful information.

CLINICAL RECOMMENDATIONS

Earlier I had posed the question of what to do with the older client who says, "Look, I am old and I am too tired to do the things that I used to do. Please, just leave me alone." Based on the literature reviewed herein, several recommendations for clinical intervention with the socially inactive client or patient can be made. First, the existing level of interaction should be assessed and compared to the levels of interaction that were typical for that individual earlier in life. As mentioned previously, optimal levels of interaction are not known for any age group, and individual differences no doubt exist. One common observation in gerontology is that the intragroup heterogeneity of samples increases with age. Thus, what is a normal level of interaction for one person will be best determined by an individual analysis, rather than by comparing the target person to others of the same age.

Next, if significant changes from earlier levels

are apparent, an examination of the person's social environment should be made. In this regard, the professional or concerned other will want to identify physical or social *barriers* to interaction. Certain environments are much more conducive to social interaction than others. Sometimes older people who maintain residence alone in the community face severe social isolation. For older individuals living alone, telephones are an absolute necessity. Not only are they needed in the event of a medical emergency, they sometimes serve as the sole link to a social network that can no longer be maintained through direct face-to-face contacts. For housebound elderly, visitation is essential, and mail is probably one of the most important ways in which family members and other significant others can offer social contact in their physical absence.

Although community residence can be most isolating in a physical sense, social withdrawal in nursing homes is extremely common. In these environments, physical isolation is not a problem, but social isolation is experienced by many. There are a number of reasons why a nursing-home setting could lead to social isolation. Entrance to a nursing-home environment, in the best of institutions, entails adjustment to a number of factors that few experience in community-based living. The size and structural homogeneity of most institutions make them difficult to navigate. Moreover, for many nursing-home residents, the diverse mixture of residents and consequent problems can lead to a great deal of anxiety. When they leave their rooms, they may encounter individuals who are confused, or they may hear screams from disoriented patients. It is not surprising that the rate of social activity is low among the institutionalized elderly. Many rarely leave their rooms.

Some steps can be taken to reduce the impact that these factors may have on withdrawal. Clear markings in corridors, repeated instructions, and assistance in navigating the environment can reduce anxiety and allow a person to venture outside his or her personal room. For the many nursing-home residents who feel that they have nothing in common with other residents, the maintenance of prior social networks is also extremely important. Telephone and mail contacts and encouraged visitation are as important for institutionalized elderly as they are for those in the community.

Reviewed earlier were a number of institution-wide strategies reported to be effective in increasing the rates of interaction among the elderly in nursing homes. Their short-term effectiveness has been demonstrated repeatedly, but long-term effectiveness is less clear. The fact that temporary increases in social contacts decline after external reinforcers are withdrawn occasions serious question about the intrinsic value of the social interactions made available by this type of intervention. It may be that global interventions do not provide valuable social contacts. Of paramount importance is the recognition that loneliness is related to the loss of confidantes, not low rates of activity per se. Thus, efforts to maintain previous contacts and to introduce residents with similar interests and backgrounds to each other may carry many more benefits than simply increasing the overall number of times a person interacts with another person.

Once obvious barriers to social interaction are removed, further intervention may be needed. At this point a case-by-case assessment of the individual's desire for social contact must be made. An interview in which significant others are identified and information about previous contacts is obtained should be conducted. Initial contacts with these persons may require assistance, but ideally a mechanism for contacting the significant other independently should be designed.

In conclusion, humans are social animals. We live most of our lives in highly complex interdependent social systems that provide us with a sense of purpose and a sense of identity. As we age, our social systems shrink. The energy and, perhaps, the inclination to continually build new ones are reduced. As a result, rates of interaction decline. But it is doubtful that age lessens the need for social contact. Rather, in old age the people with whom one interacts and the quality of the interaction may take on more importance than ever before.

REFERENCES

Arnetz, B. B., Eyre, M., & Theorell, T. (1982). Social activation of the elderly: A social experiment. *Social Science and Medicine, 16,* 1685–1690.

Arnetz, B. B., & Theorell, T. (1983). Psychological, sociological, and health behavior aspects of a long-term activation program for institutionalized elderly people. *Social Science and Medicine, 17,* 449–456.

Arnetz, B. B., Theorell, T., Levi, L., Kallner, A., & Eneroth, P. (1983). An experimental study of social isolation of elderly people: Psychoendocrine and metabolic effects. *Psychosomatic Medicine, 45,* 395–406.

Baltes, M. M., & Skinner, E. A. (1983). Cognitive performance deficits and hospitalization: Learned helplessness, instrumental passitivity, or what? Comments on Raps, Peterson, Jonas and Seligman, *Journal of Personality and Social Psychology, 42,* 1036–1041.

Barton, E. M., Baltes, M. M., & Orzech, M. J. (1980). On the etiology of dependency in older nursing home residents during morning care: The role of staff behavior. *Journal of Personality and Social Psychology, 38,* 423–431.

Bennett, R. (1968). Distinguishing characteristics of the aging from a sociological viewpoint. *Journal of the American Geriatrics Society, 16,* 127–134.

Bennett, R. (1973). Living conditions and everyday needs of the aged with specific reference to social isolation. *Journal of Aging and Human Development, 4,* 179–198.

Bennett, R. (1980). *Aging, isolation and resocialization.* New York: Van Nostrand Reinhold.

Berezin, M. A. (1980). Isolation in the aged: Individual dynamics, community and family involvement. *Journal of Geriatric Psychiatry, 13,* 3–17.

Berger, R. M., & Rose, S. D. (1977). Interpersonal skill training with institutionalized patients. *Journal of Gerontology, 32,* 346–353.

Berkman, L., & Syme, S. L (1979). Social networks, host resistance and mortality: A nine year follow-up study of Alameda County residents. *American Journal of Epidemiology, 109,* 186–204.

Berkman, L. F. (1983). The assessment of social networks and social support in the elderly. *Journal of the American Geriatrics Society, 31,* 743–749.

Blackman, D. K., Howe, M., & Pinkston, E. M. (1976). Increasing participation in social interaction of the institutionalized elderly. *Gerontologist, 16,* 69–76.

Blazer, D. G. (1982). Social support and mortality in an elderly community population. *American Journal of Epidemiology, 115,* 684–694.

Blumenthal, J. N. A., & Williams, R. S. (1982). Exercise and aging: The use of physical exercise in health enhancement. *Center Reports on Advances in Research, 6,* 1–5.

Bowlby, J. (1969). Psychopathology of anxiety: The role of affectional bonds. In M. H. Lader (Ed.), *Studies of anxiety.* London: Royal Medico-Psychological Association.

Brownfield, C. A. (1965). *Isolation—clinical and experimental approaches.* New York: Random House.

Burgio, L., Burgio, K., Engell, B., & Tice, L. (1985, November). Increasing mobility in elderly nursing home patients. Paper presented at the meeting of the Gerontological Society of America, New Orleans, LA.

Buss, A. H., & Plomin, R. (1984). *Temperament: Early developing personality traits* (pp. 63–82). Hillsdale, NJ: Erlbaum.

Carstensen, L. L., & Erickson, R. E. (1986). Enhancing the social environments of elderly nursing home residents: Are high rates of interactions enough? *Journal of Applied Behavior Analysis, 19,* 349–355.

Carstensen, L. L., & Fremouw, W. F. (1981, November). *Assessment of social isolation among the elderly.* Paper presented at the meeting of the Association for the Advancement of Behavior Therapy, Toronto, Ontario, Canada.

Cluff, P. S., & Campbell, W. H. (1975). The social corridor: An environmental and behavioral evaluation. *Gerontologist, 15,* 516–523.

Conner, K. A., Powers, E. A., & Bultena, G. L. (1979). Social interaction and life satisfaction: An empirical assessment of late-life patterns. *Journal of Gerontology, 34,* 116–121.

Corsaro. W. A. (1985). *Friendship and peer culture in the early years.* Norwood, NJ: Ablex.

Creecy, R. F., Wright, R., & Berg, W. E. (1983). Correlates of loneliness among the Black elderly. *Activities, Adaptation and Aging, 3,* 9–16.

Cumming, E. (1963). Further thoughts on the theory of disengagement. *UNESCO International Social Science Bulletin, 15,* 377–393.

Cumming, E., & Henry, W. H. (1961). *Growing old: The process of disengagement.* New York: Basic Books.

Dibner, A. S. (1980). Isolation in the aged: Individual dynamics, community and family involvement. *Journal of Geriatric Psychiatry, 13,* 3–4.

Duckitt, J. H. (1982). Social interaction and psychological well-being: A study of elderly persons living in the inner-city area of Pretoria. *Humanitas: Journal for Research in the Human Sciences, 8,* 121–129.

Duckitt, J. H. (1985). Predictors of subjective well-being in later life: An empirical assessment of theoretical frameworks in social gerontology. *Humanitas: Journal for Research in the Human Sciences, 9,* 211–219.

Eder, D. (1985). The cycle of popularity: Interpersonal relations among female adolescents. *Sociology of Education, 58,* 154–165.

Freud, A. (1946). *The ego and mechanisms of defense.* New York: International Universities Press.

Goldstein, R. S., & Baer, D. M. (1976). R.S.V.P.: A procedure to increase the personal mail and number of correspondence for nursing home residents. *Behavior Therapy, 7,* 348–354.

Goulet, L. R., & Baltes, P. B. (Eds.) (1970). *Life-span developmental psychology: Research and theory.* New York: Academic.

Graney, M. (1975). Happiness and social participation in aging. *Journal of Gerontology, 30,* 301–706.

Green, E. J., Greenough, W. T., & Schlumpf, B. E. (1983). Effects of complex or isolated environments on cortical dendrites of middle aged rats. *Brain Research, 264,* 233–240.

Greenough, W. T., & Volkar, F. R. (1973). Pattern of dendritic branching in occipital cortex of rats reared in complex environments. *Experimental Neurology, 40,* 491–504.

Gutmann, D. (1969). The country of old men: Cross-cultural studies in the psychology of later life. In W. Donahue (Ed.), *Occasional papers in gerontology* (pp. 95–122). Ann Arbor: University of Michigan Press.

Harlow, H. F., & Harlow, M. K. (1966). Learning to love. *American Scientist, 54,* 244–272.

Harris, J. E., & Bodden, J. L. (1978). An activity group experience for disengaged elderly persons. *Journal of Counseling Psychology, 25,* 325–330.

Hartup, W. W. (1984). Commentary: Relationships and child development. In M. Perlmutter (Ed.), *Parent–child interaction and parent–child relations in child develop-*

ment (Vol. 17, pp. 177–183). Hillsdale, NJ: Erlbaum.

Havighurst, R. J., Neugarten, B. L., & Tobin, S. S. (1968). Disengagement and patterns of aging. In B. L. Neugarten (Ed.) *Middle age and aging: A reader in social psychology* (pp. 161–172). Chicago: University of Chicago Press.

Heltsley, M. E., & Powers, R. C. (1975). Social interaction and perceived adequacy of interaction of the rural aged. *Gerontologist, 15,* 533–536.

Hogue, C. C. (1985). Mobility. In E. L. Schneider (Ed.), *The teaching nursing home* (pp. 231–243). New York: Raven.

Hoyer, W. J., Kafer, R. J., Simpson, S. C., & Hoyer, F. W. (1974). Reinforcement of verbal behavior in elderly mental patients using operant procedures. *Gerontologist, 14,* 149–152.

Juraska, J. M., Greenough, W. T., Elliot, C., Mack, K. J., & Berkowitz, R. (1980). Plasticity in adult rat visual cortex: An examination of several cell populations after differential rearing. *Behavioral and Neural Biology, 29,* 157–167.

Kalish, R. A., & Knudtson, F. W. (1976). Attachment versus disengagement: A life-span conceptualization. *Human Development, 19,* 171–181.

Konarski, E. Q., Johnson, M. R., & Whitman, T. L. (1980). A systematic investigation of resident participation in a nursing home activities program. *Journal of Behavior Therapy and Experimental Psychiatry, 11,* 249–257.

Levi, L. (1972). *Stress and distress in response to psychosocial stimuli: Laboratory and real-life studies on sympatho-adreno-medullary and related reactions.* Elmsford, NY: Pergamon.

Lopez, M. A. (1980). Social-skills training with institutionalized elderly: Effects of pre-counseling structuring and overlearning on skill acquisitions and transfer. *Journal of Counseling Psychology, 27,* 286–293.

Lowenthal, M., & Haven, C. (1968). Interaction and adaptation: Intimacy as a critical variable. In B. L. Neugarten, *Middle age and aging: A reader in social psychology* (pp. 390–400). Chicago: University of Chicago Press.

Luke, E., Norton, W., & Denbigh, K. (1981). Medical and social factors associated with psychological distress in a sample of community aged. *Canadian Journal of Psychiatry, 26,* 244–250.

MacDonald, M. L. (1978). Environmental programming for the socially isolated aging. *Gerontologist, 18,* 350–354.

MacDonald, M. L., & Butler, A. K. (1974). Reversal of helplessness: Producing walking behavior in nursing home wheelchair residents using behavior modification procedures. *Journal of Gerontology, 29,* 97–101.

Maddox, G. L. (1963). Activity and morale: A longitudinal study of selected elderly subjects. *Social Forces, 42,* 195–204.

Maddox, G. L. (1968). Persistence of life style among the elderly: A longitudinal study of patterns of social activity in relation to life satisfaction. In B. L. Neugarten (Ed.), *Middle age and aging: A reader in social psychology.* Chicago: University of Chicago Press.

Maddox, G. L. (1970). Themes and issues in sociological theories of human aging. *Human Development, 13,* 17–27.

Malatesta, C. Z. (1981). Affective development over the lifespan: Involution or growth? *Merrill-Palmer Quarterly, 27,* 145–173.

Malatesta, C. Z., & Izard, C. E. (1984). The facial expression of emotion: Young, middle-aged, and older adult expressions. In C. Z. Malatesta & C. E. Izard (Eds.), *Emotion in adult development.* Beverly Hills, CA: Sage.

Matatesta, C. Z., & Kalnok, M. (1984). Emotional experience in younger and older adults. *Journal of Gerontology, 39,* 301–308.

McClannahan, L. E., & Risley, T. R. (1973). A store for nursing home residents. *Nursing Homes, 22,* 10–11.

McClannahan, L. E., & Risley, T. R. (1974). Design of living environments for nursing home residents: Recruiting attendance at activities. *Gerontologist, 14,* 236–240.

McClannahan, L. E., & Risley, T. R. (1975). Design of living environments for nursing home residents: Increasing participation in recreation activities. *Journal of Applied Behavior Analysis, 8,* 261–268.

Miller, P., & Ingham, J. G. (1976). Friends, confidents and symptoms. *Social Psychiatry, 11,* 51–58.

Mueller, D. J., & Atlas, L. (1972). Resocialization of depressed elderly residents: A behavioral management approach. *Journal of Gerontology, 27,* 390–392.

Mulligan, Sr. M. A., & Bennett, R. (1978). Assessment of mental health and social problems during multiple friendly visits: The development and evaluation of a friendly visiting program for the isolated elderly. *Journal of Aging and Human Development, 8,* 43–65.

Neugarten, B. L., Havighurst, R. J., & Tobin, S. S. (1968). Personality and patterns of aging. In B. L. Neugarten (Ed.), *Middle age and aging: A reader in social psychology* (pp. 173–177). Chicago: University of Chicago Press.

Peterson, R., Knapp, T. J., Rosen, J. C., & Pither, B. F. (1977). The effects of furniture arrangement on the behavior of geriatric patients. *Behavior Therapy, 8,* 464–467.

Quattrochi-Tubin, S., & Jason, L. A. (1980). Enhancing social interactions and activity among the elderly through stimulus control. *Journal of Applied Behavior Analysis, 13,* 159–169.

Rathbone-McCuan, E., & Levenson, J. (1975). Impact of socialization therapy in a geriatric day-care setting. *Gerontologist, 15,* 338–342.

Revenson, T. A. (1984). Social and demographic correlates of loneliness in late life. *American Journal of Community Psychology, 12,* 71–85.

Rook. K. S. (1984). The negative side of social interaction: Impact on psychological well-being. *Journal of Personality and Social Psychology, 46,* 1097–1108.

Schulz, R. (1985). Emotion and affect. In J. E. Birren & K. W. Schaie (Eds.), *Handbook of the psychology of aging* (2nd ed.,) pp. 531–543). New York: Van Nostrand Reinhold.

Simpson, S., Woods, R., & Britton, P. (1981). Depression and engagement in a residential home for the elderly. *Behavior Research and Therapy, 19,* 435–438.

Sommer, R., & Ross, H. (1958). Social interaction on a

geriatric ward. *International Journal of Social Psychiatry, 4*, 128–133.

Spitz, R. A. (1954). "Hospitalism": An inquiry into the genesis of psychiatric conditions in early childhood. In *Psychoanalytical study of the child* (pp. 53–74). New York: International Universities Press.

Tec, N., & Granwick (Bennett), R. (1959–1960). Social isolation and difficulties in social interaction in residents of a home for the aged. *Social Problems, 7*(1), 226–232.

Troll, L., & Smith, J. (1976). Attachment through the life span: Some questions about dyadic bonds among adults. *Human Development, 19*, 156–170.

Weinstock, C., & Bennett, R. (1971). From "waiting on the list" to becoming a "newcomer" and an "old-timer" in a home for the aged: Two studies of socialization and its impact upon cognitive functioning. *International Journal of Aging and Human Development, 2*, 46–58.

Wisocki, P. A., & Mosher, P. M. (1980). Peer-facilitated sign language training for a geriatric stroke victim with chronic brain damage. *Journal of Geriatric Psychiatry, 13*, 89–102.

Zingg, R. M. (1940). Feral man and extreme cases of social isolation. *American Journal of Psychology, 53*, 487–517.

Chapter 18

Sleep Disturbances

Richard R. Bootzin and Mindy Engle-Friedman

Sleep disturbances, such as difficulty in falling asleep, frequent or prolonged awakenings during the night, early-morning awakenings, or subjective experience of poor quality sleep, are common complaints among older adults. Next-day effects on mood, performance, fatigue, and motivation are also reported. For example, in a national survey conducted in 1979 (Mellinger, Balter, & Uhlenhuth, 1985), the prevalence of "serious" insomnia (defined as considerable difficulty in falling asleep or staying asleep within the last 12 months) increased from 14% for the 18–34 age group to 25% for the 65–79 age group. The number of individuals with "less severe" insomnia also rose with increasing age. All told, 45% of those persons aged 65 to 79 years had some difficulty with insomnia in the previous 12 months.

The disproportionate use of sleep medication in older adults corroborates the survey reports of sleep disturbances. Sixty-nine percent of those taking prescription medication for sleep were individuals aged 50 to 79 (Mellinger, Balter, & Uhlenhuth, 1985). The use of hypnotics is even greater among the institutionalized elderly. For example, a U.S. Public Health Service survey of prescribing patterns in skilled nursing facilities found that prescriptions for hypnotics had been written for 94.2% of the 98,505 patients studied (U.S. Public Health Service, 1976). In an intensive study of 180 nursing-home residents, it was found that 39% received hypnotics daily (Cohen, Eisdorfer, Prinz, Breen, Davis, & Gadsby, 1983). An examination of the patients' charts revealed that no notations had been made concerning either a diagnosis of sleep disturbance or the type of sleep problem. In addition, there was no relationship between the occurrence of sleep problems as rated by either the patients or the nurses and the use of hypnotics. Not only do older adults consume disproportionate amounts of sleep medication, but persons living in institutions may be using these medications without sleep disturbance.

Despite the heavy reliance on sleep medication, the use of hypnotics is both ineffective and potentially dangerous for the chronic insomniac. Most hypnotics lose their effectiveness within 2 weeks of continuous use (Kales, A., Allen, Scharf, & Kales, 1970). Only one hypnotic, flurazepam (Dalmane), has been found to retain its effectiveness throughout 1 month of continuous use (Kales, A., Kales, Bixler, & Scharf, 1975). Tolerance to hypnotics develops rapidly, so larger and larger doses are required to produce an effect and continuous use results in less deep sleep and more light, fragmented sleep. In addition, most hypnotics are rapid-eye-movement (REM) sleep-depriving and produce a marked REM rebound on subsequent nights. REM sleep is the stage of sleep typically associated with dreaming. REM-rebound nights are often spent in restless dreaming, nightmares, and fitful sleep. The insomniac may conclude that the hypnotics are needed to avoid the rebound effect; thus, hypnotics may lead to drug dependence (Kales, A., Scharf, & Kales, 1978).

Besides their disruptive effect on sleep, hypnotics have a number of deleterious side effects. As central nervous system depressants, they affect respiration (Carskadon, Brown, & Dement, 1980;

Dolly & Block, 1982). They also produce drug hangover during awakenings at night and can affect functioning the next day. Dysphoric mood, impaired motor and intellectual functioning, and daytime sleepiness all have been reported as daytime side effects of hypnotics.

These daytime effects are likely due to the fact that most hypnotics remain in the blood stream for days. For example, flurazepam has a plasma half-life of 50 to 100 hours. Thus, the daytime side effects of hangover, sleepiness, impaired motor and intellectual functioning, and dysphoric mood are evidence of continued pharmacological action of a central nervous system depressant. In addition, the long half-lives of these drugs mean that side effects may be observed for days, and even weeks, after the individual has stopped taking sleep medication.

Recently, hypnotics with short elimination half-lives (less than 5 hours) have been introduced, such as triazolam (Halcion). Although they have been found to be effective for transient and short-term sleep onset problems, they are also REM-depriving and produce more wakefulness in the last third of the night, that is, rebound insomnia the very same night the medication was taken. In addition, continuous use has resulted in memory deficits and daytime anxiety (Morgan & Oswald, 1982; Soldatos, Bixler, & Kales, 1985).

The elderly are particularly vulnerable to deleterious side effects because they are more likely to have disorders aggravated by hypnotics, such as respiratory, hepatic, renal, or cardiac disorders (Institute of Medicine, 1979). For example, flurazepam increases the frequency and duration of apneic events in healthy elderly subjects (aged 66–77 years). The respiratory response to hypnotics in individuals experiencing sleep apnea prior to drug use is even more severe (Dement, Miles, & Carskadon, 1982). In addition, the decreases associated with aging in protein-binding ability, circulation time, and kidney and liver metabolism lengthen the time drugs remain in the body, extending the period of potential toxicity (Albert, 1981). The elderly are also likely to have increased risk of toxic interactions from multiple drug use (Miles & Dement, 1980). This is exacerbated by the fact that older persons are more likely to substitute one drug for another, exchange drugs with friends, consult a number of physicians, and use drugs beyond their expiration date (Hemminki & Heikkila, 1975).

In a recent National Institutes of Health con-sensus conference, the recommendation was made that hypnotics should not be used for chronic sleep disturbances (National Institutes of Health, 1983). Consequently, it is critical to evaluate nonpharmacological interventions for persistent sleep disturbances. Possible alternatives to drugs will be discussed later in the chapter.

CAUSES OF SLEEP DISTURBANCES

Sleep disturbances may result from a number of factors, including developmental changes associated with aging, physical pathology, prescription and nonprescription medication, alcohol, caffeine, nicotine, stress and anxiety, psychopathology, inactivity, sleep environment factors, poor sleep habits, and reinforcement for sleepiness (see also Bootzin, Engle-Friedman, & Hazlewood, 1983). A thorough assessment of each is required in order to implement effective interventions.

The Effects Of Aging on Sleep

The most frequent sleep complaints of older adults are increased frequency and duration of nocturnal awakenings, frequent early-morning awakenings, increased latency to sleep onset, and excessive daytime sleepiness (Dement, Miles, & Carskadon, 1982; Gerard et al., 1978; Karacan et al., 1976; McGhie & Russell, 1962; Miles & Dement, 1980; Strauch & Wollschlaeger, 1973). Many of these complaints parallel developmental changes in psychophysiological sleep parameters that occur with advancing age.

The measure of sleep that has been generally accepted as most reliable and valid is polysomnography (Bootzin & Engle-Friedman, 1981). Polysomnography consists of the all-night recording of the electroencephalogram (EEG), the electrooculogram (EOG), and the electromyogram (EMG). Other physiological parameters such as temperature, respiration, galvanic skin response, and heart rate, can be measured for special purposes.

One of the most consistent findings associated with aging, documented through polysomnography, is an increase in the frequency of awakenings, particular during the latter half of the night (Agnew, Webb, & Williams, 1967; Feinberg, Koresko, & Heller, 1967; Hayashi & Endo, 1982; Kahn & Fisher, 1969; Kales et al., 1967; Webb, 1982; Williams, Karacan, & Hursch, 1974). Older adults also have more difficulty falling back to sleep than younger individuals. For example,

Webb and Campbell (1980) found that individuals 50 to 60 years old took longer to fall asleep when awakened after the first 80 minutes of the night than subjects 21 to 23 years old. This increased difficulty in falling back to sleep later in the night may account for the increased frequency of early-morning awakenings among the elderly.

In addition to difficulty falling back to sleep once awakened, many older adults also have difficulty falling asleep initially (Feinberg et al., 1967; Hayashi & Endo, 1982; Webb, 1982; Williams et al., 1974). For example, Webb (1982) found that sleep latency was more than twice as long in women aged 50 to 60 years that in women aged 20 to 30.

Sleep onset latency and awakenings are reflected in a commonly used measure—*sleep efficiency*. Sleep efficiency is the ratio of total time asleep divided by the total time in bed after the lights are turned off. As would be expected from the results on sleep onset latency and awakenings, sleep becomes substantially less efficient with age. For example, mean sleep efficiency was 80% in individuals 30 to 54 years of ages and only 67% in individuals 60 to 85 years of age (Coleman, Miles, Guilleminault, Zarcone, van den Hoed, & Dement, 1981).

As a consequence of increased time awake and difficulty falling back to sleep, older adults get less total sleep at night than younger adults (Hauri, 1977). Because daytime naps increase in frequency with age (Zepelin, 1973), the total sleep of the elderly is about equivalent to that of younger individuals if the sleep distribution throughout the entire 24-hour day is considered (Webb & Swinburne, 1971; Zepelin, 1973).

A marked reduction in deep (also known as slow-wave) sleep (Stages 3 and 4) is observed with aging (Coleman et al., 1981; Hayashi & Endo, 1982; Reynolds, Kupfer, Taska, Hoch, Sewitch, & Spiker, 1985). One fourth of the population over the age of 60 may have little or no Stage 4 sleep, although this deficit is much more likely in males than in females (Webb, 1974; Williams et al., 1974). The reduction in the amount of Stages 3 and 4 is due primarily to the reduction in amplitude of the EEG waves to the point where they do not meet the amplitude criterion to be scored as slow-wave sleep (Agnew, Webb, & Williams, 1967; Feinberg et al., 1967; Kales, 1975; Prinz, Obrist, & Wang, 1975; Miles & Dement, 1980; Webb & Dreblow, 1982). Thus, slow EEG-frequency sleep still occurs in the elderly, but there is

a marked loss in EEG amplitude. When the amplitude criterion is modified, older adults have the same amount of slow-wave sleep as younger adults (Feinberg, Fein, Floyd, & Aminoff, 1982; Smith, Karacan, & Yang, 1977; Webb, 1982).

REM sleep occurs every 90 to 100 minutes and is the stage of sleep typically associated with dreaming. The largest proportion of REM sleep occurs in the latter half of the night because REM periods tend to increase in duration throughout the night. There are small decreases in REM sleep with aging (Coleman et al., 1981; Williams et al., 1974). Unlike younger individuals, older adults have REM periods that remain uniform or decrease in duration during the night (Hayashi & Endo, 1982; Reynolds et al., 1985). Increased REM early in the night's sleep is often associated with depression. In addition, Feinberg, Koresko, and Heller (1967) found that shortened latency to REM sleep and lower amounts of REM were associated with intellectual decline.

Variability in a number of sleep parameters, including time in bed, total sleep time, sleep latency, number of awakenings, and time awake after sleep onset, increases with age (Williams et al., 1974). In addition, older adults are likely to have more deleterious effects from sleep loss on next-day performance and mood. Webb and Levy (1982) found that in comparison to 18- to 22-year-olds, 40- to 49-year-olds showed significantly poorer performance on auditory vigilance, addition, and mood scales following 2 nights of sleep deprivation.

The differences that occur as a consequence of aging are much the same as the differences between nonelderly insomniacs and normal sleepers. Insomniacs show decreased slow-wave sleep and total sleep, as well as increases in sleep onset latency and in the number and duration of awakenings (e.g., Engle-Friedman & Bootzin, 1981; Frankel, Coursey, Buchbinder, & Snyder, 1976; Monroe, 1967). It should be emphasized that while there are substantial changes in sleep associated with aging, these changes do not always result in a subjective complaint of sleep disturbance. Changes in slow-wave sleep and REM sleep, for example, may not influence judgments about the quality of sleep, while frequent awakenings will (Bonnet & Johnson, 1978). However, the changes in sleep parameters observed in the older adult may be due to a degradation of the central nervous system. Changes in the brain, including decreases in neurons, metabolic rate, and blood flow, may impact on both sleep and intellectual performance (Prinz, 1977). For example, there are striking sleep changes in persons with dementia, including frequent nocturnal awakenings and decreased REM sleep. These changes parallel but exceed in magnitude the changes of "normal aging" (Prinz et al., 1982).

Physical Disorders

The most common physical disorders that affect sleep are sleep-related respiratory disturbances, including *sleep apnea* (a cessation of airflow for 10 seconds or longer) and *hypopnea* (50% or greater reduction of airflow for 10 seconds or longer). Sleep-related respiratory disturbance is considered abnormal when it exceeds 5 apneas per hour. Sleep apnea is the most common diagnosis of older adult patients seen in sleep disorder clinics, accounting for 39% of older patients (Coleman et al., 1981).

Respiratory pauses and sleep apnea increase with age (Ancoli-Israel, Kripke, Mason, & Messing, 1981; Carskadon, et al., 1981; Krieger, Turlot, Mangin, & Kurtz, 1983). Respiratory disturbances have been found in both asymptomatic older persons (McGinty, Littner, Beahm, Ruiz-Primo, Young, & Saver, 1982) and symptomatic older adults. (Ancoli-Israel et al., 1981). When oxygen consumption was measured, nocturnal respiration was found to become increasingly more irregular with increasing age. A rare longitudinal study found that sleep apnea increases as the individual ages (Bliwise, Carskadon, Carey, & Dement, 1984). Of particular relevance to the sleep process are the arousals that must occur for a respiratory pause or apnea to be terminated. Thus, as one ages, there is likely to be an increase in arousals to terminate apneas. In addition to producing frequent arousals, sleep-related respiratory disturbances produce excessive daytime tiredness, headaches, dry mouth, and cognitive and perceptual-motor deficits (Guilleminault & Dement, 1978; Yesavage, Bliwise, Guilleminault, Corskadon, & Dement, 1985). They have also been implicated in pulmonary and arterial blood pressure increases, cardiac arrhythmias, increased decompensation of impaired cardiovascular systems, and possibly death (Dement et al., 1982).

Two muscular disorders—*nocturnal myoclonus* and *restless legs*—can also impair sleep. In nocturnal myoclonus, leg twitches occur repeatedly throughout the night (Lugaresi, Coccagna, Berti-Ceroni, & Ambrosetto, 1968), whereas in restless legs, the person feels a deep itching in the legs and the need to move them in order to stop the sensation. Both disorders increase with age and account for between 18% and 25% of diagnoses of older adults in sleep disorder clinics (Ancoli-Israel et al., 1981; Coleman et al., 1981; Roehrs, Zorick, Sicklesteel, Wittig, & Roth, 1983).

A number of other physical disorders experienced by the older adult can interfere with sleep. Physical illness can disrupt sleep because of discomfort, such as back pain, gastric pain from ulcer, or cardiac pain. The experience of pain, especially that associated with arthritis, constitutes one of the most frequent sleep disruptions among older adults (Prinz & Raskind, 1978). Diabetes may also interfere with sleep through underregulation of blood sugar, resulting in glycosuria and nocturia, or through overregulation, leading to hypoglycemia (Prinz & Raskind, 1978).

Medication

Both prescription and nonprescription drugs can cause sleep disturbances. Asthma medication (e.g., theophylline) can contain adrenaline, which interferes with sleep if taken at night. Tricyclic antidepressants suppress REM sleep and can exacerbate nocturnal myoclonus. Some antiseizure, antiparkinsonian, and antihypertensive medications can increase nighttime wakefulness (Karacan & Williams, 1983). Diuretics, often used in conjunction with antihypertensive medication, can increase nighttime urination, causing the individual to awaken more frequently.

As discussed earlier, the elderly are major consumers of sleep medication. Nevertheless, the persistent use of hypnotics is ineffective and can produce drug-dependent insomnia, increased respiratory problems, dysphoric mood, impaired motor and intellectual functioning, and daytime sleepiness. The same side effects, multiple drug interactions, and disrupted sleep that are associated with hypnotics also apply to tranquilizers, such as diazepam (Valium). Neither hypnotics nor tranquilizers are an appropriate treatment for chronic sleep disturbance.

The active ingredient in most over-the-counter sleep medication is an antihistamine. Because drowsiness is a side-effect of antihistamines, over-the-counter medications have been promoted as facilitating the onset of sleep by making the person drowsy. However, polysomnographic investigations of these medications have not found them to be more effective than placebos (e.g., Kales, Tan, Swearingen, & Kales, 1971). In addition to ineffectiveness, a number of hazards are associated with them. As depressants, they potentiate the effects of alcohol, hypnotics, and tranquilizers. They can also produce side effects—confusion, disorientation, and memory disturbance (Institute of Medicine, 1979).

There is now considerable consensus that sleep medication is not the appropriate treatment for the chronic insomniac of any age, particularly the elderly insomniac (National Institutes of Health, 1983). If hypnotics are to be replaced as the primary means of treating elderly insomniacs, viable short-term alternatives must be evaluated.

Alcohol

The problems associated with hypnotics and tranquilizers are true for alcohol as well. Like other depressants, alcohol is REM-sleep-depriving. Habitual heavy drinking results in fragmented sleep, with frequent awakenings. Withdrawal produces REM rebound, with fitful sleep and nightmares. Although there is no evidence that an occasional glass of wine or its equivalent should be avoided, habitual heavy drinking before sleep will produce sleep disturbance rather than improved sleep.

An important additional danger is that alcohol potentiates the effects of hypnotics and other depressants. Thus, the combination of alcohol and sleeping pills may intensify and prolong deleterious side effects to produce lethal levels of overdose (Institute of Medicine, 1979). It is likely, too, that alcohol will be less well tolerated by the older than the younger adult since toxic substances remain in the body for extended periods of time in the older adult.

Caffeine and Nicotine

Caffeine and nicotine are central nervous system stimulants that produce lighter and more fragmented sleep (Bonnet, Webb, & Barnard, 1979; Soldatos, Kales, Scharf, Bixler, & Kales, 1980). Caffeine is contained in many foods and beverages, including coffee, tea, soft drinks, and chocolate. Complaints of insomnia and/or anxiety may be due to excessive ingestion of caffeine and/or nicotine. Since caffeine has a plasma half-life of approximately 6 hours, the older adult might con-

tinue to experience its effects long after it was ingested. Reducing or eliminating the intake of caffeine, particularly in the afternoon and evening, and quitting smoking can lead to substantial improvement in sleep.

Stress

Sleep disturbances not caused by physical disorders are usually seen as the symptom of some psychological problem. There is support for this intuition, because people who ordinarily have no trouble sleeping often develop insomnia during periods of stress (Healey, Kales, Monroe, Bixler, Chamberlin, & Soldatos, 1981). As a person ages, many important life events occur that may be difficult to adjust to and thus may affect sleep. For example, a spouse may die, the person may retire, living arrangements may change, or the individual may become aware of changes in his or her own physical and intellectual functioning.

Psychopathology

There is a large literature on the relationship between psychopathology and sleep disturbance, particularly with regard to anxiety and depression. On self-report personality inventories, insomniacs have been found to be more introverted, anxious, neurotic, and depressed than normal sleepers (Costello & Smith, 1963; Coursey, Buchsbaum, & Frankel, 1975; Haynes, Follingstad, & McGowan, 1974; Kales, Caldwell, Preston, Healey, & Kales, 1976; Nicassio & Bootzin, 1974). Older insomniacs have been found to be less depressed and anxious than their younger insomniac counterparts (Roehrs et al., 1983).

A number of studies have focused specifically on the sleep of patients diagnosed as depressed (Kupfer & Foster, 1978). Nearly all studies of depressed patients have found that slow-wave sleep is reduced (Mendelson, Gilling, & Wyatt, 1977), and many have suggested that shortened REM latency is symptomatic of major depression (e.g., Hartmann, 1968; Snyder, 1966). Kales and Kales (1970) recommended that antidepressant medication should be prescribed for those patients whose insomnia is diagnosed as *resulting from* depression. It is difficult, if not impossible, however, to determine that depression (or anxiety) is directly causing insomnia, because all that is observed is covariation (Bootzin & Nicassio, 1978). In cases in which psychological problems accompany sleep disturbance, separate therapeutic attention should be given to each. The therapist should not assume that improvement in one will automatically produce improvement in the other.

Inactivity

A major problem of the elderly is an inactive life-style. This is particularly true for the institutionalized elderly, but it is also applicable to many healthy, adaptive, noninstitutionalized elderly individuals. In addition to being inactive, the elderly frequently nap during the day. Sleep onset latency is inversely related to the length of time since the individual last slept (Webb, 1975). In addition, the night's sleep following an afternoon or evening nap continues as if the nap were part of the night's sleep. Because afternoon and evening naps contain more deep sleep and less REM sleep, the entire night's sleep is similar to the latter half of a typical night's sleep, with more light and REM sleep and more frequent awakening (Webb, 1975). A morning nap, on the other hand, is a continuation of the previous night's sleep and has minimal effect on the subsequent night's sleep architecture.

Hauri (1975) has noted that insomniacs who fall into the habit of sleep late in the morning or taking naps whenever fatigue overwhelms them are likely to develop circadian rhythm disturbances. If circadian cycles become desynchronized, an optimal time for sleeping may never exist. Webb (1975) pointed out that with aging there is a breakdown in the biphasic pattern of sleep and wakefulness. Older adults appear to return to the polyphasic alternation of sleep and wakefulness of infancy. Disruptions of circadian wake-sleep schedules have been found to be particularly common in institutionalized elderly (Wessler, Rubin, & Sollberger, 1976).

Sleep Environment

There are many sleep environment factors, such as the temperature of the room, firmness of the mattress, noise, and whether the bed or bedroom is shared, that may influence the quality of an individual's sleep. There is no ideal room temperature or degree of mattress firmness. People can learn to sleep comfortably in a wide range of temperatures and on many different surfaces. However, individuals may have developed strong preferences to the point where sleep is disrupted if the sleep environment does not correspond to those preferences. This problem is frequently observed when people move to a new setting. The unfamiliarity of the setting and the lack of familiar personal belongings may cause a prolonged period of disrupted sleep.

The effect of noise on sleep is to decrease the amount of deep sleep and increase the frequency of awakenings. Even people who habitually sleep in noisy environments do not fully adapt to the noise (Sanchez & Bootzin, 1985). Because the elderly are more easily awakened (Zepelin, McDonald, & Zammit, 1984) and have more difficulty falling back to sleep once awakened (Webb & Campbell, 1980), noisy environments are likely to be particularly troublesome.

Sleep Habits

Insomniacs may engage in activities at bedtime that are incompatible with falling asleep (Bootzin, 1972, 1976, 1977; Bootzin & Nicassio, 1978). Insomniacs may, for example, use their bedrooms for reading, talking on the telephone, watching television, snacking, listening to music, and probably, most disturbing of all, worrying. The result is that the bed is no longer just a cue for sleeping; instead it becomes a cue for physiological arousal.

Cognitive intrusions may be particularly disruptive. Worries and concerns are often accompanied by emotional upset, yet they may appear in the absence of excessive physiological arousal (Starker & Hasenfeld, 1976). The content of the insomniac's concerns may shift from the general pressures of current and future problems to persevering worries regarding the inability to fall asleep or to get enough sleep during the night (Hauri, 1975).

The bedroom, then, can become a cue for the anxiety and frustration associated with trying to fall asleep. Insomniacs often sleep well any place other than in their own beds. For example, they often sleep better in a sleep laboratory than they do at home (de la Pena, 1978). In contrast, people who have no difficulty falling asleep in their own beds often have difficulty doing so in strange surroundings.

Poor sleeping habits may help maintain insomnia even if the sleeping difficulties were initially caused by physical illness or situational stress. For the chronic insomniac, sleeping difficulties usually continue long after the initial causes have disappeared.

Reinforcement

Finally, sleep complaints may be reinforced by their consequences, such as the attention of sympathetic listeners. Some insomniacs may find that others are more tolerant of their shortcomings when they appear fatigued, groggy, and irritable as a result of lack of sleep. The inadvertent reinforcement of "sick" behavior has been found to play a prominent role in other disorders as well (e.g., Fordyce, 1976).

TREATMENT OF SLEEP DISTURBANCES

During the past 15 years, a number of short-term nonpharmacological interventions for insomnia have been evaluated (for reviews, see Bootzin & Nicassio, 1978; Borkovec, 1982; Youkilis & Bootzin, 1981). Only recently, however, has there been any systematic attempt to evaluate the effectiveness of such treatments with older adults. Because of the marked changes in sleep associated with aging, many professionals in the past assumed that psychological interventions would be ineffective. This is often the attitude regarding many different problems of the elderly. Consequently, various treatable problems often go untreated (Rowe, 1985; Zarit & Zarit; 1983).

Although systematic evaluation of nonpharmacological treatments for sleep disturbance in the elderly has only recently begun, there has been no lack of general advice. Recommendations have included reassurance by the physician (Prinz & Raskind, 1978), changes in the sleep environment, for example by decreasing the noise and increasing the privacy of the bedroom (Miles & Dement, 1980), establishment of prebed rituals (Butler & Lewis, 1973), use of nonsleeping time at night for unfinished business (Raskind, 1977), psychotherapy (Berlin, 1985), and nonintervention in the sleep of the older adult (Pfeiffer, 1977).

We recently completed the first controlled evaluation of alternate psychological interventions for the treatment of insomnia in the elderly (Bootzin et al., 1983; Engle-Friedman, 1985). We evaluated three treatments. Two of them— progressive relaxation training (Bernstein & Borkovec, 1973) and stimulus control instructions (Bootzin, 1972, 1976, 1977)—have been thoroughly evaluated with younger adults and therefore were quite promising for use with the elderly. The third treatment, information and support, is usually a component of all treatment. Thus, we evaluated whether specific relaxation or stimulus control instructions added significantly to what can be accomplished by providing support and sleep hygiene information.

Information and Support

An important component of effective therapy for a variety of problems is the extent to which the individual stops perceiving himself or herself as a victim of the problem and begins to believe that he or she can cope with it (Bootzin, 1985). The insomniac's appraisal of the problem is often an important component in its persistence. Perseverant worry about why one cannot sleep, as well as preoccupation with one's inability to sleep and the consequences of sleeplessness, is likely to intensify any existing problem (Youkilis & Bootzin, 1981). The goal of the information and support treatment in our study (Bootzin et al., 1983) was to reverse the cycle by helping the insomniac change his or her appraisal of the problem.

Support and sleep hygiene information was provided in all treatments. Thus, all subjects were informed about sleep stages and the developmental changes that occur with age, as well as the effects on sleep of physical illness, prescription and nonprescription medication, alcohol, caffeine, nicotine, stress, inactivity, naps, sleep environment factors, and reinforcement for sleeplessness. In other words, the type of information that is contained in the first section of this chapter was discussed in the context of each individual's problem.

Two additional points were stressed. First, there are large individual differences in sleep needs. Some people have lived long, productive, satisfying lives getting less than 2 hours of sleep a night for as long as they can remember (Meddis, 1977). In general, the body will get the amount of sleep that it needs. One possibility is that patients may not need as much sleep as they believed necessary.

Second, it is not a calamity to go without sleep. Although some small performance deficits have been demonstrated after sleep deprivation, other studies have failed to find such effects. There is very little performance deficit following prolonged periods of reduced sleep (Freidmann, Globus, Huntley, Mullaney, Naitoh, & Johnson, 1977; Webb & Agnew, 1974) or even following total sleep deprivation for as long as 8 days (Pasnau, Naitoh, Stier, & Kollar, 1968). Even studies of sleep deprivation with the elderly indicate that the effects on performance are small (e.g., Bonnet, 1984).

The major effects of sleep deprivation are fatigue and irritability. Fatigue, however, follows a daily circadian rhythm even if the individual goes without sleep entirely (Kleitman, 1963). A person will be fatigued and have a low body temperature at times when he or she would ordinarily be asleep. On the other hand, the individual will be alert even after sleep deprivation at times when he or she is ordinarily awake. Thus, the day's performance is not as dependent on the previous night's sleep as many patients expect.

The goal of the information and support treatment in our study was to help the insomniac put the problem in a coping context. The therapist explored with the patient the nature and severity of the problem, possible causes, and alternative solutions.

Stimulus Control Instructions

The goals of stimulus control instructions are to help the insomniac acquire a consistent sleep rhythm, to strengthen the bed as a cue for sleep, and to weaken it as a cue for activities that might interfere with sleep. As discussed in the earlier section on causes, poor sleep habits can contribute to sleep disturbance. One part of this problem is that the person may never allow himself or herself to acquire a consistent sleep rhythm. This may occur as a result of inconsistent bedtime and/or time of arising in the morning.

As mentioned earlier, another part of the problem is that insomniacs may engage in activities in the bedroom at bedtime that are incompatible with falling asleep, such as reading, watching television, or worrying. The result is that the bed and bedroom become cues for arousal rather than cues for sleep.

From the preceding anaylsis, a stimulus control treatment for insomnia has been developed (Bootzin, 1972, 1976, 1977) to strengthen the cues for falling asleep and separate them from the cues for other activities. The following rules constitute the stimulus control instructions.

1. Lie down intending to go to sleep only when you are sleepy.
2. Do not use your bed for anything except sleep; that is, do not read, watch TV, eat, or worry in bed. Sexual activity is the only exception to this rule. On such occasions, the instructions are to be followed afterward when you intend to go to sleep.
3. If you find yourself unable to fall asleep, get up and go into another room. Stay up as long as you wish and then return to the bedroom to sleep. Although we do not want you to watch the clock, we want you to get out of bed if you do not fall asleep immediately. Remember, the goal is to associate your bed with falling asleep *quickly*! If you are in bed more than about 10 minutes without falling asleep and have not gotten up, you are not following this instruction.
4. If you still cannot fall asleep, repeat Step 3. Do this as often as is necessary throughout the night.
5. Set your alarm and get up at the same time every morning irrespective of how much sleep you got during the night. This will help your body acquire a consistent sleep rhythm.
6. Do not nap during the day.

Stimulus control instructions have been shown to be highly effective in case studies and controlled evaluations (Bootzin, 1972, 1975; Haynes, Price, & Simons, 1975; Lacks, Bertelson, Gans, & Kunkel, 1983; Turner & Ascher, 1979, 1982). Although the focus of most evaluations has been on sleep onset latency, improvement in total sleep (Bootzin, 1975) and number and duration and arousals (Lacks, Bertelson, Sugerman, & Kunkel, 1983; Toler, 1978) has also been reported.

Six studies have compared stimulus control instructions and progressive relaxation training. Stimulus control instructions were found to be superior in four studies (Bootzin, 1975; Lacks et al., 1983; Lawrence & Tokarz, 1976; Slama, 1975), and there were no significant differences between the two treatments in two other studies (Turner & Ascher, 1979, 1982). At present, stimulus control instruction appears to be the most effective psychological intervention for insomnia (Borkovec, 1982) and holds considerable promise as a treatment for the elderly. In the only published study of stimulus control instructions with elderly insomniacs, they were found to be effective in a between-subject multiple baseline design with 16 sleep-onset insomniacs over the age of 60 (Puder, Lacks, Bertelson, & Storandt, 1983).

In our evaluation (Bootzin et al., 1983), patients received support and sleep hygiene information in addition to stimulus-control instructions. Therapist and patient met weekly to discuss difficulties in carrying out the instructions. A common problem was the disturbance of the spouse's sleep when the insomniac got out of bed. Sometimes discussion of the problem directly with the spouse was useful in ensuring full cooperation. During the winter, some elderly participants were reluctant to leave the warmth of their beds. Suggestions for keeping warm robes near the bed and keeping an additional room warm through the night, along with encouragement to try to follow the instructions, were usually effective in promoting compliance.

Progressive Relaxation Training

The most frequently recommended nonpharmacological treatment for insomnia is some type of relaxation training (Bootzin & Nicassio, 1978). This includes a variety of training procedures, such as progressive relaxation, autogenic training, transcendental meditation, yoga, hypnosis, and EMG biofeedback. As treatments for insomnia, all of these procedures are based on the same premise: If people can learn to be relaxed at bedtime, they will fall asleep faster. The different types of relaxation procedures have all achieved about the same degree of effectiveness.

Progressive relaxation, developed by Edmund Jacobson (1938, 1964), has been the most thoroughly evaluated relaxation method for treating insomnia. A number of studies provide evidence for its superior effectiveness when compared to placebo control and no-treatment conditions (Borkovec, 1982). As with stimulus control instructions, most evaluations have focused on sleep onset insomnia. However, case studies have indicated that relaxation training can be effective with sleep maintenance problems (Coates & Thoresen, 1979), and other studies have reported improvement in total sleep or number of awakenings (e.g., Borkovec & Fowles, 1973; Lick & Heffler, 1977).

One common problem in using relaxation with the elderly is that the patient may experience arthritic pain as a result of tensing and releasing particular muscle groups (Bootzin et al., 1983). In such instances, the patients are instructed not to tense that muscle group but to just release the tension from whatever level of tension is already present. In our evaluation, we discouraged the use of tape-recorded relaxation instructions. The goal of relaxation training is to teach the patient a new coping skill that can be available whenever it is needed. We did not want the patient's relaxation

response to be dependent upon the availability of a tape recorder.

Because many insomniacs are aroused and anxious, relaxation training may provide a double benefit—first, as a means of helping to induce sleep, and second, as a general coping skill to be used to deal more effectively with the stresses of the day.

Evaluation

Fifty-three insomniacs aged 47 to 76 years were recruited for our study (Bootzin et al., 1983) through contact with local seniors clubs, media advertisements, and physician referrals. Patients were selected for participation if they met at least one of the following three criteria: (a) sleep latency of more than 45 minutes at least 3 nights per week, (b) more than 3 awakenings at least 3 nights per week, or (c) a period of more than 30 minutes awake after sleep onset at least 3 nights per week. Twenty-two patients met the criterion for sleep onset insomnia (6 men and 16 women; mean age, 61.4 years), and 31 met the criterion for sleep maintenance insomnia (12 men and 19 women; mean age, 57.7 years).

The insomniacs were randomly assigned to short-term individual nonpharmacological treatment of (a) support and sleep hygiene information alone; (b) support and information plus progressive relaxation training; (c) support and information plus stimulus control instructions; and (d) no treatment. Participants received 2 weeks of baseline, 4 weeks of weekly individual treatment sessions, and 2 weeks follow-up.

During the initial interview, participants completed questionnaires regarding general sleep habits, personality characteristics, psychopathology, and medical history. At the final interview, they completed the questionnaires for the second time, rating their improvement and the extent to which sleep continued to be a problem for them. All participants completed a sleep diary each morning upon awakening and provided a rating of daytime functioning each evening before sleep. In addition to sleep diary and questionnaire assessments, 29 of the 53 participants were assessed polysomnographically in their homes four times over the course of the study. Participants were monitored twice during baseline, once at the end of treatment, and once during follow-up. All participants were required to refrain from taking sleep medication for 2 weeks prior to and during the course of the study itself.

The results were that all three treatments resulted in significant improvement ($p < .05$). Participants reported fewer awakenings, almost 50% less nap taking, increased feelings of being refreshed in the morning, increased self-efficacy with respect to sleep, decreased concern about being able to fall asleep, and decreased depression on the Beck Depression Inventory (Engle-Friedman, 1985).

It is particularly noteworthy that awakenings were reduced by the treatment, because increased awakenings are among the sleep changes most associated with aging (Hayashi & Endo, 1982; Webb & Campbell, 1980). The polysomnographic evaluation supported the results on awakenings. While only marginally significant ($p < .10$), awakenings lasting more than 1 minute decreased from a mean of 9.8 awakenings during baseline to a mean of 7.2 after therapy.

The finding of reduced nap taking also runs counter to the general findings associated with advancing age (Miles & Dement, 1980). In addition, nap taking has been implicated in increased sleep onset latency, increased awakenings (Webb, 1975), and disruption of circadian rhythms (Hauri, 1975). Although the elderly may be more vulnerable to increased nap taking and polyphasic sleep/wake patterns, the observed decrease in nap taking indicates that these patterns may be reversible.

Particularly encouraging were the results of increased self-efficacy and decreased concern regarding sleep. The goal of all of our therapies was to help the insomniacs see themselves as people who could cope wth their sleep disturbance rather than be victims of it. People who feel they are in control of their problems should find less need to seek additional therapy.

The finding of decreased depression following treatment of sleep disturbance is also intriguing. 15 to 20% of older adults have been found to experience depression of sufficient severity to seek psychological or psychiatric intervention (Shamoian, 1983). The finding of reduced depression suggests that treatment for sleep not only improves the sleep process but may generalize to improved mood. In either case, improved mood may be a benefit of effective treatment.

As reported above, all treatments were effective, resulting in significant improvements. However, some differential effects did emerge. The amount of improvement from baseline to the end of treatment on reported sleep latency was 35% for stimulus control instructions, 23% for support and information and 8% for progressive relaxation training ($p < .10$). An analysis of covariance of the posttherapy polysomnographic assessment, with the baseline as a covariate, indicated that the addition of either stimulus control or relaxation training to support and information resulted in improved sleep efficiency ($p = .10$). The adjusted sleep efficiency means were 77.3% for stimulus control instructions, 78.6% for progressive relaxation training and 60.3% for support and information. These results are due to a reduction of almost 50% of time spent in stage wake for both stimulus control instructions and progressive relaxation training; there was no reduction for support and information. These sleep efficiency results are impressive since sleep efficiency was found to average 67% in 60 to 85-year-old non-insomniacs (Coleman et al., 1981).

To evaluate whether the results were maintained, a 2-year follow-up via telephone interviews and sleep diaries was conducted (Tsao, Bootzin, Hazlewood, & Engle-Friedman, 1985). Forty-two of the original 53 subjects participated in the telephone interview, and 21 of these completed sleep diaries for 1 week. Most important, subjects maintained or improved upon the results obtained in treatment on measures of total sleep and sleep onset latency. Similar to the analyses of immediate effects, there were few differential treatment effects in the 2-year follow-up. However, insomniacs who received stimulus control instructions were found to have continued using components of the treatment more than those receiving other treatments ($p < .01$). In addition, they reported the most improvement on sleep onset latency in sleep diaries ($p < .01$), and they reported that their sleep was least affected negatively by changing life events ($p < .01$). Thus, although all treatments were effective immediately after treatment and 2 years later, stimulus control instructions were more effective than other treatments on those few measures on which differential effects emerged.

CONCLUSION

The major outcome of the preceding evaluation is that chronic insomnia in the elderly can be effectively treated with short-term nonpharmacological therapy. The magnitude of improvement in older individuals, particularly on the polysomnographic measures, was not as large as in younger insom- niacs. Nevertheless, improvement was substantial and occurred on some measures (such as awaken- ings) that are commonly associated with aging and would be expected to be difficult to treat.

The evaluations presented here were of single treatment components. Although it is essential to evaluate the efficacy of individual treatment elements, treatment components can be combined. Thus, a multicomponent treatment combining sleep hygiene information, relaxation training, and stimulus control instructions may be appropriate for some patients. In addition, because many insomniacs lack the skills to deal effectively with the stresses of their environments, training in cop- ing skills, such as cognitive restructuring, social- skills training, and stress management, may be important supplements to direct treatment of the sleep disorder.

We have a good understanding of the treatment of sleep disturbances in younger populations and the evaluations presented in this chapter indicate that the same procedures hold considerable pro- mise for the elderly.

REFERENCES

Agnew, H., Webb, W., & Williams, R. L. (1967). Sleep patterns in late middle-aged males: An EEG study. *Electroencephalography and Clinical Neurophysiology, 23,* 168–171.

Albert, M. S. (1981). Geriatric neuropsychology. *Journal of Consulting and Clinical Psychology, 49,* 835–850.

Ancoli-Israel, S., Kripke, D. F., Mason, W., & Messing, S. (1981). Sleep apnea and nocturnal myoclonus in a senior population. *Sleep, 4,* 349–358.

Berlin, R. M. (1985). Psychotherapeutic treatment of chronic insomnia. *American Journal of Psychotherapy, 39,* 68–74.

Bernstein, D. S., & Borkovec, T. D. (1973). *Progressive relaxation training.* Champaign, IL: Research Press.

Bliwise, D., Carskadon, M., Carey, E., & Dement, W. (1984). Longitudinal development of sleep-related respiratory disturbance in adult humans. *Journal of Gerontology, 39,* 290–293.

Bonnet, M. H. (1984). The restoration of performance following sleep deprivation in geriatric normal and insomniac subjects. *Sleep Research, 13,* 188.

Bonnet, M. H., & Johnson, L. C. (1978). Relationship of arousal threshold to sleep stage distribution and sub- jective estimates of depth and quality of sleep. *Sleep, 1,* 161–168.

Bonnet, M. H., Webb, W. B., & Barnard, G. (1979). Effect of flurazepam, pentobarbital and caffeine on arousal threshold. *Sleep, 1,* 271–279.

Bootzin, R. R. (1972, September). *Stimulus control treat- ment of insomnia.* Paper presented at the meeting of the American Psychological Association, Honolulu.

Bootzin, R. R., (1975). A comparison of stimulus control instructions and progressive relaxation training in the treatment of sleep onset insomnia. Unpublished monograph. Evanston, IL: Northwestern University.

Bootzin, R. R., (1976). *Self-help techniques for controlling insomnia.* New York: BMA (audio cassette recording).

Bootzin, R. R. (1977). Effects of self-control procedures for insomnia. In R. B. Stuart (Ed.), *Behavioral self- management: Strategies, techniques, and outcomes.* New York: Brunner/Mazel.

Bootzin, R. R. (1985). The role of expectancy in behavior change. In L. White, G. Schwartz, & B. Tursky (Eds.), *Placebo: Clinical phenomena and new insights.* New York: Guildford.

Bootzin, R. R., & Engle-Friedman, M. (1981). The assessment of insomnia. *Behavioral Assessment, 3,* 107–126.

Bootzin, R. R., Engle-Friedman, M., & Hazelwood, L. (1983). Insomnia. In P. M. Lewinsohn & L. Teri (Eds.), *Clinical geropsychology: New directions in assess- ment and treatment.* Elmsford, NY: Pergamon.

Bootzin, R. R., & Nicassio, P. M. (1978). Behavioral treatment for insomnia. In M. Hersen, R. M. Eisler, & P. M. Miller (Eds.) *Progress in behavior modification* (Vol. 6). New York: Academic.

Borkovec, T. D. (1982). Insomnia. *Journal of Consulting and Clinical Psychology, 50,* 880–895.

Borkovec, T. D., & Fowles, D. (1973). Controlled inves- tigation of the effects of progressive relaxation and hypnotic relaxation on insomnia. *Journal of Abnormal Psychology, 82,* 153–158.

Butler, R., & Lewis, M. (1973). Treatment of specific conditions. In R. Butler (Ed.), *Aging and mental health: Positive psychosocial approaches.* St. Louis, MO: Mosby.

Carskadon, M., Brown, E., & Dement, W. (1980). Res- piration during sleep in the elderly. *Sleep Research, 9,* 99.

Coates, T. J., & Thoresen, C. E. (1979). Treating arou- sals during sleep using behavioral self management. *Journal of Consulting and Clinical Psychology, 47,* 603–605.

Cohen, D., Eisdorfer, C., Prinz, P., Breen, A., Davis, M., & Gadsby, A. (1983). Sleep disturbances in the insti- tutionalized aged. *Journal of the American Geriatrics Society, 31,* 79–82.

Coleman, R. M., Miles, L. E., Guilleminault, C. C., Zar- cone, V. P., van den Hoed, J., & Dement, W. C. (1981). Sleep wake disorders in the elderly: A poly- somnographic analysis. *Journal of the American Geri- atrics Society, 29,* 289–296.

Costello, C. G., & Smith, C. M. (1963). The relation- ships between personality, sleep and the effect of sedatives. *British Journal of Psychiatry, 109,* 568–571.

Coursey, R. D., Buchsbaum, M., & Frankel, B. C. (1975). Personality measures and evoked responses in chronic insomniacs. *Journal of Abnormal Psychology, 84,* 239–249.

de la Pena, A. (1978). Toward a psychophysiologic con- ception of insomnia. In R. L. Williams & I. Karacan (Eds.), *Sleep disorders: Diagnosis and treatment.* New York: Wiley.

Dement, W. C., Miles, L. E., & Carskadon, M. A. (1982). "White paper" on sleep and aging. *Journal of the American Geriatrics Society, 30,* 25–50.

Dolly, F. R., & Block, A. J. (1982). Effect of flurazepam on sleep disoriented breathing and nocturnal oxygen desaturation in asymptomatic subjects. *American Journal of Medicine, 73*, 239–243.

Engle-Friedman, M. (1985). *An evaluation of behavioral treatments for insomnia in the older adult*. Unpublished doctoral dissertation, Northwestern University, Evanston, IL.

Engle-Friedman, M., & Bootzin, R. R. (1981). The effect of mood on sleep on insomniac and normal sleepers. *Sleep Research, 10*, 193.

Feinberg, I., Fein, E., Floyd, T. C., & Aminoff, M. J. (1982). Delta (0.5–3Hz) EEG waveforms during sleep in young and elderly normal subjects. In E. Weitzman (Ed.), *Advances in sleep research*. New York: Plenum.

Feinberg, I., Koresko, R., & Heller, N. (1967). EEG sleep patterns as a function of normal and pathological aging in man. *Journal of Psychiatric Research, 5*, 107–144.

Fordyce, W. F. (1976). *Behavioral methods for chronic pain and illness*. St. Louis, MO: Mosby.

Frankel, B. L., Coursey, R. D., Buchbinder, R., & Snyder, F. (1976). Recorded and reported sleep in chronic primary insomnia. *Archives of General Psychiatry, 33*, 615–623.

Friedmann, J., Globus, G., Huntley, A., Mullaney, D., Naitoh, P., & Johnson, L. (1977). Performance and mood during and after gradual sleep reduction. *Psychophysiology, 14*, 245–250.

Gerard, P., Collins, K., Dore, C. et al. (1978). Subjective characteristics of sleep in the elderly. *Age and Ageing* (Suppl.), *7*, 55.

Guilleminault, C., & Dement, W. C. (1978). Sleep apnea syndromes and related sleep disorders, In R. L. Williams & I. Karacan (Eds.), *Sleep disorders: Diagnosis and treatment*. New York: Wiley.

Hartmann, E. (1968). Longitudinal studies of sleep and dream patterns in manic-depressive patients. *Archives of General Psychiatry, 19*, 312–329.

Hauri, P. (1975, September). *Psychology of sleep disorder: Their diagnosis and treatment*. Paper presented at the meeting of the 83rd Annual Convention of the American Psychological Association, Chicago.

Hauri, P. (1982). *The sleep disorders*. Kalamazoo, MI: Upjohn.

Hayashi, Y., & Endo, S. (1982). All-night sleep polygraphic recordings of healthy aged persons: REM and slow-wave sleep. *Sleep, 5*, 277–283.

Haynes, S. N., Follingstad, D. K., & McGowan, W. T. (1974). Insomnia: Sleep patterns and anxiety level. *Journal of Psychosomatic Research 18*, 69–74.

Haynes, S. N., Price, M. G., & Simons, J. B. (1975). Stimulus control treatment of insomnia. *Journal of Behavior Therapy and Experimental Psychiatry, 6*, 279–282.

Healey, E. S., Kales, A., Monroe, L. J., Bixler, E. O., Chamberlin, K., & Soldatos, C. R. (1981). Onset of insomnia: Role of life-stress events. *Psychosomatic Medicine, 43*, 439–451.

Hemminki, E., & Heikkila, J. (1975). Elderly people's compliance with prescriptions and quality of medication. *Scandinavian Journal of Social Medicine, 3*, 87–92.

Institute of Medicine. (1979). *Sleeping pills, insomnia, and medical practice*. Washington, DC: National Academy of Sciences.

Jacobson, E. (1938). *Progressive relaxation*. Chicago: University of Chicago Press.

Jacobson, E. (1964). *Anxiety and tension control*. Philadelphia: Lippincott.

Kahn, E., & Fisher, C. (1969). The sleep characteristics of the normal aged male. *Journal of Nervous and Mental Disease, 148*, 474–494.

Kales, A., Allen, W. C., Scharf, M. B., & Kales, J. D. (1970). Hypnotic drugs and effectiveness: All-night EEG studies of insomniac subjects. *Archives of General Psychiatry, 23*, 226–232.

Kales, A., Caldwell, A. B., Preston, T. A., Healey, S., & Kales, J. D. (1976). Personality patterns in insomnia. *Archives of General Psychiatry, 33*, 1128–1134.

Kales, A., & Kales, J. D. (1970). Evaluation, diagnosis and treatment of clinical conditions related to sleep. *Journal of the American Medical Association, 213*, 2229–2334.

Kales, A., Kales, J. D., Bixler, E. O., & Scharf, M. B. (1975). Methodology of sleep laboratory drug evaluations: Further considerations. In F. Kagan, T. Harwood, R. Rickels, A. D. Rudzik, & A. Soyers (Eds.), *Hypnotics: Methods of development and evaluation*. New York: Spectrum.

Kales, A., Scharf, M. B., & Kales, J. D. (1978). Rebound insomnia: A new clinical syndrome. *Science, 201*, 1039–1040.

Kales, A., Wilson, T., Kales, J., Jacobson, A., Paulson, M., Kollar, E., & Walter, R. O. (1967). Measurements of all-night sleep in normal elderly persons: Effects of aging. *Journal of the American Geriatrics Society, 15*, 405–414.

Kales, J. (1975). Aging and sleep. In R. Goldman & M. Rickstein (Eds.), *Symposium on the psychology and pathology of aging*. New York: Academic.

Kales, J., Tan, T., Swearingen, C., & Kales, A. (1971). Are over-the-counter sleep medications effective? All-night EEG studies. *Current Therapeutic Research, 13*, 143–151.

Karacan, I., Thornby, J., Anch, M., Holzer, C. E., Warheit, G. J., Schwab, J. J., & Williams, R. L. (1976). Prevalence of sleep disturbance in a primarily urban Florida county. *Social Science Medicine, 10*, 239–244.

Karacen, I., & Williams, R. L. (1983). Sleep disorders in the elderly. *American Family Physicians, 27*, 143–152.

Kleitman, N. (1963). *Sleep and wakefulness*. Chicago: University of Chicago Press.

Krieger, J., Turlot, J., Mangin, P., & Kurtz, D. (1983). Breathing during sleep in normal young and elderly subjects: Hypopneas, apneas, and correlated factors. *Sleep, 6*, 108–120.

Kupfer, D. J., & Foster, F. G. (1978). EEG sleep and depression. In R. L. Williams & I. Karacan (Eds.), *Sleep disorders: Diagnosis and treatment*. New York: Wiley.

Lacks, P., Bertelson, A. D., Gans, L., & Kunkel, J. (1983). The effectiveness of three behavioral treatments for different degrees of sleep onset insomnia. *Behavior Therapy, 14*, 593–605.

Lacks, P., Bertelson, A. D., Sugerman, J., & Kunkel, J. (1983). The treatment of sleep-maintenance insomnia with stimulus-control techniques. *Behavior Research and Therapy, 21,* 291–295.

Lawrence, P. S., & Tokarz, T. (1976, November). *A comparison of relaxation training and stimulus control.* Paper presented at the meeting of the Association for the Advancement of Behavior Therapy, New York.

Lick, J. P., & Heffler, D. (1977). Relaxation training and attention placebo in the treatment of severe insomnia. *Journal of Consulting and Clinical Psychology, 45,* 153–161.

Lugaresi, E., Coccagna, G., Berti-Ceroni, G., & Ambrosetto, C. (1968). Restless legs syndrome and nocturnal myoclonus. In H. Gastant, E. Lugaresi, G. Berti-Ceroni, & G. Coccagna (Eds.), *The abnormalities of sleep in man.* Bologna, Italy: Aulogaggi.

McGhie, A., & Russell, S. (1962). The subjective assessment of normal sleep patterns. *Jounal of Mental Science, 108,* 642–654.

McGinty, D., Littner, M., Beahm, E., Ruiz-Primo, E., Young, E., & Saver, J. (1982). Sleep related to breathing disorders in older men: A search for underlying mechanisms. *Neurobiology of Aging, 3,* 337–350.

Meddis, R. (1977). *The sleep instinct.* London: Routledge & Kegan Paul.

Mellinger, G. D., Balter, M. B., & Uhlenhuth, E. H. (1985). Insomnia and its treatment. *Archives of General Psychiatry, 42,* 225–232.

Mendelson, W. B., Gillin, J. C., & Wyatt, R. J. (1977). *Human sleep and its disorders.* New York: Plenum.

Miles, L. E., & Dement, W. C. (1980). Sleep and aging. *Sleep, 3,* 119–220.

Monroe, L. J. (1967). Psychological and physiological differences between good and poor sleepers. *Journal of Abnormal Psychology, 72,* 255–264.

Morgan, K., & Oswald, I. (1982). Anxiety caused by a short-life hypnotic. *British Medical Journal, 284,* 942.

National Institutes of Health. (1983). *Consensus development conference summary: Drugs and insomnia* (Vol. 4, No. 10). Bethesda. MD: Office of Medical Applications of Research.

Nicassio, P., & Bootzin, R. R. (1974). A comparison of progressive relaxation training and autogenic training as treatment for insomnia. *Journal of Abnormal Psychology, 83,* 253–260.

Pasnau, R. O., Naitoh, P., Stier, S., & Kollar, E. J. (1968). The psychological effects of 205 hours of sleep deprivation. *Achives of General Psychiatry, 18,* 496–505.

Pfeiffer, E. (1977). The patients of geriatric psychiatry. *Career Directions, 5,* 20–38.

Prinz, P. (1977). Sleep patterns in the healthy aged: Relationship with intellectual function. *Journal of Gerontology, 32,* 179–186.

Prinz, P., Obriest, W., Wang, H. (1975). Sleep patterns in healthy elderly subjects: Individual differences as related to other neurological variables. *Sleep Research, 4,* 132.

Prinz, P. N., Peskind, E. R., Vitaliano, P. P., Raskind, M. A., Eisdorfer, C., Zemcuznikov, N., & Gerber, C. J. (1982). Changes in the sleep and waking EEGs of nondemented and demented elderly subjects. *Journal of the American Geriatrics Society, 30,* 86–93.

Prinz, P. N., & Raskind, M. (1978). Aging and sleep disorders. In R. Williams & I. Karacan (Eds.), *Sleep disorders: Diagnosis and treatment.* New York: Wiley.

Puder, R., Lacks, P., Bertelson, A. D., & Storandt, M. (1983). Short-term stimulus control treatment of insomnia in older adults. *Behavior Therapy, 14,* 424–429.

Raskind, M. (1977). Why you don't sleep like you used to. *Drug Therapy, 7,* 51–52.

Reynolds, C. F., Kupfer, D. J., Taska, L. S., Hoch, C. C., Sewitch, D. E., & Spiker, D. G. (1985). Sleep of healthy seniors: A revisit. *Sleep, 8,* 20–29.

Roehrs, T., Zorick, F., Sicklesteel, J., Wittig, R., & Roth, T. (1983). Age-related sleep-wake disorders at a sleep disorders center. *Journal of the American Geriatrics Society, 31,* 364–369.

Rowe, J. W. (1985). Health care of the elderly. *The new England Journal of Medicine, 312,* 827–835.

Sanchez., R., & Bootzin, R. R. (1985). A comparison of white noise and music: Effects of predictable and unpredictable sounds on sleep. *Sleep Research, 14,* 121.

Shamoian, C. A. (1983). Psychogeriatrics. *Medical Clinics of North America, 67,* 361–378.

Slama, K. (1975). Unpublished master's thesis, University of Iowa, Iowa City.

Smith, J., Karacan, I., & Yang, M. (1977). Ontogeny of delta activity during human sleep. *Electroencephalography and Clinical Neurophysiology, 43,* 229–237.

Snyder, F. (1966). Toward an evolutional theory of dreaming. *American Journal of Psychiatry, 123,* 121–136.

Soldatos, C. R., Bixler, E. O., & Kales, A. (1985, September). *Behavioral side effects of benzodiazepine hypnotics.* Paper presented at Fourth World Congress of Biological Psychiatry, Philadelphia, PA.

Soldatos, C. R., Kales, J. D., Scharf, M. B., Bixler, E. O., & Kales, A. (1980). Cigarette smoking associated with sleep difficulty. *Science, 207,* 551–553.

Starker, S., & Hasenfeld, R. (1976). Daydream styles and sleep disturbance. *Journal of Nervous and Mental Disease, 163,* 391–400.

Strauch, I., & Wollschlaeger, M. (1973). Sleep behavior in the aged. In U. Jovanovic (Ed.), *The nature of sleep.* Stuttgart: Fischer.

Toler, H. C. (1978). The treatment of insomnia with relaxation and stimulus-control instructions among incarcerated males. *Criminal Justice and Behavior, 5,* 117–130.

Tsao, C., Bootzin, R. R., Hazlewood, L., & Engle-Fiedman, M. (1985). Long-term follow-up on the effectiveness of several behavioral treatments for older adult insomnias. Unpublished paper, Northwestern University, Evanston, IL.

Turner, R. M., & Ascher, L. M. (1979). Controlled comparison of progressive relaxation, stimulus control and paradoxical intention therapies for insomnia. *Journal of Consulting and Clinical Psychology, 49,* 500–508.

Turner, R. M., & Ascher, L. M. (1982). Therapist factor in the treatment of insomnia. *Behavior Research and Therapy, 17,* 107–112.

U.S. Public Health Service. (1976). *Physician's drug prescribing patterns in skilled nursing facilities.* Washington, DC: U.S. Department of Health, Education, and Welfare.

Webb, W. B. (1974). The rhythms of sleep and waking.

In L. Sheving, F. Halberg, & J. Pauly (Eds.), *Chronobiology*. Tokyo: Igaku Shorn.

Webb, W. B. (1975). *Sleep: The gentle tyrant*. New York Spectrum.

Webb, W. B. (1982). Sleep in older persons: Sleep structures of 50- to 60-year old men and women. *Journal of gerontology, 37*, 581–586.

Webb, W. B., & Agnew, H. W., Jr. (1974). The effects of a chronic limitation of sleep length. *Psychophysiology, 11*, 265–274.

Webb, W. B., & Campbell, S. S. (1980). Awakenings and the return to sleep in an older population. *Sleep, 3*, 41–46.

Webb, W. B., & Drebrow, L. M. (1982). A modified method for scoring slow wave sleep of older subjects. *Sleep, 5*, 195–199.

Webb, W. B., & Levy, C. M. (1982). Age, sleep deprivation and performance. *Psychophysiology, 19*, 272–276.

Webb, W. B., & Swinburne, H. (1971). An observational study of sleep in the aged. *Perceptual Motor Skills, 32*, 895–898.

Wessler, R., Rubin, M., & Sollberger, A. (1976). Circadian rhythm of activity and sleep-wakefulness in elderly institutionalized patients. *Journal of Interdisciplinary Cycle Research, 7*, 333.

Williams, R. L., Karacan, I., & Hursch, C. J. (1974). *EEG of human sleep: Clinical applications*. New York: Wiley.

Yesavage, J., Bliwise, D., Guilleminault, C., Carskadon, M., & Dement, W. (1985). Preliminary communication: Intellectual deficit and sleep-related respiratory disturbance in the elderly. *Sleep, 8*, 30–33.

Youkilis, H. D., & Bootzin, R. R. (1981). A psychophysiological perspective on the etiology and treatment of insomnia. In S. N. Haynes & L. A. Gann (Eds.), *Psychosomatic disorders: A psychophysiological approach in etiology and treatment*. New York: Praeger.

Zarit, S. H., & Zarit, J. M. (1983). Cognitive impairment. In P. M. Lewinsohn & L. Teri (Eds.), *Clinical geropsychology: New directions in assessment and treatment*. Elmsford NY: Pergamon.

Zepelin, H. (1973). A survey of age differences in sleep patterns and dream recall among well-educated men and women. *Sleep Research, 2*, 81.

Zepelin, H., McDonald, C. S., & Zammit, G. K. (1984). Effects of age on auditory awakening thresholds. *Journal of Gerontology, 39*, 294–300.

Chapter 19

Urinary Incontinence Behavioral Assessment and Treatment

Kathryn L. Burgio and Bernard T. Engel

Urinary incontinence in the elderly is a major problem with significant medical, psychological, and social consequences. Mild incontinence may be managed with only major accommodations of life-style, but moderate or severe incontinence has more serious implications. It predisposes patients to other health problems (e.g., skin breakdown, urinary tract infections) and contributes to depression, anxiety, and social isolation. Incontinence is a significant source of dependence among the elderly and a widely cited factor in nursing-home admissions. The costs of incontinence are enormous, accounting for an estimated $.5 to $1.5 billion each year in U.S. nursing homes (Ouslander & Kane, 1984).

Urinary incontinence affects individuals of every age, but it is most prevalent among the elderly. As a result, incontinence is commonly and mistakenly attributed to age. Unfortunately, both patients and their health care providers frequently accept incontinence as a natural and inevitable consequence of the aging process. In fact, the elderly are more likely to have conditions that predispose them to incontinence or contribute to the causes of incontinence. Many of these conditions may be controlled or avoided if properly identified. Urinary incontinence is not a normal aspect of aging, nor is it irreversible. Elderly

patients should be managed with the same effort afforded to younger patients with incontinence. They should be carefully evaluated, with special attention to age-related deficits, such as impaired mobility, diminished vision, or deficits in mental status. Incontinence is a multifaceted disorder, with many possible causes, each of which needs to be explored. Only through careful assessment can specific deficits be identified and rational treatment implemented.

Even as treatments for incontinence are improved and made more available, barriers to treatment will exist in the attitudes held by patients and health care providers. Because incontinence is socially unacceptable and can be embarrassing, many incontinent persons ignore or conceal the problem and avoid seeking help. Research on incontinence in the community suggests that one third to one half of all incontinent persons do not seek advice or treatment (Thomas, Plymat, Blannin, & Meade, 1980; Vetter, Jones, & Victor, 1981). Many of those who do seek help are encouraged to accept incontinence as a natural and inevitable consequence of advancing age or of childbearing. As a result, incontinence is often regarded as untreatable, and patients are managed less than optimally. One study of U.S. nursing homes found that incontinence was mentioned infrequently in physicians' notes and that less than 5% of patients received a diagnostic evaluation (Ouslander, Kane, & Abrass, 1982). In another study of three nursing homes, incontinence was included in the medical problem list of less than 5% of the incontinent residents (Ribeiro & Smith, 1985).

This chapter describes behavioral approaches to the assessment and treatment of urinary incontinence with special attention to common causes of incontinence in the elderly. Behavioral interventions are especially relevant for the elderly for two reasons: (a) Surgery for incontinence is often unacceptable to elderly patients or inadvisable because of other medical conditions and (b) pharmacologic therapy often produces side effects, such as mucous membrane dryness, constipation, confusion, drowsiness, urinary retention, blurry vision, or exacerbation of glaucoma, any of which can produce significant discomfort and lead to discontinuation of the drug. In addition, the possibility of drug interactions is always a matter of concern for many elderly people, who often take several medications. Behavioral interventions offer a potentially effective means of improving continence without the risks and side effects of the traditional approaches to this common and disturbing problem.

However, one should not infer from this that all medications are harmful or that all persons are amenable to behavioral treatment. Management of incontinence should be based on the same principles as management of any medical disorder. All incontinent patients should first be evaluated medically, and the decision to intervene behaviorally should be reached concurrently by the physician and behavioral therapist.

PHYSIOLOGY OF URINARY CONTINENCE AND INCONTINENCE

Normal micturition and urinary continence involve a complex set of physiological responses, described in depth by Bradley, Timm, and Scott (1974). As the bladder fills, stretch receptors in the bladder wall signal the sacral spinal cord. At a critical threshold volume, a spinal cord reflex (the micturition reflex) stimulates the bladder to empty. This is accomplished by rhythmic contractions of the detrusor muscle, a smooth muscle that surrounds the bladder wall, and relaxation of the external urinary sphincter, a striated muscle that surrounds the urethra. The micturition reflex stimulates bladder emptying in infants and spinal-cord-transected patients. Voluntary control over urination is accomplished through inhibition of the micturition reflex via neural circuits from the cerebral cortex. Continence requires that the individual anticipate the threshold for bladder emptying and avoid incontinence by voiding before the threshold is reached, or more commonly, by perceiving bladder distention and inhibiting reflex contractions until an appropriate setting for urination is reached. One must also be able to occlude the urethra to prevent incontinence during uninhibited bladder contraction or sudden pressure rises associated with physical activities, such as coughing or sneezing. Also important to the maintenance of continence is the ability to voluntarily empty the bladder.

Failure to emit these physiological responses at the appropriate times results in one of the following common types of incontinence: (a) urge incontinence, in which bladder contractions are not inhibited; (b) stress incontinence, in which the outflow is not effectively prevented during transient pressure rises; and (c) overflow incontinence, in which urine is lost from a chronically full bladder because the bladder does not empty fully. A fourth type of incontinence—functional incontinence—can occur in individuals who have normal physiological responses but who for other reasons, such as cognitive or mobility impairment, do not show a normal ability to reach or use the toilet reliably.

TYPES AND CAUSES OF INCONTINENCE

In up to one third of cases, urinary incontinence is a transient difficulty related to urinary tract infection or an acute illness that produces confusion or immobilizes the patient (Isaacs & Walkey, 1964; Yarnell & St. Legar, 1979). Transient incontinence is resolved with appropriate treatment of the precipitating medical condition.

Persistent incontinence, or established incontinence, can be classified as urge incontinence, stress incontinence, overflow incontinence, or functional incontinence according to the primary mechanism of urine loss.

Urge Incontinence

The category of *urge incontinence* encompasses a group of disorders including bladder instability, detrusor hyperreflexia, spastic bladder, neurogenic bladder, or uninhibited bladder. Urine loss is associated with uncontrolled contractions of the detrusor muscle.

This inability to inhibit detrusor contraction can be caused by neurological disorders or injuries that impair central nervous system control: cerebrovascular accident, brain tumor, dementia, parkinsonism, multiple sclerosis, or spinal cord injury. Bladder dysfunction can also be produced by local inflammation or irritation of the bladder or urethra resulting from such conditions as urinary tract infection, fecal impaction, benign prostatic hypertrophy, uterine prolapse, or bladder carcinoma.

It has also been asserted that bladder instability can result from poor bladder habits, such as frequent voiding. Repeated low-volume voiding prevents the bladder from accommodating normal urine volumes and is purported to decrease bladder capacity, resulting in increased urinary frequency and urgency (Frewen, 1978, 1980).

Typically, urge incontinence is characterized by large-volume urinary accidents, which can lead to embarrassment and serious restriction of activities even if such incontinent episodes are infrequent.

The primary interventions for urge incontinence are medications and behavioral procedures, such as habit training. Several pharmacologic agents have proved effective in reducing incontinence associated with bladder instability. Two drugs—oxybutynin chloride and imipramine—have been tested in a small number of elderly patients, with 60% to 70% showing improvement (Castleden, George, Renwick, & Asher, 1981; Moisey, Stephenson, & Brendler, 1980). The major disadvantage of these drugs is their side effects. In the study of oxybutynin chloride, 55% of the patients reported side effects, primarily dry mouth, and 20% discontinued the drug as a result. Imipramine is well known to behavioral therapists, because it is frequently used as an antidepressant. Its major side effects in the elderly are mucous membrane dryness, confusion, drowsiness, or urinary retention. The behavioral procedures, which are described later in the chapter, have no known side effects.

Stress Incontinence

Stress urinary incontinence is the involuntary loss of urine that occurs following a sudden rise in intra-abdominal pressure produced by such physical activities as coughing, sneezing, jogging, or lifting.

Incontinence results when a corresponding rise in bladder pressure exceeds urethral resistance in the absence of detrusor contraction. Stress incontinence is due to a defect of the bladder outlet (sphincter insufficiency, incompetent sphincter) such that the resistance provided by the urethra is inadequate to prevent leakage.

Stress incontinence occurs so commonly in women that mild incontinence is accepted as normal by many women, and a surprising number are not inconvenienced enough to accept treatment. One study of the prevalence in young, nulliparous women reports that 51% experienced stress incontinence, although only 16% had daily leakage (Wolin, 1969). In men, stress incontinence is uncommon and is usually a result of urologic surgery, such as prostatectomy.

One commonly accepted etiologic factor in female stress incontinence is perinatal damage to the supporting tissues of the pelvic floor. The precise mechanism of urine loss is a topic of debate. Anatomical explanations emphasize the loss of the vesicourethral angle due to overstretched or damaged pelvic floor tissues. A normal angle between the bladder floor and urethra provides transmission of pressure to the urethra and bladder simultaneously during physical activities. Thus, urethral pressure is increased during transient rises in bladder pressure and prevents leakage. When the position of the urethra is altered by loss of urethral support, sudden increases in abdominal pressure are transmitted to the bladder, leaving urethral pressure unaltered and thus leading to incontinence. The usual treatment for stress incontinence is surgical restoration of a normal vesicourethral angle by repositioning the urethra and improving support to the bladder. Surgical approaches are known to be effective in properly selected patients, but study patients have been predominantly younger women and little attention has been paid to effectiveness in elderly patients. Further, the presence of other medical conditions can preclude surgery in some elderly patients.

Functional explanations of stress incontinence attribute urinary leakage to a lack of awareness or voluntary control of pelvic floor muscles (Kegel, 1948, 1956) or a failure of the striated muscle of the distal urethral sphincter to contract during transient rises in intra-abdominal pressure. The usual method for improving weak muscles is physiotherapy. Behavioral methods for training patients to exercise pelvic floor muscles are described in detail later in this chapter.

Stress incontinence is commonly associated with atrophic vaginitis in postmenopausal women and may be treated with topical or oral estrogen. Studies of estrogen therapy have reported beneficial effects on urinary control (Faber & Heidenreich, 1977; Judge, 1969; Walter, Wolf, Barlebo, & Jensen, 1978). Long-term estrogen therapy carries a risk of endometrial cancer, which can be reduced or eliminated by administering the estrogen in low, cyclic doses with progestin (Harman & Robinson, 1982).

Overflow Incontinence

Overflow incontinence is the leakage of urine when pressure in a chronically full bladder exceeds urethral resistance. This may be due to an atonic (acontractile) bladder or to a functional or mechanical obstruction of the bladder outlet. Atonic bladder commonly results from spinal cord trauma or diabetes mellitus. In the elderly, outlet obstruction is often due to fecal impaction (Willington, 1980). An estimated 55.6% of constipated nursing home residents are incontinent, compared to approximately 42% of those who are not constipated (Van Nostrand, Zappolo, Hing et al., 1979). Other sources of obstruction are benign prostatic hypertrophy, carcinoma of the prostate, and bladder-sphincter dyssynergia, in which the sphincter contracts simultaneously with bladder contractions. Occasionally psychogenic retention is diagnosed when no physical cause of obstruction can be found. Cases such as these have been known to respond well to a placebo. An empirical trial of a placebo may be a useful diagnostic tool in the treatment of patients with retention of unknown etiology.

Functional Incontinence

Functional incontinence is the loss of urine resulting from an inability or unwillingness to use the toilet appropriately. In a person with normal bladder function incontinence can be precipitated by limitations that prevent the individual from reaching the toilet in time. Factors that contribute to functional incontinence may include deficits of mobility, mental status, motivation, or environmental barriers.

Arthritic pain, muscle weakness, disorders of balance, joint abnormalities, fractures, and fatigue are examples of physical conditions that limit mobility and normal toilet use. Ouslander et al. (1982) studied 299 elderly nursing-home patients with frequent incontinence and reported that only 15% were ambulatory. The other 85% suffered severe impairments of mobility, which caused them to be wheelchair-bound or bed-bound. They described the predicament of many patients who appreciate the sensation of bladder fullness but are unable to postpone urination until staff assistance is available. Continence in patients with mobility impairment depends on their ability to acquire toileting skills, the availability of caregivers to assist toileting on a regular schedule, or the promptness with which caregivers can respond to the expressed desire to void.

In patients with significant cognitive impairment, incontinence may be related to memory deficits, confusion, depression, or fears that interfere with appropriate voiding. Ouslander et al. (1982), using the Short Portable Mental Status Questionnaire (Pfeiffer, 1976), showed that most elderly incontinent nursing-home patients have some degree of cognitive impairment and that the severity of this impairment was related to the degree of incontinence.

Similarly, incontinence is occasionally a manipulative behavior for the purpose of eliciting attention or the result of indifference to the social consequences of wetting. It is not unusual in institutional or home settings for incontinence to elicit more attention than dryness. Under these circumstances, treatment may involve the rearrangement of environmental contingencies such that positive behavior (e.g., toileting, dryness) elicits attention and incontinence elicits negative consequences (e.g., disapproval, cleaning up).

Environmental factors, such as lack of privacy, uncomfortable toilet facilities, poor lighting, and physical barriers, can also contribute to functional incontinence.

Factors involved in functional incontinence are crucial variables in nursing-home patients whose lack of bladder control is often secondary to the disabilities that necessitated institutional care. Intervention is directed at improving the functional level of the patient. Based entirely on the nature of the deficit, it is aimed at reversing the conditions that impair functional level by removing environmental barriers, by introducing stimuli or devices that facilitate function, by improving skill level through training, or by introducing contingencies that encourage normal voiding habits.

ASSESSMENT

The purpose of behavioral assessment is to characterize incontinence and to identify the mechanism of urine loss. Knowledge of an underlying disease is often useful but not always sufficient to identify the mechanism or to treat incontinence. Urine loss will occur when intravesical (bladder) pressure exceeds urethral resistance regardless of the presence or the nature of an underlying disease. Further, urinary incontinence in the elderly is commonly the result of several interacting factors, any of which may be amenable to change.

Behavioral assessment should be accompanied by medical screening, including history taking and physical examination, in order to detect conditions that may not be apparent otherwise and to exclude conditions that are inappropriate for behavioral intervention. Examination of urine to detect urinary tract infection is an indispensable component of the routine medical evaluation. Post-void catheterization for residual urine will detect overflow incontinence, which usually requires medical or surgical intervention. Physical examination will reveal the presence of fecal impaction, benign prostatic hypertrophy, atrophic vaginitis, and other conditions that are reversible causes of incontinence.

The Interview

Behavioral evaluation of incontinence begins with an interview of the patient or a caregiver if the patient is unable to participate. Using carefully selected questions, the interviewer can elicit information that in many cases will provide a clear picture of the behavioral mechanisms (or correlates) of the incontinence and help formulate a preliminary diagnosis. Care should be taken to identify the antecedents of incontinence, to obtain a description of typical incontinent episodes, and to ascertain the consequences of wetting.

Patients with urge incontinence usually give a clear description of accidents that occur in the presence of a strong urge to void and an inability to reach the toilet in time. Typical antecedents of urge incontinence are the sounds of running water, thoughts about going to the toilet, the sight of a toilet, or cold weather. A common report is the occurrence of accidents as one returns home and unlocks the door of the house. This difficulty, termed *key in the door syndrome*, is partially the result

of classical conditioning in which arriving home has been repeatedly paired with bladder emptying.

Patients with stress incontinence are usually able to identify specific physical activities that precipitate incontinence. Common among these are coughing, sneezing, lifting, bending, or stooping. One must be alert to identify cases in which the physical activity is subtle. Patients occasionally report the absence of physical activity when in fact they are walking, turning, or standing up from a sitting position. Incontinence can occur with slight jarring movements (as when climbing stairs) or with changes in position of which the patient may be unaware.

Bladder Records

Bladder records, or symptom diaries, are used to document voiding habits and patterns of incontinence on a day-to-day basis. Such records serve two purposes. First, they provide a picture of the patient's behavior that, together with the interview, can be used to identify preventable causes of incontinence and formulate an accurate diagnosis and treatment plan, and second, they function as a vehicle for evaluating progress and testing the effectiveness of treatment. Self-recording eliminates an important source of error by circumventing the patient's verbal report. It is difficult for patients to judge the frequency or patterns of incontinence retrospectively, especially if the patterns are irregular. Home recording over a period of 2–4 weeks will often document such patterns of variability that the patient finds difficult to communicate. Patients are sometimes surprised at the actual number of accidents once they are required to record them. We have seen patients who profess improvement, whereas their diaries showed no change in the extent or frequency of accidents. Thus, we emphasize the importance of bladder records for preventing any tendencies patients may have to report positively on their progress for the purpose of pleasing the doctor.

A variety of record forms have been developed for documentation of bladder habits (e.g., Clay, 1980). Most have been designed for use by nurses and are complex. If patients or caregivers are expected to keep meaningful records, a simple bladder form is crucial. A form that we have used (Whitehead, Burgio, & Engel, 1984) to document the most necessary information is presented in Figure 19.1. Space is provided to record the time of voiding, the time of incontinent episodes, whether the accident was large or small based on whether the outer clothing was wet, and finally, the reason for incontinence, which is helpful in identifying the antecedents of incontinence.

Observation of Mobility and Toileting Skills

The ability to reach and use the toilet appropriately is a basic skill for the maintenance of continence. Direct observation of one or more toileting episodes is the best method of determining these skills. The time needed to reach the toilet, to undress, and to position appropriately for voiding is measured. If any of these cannot be performed independently, note is taken of the required assistance and its availability in the patient's natural environment. The type of clothing worn is also of interest, particularly if it might be modified to facilitate undressing. In physically handicapped patients, behavioral observation can help determine skill deficits, such as inadequate transfer skills, that might be overcome with training. During direct observation it will also become clear whether the patient knows where the bathroom is and whether he or she has an understanding of its appropriate use. A relevant example of the latter is from our experience with a patient who, when guided to the toilet and instructed to void, tore toilet paper from the roll, placed it in the toilet, and flushed. Over weeks of observation, he was not observed to use the toilet but voided consistently in a diaper.

Mental Status Evaluation

Appropriate voiding habits and continence can be seriously disrupted by depression or cognitive deficits, such as confusion, disorientation, and memory impairment. Although these deficits may surface in other areas of assessment, it is often useful to evaluate them using standardized tests. The Mini-Mental State Examination (Folstein, Folstein, & McHugh, 1975) is a brief test of mental status that includes assessment of orientation, alertness, memory, attention, and judgment. However, because it was designed for rapid and easy assessment of acutely ill patients, it does not fully evaluate the range of cognition, and when indicated, it should be supplemented by more elaborate neuropsychologic instruments. Depression may be evaluated using a structured device, such as the CES-D (Center for Epidemiological Study) Scale (Radloff, 1977).

Urodynamics

Physiologic measurements of bladder pressure and sphincter activity are routine methods for assessing bladder or sphincter dysfunction. The cystometrogram measures bladder pressure during rapid bladder filling and is a standard procedure in urology clinics. It is often complemented by measurement of intraurethral pressures (urethral pressure profile) or measurement of pelvic floor activity (sphincter electromyography). The cystometrogram is very useful in evaluating bladder physiology and, with modification, provides an extremely useful behavioral evaluation of incontinence.

When a behavioral analysis is made of bladder and sphincter physiology, incontinence is characterized as a behavioral deficit. Central to this approach is the acceptance of physiological responses as behavior. In a behavioral analysis, incontinence occurs when an individual (a) fails to voluntarily inhibit reflex bladder contractions, or (b) fails to adequately contract the striated (voluntary) sphincter muscles of the pelvic floor that obstruct bladder emptying. Both bladder inhibition and sphincter contraction are acquired physiological responses that preserve continence.

Because bladder function is responsive to environmental conditions, the patient should be tested in surroundings that preserve privacy and permit relaxation. The patient should be made as comfortable as possible in an unusual situation. During bladder filling, emphasis should be placed on the evaluation of bladder sensation, because sensation provides critical information about bladder function and cues voluntary inhibition of bladder contractions. It is important to determine not only the sensory threshold for bladder filling but also the amount of time between the onset of sensation and the threshold for uninhibited bladder contractions in urge incontinent patients. This is the amount of time the patient has to reach a toilet or to implement bladder inhibition before incontinence occurs. Filling the bladder slowly improves the accuracy of this assessment.

Once the patient reports bladder sensation, the response to this sensation can be observed; specifically, one should note carefully the ability to voluntarily inhibit bladder contractions and the use of periurethral muscles to occlude the urethra. The inhibition of bladder contractions cannot be observed directly but must be inferred from the threshold for uninhibited contractions. However,

Bladder Record

Name_____   Date_____

Instructions: (1) In the 1st column, mark the time every time you void
                 (2) In the 2nd or 3rd column, mark every time you accidently leaked urine.
                 (3) Write "dry" if no accident occurred in the 2-hour interval.

Time Interval	Urinated in toilet	Leaking Accident	or	Large Accident	Reason for Accident
6–8 AM					
8–10 AM					
10–12 AM					
12–2 PM					
2–4 PM					
4–6 PM					
6–8 PM					
8–10 PM					
10–12 PM					
Overnight					

Number of pads used today: _____

Comments: _____

_____

Exercises: _____

_____

_____

Total: _____

Figure 19.1 Bladder record form used by patients to document voiding, incontinent episodes, volume of accidents, and antecedents of incontinence.

one can increase the reliability of assessment by encouraging the patient throughout bladder filling to try to prevent urine loss. It should be noted that this need for patient cooperation greatly limits the usefulness of cystometrograms in the assessment of urge incontinence in patients with cognitive impairment or under conditions where there is reason to suspect that the patient will be uncooperative.

Voluntary contractions of the periurethral muscles can be measured in a variety of ways one of which is the use of an air-filled balloon at the external anal sphincter. Because the innervation of the external urethral sphincter is similar to that of the external anal sphincter, this balloon provides an index of urethral sphincter activity. To minimize the effects of motivational state, the patient is specifically instructed to contract the sphincter muscles and to hold the contractions for a specified period of time.

The test should also include a measure of intra-abdominal pressure, such as rectal pressure. The purpose of this measure is to distinguish increases in bladder pressure that are attributable to increases in intra-abdominal pressure, as well as to detect inappropriate responses to the desire to void. Many incontinent patients respond to the sensation of urgency by tensing abdominal muscles in an effort to prevent incontinence (Burgio, Whitehead, & Engel, 1985). This response increases bladder pressure and thus contributes to the likelihood of an accident.

Some investigators report that careful history and physical examination provide an accurate diagnosis of urinary tract dysfunction (Hinman, 1979). Hilton and Stanton (1981) developed a clinical algorithm for categorizing incontinent women and compared its outcome to the results of urodynamic assessment. They concluded that the algorithm provided 83% accuracy in diagnosis. Other investigators have noted significant disparities between clinical and urodynamic investigations (Katz & Blaivas, 1983). Certainly, urodynamic procedures occasionally detect urinary tract abnormalities that go unnoticed during clinical examination, and the discrepancy warrants alteration of the treatment plan. However, other discrepancies (e.g., normal urodynamic findings in patients with urge incontinence) may not necessitate changing the intervention indicated by the clinical interview (Hilton & Stanton, 1981).

In addition, the validity of urodynamic testing needs to be evaluated. Because the procedure of bladder filling is accelerated, it may produce instability in patients who otherwise have stable patterns. Abnormal patterns have been documented in patients who do not experience incontinence (Brocklehurst & Dillane, 1966), and we have seen bladder stability in patients who clearly describe urge incontinence outside the clinic setting. Clinicians are becoming increasingly aware that the test situation lacks certain components that stimulate bladder instability. It is for this reason that supine cystometry is now complemented by provocative maneuvers, such as standing or coughing, which in many cases will reveal instability otherwise masked by the quiet supine position. But there remain many antecedents of incontinence aside from bladder filling (e.g., running water, cold weather, laughing) that are usually absent from the test situation.

Urodynamic testing in patients with cognitive impairment poses a serious problem. This form of testing requires the active cooperation and understanding of the patient. First, it is necessary that patients understand that they should make every effort to inhibit urine loss, and second, they must be motivated to do so. If either criterion is not met, the mechanism of an uninhibited detrusor contraction may be uninterpretable.

One setting in which urodynamic monitoring is clearly required is during intervention using biofeedback techniques, in which patients learn to alter physiological responses.

INTERVENTION

The choice of behavioral intervention depends upon the results of the behavioral evaluation of the patient's deficits. Generally, elderly patients will fall into one of two categories: those who are capable of learning self-management procedures and those who require ongoing intervention from a caregiver. Usually, but not necessarily, the former will be community-dwelling and the latter will be institutionalized. Community-dwelling patients usually have demonstrable bladder or sphincter dysfunction but are otherwise functional in terms of self-care, often have little or no cognitive impairment, and frequently are capable of independent living. They can be managed in an outpatient setting, where the patient receives training in self-management skills in the clinic and prescribed practice is implemented at home. Institutionalized patients are often characterized by functional dependence and significant cognitive or mobility impairment, and will require assistance in the management of incontinence. Many of these will be unaware of or indifferent to their incontinence. Management requires family or institutional staff to implement treatment procedures that involve the control of environmental factors.

Habit Training

Temporal voiding schedules (habit training) are the most frequently used behavioral methods of managing incontinence in nursing homes. Ouslander and Fowler (1985) surveyed 90 Veterans

Administration nursing homes and found that 34% reported using guidelines for managing incontinence that included some form of habit training. Such training consists of the establishment of a voiding routine, usually two to four hourly, whether or not a sensation to void is present. In addition to the voiding routine, these programs usually involve careful timing of fluid intake and medications. The objective of habit training is not to modify bladder function but to keep the patient dry. A more individualized form of habit training involves adjustment of the voiding schedule to the needs of the patient. The voiding interval is shortened if incontinence persists and lengthened when the patient is consistently dry at a certain interval (Clay, 1980).

These procedures, though widely adopted and advocated, have not been tested extensively in the elderly. Sogbein and Awad (1982) used a 2-hour voiding schedule to treat 20 elderly men with bladder hyperreflexia; 85% achieved the criteria for improvement (reduction of incontinence to less than 20% of the time). Schnelle, Traughber, Morgan, Embry, Binion, and Coleman (1983), in a carefully controlled study of incontinence in two nursing homes, implemented hourly checks for incontinence, followed by prompts to void. Habit training was accompanied by social approval contingent on dry checks or requests for toileting assistance and social disapproval for incontinence. In 11 geriatric patients, most of whom were diagnosed as having senile dementia or organic brain syndrome and none of whom were independently ambulatory, correct toileting increased by 45% and incontinence was reduced by 49%.

Clay (1978) reported the results of habit training with adjustment of the voiding schedule to "catch the patient" before incontinence occurred. Among 20 male patients in an assessment and rehabilitation ward, 63% were successfully managed. Habit training in 11 female patients on a continuous care and rehabilitation ward produced success in 73%. These patients were apparently less impaired physically than those in other studies, and several of them were discharged following training. Among 4 patients who were "mentally disoriented," one had a satisfactory result and two others showed improvement.

When the goal is to keep the patient dry, temporal voiding routines have demonstrated success even with physically and mentally debilitated patients. Habit training may be self-administered by capable patients. In most instances, however, it is clear that continence is not a result of relearning on the part of the patient but alterations in the habits of the staff and that continued continence depends upon consistent involvement of the staff.

Bladder Training

The primary objective of bladder training (also termed bladder retraining or bladder drill) is to restore a normal pattern of voiding and normal bladder function. Unlike habit training, in which the voiding schedule is adjusted to the needs of the patient, bladder training encourages the patient to adopt an expanded voiding interval. By gradually increasing the intervals between voidings, it attempts to correct the bad habit of frequent voiding, improve the ability to suppress bladder instability, and eventually diminish urgency.

Frewen (1978, 1980) provided the rationale for this approach. He suggested that urinary frequency is a precursor and a precipitant of bladder instability and that urgency is not only a symptom of detrusor instability but also an initiating factor because it increases frequency of urination, which contributes to decreased bladder capacity. The Frewen bladder drill program requires patients to resist the sensation of urgency, to postpone voiding, and to urinate by the clock rather than in response to an urge. The goal is to increase bladder capacity day by day. Frewen advocates admission to a hospital for 7–10 days for a combination of bladder drill, supportive therapy, anticholinergic medication, and sedatives. He reported an 82% to 86% cure rate (i.e., absence of abnormal symptoms and normal cystometrogram) in women aged 15–77 years (Frewen, 1978, 1979, 1982).

Jarvis tested inpatient bladder drill without adjunctive medication in the treatment of women aged 17–79 with urge incontinence, obtaining cure rates of 61% to 90% (Jarvis, 1981, 1982; Jarvis & Miller, 1980). Results appear to be related to cystometric findings prior to treatment. The 61% cure rate was reported in a study of women with bladder capacities less than 400 mL (Jarvis, 1982); the 90% cure rate was among women with capacities exceeding 650 mL (Jarvis & Miller, 1980). Others reported 44% to 52% of patients cured, with an additional 25% to 34% showing improvement with bladder drill alone or in combination with other treatment (Elder & Stephenson, 1980; Pengelly & Booth, 1980; Svigos & Matthews,

1977). Symptomatic improvement was not always associated with urodynamic change.

Bladder training, like habit training, has the advantage that there are no documented side effects and the procedures are easy to implement. Research on bladder training indicates that incontinence can be reduced and bladder function altered through the modification of toileting habits.

Contingency Management

The use of rewards and punishment to improve continence has produced encouraging results. The earliest and still the most definitive study (Carpenter & Simon, 1960) compared two contingency management procedures with habit training and usual institutional care in 94 hospitalized psychotic patients between the ages of 33 and 84. Patients were ambulatory and without known urinary tract abnormalities. The experimental groups received either habit training alone (regular visits to the toilet every 2 hours), habit training plus verbal approval for successful toileting and disapproval for accidents, or habit training plus permission to wear a clean suit of personal clothing (instead of hospital fatigues) as long as they remained continent. Unfortunately, the subjects were not randomly assigned to treatment groups. The nurses heading the groups chose their own patients, and the remaining patients served as controls. As a result, only the intragroup comparisons are interpretable. The group receiving clothing privileges showed a rapid, sustained decrease in frequency of incontinence, from 4.6 incontinent episodes per week to 0.5, within the first month of training. The verbal approval/disapproval group also showed significant reductions, from 4.5 accidents per week to less than 0.5, but required more than 2 months of training. Neither the habit training group nor the control group showed consistent decreases in incontinence.

Grosicki (1968) subsequently reported an unsuccessful attempt to reduce incontinence using tokens and social interaction. The patients—20 ambulatory men (aged 63–85) in a psychiatric unit of a Veterans' Administration hospital—were checked hourly and given 3 minutes of social attention if dry. In a separate trial, tokens were awarded for proper elimination and withdrawn if the patient was incontinent. Many of the patients had "genito-urinary system impairments." Controls showed significant reduction in incontinence,

whereas the experimental subjects showed no significant change. However, it is difficult to interpret these findings since the subjects were not randomly assigned to groups.

Wagner and Paul (1970) observed positive results with a stringent program in 19 psychotic male patients aged 25–66. Dry checks were rewarded with candy, cigarettes, social approval, and progressively more comfortable sleeping conditions. Incontinence was punished by the withholding of up to two meals. All patients improved following 22 weeks of training; of these, 6 were completely continent and 8 were incontinent only at night.

An unsuccessful application of contingency management was reported by Pollock and Liberman (1974) in 6 demented ambulatory men aged 61–79 years. During 1 week, patients were required to mop up following an incontinent episode and were not changed unless they requested it. For an additional 3 weeks, dry checks were rewarded with social interaction, including praise and material rewards (candy, cigarettes). The authors note that the patients had memory deficits; 2 were unable to locate the toilet, indicating that the training may have been effective if it had included physical guidance to the toilet and shaping of appropriate toileting behavior. One cannot expect to achieve continence unless appropriate voiding habits are established.

A more sophisticated approach was used by Azrin and Foxx (1971) to toilet-train mentally retarded adults, aged 20–62. They proposed that continence be conceived as a complex chain of behaviors, each of which must be taught. By encouraging a patient to drink excessive amounts of fluids, they artificially increased the frequency of urinations and intensively trained each patient 8 hours per day. The first step involved teaching the patient to walk to the commode, remove clothing, and sit on the commode. This was accomplished by immediately rewarding the patient with a snack food for each successive approximation and by physically guiding the patient's hands and body when necessary. Prompts to go to the toilet were given every 30 minutes, and the patient was given a reward for every 5 minutes with dry clothes (detected by means of a urine detector in the patient's pants). When urination in the toilet occurred, this was rewarded. Gradually the prompts were eliminated and rewards were switched to self-initiated toileting. When self-initiations were occurring at a high frequency, the patient was moved farther and farther from the toilet and the interval between pants checks was increased from every 5 minutes to every few hours. Throughout this procedure, the patient was punished for incontinence by being required to clean up and to practice going to and sitting on the commode several times. This program resulted in a reduction of 80% or more in the frequency of accidents in an average of 6 days of training. The results were well maintained at follow-up 5 months later.

Smith, Britton, Johnson, and Thomas (1975) replicated these results in a study of five severely mentally retarded patients aged 25–56. However, they found that their patients required a lengthy maintenance program (intermittent rewards for self-initiations and punishments for accidents) to achieve an average 84% reduction in frequency of incontinence.

The Azrin and Foxx procedure was developed for mentally retarded patients with no history of successful toilet training. Its appropriateness for demented geriatric patients who have a different type of cognitive impairment and who have a history of previous continence has not been established. It is possible that the procedure in its original form would be impractical in institutional settings for the elderly because families or nursing staff would object to the punishment components of the program. However, Sanavio (1981) reported a case of a 60-year-old with urinary incontinence and a 77-year-old with fecal incontinence who achieved continence using these procedures.

Biofeedback

In the interventions described above, toileting habits are the primary targets of behavioral change. Biofeedback is a form of behavioral training that attempts to reverse incontinence by altering physiological responses of the bladder and the pelvic floor muscles that mediate incontinence. The targets of the intervention are the striated muscles of the pelvic floor or abdominal wall and the smooth detrusor muscle that mediates bladder emptying. Physiologic change is possible through the use of operant conditioning in which suitably motivated patients can learn by observing the results of their attempts to voluntarily control bladder and sphincter responses. Intraurethral resistance can be increased by training patients to contract periurethral muscles; voluntary inhibition of bladder contractions can also be relearned.

Urge Incontinence

The earliest reported use of a biofeedback procedure for urge incontinence was reported in 1948 by Wilson. He reported that 10 of 23 elderly patients with precipitancy or incontinence were improved or made completely continent, and 5 others were somewhat improved following a diagnostic cystometrogram. During cystometrograms, bladder pressure readings were available to his patients and may have provided a mechanism for feedback that allowed them to acquire better control. Wilson referred to his method as *inhibitory re-educative training*, but he clearly described a form of intervention that would now be termed *biofeedback*.

Willington (1980) has also described a method of biofeedback in which a patient's catheter is attached to a vertical tube in which the fluid level is visible to the patient. The fluid level remains low as long as the bladder remains relaxed but rises noticeably when bladder contractions occur.

Cardozo and her colleagues (Cardozo, Abrams, Stanton, & Feneley, 1978; Cardozo, Stanton, Hafner, & Allan, 1978) published a bladder-pressure biofeedback procedure for treating urge incontinence. This method provides both auditory and visual feedback of bladder pressure during repeated bladder filling. Twenty-seven women aged 18–64 with bladder instability were treated in four to eight 1-hour sessions at weekly intervals. Improvement was seen in 81% of the women; of these, 41% were judged to be cured.

In 1979 investigators at the National Institute on Aging developed a procedure that provides simultaneous feedback of bladder pressure, sphincter activity, and intra-abdominal pressure using the instrumentation shown in Figure 19.2 (Burgio, Whitehead, & Engel, 1985). The third component, intra-abdominal pressure, was added because many patients exhibit a tendency to tense abdominal muscles while trying to prevent incontinence. This behavior is counterproductive because it increases bladder pressure and consequently increases the probability of urine loss. Simultaneous feedback of the three pressures provides a mechanism for operant conditioning of bladder, sphincter, and abdominal muscle responses. Specifically, patients acquire selective responses: bladder inhibition (relaxation) or active contraction of pelvic floor muscles coupled with abdominal relaxation. The procedure was tested as an integral component in a behavioral training program for treating urinary incontinence in an outpatient clinic. After a 2-hour voiding schedule

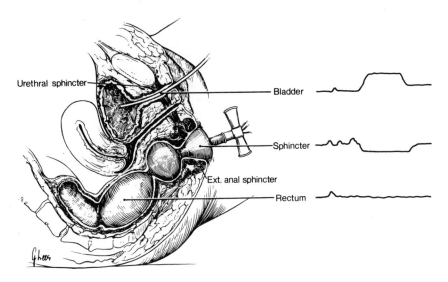

Figure 19.2 Schematic of female pelvic anatomy showing devices used to provide biofeedback information to patients. Sample polygraph tracings are shown at right.

failed to resolve incontinence in 18 elderly patients with urge incontinence, the biofeedback procedure was implemented. Patients achieved 39% to 100% reductions of incontinence following an average of four training sessions. Included in the sample were four men with bladder instability secondary to cerebrovascular accident who achieved total continence by the 6-month follow-up. This study demonstrated that biofeedback is a practical and effective approach to treating geriatric urge incontinence.

Stress Incontinence

The first report of feedback for stress incontinence was published by A. H. Kegel (1948), a gynecologist who asserted that stress-incontinent women lack awareness of function and coordination of pelvic floor muscle function. He developed what is now regarded as a biofeedback device— the perineometer—which was used by his patients to monitor the strength of pelvic floor muscle contractions during daily exercises. The perineometer consisted of an intravaginal balloon attached to an external pressure gauge that registered the strength of vaginal muscle contractions. Kegel (1956) reported 90% improvement in 455 women who were trained with this method.

Over the years Kegel exercises have continued to be prescribed, but typically without the benefit of the perineometer. Instead, the patient is instructed to squeeze her vaginal muscles around the examiner's fingers to learn the correct technique. She is then instructed to practice contracting these muscles at home without feedback. She may also be asked to practice interrupting the urinary stream. Under these conditions, the exercises are apparently less effective and their use has waned.

Burgio et al. (1985) used the instrumentation shown in Figure 19.2 to teach elderly patients how to selectively contract and relax pelvic floor muscles without increasing bladder or abdominal pressure. Following the acquisition of this skill, they were instructed in the daily exercise of these muscles at home, and also instructed in the active contraction of these muscles, to prevent leakage during physical activities, known to produce incontinence. Nineteen patients over the age of 65 were trained in an average of 3.5 one-hour sessions. An average 82% reduction in the frequency of urinary accidents was achieved. The sample included one man who experienced stress incontinence following transurethral resection of the prostate.

Two studies investigated the importance of feedback in the treatment of stress incontinence. Shepherd, Montgomery, and Anderson (1983) trained 22 stress-incontinent women aged 23–67 how to voluntarily contract their pelvic floor muscles. One group of patients was trained using a vaginal perineometer similar to Kegel's; the control group was taught without the perineometer.

Ninety-one percent of the biofeedback patients but only 55% of the control patients were cured or improved. Burgio, Robinson, and Engel (1986) treated 24 stress-incontinent women aged 24–64 using simultaneous bladder, sphincter, and abdominal pressure feedback. Results were similar, indicating that feedback improves the patient's ability to learn appropriate pelvic floor contraction and increases the likelihood of successful physiotherapy.

Overflow Incontinence

There is one report of bladder pressure biofeedback used in the treatment of atonic (acontractile) bladder. Schneider (1972) reported the case of a 5-year-old child who had suffered a traumatic spinal cord injury. Two years following the injury, visual feedback of bladder pressure was provided during attempts to elicit and then increase the strength of bladder contractions. The child learned to void and became continent. The usefulness of this procedure for elderly patients with atonic bladder has yet to be investigated.

The use of biofeedback for the treatment of bladder-sphincter dyssynergia involves feedback from the bladder and from the urethral or anal sphincter. Patients are taught to relax the sphincter and pelvic floor while the bladder is contracting in order to allow the bladder to empty fully. Wear, Wear, and Cleeland (1979) used urethral sphincter electromyographic (EMG) feedback to treat dyssynergia with the result that three of the five patients showed moderate to marked improvement. Maizels, King, and Firlit (1979) provided feedback of EMG activity of the external anal sphincter and urine flow rate during attempts to void. Two of three children showed improvement following treatment. Bladder-sphincter dyssynergia is not a common disorder among the elderly, but biofeedback may hold promise for this group of patients as well.

CONCLUSION

Research on the behavioral treatment of urinary incontinence is encouraging, but there are few systematic studies that test these methods in the elderly. Most studies of contingency management have been conducted with psychiatric or mentally retarded patients. Bladder training procedures have been tested primarily with young and middle-aged patients, and most studies of biofeed-back have included few elderly patients. Future research with independent or functionally impaired elderly persons will be helpful in reaching practical solutions to the incontinence problem in this population.

Research on incontinence will also benefit from collaboration between behaviorally trained specialists and the medical community. Geriatricians, gynecologists, and nurses are most familiar with the problems of incontinence and are often eager to form collaborative relationships to solve them.

Although it is clear that more extensive research is needed, enough data exist to justify the application of behavioral methods in clinical practice. Behavioral procedures alone or in conjunction with medical approaches are known to be effective in the treatment of the major types of incontinence.

Currently, biofeedback procedures and other behavioral techniques are not readily available to the vast majority of elderly people. Continence clinics are well established in Great Britain, where nurse continence advisers enjoy professional status. In the United States, however, such clinics are uncommon and exist primarily in research settings; this is because the concept is relatively new and much has yet to be learned about the relative effectiveness of various procedures and patient selection. What is needed now is a transfer of technology from the research setting into clinical practice, especially into nursing practice. Outpatient services, including biofeedback, could be administered by professional nurses trained in these techniques, provided that patients are medically screened and consultative services with behaviorally trained professionals are available.

One setting where such an interdisciplinary service might be offered is in existing behavioral medicine clinics. However, the biofeedback procedures usually require catheterization, a sterile procedure ordinarily performed by a nurse, and many behavioral medicine clinics do not have such service available. A more appropriate setting is the office of a family physician, geriatrician, or gynecologist. Clinics might also be established at health maintenance organizations or hospitals, where nurses are available to perform the catheterization and biofeedback procedures.

Behavioral programs to treat incontinence in the institutionalized elderly will also benefit from interdisciplinary collaboration. Despite the fact that many nurses in these settings have little or no formal training in behavioral principles, they play a critical role in the successful management of incontinent patients.

Treatment of institutionalized patients usually requires environmental control, which includes ongoing staff intervention under nursing supervision. Behavioral procedures are useful, provided they are used appropriately by adequately trained staff. Carefully implemented programs that take into account the physical and mental limitations of nursing-home patients can improve continence skills and preserve the dignity of patients.

Involvement of behavioral specialists as consultants or in teaching roles will promote the appropriate and systematic application of behavioral techniques. Behavioral specialists can enhance their effectiveness in these roles by developing a knowledge of bladder physiology and by obtaining appropriate clinical training in the behavioral treatment of incontinence.

Attitudes toward incontinence may be modified eventually when treatment services are more common and known to be effective. Continence programs established within existing health care systems may not only make current and new interventions available to more elderly patients, but will be evidence to both patients and professionals that incontinence is treatable and not a hopeless consequence of the aging process.

REFERENCES

Azrin, N. H., & Foxx, R. M. (1971). A rapid method of toilet training the institutionalized retarded. *Journal of Applied Behavior Analysis, 4,* 89–99.

Bradley, W. E., Timm, G. W., & Scott, F. B. (1974). Innervation of the detrusor muscle and urethra. In *Symposium on Neurogenic Bladder, Urologic Clinics of North America* (Vol. 1, pp. 3–27). Philadephia: Saunders.

Brocklehurst, J. C., & Dillane, J. B. (1966). Studies of the female bladder in old age: 1. Cystometrograms in non-incontinent women. *Gerontologia Clinica, 8,* 306–319.

Burgio, K. L., Robinson, J. C., & Engel, B. T. (1986). The role of biofeedback in Kegel exercise training for stress urinary incontinence. *American Journal of Obstetrics and Gynecology, 157,* 58–64.

Burgio, K. L., Whitehead, W. E., & Engel, B. T. (1985). Urinary incontinence in the elderly: Bladder-sphincter biofeedback and toileting skills training. *Annals of Internal Medicine, 104,* 507–515.

Cardozo, L. D., Abrams, P. D., Stanton, S. L., & Feneley, R. C. L. (1978). Idiopathic Bladder instability treated by biofeedback. *British Journal of Urology, 50,* 27–30.

Cardozo, L. D., Stanton, S. L., Hafner, J., & Allan V. (1978). Biofeedback in the treatment of detrusor instability. *British Journal of Urology, 50,* 250–254.

Carpenter, H. A., & Simon, R. (1960). Effect of several methods of training on long-term incontinent, behaviorally regressed hospitalized patients. *Nursing Research, 9,* 17–22.

Castleden, C. M., George, C. F., Renwick, A. G., & Asher, M. J. (1981). Imipramine—a possible alternative to current therapy for urinary incontinence in the elderly. *Journal of Urology, 125,* 318–320.

Clay, E. C. (1978). Incontinence of urine: A regime for retraining. *Nursing Mirror, 146,* 23–24.

Clay, E. C. (1980). Promoting urine control in older adults: Habit retraining. *Geriatric Nursing, 1,* 252–254.

Elder, D. D., & Stephenson, T. P. (1980) An assessment of the Frewen regime in the treatment of detrusor dysfunction in females. *British Journal of Urology, 52,* 467–471.

Faber, P., & Heidenreich, J. (1977). Treatment of stress incontinence with estrogens in postmenopausal women. *Urologia Internationalis, 32,* 221–223.

Folstein, M. F., Folstein, S. E., & McHugh, P. R. (1975). "Mini-Mental state": A practical method for grading the cognitive state of patients for the clinician. *Journal of Psychiatric Research, 12,* 189–198.

Frewen, W. K. (1978). An objective assessment of the unstable bladder of psychosomatic origin. *British Journal of Urology, 50,* 246–249.

Frewen, W. K. (1979). Role of bladder training in the treatment of the unstable bladder in the female. *Urologic Clinics of North America, 6,* 273–277.

Frewen, W. K. (1982). A reassessment of bladder training in detrusor dysfunction in the female. *British Journal of Urology, 54,* 372–373.

Frewen, W. K. (1980). The management of urgency and frequency of micturition. *British Journal of Urology, 52,* 367–369.

Grosicki, J. P. (1968). Effect of operant conditioning on modification of in neuropsychiatric geriatric patients. *Nursing Research, 17,* 304–311.

Harman, S. M., & Robinson, J. C. (1982). Common problems in reproductive endocrinology. In L. R. Barker, J. R. Burton, & P. D. Zieve (Eds.), *Principles of ambulatory medicine* (pp. 795–796). Baltimore MD: Williams & Wilkins.

Hilton, P., & Stanton, S. L. (1981). Algorithmic method for assessing urinary incontinence in elderly women. *British Medical Journal, 282,* 940–942.

Hinman, F., Jr. (1979). Urodynamic testing: Alternative to electronics. *Journal of Urology, 121,* 643.

Isaacs, B., & Walkey, F. A. (1964). A survey of incontinence in the elderly. *Gerontologia Clinica, 6,* 367–376.

Jarvis, G. J. (1981). A controlled trial of bladder drill and drug therapy in the management of detrusor instability. *Journal of Urology, 53,* 565–566.

Jarvis, G. J. (1982). The management of urinary incontinence due to primary vesical sensory urgency by bladder drill. *British Journal of Urology, 54,* 374–376.

Jarvis, G. J., & Miller, D. R. (1980). Controlled trial of bladder drill for detrusor instability. *British Medical Journal, 281,* 1322–1323.

Judge, T. G. (1969). The use of quinestradol in elderly incontinent women: Preliminary report. *Gerontologia Clinica, 11,* 159–64.

Katz, G. P., & Blaivas, J. G. (1983). A diagnostic dilemma: When urodynamic findings differ from the clinical impression. *Journal of Urology, 129,* 1170–1174.

Kegel, A. H. (1948). Progressive resistance exercise in the functional restoration of the perineal muscles. *American Journal of Obstetrics and Gynecology, 56,* 238–248.

Kegel, A. H. (1956). Stress incontinence of urine in women: Physiologic treatment. *Journal of the International College of Surgeons, 25,* 487–499.

Maizels, M., King, L. R., & Firlit, C. F. (1979). Urodynamic biofeedback: A new approach to treat vesical sphincter dyssynergia. *Journal of Urology, 122,* 205–209.

Moisey, C. U., Stephenson, T. P., and Brendler, C. B. (1980). The urodynamic and subjective results of treatment of detrusor instability with oxybutynin chloride. *British Journal of Urology, 52,* 472–475.

Ouslander, J. G., & Fowler, E. (1985). Management of urinary incontinence of Veterans Administration homes. *Journal of the American Geriatrics Society, 33,* 33–40.

Ouslander, J. G., & Kane, R. L. (1984). The costs of urinary incontinence in nursing homes. *Medical Care, 22,* 69–79.

Ouslander, J. G., Kane, R. L., & Abrass, I. B. (1982). Urinary incontinence in elderly nursing home patients. *Journal of the American Medical Association, 248,* 1194–1198.

Pengelly, A. W., & Booth, C. M. (1980). A prospective trial of bladder training as treatment for detrusor instability. *British Journal of Urology, 52,* 463–466.

Pfeiffer, E. (1976). A Short Portable Mental Status Questionnaire for the assessment of organic brain deficit in elderly patients. *Journal of the American Geriatrics Society, 23,* 433–437.

Pollock, D. D., & Liberman, R. P. (1974). Behavior therapy of incontinence in demented inpatients. *Gerontologist, 14,* 488–491.

Radloff, L. S. (1977). The CES-D scale: A self-report depression scale for research in the general population. *Applied Psychological Measurement, 1,* 385.

Ribeiro, J., & Smith, S. R. (1985). Evaluation of urinary catheterization and urinary incontinence in a general nursing home population. *Journal of the American Geriatrics Society, 33,* 479–482.

Sanavio, E. (1981). Toilet training psychogeriatric residents. *Behavior Modification, 5,* 417–427.

Schneider, R. D. (1972). Adjuvant bladder-pressure biofeedback in treating neurogenic bladder dysfunction: A case report. *Behavior Therapist, 2,* 29.

Schnelle, J. F., Traughber, B., Morgan, D. B., Embry, J. E., Binion, A. F., & Coleman, A. (1983). Management of geriatric incontinence in nursing homes. *Journal of Applied Behavior Analysis, 16,* 235–241.

Shepherd, A. M., Montgomery, E., & Anderson, R. S.

(1983). Treatment of genuine stress incontinence with a new perineometer. *Physiotherapy, 69,* 113.

Smith, P. S., Britton, P. G., Johnson, M., & Thomas, D. A. (1975). Problems involved in toilet-training profoundly mentally handicapped adults. *Behavior Research and Therapy, 13,* 301–307.

Sogbein, S. K., & Awad, S. A. (1982). Behavioral treatment of urinary incontinence in geriatric patients. *Canadian Medical Association Journal, 127,* 863–864.

Svigos, J. M., & Matthews, C. D. (1977). Assessment and treatment of female urinary incontinence by cystometrogram and bladder retraining programs. *Obstetrics and Gynecology, 50,* 9–12.

Thomas, T. M., Plymat, F. R., Blannin, J., & Meade, T. W. (1980). Prevalence of urinary incontinence. *British Medical Journal 281,* 1243–1245.

Van Nostrand, J. F., Zappolo, A., Hing, E., et al. (1979). The national nursing home survey: 1977 summary for the United States. National Center for Health Statistics, Vital and Health Statistics Series 13, # 43. Department of Health, Education, and Welfare Publications No. (PHS) 79–1794.

Vetter, N. J., Jones, D. A., & Victor, C. R. (1981). Urinary incontinence in the elderly at home. *Lancet, ii,* 1275–1277.

Wagner, B. R., & Paul, G. L. (1970). Reduction of incontinence in chronic mental patients: A pilot project. *Journal of Behavior Therapy and Experimental Psychiatry, 1,* 29–38.

Walter, S., Wolf, H., Barlebo, H., & Jenson, H. K. (1978). Urinary incontinence in postmenopausal women treated with estrogens. *Urologia Internationalis, 33,* 135–43.

Wear, J. B., Jr., Wear, R. B., & Cleeland, C. (1979). Biofeedback in urology using urodynamics: Preliminary observations. *Journal of Urology, 121,* 464–468.

Whitehead, W. E., Burgio, K. L., & Engel, B. T. (1984). Behavioral methods in the assessment and treatment of urinary incontinence. In J. C. Brocklehurst (Ed.), *Urology in the elderly.* New York: Churchill Livingstone.

Willington, F. L. (1980). Urinary incontinence: A practical approach. *Geriatrics, 35,* 41–48.

Wilson, T. S. (1948). Incontinence of urine in the aged. *Lancet, ii,* 374–377.

Wolin, L. H. (1969). Stress incontinence in young, healthy nulliparous female subjects. *Journal of Urology, 101,* 545–549.

Yarnell, J. W. G., & St. Legar, A. S. (1979). The prevalence, severity, and factors associated with urinary incontinence in a random sample of the elderly. *Age and Ageing, 8,* 81–85.

Chapter 20

Family Management of the Elderly

Roger Patterson

Recent research in social gerontology has confirmed that most elderly people in the United States today remain firmly embedded in family systems (Shanas, 1961, 1979; Shanas, Townsend, Wedderburn, Milhoi, & Stohower, 1968; Quinn & Hughston, 1984). Furthermore, family relationships are very important to both the older and younger members. These relationships usually remain intact, even when there are differences between the generations in location and other social parameters (Troll, Miller, & Atchley, 1979). In any event, most elderly individuals do live in close physical proximity to their children and other relatives (Shanas, 1961, 1979).

When elderly people are no longer able to function independently as a result of physical, mental, financial, or other deficits, it is most often family members who seek to assist them (Shanas, 1961, 1979; Quinn, Hughston, & Hubler, 1984). Such aid is often vital and very helpful.

Families have undoubtedly been assisting their needy elders for thousands of years. In recent years, however, the development of systematic empirically based principles and methodology for behavioral change have aided family interventions directed at such problems as child rearing and marital difficulties; and these offer promise for families with impaired elders. Unfortunately, the potential of the application of behavioral psychology to the family management of the problems of the elderly has been recognized only quite recently. Thus,

Haley (1983) has reported that he could not find a single published study on training family members to use behavior modification techniques with impaired elderly members. To this author's knowledge, Haley's report, a book on family care of the elderly by Pinkston and Linsk (1984), some appendices in a book by Hussian and Davis (1985), and the works of Zarit and Zarit (1983, 1984) are the first widely read publications devoted specifically to this subject.

In contrast, there have been a number of publications reporting considerable success in teaching family members to help alleviate child-related family problems (e.g., O'Dell, 1974). One reason for this lack of interest in training family members of impaired elderly has probably been the belief that the problems of the elderly are often incurable and even untreatable. As noted by Pfeiffer (1982), "That older patients can be successfully treated has only recently been recognized by professionals and by older persons themselves. That older persons can also be *taught* new skills or retaught previously existing skills constitutes even newer knowledge" (p. v).

The evidence that behavioral techniques do indeed work with the impaired elderly has come largely from institutional settings (Hussian, 1981; Patterson & Jackson, 1980; Patterson et al., 1982) and from formal day treatment settings (Dupree, Broskowski, & Schonfeld, 1984; Patterson et al., 1982). Yet there is no apparent reason that similar behavioral methods designed specifically for use in the home should not be successful in overcoming many problems relating to the elderly.

A number of general issues pertaining to the application of behavioral techniques by families and by the elderly themselves will be discussed first. Then, ways of rendering the home environment more globally supportive of adaptive behavior will be considered, followed by assessments of several key variables. Finally, the application of behavioral methods to more specific problems will be described.

GENERAL ISSUES

Many behavioral practitioners have been trained to work with parents on solving child-rearing problems. As noted by Pinkston and Linsk (1984), this training and the literature describing it can be applied in working with the families of impaired elderly. However, there are some vital differences in dealing with the elderly population.

A major issue is the attitudes of the practitioner, the family, the elderly individual, and other professionals regarding the behavioral management of family problems related to the elderly. Practitioners must make sure that their approach is viewed as that of assisting a *family* rather than of "managing" a problem-producing elder. The targeted elder is an important family member. Not many of us would like to think of ourselves as "managing" our parents, and resentment may be generated if the situation is approached in this way. The treatment goals should be agreeable to *all* concerned. Each person should see the planned outcome of the behavioral treatment as desirable.

A second important issue is related to the physical health of the elder. Older people, especially impaired individuals, often suffer chronic illnesses, and it is easy to look solely to medical care as the solution to all problems. Behavioral practitioners may find themselves faced with a referral problem whose solution entails behavior modification; however, the family may be so focused on the diagnosed chronic illness that they fail to see the potential benefit of behavioral intervention. Perhaps the ultimate tragedy of such a view occurs when an elder is sent to a nursing home—not because of a health problem necessitating nursing care but because of a behavioral problem that could have been managed by the family had they had appropriate training.

Many practical, legal, and ethical issues arise regarding who can provide assistance and what kind. The impaired elderly may live in their own homes, apart from potential caregivers. By late life, many people have accumulated a substantial amount of property, including many tangible possessions. The retention of such property can become a' major source of distress for the family, both in terms of practical issues such as caretaking and storage and in regard to the more emotion-laden issues of inheritance. Except for those few declared legally incompetent or who give power of attorney to others, older persons have legal control of their own property and affairs. The social roles of the various family members are usually well-defined but differ among families with regard to blood ties, ethnic and family customs, and personal histories. The physical strength and health status of the various family members also differ, as do time constraints and the willingness to help. Sometimes, even friends may express a desire to assist. These and other factors can make it difficult to ascertain who can and is willing to assume the role of caregiver and to what extent the prospective caregiver can influence the impaired individual and his or her environment.

A somewhat related issue is that of *control* over the person and their environment. According to Tjosvold and Tjosvold (1983), problems related to control in institutions may result in debilitating conflicts between staff and residents. For example, the staff may come to assume that, regardless of a resident's abilities, they are in complete charge and thus must regulate all aspects of the resident's everyday life. Not only does such an assumption tend to extinguish independent behavior on the part of the elderly (see chapter 16, this volume), but it also places a large and unnecessary burden on the staff. Clearly, similar problems may arise when family caregivers seek to influence an impaired elder member. They can, however, be avoided, by establishing a *collaborative* relationship between the caregiver and the elder (Tjosvold & Tjosvold, 1983). Within the family, the practitioner and the caregiver(s) should seek to assist the elders to regain and/or maintain personal control over their own environment and affairs, to the greatest extent possible. The role of the practitioner is *not* to maximize the control of the caregivers over the elders and their environment. Indeed, Rodin and Langer (1977) have found that restoring control over some aspects of the environment to elderly people, especially aspects that have been controlled almost completely by others, may in itself have important therapeutic effects.

Thus, the practitioner who is involved in assisting in the family management of the impaired elderly is one party of a three-party arrangement whose goal is to maximize the ability of the target person to remain as independent as his or her physical and mental condition will permit.

ENVIRONMENTAL SUPPORTS

One of the factors often discussed as crucial, for helping the elderly remain as independent as possible in the community, is the provision of supports. Unfortunately, the term *supports* is one that has become so ubiquitous in various uses, including discussion of the needs of the elderly, that it has lost much of its meaning. Indeed, it is often used without definition, apparently under the assumption that others will know what a particular user means. Perhaps the more common use of the term is to refer to elements of the environment that exist *in addition* to the usual environment and serve to enable an otherwise disabled elderly person to remain in his or her home and/community.

In this chapter, the term *environmental supports* will be used both with a more specific and a more broadly applicable meaning. As per Jenkins and his associates (Jenkins, 1977; Pascal & Jenkins, 1961; Witherspoon, de Valera, Jenkins, & Sanford, 1973), it will be used here to refer to *all* aspects of the environment, not just extra elements, that serve to prompt, reinforce, and otherwise maintain socially acceptable and effective social, self-care, and leisure activities. This definition will include the production and maintenance of positive attributions to oneself and one's life. The crucial implication of such a broadened definition is that it immediately leads one to examine many aspects of an elder's life to determine if proper supports are present. This definition also makes it possible to examine the quality of social relationships in order to determine which are supportive and which are not. For example, some have considered the relationship between an adult son or daughter and an elderly parent supportive if contact was sufficiently frequent and/or if some service was being supplied by the adult child. However, it may be easily seen that, in some cases, the son or daughter may be reinforcing dependence or even depression. For example, a daughter may give her father attention only when

he is manifesting helpless behavior or a son may only talk to his mother when she is expressing sadness about the loss of her husband or job. These interactions may not be supportive because they may foster undesirable "depressed" behavior rather than desirable coping behavior, especially when carried out over a period of months or years.

In caring for the elderly individual, the family should focus its efforts on maintaining a highly supportive environment. An environment that is structured to provide the necessary prompts, reinforcers, and materials to the individual for adequate and satisfying social, self-care, and leisure behavior serves to both prevent the occurrence of many problems of the aged and to remedy existing problems.

Among the factors that are important in a supportive environment are, (a) intimate personal relationships, (b) casual social relationships, (c) home, (d) income, (e) mobility, and (f) hobbies or some personal activity or activities which may involve others minimally or not at all, but that are a source of pride and satisfaction (Witherspoon et al., 1973).

Intimate Personal Relationships

Intimate personal relationships are those that endure, include affection, and involve the exchange of intimate information and material help. These are the highly desirable relationships most commonly found between family members. Obviously, a spouse (or spouse substitute), children, grandchildren, and siblings are most likely to fill these roles for an elderly person. As previously mentioned, some families may attend to the elder only when there is a problem. But in order to be supportive, a relationship must also include attendance to the elder's adaptive, prosocial, and enjoyable experiences. Families should involve the elder in pleasurable family activities and events as much as possible.

Spouse or spouse substitutes as supports deserve special attention. This is a type of intimate relationship that, apart from sexual functioning, may provide supports not encountered in any other relationship. It is this clinician's observation that a relationship between an elder and a compatible opposite-sex partner often produce a variety of very positive social and self-care behavior. In addition, elders so involved often report greater satisfaction about themselves and their lives. This may be especially noticeable in those who have lost a partner and then gained a new one. (The case of Mr. O, discussed later in this chapter, is partially illustrative of this point.)

Families may have difficulty in accepting the fact that their elders could want and benefit from a relationship with an opposite-sex partner. The traditional view is that older widowed, divorced, or never-married persons no longer desire such involvements. The elderly themselves may share this belief. Although it is true that some people make a conscious choice to avoid opposite-sex relationships, it is important that the elderly and their families recognize that age alone is not sufficient reasons for such a choice.

Casual Social Relationships

Neighbors, the ladies at the club, and the men who play dominoes every week are examples of casual relationships. One physically ill, somewhat depressed eldely woman interviewed by the author (Dupree & Patterson, 1985) illustrates this point. She was largely confined to an apartment complex to which she had recently moved because of illness and economic reasons. Although she knew no one there, she quickly discovered that women her age gathered in the laundry room, played cards, and chatted almost every day. She began to join them, and this support seemed to be important to her, helping her maintain her social behavior and her view of herself as a socially desirable person. An important point here is that casual social relationships may serve purposes different from more intimate relations, but both types of interactions are important. Families should recognize that they alone may not be able to fulfill all of an elder's needs for social contacts. If possible, they should encourage the elder to seek a variety of casual relationships. (See the case of Mr. O discussed later in this chapter.)

Home

The home environment serves a utilitarian purpose. To be properly supportive, it should also be a source of pride and enjoyment. The utilitarian purpose is largely met if the person can take care of his or her daily needs and wants within the home. Impaired elderly people are often rather ingenious in modifying their homes to meet their needs. Lawton (1984) described how disabled elderly often establish a "control center" in the home. These people locate most of the objects they use regularly within easy reach of a favorite chair, where they spend much of their day. The most crucial features of a utilitarian environment are that everything needed is easily reached or controlled and that there are necessary prompts (e.g., clocks, check-off lists) to remind the forgetful of tasks that must be done regularly, such as taking medicine.

Pride and enjoyment in the home, in behavioral terms, mean that the person can tell you things they enjoy about their home and things they enjoy doing there. In addition, pride is evidenced by attempts to maintain the appearance of the home by gardening, decorating, displaying prized objects, inviting people there, etc.

It follows, then, that families may make the home more supportive by encouraging the elder in every way to participate in decorating and maintaining the home, both to satisfy utilitarian and emotional needs. Obviously, there may be, and probably frequently are, conflicts between the elders and family members over decor and the location of various objects. Such conflicts often arise when elders move into the homes of other, particularly younger, relatives. They will most likely have their collection of favorite items of decor and furniture. They may require certain arrangements to meet practical needs. They may like to crochet doilies, carve owls, or make other ornaments. They may prefer certain colors. Any or all of these may conflict with the tastes of other family members. It is very important that the family recognize the *function* of the elder's participation in the decoration and maintenance of the home. The elderly are not just being stubborn, disagreeable, or old-fashioned if they wish to perform these activities. Instead, it is *necessary* for them to participate in this way if the home is to be supportive. Many families living in the house with an elder with different tastes and physical needs compromise by setting aside space that the elder can decorate and partially maintain according to his or her wishes.

Income

Income as a source of support seems largely self-explanatory; however, some people make the mistake of considering only necessities when calculating the desirable income of an elderly person. If the income is truly supportive, it will include money for discretionary spending on items other than necessities. The ability to purchase minor luxuries and occasional small gifts for others may be supportive to an extent that far outweighs its monetary value. Families may be counseled regarding the importance of supplying discretionary funds if possible and needed.

Mobility

Old people often have various difficulties in getting where they need to go within the home, the neighborhood, and elsewhere. Such difficulties may be due to sensory losses, a variety of medical problems, cognitive losses, economics, or a combination of these. As an obvious outcome, it is difficult for the elderly to meet physical and social needs. The major behavioral effect may be the extinction of many social and self-care behaviors. Elders with such problems may also come to view themselves and their lives negatively.

Families and others may often recognize the problems of the elders in meeting physical needs (buying groceries, going to doctors), but the undesirable psychological effects of the loss of mobility may often not be recognized or alleviated. Perhaps family members provide the obviously necessary transportation themselves or may assist the elder in obtaining prosthetic devices, such as walkers, wheelchairs, and glasses. Although such efforts are certainly useful and even necessary, the importance of other aspects of mobility, which maintain habitual behaviors and provide emotional support should also be recognized.

In order to be maximally supportive, assistance with mobility must be responsive and flexible, often necessitating the availability of more than one system. If independent and social behavior is not to be extinguished, such assistance must also be relatively *easy* not only for the elder to take care of his or her needs but also to maintain social contacts. Many elders will greatly curtail many desirable activities if they are forced to ask for favors, or if transportation is difficult to obtain.

For maximum flexibility and availability, it is important that elders be informed of all the transportation options available to them. Many elders who previously drove everywhere may feel helpless if they can no longer do so. However, many people are not aware that their communities offer van services to doctor's offices, senior citizens' centers, and other places. Some are confused by the various bus routes a city may offer. Elders not accustomed to using all these sources of transportation may need to be *taught*, not merely told, how to get where they need to go. Families may be instructed

as to how they can help the elders obtain suitable transportation. For example, they may provide the elders with the phone numbers of various transportation sources. In many cases, family members should accompany elders on public transportation until the elders demonstrate that they are knowledgeable and confident.

Hobbies

Some hobbies, such as dancing and bowling, may involve interaction with others, but the primary purpose of hobbies in general is not social activity. Indeed, it is important for older people to have enjoyable activities that they can do alone, because other people are not always available. Many very cherished and useful hobbies, such as coin collecting, needlework, and gardening, are primarily solitary. The reinforcer for these activities seems to be accomplishment (e.g., completing a set of coins, growing a new blossom) and, perhaps, its recognition by others. Such activities are undoubtedly supportive in that they provide a variety of prompts and reinforcers for realistic, organized, and purposeful activity. They also provide an opportunity for people to positively evaluate themselves and their lives.

ASSESSMENTS

The previous discussion about environmental supports leads naturally to a discussion of how to assess them. There are also other assessment-related issues that need to be considered before it is possible to develop an adequate treatment plan for the family. These include targeting the behavior of the elder, determining the relative burden caused by various problem behaviors, assessing the relative strengths and weaknesses of caregivers, and determining relevant antecedents and consequences of behaviors that might be altered.

Although it would be useful to observe the interaction of the elder with all the sources of support previously mentioned, this would obviously be a prohibitive task. A good alternative, one that has been insufficiently used in behavioral psychology, is the Behavioral Incident (BI) interviewing technique (Pascal & Jenkins, 1961; Witherspoon et al., 1973). In this technique, interviewees are asked to describe in detail their behavior and that of other relevant persons with regard to sources of support. For example, to determine if a relationship between a mother and daughter was supportive of adaptive behavior, the mother would be asked when she last saw and/or spoke with her daughter and what they said to each other or did together. Such an interview could be conducted with both parties and, if possible, could be supplemented by actual observations. Similarly, one could ask elders what they recently did with their friends, what hobbies they had, what they did to indicate pride in and control of their home, and how they were able to travel to places they needed and wanted to go.

Again, the emphasis is on detailed descriptions of the behaviors of all parties concerned. It is likely that most people will tend to give opinions, and to speak in generalities rather than to describe actual behavior. It is the interviewer's task to avoid such undesirable responses by carefully structuring the interview so that the desired behavioral descriptions are given. Such descriptions may be highly reliable (Witherspoon et al., 1973).

The author's experience is that the great majority of elders, excluding those who are seriously demented, can provide good descriptions of their support system in this way. Even if they cannot, relatives and friends can supply such information. (See Dupree & Patterson, 1985, for an example and more information regarding the use of this technique with the elderly.)

For assessing caregivers and their capabilities, Pinkston and Linsk (1984) include as part of their system the Caregiver Checklist, consisting of 20 items pertaining to the strengths and weaknesses of prospective caregivers. Included are such factors as the physical and mental health of the caregivers, the time they have spent with the elder, the degree of control they may have, their attitude toward the elder's behavior, and the kinds of help other people may provide.

The importance of measuring the relative burden imposed upon a caregiver by an impaired elder's behavior has been noted by the Zarits and their associates (Zarit, 1982; Zarit, Reever, & Bach-Peterson, 1981; Zarit & Zarit, 1983). They point out that not every caregiver responds to the same problem in the same way. Some may consider something as serious as incontinence to be less of a problem than, for example, excessive restlessness. The important point is that in developing management programs, the practitioner must take into account which behaviors are most bothersome both to the elder and the caregiver. Zarit et al. (1981) have developed the Memory and Behavior

Problems Checklist to be completed by the caregiver, which includes a measure of relative burden caused by behavior problems, as well as a list of specific target behaviors and estimates of the frequency of their occurrence. This checklist was developed specifically for use by the caregivers of dementia patients, but may be useful to others.

Several assessments have been used to target both the behavioral problems of the elder and the environmental events preceding and following them. Patterson et al. (1982) described a Behavior Analysis Form (BAF) useful for this purpose. The BAF was divided into three columns: "Antecedents," "Behavior," and "Consequences." Within the columns were prompts for observers to provide such information as place, time, who was in the area, how long the behavior lasted, and what kinds of interpersonal interactions occurred. Thus, a number of completed BAFs provided information on the frequency, duration, and type of behaviors, as well as descriptions of antecedent and consequent interpersonal and other events. Pinkston and Linsk (1984) proposed the Anecdotal Record, which provides similar information, as well as the Interview Guide, used to assess problem behavior. The latter consisted of five major topics about which family members were questioned. The questions were designed to help family describe the behavior along with the antecedents and consequences, the desired changes in behavior, and general concerns, as well as the strengths and weaknesses of the elder. Other examples of data forms used by Pinkston, Linsk, and their associates include the Daily Activity Record, designed to record specific activities in which the elder engaged at specified times, and the Family Behavior Record. The latter requires the family to note when during the day a specified behavior occurred, what preceded the behavior, and the responses made by the family after the behavior occurred.

In addition to these specific observation and interview forms, Pinkston and Linsk (1984) described two comprehensive major questionnaires, administered before and after treatment to determine the ability and disability of the elders in major areas of their lives. One questionnaire was for the targeted elder, and the other for relatives. They included measures of personality, mental status, hearing, social resources, economic resources, mental health, activities of daily living, physical health, social activities, and caregiving received, as well as four target behaviors. Patterson and Moon (1985) described a system of determining similar variables.

INTERVENTIONS IN INDIVIDUAL CASES

In considering interventions to be applied by families of the elderly, the point should be made that there are probably no behavioral problems which are unique to this population. Similarly, it is likely that the general types of intervention will be the same for this group as for any other. However, there are accepted categories of problem behaviors of the elderly that are based on reviews of the relevant literature. For example, Patterson and Jackson (1980) grouped studies of behavior modification research on the elderly into the following categories: skills in daily living, social and leisure participation, social skills, and intellectual tasks. More recently, Pinkston and Linsk (1984) classified problem behaviors of older persons into these categories: self-care, negative activities and verbalizations, positive behaviors, and social contacts. (The reader should also note the types of behavior discussed in chapters 14 and 16 of this book.)

Behavior therapists working with elders and their families should be prepared to draw upon the full range of available techniques. Skills training of the family, the elder, or both may be required. Elders may benefit from learning social and self-care skills from professionals and trained paraprofessionals (Patterson et al., 1982) and families may learn to maintain them. Families may be taught the methods of applied behavior analysis in order to act as behavioral-change agents (Pinkston & Linsk, 1984). Therapists may establish behavioral regimens in the home to manage troublesome idiosyncratic behaviors, which the families can then maintain with minimal assistance (Haley, 1983).

The essentials of any behavioral management program are that (a) the desired behaviors are well identified, (b) the approaches to altering these behaviors are defined, and (c) there is empirical confirmation of the effectiveness of the approaches used.

Three cases will now be presented that illustrate some ways in which the author and his associates have used behavioral techniques to assist elders and their concerned families. The cases were selected because they represent problems found frequently among impaired elders living with their families.

The Case of Mr. O

This case illustrates the loss of environmental supports as a result of the death of a spouse and subsequent physical relocation to another state. The central problem was that neither the client nor his family seemed to know what they *should* expect to replace the lost supports, nor have any idea how to go about it. Intervention consisted of verbal prompts provided by the therapist to the client and his family, via appropriate information and suggestions. The therapist also supplied social reinforcement (approval) to the client and his family for desired accomplishments.

Mr. O was a 75-year-old widower who had moved south from a northern state to live with his son, daughter-in-law, and grandson after the death of his wife. Mr. O had become severely depressed after the death of his wife and had attempted suicide several times before relocation. Although it had been about a year since his wife's death, and he had received psychiatric treatment, Mr. O remained moderately depressed. He was referred for individual therapy from a day treatment program he was attending at that time because the program had not been sufficient to alleviate his depression.

An examination of Mr. O's environmental support system revealed that both Mr. O and his son were financially comfortable. Mr. O had his own spacious room in the son's home. Furthermore, Mr. O was in good health and owned a late-model automobile that he was quite capable of driving wherever he wished.

Interactions with the family were supportive to the extent that Mr. O was included in all family activities and was encouraged to be active in the home. Nevertheless, the son was deeply concerned because his father remained depressed despite all efforts on his part.

In spite of these good supports, it was apparent that there were deficits in environmental supports that were especially significant in Mr. O's case, namely lack of hobbies, leisure activities, friends, and a relationship with a woman. Mr. O and his late wife had been very active in their church, particularly with music. Activities with friends also involved his late wife. These social supports had been missing since her death. In addition, Mr. O, a baseball fan, had been involved with the Little League; but he had not resumed these activities either after the death of his wife.

Interestingly, Mr. O did not appear to be grieving intensely over the death but had come to a reasonable acceptance of it. Indeed, he confided to the therapist that a middle-aged woman had shown interest in him recently, and he had wanted to respond positively but thought that "at his age" he should not be socially involved with a woman.

Mr. O and his son's family were informed that he would probably benefit from the rebuilding of a relatively *independent* social life and that he was capable of doing it. The following suggestions were made and agreed upon: (a) Mr. O would not just attend church with the family but would volunteer some service with the choir; (b) He would drive his grandson to Little League practice and stay to watch, offering to assist the coach if he felt so inclined, and (c) It would be quite acceptable if he attended social activities with a female companion.

Over the next few weeks, Mr. O took over the daughter-in-law's "chore" of driving his grandson to ball practice and began to assist the coach. He began playing piano regularly for choir practice. Furthermore, he began driving one of the widowed female choir members to practice and attended several social events with her.

The family reported great relief at Mr. O's resurrected independence. He reported feeling much happier and more useful, no longer a burden to his family. He accounted for his depression by explaining that he and his late wife had had a long and happy marriage, and after her death, it had not occurred to him that he could resume many of his previous activities. The reality of finality of the loss of his active social life seemed to be confirmed not only by the loss of his wife, but also by the move to his son's home, far removed from everything and everyone he knew. In addition, in his view the move had been for the purpose of being "taken care of" by his son in his old age, rather than to resume a normal social life.

The Case of Mr. Z

This case illustrates emotional and practical problems related to a relatively minor memory loss, and how family intervention was able to alleviate many of them. The therapists taught a family member to apply appropriate prompts on a relatively permanent basis in order to compensate for the memory loss.

Mr. Z was a 69-year-old man who was referred by his sister because he had secluded himself in his apartment and was failing to pay his bills or to go out to buy necessities. His sister, who lived just down the street, described his behavior as being very suspicious and withdrawn.

Mr. Z was a retired automobile assembly-line worker. He had never married and had lived in a rooming house with his older brother throughout his work career. The older brother had died several years before. Mr. Z had a comfortable retirement income by his standards and had managed to accumulate large savings because of frugal living habits. Mr. Z retired at the age of 65 and relocated near his sister and her family in Florida. The sister said that up until the last few months her brother had seemed to enjoy his retirement and had socialized quite freely with her family and others. The suspicion and withdrawal were uncharacteristic of him. A thorough physical examination showed that he was in good health.

When interviewed, Mr. Z appeared very anxious and depressed. He expressed much concern about his finances, explaining that he didn't trust the banks and wasn't sure what they were doing with his money. After some persuasion, he gave a social worker permission to investigate his finances. With the help of his sister, the social worker discovered that Mr. Z had good hospital insurance, a good income, and savings in several different banks. In reality, he had no financial difficulties.

Based upon this information, the social worker and the sister gathered the bankbooks and bills to show Mr. Z that his financial situation was secure. He seemed to accept the information with satisfaction. However, within a few days, Mr. Z was again acting withdrawn and depressed. When spoken to, he was once more expressing confusion and concern about his finances. Repeated explanations about his finances on several occasions produced only temporary results.

Psychological testing revealed that Mr. Z had developed some considerable deficits in his ability to assimilate new information, particularly with regard to numbers and arithmetic. Based upon this information, the social worker was able to devise a pocket notebook for Mr. Z to carry at all times that showed his bank balances in large bold figures. These balances were stated very simply. The sister agreed to see that they were kept current and to remind Mr. Z to review his notebook anytime he became concerned. She also agreed to help him to pay his bills.

This system greatly alleviated Mr. Z's anxiety and depression. As a result, he began to socialize freely once more. Mr. Z said that he had previously felt completely overwhelmed by his different bank accounts and bills, but now, with his sister's help, he was no longer greatly concerned.

It was felt by the therapist that Mr. Z's recently developed cognitive deficits might possibly indicate developing dementia. The sister was advised to observe him closely and to contact the therapist and the physician if further changes were noted.

The Case of Mrs. J

This case illustrates problems related to a real permanent disability, as well as to deficits in social skills. Intervention included professional assessment and retraining of the patient's social and physical skills, suggestions to the family of ways to assist her, and arrangement of a contractlike agreement between the family and the patient.

Mrs. J was a 71-year-old lower-class widow with little formal education. She had lived with her son, his wife, and their small children until recently, when she had been admitted to a psychiatric unit because of increasingly frequent angry outbursts and threats directed at the daughter-in-law. During these outbursts, she spoke of voodoo and used foul language. A physical examination found that Mrs. J was in good physical condition, despite the fact that one arm had been amputated below the elbow several years before.

Conversations with the son and his wife revealed that they wished Mrs. J would return to live with them, but only if the outbursts were eliminated. Mrs. J served a purpose useful to the family: She often watched the children while the mother and father worked. Mrs. J also expressed a desire to return to her son's home, but only if her daughter-in-law would stop criticizing and bossing her around. Thus, there existed apt material for a contract agreement.

Assessments of Mrs. J while she was in residential treatment revealed two primary problems. Her eating habits were somewhat disgusting to others, primarily because she had the use of only one arm: she would pile items on a piece of bread, pick it up, and bite into it, or would simply pick up large items and bite into them. She was also deficient in social skills. She was unable to ask for assistance in a polite manner, nor did she ever express gratitude for assistance. Moreover, she was unable to express dislike for anything in a socially acceptable way.

Mrs. J was provided training in more acceptable eating habits, although she would always require assistance with cutting food. She was also provided social skills training to teach her to express her wishes in acceptable ways and to express gratitude. These new skills were then demonstrated to the son and his wife. They in turn were taught how to assist her in eating, and how to respond to her and reinforce her appropriate requests. The agreement was then made that Mrs. J would return home, with the provision that the family would assist her with eating and other difficulties she might experience because of her handicap, while she would request assistance without angry outbursts and talk of voodoo. Mrs. J also agreed to resume babysitting duties, which she seemed to enjoy and which the family needed. Follow-up revealed that this arrangement was working well.

CONCLUSION

It is the author's belief that widespread, appropriate, and ethical application of behavioral approaches, to solve the variety of problems faced by the elderly and their families could be of enormous economic and humanitarian benefit. This chapter and the work of others indicate that many families wth elderly members could be helped by behavior therapists to better serve the needs of the elder members.

REFERENCES

Dupree, L. W., Broskowski, H., & Schonfeld, L. (1984). The gerontology alcohol project: A behavioral treatment program for elderly alcohol abusers. *Gerontologist, 24*, 510–516.

Dupree, L. W., & Patterson, R. L. (1985). The elderly. In M. Hersen & S. Turner (Eds.), *Diagnostic interviewing* (pp. 337–359). New York: Plenum.

Haley, W. E. (1983). A family-behavioral approach to the treatment of the cognitively impaired elderly. *Gerontologist, 23*, 18–20.

Hussian, R. A. (1981). *Geriatric psychology: A behavioral perspective*. New York: Van Nostrand Reinhold.

Hussian, R. A., & Davis, R. L. (1985). *Responsive care*. Champaign, IL: Research Press.

Jenkins, W. O. (1977). *An innovative approach to the analysis and alteration of human behavior. Behavior evaluation, treatment, and analysis (Beta)*. Montgomery, AL: Beta Systems.

Lawton, M. P. (1984, November). *Environmental design as a compensation for loss*. Paper presented at the 18th Annual Convention of the Association for the Advancement of Behavior Therapy, Philadelphia.

O'Dell, S. (1974). Training approach in behavior modification. *Psychological Bulletin, 81*, 418–433.

Pascal, G., & Jenkins, W. O. (1961). *Systematic observation of gross human behavior*. New York: Grune & Stratton.

Patterson, R. L., Dupree, L. W., Eberly, D. A., Jackson, G. M., O'Sullivan, M. J., Penner, L. A., & Dee-Kelley, C. (1982). *Overcoming deficits of aging: A behavioral approach*. New York: Plenum.

Patterson, R. L., & Jackson, G. M. (1980). Behavior modification with the elderly. In M. Herson, R. M. Eisler, and P. Miller (Eds.), *Progress in behavior modification* (Vol. 9), New York: Academic.

Patterson, R. L., & Moon, J. (1985). Special problems in assessment and treatment of the elderly. In M. Hersen & A. Bellak (Eds.), *Handbook of clinical behavior therapy with adults*. New York: Plenum.

Pinkston, E. M., & Linsk, N. L. (1984). *Care of the elderly: A family approach*. Elmsford, NY: Pergamon.

Pfeiffer, E. (1982). Foreword. In R. L. Patterson, D. A. Everly, G. M. Jackson, M. J. O'Sullivan, L. A. Penner, & C. Dee-Kelley (Eds.), *Overcoming deficits of aging: A behavioral approach*. New York: Plenum.

Quinn, W. H., & Hughston, G. A. (1984). *Independent aging: Family and systems perspectives*. Rockville, MD: Aspen.

Quinn, W. H., Hughston, G. A., & Hubler, D. J. (1984). Preservation of independence through non-formal support systems: Implications and promise. In: Quinn W. H. & Hughston, G. A. (Eds.), *Independent aging: Family and systems perspectives*. Rockville, MD: Aspen.

Rodin, J. & Langer, E. (1977). Long-term effects of a control-relevant intervention with institutionalized aged. *Journal of Personality and Social Psychology, 35*, 897–902.

Shanas, E. (1961). *Family relationships of old people*. Chicago: Health Information Foundation.

Shanas, E. (1979). Social myth as hypothesis: The case of the family relations of older people. *Gerontologist, 19*, 3–9.

Shanas, E., Townsend, P., Wedderburn, D., Milhoi, P., & Stohower, J. (1968). *Old people in three industrial societies*. New York: Atherton Press.

Tjosvold, D., & Tjosvold, M. M. (1983). *Working with the elderly in their residences*. New York: Praeger.

Troll, L. E., Miller, S. J., & Atchley, R. C. (1979). *Families in later life*. Belmont, CA: Wadsworth.

Witherspoon, A. D., de Valera, E. K., Jenkins, W. O., & Sanford, W. L. (1973). *Behavioral interview guide*. Montgomery, AL: Beta Systems.

Zarit, J. (1982). *Predictors of burden and distress for caregivers of senile dementia patients*. Unpublished doctoral dissertation, University of Southern California, Los Angeles.

Zarit, S. H., Reever, K. E., & Bach-Peterson, J. (1981). Relatives of the impaired elderly. Correlates of feelings of burden. *Gerontologist, 21*, 158–164.

Zarit, S. H., & Zarit, J. M. (1983). Cognitive impairment of older persons: Etiology, evaluation, and intervention. In P. M. Lewinsohn & L. Teri (Ed.), *Coping and adaptation in the elderly*. Elmsford, NY: Pergamon.

Zarit, S. H., & Zarit, J. M. (1984, November). *Behavioral interventions with caregivers of dementia patients*. Paper presented at the 18th Annual Convention of the Association for the Advancement of Behavior Therapy, Philadelphia.

Chapter 21

Cognitive, Behavioral and Psychosocial Sequelae of Cerebrovascular Accidents and Closed Head Injuries in Older Adults

Robert J. McCaffrey and Jerid M. Fisher

The goal of this chapter is to outline the cognitive, behavioral, and psychosocial sequelae of cerebrovascular accidents (CVAs) and closed head injuries (CHIs) in older adults. Because the likelihood of CVA increases with age, this topic holds obvious relevance for gerontology professionals. The majority of CHIs occur in the 15- to 24-year old age group; however, several factors mandate their inclusion in the chapter as well.

AGE-RELATED PHYSIOLOGICAL CHANGES

The sequelae of both CVAs and CHIs among older adults must be evaluated in light of age-related physiological changes. Some changes may affect a patient's prognosis by hampering rehabilitation efforts; other age-related physiological alterations may be erroneously attributed to the CVA or CHI. Consequently, it is important to differentiate these age-related changes from the sequelae accompanying CVAs or CHIs. For example, visual, auditory, and motor system decline may profoundly influence older adults' behavior and, in some cases, may be the underlying cause for psychiatric disturbances among these individuals. This could potentially lead to erroneous assessment and treatment efforts if these changes in the older adult were mistakenly attributed to the CVA or the CHI.

Several visual functions are adversely affected by aging. Older adults tend to exhibit decreased peripheral vision. They are also likely to have diminished dark-adaptation responsiveness, limited visual accommodation and contrast sensitivity abilities, poorer visual acuity, and less tolerance of glare (Fozard & Thomas, 1975).

Older adults are also likely to present with auditory system decline. These may include problems in comprehending normal speech, decreased ability to make pitch discrimination, and decrements in auditory acuity. Sufrin (1984) points out that paranoid ideation and concomitant agitation or depression are often present in older adults secondary to a correctable hearing deficit.

Motor system functions are also adversely affected by the aging process. One significant change is an increase in simple reaction time among older adults compared to younger adults. This is most obvious when the older individual is required to engage in a series of complex coordinated motor movements (Fozard & Thomas, 1975). The functional implications, as noted by Sufrin (1984), are likely to be marked in such situations as regaining balance after stumbling, which may contribute to the greater number of falls among the elderly than among younger individuals (Rodstein, 1983).

Age-related sensory/motor changes (see Rockstein & Sussman, 1979) provide a context for evaluating the adverse effects of CVAs and CHIs in older adults. It is worth noting that no two older adults necessarily experience identical age-related physiological decline. Moreover, rarely will two patients with comparable CVAs or CHIs demonstrate identical behavior patterns. For professionals working with older adults in rehabilitation settings, this poses a unique challenge. First, the clinical literature based on younger populations may lack external validity when applied to older adults, because of age-related physiological decline. This suggests that the recovery process may differ between younger and older populations. Second, the psychosocial, cognitive, and behavioral effects of CVAs and CHIs in older adults remains a complex issue, requiring appropriate clinical methodology (Webster, McCaffrey & Scott, 1986), and has received insufficient attention in the research literature.

CEREBROVASCULAR ACCIDENTS

Epidemiology of CVAs

Cerebrovascular accidents, or strokes, as they are commonly called, occur secondary to compromised blood supply to brain tissue. Approxi-

mately 80% of CVAs result from either a thrombus or an atheroma. The former is a blood clot, whereas the latter represents the accumulation of fatty deposits in blood vessel walls. Bleeding, consequent to the rupture of a cerebral blood vessel, accounts for the remaining 20% of CVAs (Rockstein & Sussman, 1979). Regardless of the etiology, CVAs compromise normal vascular flow, which decreases the supply of oxygen and nutrients to the brain.

A CVA rarely occurs as a discrete disorder in an otherwise healthy older adult. Autopsy data from 47 older adults, ranging in age from 50 to 91 years, who had shown signs or symptoms suggestive of a CVA revealed an average of 10.7 pathologic lesions per patient, in addition to the CVA (Howell, 1981). The lesions were found in a variety of systems: 36.5% in cardiovascular tissue, 15.8% in pulmonary, 11% in renal; 9% in cerebal; 8.3% in hepatic; 6.5% in gastrointestinal or pancreatic; 5% in genital; 3.5% in splenic; and 4.4% in other tissue. The presence of multiple pathologic lesions in older adults who have sustained a CVA may not only complicate their clinical picture, but can also affect their prognosis.

Among older adults, CVAs are a leading cause of death and disability. The incidence of CVAs increases with age. The approximate frequency of CVAs per 1,000 population is 20 for 45- to 64-year-olds, 60 for 65- to 74-year olds and 95 for 75- to 84-year-olds (Wolf, Dawber, Thomas, Colton, & Kannel, 1977). In the United States CVAs cause 275,000 deaths annually and disable another 300,000 individuals. Of CVA victims admitted to a hospital, approximately 50% die within the first 3 weeks (Goodstein, 1983), whereas almost one third remain entirely dependent upon family or institutions as a result of physical and emotional sequelae (Andrews, Brocklehurst, Richards, & Laycock, 1981).

Owing to the identification of risk-related etiologic factors, the frequency of CVAs has declined during the last 25 years. For example, it is well recognized that hypertension is a risk factor for stroke in men under 60; controlling blood pressure reduces morbidity and mortality (Veterans Administration Cooperative Study Group on Antihypertensive Agents, 1970, 1972). The benefits of controlling hypertension in women, however, are less obvious, and for adults over 75 years of age, the role of blood pressure as a risk factor for CVAs is not clear (Briggs, 1982).

Ultimately the most successful method for

reducing the occurrence of CVA is through prevention. The principal thrust of late-stage prevention programs is teaching older adults and their relatives the symptoms of *transient ischemic attacks* (Caplan, 1977). Transient ischemic attacks (TIAs) are brief, reversible neurologic episodes that may last for a few minutes but, by definition, not longer than 24 hours (Gilroy & Meyer, 1979). Episodes have an abrupt onset and are characterized by mild parasthesias, vertigo, premonitory falls, fleeting sensations of giddiness, impaired consciousness, and other subtle neurological symptoms (Howell, 1971: Kolb & Whishaw, 1985). Patients that experience TIAs are more likely to have a CVA, although the magnitude of the risk is unclear. Estimates of patients experiencing TIAs prior to a CVA range from 4% to 75% (Friedman, Wilson, Mosier, Colandrea, & Nichaman, 1969). The brief and reversible nature of the neurological deficits accompanying TIAs may be misinterpreted by the older adult as a normal consequence of aging or by family members as a hypochondriacal event, because they are brief and reversible. These factors underscore the importance of community-wide preventive education programs. In the absence of successful prevention, the patient, family, and concerned professionals from a variety of disciplines are faced with the often arduous task of formulating and implementing rehabilitation programs.

Psychosocial Reactions to CVAs

CVAs are generally not predictable events. As a result, older adults begin the process of coping and adapting at a time when they are faced with major losses and are maximally impaired (Horenstein, 1968). The constellation of losses facing the patient varies but is likely to include feelings of being out of control, fear, and loss of personal dignity and separation from family and familiar environments. Other losses may occur in the areas of finance, personal appearance, family status, and leisure and social activities. The feelings of loss of control associated with the CVA are further exacerbated by hospitalization, as well as by the uncertainty of prognosis. Fears of death and dying are reportedly common, as are fears of insanity, physical dysfunction, sexual impairment, and a subsequent CVA. Loss of self-esteem and personal dignity may lead to depression. In general, the higher the patient's premorbid level of intellectual functioning and responsibilities, the greater the

perceived loss by the patient (Griffith, 1980). In addition, the patient's interpretation of the cause of the CVA may impact adversely upon their rehabilitation program and subsequent life-style (Goodstein, 1983). For example, patients who interpret the CVA as a form of retribution for prior misconduct or who restrict physical activities to "avoid" another CVA, may not achieve maximal recovery.

The family's reaction to the patient's situation has received less attention in the literature (Bray & Clark, 1984) than other disorders such as Alzheimer-type dementia (Brown, 1985; Heston & White, 1983; Mace & Rabins, 1984; Powell & Courtice, 1983; Reisberg, 1981; Zarit, Orr, & Zarit, 1985). The ability of the family to accept changes in their injured loved one appears to be a function of the patient's premorbid emotional and social adjustment. Those who are reasonably well adjusted are more likely to be supported by family and friends than those who are not. The latter group lacks critical social support when it is most needed (Lezak, 1983).

The available data indicate that both the patient and family sense that improvement slows by 6 to 9 months after the CVA (Griffith, 1980). In terms of the psychosocial readjustment of the spouses' of CVA patients, one study (Kinsella & Duffy, 1979) found that by 12 months post-CVA, there was a general deterioration in the marital relationship, as indicated by a decrease in the frequency of social/leisure activities and a worsening sexual relationship.

The overall intrapersonal and interpersonal adjustment of the CVA patient may be significantly influenced by the cognitive, behavioral, and psychosocial sequelae associated with their CVA. Differentiation of these changes from age-related physiological decline and development of an appreciation of the potential for interaction with other coexisting disease processes are difficult, yet important, tasks. A discussion of these factors and their impact upon the patient, significant others, and the rehabilitation process follows.

Recovery of Function Following a CVA

There are a wide array of cognitive, behavioral, and emotional alterations associated with the acute period following a CVA; nevertheless, many of these are transient and dissipate within 2 to 3 months. It is the persistent, long-term changes that are most relevant to this discussion. Before examining these sequelae, however, the recovery of function process will be reviewed.

Recompensation of language, and language-related functions following CVAs has been researched extensively. There is general agreement among investigators regarding the time course for recovery (Kertesz, 1985). During the acute recovery phase, many patients experience significant functional improvements (Kohlmeyer, 1976). This recovery is generally attributed to the abatement of abnormal physiological changes associated with the CVA. Functional improvement generally peaks at 2 to 3 months; by 12 months it tends to be asymptotic (Kertesz, 1985), although recovery may continue for several years (e.g., Broida, 1977).

The resolution of hemiplegia follows a course similar to the recompensation of language functions (Newman, 1972; Van Buskirk, 1954). Those patients who recover generally have initial movement within 2 weeks of the CVA and full motion within 3 months. Continued recovery, although slow, has been reported 6 to 8 months following the CVA (Adams & Hurwitz, 1975; Carroll, 1962) and may extend beyond 8 months. There are two other noteworthy points. First, upper extremity recovery is poorer than lower extremity recovery. The second point involves the differential hemispheric effects of CVAs on the recovery of ambulation. In general, right-sided hemiplegics recover independent ambulation more frequently and sooner than left-sided hemiplegics (Kertesz, 1985). The visuospatial problems that often accompany right-hemisphere CVAs presumably act as an impediment to the recovery of ambulation in left-sided hemiplegics (Cassvan, Ross, Dyer, & Zane, 1976).

In contrast to the literature addressing the recovery of language and motor function after CVA, other functions have been less systematically investigated. Although the reasons for this are not entirely clear, one possibility is that language and motor functions are more readily assessed than many neuropsychological, personality, and affective sequelae. In addition, Kertesz (1985) notes that clinicians observing patients in the acute phase rarely have an opportunity to follow the patient through the recovery process, while rehabilitation specialists seldom interact with the patient during the acute phase. Thus, there is a dissociation between professionals during these two stages of recovery. On the one hand, rehabilitation specialists are more likely to attribute improvement to their specific treatment interventions than to underlying neurological recovery. On the other hand, professionals concerned with initial diagnoses are apt to view the patient's clinical picture as stable and thereby downplay changes in the patient's performance or the pattern of neuropsychological deficits. The absence of a continuum of contact with the patient, from the initial recovery stages through the entire recovery process, by an interdisciplinary team of rehabilitation professionals is a contributing factor to our incomplete understanding of the recovery of function process.

Variables Affecting Recovery of Function

There are several variables that may influence the recovery course: age, handedness, personality, and level of intelligence. The best prognosis is usually associated with a young, left-handed, optimistic, intelligent female (Kolb & Whishaw, 1985). This is presumably due to the fact that neuropsychological functions are not as lateralized in females and many sinistrals as they are in males and dextrals. Intelligence may influence the patient's ability to develop functional compensations, that is, the ability to acquire new solutions to old problems by relying upon residual brain structures (Luria, Naydin, Tsvetkova, & Vinarskaya, 1969). An optimistic patient attitude suggests positive motivation, which has been demonstrated to have a facilitating effect upon the recovery process (Stoicheff, 1960).

In addition to the deficits in motor and language-related functions, there may also be perceptual, intellectual, emotional, and personality alterations after a CVA. Clearly, the patient's prognosis is determined not only by the degree of physical impairment but also by the effects of intellectual impairment, emotional/personality changes, and the severity of any psychiatric disorder (anxiety and depression). These factors will largely govern the patient's ability to resume activities of daily living, as well as the ability to reestablish social and family relationships.

Affective/Personality Sequelae

The occurrence of a CVA does not necessarily result in dramatic personality alterations, although there may be an exaggeration of premorbid personality characteristics. These changes may affect the patient's social adjustment and the amount of benefit derived from treatment (Lezak, 1983).

When affective disturbances accompany a CVA, they are often shaped by the damaged cerebal hemisphere. Patients with left-hemisphere damage may be especially sensitive to their limitations; they tend to exaggerate their disabilities. Anxiety is often reported (Lezak, 1983). In addition, these patients may demonstrate what Goldstein (1948) calls the *catastrophic reaction*. This is characterized by an extremely disruptive, transient, emotional disturbance that presents as disorganizing anxiety, agitation, or tearfulness. This reaction, reportedly rare, is typically evoked when the patient is confronted with his limitations (e.g., during an assessment or in a physical or occupational therapy session). The catastrophic reaction subsides when the patient is removed from the provoking situation. To diminish the probability of eliciting such a reaction, Benson (1973) recommends blending easy items/tasks among more difficult ones during assessments.

Impairment in the right hemisphere, in contrast to left-hemisphere injury, is less likely to result in concern or excessive awareness of mistakes or limitations. During the acute period following a CVA, many patients with right-hemisphere damage may either deny the presence of their disabilities or diminish their significance (Denny-Brown, Meyer, & Horenstein, 1952; Gainotti, 1972). This phenomenon is known as the *indifference reaction*. During the acute recovery phase, patients with left-hemisphere damage may also exhibit an indifference reaction. The presence of such a reaction in left-hemisphere patients is presumably due to the initial physiological changes associated with the brain insult (Plum & Posner, 1980). As left-hemisphere damage resolves, however, this reaction usually subsides.

Many right-hemisphere-damaged patients appear to be apathetic or emotionally unresponsive. There is a growing body of clinical research suggesting that right-hemisphere-damaged patients are more likely to be deficient in the comprehension or expression of affect or both, compared to left-hemisphere-damaged patients (Heilman, Bowers, & Valenstein, 1985). Several studies have reported that, in general, right-hemisphere-damaged patients have greater difficulty comprehending affectively intoned speech than left-hemisphere-damaged patients (Heilman, Bowers, Speedie, & Coslett, 1983; Heilman, Scholes, & Watson, 1975; Ross, 1981). In addition, there are data indicating that right-hemisphere-damaged patients are more deficient in recognizing emotional states from photographs than left-hemisphere-damaged patients (Cicone, Waper, & Gardner, 1980; DeKosky, Heilman, Bowers, & Valenstein, 1980), as well as more deficient in expressing emotional intoned speech (Tucker, Watson, & Heilman, 1977), producing appropriate emotional facial expressions (Buck & Duffy, 1980), communicating emotion through the use of limb and body gestures (Ross & Mesulam, 1979), and recalling affectively laden stories (Wechsler, 1973).

It is unclear whether or not the emotional experiences of right-hemisphere patients are less intense than those of left-hemisphere patients or normals. Lezak (1983) contends that right-hemisphere-damaged patients do not experience emotions less intensely than other people; rather, they differ in terms of their ability to appreciate and transmit the nuances and subtleties of affective communication. Others suggest basic affective inhibition. Right-hemisphere patients, however, have been found to be hypoaroused, as indexed by GSR magnitude, compared to left-hemisphere patients when presented with a painful stimulus (Heilman, Schwartz, & Watson, 1978) or emotionally loaded visual stimuli (Morrow, Urtunski, Kim, & Boller, 1981). The left-hemisphere patients in these studies had greater magnitude GSRs than either the right-hemisphere or intact control group to the same stimuli. Although it is, of course, impossible to directly measure another person's subjective state, it appears that right and left-hemisphere patients physiologically experience emotions differently. The presence of hypoarousal in right-hemisphere patients has led Heilman, Bowers, and Valenstein (1985) to speculate that this state may underlie the indifference reaction while hyperarousal in left-hemisphere patients may contribute to the catastrophic reaction.

Several other, more subtle emotional changes in right-hemisphere patients may adversely affect the rehabilitation process and the patient's subsequent social adjustment. Behavioral alterations associated with right-hemisphere lesions may be misdiagnosed as poor motivation or as "bad patient" behavior (Goodstein, 1983). The right-hemisphere patient's behavioral inertia, impulsivity, distractibility, perseveration, and decreased social graces may reflect frontal lobe damage. The presence of these neuropathologically mediated behavioral deficits often overshadow other problems and may significantly impair rehabilitation efforts (Lishman, 1978; Norman, 1979). Patients who fail to dress themselves or engage in routine physical hygiene may be characterized by staff members as difficult patients when these behaviors are due to right-hemisphere dysfunction (Cohen, 1979). Moreover, right-hemisphere damage may result in the patient's neglect of left visual space (hemispatial neglect) or the left side of their own body (anosognosia) (Heilman, Watson, & Valenstein, 1985; Nichols, 1979).

Depression and Suicide

Depression is a common sequela of CVA. The development of depressive disorders does not appear to be a simple reactive response to the patient's sensory/motor deficits (Folstein, Maiberger, & McHugh, 1977; Robinson & Price, 1982; Robinson & Szetela, 1981). Instead, depression secondary to a CVA appears to be a function of both interhemispheric and intrahemispheric factors. While there are reports of a greater frequency of depressive disorders among right-hemisphere patients than among either left-hemisphere patients or controls, these results were based on a single assessment 30 days post CVA and did not consider intrahemispheric factors or long-term follow-up (Folstein et al., 1977).

A recent analysis of mood disorders in CVA patients found that intrahemispheric lesion location may be an important factor in the presence and the severity of mood change secondary to stroke (Robinson, Kubos, Starr, Rao, & Price, 1984). Specifically, Robinson et al. reported that patients with left-anterior-hemisphere lesions were more depressed than patients with lesions in any other location. Interestingly, right-posterior-hemisphere patients were more depressed than right-anterior-lesion patients, who were generally cheerful and apathetic. This study suggests that there are graduations in mood changes following CVA as a function of the affected hemisphere and intrahemispheric location.

Interestingly, none of the depressed patients examined by Folstein et al. (1977) or by Robinson and Price (1982) had been evaluated or treated for their mood disturbance at the time they were studied. These findings suggest that mood disturbances may be an unrecognized psychiatric complication following a CVA.

Based on a careful analysis of five depressed brain-damaged patients (3 right-hemisphere, 1 left-hemisphere, and 1 CHI), Ross and Rush (1981) noted several factors related to this disorder. First, the clinical picture of depression among brain-damaged patients often consists of a poor or erratic course of recovery, deterioration from a previously stable neurological state, and failure to cooperate with rehabilitation efforts or behavior management problems. Second, patients may deny vegetative signs or symptoms, and family members will need to provide this information. Third, in the absence of pseudobulbar palsy, excessive laughing or crying is suggestive of depression. Fourth, affective behaviors may be incongruent with verbal expressions of dysphoria, helplessness, and other depressive symptoms. Similarly, flattened affect may not reflect a depressive state. Fifth, an abnormal dexamethasone test may aid in establishing a diagnosis of endogenous depression in some brain-damaged patients. Ross and Rush (1981) believe that a trial of antidepressant medication in conjunction with neuroleptics may alleviate behavioral problems as well as any coexisting depression. The efficacy of antidepressant drug therapy for depression secondary to brain damage may be dependant upon the affected hemisphere. Depression in right-hemisphere patients has been reported to be more refractory to drug treatment than depression in left-hemisphere patients (Lezak, 1983), while the latter group may show improvement after a trial of antidepressant medication (Heilman, Bowers, & Valenstein, 1985).

There are two groups of CVA patients that, at present, appear to have a high risk of developing a depressive disorder (Robinson & Price, 1982). Patients who have sustained a left-hemisphere CVA involving the frontal lobe are vulnerable to developing a depressive disorder, particularly within the first 2 years following the event. The clinician should be aware that these depressions may be severe, lasting 7 to 8 months without treatment, and may lead to suicide attempts. Antidepressant medication and/or psychotherapy may be warranted. The other group of CVA patients who appear to be at risk for developing a depressive disorder includes the chronically ill, who are 10 or more years post-left-hemisphere CVA. The families of these CVA patients in high-risk categories should to be educated to recognize the onset of depression and to seek professional assistance for evaluation and possible treatment.

The presence of endogenous or reactive depression among stroke victims increases the probability of suicide. While completed suicides, attempted suicides, and suicidal gestures are reportedly rare (Benson, 1973), the clinician should be cognizant of this potential and initiate suitable precautions as with any other population.

Psychiatric Disturbances

Patients with CVAs involving the left hemisphere may present with a clinical picture that suggests a primary psychiatric disturbance. Very often, however, this reflects underlying brain pathology. A disturbance of normal brain functions involved in the comprehension of speech (e.g., Wernicke's aphasia) may predispose the patient to exhibit paranoid-like behavior. The reaction is in some ways analogous to the paranoia that accompanies a gradual hearing loss. As a result of the underlying organic involvement, the patient is unable to comprehend what others say but fails to recognize his or her problem as organically based. These patients are likely to accuse family members and hospital staff of conspiring against them. The patient may leave the hospital without authorization. In addition these patients may physically assault the medical staff, other patients, or family members (Benson, 1973).

Problems with language comprehension or expression, or both, may provoke anger and frustration among left-hemisphere patients. Anger may range from a childlike withdrawal to an absolute refusal to participate in rehabilitation or other activities to physical abusiveness with family members and the rehabilitation team.

In contrast to left-hemisphere patients, right-hemisphere patients are less likely to exhibit discrete psychiatric-like disturbances. The right-hemisphere patient may, however, show emotional lability, lack of social graces, confusion, disorientation, and rude or impulsive behavior that can potentially affect their psychosocial adjustment.

Cognitive Sequelae

The cognitive and behavioral changes in older adults who have suffered a CVA may be discrete or global. These sequelae are most marked whenever the frontal lobe is affected. The most prominent and disturbing cognitive sequelae involve disturbances in abstract reasoning abilitits, the sequential ordering of information or activities, and a disruption in complex forms of goal-directed behavior (Luria, 1966, 1973). These sequelae may

obscure other cognitive deficits. For example, ordering or sequencing deficits are often misinterpreted as disturbances in memory. Upon closer examination, however, the deficit is not in the recall of the individual elements, but rather in the ordering or sequencing of the recalled elements. Moreover, there is a discernible asymmetry in the function of the frontal lobes. Specifically, the frontal lobe of the dominant hemisphere, usually the left, seems more involved in the sequencing of verbally presented material, while the frontal lobe of the nondominant hemisphere processes the sequential ordering of nonverbal or pictoral events (Kolb & Whishaw, 1985).

The CVA patient's ability to program and execute a sequence of events either during formal assessment or within the context of daily living may be significantly disrupted. The differential diagnosis of a sequencing or memory deficit, as well as whether verbal or nonverbal material is most affected, is important in the development and implementation of rehabilitation efforts that capitalize on the patient's remaining cognitive functions. For example, a patient with a left-hemisphere CVA involving the frontal lobe would be expected to have less difficulty with sequencing pictorial material than with verbal or written material.

The behavioral characteristics of frontal lobe damage due to a CVA or other etiologies may vary as a function of the location and extent of damage. Mild frontal lobe injury is often characterized by apathy and indifference (Luria, 1966, 1973). Some patients are less spontaneous behaviorally (Jones-Gotman & Milner, 1977; Milner, 1964). In addition, there may be changes in the patient's prosocial and/or sexual behavior. In the former, the patient may demonstrate impulsivity, poor judgment, rude or abrupt behavior, or a general absence of customary social graces. Changes in a patient's sexual behavior may range from a loss of libido to uninhibited, inappropriate sexual advances directed toward staff members, other patients, or family members. Since frontal lobe damage is a common characteristic in CHIs, a more detailed discussion will be presented in that section.

Medication Factors

CVAs, as described earlier, rarely occur in healthy older adults (Howell, 1981). Instead, the presence of multiple coexisting medical conditions that require medication appears to be the most common cause among CVA patients. Thus, medication side effects may be mistakenly attributed to the CVA, or, conversely, associated CVA sequelae may be considered a side effect of medication (Goodstein, 1983). One cannot assume that older adults metabolize drugs in the same manner as younger adults (see chapter 13, this volume).

During the acute stages of a CVA, many older adults are removed from a familiar and stimulating environment and placed in a less stimulating environment—an unfamiliar hospital room, often confined to bed. There is evidence suggesting that decreased stimulation or sensory deprivation, even in mild forms, may generate "psychiatric" problems. The major symptoms of sensory deprivation include anxiety, tension, difficulty concentrating, suggestibility, vivid sensory imagery, hallucinations, somatic complaints, bodily illusions, and intense subjective emotions (Solomon & Kleeman, 1975). A study by Downs (1974) reported the presence of varying degrees of sensory deprivation symptoms in a *healthy* group of 180 subjects after only $2\frac{3}{4}$ hours of bed rest. The injudicious application of medication for acute symptoms of anxiety, depression, or agitation may worsen the symptoms for which the medication was prescribed, if the symptoms reflect sensory deprivation. The sedating or tranquilizing effects of the medication may increase sensory deprivation in the older adult by further dulling the patient's responsiveness to environmental stimulation (Oster, 1976).

CLOSED HEAD INJURIES

An overview of the cognitive, behavioral, and psychosocial sequelae of CHIs is included in this chapter for several reasons. First, in all age groups, the incidence of CHIs exceeds 1 million new cases annually (Kertesz, 1982). Second, the mortality rates for CHIs have decreased dramatically because of improved emergency transport and neurosurgical interventions, which have contributed to the near normal life expectancies of many CHI survivors. Third, cognitive and behavioral sequelae that occur after severe CHI may persist for 40 to 50 years; this has immense personal, social, and economic ramifications (Fisher, 1985). In addition, this growing patient population is likely to pose unique challenges to geriatric health care professionals.

The categories of patients represented by the term *CHI*, like those grouped under the label *CVA*, are far from homogeneous. A description of common cognitive and behavioral sequelae of minor and moderate-severe CHIs, adapted from a review by Fisher (1985), is presented in Table 21.1. Among many patients these symptoms reflect damage to the frontal lobes. The frontal lobe syndrome is often characterized by impaired judgment, inappropriate affect, apathy or anergia, disinhibition, regressive-like behaviors, aggression, and self-centeredness (Bond, 1984). In addition, these patients are likely to demonstrate significant problems in planning, organizing, and executing a sequence of behaviors to achieve a goal and/or difficulties in solving problems that involve abstract thought or complex reasoning.

There is accumulating evidence that suggests persistent affective, behavioral, and psychiatric disturbances are, more often than not, sequelae of moderate-severe CHI (Bond, 1984; Jennett & Teasdale, 1981). Moreover, behavioral disorders are ultimately more distressing to the patient's family than physical sequelae (Fisher, 1985).

Until recently, the impact of minor CHIs upon the patient's cognitive, psychological, and social functioning was afforded little attention in the literature. In fact, patients with persistent problems following minor CHI were thought to be neurotic, capitalizing on the presence of secondary gain or maintaining symptoms for purposes of litigation or disability claims. Recent investigations, however, support the genuine nature of their symptoms. Even when loss of consciousness or specific neurological deficits do not occur, patients with postconcussional head trauma may develop cognitive, behavioral, and psychological problems (Fisher, 1985). Recognition of the significance of minor CHIs is very important, especially among geriatric care providers.

A common cause for minor CHIs among older adults is falls. This event may be associated with the occurrence of a subdural hematoma. The low base rate for subdural hematomas, however, coupled with atypical clinical signs and symptoms, may obscure this crucial early diagnosis (Rosin & Van Dijk, 1980). Accurate early detection may result in an excellent prognosis, whereas delays can prove fatal or be associated with severe morbidity (e.g., coma) (Gilroy & Meyer, 1979; Rosin & Van Dijk, 1980). Among older adults, the diagnosis of a subdural hematoma may be complicated by the patient's inability to recall the precipitating event (Busse, 1959). In five cases examined by

Table 21.1. Selected Cognitive and Behavioral Sequelae Associated with Mild and Moderate to Severe Closed Head Injuries

MINOR HEAD TRAUMA		MODERATE TO SEVERE HEAD TRAUMA	
Cognitive	Behavioral	Cognitive	Behavioral
Memory deficits	Anxiety	General intellectual deficits	Apathy
Concentration difficulties	Depression	Planning/organization problems	Anxiety
Slowed rate of information processing	Irritability	Memory deficits	Aggression
		Abstraction reasoning deficits	Dependency
		Poor concentration	Disinhibition
		Slowed information processing	Depression
		Language-related deficits	Emotional liability
			Hyper/hyposexual
			Impatience
			Impulsive
			Irritable
			Poor judgment

Rosin and Van Dijk (1980), the time from the fall to the diagnosis of subdural hematoma ranged from 1 day to 3 months.

The postoperative recovery period following a hip fracture is another situation that warrants careful evaluation, because the fall responsible for the hip fracture may have also have been accompanied by an unreported minor CHI. During the postoperative hip fracture recovery period, the signs and symptoms of minor head injury may be mistakenly attributed to the sensory deprivation that often accompanies a physically limiting condition (Gates, 1984). Thus, the differentiation of CHI from sensory deprivation is crucial, especially if an occult subdural hematoma is present.

Oster (1977) examined 39 hip-fracture patients and 18 patients with multiple non hip fractures using electroencephalography, echoencephalography, and CAT scanning of the head. Five of the hip-fracture patients and two of the multiple-fracture patients who demonstrated signs of sensory deprivation had abnormal test results. Five of the seven patients had a subdural hematoma, whereas the other two had tumors. All but one of the seven had an excellent recovery. According to Oster (1977), some of these patients had a chronic subdural hematoma, presumably from an earlier fall that was not recalled by the patient. Speculatively, the neurological sequelae from this injury may have contributed to the subsequent fall that caused the hip fracture.

It is clear from the foregoing discussion that the index of suspicion for minor head trauma should be higher among older adults. A careful and thorough evaluation is indicated to ensure a reliable diagnosis.

There is evidence suggesting that CHIs may be a risk factor in the subsequent development of senile dementia of the Alzheimer's type (SDAT). It has been recognized for quite some time that repeated blows to the head may result in a dementing condition known as *dementia pugilistica*, generally in the fifth or sixth decade of life (Martland, 1928). It has also been reported that among older adults, head injury may act as a catalyst in either the development or acceleration of Alzheimer's disease (for a review, see Rudelli, Strom, Welch, & Ambler, 1982).

Rudeli et al. (1982) reported a case study in which a single severe CHI in a 22-year-old male preceded a diagnosis of SDAT by 8 years; death occurred at age 37. Histopathological studies confirmed that the patient's clinical deterioration was due to SDAT. This case, unlike previous ones, demonstrated the onset of a dementing condition after a CHI in a younger adult; this finding tentatively suggests that CHIs may predispose some head-injured survivors to the development of a dementia. One cannot rule out, however, the confounding of age, CHI, and SDAT.

The role of prior CHIs as a risk factor in the development of SDAT was also examined retrospectively (Mortimer, French, Hutton, & Schuman, 1985). Using an interview procedure in which neither the interviewer nor the respondent (usually the subject's spouse) was aware of the purpose of the study, the researchers assessed the frequency of prior CHIs in 78 patients with a confirmed diagnosis of SDAT, 76 non demented hospital controls, and 46 neighborhood controls. The control groups were matched to the SDAT group for age, sex, and race. A history of CHI with loss of consciousness was found in 25.6% of the SDAT group, compared to 5.3% and 14.6% of the hospital and neighborhood control groups, respectively. These findings are similar to those reported by Heyman, Wilkinson, Stafford, Helms, Sigmon, and Weinberg (1984), who found that 15% of 40 SDAT patients reported a history of CHI as opposed to 3.8% of 80 control subjects.

However, the literature on CHI as a risk factor in the development of SDAT must be interpreted cautiously (Mortimer et al., 1985). First, the physiological mechanisms involved in the relationship between CHI and SDAT are not well understood. Second, all of the reports to date have been based on retrospective accounts. Clearly, prospective studies of CHI survivors are needed in order to better understand the role of head trauma as a risk factor for SDAT.

SUMMARY

Geriatric health care professionals, working with CVA patients and CHI survivors, are charged with the often complex task of designing and implementing individualized rehabilitation programs. The complex relationship between compromised brain tissue and physiological age-related changes, as well as coexisting disease states, warrants an interdisciplinary geriatric rehabilitation team approach. A team approach may begin to narrow the gap in our knowledge of the recovery process, since the individual disciplines would, of necessity, become familiar with the role and contributions of the other member disciplines.

A major role of the geriatric health care team will be active participation in the education and dissemination of information regarding the sequelae of CVAs and CHIs, not only to other professionals but to family members and patients as well. This is especially true with respect to the organically based psychiatric disturbances, such as depression. Although the frequency of CVAs has decreased, and will probably continue to decline, the incidence of CHIs in the United States alone approximates 1 million new cases annually. This population will pose a unique set of challenges to geriatric health care providers in particular and to society in general.

REFERENCES

Adams, F., & Hurwitz, L. J. (1975). Rehabilitation of hemiplegia: Indices of assessment and prognosis. *British Medical Journal, 1,* 94–08.

Andrews, K., Brocklehurst, J. C., Richards, B., & Laycock, P. J. (1981). The rate of recovery from stroke— And its management. *International Rehabilitation Medicine, 3,* 155–161.

Benson, D. F. (1973). Psychiatric aspects of aphasia. *British Journal of Psychiatry, 123,* 555–566.

Bond, M. (1984). The psychiatry of closed head injury. In N. Brooks (Ed.), *Closed head injury—Psychological, social, and family consequences* (pp. 148–178). Oxford: University Press.

Bray, G., & Clark, G. (1984). *A stroke family guide and resource.* Springfield, IL: Charles C. Thomas.

Briggs, R. S. (1982). Stroke management of the elderly in Great Britain. *Postgraduate Medicine, 71,* 101–111.

Broida, H. (1977). Language therapy effects in long-term aphasia. *Archives of Physical Medicine and Rehabilitation, 58,* 248–253.

Brown, D. S. (1985). *Handle with care: A question of Alzheimer's.* Buffalo, NY: Prometheus Books.

Buck, R., & Duffy, R. J. (1980). Nonverbal communication of affect in brain damaged patients. *Cortex, 16,* 351–362.

Busse, E. W. (1959). Psychopathology. In J. E. Birren (Ed.), *Handbook of aging and the individual.* Chicago: University of Chicago Press.

Caplan, L. R. (1977). Stroke prevention—Early signs of the patient at risk. *Resident and Staff Physician, 23,* 52–65.

Carroll, D. (1962). The disability in hemiplegia caused by cerebrovascular disease. *Journal of Chronic Diseases, 15,* 179–189

Cassvan, A., Ross, P. L., Dyer, P. R., & Zane, L. (1976). Lateralization in stroke syndromes as a factor in ambulation. *Archives of Physical Medicine and Rehabilitation, 57,* 583–587.

Cicone, M., Waper, W., & Gardner, H. (1980). Sensitivity to emotional expressions and situations in organic patients. *Cortex, 16,* 145–148.

Cohen, B. S. (1979). Rehabilitation of the stroke patient. *Maryland State Medical Journal, 28,* 82–83.

De Kosky, S., Heilman, K. M., Bowers, D., & Valenstein, E. (1980). Recognition and discrimination of emotional faces and pictures. *Brain and Language, 9,* 206–214.

Denny-Brown, D., Meyer, J. S., & Horenstein, S. (1952). The significance of perceptual rivalry resulting from parietal lesions. *Brain, 75,* 433–471.

Downs, F. S. (1974). Bed rest and sensory disturbances. *American Journal of Nursing, 74,* 434–438.

Fisher, J. M. (1985). The cognitive and behavioural consequences of closed head injury. *Seminars in Neurology, 5,* 197–204.

Folstein, M. F., Maiberger, R., & McHugh, P. R. (1977). Mood disorder as a specific complication of stroke. *Journal of Neurology, Neurosurgery, and Psychiatry, 40,* 1018–1020.

Fozard, J. L., & Thomas, J. C., Jr. (1975). Psychology of aging. In J. G. Howells (Ed.), *Modern perspectives in the psychiatry of old age.* New York: Brunner/Mazel.

Friedman, G. D., Wilson, W. S., Mosier, J. M., Colandrea, M. A., & Nichaman, M. Z. (1969). Transient ischemic attacks in a community. *Journal of the American Medical Association, 210,* 1428–1438.

Gainotti, G. (1972). Emotional behaviour and hemispheric side of the lesion. *Cortex, 8*, 41–55.

Gates, S. J. (1984). Helping your patient on bedrest cope with perceptual/sensory deprivation. *Orthopaedic Nursing, 3*, 35–38.

Gilroy, J., & Meyer, J. S. (1979). *Medical neurology* (3rd ed.). New York: Macmillan.

Goldstein, K. H. (1948). *Language and language disturbances*. New York: Grune & Stratton.

Goodstein, R. K. (1983). Overview: Cerebrovascular accident and the hospitalized elderly—A multidimensional clinical problem. *American Journal of Clinical Psychiatry, 140*, 141–147.

Griffith, V. E. (1980). Observations on patients dysphasia after stroke. *British Medical Journal, 281*, 1608–1609.

Heilman, K. M., Bowers, D., Speedie, L., & Coslett, H. B. (1983). The comprehension of emotional and nonemotional prosody. *Neurology, 33*, 377–402.

Heilman, K. M., Bowers, D., & Valenstein, E. (1985). Emotional disorders associated with neurological diseases. In K. M. Heilman & E. Valenstein (Eds.), *Clinical neuropsychology* (2nd ed.). New York: Oxford University Press.

Heilman, K. M., Scholes, R., & Watson, R. T. (1975). Auditory affective agnosia: Disturbed comprehension of affective speech. *Journal of Neurology, Neurosurgery and Psychiatry, 38*, 69–72.

Heilman, K. M., Schwartz, H., & Watson, R. T. (1978). Hypoarousal in patients with the neglect syndrome and emotional indifference. *Neurology, 28*, 229–232.

Heilman, K. M., Watson, R. T., & Valenstein, E. (1985). Neglect and related disorders. In K. M. Heilman and E. Valenstein (Eds.), *Clinical neuropsychology* (2nd ed.). New York: Oxford University Press.

Heston, L. L., & White, J. A. (1983). *Dementia: A practical guide to Alzheimer's disease and related illnesses*. New York: Freeman.

Heyman, A., Wilkinson, W. E., Stafford, J. A., Helms, M. J., Sigmon, A. H., & Weinberg, T. (1984). Alzheimer's disease: A study of epidemiologic aspects. *Annals of Neurology, 15*, 335–341.

Horenstein, S. (1968). Effects of cerebral vascular disease in personality and emotionality. In A. L. Benton (Ed.), *Behavioral change in cerebral vascular disease*. New York: Harper & Row.

Howell, T. H. (1971). Premonitory falls. *Practitioner, 206*, 666–667.

Howell, T. H. (1981). Multiple lesions in stroke patients: A study in morbid anatomy. *Journal of the American Geriatrics Society, 24*, 246–250.

Jennett, B., & Teasdale, G. (1981). *Management of head injuries*. Philadelphia: F. A. Davis.

Jones-Gotman, M., & Milner, B. (1977). Design fluency: The invention of nonsense drawings after focal cortical lesions. *Neuropsychologia, 15*, 653–674.

Kertesz, A. (1982). The current neurologic burden of illness and injury in the United States. *Neurology, 32*, 1207–1214.

Kertesz, A. (1985). Recovery and treatment. In K. M. Heilman & E. Valenstein (Eds.), *Clinical neuropsychology* (2nd ed.). New York: Oxford University Press.

Kinsella, G. J., & Duffy, F. D. (1979). Psychosocial readjustment in the spouses of aphasic patents. *Scandinavian Journal of Rehabilitation Medicine, 11*, 129–132.

Kohlmeyer, K. (1976). Aphasia due to focal disorders of cerebral circulation: Some aspects of localization and of spontaneous recovery. In *Neurolinguistics: 4. Recovery in Aphasics*. Amsterdam: Sevets & Zeitlinger.

Kolb, B., & Whisaw, I. Q. (1985). *Fundamentals of human neuropsychology* (2nd ed.). New York: Freeman.

Lezak, M. D. (1983). *Neuropsychological assessment* (2nd ed.). New York: Oxford University Press.

Lishman, W. A. (1978). *Organic psychiatry*. Oxford: Blackwell Scientific.

Luria, A. R. (1966). *Higher cortical functions in man*. New York: Basic Books.

Luria, A. R. (1973). *The working brain: An introduction to neuropsychology*. New York: Basic Books.

Luria, A. R., Naydin, V. L., Tsvetkova, L. S., & Vinarskaya, E. N. (1969). Restoration of higher cortical function following local brain damage. In R. J. Vinken & G. W. Bruyn (Eds.), *Handbook of clinical neurology* (vol. 3). Amsterdam: North Holland.

Mace, N. L., & Rabins, P. V. (1984). *The 36-hour day*. Baltimore, MD: Johns Hopkins University Press.

Martland, H. S. (1928). Punch drunk. *Journal of the American Medical Association, 91*, 1103–1107.

Milner, B. (1964). Some effects of frontal lobectomy in man. In J. M. Warren & K. Akert (Eds.), *The frontal granular cortex and behavior*. New York: McGraw-Hill.

Morrow, L., Urtunski, B., Kim, Y., & Boller, F. (1981). Arousal responses to emotional stimuli and laterality of lesion. *Neuropsychologia, 19*, 65–71.

Mortimer, J. A., French, L. R., Hutton, J. T., & Schuman, L. M. (1985). Head injury as a risk factor for Alzheimer's disease. *Neurology, 35*, 264–267.

Newman, M. (1972). The process of recovery after hemiplegia. *Stroke, 3*, 702–710.

Nichols, P. J. R. (1979). Rehabilitation of the stroke patient. *Age and Ageing, 8* (Suppl.), 67–75.

Norman, S. (1979). Diagnostic categories for the patient with a right hemisphere lesion. *American Journal of Nursing, 79*, 2126–2130.

Oster, C. (1976). Sensory deprivation in geriatric patients. *Journal of the American Geriatrics Society, 24*, 461–464.

Oster, C. (1977). Signs of sensory deprivation versus cerebral injury in post-hip-fracture patients. *Journal of the American Geriatrics Society, 25*, 368–370.

Plum, F., & Posner, J. B. (1980). *Diagnosis of stupor and coma* (3rd ed.). Philadelphia: F. A. Davis.

Powell, L. S., & Courtice, K. (1983). *Alzheimer's disease: A guide for families*. Reading, MA: Addison-Wesley.

Reisberg, B. (1981). *A guide to Alzheimer's disease*. New York: Free Press.

Robinson, R. G., Kubos, K. L., Starr, L. B., Rao, K., & Price, T. R. (1984). Mood disorder in stroke patients: Importance of location of lesion. *Brain, 107*, 81–93.

Robinson, R. G., & Price, T. R. (1982). Post-stroke depressive disorders: A follow-up study of 103 patients. *Stroke, 13*, 635–641.

Robinson, R. G., & Szetela, B. (1981). Mood change following left hemisphere brain injury. *Annals of Neurology, 9*, 447–453.

Rockstein, M., & Sussman, M. (1979). *Biology of aging*. Belmont, CA: Wadsworth.

Rodstein, M. (1983). Accidents among the aged. In W. Reichel (Ed.), *Clinical aspects of aging.* Baltimore MD: Williams & Wilkins.

Rosin, A. J., & Van Dijk, Y. M. (1980). Subdural hematoma: A clinical approach. *Journal of the American Geriatrics Society, 28,* 180–183.

Ross, E. D. (1981). The aprosodias: Functional-anatomic organization of the effective components of language in the right hemisphere. *Annals of Neurology, 38,* 561–589.

Ross, E. D., & Mesulam, M. M. (1979). Dominant language functions of the right hemisphere? Prosody and emotional gesturing. *Archives of Neurology, 36,* 144–148.

Ross, E. H., & Rush, A. (1981). Diagnosis and neuroanatomical correlates of depression in brain-damaged patients. *Archives of General Psychiatry, 38,* 1344–1354.

Rudelli, R., Strom, J. O., Welch, P. T., & Ambler, M. W. (1982). Post-traumatic premature Alzheimer's disease. *Archives of Neurology, 39,* 570–575.

Solomon, P., & Kleeman, S. T. (1975). Sensory deprivation. In A. M. Freedman, H. I. Kaplan, & B. J. Sadock (Eds.), *Comprehensive textbook of psychiatry* (2nd ed.). Baltimore, MD. Williams & Wilkins.

Stoicheff, M. L. (1960). Motivating instructions and language performance of dysphasic subjects. *Journal of Speech and Hearing Research, 3,* 75–83.

Sufrin, E. M. (1984). The physical rehabilitation of the brain-damaged elderly. In B. A. Edelstein & E. T. Couture (Eds.), *Behavioral assessment and rehabilitation of the traumatically brain-damaged.* New York: Plenum.

Tucker, D. M., Watson, R. T., & Heilman, K. M. (1977). Affective discrimination and evocation in patients with right parietal disease. *Neurology, 17,* 947–950.

Van Buskirk, C. (1954). Return to motor function in hemiplegia. *Neurology, 4,* 919–928.

Veterans Administration Cooperative Study Group on Antihypertensive Agents. (1970). Effects of treatment on morbidity in hypertension (Part 2). *Journal of the American Medical Association, 213,* 1143–1152.

Veterans Administration Cooperative Study Group on Antihypertensive Agents. (1972). Effects of treatment on morbidity in hypertension (Part 3). *Circulation, 45,* 991–1004.

Webster, J. S., McCaffrey, R. J., & Scott, R. R. (1986). Single case design in clinical neuropsychology. In D. Wedding, A. M. Horton, & J. S. Webster (Eds.), *The neuropsychology handbook: Behavioral and clinical perspectives.* New York: Springer.

Wechsler, A. F. (1973). The effect of organic brain disease on recall of emotionally charged versus neutral narrative texts. *Neurology, 23,* 130–135.

Wolf, P. A., Dawber, T. R., Thomas, H. E., Colton, T., & Kannel, W. B. (1977). Epidemiology of stroke. In R. A. Thompson and J. R. Green (Eds.), *Advances in neurology* (vol. 16). New York: Raven.

Zarit, S. H., Orr, N. K., & Zarit, J. M. (1985). *Caring for the patient with Alzheimer's disease: Families under stress.* New York: New York University Press.

Part V

Social Issues

The chapters in this section provide a social context within which to view the medical, psychological, and behavioral problems discussed in the previous sections. Discussion of the function of social support, the emotional trauma of bereavement, prevention of age-related disorders, and the meaning of home to the elderly individual is contained in these chapters, as well as discussion of minority issues, the politics of aging, and ethics.

Chapter 22

Social Support, Interpersonal Efficacy, and Health: A Life Course Perspective

Toni C. Antonucci and James S. Jackson

In the last two decades the concept of social support has received increased attention. The early work included several reviews, many of them based upon clinical impressions (e.g., Cassel, 1976; Cobb, 1976). The positive role of family and friends in the promotion of health and the prevention of illness gradually became an area of increased focus. Of particular importance in these early investigations was the anthropological social network research of European scientists (Boissevain, 1974; Bott, 1957), which emphasized the importance of network ties and the mutual benefits to all network members. This emphasis on the positive role of the family, as pointed out by Heller (1979, 1986; Heller, Swindle, & Dusenbury, 1986), was a reversal from the previous research in this area. The earlier writing had emphasized the role of the family as the source of a wide variety of problems, most notably those associated with the burdens and responsibilities of family, ethnic, and social group membership.

Within the last 5 years the amount of research appearing under the rubric of social support has expanded greatly. In part, this is due to the colloquial appeal and topical importance of the social support concept. Unlike many "scientific" concepts, the term *social support* is understandable and meaningful to the lay public. Interest in this topic also comes at a time when the public formal resources available to serve the needy, that is, the old, the sick, and the frail, are inadequate to meet the increasing demands. This is a critical issue in gerontology, where the changing demographics of the country portend less public or government contribution to the service needs of the acute and chronic care of the elderly (Rathbone, Hooyman, & Fortune, 1985). Optimization of the role of informal social supports from family, friends, and neighbors has thus emerged as an important social and public policy priority (Kiesler, 1985).

Some of the same reasons for the popular interest in social support, however, have also contributed to problems in the scientific inquiry in the field. In general, researchers have been inconsistent and loose in both the definition and measurement of social support (for explicit discussions of this issue, see Antonucci, 1985a, 1985b; Berkman, 1984; House & Kahn, 1985). Because of its broad colloquial use, the term *social support* has not been rigorously defined. Similarly, researchers have not been specific about the appropriate measurement of social support. For example, some researchers have simply measured the existence of social ties, such as marriage, whereas others have actually assessed the quality and content of these relationships. This lack of specificity has created many problems in interpreting the research literature.

Potential problems also result from the fact that the concept is of interest to research investigators from a variety of disciplines— psychologists, sociologists, anthropologists, physicians, social workers, and nurses. A multiplicity of scientific fields focused on the same topic is an exciting and potentially productive process but also frequently means that the level of research inquiry can be very different. For example, the anthropologist is likely to be interested in the formation and intricacies of the network ties; the sociologist, in the variation in support relationships by demographic characteristics; and the psychologist, in the interpersonal and intrapersonal processes that make social support effective. The diversity of interests and foci attests to the importance of the concept but has contributed to a potpourri of research that has yet to yield a clear picture.

Because many researchers from various fields have offered recent and thorough reviews of the social support literature (Antonucci, 1985b; Berkman, 1984; Broadhead et al., 1983; Brownell & Shumaker, 1984; Cohen & Syme, 1985; Cohen & Wills, 1985; Ell, 1984; House, 1981; Israel & Rounds, in press; Kessler, Price, & Wortman, 1985; Sauer & Coward, 1985), we do not plan to replicate these efforts. In this chapter, we will first briefly review the methodological and conceptual issues, in order to suggest the direction future research might take to advance the field from its current early developmental stage. Next, we will present the research documenting the relationship between social support and health, including some of the recent research in psychoimmunology. Then we will briefly review the control and efficacy literature. Interpersonal efficacy is proposed as a possible mechanism through which social support affects health and well-being. Finally, we will explore the clinical implications of how the model can be used to organize and explain existing findings and how it can be used in future research and clinical programs.

CRITICAL ISSUES IN THE SOCIAL SUPPORT LITERATURE

Numerous definitions of the concept of social support have been offered in the literature. As noted earlier, this is one of the problems associated with an area of scientific inquiry that has broad appeal. This has resulted in a lack of specificity in the definition of social support. Basically, most definitions have involved the exchange or provision of supportive behaviors. Frequently, however, structural characteristics of the social network have been confused with the actual exchange of social support. In our research we have defined *social support* as those interpersonal transactions involving aid, affect, or affirmation (Kahn & Antonucci, 1980). In order for the plethora of research findings to be compared, it is critical that the entity being measured and labeled social support be comparable across studies.

The same standard must be applied with respect to measurement. Antonucci and Depner (1982), Depner, Wethington, and Ingersoll-Dayton (1984), Gottlieb (1981), House and Kahn (1985), Kasl and Berkman (1981), and Mermelstein, Cohen, Lichenstein, Baer, and Kamarck (1986), Sarason and Sarason (1985) have outlined several important issues with respect to the measurement of social support. As with most constructs, the measurement issue is critical. The term *social support* is fairly broad, and a variety of measures can and have been constructed to assess it. It is unlikely that one measure or instrument can be developed to assess social support in a way that will satisfy the needs of all the researchers and clinicians working in this field. It is critical, therefore, that the measure and its description be specific, empirically reliable, and valid, so that those reviewing the results will be able to place them within the broader framework of research findings. Some of the issues that require elucidation include the type of supports assessed (e.g., aid, affect, and affirmation), the source of supports (e.g., family, friends, and neighbors), and both the recipient's and the provider's assessment of the support (e.g., whether the recipient feels aided or smothered).

Several other general areas of research problems have been noted in the literature. We have chosen three issues to review in some detail. It is our assessment that they demonstrate certain critical gaps that remain despite the recent surge in social support research. These are the relative importance of quality versus the quantity of support relationships, the relative importance of family versus friends, and the importance of reciprocity in supportive relationships. These issues are often intertwined and are directly related to the broader etiological question, for which we offer an explanation, of the processes and mechanisms through which social supportive behaviors exert their effects.

Quality Versus Quantity of Support

Several studies have pointed to the significance of the confidant relationship and the relative importance of quality versus quantity in supportive relationships. The classic study of Lowenthal and Haven (1968) first demonstrated the role of a confidant in increasing the well-being and preventing depression among older people. More recently, Chappell (1983) and Strain and Chappell (1982) reiterated the importance of this relationship, suggesting that social relationships with nonfamily peers are critical and that the confidant relationship may be more important to the quality of life and well-being than the quantity of interactions with either family or friends. Ward, Sherman, and LaGory (1984), in a recent publication emphasizing the importance of subjectively assessed social support over more objective or quantifiable measures, made the crucial distinction between quantity and quality of social support. Heller and Mansbach (1984), however, in their study of elderly women, concluded that both quality and quantity of support are important. And finally, McFarlane, Norman, Streiner, and Roy (1984), using a nonrandom sample of Canadian Family Practice patients, found that patients reporting smaller networks felt that their networks were more helpful than patients who reported larger networks. This nonintuitive finding is consistent with earlier studies that found subjective quality of social support to be a better indicator of life satisfaction than quantity of social support (Duff & Hong, 1982) and that "quality support" is more effective in times of crisis than "quantity support" (Porritt, 1979).

Some researchers, however, have suggested that the presence of too small a network can unnecessarily strain support providers. Jones (1981) found that individuals who had experienced the loss of a significant interpersonal relationship were better off if they had many support providers than if they had only one support provider. Interestingly, she

also found that people with no supportive others were sometimes better off than those who reported only one support provider. One might argue that too much emphasis on a single network member becomes a burden on that support provider. Levitt, Antonucci, Clark, Rotton, and Finley (1985) compared the support networks of a national sample of older Americans with a less affluent sample of older Americans threatened with urban renewal in South Miami. They found that the South Miami sample reported significantly fewer people in their social network and significantly lower levels of well-being. The number of individuals reporting no one in their network was too few to analyze systematically, but this group did not look better off than their more "supported" peers. They concluded that members of the national sample who reported larger support networks were at a greater advantage, on average, than members of the South Miami sample. Similar work by Cohen and Rajkowski (1982) and Felton, Lehmann, Adler, and Burgio (1981) with elderly residents of single room occupancy hotels support this same conclusion.

Possibly related to these findings is the work of Coyne and his colleagues (e.g., Coyne & Gotlib, 1982), who have noted the frequent presence of a counterproductive cycle between depressives and family network members. He has hypothesized that the burden of providing support to a depressed family member becomes so overwhelming that the support provider begins to emit subtle cues that are not only nonsupportive but also potentially rejecting. Thus, the presence of a sole support provider may elicit this type of cyclical nonsupportive interaction. This is particularly unfortunate because depressives and people with mental illness have been generally found to have smaller networks than the population at large (D'Augelli, 1983; Greenblatt, Becerra, & Serafetinides, 1982). Similarly, a number of recent studies (Heller, 1979; Heller et al., 1986; Reis, 1984) have suggested that social competence may be a critical underlying dimension in the exchange of social support. Research by Jones, Carpenter, and Quintana (1985) has demonstrated consistent personality correlates of loneliness among samples from two different cultures. It may be that a long-term enduring personality characteristic actually represents the foundation that enables individuals to develop social relationships.

Although most research has emphasized the importance of quality over quantity of support, the question remains as to how an individual either comes to expect or actually develop a high quality of interactive relationships. There are several types of research evidence that might be informative. The attachment literature (Ainsworth, Blehar, Waters, & Wall, 1978; Antonucci & Levitt 1984; Bowlby, 1969) indicates that there is a direct relationship between the primary caretaker and his or her interactive style and the type of attachment relationship the individual develops. More recently, Cochran and Brassard (1979) and Levitt, Weber, and Clark (1986) have noted the relationship between the characteristics of the parents' supportive interactions and the child's social and emotional development. Child development researchers have also documented a fairly strong and consistent relationship between infant attachment styles and social competence in childhood (Arend, Gove, & Sroufe, 1979; Boyce, 1985; Bretherton & Waters, 1985; Matas, Arend, & Sroufe, 1978). This pattern of results is especially important when considered within the context of the notion that social support might be related etiologically to social competence (Heller, 1979). Only a life course perspective can provide the long-term view of interpersonal relationships that can integrate these findings and provide a comprehensive perspective on supportive interactions.

Similarly, a great deal of research has recently begun to emerge that points to the negative effects social support might have on an individual's health and well-being (Antonucci, 1985a; Heller, 1979; Rook, 1984). In fact, the effect of negative support is unfortunately, but clearly, stronger (at least statistically speaking) than the effect of positive support (Antonucci, 1985a). As we seek to understand the etiology of supportive relationships, the question one must raise is why some people maintain ostensibly supportive relationships that in fact have negative effects on their health and well-being. Again, a life course perspective suggests that the individual has not developed a normal, healthy standard of appropriate relationships.

The pattern of these various findings suggests that a curvilinear relationship between quality, quantity, and well-being might best fit the data. And, indeed, Heller and Mansbach (1984) have recently emphasized the multifaceted nature of social support in an elderly sample of community-dwelling women. They note that for this group, both quality and quantity of support seem to be important. Reis, Wheeler, Kernis, Spiegel, and

Nazlek (1985) hypothesize that quality more than quantity of social interactions is related to health. Additional research is necessary to disentangle these findings and to understand how social support operates. For example, it may be that the apparent importance of quality of support over quantity of support is a methodological artifact (Reis et al., 1985). Most measures of both qualitative and quantitative support are, in fact, self-report. It may be that questions asking how many people provide support permits less perceptor bias than questions asking how well one's network provides support. Thus, the higher relationship between qualitative support and well-being may be an indication of respondent evaluator bias. An individual who is likely to say his or her network provides high-quality support may be more likely to report that he or she is satisfied with life and happy. These possibilities, although probably accounting for only a small proportion of the variance (Duff & Hong, 1982), need to be explored before practical interventions can be designed.

Support from Family versus Friends

Another important issue that has unfortunately received little attention in the literature is the relative impact of support provided by family versus support provided by friends. Biegel (1985) notes that families, friends, and neighbors are important components in the care of the elderly and that social network principles may offer helpful insights in providing and organizing the care of older people. Adding to the complexity of the issue is a recent finding by Griffith (1985). A random sample of adults indicated that two-thirds of their support networks consisted of family members. Interestingly, however, this same group also reported that the most sought after support provider was a same-sex friend. Cantor (1979), in a large study of inner New York city elderly, noted that neighbors play an important support role in the everyday lives of the elderly, primarily because of their availability. This does not seem to detract, however, from the important and central role of family as support provider. She describes a hierarchy of support providers that seems to exist among the elderly, which includes family, friends, and neighbors. Litwak (1985) argues that primary groups among the elderly should be matched according to needs and resources in order to produce optimal outcomes. Perhaps Cantor's concept of a hierarchy of support providers essentially outlines the optimal match between needs and resources among primary and secondary groups.

The role of family as support providers is further elucidated by research comparing support networks by marital and parental status (Johnson & Catalano, 1981; Longino & Lipman, 1981, 1985). For example, Hanson and Sauer (1985) report that being married and having children are among the most important factors keeping older people out of institutions. Married people do seem to have consistently better support networks than unmarried people, but childless married people tend to be more isolated than childless unmarried people. Hess and Soldo (1985), in their review of husband and wife networks, indicate that although being married affects men, being *happily* married affects women. On the other hand, Arling (1976), Wood and Robertson (1978), and others have reported that support from friends is a better predictor of well-being than support from family. Over the years there has also been substantial research indicating the importance of support, especially the support of children, in coping with and adjusting to widowhood (Lopata, 1979). But Ferraro, Mutran, and Barresi (1984) found that friendship support is one of the most important factors associated with positive changes in health status among both married and widowed older respondents. Peters and Kaiser (1985) recently examined the literature with respect to the role of friends and neighbors in the provision of support among the elderly. They found that there is less likelihood with increasing age of an individual being named as a confidant, that friendships are very homogeneous, and that friends are an important source of affection.

There is some research suggesting that the relationship between structural characteristics, such as type of relationship, and outcome is not always direct. For example, Hall and Wellman (1985) indicate that network density is not necessarily associated with increased support or increased health. In this vein, Wilcox (1981) has shown that the relationship between network density and successful coping varies with life crisis. High-density networks, which usually consist of family, are helpful in coping with normative life crises, whereas low-density networks, such as friends, are helpful in coping with nonnormative life crises. Mitchell and Trickett (1980) speculated about this relationship and suggested that high-density networks lead to higher levels of perceived support, but low-density networks lead to better adap-

tation to life transitions. However, Kadushin's (1982) work indicating that stress can lead to an increase in network density, made it clear that the casual relationship between network density and coping with life crises should not be assumed. In addition, Lee (1985), in a recent report on kinship in the United States, indicated that although the elderly are receiving a great deal of support from their families, there are also frequently psychological costs associated with the receipt of this support. The observations of Coyne and Gotlib (1982) concerning the counterproductive cycle of relationships among depressives and their families provides an example.

Although most research addressing the role of family in the lives of the elderly has focused on marital relationships, there are some notable exceptions. Circirelli (1985) has reported that most older people have at least one living sibling and that more than half live within 100 miles of their siblings. Although 88% of the elderly say that they get along well with their siblings, there is some indication that negative relationships with siblings have deleterious effects on well-being.

The role that family members play and the standards by which they are judged have been hypothesized to be different from those of friends (Antonucci, 1985b). The difference is, at least in part, related to the differences in the experience and exchange of support with friends versus family over the life course. Families are important in times of crisis, especially during the course of long-term chronic illnesses. Family are those individuals to whom one turns in times of need, those people with whom one has the sense of a lifetime reciprocity. This observation is most evident among parents and children. The older person cared for their now adult children when they were young, dependent, sick, or needy. The children were the recipients of this support. Hence, when the parent becomes old, dependent, sick, or needy, it seems quite reasonable to turn to these same children for support. Interestingly enough, and as conventional wisdom often suggests, the children are seen to have an obligation to attend to the needs of the parents. Perhaps because this obligation is present, the older adult can accept, and indeed may expect, support from his or her children. In this case, the presence of the support is anticipated and probably contributes to the positive effect of social support; however, the absence of such support will have a greater negative effect on the older person. On the other hand, the role of friend is hypothesized to be one of choice, not obligation, and thus its presence is a tribute to the current relationship of the elder with his or her peers. Our work (Antonucci & Israel, 1986; Ingersoll & Antonucci, 1983a, 1983b) has shown that the norm of reciprocity is quite strong. The receipt of support from a friend may be seen as reinforcing a mutually supportive relationship and therefore serves as evidence of the individual's continued good health, good company, and usefulness. The possibly counterintuitive findings concerning family versus friends can be interpreted as indicative of the critical interpersonal and intrapersonal aspects of long-term supportive relationships.

Reciprocity

The norm of reciprocity is quite strong in this country, and we believe it has important effects on how the individual accepts, provides, and perceives the exchange of social support. The life course perspective is particularly important and helpful in examining the role of reciprocity (Schulz & Rau, 1985). Clark, Mills, and Powell (1986) suggested that there are two types of relationships: communal and exchange. The first assumes a long-term perspective of mutual benefits over time, and the second, short-term explicit reciprocity versus immediate reciprocity. Wentowski (1981) suggested a similar dichotomy of relationships on the basis of her anthropologic study of socially supportive interactions. Lee (1985) has also addressed the issue of reciprocity through his reconsideration of social networks within a social exchange perspective (see also Dowd, 1980). Longino and Lipman (1981) used the concept of life course reciprocity to explain the differences in support systems of men and women. In this regard, the work of Israel, Hogue, and Gorton (1984) is particularly enlightening. They found that affective reciprocal support was one of the few support variables from an entire battery that was significantly related to psychological well-being. In general, the concept of reciprocity has been considered, if not developed with a great deal of specificity, by several theorists (see also Knipscheer, 1985; Mitchell & Trickett, 1980; Shinn, Lehmann, & Wong, 1985; Shore, 1985).

We hypothesize that over time, as an individual grows and matures, he or she maintains an accounting system of the reciprocity that exists with supportive others. This is an important issue for the frail or needy elder, because he or she may

be able, as previously suggested, to maintain a sense of reciprocity by using a life course accounting system. Elsewhere (Antonucci, 1985b) it has been suggested that we maintain an imaginary support account, much like a bank account. We readily note deposits, that is, supports we provide to others, and withdrawals, that is, supports we receive from others. We strive to maintain a balance at minimum but preferably a support "reserve" that can be drawn on in times of need.

Findings from a recent national study of people 50 years of age and over are illustrative (Antonucci & Akiyama, in press). It had been hypothesized than older individuals would receive more support than younger people and that they would provide fewer supports to others than younger people. It was hypothesized that older people would feel, especially using the life course perspective noted above, comfortable receiving support even when they were unable to provide it. Because the data were cross-sectional, it is difficult to make a longitudinal, life course interpretation. However, it was found that older people did report that they provided fewer supports to fewer people than younger people, but they also reported that they received support from fewer people. It is plausible that older people—this appears especially true of healthy older people—maintain cross-sectional or temporal reciprocity as long as possible. They seem to do this by denying the receipt of support and maximizing their perception of the support they provide. Three-generation research is informative in this regard, because it suggests that the older generation maximizes the similarities among the generations, whereas the younger generations are more likely to minimize them. This difference in developmental stake (Bengston & Kuypers, 1971) might be rephrased as accounting system differences that permit the maintenance of a support bank reserve or balance. Once the older individual becomes frail, it may be necessary to use the more long-term life-cycle accounting system to maintain reciprocity. Thus, an older person might find herself preferring to receive support from a relative with whom she has a lifelong reciprocal relationship. Such a finding might be considered counterintuitive, depending on one's view of social support. The receipt of tangible aid, especially when it cannot be reciprocated, may be more acceptable from a family member for the frail elder because of a perception of life-course reciprocity. On the other hand, the receipt of support from a friend with whom one can assume a reciprocal relationship may be perceived as more advantageous, especially to the elderly person who values being able to continue to maintain the norm of temporal reciprocity.

Several researchers have suggested a longitudinal life course or life span perspective to study the aging process (Hagestad & Neugarten, 1985; Riley, 1985). This approach has also been applied to the study of interpersonal socioemotional relationships. Antonucci (1976) suggested applying the infant attachment theory of Bowlby (1969) across the life cycle. In this vein, Kahn and Antonucci (1980) developed the concept of convoy as a life course description of social support over time proposed by Plath (1980). Parkes and Stevenson-Hinde (1982) call for a consideration of the place of attachment in adult interpersonal relationships, and Brown (1982) has documented the early childhood psychosocial determinants of depression among adult women, namely the early loss of an important support figure. Thoits (1982), addressing the conceptual and measurement problems that have plagued the research in this field, noted particularly that the predominant emphasis on cross-sectional, crisis-orientated data collections denies the fundamental long-term component that is clearly central to the social support construct. And Jung (1984) has suggested that as we seek to understand how social support operates and how it affects health, an important component of this process is likely to be reciprocity and reciprocity needs over time.

As we seek to understand the concept of social support, a number of questions must be raised: How do individuals come to seek out, develop, and maintain "quality" relationships? Why are some supportive relationships helpful and why are others less helpful and in some cases quite destructive? Do people develop, and if so, how do they develop an awareness that certain structural characteristics, such as density, are more useful in some crisis situations but not others? In order to address these issues, future research must focus on understanding the etiology of social support.

RELATIONSHIP BETWEEN SOCIAL SUPPORT AND HEALTH

Research examining the relationship between social support and health falls into two broad categories: the relationship between social support and physical health and the relationship between social support and mental health. Much investigation has been conducted in these areas in recent years, and some relevant research results are presented below.

A growing body of literature indicates a consistent, generally positive relationship between health and social support (e.g., Minkler, 1985; Suls, 1982). Wallston, Alagna, DeVellis, and DeVellis (1983), however, have suggested that caution is necessary when reporting the positive relationship between the two. Singer and Lord (1984) have outlined several hypothesized relationships between social support and chronic or life-threatening illness that might be positive (e.g., social support as a protection against stress) or negative (e.g., the loss of support might be a stressor itself). Several epidemiological findings have documented the positive relationship between social support and morbidity/mortality, using fairly gross measures of social support (Berkman, 1984). Berkman and Syme (1979), in a now well-known prospective study of residents of Alameda County in California, found that men and women who were married and reported numerous amounts of social interactions with family and friends were less likely to have died within the 9 years of the study than those who were unmarried and reported few social contacts. House, Robbins, and Metzner (1982) found a similar relationship for men in an 11-year longitudinal study of residents of Tecumseh, MI. The relationship was the same, though not significant, for women. And Blazer (1982) found that mortality was inversely related to social support in a longitudinal study of people over 65.

Evidence has also been growing concerning the relationship between social support and physical health. A significant relationship has been shown to exist between social support and coronary heart disease (Haynes, Feinleib, & Kannel, 1980; Joseph, 1980; Medalie & Goldbourt, 1976); pregnancy complications (Norbeck & Tilden, 1981; Nuckolls, Cassel, & Kaplan, 1972; Sosa, Kennel, & Klaus, 1980); and general health (Israel, 1982; Kaplan, Atkins, & Reinsch, 1984; Lin, Simeone, Ensel, & Kuo, 1979; Schaefer, Coyne, & Lazarus, 1981), including health specifically among the elderly (Kahn, 1979; Kasl & Berkman, 1981; Parkes & Pilisuk, 1981). In addition, practical cost-effective benefits of social support have been proposed: it can decrease the need for or length of hospitalization (Wan & Weissert, 1981); prevent or postpone the need for institutionalization (Lindsey & Hughes, 1981); decrease the need for social or formal services (Brody, Poulshock, & Masciocchi,

1978; Crossman, London, & Barry, 1981; Friedman & Kaye, 1979; McKinlay, 1980; Rundall & Evashwick, 1982; Whittaker & Garbarino, 1983); increase adherence to a medical regimen (Caplan, Robinson, French, Caldwell, & Shinn, 1976; Doherty, Schrott, Metcalf, & Iasiello-Vailas, 1983); and increase the probability of an individual's attempt to engage in and maintain preventive health behaviors (Berkman & Breslow, 1983; Finnegan & Suler, 1985; Langlie, 1977). Cohen, Teresi, and Holmes (1985) recently reported that social support reduces symptoms and increases the ability of elderly residents of mid-Manhattan hotels to meet their health needs over a 1-year period. But Schaefer et al. (1981) found that neither social support nor stressful life events were related to physical health in a sample of middle-aged (45–65) Californians.

Recently Wan (1982) used four waves of prospective data from the Social Security Administration's Longitudinal Retirement History Study (Irelan, 1976) to explore the relationship between stressful life events, social support networks, and gerontological health. The uniqueness of this large, multiwave data set permitted some of the most sophisticated analyses of these relationships thus far. He concluded that social support has an effect on gerontological health during certain stressful life events, but that this relationship is considerably more complicated than had previously been suggested.

The relationship between social support and mental health is fairly well established, but not the cause and effect of this relationship (Leavy, 1983). Studies of the relationship between social support and depression (Brown & Harris, 1978; Henderson, 1980; Schaefer et al., 1981) indicate that depressives have a history of limited supportive relationships and frequently report the early loss of a significant support person, such as a parent, during childhood. Norris and Murrell (1984) found that although interactive resource relationships do not reduce the number of stressful life events experienced, they do serve to protect older adults from global stress and depressive symptoms. Similarly, a series of articles that focused on the supportive networks of schizophrenics (Beels, 1981; Hammer, 1981; Sokolovsky & Cohen, 1981) showed their networks to be smaller and generally less able to provide necessary supports. Life satisfaction, morale, and well-being have been shown to be positively related to social support (e.g., George, 1978; Hoyt, Kaiser, Peters, & Babchuk,

1980; Mancini, 1980; Noelker & Harel, 1978, 1983; Stephens, Blau, Oser, & Millar, 1978; Tesch, Whitbourne, & Nehrke, 1981). Mental illness (Meyers & Drayer, 1979), anxiety mediation (Pattison, Llamas, & Hurd, 1979), and psychopathology (Kessler et al., 1985) have also been shown to be systematically related to social support in predictable ways. However, questions about the nature of this relationship yet remain. Many researchers (e.g., Berkman, 1984; Jung, 1984; Pearlin, 1985; Thoits, 1985) have recently noted this and have suggested that future research must focus on the interactive process between the provider and recipient of social support. The model we offer later does exactly this while at the same time considering the interactive process within a life course framework.

PSYCHOIMMUNOLOGY AND SOCIAL SUPPORT

Recent research in the field of psychoimmunology has provided some important data confirming the view that psychological variables influence immunologic functioning (Jemmott & Locke, 1984; Lauderslager & Reite, 1985). This work is particularly important because it links physiological processes with social-psychological ones. In the field of behavioral medicine this is a relationship that is well accepted. In fact, Ader and Cohen (1984) recently wrote that all the major organ systems or homeostatic defense mechanisms are subject to the influence of interactions between psychological and physiological events while also noting that this relationship is not as widely accepted among immunologists. Most immunology textbooks devote no attention to either the central nervous system or to the social-psychological factors that might influence immune functioning.

An extensive amount of research has revealed a relationship between psychological stress and physiological strain. For example, French (1974) found that role ambiguity was associated with elevated serum cortisol levels among supervisors who had poor relationships with their subordinates but not among those who had good relationships. More relevant to the current subject are the findings of Bandura, Taylor, Williams, Mefford, and Barchas (1985). They reported a relationship between catecholamine secretion and coping as a function of perceived and manipulated self-efficacy. Snake phobics showed higher levels of catecholamine secretion when asked to perform tasks for which they felt inefficacious, thus demonstrating a relationship between psychological factors and physical outcomes.

But perhaps the most striking results are those reported by Kiecolt-Glaser in a series of studies that are illustrative of the relationship between psychosocial and physical factors. She and her colleagues (Kiecolt-Glaser & Greenberg, 1984; Kiecolt-Glaser, Ricker, George, Messick, Speicher, Garner, & Glaser, 1984) found that the urinary cortisol levels were higher and cellular immunocompetency lower among lonely nonpsychotic psychiatric inpatients. In another study (Kiecolt-Glaser, Garner, Speicher, Penn, Holliday, & Glaser, 1984) it was found that medical students who were stressed by exams had lower levels of immunocompetence than these same individuals at the beginning of the academic year. One interesting and important aspect of this study was the finding that this effect was mediated by self-reported loneliness. Individuals who reported that they were lonely had higher cortisol levels and lower levels of immunocompetence than individuals who scored low on a loneliness scale. Kiecolt-Glaser et al. (1985) also showed that cellular immunocompetence in a geriatric population could be enhanced through psychosocial interventions. Research suggesting a similar relationship had been reported earlier, in the naturally occuring field studies of plant closings. Unemployed plant workers showed higher levels of stress, as well as higher cortisol levels, and this relationship was mediated by the presence of social support (Cobb & Kasl, 1977).

Much of these data on physiologic functioning and health may be reinterpretable in terms of the effects of social support on the neuroimmunologic systems. Thus, the ability to recover from cardiovascular disease, to recover more quickly from surgery, and to deliver with fewer labor complications all suggest the possible effects of social psychological factors on the neuroimmunologic processes.

CONTROL, EFFICACY, AND SOCIAL SUPPORT

Evidence has been accumulating suggesting that perceived control may play an important role in individual's assessment of and adjustment to the environment (Hamburg, 1982; Janis & Rodin, 1979: Rodin, 1986). Several general social-psycho-

logical studies are informative. Jacobs, Prentice-Dunn, and Rogers (1984) reported that self-efficacy was the best predictor of persistence on difficult tasks. Thompson (1981) found that although control over painful events did not reduce the perception of pain, it did increase the amount of pain that could be tolerated. Abella and Heslin (1984) found that valuing health and having an internal locus of control were the best predictors of engaging in health preventive behaviors. Brunstein and Olbrich (1985) found a significant increase in the perception of helplessness among state-oriented people and a significant gain in competence among action-oriented people. And finally, a recent review of action, action judgments, and the structure of control experience by Skinner (1985) provides suggestive evidence for an element of life course continuity in the perception of control. However, some caution should be exercised in the interpretation of higher levels of control as a positive influence. Miller, Lack, and Asroff (1985) found that those with Type A, or coronary-prone, behavior patterns were the least likely to give up control, even in an experimental situation, where giving up control would most likely improve task outcomes.

Some research has specifically addressed the issue of control with older people (Baltes, 1982; Lachman, 1985; Rodin, 1986). Studies by Langer and Rodin (1976) and Schulz (1976) indicated that inducing feelings of autonomy and control in older institutionalized patients results in more positive outcomes, including reduced morbidity and mortality. In a lengthy review, Janis and Rodin (1979) specifically implicated feelings of control as a major variable in positive health outcomes. And more recently, O'Leary (1985) has made this point with reference to self-efficacy and health. Two studies (Ewart, Taylor, Reese, & DeBusk, 1983; Kaplan et al., 1984) all provide empirical evidence that specific efficacy expectations (Bandura, 1977, 1982, 1986) of the individual are related to health behaviors and health outcomes. We believe, however, that this research also has implications for the interindividual and social psychological process of social support. Moos and his associates (Lemke & Moos, 1981; Moos, 1981; Moos & Ingra, 1980) have shown that higher levels of perceived control are associated with increased social interaction and more positive perceptions of the environment.

A related area of research is the relationship between locus of control and self-esteem. Wallace, Cunningham, and Del Monte (1984) found that an internal locus of control was associated with higher levels of self-esteem in children. And Lefcourt, Marti, and Saleh (1984) reported that individuals with an internal locus of control derive greater benefits from social support than those with an external locus of control. However, again caution is necessary. Schulz and Hanusa (1978), after experimentally increasing the control of older people in a retirement home, showed that the immediate positive effects dissipated after the cessation of the intervention.

As noted previously, several researchers have suggested that social support might be related to some other stable personality characteristic, such as self-esteem, mastery, or personal competence (Gore, 1985; Heller et al., 1986; Jung, 1984; Pearlin, 1985; Reis, 1984; Wills, 1985). The exact role of social support has not yet been full explicated in the perceived control literature. One possibility that is incorporated into the model to be presented in this chapter is that supportive relationships foster, develop, and help maintain an individual's perception and sense of control. We believe that the social support literature needs to incorporate the social-psychological aspects of the social support situation. It may be that the processes and mechanisms through which individuals in social support networks affect the support recipient's behaviors might be best understood within more traditional social motivation and social-psychology models. The social support situation is, actually or symbolically, one of minimum social interaction—one that involves a support recipient and support provider. Larger networks are only extensions of this basic situation. The research by Lowenthal and Haven (1968) has clearly pointed out that it is the minimal social situation (i.e., confidant relationship) that is most important in the provision of social support. This finding is consistent with the support/efficacy framework that we later propose.

Once conceived as a social interaction/social influence situation, the study of social support can be incorporated within general social psychological paradigms. Particularly important is the work on social motivation and social influence (Kelman, 1958), because a core issue is how socially supportive behaviors influence the behavior of the support recipient.

The Support/Efficacy Framework

As previously reviewed, several aspects of the social support literature have raised considerable questions about current theorizing in this area. First, the effects of social support have been observed to be less than robust (e.g., Coyne & DeLongis, 1986; Suls, 1982; Wallston et al., 1983), and in some cases the relationships have not been as expected (Antonucci, 1985a, 1985b; Antonucci & Israel, 1986; Coyne & DeLongis, 1986; Gottlieb, 1981; Heller et al. 1986). Second, the social support literature does not account particularly well for observed empirical relationships that suggest negative consequences of ostensibly social supportive behaviors on the part of supportive others (Belle, 1982; Rook, 1984). And finally, previous literature has been curiously silent on the exact mechanism(s) by which social support has positive (or negative) effects on the support recipient (Berkman, 1984; Lieberman & Mullan, 1978; Minkler, 1981; Pearlin, 1985). The largely atheoretical approach to the study of social support has contributed to these three major weaknesses.

The conceptual basis of the proposed support/efficacy framework can be understood within the psychological framework of perceived efficacy and is stimulated by the research program currently being conducted by Bandura and his colleagues (Bandura, 1977, 1982, 1986; Taylor, Bandura, Ewart, Miller, & DeBusk, 1985). Their work focuses on the rehabilitation of patients who have recently experienced uncomplicated myocardial infarctions and generally have equivalent prognoses of recovery. The study by Taylor et al. (1985) suggests that the perception of the potential for health recovery of the patient by the support provider is a critical element in the process by which social support is effective. According to their findings, wives who had higher efficacy beliefs for their husbands' recovery had husbands who were more likely to recover. In fact, the wives' perceptions were more predictive of recovery than those of their husbands. One additional aspect of their finding is particularly important: wives who actually participated in the treadmill exercise testing had higher efficacy beliefs for their husbands than wives who simply observed the treadmill testing. Actually experiencing the treadmill test increased the wives' belief in their husbands' recovery. Although Taylor et al. emphasize the recovery aspect of their findings, we are especially interested in its implications as an underlying mechanism of social support. We are proposing that social support operates by transferring the beliefs of the supportive other in the ability of the target person to perform a task, thereby increasing the target person's self-efficacy. This basic mechanism must be viewed within a life-span framework that encompasses the past social interactions and experiences of the individual's supportive others.

As this work suggests, it may be that the belief of the support provider in the efficacy or ability of the target person is the important element that influences the supportive other to engage in appropriate and effective supportive behaviors. This, in turn, influences the target person by increasing his or her sense of self-efficacy or perceived ability to accomplish the behaviors in question. In more traditional psychological terminology, one might speculate that these efficacy beliefs then become internalized and eventually persist within the target person independent of the supportive other. Within a life-span perspective we further speculate that this process is continuous over the individual life course. For example, as the supportive other communicates a specific efficacy to the target person, who eventually internalizes these efficacy beliefs, the supportive other may become more positive toward the target person because of his or her subsequent success experience. This reinforces and perpetuates the supportive other's sense of the target person's efficacy and provides a basis for the continued support/efficacy interaction.

Coyne and Gotlib (1982) have suggested a compatible process with depressed persons though with perhaps opposite results. The depressed behavior of target persons causes their supportive others to feel less positively towards them. This is subtly communicated to the depressed person. The target person thus perceives supportive others as less supportive, which may serve to reinforce his or her depression.

These studies and the framework we have just outlined suggest that a fairly complex process may be operating. Figure 22.1 presents the hypothesized process of the support/efficacy relationship. The supportive other's beliefs in the efficacy of the target person (A) is influenced by the supportive other's motivations to communicate these beliefs to the target person (B). The supportive other's perceptions of the target person's efficacy and his or her motivation to communicate this belief combine to influence the performance of supportive behaviors (C). These supportive behaviors are interpreted by the target person in terms of his or her assessment of the supportive other's motivations (D) for performing the supportive behaviors. In the positive case, these positively affect the target person's self-efficacy (E), and health and well-being (F). Of course, the sequence could also have a negative effect. For example, the target person might question the supportive other's motivation and perceive the latter as insincere or self-serving in his or her support behaviors. The concluding segments of the model are reinforced by several recent studies which show that the specific efficacy beliefs of individuals are directly related to health and health outcomes (Ewart et al., 1983; Holahan, Holahan, & Belk, 1984; Kaplan et al., 1984; Taylor, Bandura, Ewart, Miller, & DeBusk, 1984).

Implications of the Support/Efficacy Framework

Most of the support literature has focused on the nature of the support network (e.g., structure, function) or on the perceived quantity or quality of support by the recipient. Less research has been conducted on the relationship between support provider and support recipient in terms of factors that may influence the nature and effectiveness of the support provider's behaviors. Thus, equivalent supportive behaviors engaged in by different support providers may be differentially perceived and effective in the support relationship (Antonucci, 1985b). This hypothesized process may account for why equivalent behaviors are differentially effective and even why tangible support may not always result in positive outcomes.

We believe that the willingness of the support provider to engage in what appear to be supportive behaviors is a complex process that begins with the support provider's beliefs about the perceived efficacy of the target person to engage in the relevant behaviors. This perception may be affected by objective indicators in the environment but also may be dependent upon the prior relationship between the provider and recipient and the ability and willingness of the recipient to engage in the behaviors.

Similarly, this approach also takes into consideration perceptual and cognitive factors in the relationships between support provider and

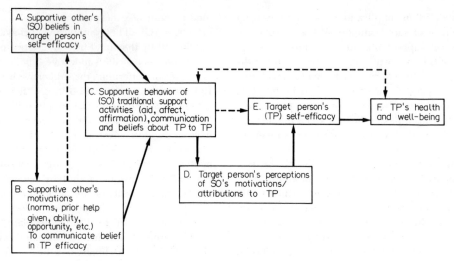

Figure 22.1 Hypothesized interpersonal support/efficacy process

support recipient. Thus, it can also explain why some ostensibly supportive behaviors can be construed as negative support (Heller, 1979; Rook, 1985). In some situations it may be that it is the perception by the support recipient regarding the legitimacy of the motivation(s) underlying the behaviors that is important. In short, not all supportive behaviors engaged in by the support provider will be positively evaluated and have positive effects on the personal efficacy of the support recipient. If these positive effects on the personal efficacy of the support recipient do not occur, then the behaviors of the support recipient are not supportive according to our definition of the concept. In fact, negative support can be construed as either the absence of a positive influence on the self-efficacy of the support recipient or a negative influence, i.e. a decrease in the self-efficacy of the support recipient.

In a more positive light, the proposed framework may help explain the greater predictive power of adequacy and perceptual over structural or functional measures, of social support. It may also help explain why quantity of support appears to be less effective, proportionately, than quality, although it is still related to positive outcomes. As the literature has often shown (e.g., Lowenthal & Haven, 1968) the quality of perceived support is important, perhaps because the confidant communicates and promotes the target person's self-efficacy.

We believe the proposed support/efficacy framework can begin to account for some of the previous atheoretical and often anomalous findings in the social support literature. The conceptualization is highly relevant to the work that has demonstrated effects of control and efficacy on behavioral outcomes, particularly health and health-related behaviors (Ewart et al., 1983; Kaplan et al., 1984; Langer & Rodin, 1976; Rodin, 1980, 1986; Schulz, 1976; Thomas, Garry, Goodwin, & Goodwin, 1985). Thus, it is generally predicted that measures based upon the proposed support/efficacy framework will be more effective in accounting for health and other successful outcomes than traditional measures of social support, such as structure and function.

CLINICAL APPLICATIONS OF THE PROPOSED MODEL

In the final analysis for the clinical gerontologist, the potential contribution of the social support literature is its practical implications for the health and well-being of the older individual. Social support researchers have now reached the point where a great deal of baseline descriptive data are available, and we are generally convinced that social support has some potential for positively affecting the lives of the elderly. However, the research data have also presented some inconsistencies, especially with respect to the magnitude of the positive effects, the situations in which these might occur, and, for the clinician, the sensitive issue of when social support might have a negative effect on the individual.

In this chapter we have suggested a life course

framework, particularly reciprocity over the life course, as an important basis for understanding the processes and mechanisms by which social support operates. We have theorized that a self-efficacy process provides the underlying basis through which social support has its effects. We believe that the derivations from this model have practical implications for clinical gerontological interventions.

Recently researchers have begun to focus on the applicability of social support to health and health promotion, especially in terms of prevention, intervention, and caretaking (Israel & Rounds, in press; Tretli, Bjartveit, Foss, Haider, & Lund-Larsen, 1985; Simson, Wilson, Hermalen, & Hess, 1983; Wan, Odell, & Lewis, 1982; Wortman & Conway, 1985). Policymakers (e.g., Kiesler, 1985) are particularly interested in this potentially cost-effective means for attending to the needs of the elderly—especially as they become sick and frail and consequently a potential burden on public services and the health care system. The changing demographics pose this issue as an increasingly pressing one. We believe that the support/efficacy model offers several guidelines to those for whom the practical application of the principles of social support is an important issue. First, an assessment of the life course relationships between the elderly person and the potential support provider is critical. To attempt an intervention program, for example, with a supportive other whom the elderly person does not trust or with whom he or she does not have a past history of a supportive relationship would be misguided, and would unnecessarily (and negatively) bias the plan. Next, one might consider the elderly individual's personal characteristics. Some people have a preference for—and a history of—control. Evidence suggests that these people may be more likely to have higher levels of self-esteem, mastery, and social competence. They are likely to have qualitatively superior support networks, and we would predict they are more likely to have a history of reciprocal relationships. A traditional intervention strategy planned for these individuals has a high probability of success. However, for individuals who do not meet these specifications, the traditional support intervention may be doomed to failure. For this group, although the task is certainly formidable, an intervention strategy that specifically highlights the enhancement of self-esteem, mastery, and social competence is likely to have a greater probability of a successful outcome.

Applications of the principles and framework

suggested in this chapter may serve several important functions for the clinician. The group where the "traditional" success of supportive relationships is likely to result can be specified. This will isolate a second group of people who are less likely to show the expected effect of support interventions unless special à priori interventions are incorporated into the support program. Thus, the clinician will be better able to anticipate the potential success and the special needs of his or her patients. In addition, the work of Bandura and his colleagues suggests a mechanism by which the strength of all supportive interventions might be enhanced. Assuming a basically positive or neutral relationship, the support provider might be involved in the intervention program, much as the treadmill-exercising wives were in the study by Taylor et al. (1985). For the older individual who has already mastered several difficult tasks, the support provider might be sensitized to the difficulty of these tasks given the elder's current condition. Examples might include the successful management of a special diet, the negotiation of steep stairs despite arthritis, or the ability to carry on a conversation through lipreading, despite severe hearing loss. The supportive other might come to appreciate the difficulty of these tasks, and the success their friend or family member has had, through simulation or experience of the actual tasks or through comparison with less successful others in similar situations. In short, the clinician can target both the older person and the support provider for efficacy-enhancing interventions, in order to optimize the positive effects of supportive relationships.

CONCLUSIONS

In this chapter we have presented data from the available literature that leads to the inescapable conclusion that social support can have facilitative influences on effective functioning and health in older persons. Thus, the social support process is of critical concern to clinicians involved in modifying the health behaviors of their clients. We have argued, both from need as well as important social policy dimensions, that social support is of increasing importance in the lives of the elderly, especially the frail elderly. Demographic trends of increased average age suggest that tomorrow's older person will be living even longer. But the morbidity data raise questions regarding the quality of that life extension and the level of health needs that will be a consequence. What is clear is that the health needs of the older population will continue to be greater than the needs of other age groups in the adult life span.

Some have made dire predictions about the rising health care costs and the ability of the population to meet these increased demands. These concerns have led policymakers and health planners to seek less costly alternatives. Thus, social support as an alternative to professional services becomes an attractive option. However, as we presented, many questions remain regarding the effects of social support on physical health and mental health functioning. The massive data that have accumulated confirm some type of direct or moderating effects on health. We have argued that the vast multidisciplinary and lay attention to the support concept has created a great deal of confusion in the literature. Definitions, measures, approaches, and theoretical frameworks differ as a function of discipline and the specific areas of inquiry. We argue that this has done a disservice to the social support concept and undoubtedly contributes to its current pretheoretical state. However, we conclude that the evidence of social support's importance is incontrovertible. What is not clear is: What is social support? How should it be measured? What are its critical dimensions? What are the exact mechanisms that underlie its important relationships to health and well-being?

Although fearful of adding to an already confusing situation, we have suggested several important aspects of the social support concept that we believe should have investigatory precedence. An overriding concern is the need to consider social support in a life span or life course theoretical framework. We have argued that the history of interactions, the nature of prior support networks and arrangements and even a concept like support bank demand a much more dynamic life course treatment than is currently provided by most theorists. Within this conception we have highlighted the importance of reciprocity relationships, the need to clearly distinguish quality from quantity of support and structural from functional relationships. Perhaps most important is the need to begin the difficult process of addressing the nature of the mechanism or mechanisms through which social supportive behaviors have their effects.

We have devoted much of this chapter to a discussion of one possible mechanism that may serve as an organizing scheme to account for the process by which behaviors of support providers affect individual support recipient responses and behaviors. We have essentially conceived of the social support situation, at its basic level, as a minimal social situation in social psychological and social interaction terms. Structurally and functionally, social support must involve the actual or symbolic interaction of at least two people. We believe then that the situation of social support can be more fruitfully studied within the traditional models of social influence and social interaction processes.

This chapter proposes that the work on self-efficacy provides a good organizing scheme in which to consider socially supportive mechanisms. We have suggested both a strong and weak hypothesis. The weak hypothesis proposes that socially supportive behaviors influence the personal efficacy of the support recipient. The strong hypothesis proposes that socially supportive behaviors are only supportive to the extent that they positively influence the personal efficacy of the support recipient to engage in the target behaviors. We believe the review of the relevant literature presented in this chapter provides fairly conclusive evidence that personal efficacy can influence behavior, including health behaviors. What is not clear at the present time, and is somewhat speculative on our part, is the exact mechanism through which social interaction and the supportive behaviors of others are internalized by support recipients. We have discussed possible mechanisms through which this may occur, based upon the general social psychological literature.

In summary we have argued that the support/efficacy mechanism can provide a unifying model of the social influence and social interaction process that we believe characterizes the social support situation. We have presented arguments that this framework can help explain the positive, negative, and null effects of ostensibly the same supportive behaviors; the superiority of quality over quantity of support; the strength of weak ties effects; the very weak effects of structural characteristics of social networks; the importance of reciprocity and life span approaches; and the fact that support is relatively enduring in certain situations and more ephemeral in others. We do not imply that the support/efficacy mechanism is the only one that may operate in the social support situation. We only propose that, at least theoretically, it may serve as a useful and broad framework to account for observed consistent and inconsistent effects in the social support literature. Work is currently under way to empirically test derivations from the model.

Finally, we turned to the major thrust of this chapter—the importance of social support in clinical gerontology. Our review indicates the importance of social support in health and effective functioning of older people. This seems indisputable. But how does this fact aid the clinician working with the geriatric patient and family? The history of social interaction and socially supportive relationships that individuals and families bring to the clinical setting poses serious challenges to the clinician who is interested in health intervention. The framework that we have proposed at least guides the clinician to possible approaches.

First, it demands that both individuals in the social support network and the potential support recipient must be involved in the intervention. Second, it demands that specific target health behaviors must be identified. Third, it suggests that accumulated credits in the "support bank" should be explored as possible beginning points. Fourth, it suggests that the historical nature of social interactions should be explored in depth. Fifth, it suggests possible interventions to increase the self-efficacy of the support recipient.

Although the intervention(s) would have to be tailored for the situation and persons involved, the model that we have proposed suggests beginning with the involvement of the supportive other in the health regimens designed to influence the support recipient. We have speculated that this will increase the expressions and performance of supportive behaviors, which in turn should influence the self-efficacy of the support recipient and finally the actual performance of the desired behaviors.

This model does not indicate the exact nature of the interventions. It does, however, suggest who should be involved and broad outlines of the intervention procedures. Further empirical testing and theoretical refinements are needed, before we are satisfied that the model can actually contribute to our understanding of the nature of social support. If the empirical results are positive, then we believe that the model can provide helpful guidelines for the work of the geriatric clinician and increase the effective functioning and quality of life of the older client.

REFERENCES

Abella, R., & Heslin, R. (1984). Health, locus of control, values, and the behavior of family and friends: An integrated approach to understanding preventive health behavior. *Basic and Applied Social Behavior*, 5(4), 283–293.

Ader, R., & Cohen, N. (1984). Behavior and the immune system. In W. Doyle Gentry (Ed.), *Handbook of behavioral medicine* (pp. 117–173). New York: Guilford.

Ainsworth, M. D. S., Blehar, M. C., Waters, E., & Wall, S. (1978). *Patterns of attachment*. Hillsdale, NJ: Erlbaum.

Antonucci, T. C. (1976). Attachment: A life-span concept. *Human Development*, 19(3), 135–142.

Antonucci, T. C. (1985a). Social support: Theoretical advances, recent findings and pressing issues. In I. G. Sarason & B. R. Sarason (Eds.), *Social support: Theory, research, and applications* (pp. 21–38). Dordrecht, the Netherlands: Martinus Nijhof.

Antonucci, T. C. (1985b). Personal characteristics, social support, and social behavior. In R. H. Binstock & E. Shanas (Eds.). *Handbook of aging and the social sciences* (2nd ed., pp. 94–128). New York: Van Nostrand Reinhold.

Antonucci, T. C., & Akiyama, H. (in press). Social Networks in Adult life and a preliminary examination of the convoy model. *Journal of Gerontology*.

Antonucci, T. C., & Depner, C. E. (1982). Social support and informal helping relationships. In T. A. Wills (Ed.), *Basic processes in helping relationships* (pp. 223–254). New York: Academic.

Antonucci, T. C., & Israel, B. (1986). Veridicality of social support: A comparison of principal and network members' responses. *Journal of Consulting and Clinical Psychology*, 54, 432–437.

Antonucci, T. C., & Levitt, M. J. (1984). Early prediction of attachment security: A multivariate approach. *Merrill-Palmer Quarterly*, 30(1), 1–10.

Arend, K., Gove, F. L., & Sroufe, L. A. (1979). Continuity of individual adaptation from infancy to kindergarten: A predictive study of ego-resiliency and curiosity in preschoolers. *Child Development*, 58, 958–959.

Arling, G. (1976). The elderly widow and her family, neighbors, and friends. *Journal of Marriage and the Family*, 38, 757–768.

Baltes, M. M. (1982). Enviromental factors in dependency among nursing home residents: A social ecology analysis. In T. A. Wills (Ed.), *Basic processes in helping relationships* (pp. 405–425). New York: Academic.

Bandura, A. (1977). Self-efficacy: Toward a unifying theory of behavioral change. *Psychological Review*, 84, 191–215.

Bandura, A. (1982). Self-efficacy mechanisms in human agency. *American Psychologist*, 37, 122–147.

Bandura, A. (1986). *Social Foundations of Thought's Actions*. Englewood Cliffs, N.J.: Prentice Hall.

Bandura, A., Taylor, C., Williams, L., Mefford, I. H., & Barchas, J. D. (1985). Catecholamine secretion as a function of perceived coping self-efficacy. *Journal of Consulting and Clinical Psychology*, 53(3), 406–414.

Beels, C. C. (1981). Social support and schizophrenia. *Schizophrenia Bulletin*, 41, 59–72.

Belle, D. (1982). Social ties and social support. In D. Belle (Ed.), *Lives in stress* (pp. 133–144). Beverly Hills, CA: Sage.

Bengston, V. L., & Kuypers, J. A. (1971). Generational

differences and the development stake. *International Journal of Aging and Human Development, 2,* 249–260.

Berkman, L. S. (1984). Assessing the physical health effects of social networks and social support. *Annual Review of Public Health, 5,* 413–432.

Berkman, L. F., & Breslow, L. (1983). *Health and ways of living.* New York: Oxford University Press.

Berkman, L. S., & Syme, S. L. (1979). Social networks, host resistance, and mortality: A nine year follow-up study of Alameda County residents. *American Journal of Epidemiology, 109*(2), 186–204.

Biegel, D. E. (1985). The application of network theory and research to the field of aging. In W. J. Sauer & R. T. Coward (Eds.), *Social support networks and the care of the elderly: Theory, research, and practice* (pp. 251–274). New York: Springer.

Blazer, D. G. (1982). Social support and mortality in an elderly population. *American Journal of Epidemiology, 115,* 684–694.

Boissevain, B. (1974). *Friends of friends.* New York: St. Martin's Press.

Bott, E. (1957). *Family and social network.* London: Tavistock.

Bowlby, J. (1969). *Attachment and loss: Vol. 1. Attachment.* New York: Basic Books.

Boyce, W. T. (1985). Social support, family relations, and children. In S. Cohen & L. S. Syme (Eds.), *Social support and health* (pp. 151–173). New York: Academic.

Bretherton, I., & Waters, E. (Eds.). (1985). Growing points of attachment theory and research. *Monographs of the Society for Research in Child Development, 50*(1–2, Serial No. 209).

Broadhead, W. E., Kaplan, B. H., Sherman, J. A., Wagner, E. H., Schoenbach, V. J., Grimson, R., Heyden, S., Tibblin, G., & Gehlbach, S. H. (1983). The epidemiologic evidence for a relationship between social support and health. *American Journal of Epidemiology, 117*(5), 521–537.

Brody, S. J., Poulshock, S. W., & Masciocchi, C. F. (1978). The family caring unit: A major consideration in the long-term support system. *Gerontologist, 18*(6), 547–555.

Brown, G. W. (1982). Early loss and depression. In C. M. Parkes & J. Stevenson-Hinde (Eds.), *The place of attachment in human behavior* (pp. 232–268). New York: Basic Books.

Brown, G. W., & Harris, T. (1978). *Social origins of depression: A study of psychiatric disorder in women.* New York: Free Press.

Brownell, A., & Shumaker, S. A. (1984). An introduction to a complex phenomenon. *Journal of Social Issues, 40*(4), 1–10.

Brunstein, J. C., & Olbrich, E. (1985). Personal helplessness and action control: Analysis of achievement—related cognitions, self-assessments, and performance. *Journal of Personality and Social Psychology, 48,* 1540–1551.

Cantor, M. H. (1979). Neighbors and friends: An overlooked resource in the informal support system. *Research on Aging, 1,* 434–463.

Caplan, R. D., Robinson, E. A. R., French, J. R. P., Jr., Caldwell, J. R., & Shinn, M. (1976). *Adherence to medical regimens: Pilot experiments in patient education and social support.* Ann Arbor: University of Michigan Institute for Social Research, Research Center for Group Dynamics.

Cassel, J. (1976). The contribution of the social environment to host resistance. *American Journal of Epidemiology, 104*(2), 107–123.

Chappell, N. A. (1983). Informal support networks among the elderly. *Research on Aging, 5*(1), 77–100.

Cicirelli, V. G. (1985). The role of siblings as family caregivers. In W. J. Sauer & R. T. Coward (Eds.), *Social support networks and the care of the elderly: Theory, research, and practice* (pp. 93–107). New York: Springer.

Clark, M. S., Mills, J., and Powell, M. C. (1986). Keeping track of needs in communal and exchange relationships. *Journal of Personality and Social Psychology, 51* (2), 333–338.

Cobb, S. (1976). Social support as a moderator of life stress. *Psychosomatic Medicine, 38*(5), 300–314.

Cobb, S., & Kasl, S. V. (1977). *Termination: The consequences of job loss* (HEW Publication No. [NIOSH] 77–224). Washington, DC: U.S. Department of Health, Education and Welfare.

Cochran, M. M., & Brassard, J. A. (1979). Child development and personal social networks. *Child Development, 50,* 601–616.

Cohen, C. I., & Rajkowski, H. (1982). What's in a friend? *Gerontologist, 22*(3), 261–266.

Cohen, S., & Syme, L. (Eds.). (1985). *Social support and health.* New York: Academic.

Cohen, C. I., Teresi, J., & Holmes, D. (1985). Social networks, stress, adaptation and health. *Research on Aging, 7*(3), 409–431.

Cohen, S., & Wills, T. A. (1985). Stress, social support, and the buffering hypothesis. *Psychology Bulletin, 98*(2), 310–357.

Coyne, J. C., & DeLongis, A. (1986). Going beyond social support: The role of social relationships in adaptation. *Journal of Consulting and Clinical Psychology, 54,* 454–460.

Coyne, J. C., & Gotlib, I. H. (1982). The role of cognition in depression: A critical appraisal. *Psychological Bulletin, 94*(3), 472–505.

Crossman, L., London, C., & Barry, C. (1981). Older women caring for disabled spouses: A model for supportive services. *Gerontologist, 21*(5), 564–570.

D'Augelli, A. (1983). Social support networks in mental health. In J. K. Whittaker, J. Garbarino, and Associates (Eds.), *Social support networks: Informal helping in the human services* (pp. 71–106). New York: Aldine.

Depner, C., Wethington, E., & Ingersoll-Dayton, B. (1984). Social support: Methodological issues in design and measurement. *Journal of Social Issues, 40*(4); 37–54.

Doherty, W. J., Schrott, H. G., Metcalf, L., & Iasiello-Vailas, L. (1983). Effect of spouse support on health beliefs on medications adherence. *Journal of Family Practice, 17*(5), 837–841.

Dowd, J. J. (1980). *Stratification among the aged.* Monterey, CA: Brooks/Cole.

Duff, R. W., & Hong, L. K. (1982). Quality and quantity of social interactions in the life satisfaction of older Americans. *Sociology and Social Research, 66,* 418–434.

Ell, K. (1984). Social networks, social support, and health status: A review. *Social Service Review*, *58*(1), 133–149.

Ewart, C. K., Taylor, C. B., Reese, L. B., & DeBusk, R. (1983). Effects of early postmyocardial infarction exercise testing on self-perception and subsequent physical activity. *American Journal of Cardiology*, *51*, 1076–1080.

Felton, B., Lehmann, S., Adler, A., & Burgio, M. (1981). Single room occupancy hotels: Their viability as housing options for older citizens. In M. P. Lawton & S. L. Hoover (Eds.), *Community housing choices for older Americans* (pp. 267–285). New York: Springer.

Ferraro, K. F., Mutran, E., & Barresi, C. M. (1984). Widowhood, health, and friendship support in later life. *Journal of Health and Social Behavior*, *25*, 245–259.

Finnegan, D. L., & Suler, J. R. (1985). Psychological factors associated with maintenance of improved health behaviors in postcoronary patients. *Journal of Psychology*, *119*(1), 87–94.

French, J. R. P., Jr. (1974). Person-role fit. In A. McLean (Ed.), *Occupational stress* (pp. 70–79). Springfield, IL: Charles C. Thomas.

Friedman, S. R., & Kaye, L. W. (1979). Homecare for the frail elderly: Implications for an interactional relationship. *Journal of Gerontological Social Work*, *2*(2), 109–124.

George, L. K. (1978). The impact of personality and social status factors upon levels of activity and psychological well-being. *Journal of Gerontology*, *33*(6), 840–847.

Gore, L. (1985). Social support and styles of coping with stress. In S. Cohen & S. L. Syme (Eds.), *Social support and health* (pp. 263–278). New York: Academic.

Gottlieb, B. (1981). *Social networks and social support*. Beverly Hills, CA: Sage.

Greenblatt, M. J., Becerra, R. M., & Serafetinides, E. A. (1982). Social networks and mental health: An overview. *American Journal of Psychiatry*, *139*(8), 977–984.

Griffith, J. (1985). Social support providers: Who are they? Where are they met? And the relationship of network characteristics to psychological distress. *Basic and Applied Social Psychology*, *6*(1), 41–60.

Hagestad, G. O., & Neugarten, B. L. (1985). Age and the life course. In R. H. Binstock & E. Shanas (Eds.), *Handbook of aging and social sciences* (2nd ed., pp. 35–61). New York: Van Nostrand Reinhold.

Hall, A., & Wellman, B. (1985). Social networks and social support. In S. Cohen & L. Syme (Eds.), *Social support and health* (pp. 23–42). New York: Academic.

Hamburg, D. A. (1982). *Health and behavior: Frontiers of research in the biobehavioral sciences*. Washington, DC: National Academy Press.

Hammer, M. (1981). Social supports, social networks, and schizophrenia. *Schizophrenia Bulletin*, *7*, 45–57.

Hanson, S. H., & Sauer, W. G. (1985). Children and their elderly parents. In W. J. Sauer & R. T. Coward (Eds.), *Social support networks and the care of the elderly: Theory, research, and practice* (pp. 41–66). New York: Springer.

Haynes, S., Feinleib, M., & Kannel, W. (1980). The relationship of psychosocial factors to coronary heart disease in the Framingham Study: Eight year inci-

dence of coronary heart disease. *American Journal of Epidemiology 111*, 37–58.

Heller, K. (1979). The effects of social support: Prevention and treatment implications. In A. P. Goldstein & F. H. Kanfer (Eds.), *Maximizing treatment gains: Transfer enhancement in psychotherapy* (pp. 353–382). New York: Academic.

Heller, K. (1986). Introduction to the series: Disaggregating the process of social support. *Journal of Consulting and Clinical Psychology*, *54*, 415.

Heller, K., & Mansbach, W. E. (1984). The multifaceted nature of social support in a community sample of elderly women. *Journal of Social Issues*, *40*(4), 99–112.

Heller, K., Swindle, R. W., & Dusenbury, L. (1986). Component social support processes: Comments and integration. *Journal of Consulting and Clinical Psychology*, *54*, 466–470.

Henderson, S. (1980). The significance of social relationships in the etiology of neurosis. In C. M. Parkes & J. Stevenson-Hinde (Eds.), *The place of attachment in human behavior* (pp. 205–237). New York: Basic Books.

Hess, B. B., & Soldo, B. J. (1985). Husband and wife networks. In W. J. Sauer & R. T. Coward (Eds.), *Social support networks and the care of the elderly: Theory, research, and practice* (pp. 67–92). New York: Springer.

Holahan, C. K., Holahan, C. J., & Belk, S. S. (1984). Adjustment in aging: The roles of life stress, hassles, and self-efficacy. *Health Psychology*, *3*(4), 315–328.

House, J. S. (1981). *Work stress and social support*. Reading, MA: Addison-Wesley.

House, J. S., & Kahn, R. L. (1985). Measures and concepts of social support. In S. Cohen & L. Syme (Eds.), *Social support and health* (pp. 83–108). New York: Academic.

House, J. S., Robbins, C., & Metzner, H. C. (1982). The association of social relationships and activities with mortality: Perspective evidence from the Tecumseh community health study. *American Journal of Epidemiology*, *116*(1), 123–140.

Hoyt, D. R., Kaiser, M. A., Peters, G. R., & Babchuk, N. (1980). Life satisfaction and activity theory: A multidimensional approach. *Journal of Gerontology*, *35*(6), 935–941.

Ingersoll, B., & Antonucci, T. C. (1983a, August). *Support networks among the elderly: Asset or liability*. Paper presented at the annual meeting of the American Psychological Association, Anaheim.

Ingersoll, B., & Antonucci, T. C. (1983b, November). *Negative social support: another side of intimate relationships*. Paper presented at the annual meeting of the Gerontological Society of America, San Francisco.

Irelan, L. M. (1976). Retirement history study: Introduction. In L. M. Irelan (Ed), *Almost 65: Baseline data from the retirement history study*, (HEW/SSA/ORS Research Report 49, HEW Publication [SSA] 76–11806). Washington, DC: Department of Health, Education, and Welfare.

Israel, B. A. (1982). Social networks and health status: Linking theory, research and practice. *Patient Counseling and Health Education*, *4*(2), 65–79.

Israel, B. A., Hogue, C. C., & Gorton, T. A. (1984). Social networks among elderly women: Implications for health education practice. *Health Education Quarterly, 10*(3/4), 173–203.

Israel, B. A., & Rounds, K. A. (in press). Social networks and social support: A synthesis for health educators. *Annual Review of Health Education.*

Jacobs, B., Prentice-Dunn, S., & Rogers, R. W. (1984). Understanding persistence: An interface of control theory and self-efficacy theory. *Basic and applied social psychology, 5*(4), 333–347.

Janis, I., & Rodin, J. (1979). Attribution, control, and decision making: Social psychology and health care. In G. Stone, F. Cohen, & N. Adler (Eds.), *Health psychology: A handbook* (pp. 487–521). San Francisco: Jossey-Bass.

Jemmott, J., & Locke, S. E. (1984). Psychosocial factors, immunologic mediation, and human susceptibility to infectious diseases: How much do we know? *Psychological Bulletin, 95,* 78–108.

Johnson, C. L., & Catalano, D. J. (1981). Childless elderly and their family supports. *Gerontologist, 21*(6), 610–618.

Jones, B. (1981). *Mental health and the structure of support.* Unpublished doctoral dissertation, University of Michigan, Ann Arbor.

Jones, W. H., Carpenter, B. N., & Quintana, D. (1985). Personality and interpersonal predictors of loneliness in two cultures. *Journal of Personality and Social Psychology, 48*(6), 1503–1511.

Joseph, J. (1980). *Social affiliation, risk factor status, and coronary heart disease: A cross-sectional study of Japanese-American men.* Unpublished doctoral dissertation, University of California, Berkeley.

Jung, J. (1984). Social support and its relation to health: A critical evaluation. *Basic and Applied Social Psychology, 5*(2), 143–169.

Kadushin, C. (1982). Social density and mental health. In P. V. Marsden & N. Lin (Eds.), *Social structure and network analyses* (pp. 147–159). Beverly Hills, CA: Sage.

Kahn, R. L. (1979). Aging and social support. In M. W. Riley (Ed.), *Aging from birth to death* (pp. 77–92). Boulder, CO: Westview.

Kahn, R. L., & Antonucci, T. C. (1980). Convoys over the life course: Attachment, roles and social support. In P. B. Baltes & O. Brim (Eds.), *Life-span development and behavior* (Vol. 3, pp. 254–283). Boston: Lexington.

Kaplan, R. M., Atkins, C. J., & Reinsch, S. (1984). Specific efficacy expectations mediate exercise compliance in patients with COPD. *Health Psychology, 3*(3), 223–242.

Kasl, S. V., & Berkman, L. F. (1981). Some psychosocial influences on the health status of the elderly: The perspective of social epidemiology. In J. McCaugh & S. Kiesler (Eds.), *Aging: Biology and behavior* (pp. 345–385). New York: Academic.

Kelman, H. C. (1958). Compliance, identification and internalization: Three processes of attitude change. *Journal of Conflict Resolution, 2,* 51–60.

Kessler, R. C., Price, R. H., & Wortman, C. B. (1985). Social factors in psychopathology: Stress, social support, and coping process. *Annual Review of Psychology, 36,* 531–572.

Kiecolt-Glaser, J. K., Garner, W., Speicher, C., Penn, G. M., Holliday, J., & Glaser, R. (1984). Psychosocial modifiers of immunocompetence in medical students. *Psychosomatic Medicine, 46*(1), 7–14.

Kiecolt-Glaser, J. K., Glaser, R., Williger, D., Stout, J., Messick G., Sheppard, S., Ricker, D., Romisher, S. C., Briner, W., Bonnell, G., & Donnerberg, R. (1985). Psychosocial enhancement of immunocompetence in a geriatric population. *Health Psychology, 4*(1), 25–41.

Kiecolt-Glaser, J. K., & Greenberg, B. (1984). Social support as a moderator of the after-effects of stress in female psychiatric inpatients. *Journal of Abnormal Psychology, 93*(2), 192–199.

Kiecolt-Glaser, J. K., Ricker, D., George, J., Messick, G., Speicher, C. E., Garner, G., & Glaser, R. (1984). Urinary cortisol levels, cellular immunocompetency, and loneliness in psychiatric inpatients. *Psychosomatic Medicine, 46*(1), 15–24.

Kiesler, C. A. (1985). Policy implications of research on social support and health. In S. Cohen & L. Syme (Eds.), *Social support and health* (pp. 347–364). New York: Academic.

Knipscheer, K. (1985, July). *The quality of the relationship between elderly people and their adult children.* Paper presented at the International Gerontology Meeting, New York.

Lachman, M. E. (1985). Personal efficacy in middle and old age: Differential and normative patterns of change. In G. H. Elder, Jr. (Ed.), *Life-course dynamics: Trajectories and transitions* (pp. 188–213). Ithaca, NY: Cornell University Press.

Langer, E. T., & Rodin, T. (1976). The effects of choice and enhanced personal responsibility for the aged: A field experiment in an institutional setting. *Journal of Personality and Social Psychology, 34,* 191–198.

Langlie, J. K. (1977). Social networks, health beliefs, and preventive health behavior. *Journal of Health and Social Behavior, 18,* 244–260.

Lauderslager, M. L., & Reite, M. L. (1985). Losses and separations: Immunological consequences and health implications. In P. Shaver (Ed.), *Review of personality and social psychology* (pp. 285–312). Beverly Hills, CA: Sage.

Leavy, R. L. (1983). Social support and psychological disorder: A review. *Journal of Community Psychology, 11,* 3–19.

Lee, G. R. (1985). Kinship and social support of the elderly: The case of the United States. *Aging and Society, 5*(1), 19–38.

Lefcourt, H. M., Marti, R. A., & Saleh, W. E. (1984). Locus of control and social support: Interactive moderators of stress. *Journal of Personality and Social Psychology, 47*(2), 378–389.

Lemke, S., & Moos, R. H. (1981). The suprapersonal environments of sheltered care settings. *Journal of Gerontology, 36*(2), 233–243.

Levitt, M. J., Antonucci, T. C., Clark, M. C., Rotton, J., & Finley, G. E. (1985). Social support and well-being: Preliminary indicators based on two samples of the elderly. *International Journal of Aging and Human Development, 21*(1), 61–77.

Levitt, M., Weber, R., & Clark, M. C. (1986). Social network relationships as sources of maternal support and well-being. *Developmental Psychology, 22*(3), 310–316.

Lieberman, M. A., & Mullan, J. T. (1978). Does help

help? The adaptive consequences of obtaining help from professionals and social networks. *Amercian Journal of Community Psychology, 6*(5), 499–517.

Lin, N., Simeone, R. L., Ensel, W. M., & Kuo, W. (1979). Social support, stressful life events and illness: A model and an empirical test. *Journal of Health and Social Behavior, 20,* 108–119.

Lindsey, A. M., & Hughes, E. M. (1981). Social support and alternatives to institutionalization for the at-risk elderly. *Journal of the American Geriatrics Society, 29*(7), 308–315.

Litwak, E. (1985). *Helping the elderly.* New York: Guilford.

Longino, C. F., Jr., & Lipman, A. (1981). Married and spouseless men and women in planned retirement communities: Support network differentials. *Journal of Marriage and the Family, 43,* 169–177.

Longino, C. F., Jr., & Lipman, A. (1985). The support systems of women. In W. Sauer & R. Coward (Eds.), *Social support networks and the care of the elderly: Theory research and practice* (pp. 219–233). New York: Springer.

Lopata, H. Z. (1979). *Women as widows: Support systems.* New York: Elsevier.

Lowenthal, M. F., & Haven, C. (1968). Interaction and adaptation: Intimacy as a critical variable. *American Sociological Review, 33,* 20–30.

Mancini, J. A. (1980). Friend interaction, competence and morale in old age. *Research on Aging, 2*(4), 416–431.

Matas, L., Arend, R. A., & Sroufe, L. A. (1978). Continuity of adaptation in the second year: The relationship between quality of attachment and later competence. *Child Development, 49,* 547–556.

McFarlane, A. H., Norman, G. R., Streiner, D. L., & Roy, R. G. (1984). Characteristics and correlates of effective and ineffective social supports. *Journal of Psychosomatic Research, 28*(6), 501–510.

McKinlay, J. B. (1980). Social network influences on morbid episodes and the career of help seeking. In L. Eisenberg & A. Kleinman (Eds.), *The relevance of social science for medical practice* (pp. 77–110). Hingman, MA: D. Reidel.

Medalie, J. H., & Goldbourt, U. (1976). Angina pectoris among 10,000 men. Psychosocial and other factors as evidenced by a multivariate analysis of a 5 year incidence study. *American Journal of Medicine, 60,* 910–921.

Mermelstein, B., Cohen, S., Lichtenstein, E., Baer, J. S., & Kamarck, T. (1986). Social support and smoking cessation and maintenance. *Journal of Consulting and Clinical Psychology, 54,* 447–453.

Meyers, J. M., & Drayer, C. S. (1979). Support systems and mental illness in the elderly. *Community Mental Health Journal, 15*(4), 277–287.

Miller, S. M., Lack, E. R., & Asroff, S. (1985). Preference for control and the coronary-prone behavior pattern: "I'd rather do it myself." *Journal of Psychiatry and Social Psychology, 49,* 492–499.

Minkler, M. (1981). Applications of social support theory to health education: Implications for work with the elderly. *Health Education Quarterly, 8,* 147–165.

Minkler, M. (1985). Social support and health of the elderly. In S. Cohen & S. L. Syme (Eds.), *Social support and health* (pp. 199–216). New York: Academic.

Mitchell, R. E., & Trickett, E. J. (1980). Task force

report—Social networks as mediators of social support: An analysis of the effects and determinants of social networks. *Community Mental Health Journal, 16*(2), 27–44.

Moos, R. H. (1981). Environment choice and control in community care settings for older people. *Journal of Applied Psychology, 11*(1), 23–43.

Moos, R. H., & Ingra, A. (1980). Determinants of the social environments of sheltered care settings. *Journal of Health and Social Behavior, 21,* 88–98.

Noelker, L., & Harel, Z. (1978). Predictors of well-being and survival among institutionalized aged. *Gerontologist, 18*(6), 562–567.

Noelker, L., & Harel, Z. (1983). The integration of environment and network theories in explaining the aged's functioning and well-being. *Interdisciplinary Topics in Gerontology, 17*(8), 84–95.

Norbeck, J. S., & Tilden, V. (1981). Life stress, social support and emotional equilibrium in complications of pregnancy: A prospective multivariate study. *Journal of Health and Social Behavior, 24,* 30–46.

Norris, F. H., & Murrell, S. A. (1984). Protective function of resources related to life events, global stress, and depression in older adults. *Journal of Health and Social Behavior, 25,* 424–437.

Nuckolls, K. B., Cassel, J., & Kaplan, B. H. (1972). Psychosocial assets, life crisis and the prognosis of pregnancy. *American Journal of Epidemiology, 95,* 431–441.

O'Leary, A. (1985). Self-efficacy and health. *Behavior Research Therapy, 23*(4), 437–451.

Parkes, C. M., & Stevenson-Hinde, J. (Eds.). (1982). *The place of attachment in human behavior.* New York: Basic Books.

Parks, S. H., & Pilisuk, M. (1981, August). *Social ties and health status in an elderly population.* Paper presented at the annual meeting of the American Psychological Association, Los Angeles.

Pattison, E. M., Llamas, R., & Hurd, G. (1979). Social network mediation of anxiety. *Psychiatric Annals, 9,* 56–57.

Pearlin, L. I. (1985). Social structure and processes of social support. In S. Cohen & S. L. Syme (Eds.), *Social support and health* (pp. 43–60). New York: Academic.

Peters, G. R., & Kaiser, M. A. (1985). The role of friends and neighbors in providing social support. In W. Sauer & R. Coward (Eds.), *Social support networks and the care of the elderly: Theory, research, and practice* (pp. 123–158). New York: Springer.

Plath, D. (1980). *Long engagements.* Stanford: Stanford University Press.

Porritt, D. (1979). Social support in crises: Quality or quantity? *Social Science and Medicine, 13*(6A), 715–722.

Rathbone, E. E., Hooyman, N., & Fortune, A. E. (1985). Social support for the frail elderly. In W. Sauer & R. Coward (Eds.) *Social support networks and the care of the elderly: Theory, research, and practice* (pp. 234–248). New York: Springer.

Reis, H. T. (1984). Social interaction and well-being. In S. W. Duck (Ed.), *Personal relationships: Repairing personal relationships* (pp. 21–45). New York: Academic.

Reis, H. T., Wheeler, M. H., Kernis, N., Spiegel, T., & Nazlek, J. (1985). On specificity in the impact of social participation on physical and psychological health. *Journal of Personality and Social Psychology, 48*(2), 456–470.

Riley, M. W. (1985). Age strata in social systems. In R. H. Binstock & E. Shanas (Eds.), *Handbook of aging and social sciences* (2nd edition, pp. 369–414). New York: Van Nostrand Reinhold.

Rodin, J. (1980). Managing the stress of aging: The role of control and coping. In S. Levine & H. Ursin (Eds.), *Coping and health* (pp. 171–202). New York: Plenum Press.

Rodin, J. (1986). Aging and health: Effects of the sense of control. *Science, 223,* 1271–1276.

Rook, K. (1984). The negative side of social interaction: Impact on psychological well-being. *Journal of Personality and Social Psychology, 46*(5), 1097–1108.

Rook, K. (1985). Research on social support, loneliness, and social isolation. In P. Shaver (Ed.), *Review of personality and social psychology* (pp. 239–264). Beverly Hills: Sage.

Rundall, T. G., & Evashwick, C. (1982). Social networks and help-seeking among the elderly. *Research on Aging, 4*(2), 205–226.

Sarason, I. G., & Sarason, B. R. (1985). *Social support: Theory, research and applications.* Dordrecht, The Netherlands: Martinus Nijhof.

Sauer, W., & Coward, R. (1985). *Social support networks and the care of the elderly: Theory, research, and practice.* New York: Springer.

Schaefer, C., Coyne, J. C., & Lazarus, R. S. (1981). The health-related functions of social support. *Journal of Behavioral Medicine, 4,* 381–406.

Schulz, R. (1976). Effects of control and predictability on the physical and psychological well-being of the institutionalized aged. *Journal of Personality and Social Psychology, 33,* 563–573.

Schulz, R., & Hanusa, B. H. (1978). Long-term effects of control and predictability-enhancing interaction: Finding ethical issues. *Journal of Personality and Social Psychology, 36,* 1194–1201.

Schulz, R., & Rau, M. T. (1985). Social support through the life course. In S. Cohen & S. L. Syme (Eds.), *Social support and health* (pp. 129–149). New York: Academic.

Shinn, M., Lehmann, S., & Wong, N. W. (1985). Social interaction and social support. *Journal of Social Issues, 40*(4), 55–76.

Shore, B. (1985). Extended kin as helping networks. In W. Sauer & R. Coward (Eds.), *Social support networks and the care of the elderly: Theory, research, and practice* (pp. 108–120). New York: Springer.

Simson, S., Wilson, L. B., Hermalen, J., & Hess, R. (1983). *Aging and prevention.* New York: Haworth Press.

Singer, J. E., & Lord, D. (1984). The role of social support in coping with chronic or life-threatening illness. In A. Baum, S. E. Taylor, & J. E. Singer (Eds.), *Handbook of psychology and health* (pp. 269–277). Hillsdale, NJ: Erlbaum.

Skinner, E. A. (1985). Action, control judgments, and the structure of control experience. *Psychological Review, 92*(1), 39–58.

Sokolovsky, J., & Cohen, C. I. (1981). Toward a resolution of methodological dilemmas in network mapping. *Schizophrenia Bulletin, 7*(1), 109–116.

Sosa, R., Kennel, J., & Klaus, M. (1980). The effect of a supportive companion on perinatal problems, length of labor and mother-infant interactions. *New England Journal of Medicine, 305,* 597–600.

Stephens, R. C., Blau, Z. S., Oser, G. T., & Millar, M. D. (1978). Aging, social support systems and social policy. *Journal of Gerontological Social Work, 1,* 33–75.

Strain, L. A., & Chappell, N. A. (1982). Confidants: Do they make a difference in quality of life? *Research on Aging, 4*(4), 479–502.

Suls, J. (1982). Social support, interpersonal relations, and health: Benefits and liabilities. In G. S. Sanders and J. Suls (Eds.), *Social psychology of health and illness* (pp. 255–277). Hillsdale, NJ: Erlbaum.

Taylor, C. R., Bandura, A., Ewart, C. K., Miller, N. H., & DeBusk, R. F. (1985). Exercise testing to enhance wives' confidence in their husbands' cardiac capability soon after clinically uncomplicated acute myocardial infarction. *American Journal of Cardiology, 55,* 635–638.

Tesch, S., Whitbourne, S. K., & Nehrke, M. F. (1981). Friendship, social interaction and subjective well-being of older men in an institutional setting. *International Journal of Aging and Human Devlopment, 13*(4), 317–328.

Thoits, P. A. (1982). Conceptual, methodological and theoretical problems in studying social support as a buffer against life stress. *Journal of Health and Social Behavior, 23,* 145–159.

Thoits, P. (1985). Coping, social support, and psychological outcomes: The central role of emotions. In P. Shaver (Ed.), *Review of personality and social psychology* (pp. 219–238). Beverly Hills, CA: Sage.

Thomas, P. D., Garry, P. J., Goodwin, J. M., & Goodwin, J. S. (1985). Social bonds in a healthy elderly sample: Characteristics and associated variables. *Social Science Medicine, 20*(4), 365–369.

Thompson, S. C. (1981). Will it hurt less if I can control it? A complex answer to a simple question. *Psychology Bulletin, 90*(1), 89–101.

Tretli, S., Bjartveit, K., Foss, O. P., Haider, T., & Lund-Larscn, P. G. (1985). Intervention on cardiovascular disease risk factors in Finnmark County: Changes after a period of three years. *Scandinavian Journal of Social Medicine, 13,* 1–13.

Wallace, J. R., Cunningham, T. F., & Del Monte, V. D. (1984). Changes in the relationship between self-esteem and locus of control. *Journal of Social Psychology, 124,* 261–262.

Wallston, B. S., Alagna, S. W., DeVellis, B. M., & DeVellis, R. F. (1983). Social support and physical health. *Health Psychology, 2*(4), 367–393.

Wan, T. T. H. (1982). *Stressful life events, social-support network and gerontological health.* Lexington, MA: D. C. Heath.

Wan, T. T. H., Odell, B. G., Lewis, D. T. (1982). *Promotions of the well-being of the elderly.* New York: Haworth.

Wan, T. T. H., & Weissert, W. G. (1981). Social support networks, patient status and institutionalization. *Research on Aging, 3,* 240–256.

Ward, R., Sherman, S. R., & LaGory, M. (1984). Informal networks and knowledge of services for older persons. *Journal of Gerontology, 39*(2), 216–223.

Wentowski, G. J. (1981). Reciprocity and the coping strategies of older people: Cultural dimensions of network building. *Gerontologist, 21*(2), 177–183.

Whittaker, J. K., & Garbarino, J. (1983). *Social support networks: Informal helping in the human services.* New York: Aldine.

Wilcox, B. L. (1981). Social support in adjusting to marital disruption, a network analysis. In B. H. Gottlieb (Ed.), *Social networks and social support* (pp. 97–115). Beverly Hills, CA: Sage.

Wills, T. A. (1985). Supportive functions of interpersonal relationships. In S. Cohen & S. L. Syme (Eds.), *Social support and health* (pp. 61–82). New York: Academic.

Wood, V., & Robertson, J. F. (1978). Friendship and kinship interaction: Differential effect on the morale of the elderly. *Journal of Marriage and the Family, 40*(2), 367–375.

Wortman, C. B., & Conway, T. L. (1985). The role of social support in adaptation and recovery from physical illness. In S. Cohen & S. L. Syme (Eds.), *Social support and health* (pp. 281–302). New York: Academic.

Chapter 23

The Challenge of Bereavement

Patricia A. Wisocki and James R. Averill

Was mich nicht umbringt, macht mich stärker. ("What doesn't kill me, makes me stronger.")
—Nietzsche, Twilight of the Idols

Bereavement is the lot of the elderly. One by one—friends, siblings, relatives, spouses—all must die. The only way to escape bereavement is to be the first to go—preferably in a sudden and unexpected manner, for one's own anticipated death can be a source of self-bereavement.

One purpose of this chapter is to review briefly the sequela of bereavement among the elderly. A second purpose is to outline the relevant clinical issues for assisting the elderly bereaved. The orientation of the chapter is largely empirical. However, owing to a paucity of research on bereavement among the elderly, extrapolation from available data is often necessary. Particularly lacking are studies of the efficacy of different strategies designed to facilitate recovery from bereavement both among the elderly and among other population groups (see Osterweis, Solomon, & Green, 1984, for an excellent in-depth review of research related to grief and bereavement). A long-range goal of this chapter is, then, to stimulate needed research on treatment interventions.

The chapter is divided into three parts. First, we will outline the typical features of normal grief, with special attention to elderly people; second, we will review research on pathological grief reactions, including the relationship of bereavement to health and mortality; third, we will discuss some of the contributions of a behavioral approach to understanding responses during bereavement.

NORMAL GRIEF

In an effort to describe responses to bereavement, various authors designated phases, or stages, of grief and have used a variety of labels to indicate them (cf. Bowlby, 1980; Gorer, 1965; Parkes, 1972). Typically, grief is depicted as developing in at least four stages:

1. *Shock.* The bereaved experiences a dazed sense of unreality or numbing that may last several hours or several days. A sense of isolation from the world is often common during this stage as well as during subsequent stages.

2. *Protest and yearning.* In this stage, the loss is recognized but not entirely accepted. The be-

reaved feels intense pain and longing for the deceased. There is protest over the fact of loss and a variety of "searching" behaviors may occur, including dreams about the dead person, the experience of "finding" him or her in familiar places, and hallucinations. Behaviorally, this is a time of agitation, heightened physiological arousal, and restlessness, sometimes alternating with a feeling of deceleration. Cognitively, there is a preoccupation with memories of the lost person and a focusing of attention on those aspects of the environment that were associated with past pleasures. This stage of protest and yearning typically lasts for several months.

3. *Disorganization and despair*. This is perhaps the most enduring, complex, and difficult stage in the grief process, often lasting for a year or more. Although the fact of loss may be accepted and attempts to recover the lost object abandoned, a bitter pining remains. Apathy, withdrawal, loss of energy, and despondency are common during this period, as are a loss of sexual interest, poor socialization, diminished appetite, sleep disturbances, and other behavioral and somatic problems. The bereaved may experience conflicting emotions and moods, such as despair, hostility, shame, guilt, anger, and irritability.

4. *Detachment, reorganization, and recovery*. The characteristics of the preceding stage are ultimately relieved when the bereaved develops new ways of perceiving and thinking about the world and his or her place within it. A person regains hope and confidence in him or herself and is able to enjoy life again. Most often, this involves the establishment of new roles and a new sense of purpose in life. Even in cases of normal grief, several years may be required before a relatively adequate readjustment occurs. And in many cases, the pain of the loss may never be alleviated completely. Feelings of bereavement may be triggered by holidays and dates that mark meaningful events.

Although recognizing that grief is a process, a way of reorganizing one's response to a painful reality, we want to caution against the notion that each bereaved individual must proceed in order through various identifiable categories. As Bugen (1977) has pointed out, presumed stages of grieving are not necessarily successive, the time limits per stage are variable, and the intensity of reactions in each stage may vary markedly as a function of individual and environmental variables. Bereavement is not a homogenous experience among any age group.

Grief Reactions Among the Elderly

The available literature dealing with ways the elderly respond to bereavement, although sparse, provides the following information. First, the affective experience of grief tends to be more subdued, or *flat*, among the elderly than among younger bereaved. Second, the elderly experience more somatic problems, such as pain, gastrointestinal disorders, and sleep disturbances than younger people. Third, the elderly bereaved often complain of a sense of inadequacy or loss of purpose of life. Other responses to bereavement that may be exaggerated in the elderly are apathy, self-isolation, and idealization of the deceased (Ball, 1976–1977; Heyman & Gianturco, 1973; Parkes, 1964; Skelskie, 1975; Stern, Williams, & Prados, 1951).

This picture is obviously mixed and allows a variety of interpretations, both optimistic and pessimistic. On the optimistic side, Heyman and Gianturco (1973) reported that the elderly may adapt to their bereavement with relative emotional stability. They based their conclusion on the observation of 41 people who were bereaved during the course of a longitudinal study at the Duke University Center for the Study of Aging and Human Development. It should be noted, however, that the majority of the subjects studied by Heyman and Gianturco held deep religious convictions and did not suffer severe disruptions in their social or financial conditions as a result of bereavement. Even so, many complained of feeling useless following bereavement.

Other investigators have portrayed a more dismal picture of bereavement among the elderly. Skelskie (1975), for example, suggested that the flattened affect often observed among the elderly may be more a sign of inhibited grief than of good adjustment. Or it may be a sign of depression induced by the death of a significant person. It even may signal the surrendering of an interest in life.

BEREAVEMENT-ASSOCIATED PATHOLOGIES

In this section, we will review some of the research on the pathological sequelae of bereavement and then examine the conditions that seem to exacerbate unfavorable consequences (e.g., circumstances surrounding the loss, social support systems, and the like).

Pathological Grief Reactions

Grief, although painful and often debilitating, is not in itself a form of pathology; it is a normal reaction to loss. Nevertheless, if some of the symtoms of grief become too exaggerated or prolonged, we may rightfully speak of grief as though it were a disease (Engel, 1961). Cases of pathological grief are generally characterized by extended periods of protest and yearning (Stage 2) and/or of disorganization and despair (Stage 3).

But signs of potential problems need not take such obvious forms. Even under the best of conditions, grief is a terribly painful experience. Not surprisingly, therefore, people who otherwise show adequate coping skills may at times become tense and short-tempered when references are made to the deceased, or they may refuse to hear any references about them at all (Bowlby, 1980). Such behavior may not only alienate others who are in a position to help, but it may also unduly prolong the time when detachment and reorganization are satisfactorily achieved.

Occasionally, the entire syndrome of grief may be delayed, as the person refuses to accept—in other than a coldly intellectual way—the fact of loss. Eventually, however, reality must intervene, and the severity and maladaptiveness of grief may only be exacerbated by its delay.

Some people seriously jeopardize their health as a result of their bereavement and require extended treatment, as will be discussed more fully below. For others, the elderly in particular, lives are changed in ways that require greater coping abilities than are realistically available. Thus, circumstances that for a younger person might not be unduly demanding may for an elderly person become pathogenic.

Clearly, recovery from bereavement will not take the same form for everyone. Criteria for recovery will vary, as will the demands of the therapeutic process.

Relationship of Bereavement to Health

Bereavement may be associated with increased mortality and morbidity from conditions unrelated to grief per se (e.g., cancer, cardiovascular disease, psychopathology). We will first review some of the relevant research and then discuss its implications.

Mortality

Epidemiological evidence from a variety of sources demonstrates an increase in mortality rates for the recently bereaved, especially widowed men between the ages of 55 and 75. The exact causes of death can vary. For example, emotional stress in response to loss has been implicated in deaths from congestive heart failure (Chambers & Reiser, 1953) and essential hypertension (Wiener, Gerber, Battin, & Arkin, 1975). In a study of sudden death during stressful times, Engel (1971) found that 21% of his sample died immediately after the death of someone close; an additional 20% died within 16 days. Engel suggested that the majority of these deaths were attributable to cardiac arrest in individuals with cardiovascular disease.

There is no conclusive evidence linking incidences of cancer and other specific medical disorders to bereavement. Those few studies from which data are available are methodologically inadequate, and often have not designated bereavement as a specific stressor different from other stressors.

Increased mortality following bereavement can also result from a variety of indirect sources. For example, following a death, there are generally marked increases in the consumption of tobacco, alcohol, and drugs (Maddison & Viola, 1968), mostly among people who are already using these substances. These poor health practices may help account for the noted increases in deaths from suicide, accidents, cardiovascular disease and some infectious diseases among widowers (Helsing, Comstock, & Szklo, 1981; Kraus & Lilienfeld, 1959). In widowed women, there is an increase in the risk of death from cirrhosis of the liver (Helsing et al., 1981), perhaps because of an increase in the use of alcohol.

Morbidity

A nonfatal deterioration in physical health is also associated with bereavement, but mainly to the extent that a preexisting condition may be aggravated by poor health practices.

A survey conducted by the National Center for Health Statistics (1976) indicated that the widowed frequented physicians' offices more often and had higher disability scores than the married. This was more true for widowers than for widows. Glick, Weiss, and Parkes (1974) found an increase in hospitalization among the widowed within a year following the loss of a spouse. Only widowers showed significantly more physical health problems, however. Clayton (1979) reported the same increase in hospitalization, but only among the younger widowed sample. She did not find differences in the number of physical problems reported by widowed and married people. Maddison and Viola (1968) found an increase in a variety of physical complaints, such as skin rashes, headaches, gastrointestinal problems, dizziness, and fainting spells among the widowed, compared to the married, as well as an overall deterioration in health.

Studies that particularly included subjects over 65 years of age have reported conflicting results. For example, Heyman and Gianturco (1973) found a small increase in depressive symptomatology in widowed women, but no change in health, leisure activities, and anxiety. Thompson, Breckenridge, Gallagher, and Peterson (1984), however, found that existing illnesses were worsened, new illnesses developed, and a greater use of medication occurred among a group of widowed elderly.

Psychological Health

A few authors have found that a substantial number of bereaved experienced depression within a year after their loss (Parkes & Brown, 1972; Paykel, Myers, Dienelt, & Klerman, 1969). Although depression precipitated by bereavement is seldom sufficiently severe to require psychiatric hospitalization, that is not always the case. Frost and Clayton (1977), for example, found 2% of 344 psychiatric inpatients reported the death of a close relative in the 6 months prior to admission, as compared with less than 1% for the control group. Even more dramatically, Paykel et al. (1969) found that 12% of a group of depressed outpatients and inpatients reported the death of an immediate family member 6 months prior to admission for treatment. Only 5% of the control group reported a similar experience.

Increased depression was also reported among elderly bereaved widows and widowers. Carey (1977) found that self-reported depression occurred *as long as* 13–16 months after the loss. The most detailed studies are those by Clayton and her colleagues, in which older widows and widowers (mean age, 61.5) showed signs of depression up to 12 months after a loss. Thirty-five percent showed depressive indicators at 1 month; 25% at 4 months; and 17% at 12 months (Bornstein, Clayton, Halikas, Maurice, & Robins, 1973; Clayton,

Halikas, & Maurice, 1972; Clayton, Herjanic, Murphy, & Woodruff, 1974).

Given the consistency of the preceding findings, it appears that there is indeed a significant relationship between depression and bereavement in all age groups.

Implications

We have not attempted an exhaustive review of the research linking bereavement to physical and mental health. (For such a review, see Stroebe, Stroebe, & Domittner, 1985). The studies cited are representative, however, and they suffice to illustrate some of the methodological and conceptual issues that beset this area. Among the methodological problems are the following:

1. As already noted criteria for distinguishing grief reactions (especially pathological or exaggerated grief reactions) and disease states are difficult to establish. For example, when do loss of appetite and sleep disturbances become medical problems?
2. The majority of studies on the relationship between bereavement and health have involved retrospective analyses, with the experience of death in a given time frame as the independent variable. Such retrospective studies do not allow the control of possible confounding third factors, as will be discussed below.
3. The prospective studies that have been conducted (i.e., following the bereaved from the time of death) have involved relatively few subjects, usually volunteers. Generalizations are thus difficult to draw.

The above methodological problems do not cast doubt on the link between bereavement and health. They do, however, make interpretation difficult. To a certain extent, the link is known to be artifactual, in the sense of being the product of common third factors. For example, when one spouse is fatally ill, the chances are better than average that the other spouse is also in poor health. But let us assume for the sake of argument that no such third factor is operating. Several questions still remain. To what extent is the link specific to bereavement and to what extent does it reflect a more general association between stress and disease? And to the extent that it is specific to bereavement, does it result from an exaggeration of typical grief reactions (literally, a "broken heart" syndrome) or is it secondary to changes in life-style that frequently accompany bereavement (e.g., loss of financial support, relocation to another home, increased alcohol or drug abuse)?

In one sense, it matters little whether a deterioration in health following bereavement is due to some third factor, whether it is due to stress in general, or whether it is specific to grief. Bereavement still represents a public health problem of major proportions. Of course, from a broader perspective—practical as well as theorectical—it matters a great deal. To be most effective, treatment interventions must be tailored to the needs of the individual, and that requires a careful assessment of the causes of the presenting symptoms.

Exacerbating Influences

Let us turn now from the links between bereavement and health to a consideration of the conditions that exacerbate such links. These include the kinship of the bereaved to the deceased (spouse, sibling, etc.), the quality of the preloss relationship, the circumstances surrounding the loss, and the availability of social support systems.

Kinship of Bereaved to Deceased

When we think of bereavement among the elderly, we usually think of the death of a spouse. There are, however, other relatives of the old who die and influence the behavior of the elderly. We will discuss those relatives shortly. For the moment, we will focus on the loss of a spouse.

The death of a spouse represents a double loss. The first loss is, of course, the person of the deceased, to whom the bereaved may have been deeply attached. The second loss is of one's role as husband or wife. Following retirement, such a role may be the primary social identity that the person has. Role loss is a major source of distress and depression in its own right, and it undoubtedly helps account for the sense of meaninglessness and lack of purpose often reported by the elderly bereaved.

Other factors affecting mortality rates following the death of a spouse include changes in residence to nursing homes, retirement homes, and institutions (already indicators of poor health) and solitary living.

In view of the above factors, it is not surprising that remarriage helps mitigate the pathogenic effects of bereavement. What is surprising is that this beneficial influence is observed mainly among widowed men, not women. In terms of material

and financial support, women usually suffer more following bereavement than men (although this may be less true for the elderly bereaved than for those who suffer a loss earlier in life). In any case, it would seem that in spite of greater material advantages, men are less able to cope with the psychological costs of bereavement than women. (For excellent and detailed reviews of studies that produced these findings, see Osterweis et al., 1984; Stroebe, Stroebe, Gergen, & Gergen, 1982.)

While the loss of a spouse is devastating, in some respects the loss of a child or grandchild may be even more painful. In a study of 14 bereaved (not elderly) parents, Sanders (1979–1980) found that when compared with the loss of a parent or spouse, the loss of a child produced more intense somatic responses, greater depression, and more anger, guilt, and despair. Although the death of adult children is a neglected topic area in bereavement research, Gorer (1965) has asserted that this type of loss is the "most distressing and long-lasting of all griefs." Older parents may feel that their dreams of self-extension to future generations have died along with their child. They may feel that a mistake in the life cycle has occurred and that the death of the young prior to the old is an "unnatural" event. They may feel keenly their loss of a future caregiver for themselves as they progress toward death.

There is also little information on the grief responses of adults to the death of a sibling or close friend. For the elderly, siblings and friends are often major sources of social support. Along with the loss of social reinforcers attendant upon these individuals, their death may exacerbate one's own fear of impending death.

In many cases, a younger sibling has acquired responsbility for the care of the older one. The effect of the caretaker sibling's death on the survivor may be as profound, in many respects, as that of the spouse's death. Deep personal bonds may be severed, and the practical problems of survival alone may arise. When the cared-for sibling dies, the sibling caretaker may feel a loss of purpose and meaning in life.

Pre-loss Relationship

The quality of the client's relationship to the deceased is an important etiological factor in bereavement disorders. Parkes and Weiss (1983) studied 68 normal widows and widowers in two groups: those with one or no conflict areas and those with two or more conflict areas. They found that those who expressed few conflicts in marriage were more than twice as likely to recover from bereavement than those in the conflict group when assessed at follow-up interviews 13 months, 2 years, and 4 years after the loss. Those widows and widowers who had been in a dependent conjugal relationship also tended to do poorly. Based on these data, Stroebe and Stroebe (in press) have predicted that the effect of a loss will be greater the more a person was dependent upon the deceased person for material aid and advice, assistance in self-evaluation, environmental assessment and structure, and unconditional positive regard.

Circumstances Surrounding the Loss

The timing and manner of death are important factors in determining the course of bereavement. For younger people, sudden loss has more deleterious consequences than an anticipated loss. That does not appear to be the case among the elderly. Of course, for elderly people, death is never completely unexpected. But of greater relevance is the fact that an anticipated death among the elderly is often due to some chronic illness. The surviving spouse may have been the major caretaker of the deceased, a task that can take its toll on the physical and mental health of the bereaved. (For a review of research related to anticipatory bereavement among the elderly, see Averill & Wisocki, 1981.)

The cause of death may also have an important effect on bereavement. This assertion can best be substantiated in the case of suicide, so we will digress briefly on this topic of growing importance.

As a group, the elderly experience a high incidence of suicide—approximately 10,000 people a year, or 25% of the suicides in the United States (Miller, 1978). The frequency is especially high among older white males, amounting to almost 4 times the average rate for the United States as a whole.

And these figures are probably underestimated, because few autopsies are done on older people, even in cases of accidental or unexplained deaths. Many suicides are probably not reported at all in order to avoid what is presumed to be public disgrace for the family or the tarnishing of a person's image.

Those who experience the suicide of a loved one have long been regarded as particularly prone to physical and psychological problems, especially increases in the use of alcohol, drugs, and nicotine and in the incidence of depression. There is also an increased likelihood of morbidity, including death by suicide for the survivor (Kraus & Lilienfeld, 1959; MacMahon & Pugh, 1965; Shepherd & Barraclough, 1974).

The survivor often feels rejected (Warren, 1972) or guilty; he or she attempts to fix blame on someone or on oneself. In some cases, the survivor worries that he or she has been tainted by another's suicide and therefore doomed to perform a self-destructive act as well. In other cases, the survivor may feel rage at being abandoned.

The survivor's reaction to suicide depends to a large extent on his or her relationship to the deceased, personality variables, cultural factors, the age and physical condition of the deceased, and the method chosen for the suicide. Contrast, for instance, an elderly person who is experiencing a painful terminal illness with no hope for recovery, commits suicide by simply refusing medication with an adolescent grandchild who with her life unfulfilled, leaps from the roof of a building. In the first case, bereavement may not be as intense; in the second case, the bereaved may be inconsolable.

The reaction of others to the suicide complicates the bereavement as well. Those who would readily comfort a person for a loss induced by illness may be reluctant to offer support to the survivor of a suicide. In fact, they may even blame the survivor for the death. Or the survivor, aware of the social stigmatization of suicide, may be reluctant to discuss the events of the death with another person. In either case, the survivor is isolated from social support systems and is cut off from a necessary therapeutic stratagem, leaving personal feelings unresolved.

Social Support Systems

Of particular importance for elderly bereaved is support gained from friends and neighbors (Arling, 1976). Although a causal relationship between social support and poor health of bereaved individuals has not as yet been determined, a correlational link does exist. Specifically, a high quality of social support has been correlated negatively with depression (Bornstein et al., 1973) and suicide (Bunch, 1972).

Social networks may not only provide support, they may also place obligations on the bereaved that can at times prolong the grief and exacerbate the suffering. For example, the bereaved may be expected to refrain from social contact "out of respect" for the deceased. In this regard, relatives and children of the deceased can be especially demanding.

On the other side of the coin, there are secondary gains to be had from bereavement, including the sympathy and attention of others and the avoidance of new responsibilities without the deceased. Thus, although the symptoms of grief can be very unpleasant, it is not uncommon for the bereaved to refuse any help in a positive direction (Parkes & Weiss, 1983).

BEHAVIORAL APPROACHES TO BEREAVEMENT

For the most part, behaviorists have not addressed themselves to a theoretical conceptualization of grief, regarding it instead as "a particular case of the more general malady of depression" (Gauthier & Marshall, 1977). They would, therefore, most likely rely on Beck's cognitive model to explain the bereaved's negative view of the world and oneself that would prolong the grief experience (Beck, Rush, Shaw, & Emery, 1979). In this section, we will examine the potential usefulness of some more traditional behavioral approaches to the problems of bereavement, that is operant and respondent conditioning paradigms. But first, a few observations should be made with regard to why behavior therapists have devoted so little attention to the study of grief and bereavement.

Averill and Wiscoki (1981) attribute this to two reasons. The first has to do more with appearance than reality. Grief is such a deep and painful experience that the most natural response is to offer unconditional nurturance. Within such an atmosphere, the application of behavioral techniques may seem to many people as inappropriate and coldly mechanistic. The appearance is deceiving, but the barrier it presents should not be underestimated. In both the popular and psychological literature, problems related to bereavement have been viewed as falling primarily within the domain of humanistically oriented psychologists, who stress the value of the theraputic relationship.

The second reason is more substantive. Behavior therapists, in the natural course of events, tend to focus attention on the specific responses demonstrated by a person within a specific context of antecedents and consequences. Historical factors, including the biological and sociocultural underpinnings of grief (Averill, 1979), may be ignored or rejected as not immediately relevant to treatment.

The precipitating event of death may also be ignored or considered irrelevant if a behavior therapist focuses exclusively on the behavioral responses. A related problem is that of straightforwardly extending existing behavioral procedures to the treatment of bereavement. Because most of the reactions during grief may be observed in other disorders, that tendency may be expected. It is important to recognize that grief reactions do form a coherent syndrome and that the relationship of each behavior to the other behaviors within the syndrome must be considered. Hence, one cannot assume that a technique effective in treating insomnia in a non-grief context will also be effective in treating the insomnia induced by bereavement. The research needed to determine the efficacy of various behavioral techniques in treating the problems of bereavement has not yet been done.

There is, however, one area in which behaviorally oriented theorists have contributed to our understanding of responses following bereavement: the role of reinforcement in the extinction and maintenance of behavior.

At least some of the symptoms of grief may be due to the extinction of previously reinforced responses, whereas other symptoms may result from the reinforcement of new and often maladaptive behavior. Extinction following bereavement may result from any one or all of the following four reasons: (a) Customary reinforcers, for example, those directly dependent on the presence of the deceased, may no longer be available; (b) Customary reinforcers, although available, may no longer be effective, as when a previously pleasurable activity becomes affectively neutral; (c) The person may no longer have the desire or ability to make the responses required to achieve reinforcement (e.g., because of apathy); or (d) The person may refrain from responding because of negative consequences (e.g., when the response serves as a painful reminder of the deceased or is a source of guilt or social criticism).

Some of the behaviors observed following bereavement are reminiscent of those occasioned by extinction. Thus, Brasted and Callahan (1985) have proposed that the searching behaviors that often occur in Stage 2 of the grieving process are examples of an extinction burst, the point at which an organism increases its response rate after reinforcement has been withdrawn. In Stage 3— disorganization and despair—the individual experiences the typical apathy and withdrawal associated with the failure to regain the lost object. And finally, in Stage 4 the individual learns new responses or develops new sources or reinforcement and begins to recover from the grief experience.

As already noted, the expressions of bereavement can also result in secondary gain (positive reinforcement). Calling for sympathy and special treatment, bereavement may provide an excuse for behaviors that are inappropriate or unacceptable at other times. For example, a person may take the opportunity to verbally chastise a daughter or son for some perceived hurt, resort to alcohol abuse, or refuse to meet social obligations. Gauthier and Marshall (1977) have suggested that behaviors that indicate excessive grieving are reinforced by significant people in the social network and result in a continuation of bereavement.

A case report by Flannery (1974) illustrates the application of reinforcement principles to eliminate the agitated depression and grief experienced by an elderly man 6 months after the death of his sister. After negotiating a specific behavioral contract with the client that set goals for the therapy, Flannery differentially reinforced the client for making positive self-statements, ignored socially aversive statements made by the client, gradually prompted him to discuss his sister's death, and rewarded him for speaking of his feelings. These techniques were generally successful in achieving the goals.

Brasted and Callahan (1985) have acknowledged the usefulness of the operant analysis but suggest an examination of the respondent model as well. Grieving in this case is likened to a conditional emotional response. As Brasted and Callahan (1985) describe it, death is similar to a non-contingent aversive stimulus that provokes the typical somatic distress signs occurring in the initial shock stage of bereavement. The individual then struggles without success to find an escape (as in the protest stage), and eventually suppresses his or her responses (ie., disorganization stage), finally developing a new response repertoire (the recovery stage). In pathological grieving the bereaved develops an effective escape or avoidance response, and extinction never occurs.

Indeed, specific treatment methods have been developed, utilizing this theoretical perspective. Ramsay (1979) has likened pathological grieving to a phobia or an obsession in which the bereaved avoids confrontation with difficult and painful experiences that may provoke grieving. His treatment program is therefore based on a foundation of flooding and prolonged exposure to the stimuli that arouse undesirable emotional reactions. During 2-hour periods, 3 days a week, clients are forced to confront situations that evoke anxiety, guilt, shame, jealousy, and the like and to remain in these situations until the undesirable reactions are extinguished. A variety of techniques, including modeling, prompting, and fantasy, are used to facilitate the flooding process. However, as Ramsay points out, this form of behavior therapy is hard on both the client and the therapist, and it should not be attempted by an inexperienced therapist. Ramsay also does not recommend it for elderly clients.

Some additional support for a respondent conditioning model is available from a study by Mawson, Marks, Ramm, and Stern (1981), who compared two groups of pathologically bereaved—subjects who experienced grief longer than 1 year. Calling their treatment condition *guided mourning*, one group of subjects was exposed to painful memories of the deceased (and not permitted to avoid them); the control group was encouraged to avoid confronting memories and to become active in life. After three 90-minute sessions, the guided mourning group improved on self-report measures of depression, anxiety, social adjustment, signs of pathological grief, and self-image. The control group showed no improvement and in some cases behavior had worsened.

In short, both operant and respondent conditioning paradigms are sources of testable hypotheses regarding the origins of some of the behaviors following bereavement. It is highly unlikely, however, that all of the symptoms of grief, no less of bereavement in general, can be accounted for in such a fashion (Averill, 1979). But regardless of the origins of a response, it is clear that *recovery* from bereavement involves a good deal of relearning. Conditioning paradigms thus suggest intervention strategies, even in instances where their explanatory power may be questioned. Unfortunately, of the few intervention studies available for review, only one has followed experimental procedure (that by Mawson et al., 1981). Hence, generalizations must be drawn with caution.

CONCLUSIONS

It is difficult to find anything nice to say about bereavement, yet it is part of the human condition. No amount of technological advancement can postpone indefinitely the loss of friends and loved ones and no amount of psychological sophistication can eliminate the pain of such loss. But even in the most dire of necessities, some virtue can usually be found. Bereavement presents a challenge as well as a loss. As old ties are severed and customary ways of behaving extinguished, new opportunities for growth are presented. "What doesn't kill me, makes me stronger." This aphorism by Nietzsche, quoted at the outset of this paper, would make a fitting motto for the bereaved.

That may be fine for the younger bereaved, a cynic might respond, but the elderly do not need such a challenge. True enough. However, we are not talking about needs, but about inevitabilities, about finding some virtue in necessity. For example, Silverman and Cooperband (1975) have reported on a group of elderly widows who evidenced dramatic personal growth in the assumption of responsibilities formerly held by their spouses. The potential for growth is present until death. Age is not the issue. But growth cannot always be achieved without assistance, and that is the challenge of bereavement for the therapist.

REFERENCES

Arling, G. (1976). Resistance to isolation among elderly widows. *International Journal of Aging and Human Development, 7,* 67–86.

Averill, J. (1979). The functions of grief. In C. Izard (Ed.), *Emotions in personality and psychopathology.* New York: Plenum.

Averill, J. R., & Wisocki, P. A. (1981). Some observations on behavioral approaches to the treatment of grief among the elderly. In H. Sobel (Ed.), *Behavior therapy in terminal care* (pp. 125–150). Cambridge, MA: Ballinger.

Ball, J. F. (1976–77). Widow's grief: The impact of age and mode of death. *Omega, 7,* 307–333.

Beck, A., Rush, J. Shaw, B., & Emery, G. (1979). *Cognitive therapy of depression.* New York: Guilford.

Bornstein, P., Clayton, P., Halikas, J., Maurice, W., & Robins, E. (1973). The depression of widowhood after thirteen months. *British Journal of Psychiatry, 122,* 561–566.

Bowlby, J. (1980). *Attachment and loss: Vol. 3. Loss: Sadness and depression.* New York: Basic Books.

Brasted, W. S., & Callahan, E. J. (1985). A behavioral analysis of the process grief. *Behavioral Therapy, 16,* 55–69.

Bugen, L. A. (1977). Human grief: A model for prediction and intervention. *American Journal of Orthopsychiatry, 47,* 196–206.

Bunch, J. (1972). Recent bereavement in relation to suicide. *Journal of Psychosomatic Research, 16,* 361–366.

Carey, R. (1977). The widowed: A year later. *Journal of Counseling Psychology, 24,* 125–131.

Chambers, W., & Reiser, M. F. (1953). Emotional stress in the precipitation of congestive heart failure. *Psychosomatic Medicine, 15,* 38–60.

Clayton, P. J. (1979). The sequelae and nonsequelae of conjugal bereavement. *American Journal of Psychiatry, 136,* 1530–1534.

Clayton, P. J., Halikas, J. A., & Maurice, W. L. (1972). The depression of widowhood. *British Journal of Psychiatry, 120,* 71–78.

Clayton, P. J., Herjanic, M., Murphy, G., & Woodruff, R. (1974). Mourning and depression: Their similarities and differences. *Canadian Psychiatric Association Journal, 19,* 309–312.

Engel, G. (1961). Is grief a disease? *Psychosomatic Medicine, 12,* 18–23.

Engel, G. L. (1971). Sudden and rapid death during psychological stress. *Annals of Internal Medicine, 74,* 771–782.

Flannery, R. B. (1974). Behavior modification of geriatric grief: A transactional perspective. *International Journal of Aging and Human Development, 12,* 197–203.

Frost, N. R., & Clayton, P. J. (1977). Bereavement and psychiatric hospitalization. *Archives of General Psychiatry, 34,* 1172–1175.

Gauthier, J., & Marshall, W. L. (1977). Grief: A cognitive-behavioral analysis. *Cognitive Therapy and Research, 1,* 39–44.

Glick, I., Weiss, R., & Parkes, C. (1974). *The first year of bereavement.* New York: Wiley.

Gorer, G. (1965). *Death, grief, and mourning.* London: Crescent Press.

Helsing, K., Comstock, G., & Szklo, M. (1981). Causes of death in a widowed population. *American Journal of Epidemiology, 116,* 524–532.

Heyman, D. L., & Gianturco, D. T. (1973). Long-term adaptation by the elderly to bereavement. *Journal of Gerontology, 28,* 359–362.

Kraus, A., & Lilienfeld, A. (1959). Some epidemiological aspects of the high mortality rate in the young widowed group. *Journal of Chronic Diseases, 10,* 207–217.

MacMahon, B., & Pugh, T. F. (1965). Suicide in the widowed. *American Journal of Epidemiology, 81,* 23–31.

Maddison, D., & Viola, A. (1968). The health of widows in the year following bereavement. *Journal of Psychosomatic Research, 12,* 297–306.

Mawson, D., Marks, I., Ramm, L., & Stern, R. (1981). Guided mourning for morbid grief: A controlled study. *British Journal of Psychiatry, 138,* 185–193.

Miller, M. (1978). Geriatric suicide: The Arizona study. *Gerontologist, 18,* 488–495.

National Center for Health Statistics. (1976). *Differentials in health characteristics by marital status: United States, 1971–72* (No. 104). Washington, DC: Author.

Nietzsche, F. *Twilight of the idols* (R. J. Hollingdale, trans.). Harmondsworth, UK: Penguin Books. (Original work published 1889).

Osterweis, M., Solomon, F., & Green, M. (Eds.). (1984). *Bereavement reactions, consequences and care.* Washington, DC: National Academy Press.

Parkes, C. M. (1964). The effects of bereavement on

physical and mental health: A study of the case records of widows. *British Medical Journal, 2,* 274–279.

Parkes, C. M. (1972). *Bereavement: Studies of grief in adult life.* London: Tavistock.

Parkes, C., & Brown, R. (1972). Health after bereavement: A controlled study of young Boston widowers. *Psychosomatic Medicine, 34,* 449–461.

Parkes, C., & Weiss, R. (1983). *Recovery from bereavement.* New York: Basic Books.

Paykel, E. S., Myers, J. K., Dienelt, M. N., & Klerman, G. L. (1969). Life events and depression: A controlled study. *Archives of General Psychiatry, 21,* 753–760.

Ramsay, R. W. (1979). Bereavement: A behavioral treatment of pathological grief. In P. O. Sjoden, S. Bates, & W. S. Dockins (Eds.), *Trends in behavior therapy.* New York: Academic.

Sanders, C. (1979–1980). A comparison of adult bereavement in the death of a spouse, child, and parent. *Omega, 10,* 303–323.

Shepherd, D., & Barraclough, B. (1974). The aftermath of suicide. *British Medical Journal, 2,* 600–603.

Silverman, P. R., & Cooperband, A. (1975). On widowhood: Mutual help and the elderly widow. *Journal of Geriatric Psychiatry, 8,* 9–27.

Skelskie, B. E. (1975). An exploratory study of grief in old age. *Smith College Studies in Social Work, 45,* 159–182.

Stern, K., Williams, G. M., & Prados, M. (1951). Grief reactions in later life. *American Journal of Psychiatry, 108,* 289–293.

Stroebe, M. S., & Stroebe, W. (in press). Social support and the alleviation of loss. In I. G. Sarason & B. R. Sarason (Eds.), *Social support: Theory research and applications.* The Hague: Martinus Nijhof.

Stroebe, W., Stroebe, M., & Domittner, G. (1985). *The impact of recent bereavement on the mental and physical health of young widows and widowers.* Report from the Psychological Institute, University of Tübingen, West Germany.

Stroebe, W., Stroebe, M. S., Gergen, K. J., & Gergen, M. (1982). The effects of bereavement on mortality: A social psychological analysis. In J. R. Eiser (Ed.), *Social psychology and behavioral medicine.* New York: Wiley.

Thompson, L., Breckenridge, J., Gallagher, D., & Peterson, J. (1984). Effects of bereavement on self-perceptions of physical health in elderly widows and widowers. *Journal of Gerontology, 39,* 309–314.

Warren, M. (1972). Some psychological sequelae of parental suicide in surviving children. In A. Cain (Ed.), *Survivors of suicide.* Springfield, IL: Charles C Thomas.

Wiener, A., Gerber, I., Battin, D., & Arkin, A. (1975). The process and phenomenology of bereavement. In B. Schoenberg, I. Berger, A. Wiener, A. Kutchner, D. Peretz, & A. Carr (Eds.), *Bereavement: Its psychosocial aspects.* New York: Columbia University Press.

Chapter 24

Prevention of Age-related Problems

Robert Kastenbaum

THE BEST OF INTENTIONS

Parr for the Course

One of the more celebrated incidents in the prehistory of clinical gerontology involved a person who first saw the light of day in the year 1482. He led the proverbial simple and industrious life. The name of Thomas Parr is not remembered because he led armies, schemed for power, or penned verses. This man's genius resided principally in his ability to survive. Warned by authorities in 1584 to keep his sexual impulses under better control, Parr searched diligently for a suitably vigorous wife. The comely young widow who took the vows with him in 1602 attested she "could discover nothing that would betray his great age" (Lorand, 1912, p. 329). According to experts of an earlier generation, Parr even died in good health. No less an authority than Harvey, first to describe the circulation of the blood, performed the autopsy and concluded that "every organ in this wonderful man was in perfect condition" (Lorand, 1912, p. 435). How, then, did death come to this man who had enjoyed such a long and active life? In his 152nd year, Parr became a guest of the king and—so the story goes—became a victim of the rich meals he could not resist after so many years of subsistence on a simple and frugal diet.

Historians have now spoiled this edifying story by casting doubt on Parr's actual age and the manner of his death. This triumph of pedantry deprives us of a choice example to preface a consideration of prevention strategies. Parr might still be flourishing today—so it would be tempting to assert—had not a well-intentioned establishment offered him such lethal enrichments. Denied this cautionary tale, one can fall back upon more recent observations that, if less spectacular, do have the advantage of better documentation:

- Frail and vulnerable elderly provided with social case work intervention had a higher mortality rate than matched peers in the control group (Blenkner, Jahn, & Wasser, 1964).
- Reducing or eliminating psychotropic drugs and sleep medications was associated with improved functional status and morale for institutionalized geriatric patients with multiple problems (Kastenbaum, Barber, Wilson, Ryder, & Hathaway, 1981).
- Private rooms have been considered more "normal" and more "therapeutic" than the open-ward accommodations common in many existing long-term-care facilities. This view has led to a campaign to transform open-ward environments into private and semiprivate accommodations. In a recent study, however, many residents expressed a preference for the companionship and stimulation of open-ward arrangements (Kayser-Jones, 1986).
- Exercise programs have become increasingly

emphasized both for older adults in the community and for those residing in long-term-care facilities. This popular form of prevention/intervention, however, has been found to carry injury and mortality risks of its own (Crandall, 1985).

These illustrative reports do not lead to the conclusions that social service interventions should be avoided, psychotropic medications withheld, privacy needs ignored, or exercise discouraged. All the authors advocate careful assessment, a balanced approach, and, of course, the obligatory "more research is needed." The point, however, is that it is not difficult to find examples of preventive and interventive efforts that have counterproductive results. Good intentions are not enough, nor does a simple additive approach (more medication, more exercise, etc.) always prove useful. It is perhaps inevitable that some prevention/intervention strategies will fail. This seems to be the fate of meliorative endeavors in all other spheres of human activity, and clinical gerontology is a relative newcomer. But there may be a more systematic concern as well—in our zeal to mitigate age-related problems we may be inclined to prematurely accept those concepts and techniques that happen to be convenient or intuitively appealing. We also seem to be having a problem in matching prevention modalities with appropriate and realistic outcome possibilities. It is not as a combined officer, judge, and jury that I offer the following observations but, rather, as a person who has made almost every possible error in his own work.

Reality Orientation and the Prevention of Prevention

If an adult day-care center or extended-care facility has any psychosocial program at all, it is likely to be *reality orientation* (RO). Introduced by Folsom and his colleagues (Folsom, 1968; Taulbee & Folsom, 1966), RO quickly became a familiar technique in geriatric settings throughout the nation. At first it was a positive and encouraging innovation. Here is a technique that (a) is employed within an interpersonal context; (b) can be used with confused, demented, and socially isolated individuals; (c) presents little risk of harmful side effects; and (d) requires relatively little expense. Some facilities utilized RO only in its small group/brief meeting format, while others also attempted to apply its principles to 24-hour

care. Apart from whatever specific benefits RO might achieve, its introduction into an institutional program represented an attempt to move in the direction of therapeutic activity. Those engaged in institutional care when RO was new will recall the pride with which administrators pointed to their state-of-the-art program, as well as the general enlivening effect among staff members who could see that something different was being tried. RO was seen as having both preventive and remedial potential. Further cognitive deterioration and social withdrawal might be halted by RO, and existing deficits perhaps overcome. Another significant potential was for the prevention or delay of institutionalization by involving vulnerable elders in this combined cognitive/social program.

The actual efficacy of RO is less important here than the way in which this treatment modality has been regarded and utilized by the caregiving system. One notes first that very few facilities have evaluated the efficacy of RO for their own participants on a systematic basis. I have asked for such data on many occasions and have invariably met with a puzzled reaction—what a strange idea, to check on the assumption that RO prevents and remediates! Further discussion yields the observation that this patient is still confused and that patient is still isolated, but such case-specific findings are not seen as bearing on the larger question (not perceived as a question) of RO's basic efficacy. Furthermore, never in more than 30 institutional inquiries did I encounter an administrator or program director who attempted to draw upon the general research literature in support of RO efficacy. Upon inquiry, several expressed the assumption that there must be substantial support for RO ("Everyone's been using it for years; there must be some studies, but I haven't read them"). The perpetuation of RO, then, has not been contingent upon either in-house studies or familiarity with published research. Actually, much of the available research is rather poor in technical quality, as Hussian (1981) has noted, not yielding dependable conclusions showing much relevance to the patients' clinical status.

A direct observational study of RO in the small group setting raises serious questions about the way in which this treatment modality may have become compromised by a rigid and insensitive approach and unrecognized assumptions. The investigators give examples such as the following from Buckholdt and Gubrium (1983):

Handbook of Clinical Gerontology

During RO sessions, therapists define reality in standard . . . terms, in response to what they see as routine questions. . . . They are not satisfied until a correct response is elicited since this formally indicates at least temporary contact with reality. Other aspects of their interaction with participants during RO therapy are seen as irrelevant to the business at hand. When a ninety year old lady complains that she is "just too tired to do this today," she is encouraged to continue. A man protests that dinner isn't always at 5 p.m., but whenever the kitchen is ready. The therapist agrees but still insists the correct answer is 5 p.m. Another man complains about being asked the same question session after session. The name of the institution doesn't matter to him. But the therapist continues to ask for the name.

. . . another lady refuses to answer the therapist. Instead she insists on talking about the upcoming visit from her son. The therapist becomes exasperated and tells the woman that her son has died. The woman weeps at the news. The therapist then races down the hall to the nursing station and quickly returns. She was wrong. The son is alive. The woman now weeps with joy and embraces the therapist. She is willing to answer the questions (p. 178, Buckholdt & Gubrium, 1983).

Buckholdt and Gubrium note that the "correctness" emphasis in RO is in harmony with the institution's continuing effort to control both resident and staff behavior, reduce individual variation, and present themselves to the world (especially to accreditation agencies) as competent. "Problems of confusion and disorientation are thus not simply individual conditions but difficulties for organizational management and control. They arise in institutions that standardize reality and thus reject alternative realities and deny the possibility of multiple realities" (p. 180). This somewhat cynical review, I must say, is consistent with my own observations. RO has often become more a tool of management and control rather than an alert and flexible modality for the prevention and treatment of age-associated problems. Buckholdt and Gubrium give a bitter title to their study: "Therapeutic Pretense in Reality Orientation." This harsh judgment should not be

applied uncritically across the broad spectrum of RO programs, but it does capture the thought that the premature enshrinement of a treatment modality can impede the development of more adequate approaches. RO deserves more appropriate and capable research attention and, probably, also some continuing place in clinical gerontology. However—and for no particular fault of its own—RO has become a case history from which cautionary lessons might well be drawn.

Reviewing or Obsessing?

Quite a different example of prevention strategies slipping their data-based links can be found in the area of life review/reminiscence therapy. This approach, in contrast to RO, started under the auspices of several converging and influential theories. The epigenetic conception of Erikson (1950) suggests that the older person needs to achieve an integrity of self by coming to grips with the actual life that one has lived. This theoretical framework has an important point of commonality with Jung (1959), who emphasized that people strive for a "completeness of being" that requires the ability to integrate opposing but complementary tendencies within the self. Butler's introduction of the life review concept into gerontology was accompanied by a similar value placed on the adaptive nature of self-scrutiny in later life (Butler, 1963).

Separately and collectively, these three conceptual orientations offered an alternative to the then prevailing notion of age as relentless deterioration. Some gerontologists found it more attractive to envision aging as part of a larger process of life span development in which every phase had its positive role to play. Certain facets of age-related experience could now be seen in a more positive and adaptive light. Reflective thought in general and concern for the past in particular found new appreciation in gerontology. There was less tendency to assume that one ought always to dote on futurity and that past orientation was necessarily unadaptive and even vaguely un-American.

The *life review* (LR) differs from RO in several other important ways:

1. LR emphasizes the uniqueness of every individual's life as compared with the RO attempt to align everybody with basic features of consensual reality.

2. Therapeutic procedures based upon LR prin-

ciples would be appropriate for a broad range of elderly adults, including the most able individuals. RO, by contrast, was developed with a primary target group of significantly impaired and institutionalized persons.

3. RO is essentially a behavior management technique that is applied to clients who are thought to require a protective and highly structured environment. By contrast, LR is defined by Butler (1963) as a "naturally occurring, universal mental process . . . " (p. 66). It is regarded as an intrinsic process that is indispensable if the individual—any individual—is to meet the challenges of aging in an adaptive manner. Older people are said to engage in LR with or without the opportunity to participate in guided reminiscence and other intervention modalities.

In both scope and details, then, LR differs significantly from RO as a strategy for preventing and/or alleviating age-associated problems. Nevertheless, the way in which LR has been perceived and utilized suggests this prevention/intervention strategy has been subjected to similar social forces. LR moved very quickly from concept to putative fact and, after gathering some momentum, has become one of the more popular approaches to psychosocial treatment. A pioneering study by McMahon and Rhudick (1964) had provided some support for the adaptational value of reminiscence, and several studies of widely varying methodology also helped dispel the lingering negative stereotype toward the older person's use of the past (Costa & Kastenbaum, 1967; Havighurst & Glaser, 1972; Kastenbaum, 1963; Lieberman & Falk, 1971). Some of these studies were designed with Butler's concepts in mind, and all were generally supportive of his emphasis on the positive aspects of reminiscence.

What tended to elude attention, however, was the fact that neither these studies nor any others provided direct and systematic information on the LR process. Do all older adults actually engage in LR? Under what circumstances is LR most likely to begin and to terminate (if it does terminate)? Precisely how is LR to be distinguished from other uses of the past? Perhaps the most relevant of the neglected questions was (and is) Under what circumstances (individual-situational interface) is LR a valuable form of prevention/intervention, and under what circumstances is it useless or potentially harmful?

Studies of reminiscence have continued to appear (e.g., Boylin, Gordon, & Nehrke, 1976; Coleman, 1974; Fallot, 1980). Although these are all useful contributions, again little has been done to subject the basic LR concept to direct and thorough investigation. The questions raised above remain unanswered, as reviewers have noted (Merriam, 1980; Molinari & Reichlin, 1984–1985). This neglect of fundamental questions about the LR concept seemingly has not interfered with its increasing use as an approach to intervention and prevention. Reports have appeared on therapeutic applications of the LR approach (e.g., Perrota & Meacham, 1981–1982; Sandell, 1978; Zieger, 1976). But even the best controlled investigation to date, by Perrota and Meacham (1981–1982), has failed to find a therapeutic effect. It is difficult to evaluate LR-oriented intervention and prevention strategies, for many reasons; perhaps the most troublesome is the lack of clear distinction between LR per se and the variety of other retrospective modalities employed by adults of all ages (Kastenbaum, 1977; LoGerfo, 1980).

With LR, as well as with RO, then, clinical gerontology has let itself be carried away by the best of intentions—seizing upon a positive idea and rushing it into practice without careful evaluation and without even seeming to recognize the need for such evaluation. In the case of LR, there has also been a lack of attention to its significant basic contention, that is, that LR is a universal process.

From this writer's clinical experience (and his opportunity to learn from other clinicians), it seems appropriate to raise the flag of caution. Some people thrive on self-reflections; others manage to have active and eventful lives without much attention to either the past or the distant future. Furthermore, among those disposed toward self-reflection, there are some with an obsessive turn of mind. Although well-intentioned, we may be intensifying the problems of an obsessive older person by encouraging the LR process. This could be a particular risk in the depressed and potentially suicidal person, as well as with the obsession-prone individual who has urgent life challenges and decisions to confront.

Despite all that could be said in favor of LR as a positive-thinking approach to intervention and prevention, it is based upon a premise that has not been carefully examined and for which differential recommendations have seldom been developed. Perhaps it is when our intentions are of the best and the concepts at hand the most appealing that we must give the most critical attention to basic assumptions and differential applications. This writer has not really been denigrating RO and LR: Clinical gerontology would be poorer without the opportunity to consider these approaches. The point is simply that the need to find and apply positive techniques too often seems to overwhelm the need to examine what we are doing with care and precision.

SOME CHARACTERISTICS OF EFFECTIVE PREVENTION

If the best of intentions are not always enough, neither are the best prevention modalities per se. The difference between effective and ineffective prevention may be contingent upon subtle and transitory factors that cannot be fully encompassed by the formal model. Give the same gourmet recipe to 10 different cooks and one will be astounded by the different procession of dishes that will emerge from the kitchen. It might be useful, then, to consider some of the little differences that can add up to significant differences in the efficacy of a preventive strategy. Examples will be drawn from a variety of content areas.

Timing, Tempo, and Intensity

A prevention program is more likely to succeed when it receives a level of intensity and a rate of action (tempo) that matches the receptivity of its intended clientele and when it is introduced at a strategic moment.

Example A

A foot-care program was initiated in a large geriatric facility based upon the recognition that helping the residents to remain mobile and pain-free would not only maintain their present quality of life but also forestall a cycle of bedfastness, isolation, and general deterioration. A competent podiatrist was engaged to run a foot-care clinic twice a week. Unexpectedly, the new program had a rocky beginning. Residents and nursing personnel both behaved as though the program constituted an imposition rather than a valuable addition. This disaffection was severe enough to threaten the continuation of the program. What was the problem? Everybody seemed to think that foot care was important. Nobody seemed to think that the physician lacked skill. The physician

recognized that things were not going well and was becoming edgy and defensive. Observation and inquiry suggested that a set of small but converging problems had built up a negative image of the prevention program:

1. The new clinic was introduced during a time period when nursing and housekeeping services were understaffed because of the heavy seasonal incidence of vacations. This predictable situation also involved a relative lack of stability on the wards because staff had been shifted about to fill the gaps. Its unquestioned virtues notwithstanding, the new program was perceived as an extra pressure and burden by many staff members. The timing was clearly disadvantageous.

2. The tempo established by the new prevention program was experienced as being at the same time both too rapid and too slow. The too-rapid aspect had two components: (a) The program was started up at full speed rather than gradually, a few people at a time, and (b) It required quick and continuous activity on the part of both residents and staff to assemble a morning's worth of clients at the specified hour. The too-slow aspect referred to the fact that many residents and some staff had to "hurry up and wait" for much of the morning.

3. The physician was an incisive and tightly organized person who was fresh from specialty training and new to geriatric practice. As a result, he had a profound fascination with feet, and—far from being biased against the elderly—he exulted in the variety of ankles and arches that were coming his way, and regarded this assignment as a worthy challenge. However, his interaction style alienated many residents and some staff. He tended to overwhelm the geriatric clientele with his intense and deadly serious demeanor. "He'd as soon shoot you as look at you," one resident confided to me. "Felt like I was back on the assembly line," reported another, "but this time it was me on the belt." Some less articulate residents expressed their discomfort by trembling, wandering off, or presenting frequent demands for the bathroom.

Despite this unpromising beginning, the program did continue and succeed in its mission of preventing mobility-related problems. Had the goal of this program been less well understood or valued, it would most likely have failed within a few weeks. The poor timing for the introduction of the program could not be reversed, but its impact was diminished as staffing returned to normal after the vacation season. The too fast/too slow tempo was modified by mutual consent and improved communication, residents no longer being rushed to the clinic, and sharp reduction in the waiting list. Open to new experience and possessed of an unsuspected keen sense of humor, the physician proved willing and able to adjust his modus operandi. Still highly intense and goal-directed in his interactions with other staff members, he now took a slower, more relaxed approach with the residents and reported enjoying this more comfortable manner himself.

Example B

At the same geriatric facility a smaller unfunded and somewhat hesitant program was introduced. The idea for this program developed over several months during informal discussions between some residents and staff members (mostly in or around the Captain's Chair, a publike setting designed to provide relief from the prevailing institutional atmosphere). Among the reoccurring themes, one became of particular interest: the anxiety and confusion of the first few hours, days, and weeks of institutionalization. "I didn't know what to expect—so I expected the worst!" "The worst days of my life." "I prayed the Lord would take me. I wanted to close my eyes and never open them again." These were typical comments for what might be called the institutional life review.

From these experiences came the idea of old-timers serving as companions for the newcomers. This plan could not be attributed to any one person; rather, it emerged from the resident/staff discussions over a period of time. Reflection was given to what kind of useful things some people had done for them and what approach might be most comforting and helpful for those newly admitted to the institution. The Welcome Program, as residents decided to call it, started slowly and only when the group felt ready to begin. No schedule was set for how many people would be welcomed and how long this process should take. "Easy does it" became the philosophy. Observing the Welcome Program in operation, one saw a quiet, low-key befriending process through which some newcomers recognized they had a special companion interested in helping them make a go of it. Using their own sense of timing to begin the program and keeping the tempo and intensity at a level that felt comfortable to them, the old-timers provided a service that proved to be a valuable supplement to the institution's more official and professional routine for orienting new admissions.

This informal program did seem to shorten the settling-in period and to reduce anxiety and confusion on the part of some newly admitted residents. Institutional staff learned not to pressure the welcome committee to see all new admissions, accept additional assignments and responsibilities, or conform to external schedules. The program worked fitfully and according to its own rhythms, but did work when appreciated and supported but otherwise left alone.

Thus, the training of clinical gerontologists might usefully include supervised experience in adjusting intensity, timing, and tempo to the particular people and situation, regardless of what substantive area of prevention is involved.

Follow-up: Immediate and Long-Term

Many prevention programs owe either their origins or their evaluations to time-limited projects. Among the problems associated with this fact are several that have become rather predictable:

1. The original project is staffed, equipped, and given special administrative protection in a manner that will not be continued over a protracted period of time or when the program is applied in other settings.
2. The situational dynamics will never again be the same as at the time the original project was introduced. (Although the halo effect is the best known facet, it is not the only process whose influence is likely to differ at different points in time—for example, resistance to the new because it *is* new is perhaps an even more common and consequential response and one that also tends to decline with time.)
3. Evaluation of the prevention program is limited to a certain realm of variables and conducted within a limited time frame. The actual fate of the program in many settings and over a prolonged time period may not be adequately investigated, as, for example, when unexpected outcomes occur that either strengthen or undermine the program's original aims, or rebound effects cancel out or compromise earlier gains. The tightly designed, cost-effective demonstration project may evaluate a project that will never again be applied in the same way and whose unexamined effects may prove more important than those subjected to formal study.

Acceptance or rejection of the program as a continuing part of the prevention/intervention spectrum is not entirely a function of its relative success in meeting the original objectives. RO is not the only treatment modality, for example, that keeps its place in many facilities without any particular evidence of efficacy. A modality may have rather limited success when given a controlled trial but still be valued as an activity that can be written up on the chart and contribute to a favorable impression at the next accreditation visit. *Self-esteem therapy* in some institutions consists only of provision of basic grooming, and possible effects on self-esteem are never seriously evaluated; nevertheless, it remains one of the personal care activities that provide the most pleasure to staff. Similarly, community-based health fairs have remained popular events even when the assessment techniques employed are of only marginal relevance to senior adults and little or no provision is made for follow-up.

Effective programs may be short-lived or limited in scope because they are not sufficiently integrated into the prevailing power structure and group dynamics.

Example

The guardianship system is intended to prevent the potentially catastrophic consequences of individuals with significant mental incapacities remaining responsible for their person and estate. These consequences include death through inability to provide self-care and nutrition; accidents to self and others; and loss of funds through defraudation. All too often, however, this system is operated with only perfunctory assessment and few safeguard procedures. As Schmidt, Miller, Bell, and New (1981) observe, "In general, there seem to be few problems in finding guardians for persons with money. What is not clear is the extent to which the rights of individuals with estates are protected" (p. 163). Those without funds seem to run a higher risk of institutional placement that almost always turns out to become a final disposition of their lives. Schmidt et al. conclude, along with most other specialists in law and aging, that once a petition for guardianship is filed, it is almost always granted, hearings are frequently waived, and guardianships are "rarely, if ever, lifted" (p. 162).

Recent discussions in Arizona between gerontologists and attorneys led to the consensus that problems of this kind are not primarily the fault of the existing statutes per se; rather, they derive from a lack of advocacy for rights of the older person whose cognitive capacity is in question. The protection built into the guardianship system by statute *could* prevent both abuse of legally mandated procedures and the risks attendant upon severe incapacity. That this double prevention apparatus too often does not work well in practice must be understood in terms of the power dynamics inherent in the situation. The general lack of adequate monitoring for guardianship dispositions is characteristic also of other problem areas in which prevention efforts are vitiated by neglect of short- and long-term follow-up.

By contrast, some geriatric physicians and gynecologists have learned to be persistent in their supervision of older women who suffer from or are strong candidates for osteoporosis. Alert care and active insistence on follow-up can be effective in preventing or postponing the occurrence of fractures (Spencer, Sontag, & Kramer, 1986). The management of osteoporosis and the prevention of its most severe consequences could serve as one useful model for the general prevention of debilitation in later life. The aim cannot be met adequately by any one preventive act or at any one moment in time—instead, caregiver and client must agree to work together regularly over an extended period of time. The preventive agenda becomes a part of the client's life-style, and regular monitoring becomes a shared responsibility.

Clinical gerontologists will be more effective as more skill is developed in the design and application of follow-up efforts. Command of the substantive facts and of an effective set of techniques does not guarantee success extended over a long period of time. One might borrow a page from experts in theatrical productions—a solid production based upon a strong script confers not the assurance but only the opportunity for an extended success. The show will be kept under a microscope, with producers looking for signs of incipient routinization, carelessness, or distortion. If the production is not always "alive," changing, and developing, even though the basic elements remain the same, then serious trouble is likely. Clinical gerontologists also have not completed their work after establishing and evaluating an intervention program—it must continue to be protected, critiqued, and developed if the positive results, and perhaps the program itself, are not to be ephemeral.

The Blessing of Ambivalence

Gerontologists have often emphasized the interdependence of functional systems and the holistic approach to care. Every prevention effort, then, might be regarded as having significant general adaptational consequences, in addition to its target effects. The 90-year-old who has received excellent foot care, for example, may find it easier to keep both his routines of daily life and his morale intact, thereby providing some insulation against the ever present threats to continued viability. The ailing widow who, by careful assessment, has been found to be depressed rather than demented and given appropriate treatment may be spared the loss of decision-making opportunity associated with guardianship and the loss of privacy associated with institutional placement. Success in some aspect of prevention, then, may lead to success in other spheres as well.

A complicating factor is frequently noticed but not quite articulated and put into perspective. In establishing an holistic plan of care, we tend to assume that the client will welcome the opportunity to reap the benefits of continued or renewed vigor and independence. But clients sometimes resist or evade "what's good for them." They may miss appointments, belittle the caregiver or themselves, and drop out of the program just when everything seems to be falling into place. Such displays of behavior, inconsistent with the prevention motif, can puzzle and perturb the clinical gerontologist, who believes that all the right moves have been made. The answer often is to be found not in any wrong moves on the part of the clinician but in a healthy display of ambivalence by the client.

The historical record suggests that the most characteristic orientation toward old age—by society in general but also by the elderly themselves—is this still underappreciated phenomenon known as ambivalence. An analysis of attitudes toward age in the ancient world has concluded that "ambivalence was never far from the surface, whether the surface itself sparkled within the Hebraic vision of the blessed and righteous old man or with Greek dread of this 'most evil of all things' " (Kastenbaum & Ross, 1975, p. 431). Manifestations of ambivalence were traced through the centuries to the present day, taking such forms as rationing of health care and other services and a less vigorous approach toward preventing suicide in the elderly. The reluctance to encourage, or even to tolerate, a large senior echelon that demands its share of power and decision-making opportunities is matched by mixed feelings on the part of many senior adults themselves. Mental health specialists were seen as having an important but neglected role in helping us all acknowledge our ambivalence toward aging—in ourselves and in others.

The fluctuations and discontinuities in the way that elderly people respond to prevention and intervention programs sometimes prove to be occasioned by the mixed signals they have been given: Their ambivalence is intensified by our own. A recent example was observed in a peer group program intended to prevent the more serious forms of depression and anxiety among widows. It was not so surprising that older widows became less involved and responsive when an observer discovered that speakers tended to restrict their eye contact with younger members of the group and to ignore problems of particular concern to the older members (Wambach, 1983). "I am here to help you" is a characteristic overt message that is often undercut by nonverbal and other covert communications. Elderly clients learn to identify such mixed messages quickly, and must then struggle with their need for help and the fear and anger that accompany rejection. It should not be surprising when the older person, well acquainted with society's ambivalence, takes the lead in shunning the prospective helping person—but without quite destroying the possibility of a viable relationship.

Some of the dynamics involved are illustrated in this excerpt from a conference workshop on intergenerational relationships. The participants were all allied health professionals and all were in their 50s or 60s.

Rhoda L.: I'm getting there myself. (*Laughs.*) All right—I am there!

R. K.: How can you tell?

Rhoda L.: They tell you. All that young stuff (*laughs*) struts in and then they see they have to deal with me and you can see them setting their faces—poor little me! I have to listen to this old prune and pretend to take her seriously. You can see it in the tight ways, the phony ways they act around you. They don't act like that around themselves.

Betty Jane S.: You can try to get through to them, you know, make them see you as a real person, not Ms. Prune Face of the Year.

Rhoda L.: I'm through with that stuff. You know what I do? I beat them to the freeze!

Harry V.: The fastest gun in the clinic!

Rhoda L.: (*Blasts Harry with her finger-guns.*) Better me than you, sweet stuff! *I'll* do the rejecting around here!

Betty Jane S.: I know what you're saying. You could still get through though.

Alexis L.: I'm sitting here and thinking. . . .

Harry V.: No thinking allowed here.

Alexis L.: You're pretty mouthy for a dead man.

(*Rhoda aims her gun at Harry again.*)

Alexis L.: I'm sitting here and thinking that our geriatric clients must feel the way you do, or more so even.

(*Several voices come in*): I mean about who's going to reject who first. We probably all look like a dish of prunes to the trainees, but then we turn around and—I'm just asking the question—don't we do approximately the same ourselves?

This group of experienced professionals, contending with their own aging, found it stimulating to remind themselves that all parties bring ambivalent thoughts and mixed feelings to significant relationships. By recognizing one's own ambivalence, it becomes easier to recognize and empathize with the other person's misgivings as well. Sharing this ambivalence openly can sometimes disarm the tensions that threaten a fragile caregiver-client relationship. I recall trying to establish rapport with a physician who had made a serious suicide attempt after being retired from his position with a large corporation and finding that nobody else seemed to want his services. The interview was not going well. He was polite, but distant and laconic.

R. K.: Would you like me to go away?

(*No response.*)

R. K.: You can kick me out of your room if you like.

Doctor: I can?

R. K.: You're the boss. I just work here.

Doctor: You must have something better to do.

R. K.: I think I'm not doing very well with you. I'm not doing my job very well.

Doctor: (*Turns toward me for the first time and inspects me searchingly with eyes that begin to moisten around the edges.*) You shouldn't tell people that.

R. K.: It's true, though. I came here not knowing if I could do anything for you and I still don't know.

Doctor: I didn't ask you to come.

R. K.: I know.

Doctor: I want to sleep, sleep. Go away.

R. K.: I want to go away because you don't want me here. But I also want to be with you awhile because you've just been through so much.

Doctor: I wouldn't be here if I had done the job right.

R. K.: You felt that bad about things. . . .

Doctor: I'll get it right next time. Don't think you can talk me out of it.

R. K.: Suppose you were me. Wouldn't you think, "Boy, I really have to find a way to keep this guy from knocking himself off!" And wouldn't you also think, "Hey, but listen, this guy knows his life a lot better than I do. Why should I even try to get in his way?" Wouldn't you have a hard time just figuring out what you really think and what you really should do?

Doctor: I've been through all that. I don't think suicide is wonderful. I'm not proud of myself for that.

R. K.: And sometimes life feels pretty good, and sometimes you could end it just like that.

Doctor: Just like that! My mind's a rusty gate. Swings back and forth.

R. K.: (*Takes a seat.*) You can't kick me out now. I won't let you. I gotta learn more about that rusty gate.

Doctor: I'll teach you then. I'll give you a lesson that will scare the daylights out of you.

R. K.: Scare away!

Doctor: The first lesson is, never get old. . . .

The dialogue had started. Had not both parties admitted to doubts and ambivalence, there might have been only a single abortive session. There was no clear resolution of the physician's suicidal thoughts, but the dialogue itself seemed to serve as one of the alternatives to converting these thoughts into an irrevocable deed.

Ambivalence is a blessing because it draws upon the realization that one can always find a reason for either continuing to face the risks and potentials of life or retreating and resigning. Strategic withdrawals can prove beneficial in the long run and are not necessarily to be despised. A prevention program that can ride the natural contours of ambivalence is likely to be more effective in its real-life outcomes than a bookish model that expects unswerving compliance on the part of caregiver and client and that interprets healthy doubts as damnable obstructions.

SOME STRATEGIES FOR PREVENTION OF AGE-RELATED PROBLEMS

Working Assumptions

All prevention efforts make a number of assumptions, whether explicit or implicit. It may be useful, then, to begin by identifying several working assumptions that seem especially relevant to prevention programs in clinical gerontology.

1. *Resources are limited and subject to all the vagaries of the political process.* Binstock, Levin, and Weatherley (1985) make it clear that political factors systematically affect not only the level but also the specific allocation of resources for older Americans. It is necessary but not sufficient to base a prevention program upon a sound data base and design it for an appropriate target population. The political process can halt or distort the program at any point. Effective prevention programs, then, should take into account not only gerontological

factors but also the political pushes and pulls that can be decisive in the program's fate.

2. *A multicause, multieffect model is most realistic for the overall approach, yet certain very specific connections must also be respected.* "Take the green pill in the morning for this, and the two orange ones in the evening for that" is a familiar way in which the simplistic one cause one effect model operates. It is not exclusively a medical model, however. Many other professionals, notably social workers, attempt to provide specific solutions to specific problems, even though they may be well aware that the client's total situation is very complex. Those functioning within a bureaucracy often expend much of their energy in the attempt to accomplish one good deed on behalf of the client, despite their realization that a holistic approach would be more realistic and effective. Many social scientists today make a strong case for a holistic approach, conducted within a model that emphasizes complex and shifting influences rather than simple cause-and-effect points (e.g., DiMatteo & DiNicola, 1982).

In clinical gerontology, however, we might be best advised to seek an integration of the two approaches. A depressive reaction, for example, can develop from many sources, including a variety of physical conditions and significant life events. The depressive reaction itself can take a variety of forms and lead to a variety of consequences. One needs a model that is complex and flexible enough to accommodate all the forces involved and yet also has the acuity and the technical knowledge to identify very specific interventions that could make a critical difference in prevention or treatment. A complex holistic model, then, may prove most heuristic as a general approach to prevention strategies, but there will be circumstances in which highly specific connections can be identified and modified.

3. *The success of prevention efforts must be considered within the framework of individual expectations as well as external criteria.* It is convenient to evaluate prevention efforts by objective outcome measures that apply equally to all members of the target population. These measures often appear both useful and convincing. A community-based program that reduces both mortality rates and the number of admissions to long-term-care facilities, for example, would probably be counted as a significant success. Nevertheless, evaluation will be incomplete and to some extent misleading if subjective well-being is neglected. Objective housing arrangements may be upgraded, for example, but with a perceived loss in "neighborhoodness" or

control over life. There are wide individual and ethnic differences in the priorities given to particular elements in maintaining self-esteem and life satisfaction (Kastenbaum, 1984). Without taking these differences into account, one can miss the opportunity to meet the distinctive needs of a particular individual or subpopulation—and never know it. A meta-analysis of the subjective well-being literature (Okun, Stock, Haring, & Witter, 1984) found that even such basic data as the ethnic composition of samples was omitted in more than half (57%) of the studies reviewed. Gerontology at present cannot pride itself in the attention given to individual and ethnic differences in subjective well-being and its correlates. Those developing and evaluating prevention programs in the future might be well advised to give as much attention to distinctive characteristics and needs of their specific subpopulations as to objective and standardized measures.

Two broad types of prevention strategies will now be briefly considered and illustrated. This is intended to be only a selective exploration, with some possible value for suggesting a wider range of strategies.

Maintenance and Strengthening of Interpersonal Support

Feeling oneself to be alone in the world is a subjective view with significant objective correlates and consequences. It has been repeatedly shown, for example, that unmarried adults are at a higher risk for suicide, a pattern that is clear among the elderly as well (Osgood, 1985). Some people do function well in the self-reliant "loner" life-style; one would not want to interfere with this kind of adaptation when it has proven successful. Nevertheless, it is likely that not only suicide but many other negative outcomes could be prevented by programs that maintain and strengthen the older person's interpersonal support network.

There is now a gradually expanding database from which prevention programs might draw in attempting to achieve this goal (e.g., literature reviews by Antonucci, 1985; Sussman, 1985). Succinct discussions can be found in *Family Relationships in Later Life* (Brubaker, 1983). Attention is given here to such topics as "The Quality of Long-Term Marriages" (Ade-Ridder & Brubaker, 1983), "Adult Children and Their Elderly Parents" (Cicirelli, 1983), "Siblings and Other Kin" (Scott, 1983), and "Family Involvement and Support for Widowed Persons" (Heinemann, 1983). Within each type of relationship—spousal, sibling, inter-generational—one can learn to identify both the warning signs of impending deterioration and the core strengths that can be built upon.

Specific prevention strategies can develop naturally as one becomes better acquainted with the interpersonal world of older people. Atchley and Miller (1983), for example, have studied elderly couples with a vital and mutually satisfying relationship. Such major life events as retirement and residential change did not diminish either their relationship or their general subjective well-being. One might think of recruiting some of these couples for programs in which they could unobtru-sively model successful "spouseship" for others. Couples who have drifted apart over the years for lack of shared activities and values might benefit from the opportunity to become acquainted with age peers for whom sharing has become second nature. I have seen this phenomenon occur spon-taneously: a subtly designed prevention program could increase the likelihood of elderly couples recognizing such alternatives and options.

Another type of strategy might be developed with the specific aim of encouraging older people to keep in more effective contact with their kin. Scott (1983), for example, found that two-thirds of her elderly respondents never wrote to their siblings, although most did maintain some telephone con-tact. Some adults go for years without putting their thoughts in writing. A program that encourages people to rediscover and cultivate this ability by writing "good, old-fashioned letters" could add a valuable dimension to relationships with those not in the immediate vicinity. As Scott has also found, older siblings are more likely to have the need to exchange assistance with each other than is the case with younger adults. Establishing regular com-munication through correspondence could main-tain and strengthen a relationship that might at any time be subject to emergent pressures.

Intergenerational discussion and counseling groups, including the possibility of extended sessions in a retreat-like atmosphere, is one of the prevention strategies that appears worth trying after examining the literature on adult parent-child relationships (e.g., Cicirelli, 1983). Marital disruption among adult children and its impact on the older generation is just one area of stress that might be managed effectively through this means. Separation, divorce, and remarriage can produce tensions that disrupt the intergenerational support network at critical points in time, but these ten-sions can often be resolved when an opportunity is provided for relaxed and thorough discussion.

Innovative strategies are needed for encouraging and legitimatizing significant relationships between older people who are not related to each other. *Friendship* is the closest term in common usage to describe these relationships, but some take on the characteristics of family relationships as well. Mat-thews (1983) makes a useful beginning in analyzing the variety of friendship relationships in later life and raises some disturbing questions about the type of relationship that is most likely to prosper in con-temporary society (basically, the shallow-opportu-nistic versus the committed). Although most close friendships start earlier in life, there are sometimes opportunities to develop new core relationships in old age. Because having a close friend or two can make a critical difference in subjective well-being, one might consider developing new strategies that will help people not only to maintain old friendships but also to develop new ones. Those who plan vari-ous types of retirement communities and services might think carefully about design and functional features that could increase the likelihood for devel-opment of new friendships.

Attention to the growing research literature on family relationships is likely to suggest many specific prevention strategies that build upon existing interpersonal strengths and that reduce the possibility of a critical relationship failing under stress.

Maintenance and Improvement of Coping Ability

A second major area for prevention efforts encompasses the older person's ability to cope and thrive. Two general types of strategy can be devel-oped: (a) focus on specific situations, problems, and challenges; and (b) focus on basic adaptatio-nal skills. There is a pressing need for innovation, evaluation, and refinement of prevention strategies in both areas, and, of course, there will be circum-stances in which situational coping and basic skills can be addressed within the same framework.

Coping with particular challenges can be illus-trated through two examples. Older adults have an excess risk for motor vehicle accidents (Brearley, 1982). Programs that reduce the likelihood of such accidents would be of clear benefit not only to the elderly themselves but to the community at large. Various proposals have been made that would require additional testing of older drivers who seek license renewal, and place restrictions upon their rights. Although there are probably instances in which the right to drive should be withheld (as with some younger adults), this would be an extreme, unfair and burdensome solution to impose on older drivers as a class. Some areas are so deficient in public transportation, for example, that a program to prevent accidents by restricting driving privileges would lead to other adverse outcomes. A promising alternative is to offer older drivers the opportunity to refresh their skills and monitor their own performance. There are now a number of such programs, including one sponsored by the Amercian Association of Retired Persons, which has the advantage of utilizing older adults as instructors. Offered as a nonstigmatizing and voluntary program and endorsed by peer groups, this kind of prevention effort has structural features that could be transferred to other substantive areas as well.

Health education is another area in which older adults can become increasingly effective in looking after their own interests. It is encouraging to note that the health care industry itself is now taking interest in such efforts, sponsoring a variety of educational programs designed to help the older person become a more knowing consumer of health-related services. Two major factors contribute to the possibility that prevention efforts can be very successful in this area: (a) the older person's self-motivated, realistic concern about health maintenance and (b) the availability of specific relevant information that can be shared with the older person. Although it is true that attitude adjustment may also be a desired outcome for some older people, there can be much benefit just from the transmission of accurate information on such subjects as drug effects and the use of medical devices.

Less has been accomplished in the realm of basic adaptational skills. Here it may be that the attitudinal component will need particular attention—one cannot make progress in compensating for memory deficits, for example, if these deficits are not acknowledged. The experimental psychology of cognitive processes in later adulthood has received considerable attention in recent years (e.g., Reese & Rodeheaver, 1985; Salthouse, 1982). Although some promising efforts have been made to bridge the gap between laboratory and everyday life (e.g., Poon, Walsh-Sweeney, & Fozard, 1980), much remains to be done. Many people fall into inefficient and unadaptive habits of perception and information processing in their earlier adult years. Difficulties that become evi-

dent in old age may owe as much to hyperhabituation and other previously established cognitive problems as they do to intrinsic age-related changes (Kastenbaum, 1980). At present, it is impossible to estimate with any confidence the true limits and the untapped potential of cognitive adaptation in later life. Much too little has been done to test the limits and to provide systematic opportunities for older adults to monitor their own cognitive processes, rediscover underutilized talents, and make optimal use of their lifelong experiences.

The American public's interest in physical fitness seems to have survived its fad stage to become a relatively enduring aspect of our consciousness. Interest in self-help books and aids has also remained high. Perhaps the most significant target for this motive has yet to come into focus: the cultivation of the human mind, not only in its early, formative years but in the culminating and challenging crest of later maturity.

REFERENCES

Ade-Ridder, L., & Brubaker, T. H. (1983). The quality of long-term marriages. In T. H. Brubaker (Ed.), *Family relationships in later life* (pp. 19–30). Beverly Hills, CA: Sage.

Antonucci, T. C. (1985). Personal characteristics, social support, and social behavior. In R. H. Binstock & E. Shanas (Eds.), *Handbook of aging and the social sciences* (2nd ed., pp. 94–128). New York: Van Nostrand Reinhold.

Atchley, R. C., & Miller, S. J. (1983). Types of elderly couples. In R. H. Brubaker (Ed.)., *Family relationships in later life* (pp. 77–90). Beverly Hills, CA: Sage.

Binstock, R. H., Levin, M. A., & Weatherley, R. (1985). Political dilemmas of social intervention. In R. H. Binstock & E. Shanas (Eds.), *Handbook of aging and the social sciences* (2nd ed., pp. 589–618). New York: Van Nostrand Reinhold.

Blenkner, M., Jahn., J., & Wasser, E. (1964). *Serving the aging: An experiment in social work and public health nursing.* New York: Community Service Society.

Boylin, W., Gordon, S. K., & Nehrke, M. F. (1976). Reminiscing and ego integrity in institutionalized elderly males. *Gerontologist, 16,* 118–124.

Brearley, C. P. (1982). *Risk and ageing.* London: Routledge & Kegan Paul.

Brubaker, T. H. (Ed.). (1983). *Family relationships in later life.* Beverly Hills, CA: Sage.

Buckholdt, D. R., & Gubrium, J. F. (1983). Therapeutic pretense in reality orientation. *International Journal of Aging and Human Development, 16,* 167–182.

Butler, R. N. (1963). The life review: An interpretation of reminiscence in the aged. *Psychiatry, 26,* 65–75.

Cicirelli, V. (1983). Adult children and their elderly parents. In T. H. Brubaker (Ed.), *Family relationships in later life* (pp. 31–46). Beverly Hills, CA: Sage.

Coleman, P. G. (1974). Measuring reminiscence characteristics from conversation as adaptive features of old age. *International Journal of Aging and Human Development, 8,* 281–294.

Costa, P. T., & Kastenbaum, R. (1967). Some aspects of memories and ambitions in centenarians. *Journal of Genetic Psychology, 110,* 3–16.

Crandall, R. C. (1985). Jogging: Road to longevity or an early death? *Gerontologist, 25,* 20 (abstract).

DiMatteo, M. H., & DiNicola, D. D. (1982). Social science and the art of medicine: From Hippocrates to holism. In H. S. Friedman & M. R. DiMatteo (Eds.), *Interpersonal issues in health care* (pp. 9–32). New York: Academic.

Erikson, E. H. (1950). *Identity and the life cycle.* New York: International Universities Press.

Fallott, R. D. (1980). The impact of mood on verbal reminiscing in late adulthood. *International Journal of Aging and Human Development, 10,* 385–400.

Folsom, J. C. (1968). Reality orientation for the elderly mental patient. *Journal of Geriatric Psychiatry, 1,* 291–307.

Havighurst, R. J., & Glaser, R. (1972). An exploratory study of reminiscence. *Journal of Gerontology, 27,* 245–253.

Heinemann, G. D. (1983). Family involvement and support for widowed persons. In T. H. Brubaker (Ed.), *Family relationships in later life* (pp. 127–148). Beverly Hills, CA: Sage.

Hussian, R. A. (1980). *Geriatric psychology: A behavioral perspective.* New York: Van Nostrand Reinhold.

Jung, C. G. (1959). *The structure and dynamics of the psyche.* London: Routledge & Kegan Paul.

Kastenbaum, R. (1963). Cognitive and personal futurity in later life. *Journal of Individual Psychology, 19,* 216–222.

Kastenbaum, R. (1977). Memories of tomorrow: On the interpenetrations of time in later life. In B. S. Gorman & A. E. Chessman (Eds.), *The personal experience of time* (pp. 194–214). New York: Plenum.

Kastenbaum, R. (1980). Habituation as a partial model of human aging. *International Journal of Aging and Human Development, 13,* 159–170.

Kastenbaum, R. (1984). *Active life expectancy: A welcome and a critique.* Paper presented at the annual meeting of the Gerontological Society of America, San Antonio, TX.

Kastenbaum, R., & Ross, B. (1975). Historical perspectives on care. In J. G. Howells (Ed.), *Modern perspectives in the psychiatry of old age* (pp. 421–449). New York: Brunner/Mazel.

Kastenbaum, R., Barber, T., Wilson, C., Ryder, B., & Hathaway, L. (1981). *Old, sick and helpless: where therapy begins.* Cambridge, MA: Ballinger.

Kayser-Jones, J. S. (1986). Open-ward accommodations in a long-term care facility: The elderly's point of view. *Gerontologist, 26,* 63–69.

Lieberman, M. A., & Falk, J. M. (1971). The remembered past as a source of data for research on the life cycle. *Human Development, 14,* 132–141.

LoGerfo, M. (1980). Three ways of reminiscence in theory and practice. *International Journal of Aging and Human Development, 12,* 39–48.

Lorand, A. (1912). *Old age deferred.* Philadelphia: F. A. Davis.

Matthews, S. H. (1983). Definitions of friendship and their consequences in old age. *Ageing and Society, 3,* 141–156.

McMahon, A. W., & Rhudick, P. J. (1964). Reminiscing: Adaptational significance in the aged. *Archives of General Psychiatry, 10,* 203–208.

Merriam, S. (1980). The concept and function of reminiscence: A review of the research. *Gerontologist, 20,* 604–609.

Molinari, V., & Reichlin, R. E. (1984–1985). Life review reminiscence in the elderly: A review of the literature. *International Journal of Aging and Human Development, 20,* 81–92.

Okun, M. A., Stock, W. A., Haring, M. J., & Witter, R. A. (1984). Health and subjective well-being: A meta-analysis. *International Journal of Aging and Human Development, 19,* 111–132.

Osgood, N. J. (1985). *Suicide in the elderly.* Rockville, MD: Aspen Systems Corporation.

Perrota, P., & Meacham, J. A. (1981–1982). Can a reminiscing intervention alter depression and self-esteem? *International Journal of Aging and Human Development, 14,* 23–30.

Poon, L. W., Walsh-Sweeney, L., & Fozard, J. L. (1980). Memory skill training for the elderly: Salient issues on the use of imagery mnemonics. In L. W. Poon, J. L. Fozard, L. S. Cermak, D. Arenberg, & L. W. Thompson (Eds.), *New directions in memory and aging* (pp. 37–59). Hillsdale, NJ: Lawrence Erlbaum.

Reese, H. W., & Rodeheaver, D. (1985). Problem solving and complex decision making. In J. E. Birren & K. W. Schaie (Eds.), *Handbook of the psychology of aging* (2nd ed., pp. 474–499). New York: Van Nostrand Reinhold.

Salthouse, T. A. (1982). *Adult cognition: An experimental psychology of human aging.* New York: Springer-Verlag.

Sandell, S. L. (1978). Reminiscence in movement therapy with the aged. *Art Psychotherapy, 5,* 217–221.

Schmidt, W. C., Miller, K. S., Bell, W. G., & New, B. E. (1981). *Public guardianship and the elderly.* Cambridge, MA.: Ballinger.

Scott, J. P. (1983). Siblings and other kin. In T. H. Brubaker (Ed.), *Family relationships in later life* (pp. 47–62). Beverley Hills, CA: Sage.

Spencer, H., Sontag, S. J., & Kramer, L. (1986). Disorders of the skeletal system. In I. Rossman (Ed.), *Clinical geriatrics* (3rd ed., pp. 523–537). Philadelphia: Lippincott.

Sussman, M. B. (1985). The family life of old people. In R. H. Binstock & E. Shanas (Eds.), *Handbook of aging and the social sciences* (2nd ed., pp. 415–449). New York: Van Nostrand Reinhold.

Taulbee, L. R., & Folsom, J. C. (1966). Reality orientation for geriatric patients. *Hospital and Community Psychiatry, 8,* 133–135.

Wambach, J. A. (1983). *Timetables for grief and mourning in widow support groups.* Unpublished doctoral dissertation, Arizona State University, Tempe.

Zieger, B. L. (1976). Life review in art therapy with the aged. *American Journal of Art Therapy, 15,* 47–50.

Chapter 25

A Place to Call Home

Graham D. Rowles

"I can't think of going anyplace as long as I can get along by myself." It was 1978. Eighty-two-year-old Nell was adamant. She had lived alone in the spacious drafty residence the family had purchased in 1944 since her husband's death several years previously. A recent attack from a "doped" youthful intruder, a flooded basement, and increasing difficulty walking up the stony rutted pathway that led up the steep incline to her house on the hill had not weakened her resolve. This was the house where her children had been raised, where her husband had spent his last years, much of it sitting on the front porch as his soot-filled lungs progressively failed.

Four years later, we discussed the same topic in her daughter Corinne's apartment, where she was recuperating following a stay in the hospital. Nell remained firm in her resolve. She talked about an offer from her son in Michigan. "They got this regular little apartment in the bottom of their basement. Paul told me five years ago when I was up there, 'This is yours whenever you're ready.'" "But you're not ready yet?" I responded, sensing her reluctance. "No, I'm not ready." On this occasion, Nell was able to return home. But a subsequent heart attack resulted once more in hospitalization. This time, she never fully recovered. After another short stay at Corinne's, she died. The house on the hill remained empty for almost a year.

Nell's story reflects an increasingly common scenario as old people and their families grapple uneasily with critical dilemmas of residential choice. From the old person's perspective, a variety of factors mitigate against residential change. Familiarity with the physical configuration of a house, reluctance to abandon longtime neighbors and friends, fear of acknowledging increased dependence, and emotional attachment to a place that may have been home for decades and the locus of many critical life experiences all reinforce inertia. At the same time, physiological decrements, failing health, reduced ability to negotiate the neighborhood environment, the death of a spouse or living companion, increasing social isolation as age peers die or move away, and reduced ability to physically maintain the residence all gradually become increasingly insistent indicators of the need to relocate.

The ongoing dilemma is not simply a problem for elderly people; it is also of major concern to their families. Increasing spatial separation of generations has raised critical issues with regard to appropriate environments for older relatives. Should Mom be supported in her wish to remain alone in the rambling old house? Should she be encouraged to move in with the family, even at the risk of separation from her friends and at the cost of disrupting the family's life-style because such a move would necessitate doubling up the children and reducing the late-night volume of the stereo? Should the family consider modifying the house to provide a separate apartment? Is building a granny cottage a viable option? Should Mom be encouraged to consider moving into an elderly housing project or to contemplate the life care facility chosen by some of her peers? At what point should institutionalization be considered? To what extent does the family have a moral obligation to provide assistance to enable her to stay in her home for as long as she chooses, regardless of the cost?

Finally, the problem of appropriate housing for the elderly has become an issue in the public domain. Is government or the private sector responsible for providing adequate housing for the elderly? How much housing and what type of housing is most appropriate?

Growing societal recognition of the multifaceted character of the elderly housing problem has resulted in a proliferation of research studies and even the creation in 1983 of the *Journal of Housing for the Elderly*. Rather, than solving the problem, this flurry of activity has served, in a counterintuitive way, to make it more complex in some respects, because old people and their families are now confronted by an almost bewildering array of alternatives.

The purpose of this chaper is, first, to provide a brief description of the changing housing needs of elderly people and some of the options available to them. Such a description provides an objective characterization of the problem. However, it fails to adequately consider the subjective meaning of the residence and the idea of *home* as more than merely a place to "hang your hat." Consequently, a major focus of the chapter will be a synthesis of an emerging literature that is attempting to understand the subjective dimensions of *dwelling* (considered as a verb) and to reveal the underlying bases of attachment to home that for many people transform a place of residence into an extension of self and a repository of meaning.

A fundamental assumption is that the quest for such understanding will provide for more informed consideration of emotional aspects of critical housing choices faced by old people and their families and will facilitate a decision-making process that is sensitive to experiential needs. Against this backdrop, a third section of the chapter reinterprets the issue of housing decision making as a *dynamic* process, extending over many years, a process that may involve a series of housing adjustments and relocation decisions as circumstances change. Sensitivity to the meaning of home and dwelling may be a significant contribution of the clinician as he or she seeks to assist old people and their families.

CHANGING HOUSING NEEDS AND OPTIONS

By middle age, many people have established a degree of congruence between personal needs and residential circumstances. Consonance has often been achieved between family size and the space and configuration of the dwelling. Furniture, appliances, and other items consonant with a preferred life-style (within the constraints of socioeconomic status) have been acquired. Characteristic patterns of use of space within the residence have become comfortable daily routines. A sense of the house as home has been achieved by a personalized style of decoration and the accumulation of pictures and other artifacts that imbue the dwelling with meaning. Often the home has been the locus of critical life events; it has acquired a history intricately intertwined with the resident's identity.

As with advancing age, both personal circumstances and environmental needs change, some discordance emerges in the person/environment "fit" that undermines this equilibrium and results in a need either to make environmental modifications or to relocate. This perspective provides the focus of several theoretical formulations, including Lawton and Nahemow's ecological theory of aging (encompassing the environmental docility hypothesis) and Kahana's environmental congruence model (Kahana, 1975; Lawton & Nahemow, 1973; Lawton, Windley, & Byerts, 1982). A fundamental assumption within both formulations is of increasing environmental vulnerability with advancing age. Such vulnerability has a variety of manifestations.

Normal physiological changes limit the ability to function effectively in an existing residence. Reduced agility makes reaching for high cupboards, climbing the stairs, or bringing in the coal for the furnace more difficult. Propensity to slip in the bathroom increases as dizzy spells and an unsteady gait begin to impair environmental competence. It becomes more tiring to maintain the house in the manner in which the individual may have been accustomed (Kellaher, 1985). Mowing the lawn becomes an increasingly taxing and unwelcome chore. Such normative transitions are often accompanied by declining health, often chronic illness, which further reduces the individual's ability to maintain herself within a home that was formerly quite manageable.

The impact of physiological and health changes

is frequently exacerbated by reduced income (a concomitant of retirement in many cases). The ability to pay for routine maintenance of the residence is reduced. As physiological and health status declines, the do-it-yourself option becomes progressively less viable. Where finances permit investments in maintenance, there is sometimes a reluctance to spend money because the old person considers her anticipated life span does not merit such expenditure (Atchley & Miller, 1979).

Environments, like people, also change over time. Thus many old people find themselves living in deteriorating neighborhoods typified by physical decay, high population turnover, and disintegration of social organization. This is particularly the case in many inner-city neighborhoods, where elderly populations have aged in place (Lawton, Kleban, & Carlson, 1973; Rowles, 1978). Many first-generation suburban neighborhoods are also becoming run down as a new generation of old people matures (Gutowski, 1981; Logan, 1985).

Finally, a potent cause of modified housing needs is the changing family status of the elderly and an associated propensity for growing social isolation. The departure of children from the family home is only one of a series of social transitions that increase the pressure for housing adjustment. The "overhousing" of elderly couples in terms of dwelling space is often justified in terms of the availability of extra rooms serving as a stimulus for children to visit (Atchley & Miller, 1979). However, when the spouse dies, the social isolation of the survivor increases the pressure to relocate. Such pressure may be reinforced by the death or relocation of elderly neighbors who may have been the focus of a viable support system (Rowles, 1983a).

The physiological, health, economic, and social decrements associated with the aging experience are rarely discrete events. Rather, they represent incremental components of a trajectory of increasing environmental vulnerability, typically extending over many years, with widely differing manifestations in individual cases and provoking a variety of responses. These responses may be considered within the framework of two sets of options: options premised upon accommodating to changing circumstances within an existing dwelling and options premised upon a change of residence.

As housing needs change, old people typically adjust by modifying the use of their residence. Upstairs rooms may be closed off, at first just for the winter, eventually permanently. Economizing on heating costs through this process may be complemented by reducing expenditure on maintenance, as less money is invested in the routine upkeep of the house. Use of extra space, increased income, and companionship (to replace departed family or a deceased spouse) may be achieved by taking in boarders or by undertaking home conversion, subdividing the house to create an income-producing apartment (Carlin & Fox, 1981). An increasing number of old people are also able to remain in their own homes by harnessing the home-equity conversion options that have grown in popularity in recent years (Jacob, 1982; Pastalan, 1983b).

Modified use of the dwelling may be supplemented by a variety of options available through the public sector. The emergence of the home care movement during the 1970s resulted in many programs oriented toward allowing old people to remain in their community residences as long as possible (Gottesman & Saperstein, 1981; Steinfeld, 1981). Chore service programs and home assistance programs reduce the likelihood of housing change, or at least delay in its occurrence, as do visiting homemakers' and visiting nurse programs and even the home-delivered-meals component of the Title III Nutrition Program.

In spite of the possibility of continuing to live within the existing residence and harnessing supportive service programs, many elderly people either choose to or are forced by changing circumstances to contemplate relocation. Numerous typologies summarizing the plethora of available options have been produced in recent years (American Association of Retired Persons, 1984; Eckert & Murrray, 1984; Lawton, 1981; Mangum, 1982; Meyer & Speare, 1985; Wiseman & Roseman, 1979). One of the more useful conceptualizations is the Nachison and Leeds' (1983) continuum of living (Figure 25.1), in which a series of residential alternatives are arrayed along a continuum of increasing need for supportive social and medical services associated with increasing functional age and degree of frailty. Within this framework the elderly person is viewed as requiring residential facilities that progress from community-based individual and multifamily *housing* options through a variety of *congregate* alternatives providing a measure of practical and social support (including dining and service facilities) to nursing homes and hospital environments, where primary emphasis is on *medical* care. A more

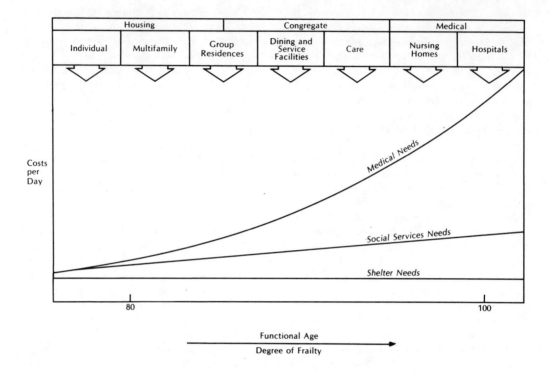

Figure 25.1 The continuum of living. (From "Housing Policy for Older Americans in the 1980's: An Overview" by J. S. Nachison and M. H. Leeds, 1983, *Journal of Housing for the Elderly*, *1*, p. 8. Copyright 1983 by The Haworth Press. Reprinted by permission.)

comprehensive list of the wide array of alternative residential settings and their numerous hybrid variations is provided in Table 25.1. Although we may think of these alternatives as arrayed along a continuum of increasing dependence and need for support, it is important to acknowledge the caution that "the amount of support (or, conversely, the degree of independence that is appropriate to residents) afforded in any one type lies within relatively wide and overlapping limits" (Lawton, 1981, p. 62).

Although Figure 25.1 and Table 25.1 suggest the complexity and multidimensional character of the objective choices confronting old people and their families, they cannot capture important subjective or phenomenological aspects of the relocation process. To develop such understanding, it is necessary to view the older person's residence as far more than a functional environment, a setting in which to engage in the activities of daily living. A growing body of research is beginning to unveil important dimensions of the house as home and, in so doing, is enabling us to develop a far more

sophisticated understanding of the experiential costs of a change of residence.

A HOUSE IS NOT A HOME

Studies spanning several decades have recorded that the elderly tend to express high levels of satisfaction with their housing, even when the physical quality of the residence leaves much to be desired (Golant, 1984; Hamovitch & Peterson, 1969; Montgomery, Stubbs, & Day, 1980; National Council on the Aging, 1975; O'Bryant & Wolf, 1983). These findings have been attributed to ego defensiveness, the familiarity generated by considerable length of residence (Taylor & Townsend, 1976) and to the development of emotional attachment to the residence as home. Such intuitively appealing explanations express a widely accepted societal image, reinforced by anecdotal evidence (Gelwicks, 1970; Townsend, 1963). The question of satisfaction is distinctive from, although related to, the question of meaning. It is apparent that simplistic explanations of attach-

Table 25.1. Residential Options for the Elderly[a]

Community-based Housing	Independence
Basic Types	
Single-family residences	
Apartments	
Mobile homes	
Independent planned housing	Increasing
Public housing	
Section 202 housing	
Section 8 housing	
Retirement Communities with few supportive services	
Alternative Housing	
Condominiums	
Single-room occupancy hotels	
Rooming houses	Levels
Boardinghouses	
Cooperative housing and communes	
House sharing	
Granny flats and ECHO housing	
Congregate Alternatives	
Basic Types	
Planned Housing offering meals in a common dining room and supportive services	
Retirement communities offering supportive services	of
Domiciliary care homes (limited personal care services)	
Personal care homes (more comprehensive personal care services)	
Alternative Housing	
Community housing (Philadelphia Geriatric Center)	
Group homes	
High-support	
Low-support	
Share-a-Home (Winter Park, FL)	Support
Foster homes	
Medically Oriented Environments	
Continuing-care or life-care retirement communities	
Nursing homes	
Hospitals	Dependence

[a] Compiled from "Alternative Modes of Living for the Elderly: A Critical Review" by J. K. Eckert and M. I. Murrey, 1984, in *Human Behavior and Environment: The Elderly and Physical Environment* (pp. 95–128), edited by J. Altman, M. P. Lawton, and J. K. Wohlwill, New York: Plenum; and from "Alternative Housing" by M. P. Lawton, 1981, *Journal of Gerontological Social Work*, 3, 61–80.

ment do not effectively communicate the complexity of this question. However, a growing body of work on the meaning of home is beginning to reveal some dimensions of this complexity.

A considerable volume of research outside of mainstream social gerontology has explored the meaning of home to the general population as an experiential phenomenon (Bachelard, 1969; Bollnow, 1967; Buttimer, 1980; Dovey, 1978; Eliade, 1961; Hayward, 1975; Porteous, 1976; Rakoff, 1977). Much of this research has suggested the need for a home is a fundamental human imperative, providing a locus of order and control in a world of chaos. As Ruskin wrote, the true nature of home is "the place of Peace; the shelter, not only from injury, but from all terror, doubt and division." Home imparts a sense of identity, security, and belonging. It is space differentiated from a world outside that is often viewed as hostile. Crossing the threshold to depart involves a transition from the sacred to the profane (Eliade, 1961). Indeed, an individual's life is characteristically experienced in terms of the ebb and flow of moving away and returning to the place where his or her roots are implanted (Bachelard, 1969; Bollnow, 1967; Seamon, 1981). Only recently have researchers begun to explore the implications of these generic themes as they apply to the elderly. *What, specifically, does home mean to an elderly person?*

For many elderly people home is a setting that maximizes a sense of personal competence (O'Bryant, 1982, 1983, in press). Intimate familiarity with the physical configuration of rooms, the placement of furniture, and places to hold on to when a dizzy spell occurs provides reassurance of the ability to maintain independence despite failing physiological and sensory capabilities. Indeed, the individual may develop a body awareness of the setting, a kind of automatic pilot based on an established daily routine developed over many years (Rowles, 1980; Seamon, 1979). Such awareness facilitates continuing effective functioning in a house that would otherwise impose environmental constraints beyond the competence of the old person.

Competence in a familiar environment is closely linked to the meaning of home as a place of protection, a refuge. Home may fulfill a critical need for security and a place of withdrawal from the buzzing cacophany of the world outside. As sensory capabilities decline, the environment may become threatening: a sense of "separation from the world" may result. This, in turn, may generate anxiety and provide a stimulus to withdrawal to the more supportive setting of the home. As Pastalan (1979) wrote in describing the results of an elderly sensory simulation research program:

> A feeling of being strongly insulated from the rest of the world was complemented by the feeling of vulnerability to the rest of the world. The outside world seemed to be farther away and more threatening. Elements comprising the feeling of insulation included a preoccupation with bodily sensations, greater amounts of time spent in fantasy, and reduced social contact. (p. 123)

The need for home as a protective environment and a place of withdrawal is reflected in a propensity for many people to clearly view their home as *inside*, as a place of *enclosure* (Boschetti, 1984) and to differentiate this space from the world *outside* (Bollnow, 1967; Relph, 1976; Rowles, 1980; Seamon, 1981). From this experiential perspective the house becomes a point of orientation for the individual, "the central reference point of human existence" (Relph, 1976, p. 20). It assumes meaning as the fulcrum of "dwelling" and as the origin of all "outgoing" and destination of all "incoming"— an arena in which the individual is in control and over which he or she has mastery.

Control and mastery are implicit dimensions of a third aspect of the meaning of home for many elderly home owners. Ownership may become a symbol of status. American culture, particularly in the era in which many of today's elderly were raised, has placed considerable status value on home ownership. The home into which so much has been invested may become a symbol of success and achievement of the American dream. In discussing the importance of this dimension, which emerged in a factor analysis of 276 responses to a survey instrument designed to investigate the subjective value of home to elderly homeowners, O'Bryant (1983) comments:

> It is interesting to note that little attention has been paid to this idea when considering what relocation might mean to elderly home owners. If the role status provided by being a home owner explains some of the older person's desire to remain in his/her home, then stepping down to the role of "tenant," "occupant," "resident," or "patient" might affect the person's self-concept. (pp. 39–40)

O'Bryant's research also revealed that the subjective value of home to elderly homeowner's involved an important "cost versus comfort trade-off." Many old people live in homes that no longer necessitate mortgage payments. Remaining in a longtime residence may be the least expensive housing option, especially if maintenance can be delayed. As O'Bryant (1983) notes, "Such a home may not represent the most comfortable surroundings; nevertheless it is a 'bargain' considering its costs to the homeowner" (p. 39).

The most significant factor to emerge from O'Bryant's factor analysis was one she termed "traditional family orientation." This factor subsumed a variety of themes pertaining to the role that home fulfilled in sustaining a sense of continuity with the future. Respondents in O'Bryant's study viewed their homes as part of family tradition, and many envisaged that after their death the residence would be passed on to their children. Other researchers have also commented on the sense of pride and accomplishment in being able to leave a physical legacy to one's children and suggested that this may constitute a form of "ego transcendence" (Boschetti, 1984; Sykes, 1980).

The idea of family continuity is only one facet of many old people's emotional identification with their residence. Through a variety of processes, as yet incompletely understood, residence in a place construed as home also plays a critical role in maintaining a sense of self-identity (Boschetti, 1984; Howell, 1983; Kellaher, 1985; Rowles, 1983b; Rubinstein, 1985, 1986). A subtle interweaving of self and place evolves through both length of residence and the accumulation of life experiences within the social context of the home. The residence becomes an accessory in the reconstruction of self-identity, as the individual engages in the ongoing creation and modification of home as a symbol of the self. In this regard the idea of home may transcend the physical setting and may remain as part of the individual's inner being in situations where the material fabric of the residence has disintegrated or when the individual has relocated. Indeed, home as a symbol of identity may be a composite outcome of cumulative experiences in all the residences of the individual's life: It becomes a concept transcending place (Boschetti, 1984; Kellaher, 1985; Rubinstein, 1985).

Fundamental within the conception of home as a focus of self-identity is the theme of connection. As has been discussed, home may be imbued with meaning as a symbol of family continuity and connection to the future. It may also be a repository of memories and provide a link with the past, either through meanings accumulated from the recollection of events that took place within the physical setting (the death of a spouse, a fondly remembered party, announcement of an impending marriage) or through the memories and sense of self that are evoked through personal possessions and artifacts maintained within the home. Such connections provide a sense of *autobiographical insideness* (Rowles, 1983b).

Both the residence itself and the possessions it contains may serve as a museum of life history, the physical manifestations of a path traversed (Boschetti, 1984; Csikszentmihalyi & Rochberg-Halton, 1981, Kalymun, 1983; Rowles, 1983b, Sherman & Newman, 1977). As Boschetti (1984) eloquently expresses this:

> Out past belongs to us. And personal possessions are tangible parts of that past. The silver, crystal, fine china, linens, odd pieces of furniture—mostly wood because it withstands the rigors of time—scrapbooks, photo albums, family portraits, and other random memorabilia of a person's life on earth, which get passed on, are the tangible parts of a person's life. During a life these items by their daily presence serve to remind the person who she/he is; when handed down they carry with them the giver's tangible presence into the future. (p. 39)

Boschetti develops this theme further by noting that possessions in the home are more than mere markers—they are linked to a social identity. The basis of this link is revealed in my own research in rural Appalachia (Rowles, 1983b) in a description of the rationale underlying an elderly woman's attachment to artifacts in her home:

> A primary theme within Audrey's perception of her life's contribution is the role she played in caring for her mother who became blind and disabled before her death in her nineties. This care was provided at great personal sacrifice. She recalls that such behavior was expected:
>
> > "People stayed together as families. you know, they took their father and mother and grandma and grandfather. I've known families where the grandmother, grandfather and the mother and father, they take them all in."
>
> This ethos of the obligation and nobility of family care and support remains a focal motif in Audrey's life; its preservation gives meaning to her existence. Consequently, it is not surprising that she has surrounded herself with artifacts that reinforce her perception and serve as cues to reimmersion in the places where she spent time with her mother—the photographs, the old chair and other remembrances. (p. 307)

Photographs and photograph albums containing many pictures of her mother were frequently identified as Audrey's most treasured personal possessions. The chair in question was a rocking chair in which her mother used to sit. Some of the lacquer and stain had worn away, as a result of her mother's propensity to constantly rub the curving wooden arms. Audrey had refused to have the chair refinished. Indeed, the chair was only one of many items that served as reminders of her mother's former presence, provided a temporal depth of meaning to the place she called home, and reinforced her self-image of having fulfilled her obligations as a loving and selfless caregiver.

Although most studies of the meaning of home to old people have focused on the interior of the dwelling, it is also important to view the home in context and to understand its link to the world outside. The exterior walls of the home constitute a sheltering cocoon, but they also contain openings providing points of contact with the outside. Doors mark a threshold, a point of transition from the sacred to the profane. Windows provide visual access to the world outside (Blytheway, 1982; Boschetti, 1984; Howell, 1976). Lozier and Althouse (1975) have illustrated the role of the porch and its social significance as an intermediary space between the house and community. As physical capabilities decline and more time is spent at home, the porch may become the primary focus of social transactions with the community; it can begin to assume meaning as an extension of the dwelling. Doors, windows, and porches provide points of contact with the surveillance zone, space within the visual field of home (Rowles, 1981). This space may become the arena for "watching" events outside, and in turn, "being watched" by neighbors and others who pass by on a regular basis. It may become the focus of sustaining reciprocal social networks. As more and more time is spent at home, this space may come to assume special meaning as a focus for vicarious participation in the world beyond the threshold. Finally, it can be argued that the ambience of the neighborhood context in which a residence is located—the space beyond the surveillance zone—plays a critical role in contributing to the meaning of home to many old people.

In summary, the meaning of home involves the complex interaction of a plethora of themes. These themes, constituting the essence of "dwelling," are often difficult to distinguish and tend to be taken for granted. They also represent the outcome of distinctive processes through which environments acquire meanings (see Rubinstein, 1985, 1986). As a consequence, it is frequently difficult for the elderly person to articulate the basis of his or her attachment to a familiar home and to rationalize reluctance to relocate when, from an outsider's perspective, such a move would appear to be necessary. However, clinicians have an obligation to attempt to understand the nature of home from a humanistic vantage point, as a locus of "dwelling," and to use such understanding as a baseline when considering the critical issue of relocation to which we now turn our attention.

RELOCATION

Although relocation is often conceived of as a discrete event—and the physical move from one residence to another may take place in a single day—from an experiential perspective the housing adjustment of an elderly person is a process involving the reconciliation of conflicting needs and emotions over a considerable period of time. Giving up a residence that may have assumed any or all of the meanings described in the preceding section is not a decision made lightly. Indeed, old homes are never completely abandoned: Their aura is psychologically carried over into the ambience of the new residence. Nor is the decision to move made independently of the social context. Rather, the decision-making process embraces a variety of actors, each of whom may have input into what is often an agonizing and drawn-out process. In most cases, it is the elderly individual who is the primary determinant of the choices. With advancing age, as vulnerability increases and personal competence declines, other actors, including family, physicians, and public officials, may assume an increasing role in determining the individual's residential trajectory. While there is a large literature on the causes and consequences of elderly relocation, little attention has been paid to understanding experiential aspects of the decision-making process. Nor has an attempt been made to place the experience of moving in longitudinal context, to view it as a series of moves over time in which each relocation is linked to moves that occurred previously and to those that are anticipated to follow. In this discussion, the experience of elderly relocation is explored from such a perspective, as a dynamic process often extending over many years.

A starting point in considering the relocation process is an assumption of residential inertia. More than 30 years ago Rossi (1955) concep-

tualized a normative model of residential mobility as "a mechanism by which a family's housing is brought into adjustment to its housing needs" (p. 122). This model does not seem to apply to many elderly people. In part, because of the meaning of house as a home and a symbol of independence, the elderly typically resist relocation; at first sight, they often do not exhibit what would appear to be rational responses to changing housing needs. They may acknowledge their housing to be inferior, to be lacking in facilities, and unsuitable in terms of their physiological, economic, and social circumstances. However, even if they nominally profess a wish to move, such aspirations are frequently not translated into behavior. There is often little correspondence between dissatisfaction with housing (stemming from its functional inappropriateness), moving preference, and actual relocation (Lawton et al., 1973; Newman & Duncan, 1979; Wiseman, 1980). In a major recent study of 400 relatively healthy elderly community residents in Evanston, IL, Golant found that the large majority "expected and preferred" to remain in their present dwelling: 80% preferred not to move and 73% reported "they definitely or probably will not move within the next two years." Of the persons who reported that they "definitely expect to move" in the next 2 years, 18% expressed a preference to remain in their present homes. Of those reporting that they "probably will move," 44% expressed a preference for not relocating (Golant, 1984, pp. 181–182).

Golant's findings indicate that, in spite of their reluctance, many old people gradually come to realize that their physical frailty, economic circumstances, and family situation necessitate housing adjustment. This realization may initiate an evaluation of residential alternatives. As vulnerability increases, the urgency of the search may intensify, particularly if other actors, including family members and medical practitioners, noting the declining ability of the individual to function effectively, become involved in the decision-making process. What are the options, and how does the decision-making process unfold?

It is useful to consider three overlapping classes of elderly people arrayed along a continuum of environmental competence. The *active old*, primarily the young-old (persons 65–74 years of age), represent a population in the immediately post-retirement phase of life. These individuals tend to be healthy, often have a living spouse, and are relatively mobile. They require minimal supportive assistance in maintaining an active life-style. Housing changes are often voluntary and frequently reflect reduced household size (as a result of the departure of children) and an inclination toward a leisure-oriented life-style. Changes necessitated by declining health, social losses, and physiological decrements are less characteristic of this group. There is also less propensity toward housing options providing a wide array of medical or supportive service facilities (although the decision-making process may acknowledge this as a future need). Instead, as Rosow (1967) forcefully argued, the need of the vast majority of the active elderly is not so much for housing with a wide array of special design features as for decent ordinary housing in the community at a price they can afford.

Although the majority of the active elderly do not relocate (Newman, Zais, & Struyk, 1984), those who elect to do so are provided with a variety of options. Some retire to the countryside, a phenomenon that emerged during the 1970s as part of a national urban to rural population turn-around (Fuguitt & Tordella, 1980; Heaton, 1983; Heaton, Clifford, & Fuguitt, 1980; Kim & Hartwigsen, 1983). Such relocation often brings relatively affluent urban retirees into conflict with established rural elderly populations as a result of differing values, expectations, and willingness to pay for supportive services (Aday & Miles, 1982; Heaton, 1983).

A second option is return migration. A growing number of retirees are returning to regions where they were born or lived during their early years (Longino, 1979; Serow, 1978). This option tends to be selected by less affluent long-distance migrants (Cribier, 1982).

A third option is to relocate to "amenity" retirement areas, often located in the Sunbelt states. Such moves tend to be made in the period immediately adjacent to retirement (Warnes, 1983). Young-old retirement migration to Florida or Arizona has become widespread. Often such relocations are preceded by several years of seasonal visits as a "snowbird" (Krout, 1983; Sullivan & Stevens, 1982). Recent years have seen a trend toward a diversification of amenity retirement destinations, with western North Carolina, the Ozarks region of Arkansas, rural Vermont, the lakeshore regions of Michigan, and the Olympic peninsula of Washington state emerging as popular choices (Bohland & Treps, 1982; Flynn, Longino, Wiseman, & Biggar, 1985).

Increasing numbers of active young-old couples are relocating to age-exclusive retirement communities (Gober, 1985; Hunt, Feldt, Marans, Pastalan, & Vakalo, 1983; Longino, 1982; Marans, Hunt, & Vakalo, 1984). Such moves are frequently influenced by a strong wish to follow a leisure-oriented life-style among age peers who share a similar desire to segregate themselves from younger populations and youth-oriented societal values. Indeed, as Golant (1985) notes, almost 2 million elderly people (approximately 6% of the elderly population) now reside in age-segregated environments.

Not all such environments are retirement communities. Many people, often widows and widowers who are less affluent but still active, choose relocation to age-segregated planned housing projects within their local community over long-distance relocation. The 1960s and early 1970s witnessed a construction boom in federally funded housing under a variety of HUD-assisted programs, including Public Housing, Section 202, Section 236, Section 231 and Section 8 housing (for a useful discussion and review of these programs, see Lawton, 1980; Lawton & Hoover, 1981). In England similar options were provided, under the designation "Category I Sheltered Housing," designed to serve "old people of the more active kind" (Blytheway, 1982, p. 225).

The increasing popularity of retirement communities and planned housing projects (many with long waiting lists) has fueled the long-standing debate in gerontology between advocates and critics of segregated environments, a debate spanning more than three decades (Golant, 1985; Mumford, 1953; Sherman, 1971). Advocates point to the various positive features of segregated environments: (a) a sense of privacy; (b) a slower pace of life; (c) a setting that facilitates the replacement of deceased friends with individuals of similar age; (d) a peer group culture and value system; (e) a supportive milieu to ease role transition; and (f) a sufficient population threshold to justify the provision of a wide array of supportive services. Critics stress the negative features, including the social and emotional costs of isolation from society's mainstream and the depressing consequences of residence in an environment where the death of neighbors is a frequent occurrence.

Although the underlying rationale of the housing-choice process for the active old tends toward a leisure-oriented life-style, this population group is not oblivious to its future needs. Accessibility to kin, supportive services, and health care facilities is often a factor in the evaluation of alternative options, including retirement community residence (Gober & Zonn, 1983; Law & Warnes, 1982; Meyer & Speare, 1985).

Research devoted to the housing adjustments of the active old suggests that relocations are viewed positively and result in generally high levels of housing satisfaction and well-being (Carp, 1966, 1975; Kahana & Kahana, 1983; Longino, 1982). Relocation stresses are limited in most cases, as the decision is characteristically made by the individual or couple with minimal input from children, physicians, or other actors. As Longino (1982) notes, "Most [old people] do not involve their children in the decision at all" (p. 253).

There is very little literature on relocation of the active elderly that considers the experiential costs of giving up a home. In moves to retirement communities, individuals are often able to transfer much of their furniture and most of their prized possessions to the new residence. However, in moves from a community residence to an apartment in a housing project, individuals are often forced to give up some items. A study by Carp (1966) indicated little reluctance to give up furniture upon relocation to a better quality residence. Improved housing in this case appeared to provide adequate compensation for the loss of the space needed to accommodate all the furniture and possessions from the abandoned home. Research on "breaking up housekeeping" has suggested the existence of significant class differences in attachment to possessions, with middle-class individuals attaching greater significance to archival items (photographs and memorabilia), which serve to preserve a sense of identity within a historical family context, and individuals of lower socioeconomic standing attaching greater significance to functional items, including furniture and appliances (Redfoot, 1985; Redfoot & Back, in press). A sense of the aura and value of the abandoned home may also be psychologically preserved by giving away artifacts that cannot be transferred to the new residence to children, thus sustaining the traditional family orientation sense of continuity identified by O'Bryant. However, there is a need for systematic studies on the degree to which the active elderly, who relocate voluntarily, evaluate and incorporate within their decision making process the necessity of giving up longtime homes, and compensate for any sense of loss or separation.

As individuals grow older and the range of losses described earlier begin to have a greater impact on their life-style and ability to function independently, the community-dwelling elderly gradually assume the characteristics of a second group, the *vulnerable old*. The vulnerable old are persons requiring a supportive physical environment or some degree of practical or social assistance in order to maintain an independent life-style. The term *vulnerable* is used because, for this population, a relatively small change in health status or life circumstances can result in major difficulty in maintaining independence.

The death of a spouse may result in increasing reliance upon children and outside agencies to sustain the individual at home. Indeed, during this phase, the modified extended family may become a critical feature of the elderly person's life (Day, 1985). A relationship develops that is best described as *intimacy at a distance* (Rosenmayr & Kockeis, 1963). Independence remains a primary focus of old people's lives, but increasingly they acknowledge increased reliance on their children and or on neighbors, who may become surrogate family (Rowles, 1983a). A pattern may emerge where geographically proximate children visit or telephone on a daily basis and provide a wide range of practical services to the old person. A grandson may mow the lawn. A son may service the furnace. A daughter may undertake shopping, set the old person's hair, and provide constant social support. Neighbors may keep an eye on the person and act as intermediaries between the person and his or her children. As vulnerability and dependence increase and stresses on the family and neighborhood support system become more severe, options may be contemplated that serve to maintain and reinforce intimacy at a distance. These range from supplementing family support with social services, such as home care, chore services, or home delivered meals, to instituting a variety of housing adjustments.

Some elderly relocate within the community closer to the home of the child, often a daughter, who has emerged as the primary caregiver. Other families make use of the Granny Flat or ECHO (Elder Cottage Housing Opportunity) option, a concept originating in Australia and in Amish communities in the United States (Hare, 1982; Hare & Hollis, 1983; Nusberg, 1978). This involves either the subdivision of a son's or daughter's home to provide an apartment for the older person or the construction of an adjacent separate residence. An essential feature of ECHO housing is that it can be moved to a new location when no longer needed, leaving the owners of the main house with no resale worries. The vulnerable old are also prime candidates for both governmentally and privately funded housing alternatives that provide an array of supportive services. In England such housing, designated "Category II Sheltered Housing", is designed "to meet the needs of less active elderly people" (Blytheway, 1982, p. 225). Some communal facilities are required in such housing, and individual units are accessible to one another by way of enclosed and heated circulation areas. In the United States, a plethora of options, including Share-A-Home, Community Housing, Domiciliary Care, and Personal Care Facilities, provide a variety of small-scale living environments with a wide range of supportive services to the vulnerable old (Brody, 1979; Lawton, 1980, 1981; Sherwood, Greer, & Morris, 1979; Streib, 1978).

Although most research suggests that relocation to such accommodations results in high levels of residential satisfaction, relocation of the vulnerable old is frequently less voluntary than that of the active elderly, in that it expresses more conscious acknowledgment of declining physical capabilities and increased dependence on external rather than personal resources. In general, such housing adjustments of the vulnerable old are associated with relocation to a smaller living space and with a less independent life-style. They frequently entail giving up furniture and some treasured personal possessions. Relocation becomes increasingly associated with acknowledgment of one's own mortality. The move may involve some anguish as future considerations of increasing frailty become openly incorporated into the decision-making process. Indeed, reasons provided for choosing such housing frequently include easier access to medical facilities. Hence, many of the well-known and successful supportive community-based housing programs, including the Highland Heights Apartments, in Fall River, Massachusetts, studied by Sherwood and her associates, and the Philadelphia Geriatric Center's Community Housing, are located adjacent to hospitals or medical facilities (Brody, 1979; Sherwood et al., 1979).

As elderly people become more vulnerable, the role of the family and other actors in the relocation decision process becomes more significant. Indeed, for many old people the decision to move is the outcome of a lengthy process of negotiation with their conscience, with family members, and with health care professionals. The choice becomes increasingly stressful not only for the individual but also for members of the family, as they grapple with the vast array of possibilities or, in some cases, with the absence of noninstitutional alternatives, as well as with the dilemma of assessing the point at which family resources and available community services are no longer adequate. The decision-making process at this stage is especially problematic for those children who, as a consequence of today's more mobile society, have relocated hundreds of miles from their vulnerable parent's home (Rowles, 1983a; Warnes, Howes & Took, 1985). There is also some potential for intra-family conflict between children who live far away and those who live nearby over sharing caregiving and decision-making responsibilities.

Sometimes, the decision process is accelerated by a series of incidents. The furnace may break down and require expensive replacement. The old person may experience fainting spells or trip over a rug. Family members may discover their elderly relative is not eating properly, or is no longer able to cook for himself or herself or manage appliances. There may be a growing reluctance to leave the older relative by himself or herself for extended periods of time. At other times, the decision to relocate is precipitated by a crisis. The old person may suffer a heart attack or stroke, requiring temporary hospitalization, which in turn brings into sharp focus the question of appropriate residence after discharge; or the spouse of a primary caregiver may be offered an attractive career opportunity in another state. In such circumstances, the needs of the family and of the older person come into direct conflict. Indeed, the vulnerable old, on the cusp between dependence and independence, provide the basis of much family stress.

Research on housing adjustments of the vulnerable old indicates, with some ambivalence, that high levels of life satisfaction can be achieved in the new residence (Brody, 1979; Lawton, 1981; Lawton, Brody, & Turner-Massey, 1978; Sherwood et al., 1979). Although there is a need for far more empirical research on this topic, it would seem logical to suppose that, consistent with research on institutional relocation (Pastalan, 1983a), adjustment may be influenced by the pre-relocation status of the elderly person, the degree to which relocation decisions are voluntary rather than forced, and the degree to which the old person participates in the process itself. As the individual becomes progressively more vulnerable and relocation becomes more strongly determined by circumstances and people beyond the individual's control, the emotional stress of relocation and separation from home and possessions tends to intensify.

A third group of old people for whom relocation may be necessary can be referred to as the *frail old*. The frail old constitute a population for which reduced physical competence, declining health, and the need for constant care has reached the point where independent residence is no longer possible. Environments providing partial support are no longer viable options. Indeed, the individual has reached a point where almost constant medical or nursing care is necessary. A move to "the last new home," often a medically oriented long-term-care facility or hospital, represents a final relocation (Rowles, 1979; Tobin & Lieberman, 1976).

The decision-making process in such cases frequently involves minimal input from the old person. A heart attack, stroke, or other medical emergency may lead to hospitalization. For many, the hospital becomes the final residence. Those who recover, however, are often relocated to a nursing home or other long-term-care facility, where they end their days. Within this common scenario, the family, in a process frequently involving great anguish and feelings of guilt and failure, makes the decision to institutionalize. Often this is not a decision made independently (McAuley & Prohaska, 1981; Prohaska & McAuley, 1983). Families may defer to the advice of professionals, physicians, social workers, and hospital discharge planners, who often are in a position not only to recognize when a family and community support system is no longer able to cope but also to provide reinforcement to the family's decision and to arrange the details of institutional placement.

In the majority of cases, this last relocation is made with great reluctance by old people because it represents clear acknowledgment of mortality and a final break with home and the possessions of a lifetime. On the other hand, many frail old people acknowledge the burden that their care imposes upon family members and neighbors and are anxious to mimimize the destructive impact of their incapacity upon loved ones. Consequently, some old people, in spite of their great reluctance, choose institutionalization voluntarily. Indeed, contrary to the increasingly discredited popular

myth that old people are placed in institutions by uncaring family members, they are often kept at home or maintained in independent residences by family long after this has ceased to be a viable option in terms of either the family's or the old person's well-being. In my own research in rural Appalachia, I have discovered old people who are kept out of institutions against their wishes! One 94-year-old, Asel, when I visited him shortly after he had inadvertently spilled a pan of boiling water over his foot, confided that he could not understand why his family insisted on maintaining him in his home (with either his son-in-law or daughter sleeping over each night) when he felt he would be far better off receiving institutional care.

Although some old people, like Asel, accept the necessity for institutionalization, such a relocation is viewed as a negative adjustment and is associated with some trauma. In contrast to relocations of the active and vulnerable elderly, the move is far more likely to be viewed pessimistically and with foreboding. Moreover, as the literature on the consequences of institutional relocation has revealed, such foreboding is often justified, particularly if the move is involuntary (for excellent reviews and discussion of this large and controversial literature, see, Borup, 1983; Coffman, 1981; Horowitz & Schulz, 1983; Pastalan, 1983a; and Tobin & Lieberman, 1976). There is often a sense of resignation mixed with trepidation as the individual comes to accept the necessity of giving up home, at least as a physical entity and in the possessive sense of a place of one's own. This raises the ultimate question: Can any sense of "home" or "dwelling" be created and maintained following such a move?

The distinction among active, vulnerable, and frail elderly is somewhat arbitrary. Clearly, the three groups represent points on a continuum. Transition from one group to another may be associated with a wide array of both personal and contextual circumstances. Thus, some individuals who might be classified as frail in terms of physiological capabilities, health status, and personal capacity for independent living may remain in community environments long after they might have been expected to be institutionalized because of a particularly resilient self-sacrificing family support system. This is in contrast to other individuals who, although they are relatively mobile, in good health, and at the fulcrum of an extensive network of family members and friends, may choose to relocate to a supportive residential environment long before such a move is warranted. Such individuals may be particularly forward-looking and may wish to anticipate what they perceive to be future needs. Between the two extremes are the numerous old people and their families wrestling uneasily with the dilemma. The result is a pattern of residential adjustments and accommodation to changing circumstances about which it is difficult to make generalizations beyond an assertion that relocations along the continuum tend to involve a transition from a predominently positively construed to a predominantly negatively construed experience. Indeed, this domain appears to be an excellent example of the widely accepted gerontological axiom of increasing experiential divergence among old people with advancing years.

In recent decades, the complexity and ambiguity of the decision-making process this diversity engenders has been somewhat ameliorated by the emergence of a *continium of care* philosophy, which has provided a number of new residential options. One approach is characterized by the development of an integrated network of services, which allow elderly people of differing levels of competence and capacities for independent living to remain in community settings, by providing progressively greater input of service support as they become more vulnerable. Another option, for those choosing relocation, is the creation of destination environments, which provide services ranging from the minimal support needed by the active to the partial support needed by the vulnerable to the constant medical support required by the frail. Thus, many retirement communities are now characterized by varied resources, ranging from the numerous golf courses and recreational facilities provided by Arizona's Sun City for its active elderly to the nursing home and hospital facilities that are available for its most frail residents. One of the most attractive features of such a residential continuum is that it provides the potential for movement in both directions along the continuum; relocation is not inevitably a process of inexorable progress toward more restrictive environments (Grant, 1970).

Among the more innovative options to have emerged from this trend have been Continuing Care or Life Care Centers. Upon an investment of a substantial endowment fee and with a regular monthly payment, individuals can now contract for care throughout the remainder of their lives in a setting providing facilities ranging from independent cottages or apartments to accommodations with an array of supportive services, including housekeeping and meals, to a nursing home providing comprehensive medical care (Longino, 1982; Marans et al., 1984; Winklevoss & Powell, 1984). While such an option provides guarantees and reassurance to the elderly individual that he or she will be cared for regardless of changing circumstances and longevity, it constitutes something of a gamble for both the individual and the family. A major initial investment will be lost should the person die within a short period of time. There is generally little choice as to who will provide services and care (the individual is obliged to use the Continuing Care Corporation's own facilities), and after a relatively short time it is difficult to withdraw from such an arrangement without extremely severe penalties. Finally, entering a life care facility implies giving up resources that might otherwise have been passed on to the children. On the other hand, such an arrangement can be advantageous should the individual live for many years, perhaps decades. In summary then, the emergence of the continuing care approach, with its new residential alternatives, has further complicated the already difficult decision-making process confronting old people and their families.

EASING TRANSITIONS

While the residential choices faced by the elderly and their families are complex, there are a variety of ways in which potentially negative consequences of relocation can be minimized. These may be summarized under the rubric of three overlapping objectives: creation of an attractive destination environment that facilitates a comfortable life-style and engenders a sense of home; provision of support to the old person and the family during the relocation decision-making process, which may span lengthy time periods and vary from months or even years before each move to many years after each change of residence; and promotion of an ongoing sense of continuity with past environments.

What constitutes an appropriate destination environment clearly depends on the level of competence of the old person and his or her ability to actively transform a new setting into a place that can be called home (see chapter 3, this volume). The ability to undertake necessary activities of daily living in a safe and supportive setting is clearly a prerequisite. Consequently, environmental design considerations become of extreme importance, particularly as the individual becomes increasingly frail. There is a large and ever growing literature on the design of environments for the elderly that attempts to take into account the special needs of this population at different levels of vulnerability and frailty. This literature includes studies on innovative designs in community-based housing (Lawton, 1980; Regnier & Bonar, 1981), analyses and evaluations of optimal design for congregate housing options (Gelwicks & Newcomer, 1974; Howell, 1980; Lawton, 1980; Regnier & Byerts, 1983), and guidelines for the construction of long-term-care facilities that maximize life-style potential for the frail elderly (Koncelik, 1976; Rowles, 1979). In recent years attention has also been paid to the environment beyond the residence and to siting facilities for the elderly in supportive locations (Kelen & Griffiths, 1983; Newcomer, 1976; Regnier, 1985a; Rowles, 1981). There has been increasing recognition of the need to locate elderly facilities outside high-crime areas, in settings where the surrounding environment is traversible by the frail (i.e., has a minimum of cracked sidewalks or steep inclines) and where medical facilities, stores and recreational opportunities are within easy access.

The creation of an environment in which an older person can function effectively does not make a home, a process involving more than a sensitive architect. Making a home may be facilitated by the transference of artifacts and memorabilia that are important to the preservation of an individual's sense of identity and links to both a past (archival relics of an ancestry and life history) and a future (items to be passed on to future generations to preserve a sense of continuity). Recognition of the importance of Jean-Paul Sartre's declaration that the "totality of my possessions reflects the totality of my being. I am what I have" (Sartre, 1956, p. 754; cited in Redfoot, 1985) has been incorporated into management policy statements in many residential environments, as part of an acknowledgment of the need to facilitate the personalization of space.

Providing support during the relocation process constitutes a second strategy for constructive intervention in the process of elderly residential change. There is some evidence that much of the trauma of relocation takes place before the actual physical displacement and is a function of the anticipation of change (Tobin & Lieberman,

1976). This is particularly the case with the vulnerable and the frail. Significant support can be provided by supplying the old person with as much information as possible regarding available alternatives and the consequences, both positive and negative, of change. Active involvement of potential future residents in the design of special housing options is an important innovation in this regard (Regnier, 1985b). This approach is paralleled on the more interpersonal level of the family by the need to involve the old person as much as is feasible in the ongoing process of decision making with respect to future accommodation (Pastalan, 1983a).

Relocation stress can also be ameliorated by advanced preparation, including careful selection of roommates in situations where shared quarters are necessary (Gutman & Herbert, 1976), and by several visits to the new residence prior to the actual move (Pastalan, 1976, 1983a). Such visits are comparable to the observed propensity of many active elderly to make a series of preliminary vacation visits to potential retirement destinations before committing themselves to a permanent relocation decision (Gober & Zonn, 1983). Other options in this domain include personal counseling programs and involvement in group discussions on the implications and consequences of alternative moves (Pastalan, 1983a).

Perhaps the most important contribution to limiting the stress of severance from home can be made by families and professionals acknowledging the critical need during the relocation decision process to maintain a sense of environmental and temporal continuity in the elderly person's life-world. In most cases, there is no need for physical relocation to be attended by complete psychological and emotional separation from home and neighborhood. For those elderly people who relocate to congregate or institutional environments, a sense of ongoing involvement with the outside world can be sustained by enhancing residential permeability through environmental design, as in providing windows that facilitate surveillance of outside space, return visits to former homes and neighborhoods, frequent family visits to the elderly relative, exchange of letters and telephone calls, and encouragement of reminiscence and vicarious return to former homes (Rowles, 1979). Such reinforcement facilitates maintaining the aura of former homes in the new setting. The maintenance of the temporal continuity of home as a repository for meaning and personal identity is also enhanced by the presence of artifacts and possessions transferred from previous residences, as these provide tangible manifestations of the individual's past and cues to the resurrection of that past via reminiscence.

CONCLUSION

The account of Nell's final days with which this chapter opened reveals the way in which many old people and their families implicitly recognize a relationship between well-being and dwelling within a place with the attributes of home. The conflict between attachment to a familiar residence and increasing need for a more supportive environment is clearly revealed. So, too, is the dilemma faced by children and other relatives. Although Corinne was reluctant to allow Nell to return to the house on the hill following recuperation from her first hospitalization, she acknowledged the importance to her mother of dwelling in the family residence, and the meaning of this home to her as a symbol of continuing independence and self-identity. Paul also acknowledged that his basement apartment in a distant state was a distinctly inferior substitute for her home as far as his mother was concerned. Yet although both Corinne and Paul understood the importance of her need to be at home, they were concerned about their mother's ability to care for herself in a setting that was increasingly inhospitable to her changing physical capabilities. Like many—perhaps the majority of—children with aging parents, they considered a variety of alternative residential arrangements and suggested these to their mother during her last years. In Nell's case, only the alternative of living with her daughter was taken up, and even then only as a temporary medical exigency. However, many old people and their families are obliged to adopt one of the options described in the previous pages. In seeking to place the process whereby such residential adjustments occur in a more general context, it is possible to draw several conclusions with implications for clinical practice.

First, a degree of caution must be exercised in the unequivocal acceptance of the link between attachment to home and well-being that has been the focal motif of this chapter. Some old people do not reveal strong emotional attachment to their residence. In my own Appalachian research I encountered several individuals, mainly men, who

professed that their homes, characteristically sparsely decorated and soulless abodes, did not hold any special meaning for them (Rowles, 1980, 1983b). Although it is tempting to conclude that these individuals' apparent alienation from place was a manifestation of deprivation and, somewhat paradoxically, reflects the importance of home, it is important to guard against undue romanticism concerning a concept that has only recently begun to be subjected to rigorous rather than anecdotal research.

Second, the ongoing process of residential adjustment involves the need for constant reconciliation of the sometimes conflicting needs of the elderly and their families. Almost inevitably, this process involves some measure of stress for all concerned.

Third, although in theory there are a plethora of residential options, in reality many of the more innovative alternatives are pilot ventures, available only in selected parts of the country and accessible to relatively few individuals. Because of these "enabling" factors (Lawton, 1981, p. 66) it is important for those concerned with providing support to old people and their families to familiarize themselves with alternatives available within their own community.

Fourth, it is important to accept that the residential needs of old people are constantly changing as capabilities and resources change. The development of appropriate support to sustain residence in the community or the selection of residential alternatives is an ongoing process. It involves a dynamic trajectory of negotiated decisions, frequently involving multiple actors and extending over many years, with each choice contingent upon what has gone before and what is anticipated to follow. A completely definitive solution, short of institutionalization, is rarely achieved.

Fifth, contrary to the impression that might have been given in this chapter, most old people do not progress in a linear fashion along a continuum of living environments. Instead, most follow a trajectory in which only a few of the many options are involved. Many, indeed the majority, move from a community residence (where they may have received progressively greater levels of support from family members and friends) directly to a hospital or long-term-care facility, which constitutes their final home. While diversity characterizes individual residential trajectories, all share in an underlying motif of either the need for environmental modification or the necessity of relocation.

It is in the context of this shared experience that a sixth, and perhaps the most important, conclusion of this chapter assumes its significance. While attachment to home is not necessarily a universal phenomenon, architects, health care professionals, families, and other caregivers can considerably enhance the quality of life or ease relocation trauma, at least for many individuals, by developing a sensitivity to the meaning of home and acknowledging this as a focal concern as they plan for or negotiate the residential future of elderly clients or relatives. In this context, a diligent effort to understand the underlying dimensions of attachment to place and the meaning of home to an elderly person becomes far more than a mere intellectual exercise.

Acknowledgements—Thanks are due to Shirley L. O'Bryant and Robert L. Rubinstein for helpful comments on early drafts of segments of this chapter.

REFERENCES

Aday, R. H., & Miles, L. A. (1982). Long term impacts of rural migration of the elderly: Implications for research. *Gerontologist, 22,* 331–336.

American Association of Retired Persons (1984). *Housing options for older Americans.* Washington, DC: Author.

Atchley, R. C., & Miller, S. J. (1979). Housing and households of the rural aged. In T. O. Byerts, S. C. Howell, L. A. Pastalan (Eds.) *Environmental context of aging: Lifestyles, environmental quality and living arrangements* (pp. 62–79). New York: Garland STPM Press.

Bachelard, G. (1969). *The poetics of space.* Boston: Beacon.

Blytheway, W. R. (1982). Living under an umbrella: Problems of identity in sheltered housing. In A. M. Warnes (Ed.), *Geographical perspectives on the elderly,* (pp. 223–238). New York: Wiley.

Bohland, J. R., & Treps, L. (1982). County patterns of elderly migration in the United States. In A. M. Warnes (Ed.), *Geographical perspectives on the elderly* (pp. 139–158). New York: Wiley.

Bollnow, O. (1967). Lived space. In N. Lawrence & D. O. O'Connor (Eds.), *Readings in existential phenomenology* (pp. 178–186). Englewood Cliffs, NJ: Prentice-Hall.

Borup, J. H. (1983). Relocation mortality research: Assessment, reply, and the need to refocus on the issues. *Gerontologist, 23,* 235–342.

Boschetti, M. A. (1984). *The older person's emotional attachment to the physical environment of the residential setting.* Unpublished doctoral dissertation, University of Michigan, Ann Arbor.

Brody, E. M. (1979). Service supported independent living in an urban setting: The Philadelphia Geriatric Center's Community Housing for the elderly. In T. O. Byerts, S. C. Howell, & L. A. Pastalan (Eds.), *Environmental context of aging: Lifestyles, environmental quality and living arrangements* (pp. 191–216). New York: Garland STPM Press.

Buttimer, A. (1980). Home, reach and the sense of place. In A. Buttimer & D. Seamon (Eds.), *The human experience of space and place* (pp. 166–187). London: Croom Helm.

Carlin, V., & Fox R. (1981). An alternative for elderly housing: Home conversion. In M. P. Lawton and S. L. Hoover (Eds.), *Community housing choices for older Americans* (pp. 259–266). New York: Springer.

Carp, F. M. (1966). *A future for the aged.* Austin: University of Texas Press.

Carp, F. M. (1975). Impact of improved housing on morale and life satisfaction. *Gerontologist, 15,* 511–515.

Coffman, T. L. (1981). Relocation and survival of institutionalized aged: A reexamination of the evidence. *Gerontologist, 21,* 483–500.

Cribier, F. (1982). Aspects of retired migration from Paris: An essay in social and cultural geography. In A. M. Warnes (Ed.), *Geographical perspectives on the elderly* (pp. 111–137). New York: Wiley.

Csikszentimihalyi, M., & Rochberg-Halton, E. (1981). *The meaning of things: Domestic symbols and the self.* Cambridge, UK: Cambridge University Press.

Day, A. T. (1985). *Who cares? Demographic trends challenge family care for the elderly* (Occasional Paper No. 9). Washington, DC: Population Reference Bureau.

Dovey, K. (1978). Home: An ordering principle in space. *Landscape, 22,* 27–30.

Eckert, J. K., & Murrey, M. I. (1984). Alternative modes of living for the elderly: A critical review. In I. Altman, M. P. Lawton, & J. F. Wohlwill (Eds.), *Human behavior and environment: The elderly and the physical environment* (pp. 95–128). New York: Plenum.

Eliade, M. (1961). *The sacred and the profane.* New York: Harper & Row.

Flynn, C. B., Longino, C. F., Wiseman, R. F., & Biggar, J. C. (1985). The redistribution of America's older population: Major national migration patterns for three census decades, 1960–1980. *Gerontologist, 25,* 292–296.

Fuguitt, G. V., & Tordella, S. J. (1980). Elderly net migration: The new trend of nonmetropolitan population change. *Research on Aging, 2,* 191–204.

Gelwicks, L. E. (1970). Home range and the use of space by an aging population. In L. A. Pastalan & D. H. Carson (Eds.), *Spatial behavior of older people.* Ann Arbor, MI: University of Michigan–Wayne State University, Institute of Gerontology.

Gelwicks, L. E., & Newcomer, R. J. (1974). *Planning housing environments for the elderly.* Washington, DC: National Council on the Aging.

Gober, P. (1985). The retirement community as a geographical phenomenon: The case of Sun City, Arizona. *Journal of Geography, 84,* 189–198.

Gober, P., & Zonn, L. E. (1983). Kin and elderly amenity migration. *Gerontologist, 23,* 288–294.

Golant, S. M. (1984). *A place to grow old: The meaning of environment in old age.* New York: Columbia University Press.

Golant, S. M. (1985). In defense of age segregated housing. *Aging, 348,* 22–26.

Gottesman, L. E., & Saperstein, A. (1981). The organization of an in-home services network. In M. P. Lawton & S. L. Hoover (Eds.), *Community housing choices for older Americans* (pp. 170–179). New York: Springer.

Grant, D. P. (1970). An architect discovers the aged. *Gerontologist, 10,* 275–281.

Gutman, G. M., & Herbert, C. P. (1976). Mortality rates among relocated extended care patients. *Journal of Gerontology, 31,* 352–357.

Gutowski, M. (1981). Housing related needs of the suburban elderly. In M. P. Lawton & S. L. Hoover (Eds.), *Community housing choices for older Americans* (pp. 109–122). New York: Springer.

Hamovitch, M. B., & Peterson, J. E. (1969). Housing needs and satisfactions of the elderly. *Gerontologist, 9,* 30–32.

Hare, P. H. (1982). Why Granny Flats are a good idea. *Planning, 48,* 15–16.

Hare, P. H., & Hollis, L. E. (1983). *ECHO housing: A review of zoning issues and other considerations.* Washington, DC: American Association of Retired Persons.

Hayward, D. G. (1975). Home as an environmental and psychological concept. *Landscape, 20,* 2–9.

Heaton, T. B. (1983). Recent trends in the geographical distribution of the elderly population. In M. Riley, B. Hess & K. Bond (Eds.), *Aging in society: Selected reviews of recent research* (pp. 95–137). Hillsdale, NJ: Erlbaum.

Heaton, T. B., Clifford, W. B., & Fuguitt, G. V. (1980). Changing patterns of retirement migration. *Research on Aging, 2,* 93–104.

Horowitz, M. J., & Schulz, R. (1983). The relocation controversy: Criticism and commentary on five recent studies. *Gerontologist, 23,* 229–234.

Howell, S. C. (1976). *Designing for the elderly: Windows design evaluation project.* Cambridge MA: Department of Architecture, Massachusetts Institute of Technology.

Howell, S. C. (1980). *Designing for aging.* Cambridge, MA: MIT Press.

Howell, S. C. (1983). The meaning of place in old age. In G. D. Rowles & R. J. Ohta (Eds.), *Aging and milieu: Environmental perspectives on growing old* (pp. 97–107). New York: Academic.

Hunt, M. E., Feldt, A. G., Marans, R. W., Pastalan, L. A., & Vakalo, K. L. (1983). *Retirement communities: An American original.* New York: Haworth.

Jacobs, B. (1982). *An overview of the national potential for home equity conversion into income for the elderly.* Rochester, NY: University of Rochester Press.

Kahana, E. (1975). A congruence model of person-environment interaction. In P. G. Windley, T. O. Byerts, & F. G. Ernst (Eds.), *Theory development in environment and aging.* Washington, DC: Gerontological Society.

Kahana, E., & Kahana B. (1983). Environmental continuity, futurity and adaptation of the aged. In G. D. Rowles & R. J. Ohta (Eds.), *Aging and milieu: Environmental perspectives on growing old* (pp. 205–228). New York: Academic.

Kalymun, M. (1983). Factors influencing elderly women's decisions concerning living room items during relocation. *EDRA: Environmental Design Research Association, 14,* 75–83.

Kelen, J., & Griffiths, K. A. (1983). Housing for the

aged: New roles for social work. *International Journal of Aging and Human Development, 16,* 125–133.

Kellaher, L. A. (1985, July). *The meaning of home for older people.* Paper presented at the XIIIth International Congress of Gerontology, New York.

Kim, J., & Hartwigsen, G. (1983). The current population shift among elderly migrants. *Research on Aging, 5,* 269–282.

Koncelik, J. A. (1976). *Designing the open nursing home.* Stroudsburg, PA: Dowden, Hutchinson and Ross.

Krout, J. A. (1983). Seasonal migration of the elderly. *Gerontologist, 23,* 295–299.

Law, C. M., & Warnes, A. M. (1982). The destination decision in retirement migration. In A. M. Warnes (Ed.), *Geographical perspectives on the elderly* (pp. 53–81). New York: Wiley.

Lawton, M. P. (1980). *Environment and aging.* Monterey: Brooks/Cole.

Lawton, M. P. (1981). Alternative housing. *Journal of Gerontological Social Work, 3,* 61–80.

Lawton, M. P., Brody, E. M., & Turner-Massey, P. (1978). The relationships of Environmental factors to changes in wellbeing. *Gerontologist, 18,* 133–137.

Lawton, M. P., & Hoover, S. L. (Eds.). (1981). *Community housing choices for older Americans.* New York: Springer.

Lawton, M. P., Kleban, M., & Carlson, D. (1973). The Inner City Resident: To Move or not to Move. *Gerontologist, 13,* 443–448.

Lawton, M. P., & Nahemow, L (1973). Ecology and the aging process. In C. Eisdorfer and M. P. Lawton (Eds.), *The psychology of adult development and aging.* Washington, DC: American Psychological Association.

Lawton, M. P., Windley, P. G., & Byerts, T. O. (1982). *Aging and the environment: Theoretical approaches.* New York: Springer.

Logan, J. R. (1985). The graying of the suburbs. *Aging, 345,* 4–8.

Longino, C. F. (1979). Going home: Aged return migration in the United States, 1965–70. *Journal of Gerontology, 34,* 736–45.

Longino, C. F. (1982). American retirement communities and residential relocation. In A. M. Warnes (Ed.), *Geographical perspectives on the elderly.* (pp. 239–262). New York: Wiley .

Lozier, J., & Althouse, R. (1975). Retirement to the porch in rural Appalachia. *International Journal of Aging and Human Development, 6,* 7–15.

Mangum, W. P. (1982). Housing for the elderly in the United States. In A. M. Warnes (Ed.), *Geographical perspectives on the elderly* (pp. 191–221). New York: Wiley.

Marans, R. W., Hunt, M. E., & Vakalo, K. L. (1984). Retirement communities. In I. Altman, M. P. Lawton, & J. F. Wohlwill (Eds.), *Human behavior and the environment: The elderly and the physical environment* (pp. 57–93). New York: Plenum.

McAuley, W. J., & Prohaska, T. R. (1981). Professional recommendations for long term care placement: A comparison of two groups of institutionally vulnerable elderly. *Home Health Care Services Quarterly, 2,* 41–57.

Meyer, J. W., & Speare, A. (1985). Distinctively elderly

mobility: Types and determinants. *Economic Geography*, *61*, 79–88.

Montgomery, J. E., Stubbs, A. C., & Day, S. S. (1980). The housing environment of the rural elderly. *Gerontologist*, *20*, 444–451.

Mumford, L. (1953). For older people—not segregation but integration. *Architectural Record*, *119*, 191–194.

Nachison, J. S., & Leeds, M. H. (1983). Housing policy for older Americans in the 1980's: An Overview. *Journal of Housing for the Elderly*, *1*, 3–13.

National Council on the Aging. (1975). *The myth and reality of aging in America*. Washington, DC: Author.

Newcomer, R. (1976). An evaluation of neighborhood service convenience for elderly housing project residents. In P. Suedfeld & J. Russell (Eds.), *The behavioral basis of design*. Stroudsburg, PA: Dowden, Hutchinson and Ross.

Newman, S. J., & Duncan, G. J. (1979). Residential problems, dissatisfaction, and mobility. *Journal of American Planning Association*, *45*, 154–166.

Newman, S. J., Zais, T., & Struyk, R. (1984). Housing older America. In I. Altman, M. P. Lawton, & J. F. Wohlwill (Eds.), *Elderly people and the environment* (pp. 17–55). New York: Plenum.

Nusberg, C. (1978). "Granny Flats"—Increasing housing options for the elderly. *Ageing International*, *4*, 8–10.

O'Bryant, S. L. (1982). The value of home to older persons and its relationship to housing satisfaction. *Research on Aging*, *4*, 349–363.

O'Bryant, S. L. (1983). The subjective value of "home" to older homeowners. *Journal of Housing for the Elderly*, *1*, 29–43.

O'Bryant, S. L. (in press). The psychological significance of home ownership to older women. *Psychology of Women Quarterly*.

O'Bryant, S. L., & Wolf, S. M. (1983). Explanations of housing satisfaction of older homeowners and renters. *Research on Aging*, *5*, 217–233.

Pastalan, L. A. (1976). *Report on Pennsylvania Nursing Home Relocation Program*. Interim Research Findings. University of Michigan, Institute of Gerontology, Ann Arbor.

Pastalan, L. A. (1979). Sensory changes and environmental behavior. In T. O. Byerts, S. C. Howell, & L. A. Pastalan (Eds.), *Environmental context of aging: Lifestyles, environmental quality and living arrangements* (pp. 118–126). New York: Garland STPM Press.

Pastalan, L. A. (1983a). Environmental displacement: A literature reflecting old person-environment transactions. In G. D. Rowles & R. J. Ohta (Eds.), *Aging and milieu: Environmental perspectives on growing old* (pp. 189–203). New York: Academic.

Pastalan, L. A. (1983b). Home equity conversion: A performance comparison with other housing options. *Journal of Housing for the Elderly*, *1*, 1983, 83–90.

Porteous, J. D. (1976). Home: The territorial core. *Geographical Review*, *66*, 383–390.

Prohaska, T. R., & McAuley, W. J. (1983). The role of family care and living arrangements in acute care discharge recommendations. *Journal of Gerontological Social Work*, *5*, 67–80.

Rakoff, R. M. (1977). Ideology in everyday life: The meaning of the house. *Politics and Society*, *7*, 85–104.

Redfoot, D. L. (1985 April). *The broken dish: Old age, class and the archival function of the family*. Paper presented at the meeting of the Southern Sociological Society, Charlotte, N. C.

Redfoot, D. L., & Back, K. W. (in press). The perceptual presence of the life course. *International Journal of Aging and Human Development*.

Regnier, V. (1985a). Design criteria for outdoor space surrounding housing for the elderly. In T. Voniar (Ed.), *Research and design 85: Architectural applications of design and technology research* (pp. 1–9). Washington, DC: American Institute of Architects.

Regnier, V. (1985b). Planning congregate housing for the elderly: An integrative research and participatory planning model. In T. Voniar (Ed.), *Research* (pp. 1–9). Washington, DC: American Institute of Architects.

Regnier, V., & Bonar, J. (1981) Recycling buildings for elderly housing. In M. P. Lawton & S. L. Hoover (Eds.), *Community housing choices for older Americans* (pp. 286–298). New York: Springer.

Regnier, V., & Byerts, T. O. (1983). Applying research to the plan and design of housing for the elderly. In M. F. Spink (ed.), *Housing for a maturing population* (pp. 24–79). Washington, DC: Urban Land Institute.

Relph, E. (1976). *Place and placelessness*. London: Pion.

Rosenmayr, L., & Kockeis, E. (1963). Propositions for a sociological theory of aging and the family. *International Social Science Journal*, *15*, 410–426.

Rosow, I. (1967). *Social integration of the aged*. New York: Free Press.

Rossi, P. H. (1955). *Why families move*. Glencoe, IL: Free Press.

Rowles, G. D. (1978). *Prisoners of space? Exploring the geographical experience of older people*. Boulder, CO: Westview Press.

Rowles, G. D. (1979). The last new home: Facilitating the older person's adjustment to institutional space. In S. M. Golant (Ed.), *Location and environment of the elderly population* (pp. 81–94). New York: Wiley.

Rowles, G. D. (1980). Growing old "inside": Aging and attachment to place in an Appalachian community. In N. Datan & N. Lohman (Eds.), *Transitions of aging* (pp. 152–170). New York: Academic Press.

Rowles, G. D. (1981). The surveillance zone as meaningful space for the aged, *Gerontologist*, *21*, 304–311.

Rowles, G. D. (1983a). Between worlds: A relocation dilemma for the Appalachian elderly. *International Journal of Aging and Human Development*, *17*, 301–314.

Rowles, G. D. (1983b). Place and personal identity in old age: Observations from Appalachia. *Journal of Environmental Psychology*, *3*, 299–313.

Rubinstein, R. L. (1985, November). *The environment as a source of meaning in late life—an anthropological view*. Paper presented at 38th annual Scientific Meeting of the Gerontological Society of America, New Orleans.

Rubinstein, R. L. (1986). *The meaning and function of home for the elderly*. Unpublished manuscript.

Sartre, J. P. (1956). *Being and nothingness*. Hazel Barnes (Trans.) New York: Washington Square Press.

Seamon, D. (1979). *A geography of the lifeworld: Movement, rest and encounter*. New York: St. Martin's Press.

Seamon, D. (1981). Newcomers, existential outsiders and insiders: Their portrayal in two books by Doris Lessing. In D. C. D. Pocock (Ed.), *Humanistic geography and literature* (pp. 85–100). London: Croom Helm.

Serow, W. J. (1978). Return migration of the elderly in the USA: 1955–1960 and 1965–1970. *Journal of Gerontology, 33,* 288–295.

Sherman, E., & Newman, E. S. (1977). The meaning of cherished personal possessions for the elderly. *International Journal of Aging and Human Development, 8,* 181–192.

Sherman, S. R. (1971). The choice of retirement housing among the well elderly. *International Journal of Aging and Human Development, 2,* 118–138.

Sherwood, S., Greer, D. S., & Morris, J. N. (1979). A study of the Highland Heights Apartments for the physically impaired and elderly in Fall River. In T. O. Byerts, S. C. Howell, & L. A. Pastalan (Eds.), *Environmental context of aging: Lifestyles, Environmental Quality and Living Arrangements* (pp. 177–190). New York: Garland STPM Press.

Steinfeld, E. (1983). The scope of residential repair and renovation services and models of service delivery. In M. P. Lawton & S. L. Hoover (Eds.), *Community housing choices for older Americans* (pp. 201–220). New York: Springer.

Streib, G. F. (1978). An alternative family form for older persons: Need and social context. *Family Coordinator, 27,* 413–420.

Sullivan, D., & Stevens, S. (1982). Snowbirds: Seasonal Migrants to the Sunbelt. *Research on Aging, 4,* 159–177.

Sykes, J. T. (1980). Comments on marketing. In K. Scholen & Y. P. Chen (Eds.), *Unlocking home equity for the elderly.* Cambridge, MA: Ballinger.

Taylor, C. C., & Townsend, A. R. (1976). The local "sense of place" as evidenced in north-east England. *Urban Studies, 13,* 133–146.

Tobin, S. S., & Lieberman, M. A. (1976). *Last home for the aged.* San Francisco: Jossey-Bass.

Townsend, P. (1963). *The family life of old people.* London: Pelican Books.

Warnes, A. M. (1983). Variations in the propensity among older persons to migrate: Evidence and implications. *Journal of Applied Gerontology, 17,* 20–27.

Warnes, A. M., Howes, D. R., & Took, L. (1985). Residential locations and intergenerational visiting in retirement. *Quarterly Journal of Social Affairs, 1,* 231–247.

Winklevoss, H. E., & Powell, A. V. (1984). *Continuing Care retirement communities: An empirical, financial and legal analysis.* Homeland, Ill: Richard D. Irvin.

Wiseman, R. F. (1980). Why older people move: Theoretical issues. *Research on Aging, 2,* 141–154.

Wiseman, R. F., & Roseman, C. C. (1979). A typology of elderly migration based on the decision making process. *Economic Geography, 55,* 3244–3337.

Chapter 26

Clinical Issues for Assessment and Intervention with the Black Elderly

Brenda F. McGadney, Robin Goldberg-Glen, and Elsie M. Pinkston

The total population of black Americans in 1980 was 26,448,000, representing a 16% increase since 1970. By contrast, the population of blacks who were 65 or older increased by 34% from 1,556,000 in 1970 to 2,085,825 in 1980 (Watson, 1982). Although the black elderly are a rapidly growing segment of the elderly population, they have been largely understudied. In addition, socioeconomic conditions perpetuate inequalities in health care, resulting in the serious neglect of their physical and mental health.

Attempting to treat age-related mental health problems of the black elderly without a clear understanding of the historical, social, and environmental events that have shaped their lives can lead to continued negative characterization, stereotyping and misguided efforts at intervention. A more complete view of the black elderly will suggest more specific and richer options for mental health intervention. In this chapter, the authors draw a picture of how the black elderly interact with the medical and mental health communities, and then provide an overview of black elderly cul-

ture, development, social structure, and physical and mental health. With an understanding of how the black elderly relate to family and community, particularly in light of the role of the church in their lives, the clinician will have a broader perspective about their problems associated with old age.

It is not known to what extent the distinctive personal histories and life-styles of the black elderly influence clinicians' intervention efforts or how effective those interventions are. Jackson (1981), in her review of the research of ethnicity and medical care, notes that research on the effects of demographic characteristics, such as sex, age, marital status, race, and education are scant, fragmented, and inconclusive. Therefore, owing to the ambiguity of the research that compares mental health outcomes of black and white elderly clients, the focus of this chapter will be on issues that are likely to help those clinicians who provide mental health services for the black elderly.

CLINICAL IMPLICATIONS OF AGEIST AND RACIST BIASES

Ageism is a form of discrimination that promotes negative attitudes toward the elderly and places greater value on youth in society (Butler, 1969). This set of biased values assumes, contrary to the evidence, that old age is characterized by senility and dependence, which therefore devalues and dehumanizes elderly individuals (Butler, 1975; 1982). Ray, Raciti, and Ford (1985), in a review of ageism research, note that ageist attitudes are prevalent across professional disciplines.

The consequences of these biases can include: (a) an impaired therapeutic relationship with the client who may feel less inclined to trust the professional and to cooperate in therapy; (b) the preference of medication over psychotherapy as the treatment of choice (Ray et al., 1985); (c) greater readiness to consider institutionalization as a viable option and; (d) avoidance of elderly clients (Butler & Sullivan, 1963; Gurland & Cross, 1982).

Dancy (1977), a major social critic of the treatment of black elderly, notes that ageism among clinicians may engender discrimination against the elderly and decrease the likelihood that they will receive the necessary services. This view of the elderly population is further supported by Ray et al. (1985), who indicate that psychiatrists prefer elderly patients the least, a fact that can limit service availability in spite of Medicare and Medicaid, which have attempted to eliminate barriers in health care delivery. The problem involves underlying social attitudes and values that characterize our society's views toward aging and the black elderly. To be old, poor, and black is to live in jeopardy.

Although as a group the black elderly are worse off economically than their white counterparts, there exists much diversity among them. Data are not available that would allow adequate evaluation of their collective experience of being black during a period of mixed racial discrimination and civil rights progress. However, the black elderly share the experience of being old and part of the collective memory of the older community. Therefore most of the information in the literature will hopefully add meaningful pieces to the puzzle that represents the life of the black elderly person. This chapter is designed to incorporate information from the literature on both black and white elderly

to aid practitioners in understanding the possible alternatives for the mental treatment of the black elderly person.

HEALTH SERVICES

Medical Health

In order to understand the attitudes of the black elderly toward mental health professionals, it is important to have some knowledge of the experience of blacks with the medical health care system, one of the areas in which the past history of discrimination has left its mark. A 1971 survey for the Special Committee on Aging of the U.S. Senate linked limited income with the health deficits of the black elderly. Too frequently, the aged minority person lacks the money to pay the deductibles of premiums required for the total Medicare plan, even though hospital and clinic facilities are technically available to them. Further, the Senate report stated, "The majority of Negroes over 65 are less educated, and have less income, suffer more illnesses and earlier death, have poorer quality housing and less choice as to where they live and where they work, and in general, have a less satisfying quality of life" (Lindsay, 1971, p. 10).

The needs of many elderly black persons are indeed serious; 24% live in substandard housing, which may aggravate chronic health conditions (Urban Resources, 1978). In 1969, 19.9% of blacks 65 years and over could not work because of poor health, compared to 9% of whites in the same age group (Sowder, 1972). The issue of insufficient income translates into fewer visits to the doctor and an inability to purchase prescribed medication, which reduces effective health care for the black elderly.

Although the number of practicing black physicians is increasing, there are still few doctors of any race in the inner city, where many of the black elderly live. Consequently, the black elderly are often forced to seek medical attention at great distances from their homes. Public transportation is often poor or erratic. These impediments mean that a visit to a doctor is something to be put off as a last resort. Many low-income blacks treat themselves with home remedies or consult druggists or folk healers, seeking the advice of a physician only in the advanced stages of illness, when pain or disease have become too much to bear untreated (Jackson, 1981; Bullough & Bullough, 1982).

Barriers to seeking health care include the absence of black physicians, inaccessibility of medical facilities, fear of cost, lack of information, fear of treatment, and suspicion of the white society that controls medical and other services. Indeed comparisons have revealed that on the average, black elderly visit physicians less frequently than their white counterparts. Based on estimates from the 1970 census, elderly blacks over 65 years of age visited physicians about 4.5 times per year, as compared to 6.9 times per year for elderly white Americans. Two thirds of older blacks do not use Medicare, particularly the costlier Part B which covers outpatient services (Hill, 1971). When they do see a doctor, their health condition has usually deteriorated, requiring costly and lengthy treatment. Research efforts by the American Association of Retired Persons (Agee, 1985) provide further evidence of these inequities:

> Black elderly are more likely to be sick and disabled, and to see themselves as being in poor health than white elderly. They have higher rates of chronic disease, functional impairment, and indicators of risk, such as high blood pressure. At age 65–75, mortality of Blacks is higher than whites. Blacks of extreme old age (75+) have lower mortality rates but higher rates of poverty and illness. (p. 3)

Differential Longevity and the Crossover Phenomenon

Life expectancy statistics of whites and non-whites (blacks, Hispanics, and Native Americans) are very revealing. The average life expectancy for the individual born in the United States is 73.3 years: it is 70.2 years for a white male, 77.8 for a white female, 65.0 for a nonwhite male, and 73.6 for a nonwhite female (Kelly, Landsiedel, Owings, Sowder & Chambers, 1978).

However, one point of interest with intriguing implications for health service providers is the observation that both male and female blacks in this very aged group live longer than whites. This reversal in average life expectancy occurs between 75 and 80 years of age. For example, a black man at age 75 can expect to live another 9.5 years whereas a white man of the same age can expect to live only 4.5 years. Manney (1974) noted that blacks constituted 12.5% of the 7,000 centenarians receiving Social Security benefits in 1971, even though they represented only 7% of the total

population aged 65 and over. Some authorities have speculated that older minority persons who are able to survive early hardships may be especially "hardy and durable." However, attention should be focused on these "survivors", whose longer life expectancy may make them more vulnerable to such problems as lower income and declining social supports.

Mental Health Care

A dominant theme of this chapter is that aging and ethnic identity are important factors in any explanations of age-related mental health problems among the black elderly. This is just as true for medical health problems. Practitioners and policymakers turned their attention to this issue in 1978, when the President of the United States convened the Commission on Mental Health. The commission report estimates that up to 25% of older persons have significant mental health problems.

In a major review of the rates of admission and the total services offered in psychiatric facilities, Kramer, Taube, and Redick (1973) showed that only a small proportion of all aged persons receive community psychiatric care. In outpatient clinics, 10% of the clients are between 45 and 55 years of age, 54.4% are between 55 and 65 and 2% are over 65. These figures contrast with census figures showing that 10% of the population is over 65 (Zarit, 1980). The consequence is that mental health problems remain undiagnosed and untreated. Several factors contribute to the gap between the need for and provision of psychiatric services to the black elderly, such as limited access, differential desire for services, ageism, racism, and therapist characteristics. The mental health profession has been largely unaware of and unresponsive to the need for services to the elderly (Walsh, 1980; Zarit, 1980); and it also has been evidenced, in reviewing ethnic differences in the utilization of mental health services, that some elderly have negative attitudes toward mental illness and the handicaps of aged peers, which may ultimately influence their own help-seeking behavior in response to mental disorders (Watson, 1970).

Factors affecting the care of the elderly include the negative beliefs held by therapists about old age, attitudes of older persons about mental health, and the lack of training programs for professionals who work with the aged (Zarit, 1980).

Furthermore, Walsh (1980) argues that stereotyping of older people and their families by mental health systems and professionals has led to assumptions that they are a poor investment for therapy—too resistant to change, or simply untreatable. Ray et al. (1985), in research on psychiatrists' attitudes, note that in general, psychiatrists do not consider the elderly good candidates for therapy. In the mental health field, this negative view of the elderly can be traced to Freud (1904), who cautioned his followers not to waste their time on the aged because their defenses were too rigid. However, as Lawton and Gottesman (1974) noted one cannot remain rigid and still adapt to all the biological and social changes that occur with aging.

Most social scientists agree that racism has greatly influenced the degree and types of mental health services available to the black elderly (Cannon & Locke, 1976; Greeson, 1978). They acknowledge that some of the problems encountered by black elderly in obtaining mental health services result directly from professional prejudice and race discrimination in psychiatric referrals (Cohen, 1976). Yet, McCaslin and Calvert (1975) and other researchers have identified circumstances in which blacks use mental health services more than whites, although outcome has not been evaluated (Cannon & Locke, 1976; Crawford, 1960; Kadushin, 1957; Kalish, 1971; Maas, 1972).

Existing stereotypes have been known to influence clinicians, diagnoses and choice of treatment. For example, a New Haven, Connecticut, study, started in 1950 by a team of sociologists and psychiatrists headed by Hollingshead and Redlich (1953, 1958), found that patients who were diagnosed as mentally ill by mental hospitals, private psychiatrists, and clinics received different types of treatment depending on their social class. Middle- and upper-class patients were more likely to have received psychotherapy or somatotherapy, administered on an outpatient basis or in the physician's office, whereas lower-class patients were more likely to have been committed to a long-term public facility. Generally, they received ineffective therapy—custodial care combined with minimal drug therapy. These differences in treatment patterns are important in explaining the higher overall percentage of mental illness among people of low income. When these patients—old, poor, and often black—were deinstitutionalized in the 1970s, they returned to communities with limited

services. Less than 2% of the funding for Medicare is allocated for mental health coverage for the elderly and the disabled (Allen, 1983). Community mental health centers are reimbursed only a little more than 0.01% for both inpatient and outpatient care (Kreuger, 1977). As a result, it is very difficult for the black elderly to obtain affordable mental health services.

Finances are not the only barriers between lower-class clients and psychotherapists. Most psychiatrists, clinical psychotherapists, and psychiatric social workers come from middle and upper-class backgrounds, and until recently, the only ethnic minority well represented in the group were Jews (Bullough & Bullough, 1982). Some degree of class and racial ethnocentrism among therapists is inevitable. This is evident in the types of clients whom psychotherapists choose for therapy. Psychiatrists tend to avoid clients whose education and verbal skills are meager or whose occupations are unskilled, justifying this on the grounds that lower-class clients lack the necessary verbal and cognitive skills to participate in the therapeutic process (Ray et al., 1985). It is clear that practitioners need evaluation and therapeutic techniques designed specifically for the black elderly. In addition, all training programs should provide more education above racial and ethnic differences (for review, see Chunn, Dunston, & Ross-Sherriff, 1983).

Black elderly represent a disproportionate share (17%) of those institutionalized in mental hospitals (Kramer, 1977). One explanation is improper institutionalization due to diagnostic errors. In a 4-year retrospective study by black psychiatrists of black patients admitted to Howard University Hospital, the researchers reported that 32.5% of the patients were diagnosed as schizophrenic; during the same period, 46.5% of all nonwhites in hospitals other than Veterans' Administration hospitals were diagnosed schizophrenic (Bullough & Bullough, 1982). Even more striking was the comparison of the Howard figures with those from the Walter Reed Army Medical Center, where 58% of the black patients were diagnosed as schizophrenic (Collins, Bickman, & Mathura, 1980; Simon, Fleiss, & Gurland, 1973). The explanation offered for the differences is that the black physicians at Howard diagnosed a larger proportion of their patient population as suffering from other less debilitating mental illnesses. Although these findings are not conclusive, they nevertheless indicate an area of possible caution in diagnostic procedures.

The problem of misdiagnosis can be caused by either the client or the practitioner. Sometimes professionals overestimate the seriousness of the black elderly patient's illness based on idiosyncratic cues presented. At other times, the patient may disclose little personal information to a non-black therapist (Bullough & Bullough, 1982). To document the latter, Carkuff and Pierce (1970) examined the initial clinical interviews of hospitalized black and white females diagnosed as schizophrenics and found that patients are more self-exploratory with therapists whose race and social class are more similiar to their own. The question that remains is whether therapists can compensate for these differences through proper training or whether different treatment methods are needed.

Service Issues

Basic services in such areas as residential housing, security, expanded coverage in health insurance, transportation, and home-based care have the potential to greatly improve mental health and a sense of well-being. The black elderly population will experience significant growth in the next few decades as the middle-aged black population, which is healthier, better educated, better nourished, and less isolated, begins to close the life expectancy gap between blacks and whites (Soldo, 1980). Geographic location and migration patterns also influence services to the poor elderly, particularly the poorest of the aged.

The black aged are relocating to the "black belt" states—Texas, Louisiana, Mississippi, Georgia, and Arkansas—for a variety of reasons, including improved living conditions in the wake of civil rights legislation, integration, and the election of black politicians. Upward mobility and good jobs have provided them with the necessary resources to relocate and the desire to reestablish connections with their Southern roots, where family homes are often located. This has become a major problem in states like Texas where revenue shortages engendered by the oil recession cannot keep up with population growth (300,000 to 400,000 a year). Dr. Jared Hazelton of the nonpartisan Texas Research League, stated that Texas, a low-tax state, is attracting people from Northern states, who arrive expecting social services (*New York Times*, May 22, 1985). Their expectations contrast sharply with the reality—Texas has one of the lowest levels of state services in the United

States. For example, its 2-year budget of about $36 billion is less than half the $39 billion annual budget of New York State, which is only slightly larger in population. Thus, elderly persons who retire with significantly reduced incomes, particularly those who are poor or widowed, may face severe hardships by relocating to states where historically they have been economically deprived. These states have limited revenues to expand such programs as Medicare, Medicaid, and comprehensive services provided by the Older Americans Act of 1965 (i.e., nutrition programs, multipurpose senior centers, and volunteer service programs, such as Foster Grandparents).

The black elderly are more likely to live in metropolitan areas concentrated in the central states. The inner city, however, is not kind to the elderly (Hawkins, 1978). They must endure the noise, dirt, smog, and social tension of the ghetto, substandard housing, and inadequate medical care. In a study of geriatric ghettos in Philadelphia, Lawton (1971) concluded that "it was not an easy life for older people. They were prime targets for purse snatchings, armed robberies, mugging, rape, and murder, which kept fear alive among the elder residents" (p. 227). Others have reported similar findings. Hawkins (1978) reported that inner-city tenants reported high levels of fear, reluctance to leave their apartments, and feelings of isolation. The suburban tenants felt more secure and comfortable, being less afflicted by crime; however, housing costs frequently prevented the black elderly from living there (Dancy, 1977).

Regardless of whether elderly blacks migrate to inner cities or Southern states, they will encounter the need for support services. Clinicians and policymakers must keep in mind that the residential environment plays a major role in the social adjustment of older persons. Improved living conditions are associated with improved functioning (Jackson, 1972), whereas poor living conditions contribute to physical and psychological impairment of both black and white older persons (Lowenthal & Frier, 1967). Therefore, mental health services should include crime prevention programs, such as neighborhood watch, escort service, and direct-deposit banking, which should be expanded to reduce the isolation and victimization of the elderly. Additional support services should be expanded to increase funding for elderly housing and rent supplements, reduce Medicare gaps, and include more health-related services, particularly focusing on alternatives to institutionalization. Finally, lifting rigid eligibility guidelines for Medicaid, nutrition programs and transportation services and providing better basic services in housing will help improve the quality of life for the elderly.

FAMILY STRUCTURE

No matter where they live, most aged blacks have Southern roots. These roots have greatly affected many black cultural patterns, including religion, culinary habits, language, and life-style (Dancy, 1977). Thus, it is important to understand the family structure and caretaking behavior of the black family.

History of the Black Family in America

Clinicians may view black families as a therapeutic ally and, as with the church, use them as a major resource for intervention. Clinicians often perpetuate the myth that the elderly are isolated and alone, abandoned by their families during times of illness and crisis despite data to the contrary (Hartman & Laird, 1983; Shanas, 1979). In the United States, approximately 75% of the elderly live within 30 minutes of their adult children and 85% live within an hour's drive (Butler & Lewis, 1982; Puner, 1974). The black elderly, like others, expect the first line of assistance to come from their children and relatives (Taylor, 1985).

In spite of slavery and social, economic, and political hardships, an aspect that pervades all areas of black family life is the general respect for and bond with elders (Hines & Boyd-Franklin, 1982; Watson, 1982). Blacks often empower themselves by creating an environment in their communites to cope with the problems of the impaired elderly (Billingsley, 1968; Dancy, 1977; Pinderhughes 1982; Soloman, 1976; Watson & Maxwell, 1977).

It is also important for practitioners and policymakers to understand cultural variations in black families in later life, particularly when defining the black family; the validity of kinship ties; social networks; and social supports. Defining the black family is not an easy task. Although the definition of family varies, one traditional definition posed by Pinderhughes (1982) is that the family is a group of individuals, usually related by blood, who live together to obtain protection, socialization, resources, and support. Hines and Boyd-Franklin (1982), however, state emphatically that there is no such entity as "the black family": "The diversity that exists among black families and communities is a reality determined by a complex interplay of variables. Black families have come to the United States from many different countries over the last four centuries. By far, however, the largest groups of blacks in the United States are those of African origin whose ancestors were brought directly here as slaves" (p. 84). Similarly, Billingsley (1968), in his search to identify variations of the nuclear family, identified 12 different types of family structures in the black family, with no single category holding a large majority. When black clinicians speak of the black family, they may mean a multigenerational extended family, which is an interdependent kinship system bound together by a sense of obligation to relatives. It is generally presided over by a dominant family figure. It can include nonblood members. It can extend across geographical boundaries to connect family units (Billingsley, 1968; Martin & Martin, 1978; Pinderhughes, 1982).

However, according to Hawkins (1978), this liberal view of the extended family is not a reality for more than half the black elderly in this country. Less than 50% of the black elderly live in an extended family situation. The rest live alone or with one other person, relative or nonrelative (Butler & Lewis 1973). Thus, it is extremely important that therapists remain flexible in their definitions of family and embrace the notion that the majority of black families are embedded in a complex kinship network of blood and nonrelated persons and ecological communities. This network is important as we examine extended kinship ties of caregiving and mutual aid.

Extended Kinship Ties

In recent years, ethnographic research (Aschenbrenner, 1975; Chatters, Taylor, & Jackson, 1985, 1986; Jackson, Tucker, & Bowen, 1982; Martin & Martin, 1978; McAdoo, 1979; Shimkin & Frate, 1978; Stack, 1974; Willie, 1974) has provided important information on informal social supports operating in the black family.

Several studies provide significant information for understanding the black family (Jackson, 1970, 1972; Taylor, 1985; Taylor, Jackson, & Quick,

1982; Willie, 1974). Jackson provides the broadest understanding of the subject, writing that the family ties of elderly blacks consist of mutual sharing, a sense of affectionate closeness, satisfaction with family relations, frequent interaction with family members, and a sense of family identification. Additional findings on helper networks provide some understanding of the concepts of family ties among black families as they relate to social class. The findings by Willie (1974) indicate that the higher the family's social class, the greater the family ties tend to be. According to Willie, family ties in middle class families are based on cooperation between spouses, family ties in the working class emanate from cooperation between parents and adult children, and family ties among lower-class blacks are weaker than those in the working or middle classes. Collectively these results are consistent with existing literature on kinship interaction patterns and support networks of older blacks and the general black population (Cantor, 1979; McAdoo, 1979; Shanus, 1979; Stack, 1974; Stanford, 1978). In fact, the analysis by Taylor et al. (1982) of the support elderly blacks (aged 55 and over) received from family members showed that respondents with less income reported receiving support less often than those with higher incomes (obtained from the first national data on the black elderly, the National Study of Black Americans, Jackson et al., 1982).

In a recent study, Taylor (1985) examined family ties more directly by focusing on the reported frequency of informal support that black elderly receive from extended family members. His findings indicate that the black elderly are active participants in family networks, with the elderly reporting significant levels of interaction with family, relatively close residential proximity to immediate family, extensive familial bonds, and a high degree of satisfaction derived from family life. In addition, over half of the respondents indicated receiving assistance from family members. A study conducted by Jackson (1980) on the social support interchange between children and elderly members of the family showed that the most frequent aid received by the elderly were gifts, assistance when ill, and transportation.

Martin and Martin (1978) note that the extended family continues to play an important role in sustaining its members. They also note that the extended family values caring, sharing, and helping, which are humanistic and people-orientated qualities. Dancy (1977) also supports the

notion that the matter of cooperation and support has been crucial for the survival and strength of the black family. In many instances, family and community networks have linked the various households in a supportive manner.

It is important, however, not to develop another stereotype. Hawkins (1978) warns that some black elderly are not happy in an extended family setting when they are:

> forced into congregate family housing as an economic necessity and may experience a loss of privacy, independence, and even identity. In some cases, they must carry on the energy-consuming household work for larger families and care for young children at an age when the older person's health is poorest, energies are lowest, and need for less stress is greatest. (p. 172)

It is important for the practitioner to know and understand these complex issues in order to make realistic use of family resources.

The literature validates the notion that black families develop strong kinship networks and coping skills as their major resource in times of trouble (McAdoo, 1979; McGoldrick, 1982; Billingsley, 1968). Often, extended households are the most stable and enduring form of family unit (Allen, 1983; Stack, 1974). Thus, the high degree of sharing among black families in part reflects society's failure to adequately meet the needs of black Americans (Hildreth & Dilworth-Anderson, in press). Black people have developed a system of cooperation and interdependence that provides the basis for a sharing and caring network (Willie, 1974).

Caregiving

Watson (1980) noted that in his research family support was preferred by blacks as the primary source of caregiving in the case of illness. His study showed that family caregiving was primary because most illnesses were sufficiently mild and family care was advisable, affordable, and sufficient to meet the needs of the older person. Watson (1982) also found that older blacks feel they should be cared for at home by their offspring rather than in specialized institutions for the aged or through public service agencies. A recent survey conducted by Taylor (1985) of 581 elderly black respondents also supports these findings, noting that the order of preferences for receiving help, from first to last are children, relative, non-kin, and formal organization. A further observation that the black elderly constitute less than 6% of the residents of old-age and nursing homes even though they make up about 8% of the general population (U.S. Bureau of Census, 1979).

Finally, there are considerable differences among various ethnic and racial groups, structures, and norms with respect to intergenerational relations. For example, there is much evidence that blacks expect greater familial responsibility than whites (Hill, 1971; Schorr, 1960; Seelbach & Sauer, 1977). According to Seelbach and Sauer, the black elderly experience much lower morale than white elderly when adult children fail to meet their expectations for care. The culture and kinship patterns of black families provide strong support for impaired or ill elderly, and the family-centred practitioner should make every effort to be aware of these variables and how they influence the planning and delivery of services.

Mutual Aid

The built-in mutual aid of the black elderly's extended family provides its members with a sense of identity, emotional security, and actual attainment of necessary resources (Pinderhughes, 1982). Kinship networks, including both family and close friends, share resources, household tasks, and housing in a system characterized by mutual obligation (Stack, 1974). Various patterns of mutual aid can develop among its members as illustrated in research by Hill (1977). The sample in his study was comprised of modified extended families, linked through three generations of nuclear families, including 312 nuclear families living within 50 miles of Minneapolis and St. Paul, MN. The findings revealed that the parent generation tended to give more help than it received and the grandparent generation received more help than it gave in all areas except child care. In addition the married-child generation gave more than it received to grandparents in emotional gratification, household management, and aid during illness. On the other hand, that generation received more help than it gave in economic assistance and child care. In an earlier study, Hill (1971) reported that 48% of elderly black women have related children living with them in contrast to only 10% of similar white families. Another study showed that 20% of the black aged took grandchildren into their homes, compared to 15% of the white aged (Jackson & Wood, 1976). The giving and receiving of aid between members of a kin network is one of the most significant bonds between them (Watson, 1982). In this context, various people interchange roles, jobs, and family functions. Thus, another attribute of the black family in response to physical, emotional, and economic stress is adaptability of family roles (Hill, 1971; Hines & Boyd-Franklin, 1982).

BROADLY BASED TREATMENT PERSPECTIVE

A broad treatment approach includes the family's environment and the community. The formal and informal support networks in the environment provide a cushion and necessary sense of belonging, as well as extend available resources (Harris & Balgopal, 1980; Solomon, 1976). These networks include groups of all kinds—church, peer groups, extended family, and neighbors.

Church

Religion and the black church have played a vital role in the survival and advancement of blacks. In considering the unique aspects of the black cultural experience, the practitioner should attune herself/himself to the religious experience of the black elderly and assess the latter's expectations regarding their church and the supports it provides.

Numerous activities offered by churches, such as dinners and trips sponsored by ushers, various choirs, and Sunday school, provide social life for the entire family, which extends far beyond the Sunday church services, and supply a network of people who are available to the family in times of trouble or loss (Hines & Boyd-Franklin, 1982). The church also functions as a vehicle for reintegrating individuals into the community following illness. The mental health worker might consider establishing religious support groups for the elderly or using the church as a location for delivery of mental health services. Studies by Tobin, Ellor, and Anderson-Ray (1986) indicate that the storefront church can function as a support delivery system for the black elderly.

The black church provides other opportunities for the black elderly as well. A study conducted in Philadelphia by Hirsch (1972) among lower-income people showed that older blacks maintained their church affiliations far more extensively than older whites. One possible explanation offered by the authors was that local black churches have always been quick to provide for the needs of the aged. For example, when vital social services were not available to its parishioners, the black church provided the counseling, the needed care (e.g., food and clothing banks, employment opportunities, credit unions, nutrition and outreach services and a spiritual framework. It also has been an organizing force and a service center for its members. More important, Watson, Knox, and Thorne (1978) found a wide range of caregiving duties taken on by black churches when illness affected older members. For example, the churches used money collected from their members as the primary form of aid offered to the infirmed elderly. Church members made friendly visits to the home of the older person and gave aid relative to the needs of the infirmed. The church usually organized and took part in visiting the home, praying for the infirmed, and giving communion. Providing material gifts was the least frequent of all the responses initiated by church members on behalf of older infirmed people (Watson, 1982).

The Hartford Memorial Baptist Church, under the direction of Rev. Charles G. Adams, is illustrative of a church that offers a wide range of vital services for both the black elderly attending the church and those in the community. The comprehensive support system includes:

1. Ministers and the lay staff, volunteers providing escort, transportation, and visitation services.
2. Social services and mental health counseling with the AGAPE House Outreach Center with two full-time social workers, crises support line.
3. Daily food and friendship, nutritional program, mission and hunger task force, food co-op, free clothing shop.
4. Free medical clinic.
5. Hartford attorneys, the Nurses and Ladies Aid Society, and credit union.

Under the direction of Rev. Jeremiah A. Wright, the Trinity United Church of Christ in Chicago has, in addition to its senior citizen housing and social services, an employment ministry that screens and retains the elderly for jobs and provides family, personal, or marriage counseling through their counseling and legal ministry.

An action plan was developed in 1981 at the 11th Annual Conference of the National Caucus and Center on Black Aged, Inc., located in Washington, DC, to promote black churches as primary service delivery centers with the following main objectives:

1. To conduct an Education and Awareness Program throughout the black church regarding the national crisis that presently confronts older black Americans and responsibility of the church community to take an active role in addressing this crisis.
2. To establish black church organizations at the national, regional, state, and local levels as a primary advocate for older blacks, and particularly the elderly poor.
3. To develop a series of strategies and technical assistance efforts that would enable local black churches and ministerial alliances to become a major focus in the coordination and delivery of services to the black elderly and their families.

In short, the benefits that some black church groups provide appear limitless. Moreover, these organized efforts serve not only as a means of addressing the service needs of the elderly but are also viable mechanisms for improving and stabilizing the conditions of the entire community.

LIFE CYCLE ISSUES

In addition to declining health, the older person experiences a change of social roles. Ethnicity interacts with the family life cycle at every stage, and for a large number of black elderly these stresses are compounded by the lack of necessary economic and personal resources to maintain an active and meaningful social life (Hawkins, 1978). Thus, changes in status (e.g., retirement, death of a spouse, birth of a grandchild, and failing health) will affect family members differently, depending on their life cycle stage, past coping styles, and family bonds (Neugarten & Weinstein, 1968; Walsh, 1983). It is important for clinicians planning interventions with families in later life to keep in mind that the salient transactions and tasks of later life hold potential for loss and dysfunction, as well as for transformation and growth (Walsh, 1980).

Retirement

Retirement represents a significant milestone and adjustment for the elderly. In a sociopsychological sense, retirement from gainful employment can be thought of as a role loss and adjustment can be difficult for many people, although most studies show that the majority of people do so reasonably well. Finances, health, physical mobility, and social involvement appear to lead the list of factors that may affect adjustment to retirement (Kart, 1981). The work histories and educational opportunities of many blacks have clearly influenced their adjustment to retirement, particularly when faced with reduced income.

Aged blacks are much less likely to have good retirement plans and pensions. Those employed in unskilled and domestic jobs are left without Social Security coverage. Black workers hired at the entry level advance more slowly than their white counterparts (Bullough & Bullough, 1982), resulting in a gap between the retirement income of black and white workers.

Income

The lack of income is probably the most serious problem facing aged blacks in the United States. According to Hawkins (1976), the black aged are disproportionately represented among the aged poor. In 1975, 52.9% of the black elderly population was classified as poor, compared to 25% of the white elderly. Being old, black, and female exposes the person to a higher risk of poverty than being old, white, and male (Lindsay, 1971; Rubenstein, 1971; Watson, 1980). This often markedly affects the quality of their lives. Approximately 36% of the black aged, for example, fall below the federal poverty level, as compared to 30% of all black Americans and 14% of aged whites (Zarit, 1980). Black women experience severe deprivation in old age; according to the U.S. Department of Commerce (1979), they were 5 times more likely than others to live in poverty. One source estimated that 96% of older black women live in poverty (Atchley, 1977). On the average, black women receive lower wages than black men, and the gaps in their work histories translate into low Social Security payments (Campbell, 1979; Kart, 1981). In 1981, black men had a median income of $4,900, and black women $3,500, which compared unfavorably with white males, whose median income was $8,600.

Indirect sources of income for the elderly include rent subsidies, Medicare, Medicaid, food stamps, congregate and home-delivered meals, and a variety of social service programs.

Widowhood

The majority of aged women are widows, who outnumber widowers by a ratio of about 5 to 1

(Kart, 1981). Women outnumber men in both races because of the higher mortality rates for men in general (Hawkins, 1978). Moreover, the reduced life expectancy of black males subjects a larger proportion of black women to widowhood and poverty at an earlier age, still with many years of life ahead.

The effects of widowhood vary somewhat by class, sex, and ethnic background (Troll, Miller, & Atchley, 1979). Social and family contacts are often disrupted for men, since it is usually the wife who links her husband to the family and social community, especially after retirement (Walsh, 1980). Moreover, working-class older black women (26% of the elderly wives in black families) report feeling less distress when widowed than their white counterparts, perhaps because they have played a more dominant role in the family (Staples, 1977; Troll et al., 1979).

Grandparenthood

Clinicians also need to focus on issues related to multigenerational families. Lower mortality rates at birth, increased life expectancy, teenage pregnancies, and advances in medical technologies have enhanced the chances of intergenerational relationships between parents, children, grandparents, grandchildren, and great-grandchildren. According to Hagerstad (1981), more than a 50-year overlap is likely to occur between parents and their children. Moreover, Troll et al. (1979) estimate that 1 out of 10 individuals over 65 years of age also have a child over the age of 65. Hence it is important for clinicians to focus on issues surrounding the aging of parents and children together and on family situations where grandchildren and/or great-grandchildren care for their elder relatives.

According to Atchley (1977), at least three out of four older people in the United States have at least one living child. Some studies have shown that 50% or more of the elderly persons who have living offspring reported seeing one or more of their children, at least once a week (Townsend, 1976). Also, grandparenting has become a middle-aged event. Early marriage, earlier childbearing, and longer life expectancy are producing grandparents in their forties (Troll et al., 1979). Also, Troll et al. point out that many find their loyalties split between helping to care for their grandchildren and helping to care for their aged parents.

A study conducted by Neugarten and Weinstein

(1968), which focused on various aspects of role behavior of grandparents, found a variety of role possibilities and meaningful relationships for many older people. For many, role change is a meaningful alternative to the "empty nest" period of life; for example, they can take care of grandchildren without being burdened by the responsibilities, obligations, and conflicts inherent in the parent–child relationship (Walsh, 1980). An investigation by Jackson (1980) on the type of support exchanged between the elderly and their children and grandchildren revealed that higher-income elderly blacks were much more likely than white elderly to give child-rearing assistance and financial help to their children and grandchildren.

In the black family, intergenerational conflicts can emerge between the aged parent, children, and grandchildren even though the aged are generally among the most respected individuals in the extended family. Although there is little ethnically oriented research in this area, Martin and Martin (1978) state that in some cases conflict stems from the "old-fashioned" beliefs of older black persons in preparing younger members for living in American society. They seek to impart these ways to them because these values (religious preference and disciplinary practices, for example) have "always" maintained the family. In this youth-oriented society, the elderly may be frustrated by their offspring's mechanistic conformity to fads, particularly when their own influence seems to be ignored. To the aged, old-fashioned ways are the cornerstone of black family stability. The desire to protect their children and grandchildren from illegal, immoral, and violent acts of society is not always maladaptive; but for the most part, the elderly are powerless to do so. The behavior of the grandparent, frequently the black grandmother, becomes dysfunctional when he/she becomes more controlling and authoritarian by increasing family enmeshment and fusion in response to personal threat to his/her role. The therapist should consider viewing this role adaptation as compensation for the effects of stresses from both outside and inside the family.

Finally, it is not unusual to find grandparents living in a congregate situation. Often, they provide financial support to unemployed children and grandchildren who live with them. Frequently, they are deprived of privacy, independence and identity. Many of their responsibilities include energy-consuming housework (e.g., cooking, cleaning, babysitting), and sometimes they are still engaged in domestic work outside the home. Much research needs to be done on the emotional and financial supports necessary for the elderly's caretaking responsibilities and the multiple domestic burdens of these multigenerational families.

Declining Health and Impending Death

Declining health promotes further problems in relationships between aged parents and adult children. These are likely to fall into one of two patterns: (a) parents relying increasingly on support from children when declining health limits their capacity to function and (b) parents suffering from physical and psychological impairments, especially depression (Simon et al., 1973; Zarit, 1980). In fact, increased incidence of disturbance in the activities of daily living result in more frequent role reversals between parents and offspring. For those adult children who adopt role reversal and treat their parents as children, it is inevitable that the parent will be placed in a negative light (Hendricks & Hendricks, 1977). Conflicts generally arise when parents resist their children's assumption of supervisory responsibility. Excessive resistance may occur because they feel the children are being overprotective and presumptuous. In this situation, the therapist should consider a treatment plan approach for such a family that would involve them in selecting the necessary care and resources (Zarit, 1980). In addition the family should be placed in touch with supplementary resources that are available to provide home-care services (e.g., visiting nurse, escort service, respite care, friendly visitor, missionary society). Other goals may include helping the parent adapt to the incapacity when passing and facilitating a better understanding between parent and child.

Another important life cycle issue related to family and kinship studies is how elders cope with the deaths of family members. In old age, grief becomes a common emotional expression because it is a constant companion. Butler and Lewis (1982) define the primary purpose of grief and mourning as "adaptive emotion which helps us to accept the reality of the loss of significant and loved people and to find ways of filling up the emptiness caused by the loss, through identifying with a new style of life and new people" (p. 41). Although there is little empirical data that focuses on the grief of the black elderly, the assumption made by Hawkin's (1978), about how they handle grief seems to be right on target:

> The black elderly as a group have shown amazing fortitude in the fact of overwhelming deprivation. Their strength may be attributed to a lifetime struggle for survival and/or their very close involvement with the church. Regardless of the reason, the majority of them have been able to compensate for their losses in a very positive and healthy manner. There is evidence that they have a strong capacity for establishing new relationships with friends and neighbors that take on greater importance for them than relationships with relatives who live far away or do not maintain frequent contact. (p. 172)

However, the results of sustained stress are evidenced by the fact that black elderly reflect "a higher degree of sustained unhappiness" (Rubenstein, 1971). As Hawkins (1978) aptly states:

> It matters little that the "official" suicide rate for older whites is three times that for older blacks. The fact that the black elderly endure and "keep the faith" does not suggest that they suffer any less from the experience of being old and deprived; rather they choose a less dramatic form of protest. In fact, suicide more broadly defined might easily include more indirect self-destructive behavior: alcoholism, drug abuse, starvation, and self-imposed isolation, all of which are commonly seen in the elderly black population. (p. 173)

Thus, it is important for clinicians to acquire a broad perspective of black families in later life, including the influences of family structure, strengths, life cycle events, and ecological supports, both external and internal.

ASSESSMENT AND INTERVENTIONS

Ecological System Approach

The ecological system includes the physical, social, and cultural aspects of the environment, with the aging persons and their families as the primary agents of change. The multigenerational family system may be the resource or target for change (Hartman & Laird, 1983). As with other groups of elderly, adequate assessment includes appraising all systems that are part of the black elderly person's life to determine the most useful point of intervention. This is particularly important for the most impoverished older people because their current use of existing systems may not provide adequate resources to support an intervention effort. Many minority families have multiple problems and are poor; therefore, supplementary services may be necessary before psychological procedures will have any value.

Pinderhughes (1982) expands this definition of the environment to include all that is external to the family — neighborhood, peer groups, church, school, and work. Unfortunately, owing to social and economic circumstances, the extended family of today is often unable to be the sole resource available to meet the needs of the aged. Inadequate environmental resources strongly affect the quality of life and influence the ability of the elderly to cope and adapt to the stresses of life cycle events. The result may be the failure of individual family members to cope with the environment and to handle the stress and conflict within the family (Germaine, 1979).

In the past, treatment has all too often been of little benefit to the black elderly, and their many health and mental health problems have been viewed as hopeless (Allen, 1983). Instances of poor assessment and treatment are unfortunately all too common, and potentially treatable problems are sometimes ignored. Older persons, for example, are rarely evaluated for reversible causes of dementia or what are sometimes referred to as acute brain syndromes (Zarit, 1980). These disorders, which cause severe behavior problems, can in many instances be treated effectively. Another difficulty that sometimes goes undiagnosed and untreated is depression (Zarit, 1980). Older depressed persons are often regarded by therapists as too old to change, so no treatment is undertaken to alter this potentially reversible situation (Ray et al., 1985). Matching the appropriate treatment to the needs of the elderly can improve both physical and mental functions. The clinician needs to acquire knowledge of aging, cultural variability, and ethnicity factors that influence blacks functioning in the family, both internally and externally in later life (Chunn et al., 1983).

Ethnosystems Approach

For the family therapist and other professional clinicians, the most important part of ethnicity training in later life involves the elderly understanding their own ethnic identity and manner of aging in a differential way. Thus, they can more efficiently and effectively select appropriate practice models when they understand the variety of family systems that are encountered in their work. Giordano and Pineiro-Giordano (1977) support this notion when they write that "significant gaps in theory, knowledge, and methods of dealing with ethnicity remain. There is an obvious need to develop an overall conceptual and ideological approach that integrates the ethnocultural factor in all aspects of mental health practice" (p. 17).

Thus, clinicians should consider the notion that culture may determine whether a system is a large component of a problem (Walsh, 1980). As stated earlier, if clinicians don't understand the stresses encountered by the black elderly and their families in the total environment, then interventions may be more destructive than constructive. Moreover, as long as blacks must function in two environments, then the goal of family treatment must be to enable the family scope constructively with these stresses and to counteract their pervasive influence. "Treatment must be directed toward strengthening family structure (and resources), enhancing flexibility, and reinforcing the ability of friends, community, and larger social systems to offer effective and appropriate support" (Pinderhughes, 1982, p. 114). In fact, Minuchin, Montalvo, Rosman, and Shumer (1967), in providing a useful model of short-term family therapy with multiproblem black poor families, used social services as a support system. Clinicians of this structural method move in "rapidly to shore up the family's sagging hierarchy (usually reliant on only mother or grandmother) and define the generational boundaries" (Aponte, 1974, 1976; Colon, 1980).

Thus, the ecological system therapist influences the external social system in a positive manner by directly negotiating with other organizations, like the church housing authority, nutrition programs, or social security agency (Aponte, 1976, 1979; Pinderhughes, 1982). When a family is black and poor, the social system is not an occasional concern. "Therapists must know the social service system and be willing to make contacts with various service providers and include them in family sessions when necessary" (Hines & Boyd-Franklin, 1982, p. 99).

Practitioners working with the black elderly can use several treatment approaches in addition to the ecostructural and systems models. Even though systematic guidelines for treating the black elderly are largely absent, clinicians have available a variety of potentially useful approaches. Zarit (1980) notes that direct and problem-oriented behavioral and cognitive therapies are the most effective in treating all older people with psychological problems:

> The psychological disorders of older persons are generally associated with certain habits or thoughts, and tend to be more frequent in specific contexts. Even in cases of senile dementia or other physiological disorders, behavior problems are more frequent in particular situations, and also vary depending on the affected person's habits and beliefs. By focusing on specific habits, thought, or social interactions, the clinician can have a more direct impact on what is immediately troubling the individual. (p. 119)

This direct approach is also more appealing to many older persons, who conceptualize the problems they are having as specific to their current situation and circumstances.

One advantage of a behavioral approach is that by focusing on the specific problems presented by clients and the contexts in which they occur, it is often possible to identify what factors in the person's environment are influencing them. These factors can be manipulated to lead to improvement in the presented symptoms (Pinkston & Linsk, 1984a, 1984b; Zarit, 1980).

The innovative aspects of the structural and problem-solving methods are often at odds with traditional psychodynamic theory. Sobel (1981) suggests that older persons are unable to benefit from insight-oriented therapies, often viewed as treatments of choice with younger people. However, Hines and Boyd-Franklin (1982) suggest that black clients can benefit from "talking" therapies if the therapy is problem-focused on life change events that pose adaptive challenges and are culturally sensitive for individuals and their families.

Role of Therapist

Clinicians are often faced with overwhelming socioeconomic problems when working with black families and elderly, and they must be able to negotiate the complexities of bureaucratic social service systems and become oriented with the mental health system. It takes a great deal of time and energy to get appropriate resources for the clients' needs, although clinicians should avoid taking over family responsibilities and carefully give instructions and directions that can affect change in their situation (Foley, 1975).

Hines and Boyd-Franklin (1982) offer additional suggestions on how to develop a successful role in order to work effectively with black families:

> 1. . . . therapists must be willing to expand the context of their therapy and the definition of their own role. They must be open to exploring the impact of the social, political, socioeconomic, and broader environmental conditions on the families they treat. (p. 99)
> 2. . . . communicating respect. Therapists should openly acknowledge the family's strengths. They should avoid professional jargon and relate to the family in a directive but supportive manner. Assuming familiarity with adult members before asking their permission should be avoided. The therapist who assumes the privilege of using first names prematurely may elicit unverbalized negative reactions. . . . (p. 103)
> 3. It may sometimes be desirable for the therapist to acknowledge his or her difference in ethnic background and to discuss the family's feelings on this matter early in therapy, particularly if the therapist is not Black. (p. 103)
> 4. . . . the first step for therapist is becoming familiar with the culture and accepting its rules despite the differences. (p. 103)

Finally, Dancy (1977) makes several suggestions that augment the above list in working with the black elderly, specifically:

> 1. . . . stereotype may prevent practitioners from seeing real needs, or negative attitudes may block them from establishing an essential relationship with elderly black clients or patients. An even more subtle level of stereotype influence is a tendency for some workers in the field of aging to show a crippling oversolicitude for the black elderly. . . . an overprotective practitioner may inadvertently contribute to the client's feelings of dependency and helplessness. The black elderly need to maintain a strong sense of pride, independence, and respect. . . . (p. 5)
> 2. . . . Members of minority groups have repeatedly experienced rejection from the larger society. They need to be assisted by workers . . . who can communicate and assist in a supportive and sensitive manner. (p. 5)
> 3. Practitioners who work with the elderly must assess their acceptance of their own aging. Workers who have difficulty coming to terms with their own aging may find working with the elderly a painful reminder of what they cannot accept or face about themselves. This can seriously impair the relationship between these practitioners and their clients. (p. 7)

In conclusion, the potential difficulty for the therapist is heightened when working with black families who live under oppressive life circumstances. However, the work is challenging, and the therapist, when possible, should utilize the multi-disciplinary team approach and consult with other therapists in obtaining feedback regarding planning and implementing treatment strategies.

Clinical Services

A community model of mental and physical health services includes an integration of clinical and supportive services. The incidence of physical and mental disabilities sufficiently severe to warrant home care increases with age. Few older persons have received mental health services, even from agencies such as community mental health centers, whose staff are now more sensitive about serving the needs of the black elderly and other special groups. This may partially account for the rising number of older persons entering long-term care for both black and white elderly (Redlick, 1974; Watson, 1982).

The black elderly were underrepresented among nursing-home residents relative to their proportions in the general population in 1977; of the 12% of the general population over 65 years of age, they accounted for only 6% of the nursing-home population (U.S. Department of Health, Education, and Welfare, 1979). Lower nursing-home utilization rates for elderly blacks may be related to their greater access to informal home care. A 1968 study of home care use showed that proportionately more blacks and minorities received home care than whites. The noninstitutionalized elderly in the United States aged 75 years and over who were receiving home care comprised 17% blacks and other minorities, compared with 13% white elders. Other factors affecting blacks using nursing homes include prior living arrangements, marital status, cost, reason for care, familial responsibility, and extent of kinship network.

For many black families, home-based clinical and supportive services are a viable alternative to institutionalization of elderly relatives. Often they are unaware of the resources available to them. Therapists may need to assist them in negotiating the system by arranging support and clinical services so they can be given effective assistance.

In developing a comprehensive model of community care stressing the integration of clinical and supportive services, Zarit (1980) and Glasscote, Gudeman, and Miles (1977) evaluated innovative mental health programs for the elderly and recommended that treatment may be categorized on three levels: (a) accommodation (support services for physical maintenance of the individual, including housing), (b) clinical services, and (c) preventive, support, and life-enhancing programs.

Zarit (1980) supports the expansion of traditional clinical services because "the problems of many older persons are in part the result of social circumstances or physical illness, so that successful interventions may involve such things as arranging for economic supports, helping to coordinate different aspects of medical care, finding home services for those with physical impairments, or developing an informal support network, consisting of neighbors and friends of the patient, to call or drop by at regular times, to see that everything is all right" (p. 256). Where comprehensive programs have been introduced, the need for long-term institutional care has been greatly reduced, and the programs appear to provide better quality of services that leave the clients in as much control as possible over their own lives (Zarit, 1980).

Finally, in providing viable alternatives to institutionalization so as to maximize independent functioning of the black elderly, professionals should emphasize ethnically oriented comprehensive programs, ranging from minimal aids to extensive interventions (Kahn, 1975). These clinical programs could incorporate *church*-based programs, including mental health outreach (Solomon, 1972), missionary visitation, telephone reassurance; *home*-based services, including health aids, visiting nurses, housekeeping, and behavioral family intervention with impaired elderly; *outpatient* programs of occupational and physical therapy; *mental health* programs, including individual and family psychotherapy; and a *therapeutic day-treatment* program oriented toward prevention of illness, maintenance, rehabilitation, and restoration of health and social contacts to overcome isolation associated with illness and disability (Rathbone-McCuan & Weiler, 1978).

Mapperly Hospital in Nottingham, England, has established a successful comprehensive community mental health program. By emphasizing community treatment, MacMillan (1967) found that only a small percentage of persons required continuous long-term care. In one year, for example, 439 persons were admitted for inpatient treatment, but by the end of the year only 49 were still in the hospital. Similar programs in Britain and the United States have effectively reduced long-term institutional care (Perlin & Kahn, 1968; Whitehead, 1970).

Behavioral interventions in home-based and therapeutic day programs can also reduce the

number of elderly entering long-term-care institutions. Previous research has indicated the usefulness of behavior modification both in older persons and in the families of younger persons with behavioral difficulties (Reidel, 1981). Pinkston and Linsk (1984), through the Elderly Support Project (ESP), evaluated the effectiveness of applying home-based behavioral procedures as an independent intervention with elderly persons who had a variety of behavioral and interactional problems likely to lead to institutional care. These problems included repetitive behaviors, poor self-maintenance, low rates of social activities, and bizarre conduct. The behavioral technology taught to caregivers to improve their responses to the problem behaviors of their elderly relatives proved to be helpful in treating a wide range of problems in institutions. These included self-care behaviors (Baltes & Zerbe, 1976), incontinence (Atthowe, 1972; Pinkston, Howe, & Blackman, in press), adherence to medical regimens (Dapcich-Miura & Howell, 1979), walking (MacDonald & Butler, 1974), and improving positive social activities (Hoyer, Kafer, Sampson, & Hoyer 1974; McClannahan & Risley, 1974). Researchers found the procedures valuable for promoting continued home care, improving the mental status and behavior of elderly clients, and reducing caregiver stress by offering families alternative responses.

Throughout this chapter we have offered an overview of information about the older black American, including both the ethnic and cultural roots that have shaped blacks' kin network responses to their larger environment. We have also noted the gaps in the literature addressing integrated material on ethnicity, cross-cultural counseling, and the elderly. The Elderly Support Project, a community-based intervention that includes families in the treatment of elderly individuals, is offered as an example of a treatment model using multiple levels of intervention (for a complete model, see Pinkston & Linsk, 1984, 1984b) that takes into consideration the relevant cultural and ethnic issues.

INTERVENTION METHODS

Elderly Support Project Practice Illustration

The following case illustration was achieved by combining casework practice and behavioral intervention and also considering ethnic issues. This case examines the life-style and needs of an elderly black male within his kin network. From a clinical point of view, this case is especially relevant because it illustrates how a behavioral intervention can be an ethnically sensitive model for social work practice. Moreover, it illustrates how a pratitioner places aside her own prevailing ethnocentric values and preferences and explores the meaning and significance of her client's ethnic identity, history, kin system, and surrounding community resources. Finally, it illustrates how the church as well as neighbors and the extended family all shared resources, household tasks, housing, and a role in implementing the interventions outlined below.

Mr. R., an 83-year-old black man diagnosed as having senile dementia, was referred to the Elderly Support Project by an adult day care center for the elderly. Mr. R. was originally referred to the day center by his church; however, the day center reported that they could no longer work with Mr. R. because of such behavioral problems as incontinence, confusion, and wandering.

Mr. R., a retired railroad man, lived in a small five-room apartment with his 62-year-old niece, Mrs. B., who was his primary caregiver, and his sister, who was 90 years old. A home health aide, Mrs. N., who was a friend from the family's parish, worked in the home 5 days a week while Mr. M., a young adult male neighbor living in the building, frequently provided evening and weekend respite care for Mrs. B. This neighbor referred to Mr. R. as "uncle."

Initial assessments revealed that Mr. R. was incontinent and severely disoriented. His dressing skills had deteriorated and his rate of desirable physical and social activities was low. Mr. R. had been prescribed 15 ml of Haldol by a local family physician, which appeared to be affecting his behavior. The family was referred to a hospital geriatric clinic for a medical evaluation. After receiving a comprehensive medical examination, Mr. R. was taken off this medication. This evaluation revealed no physical causes for Mr. R.'s incontinence.

Related problems included caregiver burden and poor provision of services from the community case management unit. After the family and worker made numerous attempts to contact their assigned case manager and central office, the family and worker agreed that the family's church would be a more reliable souce of help. Mrs. B., in

particular, appeared to be experiencing caregiver burden. She expressed that she was fatigued and had relinquished all participation in leisure activities. Consequently, maintenance plans for Mrs. B. included community links with a hospital therapist, church, and enrollment in exercise and calligraphy classes. Through these interventions, the clinician acted as a systems guide, helping the family arrange supportive and clinical services so that they could be given effective help. The clinician effectively avoided taking over the family's responsibilities but carefully gave instructions that could effect change in their situation.

Intervention procedures to reduce incontinence included modeling, coaching, rehearsal, social praise, stimulus control, differential attention, and reinforcement (Pinkston & Linsk, 1984). Environmental modifications, such as the placement of fluorescent tapes and arrows on the floor and walls, provided the cues Mr. R. needed to find his way from the bedroom to the toilet. Interventions used to increase Mr. R.'s involvement in positive activities included modeling, cueing, contracting, and social praise (Pinkston & Linsk, 1984). Here, Mr. R. chose three activities: listening to music, gardening, and conversation with the family.

When working with kin networks, implementing an intervention can become complex as a result of the shared caregiving responsibilities. Mr. R.'s caregivers' work schedules varied, and they arranged their hours with Mr. R. accordingly. In response to this problem, the practitioner made efforts to arrange sessions where all caregivers were present. However, scheduling group meetings failed, so the worker began to train each caregiver individually. For the most part, Mrs. N. received the greatest amount of training due to availability and frequent contact with the client. Possibly as a result, she became the most reliable data collection and behavior change agent.

The results of the intervention were as follows:
Incontinence: In Figure 26.1, it can be seen that Mr. R.'s incidences of incontinence declined from an average daily frequency of .4 to .27 occurrences per week. Independent toilet use after the intervention had been implemented increased from an average daily frequency of 1.14 to 2.22 times per week.

Positive Activities: Figure 26.2 illustrates that during baseline this client engaged in an average daily frequency of 1.15 activities, whereas after the intervention an average daily frequency of 4.14 activities occurred per week. Figure 26.3 rep-

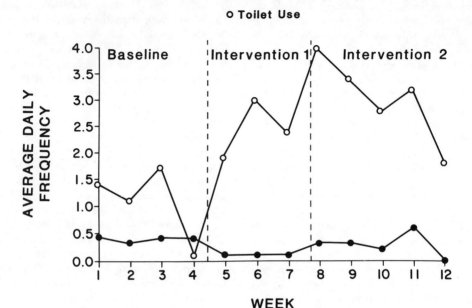

Figure 26.1 Mr. R.'s urination behavior.

resents the weekly occurrence of conversation between the client and his family. Total communication and conversations with the family had increased from an average of 24 conversations per week to a weekly average of 79. Using music as an activity initially failed. However, during a follow-up visit, Mrs. B. reported that when she changed Mr. R.'s Duke Ellington tape to gospel singer Mahalia Jackson, Mr. R. began to use the tape recorder to listen to music. Moreover, a follow-up 2 years later revealed that Mr. R. had been reintegrated into the day center.

Implications

The implication for clinical programs is that interventions should be broadly based and emphasize community services and ongoing support. Clinicians and policymakers willing to incorporate this comprehensive approach to the treatment of the black elderly should consider paying particular attention to the ecological perspective and broaden clinical services to include the church and family.

It is important that therapists expand their defi-

nitions of family and caregiver roles and embrace the notion that the majority of black families are embedded in a complex kinship network of blood and nonrelated persons and an ecological community. It is apparent that the culture and kinship patterns of many black families provide strong support for caring for impaired or ill elderly, and clinicians should make every effort to be aware of these variables and how they influence planning and delivering services. The resulting benefits to the family will include an observable way to measure progress with a method that is personalized to their environmental needs and skills.

Finally, in an effort to strengthen this model and obtain data on how ethnicity impacts outcome, the Elderly Support Project's new research initiatives utilized the Older Americans Resources and Services (OARS) instrument, which includes instruments for informal supports, for example, kinship ties, quality and density, and church supports.

Other Programs

Therapeutic day programs, often referred to as day care centers, social day care centers, and geri-

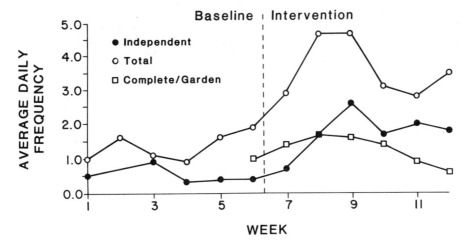

Figure 26.2 Mr. R.'s participation in positive activities including gardening, listening to music, and family conversations.

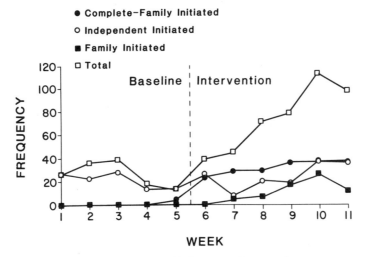

Figure 26.3 Mr. R.'s weekly frequency of conversations.

atric day programs, have expanded dramatically in the past 10 years. Day care is available to older people who have some mental and/or physical impairment but who can remain in the community if support services assist them in more independent functioning. Generally, these centers are appealing to black families because they are accessible, free or economically affordable, and provide transportation and meals. Services range from supplying appropriate social functioning and networking with other mental health services to recreation, speech, physical therapy, and counseling.

In addition to coordinated family and day care center resources, the resources of the church can be integrated in a consistent way to enhance the quality of life for older clients and reduce confu-

sion, increase positive activities, and increase the opportunity for clients to receive positive consequences for their behaviors.

Religion, which sometimes fortifies the ethnic identity of the elderly and is a source of strength in times of stress, is ignored by therapists (McGoldrick, 1982). As stated previously, religion has been a major formal institution, source of status, and community support available to black families, particularly the elderly. Therefore, they are more likely to turn to religion before they think of therapy to resolve their problems (McGoldrick, 1982). Thus, a therapist's greatest resource to mobilize a religiously oriented family with an impaired elderly member may be the minister or friends from the church group.

As stated above, it is crucial that any clinical program designed to assist the black elderly be broadly based and emphasize community services and ongoing support. It is important not to move directly to medication or psychotherapy before establishing the degree to which individuals are supported by their families and community agencies. Inadequate personal care, nutrition, and social isolation may lead to behaviors often treated by medication, psychotherapy, and institutional care rather than direct environmental intervention. The first line of assessment is to understand the overall life situation of individuals, and whether or not their current social and physical needs are being met.

Further, it is important to understand the historical significance of what it has meant to be a member of a group that has experienced poverty and discrimination, in order for clinicians to be empathic and sensitive to the needs of the black elderly.

Acknowledgements—The authors wish to express their appreciation to Jaime Roberts, administrative assistant at the University of Chicago's School of Social Service Administration, for assistance in the preparation of this chapter. The research for the case illustration was supported by the National Institute on Aging (Grant Number R01AG0212).

REFERENCES

Agree, E. M. (1985). A portrait of older minorities. In *Minorities affairs initiative: Population research*. Washington, DC: American Association of Retired Persons.

Allen, J. A. (1983). Mental health, service delivery in institutions, and the minority aged. In R. L. McNeeley & J. N. Cohen (Eds.), *Aging in minority groups*. Beverly Hills, CA: Sage.

Aponte, H. J. (1974). Psychotherapy for the poor: An eco-structured approach to treatment. *Delaware Medical Journal, X*, 1–7.

Aschenbrenner, J. (1975). *Lifelines: Black families in Chicago*. New York: Holt, Rinehart and Winston.

Atchley, R. C. (1977). *Social forces in later life*. Belmont, CA: Wadsworth.

Atthowe, J. (1972). Controlling nocturnal enuresis in severely disabled and chronic patients. *Behavior Therapy, 3*, 232–239.

Baltes, M. M., & Zerbe, M. B. (1976). Independent training in nursing home residents. *Gerontologist, 16*, 428–432.

Billingsley, A. (1968). *Black families in white America*. Englewood Cliffs, NJ: Prentice-Hall.

Bullough, V. L., & Bullough, B. (1982). *Health care for the other Americans*. New York: Appleton-Century-Crofts.

Butler, R. N. (1969). Ageism: Another form of bigotry. *Gerontologist, 9*, 243–246.

Butler, R. N. (1975). Psychiatry and the elderly: An overview. *American Journal of Psychiatry, 132*, 893–900.

Butler, R. N., & Lewis, M. I. (1973). *Aging and mental health: Positive psychosocial approaches*. St. Louis, MO: C. V. Mosby.

Butler, R. N., & Lewis, M. I. (1982). *Aging and mental health*. St. Louis, MO: C. V. Mosby.

Butler, R. N., & Sullivan, L. G. (1963). Psychiatric contact with the community-resident emotionally disturbed elderly. *Journal of Nervous and Mental Disease, 137*, 180–186.

Campbell, S. (1979). Delayed mandatory retirement and the working woman. *Gerontologist, 19*, 257–263.

Cannon, M. S., & Locke, B. Z. (1976, December). *Being black is detrimental to one's mental health: Myth or reality?* Paper presented at the W. E. B. Dubois Conference on Black Populations, Atlanta University, Atlanta, GA.

Cantor, M. H. (1979). The informal support system of New York's inner city elderly: Is ethnicity a factor? In D. E. Gelfand & A. J. Kutzik (Eds.), *Ethnicity and aging*. New York: Springer.

Carkuff, R. R., & Pierce, R. (1970). Differential effects of therapists' race and social class upon patient depth of self exploration in the initial interview. *Journal of Counseling Psychology, 31*, 632–634.

Chatters, L. M., Taylor, R. J., & Jackson, J. S. (1985). Size and composition of the informal helper networks of elderly blacks. *Journal of Gerontology, 40*, 605–614.

Chatters, L. M., Taylor, R. J., and Jackson, J. S. (1986). Aged blacks' choices for an informal helper network. *Journal of Gerontology, 41*, 94–100.

Chunn, J. C., II., Dunston, P. J., & Ross-Sheriff, F. (1983). *Mental health and people of color: Curriculum development and change*. Washington, DC: Howard University Press.

Cohen, G. (1976). Mental health services and the elderly: Needs and options. *American Institute of Psychiatry, 133* (1) 65–68.

Collins, J. L., Rickman, L. E., & Mathura, C. B. (1980). Frequency of schizophrenia and depression in a Black inpatient population. *Journal of the National Medical Association, 9*, 851–856.

Colon, F. (1980). The family life cycle of the multiproblem poor family. In E. A. Carter & M. McGoldrick (eds.), *The family life cycle: A framework for family therapy*. New York: Gardner.

Crawford, F. (1960). Variations between Negroes and whites in concepts of mental illness and its treatment. *Annals of the New York Academy of Sciences, 84* (17), 918–937.

Dancy, J. (1977). *The black elderly: A guide for practitioners*. Ann Arbor, MI: University of Michigan–Wayne State University Institute of Gerontology.

Dapcich-Miura, E., & Howell, M. F. (1979). Contingency management of adherence to a complex medical regimen in an elderly heart patient. *Behavior Therapy, 10*, 193–201.

Foley, V. (1975). Family therapy with black disadvantaged families: Some observations on roles, communications, and techniques. *Journal of Marriage and Family Counselling, 1*, 29–38.

Freud, S. (1904). On psychotherapy. In *Collected Papers* (Vol. 1). London: Hogarth Press.

Germaine, C. (1979, December). *Systems theory, ego psychology and social work practice.* Paper presented at meeting of the Massachusetts Chapter of the National Association of Social Workers, Boston, MA.

Giordano, J., & Pineiro-Giordano, G. (1977). *The ethnocultural factor in mental health, literature review and bibliography.* New York: Institute on Pluralism and Group Identity of the American Jewish Committee.

Glasscote, R., Gudeman, J. E., & Miles, D. G. *Creative mental health services for the elderly.* Washington, DC: Joint Information Service.

Greeson, A. D. (1978, May). *Creativity, mental healthiness and the black aged person: Toward a heuristic model of clinical socio-intervention.* Paper presented at the Sixth Annual Conference of the National Center on Black Aged, Dayton, OH.

Gurland, B. J., & Cross, P. S. (1982). Epidemiology of psychopathology in old age. *Psychiatric Clinics of North America, 5,* 11–26.

Hagerstad, G. O. (1981). Problems and promises in social psychology of intergenerational relations. In R. Fogel, E. Hatfield, S. Kiesler, & E. Shanas (Eds.), *Aging: Stability and change in the family.* New York: Academic.

Harris, O., & Balgopal, P. (1980). Interviewing with the black family. In C. Jansen & O. Harris (Eds.), *Family treatment in social work.* Itasca, IL: Peacock.

Hartman, A., & Laird, J. (1983). *Family-centered social work practice.* New York: Free Press.

Hawkins, B. (1976). Social participation of the Black elderly in two communities. Unpublished Ph.D. dissertation, Brandeis University, Waltham, MA.

Hawkins, B. (1978). Mental health of the black aged. In L. Gary (Ed.), *Mental health: A challenge to the black community.* Philadelphia: Dorrance.

Hendricks, J., & Hendricks, C. D. (1977). *Aging in mass society: Myths and realities.* Cambridge, MA: Winthrop.

Hildreth, G. J., & Dilworth-Anderson, P. (1986). Family ties of black Americans. In D. Baptiste & L. Johnson (Eds.), *Studies and essays about minority families in America.* Unpublished manuscript.

Hill, R. B. (1971). *The strength of black families.* New York: Emerson Hall.

Hill, R. B. (1977). *Informal adoption among black families.* Washington, DC: National Urban League, Research Department.

Hines, P. M., & Boyd-Franklin, N. (1982). Black families. In M. McGoldrick, J. K. Pearce, & J. Giordano (Eds.), *Ethnicity and family therapy.* New York: Guilford.

Hirsch, C. (1972). A review of findings on social and economic conditions of low-income black and white aged in Philadelphia. In *Proceedings of the research conference on minority group aged in the south* (pp. 63–91). Durham, NC: Duke University Medical Center.

Hollingshead, A. B., & Redlich, F. C. (1953). Social stratification and psychiatric disorders. *American Sociological Review, 18,* 163–169.

Hollingshead, A. B., & Redlich, F. C. (1958). *Social class and mental illness.* New York: Wiley.

Hoyer, W. J., Kafer, R. A., Simpson, S. C., & Hoyer, F. W. (1974). Reinstatement of verbal behavior in elderly clients using operant procedures. *Gerontologist, 14,* 149–152.

Jackson, J. J. (1970). Aged Negroes: Their cultural departures and statistical stereotypes and rural–urban differences. *Gerontologist, 10,* 140–145.

Jackson, J. J. (1972). Kinship relations among older Negro Americans. *Journal of Social and Behavioral Science, 16,* 8–17.

Jackson, J. J. (1980). *Minorities and aging.* Belmont, CA: Wadsworth.

Jackson, J. J. (1981). Urban black Americans. In A. Harwood (Ed.), *Ethnicity and medical care.* Cambridge, MA: Harvard University Press.

Jackson, J. S., Tucker, M., & Bowman P. J. (1982). Conceptual and methodological problems and survey research on black Americans. In W. T. Liu (Ed.), *Issues in minority research* 11–38. Chicago, IL: Asian–American Mental Health Center.

Jackson, M., & Wood, J. L. (1976). *Aging in America: Implications for the black aged.* Washington, DC: National Council on the Aging.

Kadushin, A. (1957). Opposition to referral for psychiatric treatment. *Social Work, 14,* 81–83.

Kahn, R. L. (1975). The mental health system and the future aged. *Gerontologist, 15* (1), 24–31.

Kalish, R. A. (1971). A gerontological look at ethnicity, human capacities, and individual adjustment. *Gerontologist* (Spring), 78–87.

Kart, C. S. (1981). *The realities of aging.* Boston: Allyn & Bacon.

Kramer, M. (1977). *Psychiatric services and the changing institutional scene 1950–1955.* U.S. Department of Health and Human Services, National Institute on Mental Health (Series B, No. 12, 24–25, 32–33, 38–39). Washington, DC: U.S. Government Printing Office.

Kramer, M., Taube, A., & Redick, R. N. (1973). Patterns of use of psychiatric facilities by the aged: Past, present and future. In C. Eisdorfer & M. Lawton (Eds.), *The psychology of adult development and aging.* Washington, DC: American Psychological Association.

Kreuger, G. (1977). *Financing of mental health care of the aged.* Paper Prepared under the National Institute of Mental Health (NIMH) contract for the Committee on Mental Health and Mental Illness of the Elderly.

Lawton, M. The aged resident of the inner city. *Gerontologist, 7,* 277–283.

Lawton, M. P., & Gottesman, L. E. (1974). Psychological services to the elderly. *American Psychologist, 29,* 689–693.

Lindsay, I. B. (1971). *Multiple hazards of age and race: The situation of aged black in the U.S.* Washington, DC: U.S. Government Printing Office.

Lowenthal, M., & Frier, M. (1967). The elderly ex-mental patient. *International Journal of Psychiatry, 13,* 103–106.

Maas, J. P. (1972). Incidence and treatment variations between Negroes and Caucasians in mental illness. In D. G. Bromley & C. F. Longine, IV (Eds.), *White racism and black Americans.* Cambridge, MA: Schenkman.

MacDonald, M. L., & Butler, A. K. (1974). Reversal of helplessness: Producing walking behavior in nursing home wheelchair residents using behavior modification procedures. *Journal of Gerontology, 29,* 94–101.

MacMillan, D. (1967). Problems of a geriatric mental health service. *British Journal of Psychiatry, 113,* 175–181.

Manney, J. D. (1974). Aging in American society: An examination of concepts and issues. Ann Arbor, MI: University of Michigan–Wayne State University Institute of Gerontology.

Martin, E. P., & Martin, J. M. (1978). *The black extended family.* Chicago: University of Chicago Press.

McAdoo, H. (1979). Black kinship. *Psychology Today, 12,* 67–69.

McCaslin, R., & Calvert, W. R. (1975). Social indications in black and white: Some ethnic considerations in delivery of service to the elderly. *Journal of Gerontology, 30* (1), 66–72.

McClannahan, L. E., & Risley, T. R. (1974). Designs of living environments for nursing home residents: Recruiting attendance in activities. *Gerontologist, 14,* 236–240.

McGoldrick, M. (1982). Ethnicity and family therapy: An overview. In M. McGoldrick, J. K. Pearce, & J. Giordano (Eds.), *Ethnicity and family therapy.* New York: Guilford.

McNeeley, R. L., & Cohen, J. N. (Eds.) (1983). *Aging in minority groups.* Beverly Hills, CA: Sage.

Minuchin, S., Montalvo, B., Rosman, B. L., & Shumer, R. (1967). *Families of the slums.* New York: Basic Books.

Neugarten, B. L., & Weinstein, K. K. (1968). The changing American grandparent. In B. L. Neugarten (Ed.), *Middle age and aging: A reader in social psychology.* Chicago: University of Chicago Press.

The oil crises (May 22, 1985). *New York Times,* p. 45.

Perlin, S., & Kahn, R. L. (1968). A mental health center in a general hospital. In L. J. Duhl & R. L. Leopold (Eds.), *Mental health and urban social policy: A casebook of community actions.* San Francisco: Jossey-Bass.

Pinderhughes, E. (1982). Afro-American families and the victim system. In M. McGoldrick, J. K. Pearce, & J. Giordano (Eds.), *Ethnicity and family therapy.* New York: Guilford.

Pinkston, E. M., Howe, M. W., & Blackman, D. K. (in press). Behavioral management of urinary incontinence of the elderly. *Journal of Social Service Research.*

Pinkston, E. M., & Linsk, N. L. (1984). *Care of the elderly: A family approach.* Elmsford, NY: Pergamon.

Puner, M. (1974). *To the good life: What we know about growing old.* New York: Universe Books.

Rathbone-McCuan, E., & Weiler, P. G. (1978). *Adult day care.* New York: Springer.

Ray, D. C., Raciti, M. A., & Ford, C. V. (1985). Ageism in psychiatrists: Associated with gender, certification, and theoretical orientation. *Gerontologist, 25,* 496–497.

Redlick, R. W. (1974). *Patterns in use of nursing homes by the aged mentally ill* (Statistical Note 107). Rockville, MD: Biometry Branch, National Institute of Mental Health.

Reidel. R. G. (1981). Behavior therapies. In C. Eisdorfer (Ed.), *Annual review of gerontology and geriatrics.* New York: Springer.

Rubenstein, D. I. (1971). *An examination of social participation found among a national sample of black and white elderly.* Unpublished manuscript.

Schorr, A. L. (1960). *Filial responsibility in the modern Ameri-*

can family. Washington, DC: U.S. Department of Health, Education and Welfare.

Seelbach, W. C., & Sauer, W. J. (1977). Filial responsibility expectations and morale among aged parents. *Gerontologist, 19,* 169–174.

Shimkin, D., Shimkin, E., & Frate, D. (1978). *The extended family in black societies.* New York: Aldine.

Simon, R. J., Fleiss, J. L., & Gurland, B. J. (1973). Depression and schizophrenia in hospitalized black and white mental patients. *Archives of General Psychiatry, 28,* 509–512.

Sobel, E. F. (1981). Anxiety and stress in later life. In I. Kutash, L. B. Schlesinger, & associates (Eds.), *Handbook on stress and anxiety: Contemporary knowledge, theory, and treatment.* San Fransisco: Jossey-Bass.

Solomon, B. (1970). *Ethnicity, mental health, and the older black aged.* Los Angeles: University of Southern California Press.

Solomon, B. (1972). Social and protective services. In *Community service and the black elderly.* Los Angeles: Ethel Percy Andus Gerontology Center, University of Southern California.

Solomon, B. (1976). *Black empowerment.* New York: Columbia University Press.

Sowder, B. J. (1972). Socialization and determinants in the developments and modification of intergroup and intragroup attitudes and behaviors. In B. J. Sowder & J. B. Lazar, *Research problems and issues in the area of socialization.* Washington, DC: Social Research Group.

Stack, C. *All our kin: Strategies for survival in a black community.* New York: Harper & Row.

Stanford, E. P. (1978). *The elder black.* San Diego: San Diego State University Center on Aging.

Staples, R. (1977). The black American family. In C. H. Mindel & R. W. Habenstein (Eds.), *Ethnic families in America: Patterns and variations* (pp. 221–247). New York: Elsevier.

Taylor, R. J., Jackson, J. S., & Quick, A. D. (1982). The frequency of social support among black Americans: Preliminary findings from the National Survey of Black Americans. *Urban Research Review, 8,* 1–4.

Taylor, R. J. (1985). The extended family as a source of support to elderly blacks. *Gerontologist, 25,* 488–495.

Tobin, S. F., Ellor, J. W., & Anderson-Ray, S. M. (1986). *Enabling the elderly: Religious institutions within the community service system.* New York: State University of New York.

Townsend, P. (1976). Integration and family. In R. C. Atchley & M. M. Seltzer (Eds.), *The sociology of aging: Selected readings.* Belmont, CA: Wadsworth.

Troll, L. E., & Bengston, V. L. (1979). Generations in the family. In W. R. Burr, R. Hill, F. I. Nye, & I. L. Reiss (Eds.), *Contemporary theories about the family* (Vol. 1). New York: Free Press.

Troll, L., Miller, S., & Atchley, R. (1979). *Families in later life.* Belmont, CA: Wadsworth.

Urban Resources Consultants (1978). Issue paper on the minority aging. Washington, DC: Author.

U.S. Bureau of the Census (1978). The social and economic status of the black population in the United States: An historical view, 1970–1978. *Current population reports: Special studies* (Series P-23, No. 80). Washington, DC: U.S. Government Printing Office.

U.S. Bureau of the Census (1979). Persons of Spanish origin in the United States. In *Current population reports* (Series P-20, No. 339). Washington, DC: U.S. Government Printing Office.

U.S. Bureau of the Census (1982). *Money, income and poverty status of families and persons in the United States: 1981 current population report* (Series P-60, No. 134, p. 22). Washington, DC: U.S. Government Printing Office.

U.S. Bureau of the Census (1983). America in transition: An aging society. *Current population reports* (Series P-23, No. 128). Washington, DC: U.S. Government Printing Office.

U.S. Department of Health, Education and Welfare, National Center for Health Statistics (1979). Home care for persons 55 years and older, United States, July 1966–June 1968. In *National health survey* (Series 10, No. 73). Washington, DC: U.S. Government Printing Office.

U.S. Department of Health, Education, and Welfare (1979). *National Nursing Home Survey.* 1977 Summary for the U.S., Vital and Health Statistics, Nat'l Health Survey Series 13, No. 43. Washington, DC: U.S. Government Printing Office.

U.S. Senate Special Committee on Aging (1982). *Developments in aging.* Washington, DC: U.S. Government Printing Office.

Walsh, F. (1980). The family in later life. In E. A. Carter & M. McGoldrick (Eds.), *The family life cycle: A framework for family therapy.* New York: Gardner.

Walsh, F. (1983). The timing of symptoms and critical events in the family life cycle. In J. C. Hansen (Ed.), *Clinical implications of the family life cycle.* Rockville, MD: Aspen.

Watson, W. H. (1970). Body image and staff-to-resident deportment in a home for the aged. *Age and Human Development, 1* (3), 354–359.

Watson, W. H. (1980). *Informal social networks in support of elderly blacks in the blackbelt of the United States: Final report.* Washington, DC: National Center on Black Aged.

Watson, W. H. (1982). *Aging and social behavior; An introduction to social gerontology.* Belmont, CA: Wadsworth.

Watson, W. H., & Maxwell, R. J. (1977). *Human aging and dying: A study in sociocultural gerontology.* New York: St. Martin's Press.

Watson, W. H., Knox, D., & Thorne, C. (1978, November). *Informal social supports for older blacks in rural South.* Paper presented at meeting of the Gerontological Society, Dallas, TX.

Watson, H. M., Carner, E. A., & Klein, M. (1984). Underutilization of mental health professionals by community elderly. *Gerontologist, 24,* 23–30.

Whitehead, A. (1970). *In the service of old age: The welfare of psychogeriatric patients.* Baltimore, MD: Penguin Books.

Willie, C. V. (1974). The black family and social class. *American Journal of Orthopsychiartry, 44,* 50–60.

Zarit, S. H. (1980). *Aging and mental disorders: Psychological approaches to assessment and treatment.* New York: Free Press.

Chapter 27

Politics and Aging: The Gray Panthers

Maggie Kuhn

THE GRAY PANTHERS' PERSPECTIVE

Simone de Beauvoir, philosopher and author, has observed that "the issues of age challenge the whole society and put the whole society to the test." The politics of age must be understood in the societal context of our changing world, which de Beauvoir perceived so clearly.

Issues pertaining to old age and aging constitute an enormous challenge to the whole society and raise basic moral and ethical questions about social justice and the survival of our society. The problems of age are basically societal, not merely personal and individualistic. Most of us live highly private lives with family and close friends, failing to see ourselves as social beings personally imprinted by the people we live and work with, powerfully conditioned by social class and the economic forces that shape our attitudes, feelings, and behavior. These forces victimize us or empower us. They pre-dispose us to health and well-being or to sickness of mind, body, and spirit.

Instead of seeing the issue of age in a societal context, we view the aging process as one of fore-ordained personal degeneration tied to a biological clock. Medically we often distinguish between the young-old (65–74 years), the old (75–84 years), and the old-old (85 and over). These are statistical time cycles for the appearance of multiple chronic ailments or terminal diseases. We view these as *personal*, individual problems. Rarely do we see them in relation to the issues of society and its stresses and hazards.

By the very nature of the economic issues that impact on older Americans, we cannot separate local concerns from global concerns. Early retirement pressures exerted by American corporations upon workers even in midlife are directly related to corporate moves to the Third World and the loss of thousands of jobs in the United States. The industrialization and urbanization of the Third World is destabilizing tribal societies and changing life-styles and relationships.

The most obvious contemporary example of the connection between domestic and international issues is the massive attack on social programs by President Reagan and a reactionary Congress and the simultaneous burgeoning of the biggest peace-time military budget in U.S. history. The millions of dollars going to train Salvadoran and Nicara-guan troops in more effective ways to kill their neighbors are the same millions that were snatched from CETA programs, funds meant to train our neighbors in useful, peaceful skills to improve our neighborhoods and arrest the blight and decay in depressed cities. We come to realize that ageism, sexism, and racism are all social sicknesses rooted in a competitive, materialistic, economic system; they are all oppressive, divisive, dehumanizing.

With this holistic perception, we must also

include in our social analysis the link between American policy in an urban ghetto and security troops in South Africa—the anti-redlining campaigns of People's Action groups successfully exposed the lending policies of the banks that refused neighborhood loans in favor of international loans in places like South Africa. Ours is indeed *one world* and we better not divide it.

Old people have the historical perspective to see these local/global connections and speak out about them. Peace and social justice are urgent and appropriate concerns for us and for our survival as a society. They go far beyond special-interest organizing around "old folks' issues." A Gray Lobby would be divisive and contrary to the public interest. Our legacy should be a just and peaceful world.

In my retirement years I have been assessing the political roots and realities of the ageism that stereotypes, victimizes, violates, and segregates people and groups by chronological age. Ageism, like racism and sexism, is a pervasive social sickness that contributes to the fears and conflicts in late life and is extremely hazardous to mental health and physical well-being.

I am convinced that mass education is required to sensitize Americans to the evils and social consequences of ageism. But it will not be eradicated without radical social and economic change in our competitive, profit-centered, class-divided society. Personal experience, social research, and nationwide contacts with many groups and organizations have brought me to this view of our world.

In 1970, when I faced mandatory retirement at the age of 65, I was anxious and depressed. I was leaving a job that I loved for an isolated retirement, caring for my 90-year-old mother, who was wheelchair-bound by arthritis, and a 60-year-old brother with many emotional problems. They were financially and emotionally dependent on me. With reduced income and without the support of professional colleagues, I felt bereft.

To ease my anxiety, I wrote a memo to five of my friends who were in a similar situation, asking this question: "What do we do with the rest of our lives?" As we met to consider the question, it was clear that we needed one another to regroup our lives and that we were at a juncture of life when we could begin something new. We could take risks together in our own supportive community. We could reach out to others and organize for change. We could be risk takers with nothing to lose but our fears and isolation!

The memo is now in the Gray Panther archives, along with exciting records of those early years when we launched an intergenerational organization committed to social justice and peace. It was to oppose the war in Vietnam that brought us old people to stand with the young who opposed the war and resisted the draft. We participated in antiwar vigils and marches and were arrested in antidraft demonstrations. Two Gray Panthers went to Sweden to support draft resisters who had sought asylum abroad. Two Gray Panthers went to Vietnam to observe the devastating military policies of the United States in Southeast Asia.

"Age and Youth in Action" was our slogan then and it is important to us in 1987. We have successfully built a coalition of people of different ages to work not for special interests but for the larger public interest. Our priorities are not old folks' issues but issues that affect all of society. It has been gutsy and exciting, but not easy. The American political system has been rooted in compromise with and accommodation to conflicting, colliding special interests. Large organizations of older Americans have brought to the political scene what some have called *the Gray Lobby*. They have followed special interest strategies and appeals: "We the Seniors unite. We are working for *our* rights. We have earned them!"

The Gray Panthers believe that such organizing is self-serving and contrary to the interests of society and the continuity of life. The issues of age and the needs of old people will be resolved with justice and equity and compassion only by basic social and economic change in our political system, not by piecemeal services and age-segregated programs that divide the human family and perpetuate social conflict and need.

We know from our members and our social analysis that old people and children suffer the same deprivations under the Reagan administration, which has shifted billions of tax dollars from human services and education to the production of supertech missiles and military expansion around the world.

We know that many American workers (some estimate more than 70%) hate their jobs and work only for the paycheck. Many jobs are drudgery. Many are hazardous to safety and health. Many workers come to their seniority failing in health and impoverished by an inadequate, unfair pension system. They look forward to retirement as a time for release, but not as a time to regroup and begin to work for change, social justice, and peace.

The mobilization of older Americans to heal and humanize our society and make society safe for their survivors should be the goal of Gray Power. The Gray Panthers and other advocates are reaching out to organize the victims of our economic system and enlist and empower them for the public interest as well as their own!

A safe, just, and peaceful world is the legacy that we seek for those who will come after us. That's the transcending Gray Power that our hate-torn world desperately needs.

The effectiveness of present social theories, policies, and programs about old age politically supported in America has been analyzed by a growing number of social scientists. The Gray Panthers have especially appreciated the work of the sociologist Carroll Estes (1984) and her associates at the Institute on Health and Aging at the University of California. The Estes studies of the issues of age show how the political economy of aging has both personal and societal impact. How old people fare as individuals is determined by their social class, status, and income. Their health, social outlook, and relationships are shaped by these forces. The structure and operations of major social institutions—the family, the workplace, and medical and welfare institutions—are directly related to the state of our society, which is built around private enterprise, private property, and the power derived from these private pursuits.

Public policies for the aged and the distribution of public resources to assist them reflect and reinforce American class structures and differences and the power relationships operating in our competitive economic system. Robert N. Butler, the psychiatrist and educator, coined the term *ageism* to describe the societal-economic aspects of the rejection of old age. His book *Why Survive?: Growing Old in America*, a classic resource for the study of gerontology, won a Pulitzer prize in 1976.

Butler (1975) has identified six widely held myths about old age: (a) old age is a disease and pathological; (b) old age is a mindless state where cognitive processes slow down, learning stops, and so-called *senility* is inevitable; (c) old age is sexless without the capacity or the need for intimacy and love; (d) old age is useless, with obsolescent skills and irrelevant experience; (e) old age is a powerless state with increasing dependence and disinclination for activity or social involvement; and (f) all old people are alike—a homogeneous population, a class unto themselves, without diversity or external interests. The Gray Panthers are working to

eradicate these myths and bring the old and young together. The myths are destructive to people and divisive in society, but they are reinforced by our economic system.

Despite the fact that aging is a universal experience for all of us—beginning with the moment when life begins and continuing to its closure—there is widespread fear of aging, as well as self-hatred and self-deception. "It can never happen to me," "You're only as old as you feel," "I'm really 70 years young," are common expressions of these fears.

The sociologist Joseph H. Bunzel, who taught at the State University of New York until his death in 1980, stated that our society is afflicted with *gerontophobia*, defined as the unreasonable fear and irrational hatred of old people by society and the irrational psychological fear of growing old. Gerontophobia is widespread among people of all ages and classes in the United States, especially among women. The anxieties and self-hatred so characteristic of the disease are compounded and reinforced by our rigid separation of people and groups by chronological age and by the *ageism* that stigmatizes and stereotypes people by chronological age. Ageism, like sexism and racism, can be eliminated only by mass education and massive changes in society, personal attitudes, and social structures.

TWO REVOLUTIONS COLLIDE: DEMOGRAPHY AND TECHNOLOGY

From my own experience and historical perspective, we are living in the midst of two colliding revolutions: (a) the demographic revolution and (b) the technological revolution. The sweeping changes engendered by these revolutions present Americans of all ages, backgrounds, and classes with challenges that involve political and structural change. The effects of these revolutions are societal. They are also personal in terms of the basic needs of old people for adequate income, health care, and useful roles and responsibilities in our communities. They powerfully influence how we think and act, what we believe about ourselves and our world, and how we respond to issues and events.

The demographic revolution documents that more people are living longer than in any period in human history. Yet in our ageist society, old age is deemed a disaster, a problem. But in fact, the demography is a triumph of public health. It represents a reversal of the population pyramid: a small base of the numbers of children and young people, and a burgeoning number of old people at the top. In the United States today we have nearly 28 million people over 60 years of age. In 1900 the average life span was 45 years of age, and in 1985, approximately 72 years. A corresponding population change is occurring in the world population, with 291 million people over the age of 60; it is estimated that by 1990 this number will rise to 595 million and by the year 2020, to approximately 600 million, an explosive situation for developing countries!

In the United States, women outlive men: for every 100 men aged 65, there are 140 women. At age 75, for every 100 men there are 150 women. The imbalance grows with every decade. At age 85 women outnumber men 2 to 1. Loss of spouses, children, friends, and neighbors—all make women very vulnerable to depression, loneliness, and poverty.

Other societal factors that influence aging are rigid segregation by chronological age and various social theories about aging. Beginning with nursery school and ending in the isolation of the frail and old people in nursing homes, we keep the old and the young separated from each other. We do violence to the essential wholeness of life and the integrity of persons when we segregate and isolate the old and the young from the mainstream. The fabric of society is weakened. The young believe they have no future, and midlife people have little life satisfaction but much stress, frustration, and burnout.

A number of social theories have been developed in response to the demographic revolution. The Gray Panthers have assessed such current theories as the activity theory and the developmental theory and believe that we need a new theoretical base for age in this new age. Gerontologists have generally discredited the disengagement theory as a useful basis for policy. But its influence lives on. We believe that it has probably provided the rationale for mandatory retirement, the Older Americans Act, and the proliferation of age-segregated institutions and services, and has influenced the growth of retirement communities where no children are allowed.

The technological revolution has the potential for great benefits for the health and well-being of human beings everywhere, but, in the context of population change, it has created economic and political dislocation and conflict. The technologi-

cal developments of the past have been gradual. The industrial revolution in England and the United States created a whole new economy and a shift from an agrarian base to our industrial urban base. But the changes occurred over a period of 300 years. The current technological revolution brought sweeping changes in a decade. Automation put robots on assembly lines and significantly changed the nature of work from industrial production to a service society. It profoundly and directly affected older workers in the United States, changing their lives, their jobs, their status, the widened the class differences between the rich and the poor and separated young workers from old workers. There is discontinuity, even conflict, between generations.

Furthermore, super technology in offices and service organizations has computerized jobs and changed work for tens of thousands of office workers. The new computers expose the employed to new hazards. They are just beginning to organize to safeguard their health and their jobs— against strong opposition from top managers. The changes in the structure of work will have profound influence on workers in late life.

As we know, multinational corporate investment and industrialization are spreading the high technology of the Western nations to all parts of the developing world, bringing sweeping changes in their wake. Peasants have left the land and young people have left older family members for jobs in the new industries. Sanitation and living conditions have been improved, but many societies have been destabilized and are in social conflict as the traditional social fabric is torn apart.

We do not have adequate and effective structures or methods for defining what technologies are "appropriate" for the enhancement of the lives of older people, nor do we have the public will to put the decisions in place in the U.S. economic system and in the economic and social systems that are spreading to the developing world.

To summarize, shock waves of technological advances are changing lives and society. The turbulence in the wake of these changes requires the following: (a) greater public awareness of the scope of technological change, (b) thorough assessment of the effects of technological change in the lives of people over 40 by governmental and nongovernmental groups, (c) analysis of the roots of technological change in the United States and elsewhere in our profit-centered economic system, (d) concern for the long-range social consequences of the technological revolution both in and outside the United States, and (e) some agreement on how new technologies can be made appropriate and socially responsible for the common good and humane and peaceful ends.

Thus, I see that technological change linked with demographic change introduces new elements of social change that profoundly influence the personal lives of old people in the United States and throughout the world, altering their roles and status, widening social class division between the rich and the poor, and separating the old from the young.

The demographic revolution has had many different responses. A positive view (my own) is that it is a triumph of survivorship and adaptation to change. My generation has lived through and initiated more changes than any other generation. The telephone, the radio, the television, are 20th-century marvels of communciation, augmented by satellite explorations of space; computers of infinite variety and transworld transport that approaches the speed of sound are other marvels of technology. They have come to be accepted realities in my lifetime.

The negative response to long life deems growing old and being old a problem. Old age is a distasteful condition that prompts many to deny their age, disguise it by hair dyes and facelifts, lie about it. The myths about age described by Butler (1975) are pervasive and even epidemic, particularly in medical circles.

An economic system that values profits and worships the bottom line needs these myths to support early retirement and the hiring of young workers at lower salaries; such a society is not a healthy society, nor is it a stable human society. It generates competition between old and young workers, which could lead to conflict.

In 1982 the mayor of Philadelphia appointed a Commission to Study the Health Care System of the City. The commission worked for 2 years through 11 committees and reported to the mayor in June 1984. I had the privilege of serving on the commission, along with physicians, nurses, social workers, planners, and consumers. Environmental hazards were studied, as well as health and safety factors. Over 400 recommendations were presented and rated for priority. An important by-product was the opportunity for members to know and interact with one another and to plan for continuing collaboration.

Mental health services were evaluated by the commission, and it was found that the deinstitutionalization of mental patients had put thousands of older patients literally on the streets. Little or no efforts had been made to involve community mental health centers in continuing counsel and assistance. Many were warehoused in boarding homes that were not licensed or inspected. Community mental health centers had limited or no outreach programs. Older patients had to come on their own. As a consequence, the average over 60 patient load was about 4%.

Philadelphia, New York, Washington, and other metropolitan centers are becoming aware and concerned about the homeless. The "bag ladies and vent men" roam the streets by the thousands. They are uncounted and destitute. Many are former patients of mental hospitals that closed their geriatric wards.

What was intended as an enlightened "humane" policy has had immense social consequences for American cities. Deinstitutionalization is a glaring example of the lack of long-range planning and coordination of health and human services. It also typifies what happens when our society gives priority to so-called "cost effectiveness." This failed policy began in California when Ronald Reagan discovered what it could save the state in welfare costs. The human suffering and malaise generated by the policy is presently beyond limits of relief or cure.

In a societal context we see new coalitions and networks of consumers of Medicare raising questions and challenging the medical establishment and its policies and presumptions. The Gray Panthers, among these challengers, have made health care a national priority for more than a decade. Alternatives to scientific medicine are gaining national support. Public and private agencies and organizations are campaigning against the spiraling costs of health services. The Washington Business Group on Health has brought together a number of America's largest corporations to fight the increased costs of health benefits with campaigns for health promotion. Patients and doctors are sharing the same apprehension about the corporatization of medical care by powerful multinational chains of hospitals, nursing homes, and providers of home services. Health care for profit seems to be the order of the day.

These developments must be recognized as structural developments, and, hopefully, patients and professionals, the people who are concerned about mental health and illness, will collaborate. They transcend present biomedical research and address society itself.

RESPONSE TO REVOLUTION

How do we respond to the challenge of the demographic and technological revolutions in the 1980s? I believe that we need a fundamental understanding of the intimate connection between our private lives and personal needs, on the one hand, and the complex structures and forces in society, on the other. Our personal problems require involvement in some aspect of social change to be fully resolved, and the public will to tackle societal issues, like the threat of nuclear war, U.S. intervention in Central America, and unemployment and hunger, can be mobilized only when we perceive how these issues affect human beings.

The injustices of our present American health care system illustrate some of the responses needed in this age of change.

We have privatized and individualized sickness in our country. We traditionally isolate patients from their social environment. We examine and test and treat them in clinics, doctors' offices, and hospitals, quite removed from where they live and work. The examining professional looks at our body parts and fluids, tests our reflexes and heartbeat, conducts a brain scan, works out a medical treatment plan and diagnosis—all without direct observation and firsthand knowledge of our human habitat and the factors and forces that predispose us to health or sickness. Furthermore, American gerontologists have been inclined to consider aging as a biological process of decline and to link old age with the need for medical care. The medicalization of old age has proven to be costly to people personally and to society as a whole. Without the knowledge of societal-environmental hazards to physical and mental health and well-being, I dare to observe that the diagnosis and the treatment are incomplete and inadequate. Holistic/social/economic/political forces must be taken into account and the energies and attention of health professionals given to the healing of our sick society.

Some parts of our society are dead and dying— blighted, declining neighborhoods; rotting slums; dead-end jobs; dying industries; exploited, worked-out farmland; polluted streams and lakes. Deadened politics, Reaganomics, and Cold War

games have eradicated many social programs and put the old and the young at risk.

For more than a decade the Gray Panthers have given priority to health care and the establishment of a national health service. We view health as a basic human right for all, not a privilege for a few. We recognize the need to correlate private health care with public health measures and programs of sanitation, waste disposal, as well as with occupational health and safety, safe, decent housing, full employment. Health in old age is the test of such coordination. We are working to secure and maintain the health of the body, mind, spirit, and environment in which we live and work. We challenge and oppose the expensive, fragmented, specialized individualistic systems that provide "sickness" care. Our analysis shows ways in which the current health programs in the United States reflect societal attitudes and myths about growing old. These societal biases are especially prevalent in the response to the mental and emotional needs of the aged.

In many instances, mental illness is deemed untreatable, and inevitable. In 1978 I served on a panel on Mental Health and the Elderly (part of a Commission on Mental Health appointed by President Carter), which examined the correlation between physical and mental health. It found that much so-called *senility* is preventable and treatable and is reversible if promptly diagnosed. We also discovered that over 100 physiological conditions could impair the supply of blood to the brain and result in irreversible brain damage. Among these conditions were malnutrition, constipation, an undiagnosed heart attack, or kidney infection. We reviewed the curriculum of leading medical schools, and found that courses in geriatrics and gerontology were shockingly absent. Our panel also observed the age range of patients in community health centers and in the private practice of psychiatrists. People 65 years of age and older made up about 4% of the patients served in our community mental health centers and about 2% of the patients under private psychiatric care. Conclusion: concern for the mental health of the elderly and the poor has been ignored and neglected.

My generation has not been conditioned to seek psychiatric counsel. "Who, me? I'm not crazy, I'm just depressed" is the frequent response. The investigative research we have done in nursing homes has shown the improper and ill-advised use of drugs. "Chemical restraints" turn out to be chemical lobotomies. Butler has repeatedly called for research and reforms in medical education to provide mental health care so urgently needed. With wider public awareness of the devastating effects of Alzheimer's disease, there is now a long overdue interest in the research and treatment procedures advocated by Butler. Change comes slowly, and requires persistence and patience on the part of its advocates.

MEDICATION, MENTAL HEALTH, AND OLDER AMERICANS

Societal attitudes and myths about age have strongly influenced the practice of medicine and the attitudes of health professionals, especially doctors.

As recently as 1984, Coccaro and Miles made the following assessment of the attitudes of the medical profession toward the care of the elderly:

> Over the past decade and a half no fewer than 17 surveys have documented the presence of negative (or indifferent) attitudes toward geriatric care or education among students, educators, and practitioners of medicine. These attitudes, which resemble those of society in general, are often thought to be the cause of suboptimal geriatric health care and of the inertia of medical educators in incorporating a gerontologic/geriatric knowledge base into the medical school curriculum. (p. 762)

These attitudes are reinforced by an inadequate knowledge base in geriatrics in general and geriatric pharmacology in particular. Steel (1984) notes that in 11 standard texts on history taking and physical diagnosis only one of the numerous examples dealt with a person over 65, a 67-year-old man. There is no reason to believe that psychiatric medicine is any more attentive to the problems of the elderly. It should, therefore, come as no surprise that the combination of negative attitudes and an inadequate knowledge base results in a variety of paradoxical, inappropriate modes of prescribing for elderly patients with mental health problems.

Margaret Ferry, a member of our Health Task Force, completed a doctoral thesis on medication, mental health, and the elderly. Her analysis addressed the negative attitudes held by physicians about old age and their older patients, attitudes reinforced by inadequate knowledge about geriatrics and, perhaps most notably, about geriatric pharmacology. The study shows how bio-pharmaceutical properties affects the rate and extent to which an active drug is absorbed into a patient's bloodstream. The extent and rate of absorption are of the greatest importance in prescribing a drug. Using a different form of the drug with a different rate of absorption can produce a toxic reaction.

Improvements in technological and biological research have shown that children and old people differ biologically both from each other and from young adult patients. This research now enables us to analyze minute quantities of a substance and its interaction with the body. It has significant implications for the practice of clinical medicine.

Although such age differences hold obvious relevance to the practice of clinical medicine, they have been virtually ignored by clinical practitioners. Instead, lack of attention to age differences in drug effects has lead to grossly inappropriate use of psychotropic drugs with elderly patients. Psychotropic drugs are over-prescribed in some cases, and in other cases not prescribed even when indicated. Perlick and Atkins (1984), for example, observed that among depressed patients, the older patients are perceived as less severely depressed and therefore less responsive to antidepressant treatment than younger patients. Thus, in the case of depression, treatment for old people may be less aggressive than for the young.

Ironically, when psychotropic treatment is provided, it is often inappropriately administered, in doses that function as chemcial straitjackets rather than health-enhancing tools. This type of treatment is typically aimed at maximizing convenience of institutional caretakers rather than enhancing the well-being of the patient (Whittington, Petersen, & Beer, 1978). Sadly, families often conspire unwittingly in attempts to reduce the older persons range of function, in order to promote docility and thus avoid subsequent embarrassment.

Moreover, drug treatment with the elderly has been used as an end in itself, rather than a means by which to return the person to a more optimal level of functioning. Too often, it is the sole treatment effort. Zimmer, Watson, and Treat (1984) found that in their random sample of nursing home residents, 58% of those who displayed a behavior problem were treated with psychoactive drugs, yet only 15% had received a psychiatric evaluation since his or her admission. It is important to underscore the potency of these drugs. A short list of the possible side-effects of trifluoperazine hydrochloride (Stelazine), a classic antipsychotic, reads like a litany of terrors. Included are: persistent tardive dyskinesia, grand mal and petit mal convulsions, catatonic-like states, cardiac arrest, and hypotension (sometimes fatal). Thus, use of these drugs without careful consideration of the costs and benefits to the patient is irresponsible at best. Davidson (1973) eloquently summarized the problem:

> For the elderly patient, the paradox remains. Expertly prescribed by caring physicians, medications may be life-saving and life-enhancing. In the hands of the hasty and uncaring, "an appropriate prescription" reduces the frail but functioning human being to a chairfast, confused, incontinent wreck. (p. 634)

In the early 1970s, two young Gray Panthers were at work as advocates in the Health Law Project of the University of Pennsylvania. They observed the need to adopt a humane patient and consumer-oriented set of hospital regulations. After more than 8 years of discussion and controversy, new regulations were finally adopted. Clearly there was continuing evidence of the need for interpretation and affirmation of the rights of patients in hospitals and extended-care facilities.

Despite efforts of the Hospital Association of Pennsylvania to discourage the bill, a Patients' Bill of Rights was established and adopted by the commonwealth of Pennsylvania. The legislature authorized the Department of Health to promote and enforce the bill through "all lawful and appropriate means," and instructed the hospital governing bodies to establish a Patients' Bill of Rights not less in substance and coverage than the minimal Patients' Bill of Rights provided by the state.

The Gray Panthers in different parts of the country have monitored the use of the Patients' Bill of Rights—where it is displayed and how it is interpreted to patients and staff. Implementation has been minimal. Seldom is the bill displayed where it can be seen and easily read, and it is seldom explained to patients.

Here are the 22 provisions of the Patients' Bill of Rights:

1. A patient has the right to respectful care given by competent personnel.
2. A patient has the right, upon request, to be given the name of his attending physician, the names of all other physicians directly participating in his care, and the names and functions of other health care persons having direct contact with the patient.
3. A patient has the right to every consideration of his privacy concerning his own medical care program. Case discussion, consultation examination, and treatment are considered confidential and should be conducted discreetly.
4. A patient has the right to have all records pertaining to his medical care treated as confidential, except as otherwise provided by law or third-party contractual arrangements.
5. A patient has the right to know what hospital rules and regulations apply to his conduct as a patient.
6. The patient has the right to expect emergency procedures to be implemented without unnecessary delay.
7. The patient has the right to good quality care and high professional standards that are continually maintained and reviewed.
8. The patient has the right to full information, in layman's terms, concerning his diagnosis, treatment, and prognosis, including information about alternative treatments and possible complications. When it is not medically advisable to give such information to the patient, the information shall be given on his behalf to the patient's next of kin or other appropriate person.
9. Except for emergencies, the physician must obtain the necessary informed consent prior to the start of any procedure or treatment, or both. Informed consent is defined in p. 103 of the Health Care Services Malpractice Act (40 P.S. P. 1301.103).
10. A patient, or in the event the patient is unable to give informed consent, a legally responsible party has the right to be advised when a physician is considering the patient as a part of a medical care research program or donor program, and the patient, or legally responsible party, must give informed consent prior to actual participation in such a program. A patient, or legally responsible party, may, at any time, refuse to continue in any such program to which he has previously given informed consent.
11. A patient has the right to refuse any drugs, treatment, or procedure offered by the hospital, to the extent permitted by law, and a physician shall inform the patient of the medical consequences of the patient's refusal of any drugs, treatment, or procedure.

12. A patient has the right to assistance in obtaining consultation with another physician at the patient's request and own expense.
13. A patient has the right to medically appropriate services without discrimination based upon his race, color, religion, sex, sexual preference, national origin, or source of payment.
14. The patient who does not speak English should have access, where possible, to an interpreter.
15. The hospital shall provide the patient, upon request, access to all information contained in his medical records, unless access is specifically restricted by the attending physician for medical reasons or is prohibited by law.
16. The patient has the right to expect good management techniques to be implemented within the hospital considering effective use of the time of the patient and to avoid the personal discomfort of the patient.
17. When medically permissible, a patient may be transferred to another facility only after he or his next of kin or other legally responsible representative has received complete information and an explanation concerning the need for an alternative to such a transfer. The institution to which the patient is to be transferred must first have accepted the patient for transfer.
18. The patient has the right to examine and receive a detailed explanation of his bill.
19. The patient has a right to full information and counseling on the availability of known financial resources for his health care.
20. A patient has the right to expect that the health care facility will provide a mechanism whereby he is informed upon discharge of his continuing health care requirements following discharge, and the means for meeting them.
21. A patient has the right of access to an individual or agency who is authorized to act on his behalf to assert or protect the rights set out in this section. This person shall not be employed by the health care facility.
22. A patient has the right to be informed of his rights at the earliest possible moment in the course of his hospitalization.

We want hospital administrators to display these rights and interpret them as patients are admitted. As American hospitals operate on the proscriptive payment system, based on diagnostic related groups, patients need to be their own advocates to secure the treatment they require.

Since the Gray Panthers have been involved with the issues of age and strategies for stamping out ageism, we have observed how gerontologists frequently regard aging as a biological process of decline and decreptitude, to be equated with sickness and the need for medical care. We oppose the medicalization of late life, just as we oppose the individualistic biomedical methods of care and treatment that ignore the environmental, social, and occupational sources of disease, as well as the political and economic systems that shape our lives and societal relationships.

Social status and class do influence health and well-being. Children born into poverty are often nutritionally deprived. Unhealthy living and working environments in youth and midlife predispose to poor health in old age.

Social class and income also determine access to health care. We have seen urban public hospitals closing across the country and nonprofit hospitals taken over by the ever more powerful chains of corporate owners and operators providing health care for *profit*. With these *for-profit* developments we see the gross inequities in the health care system and the stratification of medicine that allow two-tiered care, depending on income and insurance coverage benefits (Estes, 1984).

With dismay and outrage, we recognize that health care is big business, viewed now by corporate America and government as an economic product instead of a basic human right and a social good!

To respond to such practices, the Gray Panthers Health Task Force is expanding its membership and working with a number of scholars and health policy advisers. We are studying the proscriptive payment system for hospitals based on diagnostic-rated care. Although it is still too early to analyze the social consequences, there is evidence that the hospitals have a windfall. We are developing new strategies for monitoring and patient advocacy to assess the political economy of the diagnostic-related groups, out of our concern for the right to care, and the quality of care. Who is admitted to for-profit hospitals? Who is refused care? What about discharge policies and planning? Are patients discharged before they are recovered, to meet the proscribed period of care? These are urgent questions for all of society, not only for the elderly.

Old people usually suffer from more than one ailment. The proscriptive payment system would reimburse hospitals admitting for only *one* diagnosis at a time. The Gray Panther Health Task Force questions whether the system is appropriate for care of the complex, multiple health problems of elderly populations.

As we plan our strategy for understanding and dealing with the profitization and corporatization of hospital care, we see many challenges and opportunities for building alternative models of health care: wellness centers, health co-ops, alternative forms of healing.

Our strategy will not be based on Gray Power. It will include allies from the American Medical Students Association, Nurses for Social Responsibility, and other concerned and perceptive groups that want to heal our "sickness care" system. There will be opportunity for thoughtful social criticism, as well as action and outrage! This is a new age!

OUR PRESCRIPTION: "INTERGENERATE"

The Gray Panthers have a unique perspective about young people and old people. We believe the two groups belong together and that separation has deprived us and torn apart the social fabric of society. Despite the age segregation and isolation fostered by our ageist society and codified in government statutes, the Gray Panthers have forged an intergenerational organization based on the needs and concerns that bring old people and young people together in a common strategy and search for justice and peace. It reflects our concern about what is happening to the young today. Growing up has never been easy. But these times of tumult complicate the process, and we are probing some of the pressures and forces that influence young people and make them fearful and confused about the future. Some are not so sure that they will have a future, as recent studies documenting children's fears about nuclear war have shown.

It seems all too clear that the primary institutions responsible for the nurture and training of the young—the family and the public school—are in trouble. We read daily accounts of the neglect and abuse of children, the struggle and the poverty in single-parent households. Teenage suicide has quadrupled in the last 40 years. Addiction to drugs and alcohol is on the rise, involving younger and younger children. "Are we," a colleague asked, "a nation at war with our kids?"

Ageism, like racism and sexism, is rooted in our competitive, materialistic economic system, which gives priority to profits not people. Old people and young people are marginalized in America today because both groups are deemed nonproductive. To be told "you're too young" is just as disheartening as to be told "you're too old."

The politics of the present administration have further exacerbated the ageism that stigmatizes and diminishes young and old in our society. Based on the rationale that the young don't have the experience and should be grateful to have a job, President Reagan has supported and continues to press for a substandard wage.

Reaganomics, or "voodoo" economics, as Vice President Bush once observed, has successfully made the rich richer and the poor poorer. It has increased class differences and stratifications in America, and created what may well be a permanent "underclass." It leaves little hope for minority young trapped in poverty. Forced to compete for jobs, status, and dwindling resources, young and old are pitted against one another, and the human family is divided. Recent technological changes have further separated younger workers from older workers and created conflict between them.

We have seen the commonalities and natural affinities that unite us. The bonding is not accidental: It is life! The Gray Panthers believe that life is a continuum from birth to death. It has an essential wholeness and continuity that age segregation has violated. Aging is a process and an experience human beings share with all living things, including the plants. All of us are born of seeds that are fertilized and nurtured to grow, flower, produce progeny, wither, and die. All of us are part of an amazing cycle of life to be celebrated and revered.

It has not been easy for the Gray Panthers to organize on an intergenerational basis, and follow our goal of "Age and Youth in Action." In the press and on television, the Gray Panthers are often lumped with senior organizations and regarded as senior activists and senior advocates. Some of our local networks have difficulty establishing contacts and relationships with young people. So pervasive is the separation that senior citizens' centers, retirement communities, and Golden Age Clubs have been the usual order of the day. But our continued concern for eradicating segregation and stereotyping has brought significant changes in public policy. Our perspective has changed attitudes and lives, including our own.

Month by month, year by year, we're working to close the ranks between old and young. We need each other, and we can't afford to be apart if society is to be whole.

REFERENCES

Butler, R. (1975). *Why survive?: Growing old in America*, New York: Harper & Row.

Coccaro, E. F., & Miles, A. M. (1984). The attitudinal impact of training in gerontology/geriatrics in medical school. *Journal of the American Geriatrics Society, 32*, 762–768.

Davidson, W. (1973). The hazards of drug treatment in old age. In J. C. Brockenhurst (Ed.). *Textbook of geriatric medicine and gerontology*. London: Churchill Livingstone, pp. 632–648.

Estes, C. (1984). *Political economy, health and aging*. Boston: Little & Brown.

Ferry, M. (1984). *Factors associated with physicians knowledge of prescribing for the elderly*. Unpublished dissertation. Temple University. Philadelphia, PA.

Perlick, D., & Atkins, A. (1984). Variations in the reported age of a patient: A source of bias in the diagnosis of depression and dememtia. *Journal of Consulting and Clinical Psychology, 52*, 812–820.

Steel, K. (1984). Iatrogenic disease on a medical service. *Journal of the American Geriatrics Society, 32*, 445–449.

Whittington, F. J., Petersen, D. M., & Beer, E. T. (1978, November). Drug misuse among older people. Paper presented at the meetings of the Gerontological Society of America, Dallas, TX.

Zimmer, J. G., Watson, N., & Treat, A. (1984). Behavioral problems among patients in skilled nursing facilities. *American Journal of Public Health, 74*, 1118–1121.

Chapter 28

Ethics and the Elderly

William T. O'Donohue, Jane E. Fisher, and Leonard Krasner

What kinds of ethical questions are relevant to the elderly and to the professional who interacts with the elderly? What do we know about the ethical standards of the elderly? Why might it be important to know this? Given that the elderly are sometimes religious what is the relationship between religious claims and ethical claims? Are there ethical issues unique to the elderly, in contrast to other populations of individuals? Since professionals receive training mainly in the sciences, this gives rise to questions about the relationship between factual claims of science—*is-statements*—and the normative claims of ethics—*ought-statements*. What is the relationship between professional ethics as embodied in a professional ethical code and ordinary morality? What ethical issues need concern the therapist and researcher dealing with the elderly? How can the professional properly respond to these issues?

These are the major questions that we will address in this chapter. We review empirical research when relevant, but we also present, in some detail, distinctions and arguments taken from 20th-century analytic philosophy. We proceed in this way because, as we shall argue, there is a great deal concerning ethics that the empirical investigations of science cannot answer. Further, our own view is that science and issues of ethics are intricately interrelated (Krasner & Houts, 1984). We hope to show that argumentation and conceptual analysis, the methods characteristic of analytic philosophy, can provide valuable insights into some of these questions. We present some arguments in detail not only because we think that

their conclusions are important for gerontologists and therapists, but also to illustrate a method that these professionals may use to help them investigate other ethical concerns.

Two points regarding our use of terms: By *the elderly* we mean roughly anyone who is 65 or older and we shall use the words *values* and *ethics* interchangeably.

A distinction must be made between different *kinds* of ethical questions. Ethics can be considered to have three distinct levels of discourse: *descriptive ethics*, *normative ethics*, and *metaethics* (Nielsen, 1967). Elaboration is provided below.

CONCEPTUAL FOUNDATIONS

Descriptive Ethics

Descriptive ethics is wholly empirical. It seeks to answer such questions as, What acts do people ethically value or condemn? What ethical standards do individuals use for judging acts to be ethically good or bad? Because descriptive ethics seeks empirical information, it is approached at the level of the social and biological sciences.

There appears to be an absence of systematic studies of the elderly's actual ethical judgments and standards. Certainly stereotypes exist, for example, that the elderly hold more conservative positions regarding ethics. However, such suppositions need to be critically evaluated with respect to actual data. Many interesting but unanswered questions that can be investigated by the methods commonly used by behavioral scientists: Do ethical judgments and standards change as an individual ages? Do elderly individuals now have different ethical standards and judgments than younger individuals, not because of the aging process per se but because of other factors? Are there subgroups of the elderly that hold different ethical standards or make different ethical judgments from the group as a whole? Are there differences between the ethical standards and judgments of the elderly and those of the professionals who interact with the elderly? To what degree, if any, is age useful as a predictor of an individual's ethical standards and judgments? In sum, little seems to be known regarding the descriptive ethics of the elderly.

Knowledge of descriptive ethics can also be important for normative ethics, the next level of ethical discourse to be discussed. It is sometimes the case that normative claims are either derived from descriptive claims, for example, the ethical beliefs of the majority are such and such and therefore such and such is what ought to be valued (witness the statistical approach to defining normality); or normative systems are first formulated only to be "tested" by their agreement with certain descriptive claims.

Normative Ethics

Normative ethics does not have as its task to discover that we actually value, but rather what we *ought* to value, or what we *should* do. It attempts to define both the morally acceptable ends of human actions, as well as the means by which these ends can be ethically pursued. We will concentrate here on ethical issues relating to psychotherapy with the elderly. In a later section, we will examine ethical issues relevant to research with the elderly.

Normative Ethics and Psychotherapy With the Elderly

Following the definition offered by Bandura (1969), psychotherapy is taken to be a process in which the therapist arranges stimulus conditions to produce desired behavioral changes in the client. Bandura's definition suggests that a means-end distinction can be made in psychotherapy. That is, psychotherapy can be thought to consist of means—the methods and principles that the therapist uses to influence behavior (the arrangement of stimulus conditions)—and also of ends—desired outcomes of the application of these means (desired behavioral change). Thus, each approach

to psychotherapy can be thought to consist of means (Freudian free association, behavioral contingency management, or Rogerian unconditional positive regard) and of ends (insight, an attainment of competency at certain skills, or self-actualization). Indeed, a particular approach to psychotherapy can be defined by the means by which it pursues its particular ends.

There is wide agreement that values play a large role in both the selection of the means and the ends (goals) of psychotherapy. Regarding ends, recall that in Bandura's definition the change that psychotherapy attempts to produce is a *desirable* one. Bandura's definition is not unique in this regard, for a true lexical definition of psycho*therapy* must accurately reflect that *therapy* is not used to signify all changes—for example, it is not used to signify a change that is viewed by the speaker as undesirable. Rather, *therapy* is used by the speaker to signify what is for him or her a good change. The *Oxford English Dictionary* indicates that etymologically *therapy* is derived from the Latin "*therapia*", which means "healing". In turn, *healing* signifies, according to the same dictionary, a restoration to health, well-being, or welfare. Therefore, psychotherapy, to the extent that it is actually therapy, involves a change from an initial state to some more highly valued state.

Further, the means that are actually used for producing these more highly valued end states are also value-laden. Although it is true that the means are constrained by empirical realities, that is, their actual efficacy for producing the desired end state, it is often the case that some of these means are eliminated on ethical grounds. For example, even though sexual contact between the therapist and the client might be an effective means to a desired end state (e.g., decreased sexual inhibitions), it is eliminated on ethical grounds by the ethical code of the American Psychological Association 1977).

Let us turn to examine in more detail how statements about the ends, the goals, or the outcomes of therapy involve values. There are at least two principal actors in any psychotherapy with the elderly as it has been characterized here: the elderly client and the therapist. However, there is often a third class of actors involved—the significant other(s), such as the spouse, the child, the employer, and (writ large) the society. Next, it is important to recognize that a necessary point of departure for any particular therapy case is dissatisfaction with the present state of affairs, with respect to a particular person or set of persons (or instead, stated positively, an interest in bringing about another state of affairs relevant to the same). That is, psychotherapy is not initiated if no one wants anything changed.

If the above is correct, then for psychotherapy to be initiated in any particular case, an alternative state of affairs has to be desired by at least one of the actors in the psychotherapeutic situation: the potential client, some significant other(s), or the psychotherapist.

It seems to be the case that, at times, the dissatisfaction of the therapist is sufficient to initiate psychotherapy with the elderly. O'Donohue, Fisher, and Krasner (1986) found that the elderly individual is at times treated without his or her involvement in the determination of treatment goals and even without his or her consent. They examined 29 published reports of studies using a behavioral approach to clinical problems of the elderly. They found that the elderly individual was involved in the determination of treatment goals in only 3 of the 29 studies reviewed. For example, Atthowe (1972) reported the establishment of a treatment program designed to modify enuresis in institutionalized geriatric clients:

> The authors met two or three times a week with the three nursing assistants who worked the 11:00 p.m.–7:00 a.m. shift. It was decided that one of the main problems we would try to control was excessive bedwetting. The four of us designed the following program in which the contributions of each were included. Eighteen of the 86 patients on the ward were selected as bedwetters by the ward staff . . . the first phase of the intervention involved the creation of an aversive environment, a therapeutic regimen requiring a much more costly expenditure of effort on the part of each patient . . . this aversive and effortful routine was carried out for two months. Escape or avoidance was not possible. (pp. 234–235)

It seems here that the therapists unilaterally determined all of the goals, the "client" and the "therapy."

Of course, it is optimal when the views of the client, the significant others, and the therapist are aligned. The situation becomes more complex when the significant others are so situated that they can force an unwilling elderly individual into therapy, or when significant others can employ legal means to force unwilling individuals into therapy, as with involuntary commitment of adults to mental hospitals. As Szasz (1973) has said, "All hospitals are medical, but some hospitals are more medical than others" (p. 11).

However, a stated desire to bring about a new state of affairs for the potential client either by himself, by some significant others, or by both, is not sufficient for initiating therapy. It is not the case that the therapist is forced to provide therapy for any particular individual. Thus, another necessary condition for the initiation of therapy is the therapist's agreement to provide his or her services. In the usual case, a therapist will agree to assist an individual to obtain certain goals only if she or he agrees that the individual's goals are desirable. Therapists can, and do, refuse to provide their services to help bring about ends desired by a particular individual, because they do not agree with the individual's objectives. Suicide is a case in point: therapists usually do not judge this objective as desirable, and therefore will not usually assist an individual in gaining this end. Indeed, because therapists usually regard this goal as extremely undesirable, they will usually do everything in their power to prevent the individual from achieving this objective. Therefore, another class of value judgments necessary for initiating psychotherapy concerns the judgments made by the therapist concerning the prospective client's goals.

In sum, so far we have seen that value judgments of the therapist, the client, and significant others play a role in psychotherapy in at least three ways: (a) in eliminating some possible means to the desired ends because these means are judged to be unethical, (b) in the judgments made by the potential client or some significant others that some alternative state of affairs is more desirable than the present state, and (c) in the judgments made by the therapist regarding the desirability of the alternative state of affairs sought by the potential client.

Two other points need to be made here. First, when a mental health professional agrees to assist an individual in obtaining a certain goal, this can be construed as an expert claiming (perhaps implicitly) that this end state is superior to the initial state of affairs. This can be interpreted as an expert endorsing a certain value statement, as, for example, in the statement of a plastic surgeon that having wrinkles is less desirable than being wrinkle-free. Professionals should be aware of the ubiquity of such tacit value implications of their professional behavior.

Second, and related to the previous points, the

level at which professionals intervene also has certain value implications. Working with depressed elderly individuals in conventional individual psychotherapy can be construed to support the position that it is the individual that ought to and needs to change if he or she wants to feel happier. Yet it may be that certain societal institutions and practices are causing the individual's affective problems. Conventional individual therapy in these situations becomes tantamount to blaming the victim. Caplan and Nelson (1973) maintain that many extant psychological theories hold people responsible for all their problems, ignoring societal causes. They assert:

> 1. They [person-blaming interpretations] offer a convenient apology freeing the government and primary cultural institutions from blame for the problem. 2. Since those institutions are apparently not the cause of the problem, it may be legitimately contended that they cannot be held responsible for amelioration. If they do provide such help, they are credited with being exceedingly humane, while gaining control over those being helped, through the manipulation of problem definitions in exchange for treatment resources. 3. Such interpretations provide and legitimate the right to initiate person-change rather than system-change treatment programs. This in turn has the following functions: (a) it serves as a publicly acceptable device to control troublesome segments of the population, (b) it distracts attention from possible systemic causes, and (c) it discredits system-oriented criticism . . . 4. The loyalty of large numbers of the well-educated, melioristic-minded nonneedy is cemented to the national structure by means of occupational involvement in "socially relevant" managerial, treatment, and custodial roles required to deal with those persons designated as needing person-centered correction. (p. 210)

It is obvious that there are many plausible candidates among societal and governmental practices that contribute to the present problems of the elderly. This raises such moral questions as, Is a gerontologically oriented health professional morally obligated to act to ameliorate this situation? Is it morally wrong for the gerontologically oriented health professional to mainly or solely work with elderly individuals in treatment pursuing individual goals, in the face of such societal and governmental practices?

Normative Ethics and Religion

The ethical training of many individuals, including the elderly, has traditionally taken place in a religious context. The religiously inclined usually insist that theology must inform any correct system of ethics. For example, according to Thomas (1970), a prominent Roman Catholic theologian, "To the extent that a given religion clarifies the basic components of the conception of man held by its adherents, it furnishes the indispensable ideological foundation for their system of ethics" (p. 127).

The major tenet of theological ethics is "Whatever God wills is what ought to be done." One should note that in such theological ethics, ethics is dependent upon theology: Knowledge of what God wills—a theological matter—is required in order to know what ought to be done—an ethical matter. As previously noted, this primacy of theology is thought by the religiously inclined to be only proper.

It must also be noted that if God's will is revealed to us at all, it is only indirectly revealed, that is, through some intermediary such as holy writings. (See the arguments by Hume, 1955, against the credibility of claims of direct revelation.) Thus, to apply this standard on the basis of God's will as indirectly revealed, we need to justify some claim regarding what God wills.

However, it does not appear to be the case that ethical claims are grounded upon religious claims. Rather, ethical claims are used to justify religious claims. In any religion it is obviously of utmost importance to distinguish true religious pronouncements from false religious pronouncements. Any putative religious pronouncement containing such prescriptions as "Harm thy parents" or "Torture innocent babies" would be immediately judged not to be an actual account of God's will. These immoral claims would not become a part of church canon because these fail to pass a test of morality. Thus, we cannot ground ethical claims on religious pronouncements because we must first justify that these religious pronouncements do actually express the revealed word of God by demonstrating that they are morally correct.

This consideration does not present any insurmountable problems for the professional who interacts with the elderly. However, to the extent that some individual's ethics and theology are intimately connected in some way, one must be all the more careful when speaking about ethics with these individuals.

It should be noted that the above can be accepted by someone who believes that whatever God wills should be done. God, if all good, would always will what is morally right. However, this is to point out that if we do actually have any knowledge of God, it is ethically conditioned—it has passed a test of morality.

The Autonomy of Normative Ethics

In this section we will examine the relationship between what *is* and what *ought* to be the case. We will argue that normative ethical statements are not deducible from statements of fact. (The reader is referred to Hudson, 1969, for further discussions of this topic.) This question is important, especially for the professional with training in the empirical sciences, because at issue is whether knowledge of empirical fact is sufficient to settle normative ethical questions. If it is not, then it appears to be the case that professionals dealing with the elderly need to know other kinds of methods and other kinds of information in order to understand the normative dimensions of their work.

Hume was among the first to suggest that facts and values are distinct, that is, values, or ought-statements, cannot be derived from purely factual statements, or is-statements. In his *A Treatise of Human Nature*, Hume stated:

> In every system of morality, which I have hitherto met with, I have always remarked, that the author proceeds for some time in the ordinary way of reasoning, and established the being of a God, or makes observation concerning human affairs; when of a sudden I am surpriz'd to find, that instead of the usual copulations of propositions, *is*, and *is not*, I meet with no proposition that is not connected with an *ought* or an *ought not*. This change is imperceptible: but is, however, of the last consequence. For as the *ought*, or *ought not*, expresses some new relation or affirmation, 'tis necessary that it shou'd be observ'd and explain'd; and at the same time that a reason should be given, for what seems altogether inconceivable, how this new relation can be a deduction from others, which are entirely different from it. (p. 47)

Cornman, Lehrer, and Pappas (1982) argue that Hume is making the straightforward logical point that no ought-statement—that is, a statement that makes only an ought-claim—can be logically deducible from any number of factual is-statements—that is, statements that make only factual claims.

They demonstrate this point as follows. Consider any two propositions P & Q. Suppose that Q is logically deducible from P. If Q is deducible from P, then a self-contradiction will be deducible from the conjunction of P and not Q. For example, let P = "Indiana University is in Indiana and Stony Brook is in New York and let Q = "Indiana University is in Indiana." It should be obvious that Q is deducible from P (because P is a conjunction and Q is one of the conjuncts). Now, it also should be obvious that the conjunction of P and not Q leads to a self-contradiction. The conjunction of P and not Q is: "Indiana University is in Indiana and Stony Brook is in New York and Indiana University is not in Indiana." The self-contradiction is, of course, "Indiana University is in Indiana and Indiana University is not in Indiana."

From this we can conclude that if Q is deducible from P, then a self-contradiction is deducible from the conjunction of P and not Q.

Now suppose we have a purely factual claim, such as A, "Helping others maximizes happiness", and a normative ought-claim, such as B, "We ought not to help others." First notice that the conjunction of A and B is not a self-contradiction. Moreover, no contradiction is deducible from the conjunction of A and not B. Hence, because of our earlier conclusion, we can conclude that B is not deducible from A. Furthermore, Cornman et al. (1982) argue that what holds for propositions A and B holds generally for any pair of propositions, one of which is a pure factual claim and the other of which is a pure normative claim. Therefore, we cannot deduce that an action ought to be done—an ethical claim—from any factual claim.

The Naturalistic or Definist Fallacy

Thus, we have seen that no ought-statement or ethical standard is deducible from purely factual premises. However, it still might be possible to derive ought-statements or ethical standards from factual premises if we add to these factual premises certain analytic premises. Analytic statements, such as "A bachelor is unmarried," are known to be true by an appeal to nothing more than logic and the meanings of terms. Analytic statements are logically necessary: It is not possible for them to be false.

If, with the addition of some analytic statements to the factual premises an ought-statement or an ethical standard can be deduced, then we can conclude that if the factual premises are true, it is logically necessary that the ought-statement or ethical standard be true. For example, if we have:

1. A is an action that maximizes the total amount of happiness.
2. Whatever maximizes the total amount of happiness is what ought to be done.
   Therefore
3. A ought to be done.

This is a valid argument. Further, if 2 is an analytic statement and thus necessarily true, we can conclude that 3 is deducible from 1. Therefore, one might argue that an ought-statement can be derived from an is-statement.

However, this argument, of course, rests on premise 2. This premise can be interpreted as providing a definition of a critical ethical concept— *what ought to be done*—in terms that are purely factual, descriptive, and nonevaluative.

Moore (1960) argued that this is fallacious, that one cannot define ethical terms such as *good* or *what ought to be done* by nonevaluative terms, for, he suggests, this would make many open and debatable questions closed and trivial. As Moore states, "Whatever definition be offered, it may be always asked, with significance, of the complex so defined, whether it is itself good."

Moore argues that if we take any proposed definition of, say, *good* that employs only nonevaluative terms, such as *produces pleasure*, and we then ask if anything is good, we would be asking in effect whether it produces pleasure. However, if we ask the seemingly open and debatable question, Is that which produces pleasure good? with the previous definition of *good* our question becomes the closed and trivial question, does that which produce pleasure produce pleasure? Although the first question seems worth debating, the second question surely does not.

Also, statements that we use to condemn or praise someone would become trivially true analytic statements with no evaluative force. As Cornman et al. (1982) point out:

> . . . if I tell someone that he ought to promote the general happiness because promoting the general happiness is promoting what is good, I mean to support a certain kind of action by commending it. But if "what is good" means "the general happiness" then all I have said is that he ought to promote the general happiness because promoting the general happiness is promoting the general happiness. This latter claim is not only absurd, but it is clearly not a case of supporting something by commending it. I might just have said, "because killing is killing," or "promoting misery is promoting misery". But the original

claim is not absurd. Therefore the latter is not an adequate translation of the original claim, and any other translation which leaves out the evaluative, and thereby the moral, element will also be inadequate. (p. 297)

Thus, Moore presents some reasons to believe that moral terms such as *good* cannot be defined in terms of nonevaluative natural properties. Defining *good* in terms of such properties closes questions that would appear like they ought to be open, and renders statements used to condemn or praise someone into trivially true analytic statements. We will now turn to the third and final argument for the independence of values from empirical facts. This argument was made by the philosopher of science, Carl Hempel.

Hempel (1965) argues that science cannot establish objective standards of right and wrong that could serve as ethical norms. According to Hempel, at best science can only provide us with instrumental judgments of value. That is, science can only tell us which means are sufficient or necessary—instrumental—for bringing about certain ends.

For example, science (or more realistically, scientists) can potentially determine what factors (means) are necessary or sufficient for the reestablishment of proper cognitive functioning in an Alzheimer's patient, because this is an empirical matter that is capable of scientific test. However, even when we know which means lead to which ends, we are stil left with the question of which ends we ought to pursue. Thus, in the previous example, the unanswered question is, Should typical cognitive functioning be pursued? Hempel calls judgments that certain ends are good, or at least better than certain alternative ends, *absolute judgments of value*. Absolute judgments of value, such as "Reality contact is good," do not express assertions that can be directly tested through observation: Hence, these are incapable of scientific test.

Hempel illustrates the relevance of science for normative ethics by invoking Laplace's demon. Laplace's demon is a perfect scientific intelligence that knows all the laws of nature, everything that is going on in the universe at any given moment, and moreover can calculate with infinite speed and precision, from the state of the universe at any particular moment, its state at any other past or future moment. However, even this perfect scientist cannot help us with absolute judgments of value. As Hempel (1965) argues:

Let us assume, then, that, faced with a moral decision, we are able to call upon the Laplacean demon as a consultant. What help might we get from him? Suppose that we have to choose one of several alternative courses of action open to us, and that we want to know which of these we *ought* to follow. The demon would then be able to tell us, for any contemplated choice, what its consequences would be for the future course of the universe, down to the most minute detail, however remote in space and time. But, having done this for each of the alternative courses of action under consideration, the demon would have completed his task: he would have given us all the information that an ideal science might provide under the circumstances. And yet he would not have resolved our moral problem, for this requires a decision as to which of the several alternative sets of consequences mapped out by the demon as attainable to us is the best; which of them we ought to bring about. And the burden of the decision would still fall upon our shoulders: it is we who would have to commit ourselves to an unconditional (absolute) judgment of value by singling out one of the sets of consequences as superior to the alternatives. (pp. 88–89)

Science cannot provide answers to the questions of normative ethics: It cannot tell us what we ought to value or, ultimately, what we should do.

The three arguments presented above provide strong support for the claim that factual is-statements, which science claims to provide, are not sufficient for establishing any moral claims. This is not to say that science is irrelevant to moral decision making. For example, knowledge of empirical matters, such as whether the elderly person will be happier, safer, and physically healthier in an institution rather than at home, would be relevant to determining whether it is morally right to institutionalize the elderly individual. In consequentialist normative ethical theories, such as act or rule utilitarianism, knowledge of the empirical consequences of an act is necessary for making a moral decision. However, such facts are not sufficient—ultimately, an absolute judgment of value regarding these consquences is required.

If these arguments are correct and ethical claims are not deducible from facts, then professionals who deal with the elderly, such as psychologists and physicians, who essentially have a training in behavioral and biological sciences, need, first of all, to recognize that many of their practical decisions regarding treatment of the elderly are not purely technical, factual matters. Rather, these decisions often depend upon an absolute judgment of value that some particular end or set of ends is morally superior to some

alternative. Because it seems reasonable that professionals should be held accountable for their professional behavior, they must therefore be able to justify their moral judgments. And as we have seen, such justifications cannot be based solely on their scientific and technical expertise, but must also rely upon justification of the values they embrace. This will probably seem somewhat unreasonable, because many professionals do not receive any formal training in such matters. However, if the above is correct, then such training seems to be warranted.

Metaethics

Metaethics, the third and final level of ethical discourse, concerns itself with the meanings of ethical terms and with the function of ethical utterances. Sumner (1966) maintains that metaethical theories have five characteristics.

1. Metaethical theories are morally neutral, that is, they are neither normative ethical theories nor imply any normative theory or principle.
2. Metaethical theories are second-order (hence, *meta*) studies of the logic of normative ethical language.
3. Metaethics is propaedeutic to normative ethics in that it seeks to explicate and to criticize the presuppositions upon which normative theories are established, especially those presuppositions regarding language.
4. Metaethical theories are concerned with "matters of analysis," such as How do moral judgments differ from other kinds of judgments? What is the function of moral judgments? What are the meanings of ethical terms? Can these terms be defined in nonethical terms?
5. Metaethics is concerned with what Sumner calls "matters of justification," such as What reasons, if any, constitute a valid defense of moral judgments? How are these reasons related to the reasons given to defend statements of fact?

It is fair to say that much debate in the 20th century regarding metaethics has been concerned with whether moral terms merely express emotions (Ayer, 1936; Stevenson, 1937) or whether they are assertions that can be verified or falsified. Here, however, we will briefly review a metaethical issue more directly relevant to the ethics of researchers and therapists who interact with the elderly: Do such professionals have a morality of their own, which is distinct and perhaps even inconsistent with ordinary morality?

Freedman (1978) argues that *professional morality* (i.e., the morality attached to a professional role) is different from and can conflict with *ordinary morality*. Freedman maintains that professionals are "more constrained by their professional values than are nonprofessionals and, conversely, take into less account those considerations which ordinarily apply" (p. 1). He illustrates the difference between ordinary morality and professional morality by using the example of medical confidentiality. Freedman claims that medical confidentiality differs from confidentiality in ordinary discourse in two principal ways. First, medical confidentiality covers all information a physician or psychotherapist gains from the individual and from the course of treatment, without the need for the individual to explicitly indicate that such information is to be kept confidential. In contrast, in order to have a claim to confidentiality in ordinary discourse, it is usually the case that the divulger must explicitly indicate that the information should be kept confidential. Second, professional confidentiality is more binding than ordinary confidentiality. That is, it takes reasons of greater seriousness and validity to override, or to morally justify a departure from, professional confidentiality than from ordinary confidentiality.

> Because medical confidentiality is more stringent than is ordinary confidentiality, and because medical confidentiality is part of the professional morality of physicians, it appears that professional morality can be inconsistent with ordinary morality. Reasons which suffice to require a breach of ordinary confidentiality will not suffice to require a breach of medical confidentiality. Yet the reasons which justify breaches of ordinary confidentiality—to protect the divulger, to protect others, to serve the public interest—are moral reasons, sufficient to reach a practical conclusion (divulge!) in ordinary morality but not sufficient in professional morality. (Freedman, 1978, p. 4)

This indicates that confidentiality is a stronger value in professional morality than in ordinary morality. Thus, professional morality with its different heirarchy of values can lead professionals to resolve value conflicts in different ways than ordinary morality would recommend.

Freedman believes that a professional value hierarchy skewed in favor of values such as confi-

dentiality is useful for the practice of medicine and psychotherapy. Strong confidentiality of the professional increases the likelihood that clients will readily divulge personal information critical for these professionals to function successfully.

However, Freedman suggests that a deviation from ordinary morality can be construed as evil. After all, it is a deviation from the commonly accepted norms concerning what is morally good and bad. When one promises to abide by professional morality, one is also promising to contravene ordinary morality.

Freedman claims, however, that the deviation of professional morality is formed from the zealous attachment to one value with which the practitioner is professionally identified, the medical maxim "to above all do no harm." Society commits itself to a placing a value on health, by allocating its safeguarding to certain professionals in that society. A corollary of fanatical adherence to "above all do no harm" is professional confidentiality, as such strict confidentiality both promotes successful treatment—by increasing the likelihood that the individual will accurately and fully disclose relevant information—and decreases the likelihood of any iatrogenic (social) effects. The general public countenances such ideals, because of the obvious public benefit.

Martin (1981) disagrees with Freedman's claim that professional morality is distinct from ordinary morality; he states that both are grounded in individual's rights. Professional morality has to do with the same individual rights but in a professional context. People have certain rights to have personal and medical information kept confidential—that is, their general right to privacy has special importance in the medical context. Martin asserts:

> A number of considerations combine to make the right to privacy have special force in the medical context and apply to all medical information. (a) Medical information is often extremely personal, especially psychiatric information. If there is any area where a person has a right to determine what shall be revealed to whom, it is here. (b) The patient is in an especially vulnerable position with respect to the doctor upon whom he or she must rely for help. There are special needs for safeguards to protect the patient. (c) The patient's health and life is at stake in being able to openly convey information to the doctor without an inhibiting anxiety that the information may be misused. (d) There is always uncertainty as to how medical information may be misused. Because of its general importance, only a general ban on revealing it can maximally protect

patients' rights. (e) The doctor is providing a service which the patient pays for directly or through insurance (and pays dearly!). The transaction of information involved is part of the service, which the patient has a right to control within limits. (pp. 624–625).

Thus this discussion points to several issues not commonly raised regarding professional ethical codes. First, we need to understand their nature, including how they are related to ordinary morality. Second, we need to critically examine these ethical codes. They are not beyond criticism: They are not revealed truth or epistemologically incorrigible statements, although sometimes it seems that they are treated as such. Part of such a critical evaluation should examine whether they are adequate for special populations, such as the elderly (then, of course, an important question is: What are proper criteria of adequacy for professional codes?). This criticism is essential to the growth of knowledge regarding normative ethics. In fact the training of the professional, both therapist and researcher, who will be working with the elderly must emphasize that science and ethics are intricately interrelated.

PRACTICAL ISSUES

The remaining part of this chapter will address some practical issues realted to the ethics of research and therapy with the elderly. As mentioned earlier, a pertinent question to address when discussing these issues is whether there are ethical considerations unique to this age group. After reviewing the scant literature addressing this question, we are inclined to conclude that there are not. As Young states (1978), "While it is true that the aged have special needs, it is not clear that special ethical principles are needed to respond to the moral dilemmas raised by health care and biomedical research in the aged" (p. 68).

Rather than presenting a comprehensive review of varying views regarding this issue, we will present a discussion of problematic ethical issues a practitioner or researcher is likely to face when working with this population. Following this discussion, some ethical guidelines are presented.

The Ethics of Research

The most comprehensive statement of an ethical code concerning human experimentation is contained in the Nuremberg Code, which is described in a court opinion involving the trial of 23 German physicians for "war crimes and crimes against humanity" during World War II. Of the 10 criteria that must be met in order for an experiment to be considered ethical, the Nuremberg Code emphasizes the importance of voluntary consent. The code requires that the consent of an experimental subject have at least three characteristics: (a) the consenting individual must be mentally competent, (b) the consent must be voluntary, and (c) the consentee must be informed.

The requirement of informed consent can be problematic when one is working with the elderly because of the physiological and psychological variability of this population. The appropriate process for obtaining informed consent is even less clear when one is dealing with the institutionalized elderly. Factors such as diminished competence and possible coercion inherent in institutionalization contribute to the difficulty of obtaining informed consent from the institutionalized. These issues will be discussed in the following sections.

Autonomy

The elderly individual, whether institutionalized or not, often leads a dependent life. Dependence on relatives, social services, and financial resources, such as health insurance and social security, may all lead to the reduced autonomy of the elderly individual. Less attention to the issue of voluntariness and informed consent has been given to the community-based independently living elderly than to the institutionalized elderly. This is presumably because the former are viewed as better able to give truly informed consent to research participation and less likely to acquiesce because of external pressures. In contrast, some view the institutionalized as having so little autonomy that truly informed consent is impossible to obtain. As Ratzan (1980) suggests, "Peer pressure; institutionalization; and physical, mental, and financial vulnerabilities often subtly erode elderly subjects' autonomy to the degree that they need special protection—not so much from their vulnerabilities but from the loss of liberty which is a consequence of their vulnerabilities" (p. 36).

Although there are no specific legal guidelines dealing with the unique circumstances of elderly research subjects, a great deal of debate about the ethical difficulties raised by research involving other economically and socially disadvantaged groups (e.g., children and prisoners) has occurred (for discussions regarding experimentation with these groups see Cohen, 1978; McCormick, 1981; Ramsey, 1970). Following a discussion of the issue of competence and the elderly research subject, suggestions from these sources as well as those specifically addressing elderly research subjects will be presented.

To date, there has been little information available to determine precisely how the issue of autonomy affects research participation by institutionalized elderly individuals. A review of two published studies reporting rates of refusal to participate in research by elderly nursing-home residents was presented by Weintraub (1984) in an attempt to assess the degree of autonomy operating within these groups. In one of the studies reviewed, the refusal rate exceeded 75%, and the researchers were forced to seek subjects at another site. At the second nursing home, 64% refused to participate and an additional 11% later dropped out of the study prior to its completion. Of the remaining sample, a further 27% chose not to continue after the study had begun. Weintraub concluded that the initial rejection rate and the later dropout rates are indicative of autonomous action.

In the second study reviewed, 100% of the elderly individuals approached declined to participate. According to Weintraub (1984) the residents either refused or, more commonly, were not allowed to choose because the staff and family members were each given preemptive veto power in an attempt to protect the elderly individuals. In his view, "such excessive paternalism is degrading and dignity destroying. Autonomy includes the right of being given the choice of participation; the opportunity to choose *to* participate as well as not to do so. Paternalism reinforces dependence and decreases autonomy among elderly institutionalized people" (p. 45).

It is likely that most would agree that for those who have been determined to be incompetent, the informed consent process is inappropriate. However, this statement raises several questions regarding the determination of competence, which further complicates the issue. These questions will now be discussed.

Competence

Mental competence, an essential condition of informed consent, is rarely empirically determined but is instead often assumed. There is, in fact, much controversy over how competency should be

determined and by whom. For example, is judicial intervention necessary? Also because of the gradations of competence found between and within geriatric patients, some suggest (e.g., McCullough, 1984) that the all-or-none legal judgment of competency is inappropriate for this population.

The most difficult consent issue of the elderly concerns those who are borderline competent. Because the course of certain forms of senile dementia (e.g., senile dementia of the Alzheimer type) and its definition are so varied, the identification of minimally yet definitely impaired individuals can be extremely difficult. When they are identified, one is faced with the question of whether they are able to give legally effective informed consent. Who is best qualified to decide? And if it is decided that they are not competent, is it sufficient to rely upon the proxy consent of a relative?

According to Rozovosky (1984) an elderly person cannot participate as a research subject if in the judgment of the investigators it is determined that the person cannot give legally effective consent. Only when a mentally incompetent individual has appointed a legal representative who consents on the individual's behalf can an exception be made. Furthermore, after reviewing the relevant federal regulations, Rozovosky (1984) concludes:

> Unless a state law or other applicable provision permits a spouse or adult child to act on behalf of a person who has not been declared incompetent, neither could agree to research involving the prospective subject. A judicial determination would be necessary. Without it, participation by persons of questionable competency is risky in terms of consent and legal responsibilities. (p. 564)

These guidelines indicate how prohibitive certain types of geriatric research can be (e.g., senile dementia research). For example, it is unlikely that a judge will intervene in the absence of a health-threatening emergency. In addition, owing to the unique pathophysiology of certain forms of dementia (e.g., Alzheimer's disease) there are no acceptable animal models. So the situation involves a tremendous dilemma: Alzheimer's disease research can only be performed using demented patients, but demented patients should not, according to some, be allowed to participate because they are incompetent, whereas competent subjects cannot be effectively studied because they are not demented. Although there is a recognized need for research on senile dementia, there is at present no ethical consensus as to how best to perform it.

Research Recommendations

Taking into consideration the issues just dicussed, we recommend the following guidelines for clinical geriatric research. (For further guidelines specific to research on Alzheimer's disease, see Melnick, Dubler, Weisbard, & Butler, 1984.)

1. Because of the possibility of intermittent competence, the consent process should take place in more than one interview.
2. Consent forms should be presented in larger-face type, using simple, ordinary language.
3. Objective assessment of the subject's understanding of the experiment should be documented, possibly in the form of a questionnaire presented after obtaining consent with items regarding the procedures outlined in the consent form. If there is evidence of a lack of understanding on the part of the subject, initiation of the study should be delayed until better understanding is achieved.
4. Objective assessment of the subject's competence, when in question, should be documented. This process should be individualized, taking into consideration varying levels of competence across various tasks.
5. Researchers should attempt to employ documents, such as "durable powers of attorney" or other provisions permitted by specific state statute.

Therapy Recommendations

Previously, we discussed the role of value judgments in therapy and claimed that a necessary condition for the initiation of therapy was a dissatisfaction with the present state of affairs or, in different terms, an interest in some other state of affairs by either the elderly individual, by some significant other, or by the therapist. We think that it is desirable from an ethical point of view that therapy be initiated only if the elderly individual (or if properly determined as incompetent, some appropriate proxy) consents to treatment;

that is, the informed consent of the competent elderly individual is necessary before therapy can be ethically initiated. Again, although this may appear to be obvious, this recommendation has not always been followed (O'Donohue et al., 1986).

The informed consent process should include the following: (a) a fair explanation of the treatment methods to be followed, and their purposes, including the identification of any procedures which are experimental; (b) a description of any associated discomforts and risks than can be reasonably expected; (c) a description of the benefits that can reasonably be expected; (d) a disclosure of any alternative that might be advantageous for the individual; (e) an offer to answer any questions concerning the procedures; and (f) an explanation that the individual is free to withdraw his consent and to discontinue participation in therapy at any time without prejudice (Capron, 1981).

This upholds the right of individual autonomy—the right of self-determination. Autonomy admits of degrees (e.g., in general, a prisoner is less autonomous than a teenager, who, in turn, is less autonomous than an unimprisoned adult), and therefore its definition should reflect this. We define autonomy as a relative lack of constraints or, stated positively, the ability to choose (Krasner & Ullmann, 1973).

There are two principal factors that diminish autonomy: coercive force and some deficiency (Mappes & Zembaty, 1981). If the elderly individual is coerced or threatened into therapy, then of course that individual's autonomy is not respected. However, perhaps it is not so obvious how a deficiency can be a constraint and therefore diminish autonomy. A lack of basic resources, such as food, shelter, and funds, contrives to diminish autonomy by diminishing the person's ability to choose. One cannot choose to live in a certain place (e.g., a private nursing home or a private home) if one cannot afford it. Moreover, one cannot participate in therapy if one cannot afford it. The elderly all too often suffer from such material deficiencies, and thus their autonomy in very fundamental ways is severely curtailed. A lack of knowledge or of skills can also be a constraint that diminishes autonomy. For example, if an elderly individual does not know how to influence staff in an institution to obtain certain goals, then that individual's autonomy is diminished—that individual's choices are restricted.

Thus, maximizing the elderly individual's participation in the selection of treatment goals is consistent with respecting that individual's autonomy. This brings us to our last recommendation: Given an expressed interest and informed consent on the part of the elderly individual, therapists should conduct therapy to increase the autonomy of the elderly individual. Part of this is quite traditional: If the elderly individual wants to achieve a certain state of affairs (given that the individual is competent and the therapist is willing to participate in therapy), the therapist helps the individual to obtain this state of affairs. However, we also recommend something stronger, that is, that given the interest and informed consent, that therapists teach general skills and strategies that increase the autonomy of the elderly (O'Donohue et al., 1986). In behavioral terms, this can be achieved by increasing the ability of the elderly to change and design their environments (Krasner, 1980). This, of course, increases choices and decreases deficiencies. In the course of teaching the elderly client the particular skills relevant to achieving the specific goal, the therapist can also teach more general skills and principles that the client can use to obtain other, perhaps similar, goals.

One manner in which this can be accomplished is by "giving away" behavioral psychology (Krasner, 1982) by teaching the elderly behavioral principles and management techniques so that they can influence their own environments. Fisher and Carstensen (1985) used this approach with three elderly nursing-home residents. The three subjects reported dissatisfaction with the frequency and quality of their social interactions with the staff and with other residents. Following the determination of their treatment goals, the resident were trained in the use of specific social skills, as well as general behavioral principles in order to increase their effectiveness in social situations. Results of the study indicate that institutionalized individuals are able to formulate their own treatment goals, and to learn and apply skills that allow them to increase control over their social environment.

One important advantage of this approach is that it potentially can help the traditionally disempowered elderly individual to effectively countercontrol the influence of the empowered. As Cicero has said, "Old age is honored only on the condition that it defends itself, maintains its rights, is subservient to no one, and to its last breath rules over its domain."

REFERENCES

American Psychological Association. (1977). *Ethical guidelines for the delivery of human services.* Washington, DC: American Psychological Association.

Atthowe, J. M. (1972). Controlling nocturnal enuresis in severely disabled and chronic patients. *Behavior Therapy, 3*, 232–239.

Ayer, A. J. (1936). *Language, truth and logic.* London: Oxford University Press.

Bandura, A. (1969). *Principles of behavior modification.* New York: Holt, Rinehart & Winston.

Caplan, N., & Nelson, S. D. (1973). On being useful: The nature and consequences of psychological research on social problems. *American Psychologist, 28*, 199–211.

Capron, A. M. (1981). A functional approach to informed consent. In T. Mappes & J. Zembaty (Eds.), *Biomedical ethics,* New York: McGraw-Hill.

Cohen, C. (1978). Medical experimentation on prisoners. *Perspectives in Biology and Medicine, 21*, 357–372.

Cornman, J. W., Lehrer, K., & Pappas, G. S. (1982). *Philosophical problems and arguments: An introduction.* New York: Macmillan.

Fisher, J. E., & Carstensen, L. L. (1985). *The elderly nursing home resident as contingency manager.* Unpublished manuscript, Indiana University, Bloomington.

Freedman, B. (1978). A meta-ethics for professional morality. *Ethics, 89*, 1–19.

Hempel, C. G. (1965). Science and human values. In C. G. Hempel (Ed.), *Aspects of scientific explanation.* New York: Free Press.

Hudson, W. D. (1969). *The is-ought question.* New York: St. Martin's Press.

Hume, D. (1927). *A treatise of human nature.* Chicago: Open Court Publishing Company.

Hume, D. (1955). *An enquiry concerning human understanding.* Oxford: Oxford University Press.

Krasner, L., & Houts, A. C. (1984). A study of the "value" systems of behavioral scientists. *American Psychologist, 39*, 840–850.

Krasner, L. (1982, May). Nusquamas for sale: Confessions of a used health salesman. Invited address presented at the meeting of the Association for Behavior Analysis, Milwaukee, WI.

Krasner, L. (Ed.). (1980). *Environmental design and human behavior.* Elmsford, NY: Pergamon.

Krasner, L., & Ullmann, L. P. (1973). *Behavior influence and personality.* New York: Holt, Rinehart & Winston.

Mappes, T. A., & Zembaty, J. S. (1981). *Biomedical ethics.* New York: McGraw-Hill.

Martin, M. W. (1981). Rights and the metaethics of professional morality. *Ethics, 91*, 619–625.

McCormick, R. A. (1981). Proxy consent in the experimental situation. In T. A. Mappes & J. S. Zembaty (Eds.), *Biomedical ethics.* New York: McGraw-Hill.

McCullough, L. B. (1984). Medical care for elderly patients with diminished competence: An ethical analysis. *Journal of the American Geriatrics Society, 32*, 150–153.

Melnick, V. L., Dubler, N. N., Weisbard, A., & Butler, R. N. (1984). Clinical research in senile dementia of the Alzheimer type: Suggested guidelines addressing the ethical and legal issues. *Journal of the American Geriatrics Society*, *32*, 531–536.

Moore, G. E. (1960). *Principia ethica*. New York: Cambridge University Press.

Nielsen, K. (1967). Problems of ethics. In P. Edwards (Ed.), *The encyclopedia of philosophy*. New York: Macmillan.

O'Donohue, W. T., Fisher, J. E., & Krasner, L. (1986). Behavior therapy and the elderly: A conceptual and ethical analysis. *International Journal of Aging and Human Development*, *23*, (1), 1–15.

Ramsey, P. (1970). *The patient as person*. New Haven, CT: Yale University Press.

Ratzan, R. M. (1980). "Being old makes you different": The ethics of research with elderly subjects. *Hastings Center Report*, *10*, 32–42.

Rozovosky, F. A. (1984). *Consent to treatment*. Boston: Little, Brown.

Stevenson, C. L. (1937). The emotive meaning of ethical terms. *Mind*, *46*, 30–52.

Sumner, L. W. (1966). Normative ethics and metaethics. *Ethics*, *77*, 95–106.

Szasz, T. X. (1973). *The age of madness*. Garden City; NY: Anchor.

Thomas, J. L. (1970). The Catholic tradition for responsibility in sexual ethics. In J. C. Wynn (Ed.), *Sexual ethics and Christian responsibility*. New York: Association Press.

Weintraub, M. (1984). Ethical concerns and guidelines in research in geriatric pharmacology and therapeutics: Individualization, not codification. *Journal of the American Geriatrics Society*, *32*, 44–48.

Author Index

Aakvaag, A., 70
Abbey, H., 22
Abbott, M., 22
Abella, R., 299
Abrams, P. D., 262
Abrams, R., 89
Abrass, I. B., 253
Achong, M. R., 152
Adams, F., 279
Adams, H. E., 200
Adams, R. D., 107
Adamopoulos, P. N., 138
Aday, R. H., 343
Ade-Ridder, L., 331
Ader, R., 298
Adey, M., 79, 81
Adler, A., 293
Agnew, H., 239, 240, 244
Ainsworth, M. D., 294
Akhtar, A. J., 206, 208
Akiyama, H., 296
Alagna, S. W., 297
Alexander, F. G., 96
Algera, G., 137
Alksne, H., 57
Allen, J. A., 357, 360
Allen, M. D., 160
Allen, W. C., 238
Alonso, A., 50
Althouse, R., 341
Ambler, M. W., 285
Ambrosetto, C., 241
American Association of Retired Persons, 337
American Psychiatric Association, 78, 97, 179
American Psychological Association, 166, 388
Aminoff, M. J., 240
Amren, D. P., 136
Anand, R., 99
Ancoli-Israel, S., 241
Anderson, J. E., 37
Anderson-Ray, S. M., 361
Anderson, R. S., 263
Andreasen, N. C., 76
Andres, R., 156, 157, 159
Andresen, B. D., 153
Andrews, G. R., 206
Andrews, K., 278

Annon, J. S., 72
Antonucci, T. C., 291, 292, 294, 295, 296, 301, 331
Aponte, G. E., 70, 71
Aponte, H. J., 366
Arend, K., 294
Arkin, A., 314
Arling, G., 295, 317
Arnetz, B. B., 227, 228
Arnstein, A. F. T., 104
Arvidson, K., 26
Ashburn, W., 137
Ashenbrenner, J., 356
Asher, M. J., 254
Asire, A. J., 124, 126
Asroff, S., 299
Atchley, R. C. 267, 332, 337, 363
Atkeson, B. M., 26
Atkins, A., 79, 382
Atkins, C. J., 297
Atkinson, A. J., 164
Atkinson, R. M., 62, 63
Atlas, L., 229
Atthowe, 368
Auerbach, O., 24
Avant, G. R., 165
Averill, J., 317, 318, 319
Awad, S. A., 260
Ayer, A. J., 393
Aznin, N. H., 261

Baanders-van Halewijn, E. A., 127
Babchuck, N., 298
Bach, B., 158
Bach-Peterson, J., 272
Bachelund, G., 339
Back, K. W., 344
Baer, B., 104
Baer, D. J., 210
Baer, D. M., 229
Baer, J. S., 292
Baer, P. E., 58
Baffa, G., 90
Bagley, C. R., 49
Bahn, A., 60
Bahrick, H. P., 28
Bahrick, P. O., 28

Bailey, M. B., 57
Bailey, S., 39
Baker, H. W., 70
Baker, N., 179
Ball, J. F., 313
Ballinger, B. R., 116
Balter, M. B., 238
Baltes, M. M., 177, 206, 209, 210, 211, 212, 214, 215, 217, 229, 368
Baltes, P. B., 19, 20, 21, 27, 28, 206, 211, 217, 224
Bandura, A., 209, 298, 300, 301, 388
Baras, M., 68
Barchas, J. D., 298
Barclay, L. L., 105, 106
Barlebo, H., 255
Barnard, G., 242
Barnes, J. A., 185
Barnett, D. M., 8
Barns, E. K., 184
Barr, M. L., 190
Barraclough, B., 317
Barrow, G., 81
Barruther, A., 165
Barry, C., 298
Barry, K., 185
Barton, E. M., 177, 211, 229
Barton, R., 84
Bartus, R., 103
Bartus, R., 96
Bartus, R. T., 104
Bates, G. M., 180
Barker, R., 69
Barnes, R., 80
Battin, D., 314
Bauernfeind, R. A., 141
Baum, J., 148
Bauman, J. L., 141
Bayne, J. R. D., 152
Becerra, R. M., 293
Beck, A., 318
Beck, A. T., 79, 84, 90, 166
Beck, B., 39
Beck, P., 186
Beck, R. W., 79
Becker, L. G., 156
Becker, P. W., 63
Beckman, H., 166
Beckner, M., 127
Beels, C. C., 298
Beer, E. T., 382
Begg, C. B., 130
Beiman, I., 200
Belinda, 359
Belk, S. S., 301
Bell, B., 25, 26
Bell, W. G., 328
Bender, A. D., 152, 153, 154, 155, 156
Bengston, V. L., 296
Bennett, A. E., 206
Bennett, D., 194
Bennett, R., 226, 228
Benson, D. F., 281, 283
Beresford, 196
Berezin, M. A., 223

Berg, 115
Berg, J. W., 127
Berg, W. E., 226
Berger, K. S., 50
Berger, P. A., 104
Berger, R. K., 136
Berger, R. M., 228
Bergman, M., 26
Berkman, L. F., 225, 292, 297, 298
Berkman, L. S., 291, 292
Berkowitz, R., 227
Berlin, R. M., 244
Berlinger, W. G., 196
Berlyne, D. E., 37
Bernholz, C. D., 26
Bernstein, D. S., 244
Bernstein, J. G., 88
Berrios, G. E., 44
Bertelsen, A., 82
Bertelsen, A. D., 245
Berti-Ceroni, G., 241
Best, J. D., 156
Bhat, P., 136
Bialow, M. R., 79
Bianchine, J. R., 153, 154, 156, 159
Bibring, E., 83
Bickman, 357
Biegel, D. E., 294
Bierman E. L., 8
Biggan, J. C., 343
Biglan, A., 83
Billingsley, A., 359, 360
Binion, A. F., 250
Binstock, R. H., 330
Birren, J. E., 22, 25, 72
Bisno A. L., 136
Bisno, B., 90
Bixler, E. O., 238, 239, 242
Bj____ __K., 303
Bjorksten, J., 22
Black, R. G., 190, 193
Blackman, D. K., 229, 230, 368
Blackman, M. R., 70
Blainas, J. G., 259
Blair, P. B., 11
Blannin, J., 252
Blaschke, T. F., 164
Blass, J. P., 105, 106
Blau, Z. S., 298
Blazer, D., 49, 81, 166, 225, 297
Blehar, M. C., 294
Blenkner, M., 322
Blenkner, R., 208
Blessed, G., 54, 97, 98
Blieszner, R., 28
Bliwise, D., 241
Block, A. J., 239
Bloomfield, C. D., 130
Blum, V., 70
Blume, S. B., 64
Blumenfeld, V. G., 26
Blumenthal, J. N. A., 227
Blumenthal, M. D., 80
Blytheway, W. R., 341, 343

Bodden, J. L., 223
Bohland, J. R., 343
Boissevain, 291
Boller, F., 106, 281
Bolling, D., 22
Bollnow, O., 339, 340
Bommer, W., 136
Bonar, J., 348
Bond, M., 284
Bondareff, W., 98, 99
Bonica, J. J., 190
Bonnet, M. H., 240, 242, 245
Boone, C. W., 7
Booth, 260
Bootzin, R. R., 239, 240, 242, 243, 244, 245, 246, 247
Borkovec, T. D., 244, 245, 246
Bornstein, P., 315, 317
Bornstein, P. E., 86
Bortz, W. M., 218
Borup, J. H., 346
Boschetti, M. A., 340, 341
Botnick, L. E., 11
Bott, E., 291
Botwinick, J., 20, 26, 27, 28, 29
Boudreaux, L., 58
Bourassa, M. G., 134
Bourel, M., 8
Bouteller, J., 136
Bowens, L. M., 68
Bowers, D., 281, 282
Bowlby, J., 227, 294, 297, 312, 314
Boyce, W. T., 294
Boyd, W. D., 185
Boyd-Franklin, N., 359, 361, 366, 367
Boxlin, W., 325
Brabinski, P. Y., 196
Bradley, W. E., 253
Braida, H., 280
Branch, R. A., 157, 159
Brandfonbrener, M., 159
Brassard, J. A., 294
Brasted, W. S., 318, 319
Braun, G. W., 298
Braws, W., 152
Bray, G., 279
Brearley, C. P., 332
Breckenridge, J., 196, 315
Breen, A., 238
Breitlinger, E., 180
Breitner, J. C. S., 99
Brena, S. F., 192
Brendler, C. B., 254
Breslow, L., 298
Breslow, L. D., 118
Bressler, R., 156, 158, 165, 166, 167, 168
Bretherton, I., 294
Bridge, T. P., 55
Brien, T., 165
Briggs, R. S., 278
Briggs, W., 278
Brighton, C., 146
Brink, T. L., 79, 81
Britton, P. G., 262
Broadbent, D. E., 28

Broadhead, W. E., 292
Brocklehurst, J. C., 259, 278
Brody, E., 34, 144, 345
Brody, S. J., 297
Brody, S. S., 147
Broe, G. A., 206
Brook, P., 44, 184
Brooks, P. M., 194
Broskowski, H., 267
Brown, D. S., 279
Brown, E., 238
Brown, G. L., 80
Brown, G. W., 86
Brown, J. W., 148
Brown, P., 107
Brown, R., 315
Brownell, A., 292
Brownfield, C. A., 227
Brubaker, T. H., 331
Brunstein, J. C., 299
Buchanan, W. W., 194
Buchbinder, R., 240
Buchsbaum, M., 242
Buckholdt, D. R., 323, 324
Buckingham, T. A., 140
Buech, V. U., 19, 27
Bugen, L. A., 313
Bullough, B., 355, 357, 358
Bullough, V. L., 355, 357, 358
Bultena, G. L., 225
Bunch, J., 317
Bunney, W. E., 79
Burger, H. G., 73
Burgess, R. L., 211
Burgio, K. L., 228, 256, 259, 262, 263, 264
Burgio, L., 228
Burgio, M., 293
Burns, G., 89
Busbaum, A. I., 192
Buss, A. H., 231, 232
Busse, E., 166
Busse, E. W., 22, 113, 114, 284
Butler, A. K., 228
Butler, R., 244
Butler, R. N., 25, 73, 194, 195, 198, 324, 325, 355, 359, 364, 397
Butler, S. 196, 198
Buttimer, A., 339
Byck, R., 167
Byerts, T. O., 336, 348

Cady, B., 128
Cahalan, D., 57, 60
Caine, E. D., 113, 117
Cairns, R. S., 209
Caldwell, A. B., 242
Caldwell, J. R., 298
Callaghan, N., 180
Callahan, E. J., 318, 319
Calvert, W. R., 357
Camacho, M., 164
Cameron, P., 67
Cammarata, R. J., 155

Campbell, S., 363
Campbell, S. S., 239, 243, 247
Campbell, W. H., 182
Campeau, L., 134
Canastrari, R. E., 28
Canning, B. S., 165
Cannon, M. S., 357
Cantor, M. H., 294, 360
Caplan, N., 390
Caplan, R. D., 298
Capron, A. M., 397
Carbone, P. P., 123
Carbuff, R. R., 358
Cardazo, L. D., 262
Carey, E., 241
Carey, R., 315
Carlin, V., 337
Carlson, A., 105
Carlson, D., 337
Carney, M., 89
Carp, F. M., 344
Carpenter, M. B., 190
Carroll, D., 279
Carron, H., 198
Carp, F., 37, 38
Carpenter, B. N., 293
Carpenter, H. A., 261
Carrel, A., 6, 7, 8
Carroll, B. J., 78
Carruth, B., 58, 59
Carskadon, M., 238, 239, 241
Carstensen, L. L., 226, 230, 398
Carter, B. C., 162
Carter, W., 80
Cascardo, D., 26
Casey, J. F., 79
Casscells, W., 163
Cassel, J., 291, 297
Cassvan, 280
Castleden, C. M., 160, 163, 254
Castleden, C. N. M., 162
Catalano, D. J., 295
Cattell, R. B., 27
Caven, R. S., 73
Ceder, L., 146
Cesar, J. A., 63
Chalke, D. H., 26
Chamberlin, K., 242
Chambers, 356
Chambers, W., 314
Chaplin, W., 84
Chapman, S. L., 192
Chappell, N. A., 293
Chatters, L. M., 359
Chauqui-Kidd, P., 103
Chen, L., 106
Cherubin, C. F., 58
Chien, C., 63
Chippendale, T., 179
Christenson, R., 49
Christie, J. E., 104
Chunn, J. C., 365
Chrysanthakopaulos, S. G., 138
Cicero, 398

Circirelli, V., 331, 332
Cicone, M., 281
Cieciura, S. J., 7
Ciompi, L., 43
Circirelli, V. G., 295
Cisin, I. A., 57
Citrin, R. S., 184, 185
Clark, A. N. G., 48
Clark, G., 279
Clark, M., 204, 205, 208
Clark, M. C., 293
Clark, M. S., 296
Clark, W. W., 98
Clarkson, B., 130
Clay, E. C., 256, 260
Clay, P. M., 87
Clayton, P., 85, 86
Clayton, P. J., 86, 314, 315
Cleeland, C., 264
Clifford, W. B., 343
Clithero, E., 49
Cluff, L. E., 152
Cluff, P. S., 182
Coates, T. J., 246
Cobb, F. R., 133, 153
Cobb, S., 35, 79, 291, 299
Coccagna, G., 241
Coccaro, E. F., 382
Cochran, M. M., 294
Cockroft, D. W., 157
Coffman, G. D., 70
Coffman, T. L., 346
Cohen, B. H., 159
Cohen, C., 396
Cohen, C. I., 293, 298
Cohen, D., 179, 238
Cohen, G., 96, 103, 357
Cohen, J. L., 130
Cohen, N., 298
Cohen, S., 165, 292
Cohn, K., 155
Colandrea, 279
Cole, J. O., 63
Cole, K. D., 29
Coleman, A., 260
Coleman, P. G., 325
Coleman, R. E., 133, 153
Coleman, R. M., 240, 241, 247
Collins, 357
Collins, G., 107
Collinsworth, K. A., 164
Colon, 366
Coltman, C. A., 128
Colton, T., 278
Comalli, P. E., 26
Comfort, A., 3, 12
Comstock, G., 314
Conner, K. A., 225
Conrad, K., 162
Conrad, K. A., 156, 165
Constantina, R. T., 155
Conway, T. L., 303
Cook, D., 156
Cooley, D. A., 133

Coombs, D. W., 104
Cooper, A. F., 27, 50
Cooper, B., 208
Cooper, J. E., 81
Cooper, M., 60
Cooperband, A., 320
Copeland, J., 78, 81
Copeland, J. G., 136
Cornbleth, C., 184
Cornbleth, T., 178, 184
Cornman, J. W., 391, 392
Correa, E. I., 180
Corsaro, W. A., 230
Corso, J. F., 26
Corslett, H. B., 281
Costa, P. T., 70, 325
Costello, C. G., 83, 242
Coursey, R. D., 240, 242
Court, J., 70
Courtice, K., 279
Courtois, Y., 8
Cowan, D., 81
Coward, R., 292
Cowen, D., 107
Coyle, J. T., 98, 180
Coyne, J. C., 293, 295, 297, 300, 301
Craik, F. I. M., 28
Crandall, R. C., 323
Crassman, L., 298
Crawford, F., 357
Creecy, R. F., 226
Cremer, T., 5
Cribier, F., 353
Crimmins, E. M., 19
Crocetti, G., 57
Croft, L. H., 72
Crook, T., 96, 99, 102, 103, 108
Crooks, G. M., 195
Crooks, J., 152, 153, 155, 156, 158, 160, 165
Crombie, A., 206
Cronin, D., 79
Cross, A. J., 104
Cross, R. R., 68
Crossley, H. M., 57
Crow, T. J., 104
Crowley, 211
Crue, B. L., 193
Crystal, H. A., 98
Csikszentmihalyi, M., 341
Cudihee, R., 155
Cudkowicz, G., 11
Cumming, E., 222, 223, 224
Cunningham, T. F., 300
Curry, A. R., 27
Curtis, H. J., 13
Cusack, B., 162
Cutler, R. P., 79

Daily, P. O., 137
Dajani, A. S., 136
Dalderup, L. M., 26
D'Amaro, J., 50
Damlouji, M. N., 180

Damrosch, S. P., 68
Dancy, J., 355, 358, 359, 360, 367
Danes, B. S., 10
Daniel, C. W., 11
Danziger, W., 115
Dapcich-Miura, E., 368
Dask, B., 26
D'Augelli, A., 293
Davidson, S., 86
Davidson, W., 383
Davis, B. C., 68, 69
Davies, D. F., 157, 158, 165
Davies, K., 103
Davies, P., 98, 104
Davis, J., 83
Davis, J. M., 166
Davis, M., 238
Davis, R. L., 179, 183, 267
Davison, D., 49
Dawber, T. R., 140, 278
Day, A. T., 344
Day, S. S., 338
Dean, L., 108
Dean, R. L., 103, 104
DeBusk, R., 135, 299, 300, 301
deCharms, R., 37
Dee-Kelley, C., 272, 273
D'Elia, G., 89
Degun, G., 184
DeGruchy, J., 81
Dekimenjian, H., 166
Dekasky, S., 281
Dekretser, D. M., 70
de la Pena, A., 243
de Leon, M. J., 99
DeLong, M. R., 98
De Longis, A., 300
Del Monte, V. D., 300
DeMaira, A. N., 136
Dement, W., 238, 239, 240, 241, 244, 246, 247
Denbigh, K., 225
Dennish, G., 137
Denny, N. W., 29
Denny-Brown, D., 281
deOme, K. B., 11
Depace, N. L., 136
DePaula, J. R., 180
Depner, C. E., 292
DeSilva, R. A., 163
Desmarais, L., 85
Desmond, P. V., 165
de Valera, E. K., 269, 271, 172
DeVellis, B. M., 297
DeVellis, R. F., 297
DeVoe, A. G., 107
deVries, H., 218
deVries, H. A., 21
DeWaard, F., 127
Dewhurst, J. R., 26
Dibner, A. S., 223
Dienelt, M. N., 315
Dig, 85
Diggory, J., 84
Dillane, J. B., 259

Dilworth-Anderson, P., 360
DiMatteo, M. H., 331
DiNicola, D. D., 331
Dittman-Kohli, F., 20, 217
Ditunna, J., 199
Dixon, D. N., 184, 185
Dixon, R., 217
Dixon, R. A., 20
Doering, W., 162
Doherty, W. J., 298
Dolce, J. J., 192, 195, 197, 198, 199, 200
Doleys, D. M., 199
Doleys, J. J., 198
Dolly, F. R., 239
Domey, R. G., 26
Domittner, G., 315
Donaldson, G., 20, 27
Donovan, M. A., 162
Dovey, K., 339
Dowd, J. J., 296
Downs, F. S., 284
Drachman, D., 99
Drachman, D. A., 98
Drayer, C. S., 298
Drayer, D. E., 164
Dreblow, L. M., 240
Drew, L. R. H., 60
Droes, J., 50
Droller, H., 61
Drummond, L., 184
Dubler, N. N., 397
Duckitt, J. H., 225, 226
Duff, R. W., 293, 294
Duffy, G. J., 165
Duffy, M., 39
Duffy, P., 107
Duncan, G. J., 342
Dunlop, M., 70
Dupree, L. W., 267, 270, 272
Durack, D. T., 136
Dusenbury, L., 291
Duvall, H. J., 60
Dyer, 280
Dzindzio, B. S., 164

Eaton J. W., 81
Eberly, D. A., 272
Eckert, J. K., 337
Eder, D., 230
Ehrlich, G. E., 148, 194, 199
Eiler, J., 27, 28
Eisdorfer, C., 116, 179, 238
Ejd, A., 186
Elayda, M. A., 133
Elder, 260
Eliade, M., 339
Ell, K., 292
Ellerton, J., 130
Elliott, C., 227
Ellor, J. W., 361
Elmore, S., 185
Emery, C., 90
Emery, G., 318

Embry, J. E., 260
Emerson, R. M., 209, 210, 216
Enda, S., 239, 240, 247
Endicott, J., 78
Eneroth, P., 227
Engel, B. T., 256, 259, 262, 264
Engel, G. L., 314
Engle-Friedman, M., 239, 240, 244, 246, 247
Engell, B., 228
Engstrom, P., 194
Enjalbert, M., 134
Ensel, W. M., 297
Epstein, C. J., 8, 9
Epstein, L. J., 57, 78
Epstein, M., 170
Erbaugh, J., 79
Erichson, R., 130
Erickson, R. E., 230
Erikson, E. H., 324
Esquirol, J. E. D., 97
Essen-Moller, E., 81
Esterbrooks, D. J., 135
Estes, C., 278, 384
Evashwick, C., 298
Ewart, C. K., 299, 300, 301, 302
Ewy, G. A., 162
Ezra, 4

Faber, P., 255
Failla, G., 13
Falk, J. M., 325
Fallot, R. D., 325
Falls, M., 194
Fann, W. F., 167
Farmer, P. M., 98
Fassler, L. B., 165
Fastis, M., 187
Faulkin, L. J., 11
Fawcett, J. A., 166
Federman, J., 164
Fein, E., 240
Feinberg, I., 239, 240
Feinleib, M., 297
Feld, A. G., 343
Feldstein, I., 70, 71, 72, 73
Felton, B., 293
Feneley, R. C. L., 262
Fennell, R. H., 155
Fenster, P. E., 162, 163
Ferguson, J., 104
Ferris, I. N., 104
Ferris, S. H., 98, 99, 104
Ferster, C. B., 83
Festonstein, H., 50
Feuerstein, M., 200
Fichtl, B., 162
Fields, H. L., 192
Finch, C. E., 156
Finch, S., 130
Finley, G. E., 293
Finnegan, D. L., 298
Firlit, C. F., 264
Fischer, J., 72

Fisher, C., 239
Fisher, H. W., 7
Fisher, J. E., 389, 397, 398
Fisher, J. M., 284
Fisher, M. B., 26
Fisher, S. K., 103
Flammer, R., 60
Flannery, 319
Flannery, J., 130
Fleg, J. L., 156
Fleiss, J. L., 81, 357
Fleminger, J. J., 117
Fletcher, G. H., 124
Floyd, T. C., 240
Flynn, C. B., 343
Flynn, D. D., 104
Follingstad, D. K., 242
Folsom, J. C., 323
Folstein, M., 99
Folstein, M. F., 34, 99, 112, 179, 180, 257
Folstein, S. E., 34, 257
Foon, K. A., 130
Ford, C. E., 11
Ford, C. V., 355
Fordyce, W. E., 191, 192, 193, 195, 196, 197, 198, 200
Fortune, A. E., 291
Foss, O. P., 303
Fottrell, E., 152
Fountain-Gourlay, A., 81
Fowler, E., 259
Fox, J. H., 179
Fox, R., 337
Foxx, R. M., 261
Fozard, J. L., 25, 26, 278, 333
Francis, G., 137
Frankel, B. C., 242
Frankel, B. L., 240
Frate, D., 359
Fray, L. W., 127
Frecher, R. C., 156
Fredericks, M. L. C., 26
Freedman, B., 394
Freely, M. D., 180
Freeman, J. T., 68
Freeman, F. R., 194
Fremouw, W. F., 226
French, J. P. R., 35, 298
French, L. R., 25, 285
Freud, A., 223
Freud, S., 204, 357
Frewen, W. K., 254, 260
Friedfield, L., 68
Friedewald, W. T., 135
Friedman, 279
Friedman, E., 104
Friedman, R. J., 166
Friedman, S. R., 298
Friedmann, J., 244
Frier, M., 358
Fries, H., 206
Frishman, W. H., 135
Frohlich, E. D., 138
Fry, G., 135
Fuguitt, G. V., 343

Fujiward, T., 7
Fulcomer, M., 34
Fuld, P. A., 104, 105, 114
Funderburk, A. R., 60
Fung, H., 133
Furberg, C. D., 135
Furst, B. H., 70

Gadsby, A., 238
Gagnon, J., 73
Gainotti, G., 281
Gaitz, C. M., 58
Gajdusek, D. C., 107
Gale, 130
Galeazzi, R. L., 164
Gallagher, D., 29, 90, 112, 114, 115, 117, 118, 196, 206, 315
Gandy, H. M., 70
Garbarina, J., 298
Gardner, H., 281
Gardner, T. J., 180
Garfinkel, L., 24
Garnett, W. R., 162
Garralda, M. E., 117
Garrard, J., 206
Garrett, L., 136
Garry, P. J., 302
Garside, F. F., 50
Garside, R. F., 27
Garside, R., 89
Garver, D. L., 166
Gastel, B., 194, 195, 198
Gastes, S. J., 285
Gatz, M., 209
Gault, M. H., 157
Gauthier, J., 318, 319
Gaviria, M., 165
Gaylord, S., 115
Gebhard, P. H., 68
Gelwicks, L. E., 338, 348
Genesby, S., 27
Genest, J., 193
Geokas, M. C., 158
George, C. F., 160, 254
George, L. K., 209, 298
Gerard, P., 239
Gerber I., 314
Gerber, M. A., 136
Gerber, N., 153
Gergen, K. J., 316
Gergen, M., 316
Germaine, C., 365
Gersh, B. J., 133
Gershon, E. S., 82
Gershon, S., 96
Gerson, L. W., 152
Gerstenblith, G. M. D., 156
Gewirtz, J. L., 209
Gianturco, D. T., 313, 315
Gibbs, C. J., 107
Gibson, R. M., 152
Gibson, T., 159
Gilbert, J. G., 26

Gillette, J. R., 156, 158
Gilliland, B. C., 194
Gilroy, J., 279, 284
Giordana, J., 366
Giurgea, C., 104
Glaser, R., 325
Glasscote, R., 368
Glatt, M. M., 59, 61, 63
Glick, I., 314
Gleason, R. E., 8
Glen, A. I. M., 104
Globus, G., 244
Gober, P., 343, 344, 348
Gochros, H. L., 72
Golant, S. M., 338, 342
Goldbourt, U., 297
Goldberg, P. B., 153, 156
Goldberg, R. J., 140
Golde, P., 67
Golden, R., 108
Goldfarb, A. I., 34, 204, 205, 208, 209
Goldstein, G., 185
Goldstein, J., 91
Goldstein, K., 114
Goldstein, K. H., 281
Goldstein, R. S., 229
Goldstein, S., 8, 9
Golshani, S., 152
Goodin, D. S., 179
Goodrick, C. L., 12
Goodstein, R. K., 278, 279, 281, 283
Goodwin, F. K., 166, 167
Goodwin, J. M., 302
Goodwin, J. S., 302
Gordon, M., 134
Gordon, S. K., 208, 325
Gorer, G., 312, 316
Gorton, T. A., 296
Gorwitz, K., 60
Gotestam, K. G., 186
Gotlieb, I. H., 293, 295, 300, 301
Gottesman, L. E., 337, 357
Gottesman, S., 22
Gottfries, C. G., 98, 99, 105
Goulet, L. R., 224
Goulet, R. R., 211
Gove, F. L., 294
Grahame, P. S., 45, 48, 49
Graney, M., 225
Granick, R., 47, 226
Grann, V., 130
Grant, D. P., 347
Grauer, H., 77
Graves, P. E., 162
Gray, A. G., 133
Gray, I., 48
Gray, S. M., 11
Green, E. J., 227
Green, M., 312, 316
Greenough, W. T., 227
Greenberg, B., 299
Greenblatt, D. J., 159, 160, 164, 165
Greenblatt, M., 89
Greenblatt, M. J., 293

Greenblatt, R. B., 70, 71
Greene, H., 163
Greenhouse, S. W., 25
Greenwald, 104
Greenwald, B., 103
Greenwald, S. R., 64
Greer, D. S., 345
Greeson, A. D., 357
Gregory, M., 28
Gribnaw, F. W., 160
Griepp, R. B., 136
Griffith, J., 294
Griffith, V. E., 279
Griffiths, K. A., 348
Grosicki, J. P., 261
Grosser, G., 89
Grossman, J. L., 29
Gruenberg, E. M., 63
Gryfe, B. M., 196
Gryfe, C. I., 196
Gubrium, 323, 324
Gudeman, J. E., 368
Guider, R. L., 29
Guilleminault, C. C., 240, 241
Gurland, B. J., 78, 79, 81, 108, 357
Gutmann, D., 223
Gutowski, M., 337

Haberman, P. W., 57
Hachinski, V. C., 105
Hackett, E., 79
Hafner, J., 262
Hager, W. D., 162
Hagerman, S., 215
Hagestad, G. O., 363
Haider, T., 303
Hakikas, J. A., 86
Hakim, A. M., 106
Hakim, S., 107
Hale, W. E., 134, 138, 139
Haley, W. E., 177, 192, 195, 197, 198, 199, 200, 267, 273
Halikas, J., 315, 317
Halkin, H., 154, 155, 164
Hall, 196
Hall, A., 295
Hall, E., 22
Hall, R. J., 133
Hallberg, M. C., 70
Hallet, C., 160
Halpern, L. M., 190
Halter, J. B., 156
Halzman, A., 185
Hamburg, D. A., 79, 299
Hamilton, M., 77, 79, 89, 166
Hammer, M., 298
Hammond, E. C., 24
Hamovitch, M. B., 338
Hanel, Z., 298
Hanley, I. G., 185, 186
Hanley, R., 107, 116
Hanlon, T. E., 79
Hannon, E. C., 11
Hansen, E., 86

Hansen, J. M., 158
Hanson, S. H., 295
Hanusa, B. H., 300
Harbaugh, R. E., 104
Harbitz, T. B., 70
Harbrecht, J. J., 135
Hare, P. H., 344
Harker, H. O., 29
Haring, M. J., 331
Harkins, S. W., 26, 195, 196, 197
Harlow, H. F., 86, 227
Harlow, M. K., 227
Harman, D., 22
Harman, S. M., 70, 255
Harris, J. E., 223
Harris, M., 8
Harris, R., 153, 159
Harris, T., 86, 298
Harrison, D., 164
Harrison, D. C., 155
Harrison, D. E., 11
Harrison, M. J. G., 117
Hart, R. W., 12, 14
Hartley, J. T., 29
Hartman, A., 359, 365
Hartup, W. W., 208, 230
Hartwigsen, G., 343
Hartzler, G. O., 135
Harvald, B., 82
Harvey, S. C., 165
Hasenfeld, R., 243
Haskell, W. L., 135
Hassinger, M., 27, 28
Haug, E. A., 70
Haug, M. R., 118
Hauge, M., 82
Haugen, C. A., 70
Hauri, P., 240, 243, 246
Hauri, P. J., 105
Hauser, P. M., 205
Haven, C., 225, 293, 302
Haverback, B. J., 158
Havighurst, R. J., 223, 325
Haward, L. R. C., 117
Hawkins, B., 358, 361, 363, 364
Hay, R. J., 8
Hayashi, Y., 239, 240, 247
Hayer, F. W., 229
Hayer, W. J., 229
Hayes, M. J., 155
Hayflick, L., 4, 5, 6, 7, 8, 10, 11, 13, 14
Haynes, S. N., 242, 245, 297
Hayward, D. G., 339
Hazelwood, T., 239
Hazelwood, L., 247
Healy, G. S., 242
Healy, J. J., 165
Healey, S., 242
Heather, B. B., 116
Heathers, C., 208
Heaton, T. B., 343
Heersema, P., 81
Heffler, D., 246
Heidell, E. D., 115

Heidenreich, J., 255
Heikkila, J., 239
Heilman, K. M., 281, 282
Heinemann, C. D., 331
Heller, K., 291, 293, 294, 300, 302
Heller, N., 239, 240
Hellman, S., 11
Helms, M. J., 286
Helsing, K., 314
Heltsley, M. E., 225
Hemminki, E., 239
Hempel, C. G., 392, 393
Henderson, S., 298
Hendricks, C. D., 364
Hendricks, J., 364
Henkins, A., 211
Hennekens, C. H., 163
Henry, W. H., 222, 224
Hepner, G. W., 159, 160
Herjanic, M., 78, 315
Herr, H. W., 70
Hess, B. B., 295
Heston, L. L., 99, 102, 279
Heslin, R., 299
Hesp, R., 165
Hewick, D. S., 153
Heyman, A., 286
Heyman, D. L., 313, 315
Hiatt, L. G., 35
Higson, J. E., 155
Hilbert, N. M., 29, 108
Hildreth, G. J., 360
Hill, R. B., 356, 361
Hilton, P., 259
Hines, P. M., 359, 361, 366, 367
Hing, E., 255
Hinman, F., 259
Hippius, H., 89
Hirsch, C., 362
Hoberman, H., 114
Hoch, C. C., 240
Hoff, J. V., 141
Hogstel, M. O., 185
Hogue, C. C., 228, 296
Holahan, C. J., 301
Holahan, C. K., 301
Holden, V. P., 178, 184
Holick, M. F., 194
Holland, A., 180
Hollingshead, A. B., 357
Hollis, L. E., 344
Hollister, L. E., 79, 103, 156, 166, 167, 168, 169
Hollon, S., 90
Holm, J. W., 126
Holm, R., 211
Holmes, D., 298
Holzer, C. E., 79
Hong, L. K., 293, 294
Honn, S., 211
Hoover, S. L., 343
Hooyman, N., 291
Horenstein, S., 279, 281
Horn, J. L., 20, 27
Horowitz, M. J., 346

Hotson, J. R., 179
Hotvedt, M., 67
Houda, R. W., 196
House, J. S., 291, 292, 297
Houston, N., 135
Houts, A. C., 387
Howe, M., 229, 230
Howell, M. F., 368
Howell, S. C., 340, 341, 348
Howell, T. H., 278, 279, 283
Hoyer, F. W., 368
Hoyer, W. J., 177, 211, 368
Hoyt, D. R., 298
Hoyumpa, A., 165
Hradac, E., 127
Hubler, D. J., 267
Huckman, M. S., 179
Hudson, B., 70
Hudson, W. D., 391
Hughes, C. D., 179
Hughes, E. M., 297
Hughes, W. L., 11
Hughston, G. A., 267
Hulicka, I. M., 28, 29
Hultsch, D., 28, 29
Hume, D., 390, 391
Hunt, M. E., 343
Hunt, S. M., 79
Hunt, T. E., 195
Huntley, A., 244
Hurd, G., 298
Hurowitz, E., 134
Hursch, C. J., 239
Hurwitz, L. J., 279
Hurwitz, N., 152
Hussian, R. A., 177, 179, 183, 186, 211, 267, 323
Hutelmyer, C. M., 184
Hutton, J. T., 285

Iasiello-Vailas, T., 298
Imber, S., 60
Ingersall, B., 296
Ingham, J. G., 86, 227
Ingra, A., 299
Ingvar, D. H., 98
Institute of Medicine, 239, 242
Inui, T., 80
Irelan, T. M., 298
Isaacs, B., 206, 208, 253
Israel, B. A., 292, 296, 303
Issler, H., 165
Ivanyi, P., 50
Izard, C. E., 231

Jackson, G. M., 211, 267, 272, 273
Jackson, J. E., 167
Jackson, J. J., 354, 355, 358, 364
Jackson, J. S., 359, 360
Jackson, M., 361
Jacob, M., 136
Jacobs, B., 299

Jacobs, B., 337
Jacobsen, G., 99
Jacobson, E., 83, 245
Jahn, J., 322
Jahn, K., 70
Janis, I., 299
Janowsky, D. S., 179
Jarolim, L., 127
Jarvik, L. F., 12, 114, 178
Jarvis, G. J., 260
Jason, L. A., 186, 229
Jawaid, S. Q., 8
Jemmott, J., 298
Jenkins, W. O., 269, 271, 272
Jennett, B., 284
Jensen, H. K., 255
Johnson, A., 137
Johnson, C. L., 295
Johnson, J. A., 104
Johnson, L., 240, 244
Johnson, M., 262
Johnson, M. R., 230
Johnson, R., 104
Johnson, V. E., 70, 71, 72
Jonas, M., 214
Jones, B., 293
Jones, D. A., 252
Jones, H. B., 22
Jones, M., 64
Jones, R. H., 133, 153
Jones, W., 194
Jones-Gotman, M., 283
Joseph, J., 297
Joye, J., 136
Judd, H. L., 71
Judge, T. G., 152, 255
Jung, C. G., 324
Jung, J., 297, 298, 300
Juraska, J. M., 227

Kaas, M. J., 67
Kadushin, A., 295
Kadushin, C., 295
Kafer, R. A., 368
Kafer, R. J., 229
Kagan, N., 67
Kahana, B., 344
Kahana, E., 35, 38, 336, 344
Kahn, E., 239
Kahn, J., 90
Kahn, R. L., 29, 34, 108, 291, 292, 297, 368
Kaiko, R. F., 196
Kaiser, M. A., 295, 298
Kales, A., 238, 239, 242
Kales, J. D., 238, 240, 242
Kalinowsky, L., 89
Kalish, R. A., 208, 223
Kallman, E. J., 12
Kallner, A., 227
Kalnok, M., 231
Kalymun, M., 341
Kamarck, T., 292
Kamppmann, J. P., 157, 158

Kanagy, M., 185
Kanarski, E. Q., 230
Kancelik, J. A., 182
Kancelik, J. A., 348
Kandula, P., 182
Kane, R. L., 252, 253
Kanfer, F. H., 215
Kannel, W., 297
Kannel, W. B., 134, 278
Kapadia, C. G., 162
Kaplan, B. H., 297
Kaplan, E. L., 136
Kaplan, R. M., 297, 299, 302
Kaplan, S. A., 165
Karacan, I., 239, 240
Kare, M. R., 26
Karlaganis, G., 164
Karpman, R. R., 146, 149
Kart, C. S., 363
Kasl, S. V., 292, 297, 299
Kassam, Y., 194
Kastenbaum, R., 58, 186, 322, 325, 329, 331, 333
Katchadourian, H. A., 70
Katler, M. N., 136
Katz, D. A., 98
Katz, G., 79, 259
Katz, M., 166
Katz, W. A., 148
Katzman, R., 99, 105
Kaufman, I. C., 86
Kausler, D. H., 19, 20, 25, 26
Kay, C. M., 163
Kay D. W. K., 27, 48, 50
Kaye, T. W., 298
Kayser-Jones, 322
Keam, W. F., 194
Kear, K., 67
Keating, M. J., 130
Kegal, A. H., 254, 263
Kelan, J., 348
Kellaher, L. A., 336, 340
Kelleaher, M., 78, 81
Kellett, J., 81
Kelly, 356
Kelly, J. G., 162
Kelly, J. L., 200
Kendall, M. J., 153, 163
Kendall, R. E., 81
Kennedy, H. L., 140
Kennedy, L. J., 140
Kennel, J., 297
Kenshalo, D. R., 26
Kernis, N., 294
Kerremans, A. L. M., 160, 164
Kertesz, A., 280, 284
Kessler, K. A., 164
Kessler, K. M., 159, 160, 167
Kessler, R. C., 292, 298
Kidd, A. H., 114, 115
Kielcolt-Glaser, J. K., 299
Kiesler, C. A., 291, 303
Kiloh, L. G., 113
Kim, J., 343

Kim, Y., 281
Kindermann, T., 206, 211, 212, 214, 215
King, L. R., 264
Kinsey, A. C., 68
Kirchhoff, L., 184
Kirschner, M. A., 70
Kirkwood, T. B. L., 5
Kiyak, H. A., 38
Klaus, M., 297
Kleban, M. H., 34, 337
Kleeman, S. T., 284
Kleinplatz, F., 184
Kleitman, N., 244
Klenmack, D. L., 68
Klerman, G., 117, 315
Kliegl, R., 21
Kline, N. S., 79
Klocke, R. A., 24
Klotz, U., 165
Kluger, J., 164
Knapp, T. J., 186
Knapp, W. S., 133
Knesevich, J. M., 115
Knipscheer, K., 296
Knout, J. A., 343
Knox, D., 362
Knudtson, F. W., 223
Kochansky, G., 79
Kockeis, E., 344
Kohler, G., 6
Kohn, R. R., 24
Kolb, B., 279, 280, 283
Kolk, B., 86
Kollar, E. J., 244
Koncelik, J. A., 35
Koreska, R., 239, 240
Kornhauser, D., 159
Kossowsky, R., 206
Kothari, R., 152
Kovacks, M., 90
Kraft, C. A., 162
Kral, V. A., 99
Kramer, L., 328
Kramer, M., 356, 357
Kramer, N., 29
Krane, S. M., 194
Krannel, W. B., 140
Krasner, L., 387, 389, 397, 398
Kraus, A., 314, 317
Krieger, J., 241
Kripke, D. F., 241
Krishman, M., 72
Krohn, P. L., 11
Krueger, G., 357
Kubas, K. L., 282
Kuhn, M. E., 66
Kunkel, J., 245
Kuo, W., 297
Kupfer, D. J., 103, 240
Kurband, A. A., 79
Kuriansky, J., 81
Kurland, H. D., 79
Kurlychek, R. T., 185
Kurtz, D., 241

Kuypers, J. A., 296
Kwentus, J., 195

Labouvie-Vief, G., 19, 27
Lachman, J. L., 29
Lachman, M. C., 299
Lachman, R., 29
Lack, E. R., 299
Lacks, P., 245
La Gary, M., 293
Laird, J., 359, 365
Lakatta, E. G., 153, 156
Landahl, S., 208
Landowne, M., 159
Lane, J. M., 194
Lang, W. R., 70, 71
Langer, E., 37, 209, 214, 268
Langley, G. E., 89
Langlie, J. K., 298
Langman, M. J. S., 155
Langston, J. W., 179
Largo, D., 211
Larsen, H., 157
Larson, D. A., 162
Larson, E., 107, 116
Larson, H., 81
Larsson, T., 99
Lassen, N. A., 105
La Torre, R. A., 67
Latting, C. A., 134
Lauderslager, M. L., 298
Lavan, J., 162
Lawrence, P. S., 245
Lawson, I. R., 152
Lawton, M. P., 33, 34, 35, 37, 39, 270, 336, 337, 338, 342, 343, 348, 357, 358
Laycock, P. J., 278
Lazarus, R. V. S., 297
Learoyd, B. M., 156
Leavitt, J. L., 98
Leavy, R. L., 298
Lee, G. K., 295, 296
Leeds, M. H., 337
Lefcourt, H. M., 300
Lefcourt, M. M., 209
Le Guilly, Y., 8
Lehmann, H., 89
Lehmann, S., 293, 296
Lehrer, K., 391, 392
Leikola, E., 158
Leis, H., 71
Le Lieuvre, R. B., 196, 200
Lemke, S., 299
Lenhardt, M. L., 29
Le Noir, P., 8
Lerner, R. M., 210
Lesperance, J., 134
Lester, P. B., 211
Letcher, P. B., 185
Leutert, G., 70
Levenson, J., 228
Levi, L., 227
Levin, M. A., 330

Levitt, H., 26
Levitt, M. J., 293, 294
Levy, C. M., 240
Levy, G., 154
Levy, R., 49, 50, 103, 155
Levy, S. M., 206
Lew, M. F., 180
Lewinsohn, P. M., 83, 84, 90, 114, 115
Lewis, A. J., 44
Lewis, C. B., 190
Lewis, D. T., 206
Lewis, J. W., 192
Lewis, M., 244
Lewis, M. I., 73, 359, 364
Lewis, P., 26
Lezak, M. D., 114, 279, 281, 282
Libow, L. S., 112, 179
Lichenstein, E., 292
Lick, J. P., 246
Liberman, R. D., 186, 261
Lieberman, A., 106
Lieberman, M. A., 37, 325, 346, 348
Liebeskind, J. C., 192
Light, L. L., 28
Lillenfeld, A., 314, 317
Lilus, P., 206
Lima, L., 8
Lin, N., 297
Lindop, M. J., 155
Lindren, A. G. H., 107
Lindsay, I. B., 355
Lindsey, A. M., 297
Linn, B. S., 64
Linn, M. W., 64
Linsk, N. L., 177, 267, 268, 272, 273, 366, 368, 369
Lipinski, J., 78
Lipman, A., 295, 296
Lipowski, Z. J., 179
Lippincott, R., 89
Liptzin, B., 86
Lishman, W. A., 107, 282
Liston, E. H., 115, 179, 180, 184
Little, A., 103
Litwak, E., 294
Llamas, R., 298
Lloyd, R. A., 68
Locke, B. Z., 60, 357
Locke, S. E., 298
Loeb, A., 84, 85
Loeb, M. E., 68
Loeser, J. D., 192, 193
Logan, J. R., 337
Lo Gerfo, M., 325
Lomax, W., 72
London, C., 298
Long, D. M., 190, 198
Longina, C. F., 295, 296, 343, 344
Lopata, H. Z., 295
Lopez, M. A., 228
Lorand, A., 322
Lord, D., 297
Lorden, R., 26
Lowe, J. M., 162
Lowenthal, D. T., 159

Lowenthal, M., 225, 358
Lowenthal, M. F., 293, 302
Lown, B., 163
Lozier, J., 341
Lubin, B., 79
Ludeman, K., 67, 73
Lugaresi, E., 241
Luisda, A. A., 136
Luke, E., 225
Lukert, B. D., 194
Lullin, L., 162
Lum, O., 81
Lunde, D. T., 70
Lund-Larsen, P. G., 303
Luria, A. R., 280, 283
Lytle, L. D., 192

MacDonald, J. B., 195
MacDonald, M. T., 368
MacDonald, M. T., 185
MacDonald, M. L., 228, 229
MacGregor, A., 8
MacLeod, S. M., 165
MacMillan, D., 47
McAdoo, H., 359, 366
McAllister, C. J., 180
McAuley, W. J., 346
McCaffrey, R. J., 278
McCaslin, R., 357
McClannahan, T. E., 228, 229
McConahay, D. R., 135
McCormick, R. A., 396
McCullock, E. A., 11
McCullough, L. B., 396
McCusker, J., 58
McDonald, C. S., 243
McFarland, B. M., 8
McFarland, R. A., 25, 26
McFarlane, A. H., 293
McGhie, A., 239
McGivney, W. T., 195
McGoldrick, M., 360, 372
McGowan, W. T., 242
McGriffin, P., 50
McGuire, E. A., 156
McGuire, R. J., 185
McHugh, P. R., 34, 112, 257, 282
McKenna, T. J., 165
McKenna, P. J., 44
McKeown, T., 18
McKhann, G., 99
McKinlay, J. B., 298
McKinney, W. T., 86
McLachlan, M. S. F., 156, 157
McLean, W. M. R., 206
McMahon, A. W., 325
McMahon, B., 317
Maas, J. W., 166, 167
Mace, N. L., 105, 177, 279
Macieira-Coelho, A., 8
Mack, K. J., 227
Maddison, D., 314, 315
Maddox, G. L., 206, 208, 223, 225

Maguib, M., 49, 50
Maiberger, R., 282
Maier, S., 84
Maizels, M., 264
Malaise, E., 8
Malamud, N., 107
Malatesta, C. Z., 231
Maloney, A. J. F., 98
Malzberg, B. A., 60
Mancini, J. A., 298
Mangin, P., 241
Mangum, W. P., 337
Mankikar, G. D., 48
Manney, J. D., 356
Mannick, M., 194
Mansbach, W. E., 293, 294
Mappes, T. A., 397
Marans, R. W., 343, 347
Marcer, D., 160
Marco, L. A., 169
Marcus, P. I., 162
Maresh, C. M., 135
Margulies, M. K., 26
Marks, I., 319
Marks, R. G., 134, 138
Marnell, J. W. G., 253
Marsden, L. D., 117
Marsh, G. M., 104
Marshall, J., 105
Marshall, W. L., 318, 319
Marte, R. A., 300
Martin, C. E., 68
Martin, E. P., 359, 360, 364
Martin, G. M., 8, 9
Martin, J. M., 359, 360, 364
Martin, M. W., 394, 395
Martin, R. L., 115
Masciocchi, C. F., 297
Mash, D. C., 104
Masher, P. M., 229
Mason, D. T., 136
Mason, W., 241
Masters, C. L., 107
Masters, W. H., 70, 71, 72
Mastri, A. R., 99, 102
Masur, D. M., 104
Mather, L. E., 155
Mather, M., 184
Mathew, D., 52
Mathieson, G., 106
Mathur, V. S., 133
Matsuzawd, T., 20
Matthews, 260
Matthews, S. H., 332
Maurice, W., 315, 317
Maurice, W. L., 86
Mawson, D., 319
Maxwell, R. J., 359
May, F. E., 152
Mayer, D. J., 192
Maynard-Smith, J., 13
Meacham, J. A., 325
Meade, T. W., 252
Medalie, J. H., 297

Medawar, P. B., 14
Medical Council, 89
Medvedev, Z. A., 13
Meffin, P., 154
Meffin, P. J., 164
Mefford, I. H., 298
Mehlstrom, D., 208
Meichenbaum, D., 193
Meirer, J. P., 155
Meissner, W. A., 128
Melin, L., 186
Mellinger, G. D., 238
Melman, K. L., 152, 154, 155
Melmon, L. L., 152
Melnick, V. L., 397
Melzack, R., 190, 191
Mendelson, M., 79, 83
Mendelson, W. B., 165
Mendewicz, J., 82
Merchant, A., 116
Mermelstein, B., 292
Merriam, S., 325
Merry, D. A., 162
Mesavage, J., 103
Messing, R. B., 192
Messing, S., 241
Mesulum, M. M., 281
Metcalf, L., 298
Metha, D., 52
Metha, S., 52
Metzwer, H. C., 297
Meyer, J., 281
Meyer, J. S., 182, 279, 284
Meyer J. W., 337
Meyers, J. M., 298
Mezey, E., 156
Micklem, H. S., 11
Milaj, J., 206
Miles, A. M., 382
Miles, D. G., 368
Miles, L. A., 343
Miles, L. E., 239, 240, 244, 247
Milhoi, P., 267
Millan, D. J., 192
Millan, M. D., 298
Millard, H. D., 136
Miller, B. B., 73
Miller, C., 196, 200
Miller, D. R., 260
Miller, E., 26, 114, 185
Miller, K., 13
Miller, K. S., 328
Miller, M., 317
Miller, N., 99
Miller, P., 227
Miller, P. L., 58
Miller, P. M., 86
Miller, S. J., 267, 332, 337
Miller, S. M., 299, 300
Mills, C., 57
Mills, J., 296
Milner, B., 283
Milstein, C., 6
Mindham, R., 87

Minkler, M., 297
Minuchin, S., 366
Mirovics, A., 70
Mischel, W., 84
Mishara, B. L., 58, 186
Mitchell, R. E., 295, 296
Mitsui, Y., 8
Mittman, C., 24
Mizruchi, E. H., 208
Mizutani, T., 106
Mock, J., 79
Mock, M. B., 133
Moerman, E. J., 8
Moesmann, G., 148
Moffat, N., 185
Moholm-Hansen, J., 157, 165
Moisey, C. U., 254
Moleski, W. H., 39
Molinari, V., 325
Mondimare, F. M., 180
Monge, R., 28
Monroe, L. J., 240
Monsour, N., 178
Montalvo, B., 366
Montgomery, E., 263
Montgomery, J. E., 338
Moon, J., 272, 273
Moore, G. E., 392
Moore, M., 28, 29
Moorehead, P. S., 4, 6, 7, 8 10, 14
Moos, R. H., 299
Moran, E. C., 86
Moran, M. G., 156
Moreland, T. A., 153, 155
Morelli, H. F., 152
Morgan, J., 162
Morgan, K., 239
Morris, J. N., 345
Morgan, D. B.
Morgan, R., 104
Morganroth, J., 136
Morrissey, J. O., 48
Morrow, L., 281
Mortimer, J. A., 25, 97, 285, 286
Mosier, 279
Moss, M., 34
Motlik, K., 127
Motulsky, A. G., 8, 9
Moungren, M. A., 83
Mountjoy, C. Q., 98
Mueller, D. J., 229
Mueller, J., 179, 180
Muldowney, F. P., 165
Mulloney, D., 244
Mulligan, M. A., 228
Mumford, T., 343
Munnichs, J. M. A., 205, 208
Munro, A., 78
Murrell, S. A., 298
Murphy, E., 22, 51, 53
Murphy, G., 315
Murphy, G. E., 78
Murray, H. A., 38
Murray, M. I., 337

Mutram, E., 297
Munoz, R. F., 83
Myers, F. K., 179
Myers, J. K., 166, 315
Mysiac, P., 58

Nachison, J. S., 337
Nacht, M., 200
Naeim, F., 8
Nahemow, L., 35, 37, 336
Naitoh, P., 244
Namba, M., 7
Nathan, P. W., 191
Nation, R. L., 152, 153, 155, 156, 164
National Center for Health Statistics, 314
National Council on Aging, 338
National Institute on Aging, 262
National Institute on Mental Health, 89
National Institutes of Health, 242
Naydin, V. L., 280
Nazlek, J., 294
Neddis, R., 244
Nehemiah, 4
Nehrke, M. F., 298, 325
Nelson, S. D., 390
Nestadt, G., 116
Nestico, P. F., 136
Neugarten, B. L., 223, 362, 364
Neumann, E. M., 215, 217
Neville, Y., 206, 208
New, B. E., 328
Newcomes, R. J., 348
Newman, E. S., 341
Newman, M., 279
Newman, S. J., 342, 343
Newton, N., 68
Nicassio, P., 242, 243, 244, 246
Nichaman, 279
Nichols, P. J. R., 282
Nickens, H., 146
Niederehe, G., 29, 108
Nienhaus, A. J., 10
Nies, A. S., 156, 157
Nigola, P., 69
Niles, A., 83
Noel, J., 162
Noelker, L., 298
Norbeck, J. S., 297
Norman, G. R., 293
Norman, S., 282
Norris, A. H., 24, 156, 157, 159
Norris, F. H., 298
Norton, W., 225
Nott, P. M., 117
Nukolls, K. B., 297
Nurnberger, J. I., 82
Nusberg, C., 344
Nussbaum, K., 79

Obrist, P., 240
O'Bryant, S. L., 338, 339, 340, 344
Ochs, H. R., 164

O'Conner, S., 70
Odell, B. G., 206
O'Dell, S., 267
O'Donohue, W. T., 389, 397, 398
Ogura, H., 7
O'Hare, J., 180
Ojemann, R. G., 108
Okaysasu, H., 182
Okimoto, J., 80
Okun, M. A., 334
Olbrich, E., 299
Olsho, L. W., 26
Olsson, B., 186
O'Malley, K., 152, 153, 154, 160, 162
Omar-Amberg, C., 164
Orentreich, N., 22
Orgel, L E., 13
Orr, N. K., 279
Orzech, E. M., 211
Orzech, M. J., 299
Oser, G. T.,298
Osgood, N., 208
Osgood, N. J., 331
Oster, C., 285
Osterweis, M., 312, 316
O'Sullivan, M. J., 272, 273
Oswald, I., 239
Ouslander, J. G., 155, 158, 160, 252, 253, 255, 259
Overall, J. E., 79
Owens, J. F., 184

Pace, N., 218
Pappas, G. S., 391, 392
Paranjpe, M., 7
Parker, J. O., 133
Parker, M., 135
Parker, R. C., 6, 7
Parkes, C., 314, 316
Parkes, C. M., 312, 313, 315, 318
Parkes, S. H., 297
Parritt, D., 293
Parron, D. L., 165
Parson, R. L., 163
Pascal, G., 269, 271
Pasnaw, R. O., 244
Pastalan, T. A., 337, 340, 343, 345, 348
Patterson, G. R., 211, 214, 216
Patterson, R. L., 177, 267, 270, 272, 273
Patterson, W. B., 123
Pattison, E. M., 298
Patwardhan, R. V., 165
Paul, G. L., 261
Paykel, E. S., 85, 86, 315
Pearce, J., 114
Pearl, R., 12
Pearl, R. de W., 12
Pearlin, L. I., 298, 300
Peck, A., 34, 98, 105
Pelroth, F., 164
Pengelly, 260
Penner, L. A., 272, 273
Percy, C. L., 124
Perez, G. L., 136

Perlick, D., 79, 382
Perlmutter, M., 22
Perroth, P., 325
Perry, E. K., 98
Perry, R. H., 98
Peruzza, M., 69
Peters, G. R., 295, 298
Petersen, D. M., 382
Peterson, B. A., 128, 130
Peterson, C., 214
Peterson, J., 315
Peterson, J. E., 338
Peterson, K. L., 137
Peterson, L., 196
Peterson, L. P., 185
Peterson, R. E., 70
Peterson, R.G., 186
Pfeifer, M. A., 156
Pfeiffer, E., 68, 69, 72, 166, 244, 255, 267
Pfeiffer, R. F., 196, 197
Pflug, A. E., 155
Piatt, C., 90
Pierce, R., 358
Pilisuk, M., 297
Pilnick, S., 71
Pinderhughes, E., 359, 361, 364, 366
Pineiro-Giordano, G., 366
Pinkston, E. M., 177, 229, 230, 267, 268, 272, 273, 366,
    368, 369
Pither, P. F., 186
Plomin, R., 231, 232
Plum, F., 281
Plymat, F. R., 252
Podolsky, S., 25
Pokorny, A. D., 79
Polk, J. G., 162
Pollack, D. D., 186, 261
Pollack, E. S., 126
Pollack, M., 34
Pollack, R. H., 26
Pomery, W. B., 68
Pond, S. M., 164
Ponten, J., 8
Poon, L. W., 333
Pope, H., 78
Popkin, S. J., 26, 29
Port, S., 133, 153
Porteaus, J. D., 339
Porter, R., 50
Posner, C. M., 193
Posner, J. B., 281
Post, F., 43, 45, 47, 48, 50, 53, 54, 77, 78, 112, 113, 114
    167
Post, R. M., 166
Potter, L. T., 104
Poulshack, S. W., 297
Poulson, M., 116
Powell, 162
Powell, A. V., 347
Powell, L. S., 279
Powell, M. C., 296
Powell-Proctor, L., 185
Powers, E. A., 225
Powers, R. C., 225

Prados, M., 313
Prentice-Dunn, S., 299
Preskom, S. H., 180
Preston, T. A., 242
Price, D., 99, 195
Price, D. D., 192
Price, D. L., 98, 107
Price, M. G., 245
Price, R. H., 292
Price, T. R., 282
Prinz., P., 238, 240, 241, 244
Prohaska, T. R., 346
Puck, T. T., 7
Puder, R., 245
Pugh, T. F., 317
Puner, M., 359
Pye, D., 8

Quattrachi-Tubin, S., 186, 229
Quick, A. D., 360
Quinn, W. H., 267
Quintana, D., 293

Rabin, D. L., 88
Rabins, P. V., 105, 112, 116, 117, 179, 279
Raciti, M. A., 355
Raczynski, J. M., 198, 200
Radloff, L.S., 115, 257
Rae, D., 112, 115
Raftery, E. B., 165
Raizes, G. S., 163
Rajkowski, H., 293
Rakoff, R. M., 339
Ramm, L., 319
Ramsay, R. W., 319
Ramsey, P., 396
Randels, P. M., 169
Ransen, D. L., 218
Rao, 136
Rao, K., 282
Raotma, H., 89
Raps, C. S., 214
Raskin, A., 79, 112, 115, 178
Raskind, M., 80, 241, 244
Rasman, B. L., 366
Rasmussen, S. H., 158
Rathbone, E. E., 291
Rathbone-McCuan, E., 228, 368
Ratzan, R. M., 395
Rau, M. T., 296
Ravaris, C., 83
Ray, D. C., 355, 357, 365
Redd, W. H., 193
Redick, R. N., 356
Redfoat, D. L., 344
Redlick, F. C., 357, 367
Reenan, A., 156
Reese, H. W., 333
Reese, L. B., 299
Rees, J., 26
Reever, K. E., 272
Regnier, V., 348

Reichard, G., 155
Reichel, W., 152, 156
Reichlin, R. E., 325
Reid, A. H., 116
Reidenberg, M., 159, 170
Reidenberg, M. M., 160, 164, 165
Reifler, B. V., 107, 114, 116, 117, 118
Reimann, I., 165
Reinsch, S., 297
Reis, H. T., 293, 294, 300
Reiser, M. F., 314
Reisenzein, R., 209, 211
Reisberg, B., 99, 104, 279
Reite, M. L., 298
Relph, E., 340
Rennert, K., 194, 199, 201
Rennie, G. C., 70
Renshaw, D., 71
Renwick, A. G., 254
Revenson, T. A., 226
Reynolds, C. F., 105, 240
Reynolds, L., 57
Reynolds, M. D., 147
Rnudick, P. J., 325
Richards, B., 278
Richards, C. B., 80
Richardson, J. A., 155
Richelson, E., 168
Richen, D. P., 152, 153
Ridlinger, W. F., 137
Riberiou, J., 253
Riley, M. W., 297
Rimer, B., 194
Ringering, L., 90
Risley, T. R., 228, 229, 368
Rizer, R. I., 22
Robb, S. S., 178
Robbins, A. S., 195
Robbins, C., 297
Roberts, D. W., 104
Roberts, G., 104
Roberts, R. H., 137
Roberts, J., 153, 156
Roberts, W. C., 136
Robertson, J. F., 295
Robins, E., 78, 86, 315, 317
Robinson, A., 7
Robinson, D., 83
Robinson, E. A. R., 298
Robinson, J. C., 255, 264
Robinson, R. G., 282
Rochberg-Halton, 341
Rockstein, M., 278
Rockstein, M. J., 24, 25, 26
Rodeheaver, D., 333
Rodeheffer, R. J., 156
Rodin, J., 37, 186, 268, 299, 302
Rodnan, G. P., 155
Roehrs, T., 241, 242
Roessmann, V., 106
Roff, L. L., 68
Rogers, A. G., 196
Rogers, R. L., 182
Rogers, R. W., 299

Rogers, S. C., 87
Rogers, W., 35
Rohme, D., 8
Roland, M., 157
Romach, M. K., 156
Romano, J. M., 195
Ron, M. A., 117
Rook, K., 294, 302
Rook, K. S., 227
Roos, B. E., 98
Rose, S. D., 228
Rose, T. L., 79, 81
Roseman, C. C., 337
Rosen, J. O., 186
Rosen, K. M., 141
Rosen, W. G., 105
Rosenberg, G. S., 103
Rosenblum, L. A., 86
Rosenmayr, L., 344
Rosin, A. J., 59, 61, 63, 284, 285
Rosow, I., 343
Ross, B., 329
Ross, E. H., 280, 281, 282
Ross, J., 136, 137
Rossi, P. H., 342
Rossman, I., 22, 23, 70, 71
Roth, G. S., 153, 156
Roth, T., 241
Roth, M., 27, 48, 50, 89, 97, 98, 165
Rotter, J. B., 37
Rotton, J., 293
Rounds, K. A., 292, 303
Rowe, J. W., 157, 158, 165, 244
Rowland, M., 154, 157, 164
Rowles, G. D., 337, 340, 341, 345, 346, 348, 349
Roy, R. G., 293
Rozovosky, F. A., 396
Rubenstein, D. I., 363, 364
Rubenstein, L. Z., 195
Rubin, M., 243
Rubinstein, R. L., 340
Rudelli, R., 285
Rundall, T. G., 298
Rush, A., 282
Rush, A. J., 90
Rush, J., 318
Russell, S., 239
Rutherford, B. D., 135

Sacher, G. A., 13, 14, 15
Sackett, G. P., 211
Sacks, A., 184
St. Tegan, A. S., 253
Salazar, A. M., 107
Saleh, W. E., 300
Salthouse, T. A., 333
Salzman, C., 59, 61, 78, 79, 86, 103, 156, 165
Salzman, F. A., 128
Sanadi, D. R., 22
Sanavia, E., 262
Sanchez, R., 243
Sand, T., 70
Sandell, S. L., 325

Sanders, C., 316
Sanders, W. E., 136
Sandholzer, H., 207
Sandford, W. L., 269, 271, 272
Saperstein, A., 39, 337
Sartre, J. A., 348
Sasa, R., 297
Satariano, W. A., 22
Sauer, W., 292, 295
Sauer, W. J., 361
Saved, I., 152
Scarbrough, D. 185
Scarbrough, D. R., 184
Schaefer, C. A., 199
Schaefer, C., 297, 298
Schaie, K. W., 19, 20, 27
Scharf, M. B., 238, 242
Schenker, S., 165
Schildkraut, J. J., 166
Schlumph, B. E., 227
Schmid, U., 211
Schmidt, C. W., 166
Schmidt, W. C., 328
Schmucker, D. L., 154
Schneck, M. K., 99
Schneider, E. C., 70
Schneider, E. L., 8
Schneider, R. D., 264
Schnelle, J. F., 260
Schofield, C. B., 72
Scholes, R., 281
Schon, A. L., 361
Schonfeld, L., 267
Schonfield, D., 20
Schreuder, U. M. T. H., 50
Schrott, H. G., 298
Schuckit, M. M., 58
Schuessler, P., 144
Schultz, A. L., 8, 9
Schultz, E., 60
Schulz, R., 37, 209, 231, 296, 299, 300, 340
Schuman, L. M., 215, 285
Schurmann, K., 190
Schuyler, D., 166
Schwab, J.J., 79
Schwartz, R. H., 136
Schwenk, M. A., 185
Scott, F. B., 253
Scott, J. P., 331, 332
Scott, R. R., 278
Scowden, E. B., 186
Seamon, D., 339
Seay, B. M., 86
Secunda, S. K., 166
Sedgwick, C. E., 128
Seelbach, W. C., 361
Seidl, L. G., 152
Selesick, S. T., 96
Selig, M., 164
Seligman, M. E., 37, 84, 209, 214
Sellers, E. M., 156, 159
Selmanowitz, V. J., 22
Serafetnides, E. A., 293
Serow, W. J., 343

Setlow, R. B., 12, 14
Settin, J. M., 185
Sewitch, D. E., 240
Sexauer, J., 169
Shader, R., 59, 78, 79, 156, 159, 160, 165
Shamoian, C. A., 246
Shanas, 359, 360
Shanas, E., 267
Shanas, E. P., 206
Shand, D. B., 156, 159
Shand, D. G., 157
Sharp, A., 39
Sharpe, L., 78, 81
Sharpless, N. S., 104
Shaw, B., 318
Shaw, B. F., 90
Shaw, P., 47
Shaw, T. G., 182
Shawchuck, C., 187
Shearer, G. M., 11
Sheikh, M., 152
Shepard, A. M., 153
Shepherd, A. M., 263
Shepherd, D., 317
Shering, A., 104
Sherman, E., 341, 343
Sherman, K. A., 104
Sherman, S. R., 293
Sherwood, S., 345
Shimkin, D., 359
Shinn, M., 296, 298
Shock, N., 195
Shock, N. W., 19, 23, 24, 157, 158, 159, 163, 165
Shopsin, B., 77, 83
Shore, B., 296
Shore, H., 184
Short, A. H., 155
Short, M. J., 80
Shuler, G., 137
Shulman, S. T., 136
Shumaker, S. A., 292
Shumer, R., 366
Shumay, N. E., 136
Siassi, I., 57
Sickelsteel, J., 241
Siedler, H., 107
Siegler, I. C., 209
Sigmon, A. H., 286
Silberstein, J., 206
Silverfarb, P. M., 180
Silverman, M. E. 134
Silverman, P. R., 320
Simeone, R. L., 297
Siminovitch, L., 11
Simon, A., 57, 58, 59
Simon, B., 33
Simon, M., 8
Simon, R., 261
Simon, R. J., 81, 357, 264
Simons, J. B., 245
Simpson, G. M., 79
Simpson, S., 180
Simpson, S. C., 229, 368
Sinex, F. M., 22

Singer, J. E., 297
Singer, K., 79
Sipahioglu, I. B., 70, 71
Sjogren, H., 107
Sjogren, T., 99, 107
Skelskie, B. E., 313
Sketch, M. H., 135
Skinner, B. F., 105, 218
Skinner, E. A., 209, 214, 229, 299
Skovstad, L., 158
Skre, H., 26
Slater, E., 49
Slevin, A. E., 29
Small, R. E., 162
Smith, C. M., 242
Smith, J., 21, 223, 240
Smith, J. W., 152
Smith, K., 179
Smith, P. S., 262
Smith, R. C., 104
Smith, S. R., 253
Smith, T. W., 164
Snyder, F., 240
Snyder, L. H., 178
Sobel, E. F., 366
Soeldner, J. S., 8
Sogbein, S. K., 260
Sokoloff, L., 25
Sokolovsky, J., 298
Soldatos, C. R., 239, 242
Soldo, B. J., 295, 358
Sollberger, A., 243
Solnick, R. L., 72
Soloman, B., 359, 268
Soloman, F., 165
Solomon, F., 312, 316
Solomon, P., 284
Sommer, R., 39
Sones, D A., 148
Sontag, S., 67
Sontag, S. J., 328
Sowder, 356
Speare, A., 337
Spector, R., 196
Speedie, L., 281
Speeg, K. V., 165
Speicher, C. E., 299
Spencer, H., 328
Spiegel, T., 294
Spiker, D. G., 240
Spiro, H. R., 57
Spitz, R. A., 227
Spitzer, L., 186
Spitzer, R. L., 78
Sprague, C. A., 8
Sprague, M. K., 140
Spurgeon, H. A., 163
Squires, K., 179
Sroufe, L. A., 294
Stack, C., 359, 360
Stadlam, E. M., 99
Stafford, J. A., 286
Stamier, R., 137
Stamler, J., 137

Stanley, J. F., 8
Stanton, S. L., 259, 262
Starker, S., 243
Starr, A., 179
Starr, L. B., 282
Staunch, I., 239
Steel, K., 123, 382
Stehouwer, J., 206
Steinberg, F., 144
Steinbrunn, W., 155
Steinburg, F. U., 190
Stenson, R. E., 155
Stephens, R. C., 298
Stephenson, T. P., 254, 260
Stern, K., 313
Stern, R., 319
Sternbach, R. A., 193
Stevenson, C. L., 393
Stevenson, I. H., 152, 153, 160
Stevenson-Hinde, J., 297
Stewart, R., 211
Stewart, R. B., 134, 138, 152
Stier, S., 244
Stinson, E. B., 136
Stiller, P., 81
Stock, W. A., 331
Stohower, J., 267
Stoicheff, M. L., 280
Stone, V., 19, 27, 90
Stone, W. J., 180
Storandt, M., 28, 29
Stotsky, B. A., 63
Stoudemire, A., 179
Strain, L.A., 293
Strasberg, B., 141
Strauss, M. E., 180
Strecten, B., 107
Strehler, B. L., 8, 12
Streib, G. F., 345
Streiner, D. L., 293
Stroebe, M., 315, 316, 317
Stroebe, W., 315, 316, 317
Strom, J. O., 285
Strong, J. M., 164
Struble, R. G., 98
Stubbs, A. C., 338
Sturgis, E. T., 199
Stuyk, R., 343
Subcommittee on Taxonomy, 191
Sufrin, E. M., 278
Sugerman, J., 245
Suler, J. A., 298
Sullivan, D., 343
Sullivan, L.G., 355
Suls, J., 297, 300
Summers, W. K., 104
Sumner, L. W., 393
Surdy, T. M., 187
Sussman, M. 24, 25, 278
Sussman, M. B., 331
Svanborg, A., 208
Svigos, 260
Sviland, M. A., 69, 72, 73
Swearington, C., 242

Swerdlow, M., 194
Swim, H. E., 7
Swinburne, H., 240
Swindle, R. W., 291
Swiryn, S., 141
Sykes, J. T., 340
Sylvester, D., 82
Syme, L., 225, 292, 297
Symons, D., 69
Szasz, T., 389
Szetela, B., 282
Szilard, L., 13
Szklo, M., 314

Tachibana, H., 182
Tait, C., 89
Takeda, S., 20
Takeichi, N., 7
Talbert, G. B., 70
Tam, C. F., 22
Tan, T., 242
Tan, V., 160
Tanger, E. J., 186
Tantum, K. R., 159
Tarail, M., 68
Taska, L. S., 240
Tassin, J., 8
Taube, A., 356
Taulbee, L. R., 323
Taylor, C. C., 338
Taylor, C. R., 298, 299, 300, 301, 303
Taylor, R. J., 359, 360, 361
Teasdale, G., 284
Tec, N., 226
Tendzin, O., 91
Tenkate, L. P., 10
Teresi, J., 298
Teri, L., 114, 115, 116
Terinius, L., 192
Terman, G. W., 192
Terry, R. D., 98, 105
Terry, W. D., 123
Tesch, S., 298
Thal, L. J., 104
Theorell, T., 227, 228
Thoits, P. A., 298
Thom, T. J., 134
Thomas, B., 73
Thomas, D. A., 262
Thomas, H. E., 140, 278
Thomas, J. C., 278
Thomas, J. L., 390
Thomas, P. D., 302
Thomas, T. M., 252
Thompson, L., 112, 114, 115, 117, 118, 315
Thompson, L. W., 29, 90, 196, 206
Thompson, S. C. 299
Thompson, T. L., 156, 159, 160, 165, 166, 168, 179
Thomson, P. D., 154, 155, 159, 160, 170
Thoresen, C. E., 246
Thorne, C., 362
Thornton, G. F., 152
Thornton, J. E., 104

Thronesberry, C., 29
Tice, L., 228
Tilden, V., 297
Till, J. E., 11
Timiras, P. S., 195
Timm, G. W., 260
Tinklenberg, J. R., 104
Tjosvold, D., 268
Tjosvold, M. M., 268
Tobin, J. B., 20
Tobin, J. D., 156, 157, 159
Tobin, S. F., 361
Tobin, S. S., 37, 223, 346, 348
Tokarz, T., 245
Toler, H. C., 245
Tollefson, G. D., 180
Tomlinson, B. E., 97, 98, 105
Tonna, E. A., 23
Toone, B. K., 117
Topel, J. L., 179
Torack, R. M., 96
Tordella, S. J., 343
Torgeson, W. S., 207
Torjesen, P. A., 70
Tourney, G., 115
Townsend, A. R., 338
Townsend, P., 206, 267, 364
Tozer, T. N., 164
Traughber, B., 260
Treat, A., 382
Treps, L., 343
Tretli, S., 303
Trickett, E. J., 295, 296
Triggs, 156
Triggs, E. J., 152, 153, 155, 164
Troll, L., 223, 267, 363, 364
Trungpa, C., 84, 91
Tsao, C., 247
Tsitouras, P. D., 70
Tsvetkova, L. S., 280
Tucker, G. T., 155
Tucker, M., 359
Tune, L., 180
Turk, D. C., 193, 194, 199, 201
Turlot, J., 241
Turner, J. A., 195
Turner, S. M., 185
Turner-Massey, P., 345
Tyler, F., 209
Tyrer, S., 77

Uddenberg, C. E., 81
Ueda, C. T., 164
Uhlenhuth, E. H., 238
Ullmann, L. P., 397
Ulrich, T., 187
Upton, A. C., 11
Urban, B. J., 192, 198
Urban Resources, 355
Urtunski, B., 281
U. S. Bureau of the Census, 123, 205
U. S. Department of Commerce, 361
U. S. Public Health Service, 238

U. S. Senate Special Committee on Aging, 123
Utley, J., 137

Vakalo, K. L., 343
Valenstein, E., 281, 282
Valliant, G. E., 61
Van Baars, H., 160
Van Buskirk, C., 279
Van den Heuvel, W. J. A., 205, 208
Van der Hoed, J., 240
Van der Kolk, B., 59
Van der Kolk, B. A., 156
Van Dijk, Y. M., 284, 285
Van Ginneken, C. A., 160
Van Nostrand, J. F., 255
Van Rood, J. J., 50
Vartia, K. L., 158
Vaughn, M., 105
Veale, D., 180
Veith, R., 80
Verbugge, L., 144
Verwoerdt, A., 68, 69, 72, 89, 90
Vessel, E. S., 159
Vestal, R. E., 152, 154, 155, 156, 157, 158, 159, 163
Veterans Administration Cooperative Study Group on
    Antihypertensive Agents, 278
Vetter, N. J., 252
Victor, C. R., 252
Vigneulle, R. M., 11
Viesselman, J. O., 104
Vigorita, V. J., 194
Vinacke, W. E., 208
Vinarskaya, E. N., 280
Viola, A., 314, 315
Vlietstra, R. E., 164
Voelkel, D., 185
Volkman, F. R., 227
Vracko, R., 8
Vroulis, G., 104

Wagner, B. R., 261
Walford, R. L., 8, 22, 25
Walkey, F. A., 253
Wall, P. D., 191, 192
Wall, S., 294
Wallace, J. R., 300
Wallenstein, S. L., 196
Wallston, B. S., 297, 300
Walsh, D. A., 29
Walter, S., 255
Wan, T. T. H., 206, 208, 297, 298, 303
Wandell, M., 162
Wang, C., 70
Wang, H., 72, 240
Walsh, F., 356, 357, 362, 364, 366
Walsh-Sweeney, L., 333
Wambach, J. A., 329
Waper, W., 281
Ward, C. A., 160
Ward, C. H., 79
Ward, C. W., 26
Ward, D. C., 26

Ward, R., 293
Warner, H., 159
Warnes, A. M., 343, 345
Warren, A. B., 26
Warren, M., 317
Warthen, F. J., 60
Wasow, M., 68
Wasser, E., 322
Watanakunakorn, C., 136
Waters, E., 294
Watkins, L. R., 192
Watson, N., 382
Watson, R. T., 281, 282
Watson, W. H., 354, 356, 359, 360, 362, 363, 367
Wear, J. B., 264
Wear, R. B., 264
Weatherley, R., 330
Webb, W. B., 239, 240, 242, 243, 244, 246, 247
Weber, R., 294
Webster, J. S., 278
Wechsler, A. F., 281
Wechsler, H., 89
Wedderburn, D., 267
Weddington, W. W., 180
Wederburn, D., 206
Weg, R. B., 70,71
Weil, R. J., 81
Weiler, P. G., 368
Weinberg, C. R., 156
Weinberg, T., 286
Weindruch, R., 22
Weiner, I. M., 157
Weinman, C., 186
Weinstein, K. K., 362, 364
Weinstock, C., 226
Weintraub, M., 396
Weisbard, A., 397
Weisenberg, M., 191
Weisfeld, T. M. L., 163
Weisfeldt, M. L., 156
Weismann, A., 4, 5
Weiss, R., 314, 316, 318
Weiss, R. L., 28
Weissert, W. G., 297
Weissman, M. M., 166
Welch, P. T., 285
Wellman, B., 295
Wells, C. E., 108, 112, 113, 114, 117
Wen, G. Y., 102
Wentowski, G. J., 296
Werber, J., 128
Wessler, R., 243
Wheeler, M. H., 294
Whishaw, I. Q., 279, 280, 283
Whitbourne, S. K., 29, 298
White, C. B., 67, 68
White, C. C., 165
White, G., 81
White, J., 89
White, J. A., 279
Whitehead, A., 26
Whitehead, W. E., 256, 259, 262
Whitehouse, P. J., 96, 98
Whitlock, J. A., 140

Whitman, T. L., 230
Whittaker, J. K., 298
Whittlinger, R. D., 28
Wieland, J. M., 70
Wieland, R. G., 70
Wiener, A., 314
Wigley, F. M., 194, 198
Wilcox, B. L., 295
Wilkerson, C., 155
Wilkins, M. R., 153
Wilkinson, G. R., 156, 157, 159, 165
Wilkinson, P. R., 165
Wilkinson, W. E., 286
Willems, E. D., 210
Williams, C. D., 81, 166
Williams, E. P., 58
Williams, G. C., 14
Williams, G. M., 313
Williams, L., 298
Williams, M. A., 135
Williams, R. G. A., 207
Williams, R. L., 164, 239, 240
Williams, R. S., 227
Willie, C. V., 359, 360
Willington, F. L., 255, 262
Willis, S. L., 28
Wills, T. A., 292, 300
Wilson, 279
Wilson, B., 186
Wilson, C., 194
Wilson, I. D., 54
Wilson, L. A., 152
Wilson, T. S., 262
Winakur, G., 86
Winblad, B., 98
Windley, P. G., 336
Winkle, R. A., 164
Winklevass, H. E., 347
Winn, R. L., 68
Wiseman, R. F., 337, 343
Wisniewski, H., 102
Wisniewski, K., 102
Wisocki, P. A., 177, 229, 317, 318
Witherington, R., 70, 71
Witherspoon, A. D., 269, 271, 272
Witkowski, J. A., 8
Witter, R. A., 334
Wittig, B. A., 79
Wittington, F. J., 382
Wittig, R., 241
Wohlwill, J. F., 37
Wolf, E., 25, 26
Wolf, H., 255
Wolf, J., 107
Wolf, S. L., 200
Wolf, S. M., 338
Wolfe, C. S., 184
Wolfe, P. A., 140, 278
Wolin, L. H., 254
Wollschlaeger, M., 239

Wong, N. W., 296
Wonnacott, T., 89
Woo, E., 164
Wood, A., 160
Wood, A. J. J., 157, 159
Wood, J. L., 361
Wood, R. L., 186
Wood, V., 295
Woodruff, R., 315
Woodruff, R. A., 78
Woods, K. L., 153
Woods, R. T., 178, 184, 185
Wool, M. S., 128
World Health Organization, 206
Worthington, D. J., 153
Wortis, J., 204
Wortman, C. B., 292, 303
Wright, R., 226
Writing, B., 162
Wyatt, R. J., 55

Yancik, R., 123
Yang, M., 240
Yao, L., 162
Yarrow, M., 25
Yates, J. W., 130
Yesavage, J. A., 79, 81
Yin, F. C. P., 163
Youkilis, H. D., 244
Youmans, W. B., 19
Young, J. L., 124, 126
Young, J. T., 11

Zais, T., 343
Zammit, G. K., 243
Zane, 280
Zappalo, A., 255
Zarcone, V. P., 240
Zarit, J., 22, 84, 90, 112, 117
Zarit, J. M., 244, 272, 279
Zarit, S. H., 27, 28, 29, 50, 84, 90, 108, 112, 117, 244,
     272, 279, 356, 357, 363, 364, 366, 367, 368
Zeiss, A. M., 83
Zelinski, E. M., 28
Zeman, F. D., 47
Zembaty, J. S., 397
Zepelin, H., 184, 240, 242
Zerbe, M. B., 368
Zieger, B. L., 325
Zighebaim, 130
Zimberg, S., 58, 61
Zimmer, J. G., 382
Zingg, R. M., 227
Zoin, E. M., 70
Zonn, L. E., 344, 348
Zorick, F., 241
Zung, E. M., 80, 81
Zung, W. W. K., 79, 80, 81, 89, 115, 166

Subject Index

Activities of daily living, 34, 184
  and dependence, 206–207, 212–214
Activity
  activity theory, 223
  changes with age, 223, 224
  level, 195–196
    and sleep disturbance, 223
Adaptation
  and aging, 218
Affective disorders (see also Depression and Mania),
  76–92
  and aging, 76
  classification, 76, 78
  diagnosis, 78–81, 91
  etiology, 82–86
    behavioral theories, 83
    biochemical factors, 82–83
    genetic factors, 82
    psychoanalytic theories, 83
Affective psychoses, 47
Aging
  and appearance, 22–23
  and behavioral plasticity, 211
  biological, 4–5, 12–14, 22–27
    damage theory, 22
    definitions of, 22
    and entropy, 14
    error theory of, 13–14, 22
    program theory of, 14–15, 22
    somatic mutation theory of, 12–13
  and cancer, 123–124
  cellular, 5–12
  chronic illness and plasma protein levels, 155
  and disease, 3–4, 153
  ecological theory of, 336
  and economic forces, 376
  etiology of, 4
  and generational differences, 19–20
  and genetics, 12–14, 22
  and intelligence, 27–28
  interindividual differences in, 20
  and memory, 28–29
  normal, 18, 21–25
  physiological, 21–27, 129, 195, 364–365
    cardiovascular system, 23
    and cerebrovascular accidents, 277–278
    effects of, on pharmokinetics, 125

  and politics, 376
  primary vs. secondary, 22
  psychological, 25
    primary vs. secondary changes, 25
  secondary aging, effects, of, 24
  and society, 376, 378
  and technology, 379–380
Akathesia see Wandering
Alcohol
  abuse, 57–64
    classification in elderly, 58
    diagnosis, 59–60, 64
    early vs. late onset, 59
    effects of, 61
    factors contributing to, 60
    and organic mental syndrome, 58, 59, 63
    prevalence among elderly, 57–58
    prevention of, 63–64
    prognosis, 60, 61
    sex differences in, 57
    spontaneous remission, 61–63
    treatment, 61–64
  and sleep disturbance, 242
Alzheimer's disease
  behavioral treatment, 105
  cerebral blood flow in, 98
  clinical course, 99
  and deficits in stimulus control, 182
  diagnosis, 99, 100
  genetic factors, 99, 102
  and head injury, 285–286
  neurochemical abnormalities in, 98–99
  neuropathology of, 97–98
  and Parkinson's disease, 107
  pharmocological treatment, 102–105
  and Pick's disease, 107
  prevalence, 97
Alzheimer's Disease and Related Disorders Associated
  (ADRDA), 105
American Association of Retired Persons, 123, 356
Analytic philosophy, 387
Anxiety
  and depression, 77
  drug treatment for, 165
  interaction of, with pain, 200
  phobias of falling and hip fractures, 147
  and sleep disturbance, 242

Arteriosclerosis, 23, 24
Assessment
    of activities of daily living skills, 184
    of the elderly, 21
    issues with black elderly, 365–372
    of mental status, 34
    of sensory and perceptual deficits, 26
Atherosclerosis, 23, 105
Attachment and aging (see also Social behavior), 223
Auditory perception, 26
    decreases in, 26–27
    and speech perception, 26
Autonomy (See also Dependence) 37, 38, 39, 209, 268,
    395–396, 397–398

Beck Depression Inventory, 79, 80, 91, 166
Behavioral modification
    of dementia-related behavioral deficits, 105
    of depression, 90, 200
    with the elderly, 273–276, 368–372
    of incontinence, 261–262
    of pain, 192, 193, 200
    and stimulus control, 186–187
    of wandering, 177, 184, 186–187
Bereavement
    and health, 314–316
    and illness, 196
    of kin, 316
    pathology of, 314
        treatment, 318–32
    stages of, 312–313
Black elderly, 354–372
    assessment of, 365–372
    biases in diagnosis of, 357–358
    and family structure, 359–361
    income of, 363
    interventions with, 354, 365–372
    life expectancy of, 356
    medical services for, 354–356
    mental health services for, 356–358
    needs of, 354, 358, 363
    percent of population, 354, 358
    and religion, 361–363.
Bone (see also Orthopedics)
    bone mass loss, 145
    disorders and treatment, 145–146
    hip fractures, 145, 146–147
    osteomalacia, 145
    osteopenia, 145
    osteoporosis, 23, 145, 194
    prevalence of fractures, 145
Breasts, 71
    cancer of, 127

Caffeine
    and sleep disturbances, 242
Cancer, 123–131
    age-associated risks of, 123–124, 127, 194
    and back problems, 149
    care of elderly patients, 124, 127–130
    common forms in elderly, 127
    early detection of, 126

    incidence of types, 125, 127
    pain associated with, 194–195
    prevalence, 194
    prognosis, age associated differences in, 128, 130
    and radiotherapy, 124
    staging of, 127, 130
Cardiovascular disease, 132–141, 153, 154
    arrythmias, 139
    aortic value surgery, 137
    atrial fibrillation, 139
    balloon angioplasty, 133
    cardiac catherization, 133
        congestive heart failure and diuretics, 165
        and drug metabolism, 160
        coronary artery bypass surgery, 133
        coronary artery disease, 132–134
        and diet, 134
    and disorientation, 180
    and drug use, 160
    mitral heart disease, 136–137
    mitral stenosis, 137
        mitral repair, 137
    myocardial infarction, 134–135, 139
    slowed heart rate, 141
    ventricular arrythmias, 140
Cardiovascular system, 23
    blood pressure, 24
    effects of general anesthesia on 129
    heart murmurs, 136
    output of, 23
    regional blood flow and pharmacokinetics, 155, 158
    and response to radiotherapy, 128
    and stress, 23
CAT scan
    cerebral atrophy across lifespan, 20
    in diagnosis of osteopenia, 145
    in diagnosis of spinal stenosis, 150
    sex differences in cerebral atrophy, 21
Cerebral atrophy, 20–21
    age differences, 20
    in Alzheimer's disease, 98
    sex differences, 21
Cerebrovascular accidents
    affective sequelae of, 280–281
    and age, 277, 278
    and age-related physiological changes, 277
    cognitive changes accompanying, 283
    and depression, 282–283
    epidemiology of, 278
    and hypertension, 139
    incidence note, 278
    and medication, 283–284
    personality sequelae of, 280–281
    prevalence, 278
    prevention of, 278–279
    prognosis of, 278
    psychological reaction to, 279
    recovery from, 279–283
    risk factors for, 139, 278
    and sex, 71
Closed head injuries
    and age, 277, 278
    and Alzheimer's disease, 285–286
    behavioral sequelae, 284–285

causes of, 284–285
cognitive sequelae, 284–285
diagnosis of, 284–285
incidence rates, 284
mortality rate, 284
prognosis, 284
Cohort effects
confounding: cross-sectional research
and physiological differences
and psychological differences
Cohort-sequential design, 19–20
cohort factors in, 20
and subject attrition, 20
Competence, mental, 396–397
Confidentiality, 394–395
Contraception, 69
Coping, 332–333
Cross-National Project for the Study of Mental Disorders, 81
Cross-sectional design, 19
and cohort effects, 19
Creutzfeldt–Jakob disease, 107
and deficits in stimulus control, 182
etiology of, 107

Death, 364
Delirium, 47, 179
causes of, 179–182
hallucinosis in, 47
management of, 184
paranoid symptoms in, 52
Delusions
age differences in content, 45
in Alzheimer's disease, 105
definition of, 44–45
in manic episode, 77, 78
prevalence, 48
Dementia, 29, 96–108
Alzheimer's disease, 97–105
behavior problems associated with, 105
changes in sleep patterns, 241
Creutzfeldt–Jakob disease, 107
and depression, 112–118
diagnosis of, 97, 182
and disorientation, 182
DSM-III criteria for, 97
and functional incontinence, 255, 257
history of, 96–97
multi-infarct dementia, 105–106
normal pressure hydrocephalus, 107–108
and Parkinson's disease, 106
Pick's disease, 107
pseudodementia, 108, 112–114
Dependence, 204–219
and age, 214–216
causes of, 204
conceptualization of, 204–205, 208
definition of, 206, 208
dependency ratio, 205
interventions to reduce, 217
measurement of, 205 206, 210–213
operant model of, 209–213
prevalence, 207–208

Depression
and Alzheimer's disease, 103, 105, 117
classification, 76–77, 78
and dementia, 112–118
diagnosis, 78, 91, 113
diagnostic scales, 79
etiology, 82–83
behavioral theories, 83, 91
biochemical factors, 82, 91, 166
Buddhist perspective, 84, 90–91
cognitive theories, 84, 91
environmental factors, 85–86
genetic factors, 82
psychoanalytic theories, 83
and incontinence, 257
interaction with pain, 195, 200
masked depression, 77, 114
and memory complaints, 29
and perceptual deficits, 26
prevalence, 76, 81, 117
and pseudodementia, 108, 112–114
as sequela of cerebrovascular accident, 282
and sleep disturbances, 242
and social support, 293
and suicide, 77
symptomatology, 77
age differences in, 77, 78
treatment, 86–91
behavioral and cognitive therapy, 90
drug therapies, 86–88, 92, 165–169, 180
electroconvulsive therapy, 89, 92, 180
meditation, 90–91, 92
psychotherapy, 89–90, 92
Depression Adjective Checklist, 79
Depression Rating Scale, 79
Depressive scale, 79
Diabetes
and foot problems, 150
incidence, 25
and renal function, 158
and sex, 71
Diagnostic and Statistical Manual of Mental Disorders,
78, 80, 81, 97, 99, 105, 113, 179
Diet
and cardiovascular disease, 134
dietary fat and cancer, 127
and hypertension, 138
and osteoporosis, 145–146
Digit span
age comparisons, 21
Diogenes syndrome, 48
Disengagement theory *see* Social behaviors
Disorientation, 177, 178
assessment of, 178, 182–183
etiology, 179–182
management of, 184–187
as a problem of memory, 185–186
DNA in aging, 12–14, 22
Down's syndrome, 12, 22
and Alzheimer's disease, 99
Drugs
absorption and aging, 153–154
adverse drug reactions, 152–153, 155, 156, 160, 168,
253

dose adjustment, 155, 156, 169–170
drug distribution in body, 154
effects of, on elderly, 125
elimination, 157
interactions of, 152, 156
pharmokinetics of, in elderly, 125, 152, 239
polypharmacy, 156, 196
protein binding of, 155
and regional blood flow, 155–156
renal excretion of, 157
sensitivity and age, 160
toxicity, 130, 158, 163, 196
Drug therapy
  antibiotics, 136, 158, 159
  anticholinergic drugs, 156, 169, 180
  anticoagulants, 140, 149
  antidepressants, 86–88, 92, 156, 165–169, 180, 196, 198, 242
  antihypertensive agents, 138, 139, 156
  anti-inflammatory agents, 148, 198
  antiparkinsonian drugs, 156
  arterial dilators, 138
  aspirin, 196
  beta blocking agents, 134, 138, 139, 163
  benzodiazepines, 160, 165, 241
  for coronary artery disease
    beta-blocking agents, 134
    calcium-blocking agents, 134, 139
    nitrate therapy, 133–134
  digitalis preparations, 139, 140, 162–163
  diuretics, 138, 156, 158, 164–5
  estrogen therapy, 255
    and osteoporosis, 146
  hypnotics, 238, 241
  for incontinence, 253, 254
  lidocaine, 163–164
  lithium, 180
  narcotics, 155, 196, 198
  phenothiazines, 169, 198
  procainamide, 164
  quinidine, 164
  steroids, 148, 149, 196
  sympathomimetics, 156
  for valvular heart disease
    potassium cardioplegia, 136
Duke longitudinal study, 225
Dynamic Depression Scale, 79

Elderly
  and dependence, 205
  in institutions, 206
  percent of population, 123, 152, 190
Elderly Cottage Housing Opportunity, 344
Electroconvulsive Therapy (ECT)
  and confusion, 180
  for depression, 89, 92, 180
Emotion
  conservation, 233
  control, 232
  development of, across lifespan, 231–233
Endocrine system, 25
Environment
  and aging, 33

and behavioral competence, 33–39
definition of, 35
environmental
  accessability, 35
  complexity, 38
  legibility, 35
  safely, 35
  security, 35
and interaction with impairment, 33
person-environment congruence, 35, 37–38
press-competence model, 35, 37–38
Estrogen,
  therapy 71, 146, 255
Ethics, 387–398
  descriptive ethics, 387–388
  informed consent, 389, 395, 397–398
  metaethics, 393–395
  naturalistic fallacy, 391–392
  normative ethics and psychotherapy, 388–393, 397
  professional ethics, 393–395
  and religion, 390–391
  and research, 395–397
  and science, 391–393
Excretory system, 24
  and drugs, 157, 170
Exercise
  cardiac output and drug effects, 156
  and cardiovascular functioning, 227
  and osteopenia, 146
  and psychological well-being, 227
  in treatment of pain, 199

Family
  assessment of, 271–275
  and black elderly, 359–361
  and the elderly, 267–275
Friendship *see* Social behavior

Gastrointestinal system, 24
Generational differences, 19–20
Geriatric day care, 371–372
Geriatric Depression Scale, 79, 81
Geriatric Mental Status Review, 79
Geriatric Rating Scale, 178
Global Deterioration Scale, 99, 101–102
Gonadotropins, 70
Grandparenthood, 363–364
Gray Panthers, 376–385
Grief *see* Bereavement
Group therapy for alcohol abuse, 62
Guardianship, legal, 328

Hair, 22–23
  graying of, 22
  loss of, 23
Hallucinations, 44–45, 46
  definition of, 44
  in delirious states, 47
  prevalence of types, 44, 48

Hamilton Rating for Depression, 79, 80, 81, 91, 166
Headaches *see pain*
Health care and cancer, 126, 127
Health education, 333
Hearing, 26
    deficits and paranoia, 50
    loss, 26, 278
    pitch discrimination, 26
Hobbies, 271
Hodgkin's disease and age, 128
Homosexuality, 73
Housing, 270, 335–350
    and age-related physiological changes, 336–337
    environmental needs and aging, 336
    facilitating transitions in, 347–349
    and income, 337
    options in, 337–338, 343–345
    relocation, 342–347
    retirement communities, 343
    satisfaction with, 338–339
Hutchinson–Gilford syndrome *see* Progeria
Hypertension, 137–139
    and cerebrovascular accidents, 278
    and coronary disease, 132
    definition of, 137
    essential type, 138
    increase with age, 153
    isolated systolic type, 138
    prevalence in elderly, 137
    and renal function, 158
    and sex, 71
    treatment for, 138
Hypnosis
    for treatment of pain, 201

Iatrogenic effects, 322
Income, 270–271, 363
Incontinence, 147, 177
    assessment of, 256
    biofeedback for, 262–264
    costs of, 252
    drug therapy for, 254
    etiology of, 253
    in nursing homes, 252–253
    physiology of, 253
    prevalence rates, 254
    seeking treatment for, 252
    sequelae of, 256
    treatment, 253, 254, 261–262, 265
        bladder training, 260–261
        contingency management, 261–262
        habit training, 259–260
    types of
        functional incontinence, 255
        overflow incontinence, 255, 264
        stress incontinence, 254–255, 263
        urge incontinence, 253–254, 262
Infertility, 70
Insomnia *see* sleep
Institutionalization, 346, 380
    adjustment to, 226
    deinstitutionalization, 380

and dependence, 206, 211–219
    prevention of, 346
Intelligence, 27–28
    generational differences in, 27
    influence of training, 28
    stability of, 30
    tests, 27–28
    two-factor model of, 27
International Classification of Impairments, Disabilities
    and Handicaps, 206
Inventory for Measuring Depression 79

Kidney function
    and drug excretion, 157, 170
    failure of, 180
    reductions with age, 157
    surgery on urinary system, 136

Lansing effect, 12
Learning
    influences on, 25
Life review therapy, 324–326
    vs. reality orientation, 324–325
Life satisfaction
    and activity level, 223–224
Liver
    change in size with age, 158
    and drug metabolism, 159
Longevity, 4, 12
    and evolution, 15
    and heterosis, 12
    and race, 356
Longitudinal method
    advantages of, 19
    confounding of age and period, 19
    and subject attrition, 20
Longitudinal Observation of Behavior Inventory, 79

Mania (*see also* Affective disorders)
    classification, 76, 78
    diagnosis, 78–81, 91
    diagnostic scales, 79
    drug therapy, 88–89, 92
    electroconvulsive therapy (ECT), 89
    etiology
        biochemical factors, 82–83
    genetic factors, 82
    prevalence rate, 76, 81
    symptomatology, 77–78
    treatment, 88–89
Memory, 28–29
    age differences, 28
    and depression, 29
    and disorientation, 185–186
    encoding, 29
    information acquisition and age, 28, 29
    remote memory, 28–29
    retraining, 185–186
    retrieval time and age, 29, 30
    strategies for improvement, 29

Menopause, 23, 70, 71
  effects on bone mass, 145
Mental Status Questionnaires, 34
Mini-Mental State Examination, 34, 116
Minnestota Multiphasic Personality Inventory
  (MMPI), 49, 79
Mobility, 271
Motor function, 278
Multi-infarct dementia, 105–106
Muscle, 144–145
  atrophy, 23, 24, 124, 157
  endurance and age, 144
  strength and age, 144

National Institute of Neurological and Communicative
  Disorders and Stroke, 99
National Institute on Aging, 5
Nicotine
  and sleep disturbance, 242
NIMH collaborative Depression Mood Scale, 79
Normal pressure hydrocephalus, 107–108
Nuremburg Code, 395
Nursing homes
  and dependence, 211
  incontinence in, 254
  staff training, 217, 265

Olfaction, 26
Operant behavior, 177
  behavioral plasticity, 211
  dependence as, 209–210
  incontinence as, 255, 261
  and pain, 192, 193, 200
Organic brain syndromes (see also Dementia and
  Delirium)
  and alcoholism, 58, 59, 63
  bias in diagnosis, 79
  paranoid symptomatology in, 47
  and schizophrenic symptomatology, 49
Orthopedics (see also Bone)
  arthoscopic surgery, 149
  back problems, 149
  bursitis, 148
  cartilage diseases, 23, 147–149, 194
    arthritis, 147, 148–149
    chondrocalcinosis (gout), 148
    osteoarthritis, 23, 147, 194
    prevalence, 147
    rheumatoid arthritis, 148, 149, 194
  fibrotosis, 148
  foot problems, 150–151
  joint replacement, 149
  mobilization, importance of, 147
  musculoskeletal problems, 144
  polymalgia rheumatica, 148
  spinal stenosis, 149–150
Osteopenia, 145
Osteoporosis, 23, 145, 194

Pain
  age differences in, 26, 195
  assessment of, 195–197
  classification of, 193
  causes of in elderly
    cancer, 194–195
    headache, 193–194
    osteoarthritis, 194
    osteoporosis, 194
    rheumatoid arthritis, 194
  sensitivity to, 26
  theories of
    gate control, 191
    interactive, 192
    learning, 192
    specificity, 190–191
  treatment 196–201
    electrical stimulation, 198
    exercise programs, 199
    pharmacological, 198
    psychological approaches, 199–201
Paranoia
  age of onset, 43
  etiology, 49
  paranoid delusions, 43–44
  and sensory deficits, 27, 50
  sex differences in prevalence, 45
  symptomatology, 45–47
  treatment, 51–54
Paraphrenia
  differential diagnosis, 48
  etiology, 49–50
  incidence, 49
  management and treatment, 51–54
  and premorbid personality, 49–50
  prevalence estimate, 49
  prognosis, 54
  and sensory deficits, 50
Parkinson's disease, 82, 106–107
Patients Bill of Rights, 383–384
Perception, 25–27
Period effects see longitudinal method
Philadelphia Geriatric Center Multilevel Assessment
  Instrument, 33–34
Philadelphia Geriatric Center Mental Status Question-
  naire, 178
Phobia see Anxiety
Pick's disease see also (Dementia), 107
  and deficits in stimulus control, 182
  etiology, 107
  neuropathology, 107
Premature ejaculation, 71
Prevention, 322–333
  assumptions of, 330–331
Primary Mental Abilities Test, 27
Professional training, 393
Progeria, 9, 12, 22
Progesterone, 71
Program evaluation, 323–329
Property, 268

Prostate gland and sex, 70
Pseudodementia, 78, 91, 108, 112–114
Psychiatric Judgment of Depression Scale, 79
Psychological well being, 146

Reality orientation, 184–185, 323–324
Relaxation training, 246
Religion, 361–362
Reminiscence therapy *See* life review therapy
Research Diagnostic Criteria, 78
Respiratory system, 34
Retirement, 363
Retirement communities *see* Housing

Sad–Glad scale, 79
schizophrenic disorders, 43–49
    and affective psychosis, 47
    class cultural differences in diagnosis, 81
    delusions, paranoid, 43–44
    drug treatment, 103
    genetics, 50
    hallucinations, 44–45
    HLA–A9 antigen, 50
    paranoid schizophrenic states, 46
    paranoid subtype, 48, 49
    prognosis, 43
    schizophreniform disorder, 45–46
    simple paranoid symptomatology, 45–46
Senile seclusion, 47–48
Sensory processes, 25–27
Sex education, 69, 72–73
Sexual behavior
    attitudes toward, 67–68
    attractiveness, 67, 68, 69–70
    capability, 67, 68–69
    desire, 67, 68, 70
    following cerebrovascular accident, 283
    myths of and the elderly, 66–70
    sex roles, 69
    sex therapy, 72–73
    sexual response cycle, 72
Skin, 22–23, 124
Sleep
    and anxiety, 242
    apnea, 241
    and dementia, 241
    and depression, 242, 247
    effects of environment on, 243
    habits, 243
    hypopnea, 241
    and reinforcement, 244
Sleep disturbances, 105
    and age, 238–240
    causes of, 239–244
    drug treatment, 238, 239, 241
    measurement of, 239
    non-pharmacological treatment, 244–248
    prevalence in elderly, 238

and REM sleep, 238, 240, 242, 243
    and sleep efficiency, 240
Social behavior
    activity theory, 223
    age differences in, 215, 216, 230–231
    attachment and aging, 223
    and dependence in institutions, 212–219
    disengagement theory, 222
    intimacy, 269–270
    intra vs. interindividual differences, 224
    isolation, 47, 50, 51, 226
        measurement of, 226, 227
        in children, 227, 230
    lifespan approach, 230
    and psychological well-being, 224–227, 270
    social activity, 35, 222–232
        definition of, 225
        interventions to increase, 228
        and physical health, 227–228
        skills training, 228, 398
    social competence, 226
Social support, 331–332
    among black elderly, 359–362
    definition of, 291–292
    and family, 291
    from family vs. friends, 294–296
    and health, 225, 297–299
    and the immune system, 298–299
    measurement of, 292
    and mental health, 225, 298
    quality vs. quantity of, 292, 293
    reciprocity of, 296
    and self-efficacy, 299–305
    sex differences in, 296
Sociobiology and sex, 69
Speech perception, 26
Sperm, 70
Stimulus control
    causes of deficiencies in
        acute, 179–180, 181
        chronic, 182
    enhancement of, 186–187
    functional analysis of, 182–183
    and sleep, 243, 245–246
    of social interaction, 230
    and wandering, 177
Stockton Geriatric Rating Scale, 178
Suicide, 77, 317
Surgery
    for arthritis, 149
    coronary artery bypass, 133
    for hip fractures, 147
    orthoscopic surgery, 149

Taste, 26
Teeth, 23, 136
Testes, 70
Testosterone, 70, 71
Transient ischemic attacks, 279

Uterus, 70

Vagina, 71
Vaginitis, 71
Values *see* Ethics
Verbal behavior
  interventions to increase, 229
Vision, 25–26
  cataracts, 26
  blindness and polymalgia rheumatica, 148
  deficits in, 25–26, 277–278
  glaucoma, 26
  incidence and age, 25

macular degeneration, 26
and paraphrenia, 50
speed of accommodation, 26

Wandering, 177–187
  classes of, 179, 181, 182
  consequences of, 178–179
  definition, 178
  management of, 184–187
Widowhood, 363

Zung Self-Rating Depression Scale, 79, 80, 91, 166

Rubin Bressler, MD, is Professor and Head of the Department of Internal Medicine, Chief, Clinical Pharmacology and Professor of Pharmacology in the Department of Pharmacology at the University of Arizona Health Sciences Center. He is Executive Editor of *Life Sciences* and Science Editor of *Drug Therapy*. He also serves on the editorial boards of *GeriatrX, Physicians Drug Alert, Rx Being Well, Journal of American Geriatrics Society* and *Western Journal of Medicine*.

Kathryn Larsen Burgio, PhD, is Senior Staff Fellow at the Gerontology Research Center, National Institute on Aging, and Assistant Professor of Medical Psychology in the Department of Psychiatry and Behavior Sciences at The Johns Hopkins University School of Medicine. She has authored a number of articles and chapters on behavioral interventions for urinary or fecal incontinence and other problems associated with aging.

Thomas H. Crook, PhD, is President of Memory Assessment Clinics, Inc., a company based in Bethesda, Maryland that conducts standardized, computerized memory testing and evaluates drugs designed to improve memory. He was formerly a clinical research psychologist at the National Institute of Mental Health and Director of the Institute's geriatric psychopharmacology program. Dr. Crook is the author of numerous journal articles and book chapters on the assessment and treatment of late-life memory disorders. He is on the editorial board of several journals and has been editor of a number of books, including *Assessment in Geriatric Psychopharmacology* and *Treatment Development Strategies for Alzheimer's Disease*.

Patricia C. Dickerson, PhD, is a Postdoctoral Fellow in the Division of General and Preventive Medicine at the University of Alabama at Birmingham, and a graduate of the Counseling Psychology program at the University of Southern Mississippi. Her current research interests include the modification of cardiovascular risk factors.

Jeffrey J. Dolce, PhD, is an Assistant Professor in the Division of General and Preventive Medicine at the University of Alabama, Birmingham. He is a clinical psychologist with specialty training in Behavioral Medicine. His current clinical and research interests include a variety of behavioral medicine areas: chronic pain, pulmonary medicine, and cardiovascular risk factor modification.

Bernard T. Engle, PhD, is Chief of the Laboratory of Behavioral Sciences in the National Institute on Aging, NIH. He also is a Professor of Behavioral Biology at the Johns Hopkins University School of Medicine. A recipient of the Pavlovian Society Award, he is a Fellow of the Gerontological Society of America and of the American Association for the Advancement of Science. He also has been President of the Society for Psychophysiological Research, the Biofeedback Society of America and the American Psychosomatic Society.

Mindy Engle-Friedman, PhD, is an Assistant Professor of Psychology at City University of New York. She received her masters and doctoral degrees at Northwestern University. Her research focuses on the assessment and treatment of insomnia.

Jane E. Fisher is an Assistant Professor of Psychology at the University of Maine. Her research interests include the application of behavior therapy with the institutionalized elderly, social competence and aging, and Alzheimer's disease.

Jerid M. Fisher, PhD, is Director of Neurorehab Associates, Inc., a comprehensive outpatient rehabilitation program for traumatically brain-injured patients. His clinical and research interests include head injury, neuropsychological assessment, and cognitive rehabilitation.

Susan A. Gaylord, PhD, is an instructor in the Program on Aging, School of Public Health, University of North Carolina at Chapel Hill. For 5 years she was associated with Duke University's Center for the Study of Aging and Human Development, where she was involved in research on psychological aspects of aging. She is coeditor of the book *Aging and Public Health*.

Robin Goldberg-Glen, MA, is a National Institute on Mental Health Fellow, as well as a research associate and project director for the Elderly Support Project at The University of Chicago's School of Social Service Administration. Her work experience includes casework and clinical practice in a geriatric psychiatric clinic, a rehabilitation hospital, adult day care centers, and the Veterans' Administration. Her areas of expertise include behavioral gerontology and international social welfare with refugees.

Leonard Hayflick, PhD, is Professor of Zoology and Professor of Immunology and Microbiology at the University of Florida. He is a former President of The Gerontological Society of America and currently is Editor-in-Chief of *Experimental Gerontology*. His discovery of the limited replicative capacity of normal human cells led to a major revision in conceptions about fundamental aging processes. The author of over 200 papers, chapters and books, he has received many distinguished awards for his work, including the Brookdale Award, the Kleemier Award, and the Karl August Forster Award of the Academy of Sciences and Literature and the University of Mainz, Germany. His current research is directed toward an understanding of the putative biological chronometer that governs the lifespan of normal cells.

Richard A. Hussian, PhD, is Supervising Psychologist and Acting Unit Director of the Geriatric Unit at Terrell State Hospital in Terrell, Texas. He is currently on the editorial board of the *Clinical Gerontologist* and *Behavioral Residential Treatment*. He is also the author of *Geriatric Psychology: A Behavioral Perspective* and coauthor (with Ronald Davis) of *Responsive Care: Behavioral Interventions with Elderly Persons*. His chapters and articles reflect his interest in the areas of Alzheimer's disease and related disorders, stimulus control procedures, and behavioral interventions with the elderly.

James S. Jackson, PhD, is a Professor of Psychology in the Department of Psychology and a Research Scientist in the Research Center for Group Dynamics at The University of Michigan. Dr. Jackson is currently a Ford Foundation/National Research Council Senior Postdoctoral Fellow at the Groupe D'Etudes et de Recherches Sur La Science, Ecole Des Hautes Etudes En Sciences Sociales, Paris, France. A social psychologist, his research has focused on social reinforcement processes, attitude change, self-esteem and personal and group identity development. More recently his work has shifted to national surveys of the American black population including the National Survey of Black Americans, the National Three Generation Family Study and the National Black Election Study.

Robert R. Karpman, MD, is Director of the Phoenix Orthopedic Residency Training Program and Chief of Orthopedics at Maricopa Medical Center, Phoenix, Arizona. He is also Clinical Associate Professor in the Department of Surgery at the University of Arizona and Adjunct Professor in the Department of Public Programs at Arizona State University. Over the past several years, Dr. Karpman has been involved in the orthopedic care of geriatric patients and has chaired four national multidisciplinary conferences. He is currently coediting a textbook on musculoskeletal diseases in the aged, and will serve as a member of the Board of Directors of the Western Division of the American Geriatrics Society.

Robert Kastenbaum, PhD, is Professor of Gerontology and Director of the Adult Development and Aging Program at Arizona State University. He was formerly Superintendent of Cushing Hospital for the Aged, a facility operated by the Commonwealth of Massachusetts. He is editor of the *International Journal of Aging & Human Development*, and *Omega, Journal of Death and Dying*. He has been President of the American Association of Suicidology, President of Division 20 of APA, and Chair of the Behavioral and Social Sciences Section of the Gerontological Society of America. His books include *Death, Society, and Human Experience*, and *Old, Sick, and Helpness: Where Therapy Begins*. Research interests include death-related cognitions and behaviors, time perspective, and creativity throughout the life course.

Leonard Krasner, PhD, is a Clinical Professor of Psychiatry and Behavioral Sciences at Stanford University and Professor Emeritus at the State University of New York at Stony Brook. He is involved in research in and applications of psychology, including behavior modification, behavior therapy, environmental design, token economy, "abnormal" behavior, health behavior, clinical psychology, and issues of values in science. He has published a wide variety of materials in these areas.

Margaret E. Kuhn, better known as "Maggie," is the founder and National Convener of the Gray Panthers, an intergenerational advocacy movement dedicated to promoting a positive attitude toward aging and exposing age-related inequities and injustices. She has completed graduate work at Temple University and the University of Southern California and has received nine honorary doctorates. She is former editor of *Social Progress*, now the *Journal of Church and Society*, and has authored many articles and program materials as well as the following books: *You Can't Human Alone, Let's Get Out There and Do Something About Social Injustice*, and *Maggie Kuhn on Aging*.

M. Powell Lawton, PhD, has been Director of Behavioral Research at the Philadelphia Geriatric Center for the past 20 years, as well as an Adjunct Professor of Human Development at Pennsylvania State University and a Research Scientist at Norristown State Hospital. He has conducted research on the environmental psychology of later life, assessment of the aged, the psychological well-being of older people, and evaluation of programs for the aged and for the mentally ill. He has served as President of the American Psychological Association's Division on Adult Development and Aging, and as a member of the technical committee on housing for the 1971 White House Conference on Aging and the National Academy of Science Committee on Aging. He is the author of *Environment and Aging and Planning* and *Managing Housing for the Elderly*, as well as being editor of other books. Dr. Lawton is President of the Gerontological Society of America and first editor of the American Psychological Association's new journal, *Psychology and Aging*.

Robert J. McCaffrey, PhD, is an Assistant Professor of Psychology at the State University of New York at Albany. He is also Director of the Neuropsychological Assessment Laboratory and a Research Associate at the SUNYA Center for Stress and Anxiety Disorders. His research interests include the cognitive correlates of anti-hypertensive medications, the efficacy of "cognitive rehabilitation" in traumatically brain injured patients, and post-traumatic stress disorders.

Brenda F. McGadney, MSW, is a doctoral student in the School of Social Service Administration at the University of Chicago. She is currently a NIMH fellow and Project Director of an Administration on Aging-funded Alzheimer's disease research project. In 1979 and 1981, respectively, she received fellowships from the Phelps-Stokes Foundation, Washington, DC, and the International Academic Consortium (Xavier, Dillard, and Southern University, New Orleans, L.A.) to conduct cross-cultural aging research in the Ivory

Coast, Upper Volta, and Sierra Leone, West Africa.

William T. O'Donohue, PhD, is an Assistant Professor of Psychology at the University of Maine. He is coeditor (with James Geer) of *Theories of Human Sexuality*. A clinical psychologist by training, his recent research interests have been in the conditioning of sexual behavior, and in ethical, metaphysical, and epistemological issues in clinical psychology.

Roger L. Patterson, PhD, is a staff psychologist and coordinator of the Day Treatment Program at the Daytona Beach Veteran's Administration Outpatient Clinic. He is senior author of *Overcoming Deficits of Aging: A Behavioral Approach* and editor and contributor to *Maintaining Effective Token Economies*, and has contributed to the literature many journal articles and book chapters concerning behavior modification and assessment, particularly with the elderly. He serves on the editorial board of *Behavior Modification*. His current primary interest is in the programmatic application of behavioral methods to problems of the elderly and other chronic mental health care consumers.

Elsie M. Pinkston, PhD, is a Professor in the School of Social Service Administration at The University of Chicago. She is the Principal Investigator of The Elderly Support Project, a federally funded intervention program. She has chaired the Applied Behavior Analysis Sequence at the University of Chicago and currently teaches advanced clinical practice there. During the past 10 years, she was also the principal investigator of several family-treatment research grants developing procedures for behavioral family therapy. She is the first author of *Effective Social Work Practice* and *Care of the Elderly: A Family Approach*.

Felix Post, MD, is Physician Emeritus of The Bethlem Royal Hospital and The Maudsley Hospital, London, as well as an Honorary Fellow of the The Royal College of Psychiatrists. During the 1950s, he developed the first department for patients over 60 to be established in a psychiatric teaching hospital, and most of his clinical research has been in old-age psychiatry. Among his publications have been monographs on late life affective disorders and on late paraphrenia. He wrote the first textbook on the psychiatry of late life, and has more recently edited (with Raymond Levi) a multi-author postgraduate text on the same subject, contributing chapters on functional disorders and dementias.

Burton V. Reifler, MD, MPH, is an Associate Professor in the Department of Psychiatry and Behavioral Sciences at the University of Washington. He is Director of the Geriatric and Family Services Clinic, and of the School of Medicine's Alzheimer's Research Program. He is also Associate Director of the Alzheimer's Disease Research Center. His primary research interests are the diagnosis and management of Alzheimer's disease, particularly the relationship between Alzheimer's disease and depression.

Graham D. Rowles, PhD, is Associate Professor of Geography and Associate Director for Social and Behavioral Sciences at the Sanders-Brown Center on Aging, University of Kentucky. He is author of *Prisoners of Space?: Exploring the Geographical Experience of Older People*, coeditor (with Russell J. Ohta) of *Aging and Milieu: Environmental Perspectives on Growing Old*, and coeditor (with Shulamit Reinharz) of *Qualitative Geronotology*. Much of his research over the past 10 years has employed a qualitative approach to studying the environmental experience of the elderly in both urban and rural community settings. His most recent work focuses on the lifeworlds and social support systems of the Appalachian elderly.

John T. Santinga, MD, is an Associate Professor of Internal Medicine at the University of Michigan, with joint appointments in Geriatrics and Cardiology. Areas of special interest are valvular heart disease, exercise testing for coronary disease, cardiac rehabilitation, and the effect of age on diastolic function of the left ventricle.

Ellie T. Sturgis, PhD, is an Assistant Professor of Psychiatry and Behavioral Sciences at the Medical University of South Carolina and Program Director of the Alcohol Dependence Treatment Program at the Charleston Veteran's Administration Medical Center. She was formerly Executive Director of the Pain Clinic at the University of Mississippi Medical Center. Her research interests include diagnostic and treatment issues in substance abuse, as well as the assessment and management of chronic pain and psychophysiological disorders.

Linda Teri, PhD, is an Assistant Professor in the Department of Psychiatry and Behavioral Sciences and Chief Psychologist of the Geriatric and Family Services Clinic at the University of Washington Medical School. Since receiving her doctorate in psychology from the University of Vermont in 1980, she has been active in teaching, research, clinical work, and supervision in the areas of depression, dementia, and geropsychology. She is the author of numerous papers, and coauthored (with Peter Lewinsohn, PhD) *The Coping with Depression Course, Clinical Geropsychology*, and *Geropsychological Assessment and Treatment*.

Hans Werner-Wahl, MA, is a doctoral student at the Free University of Berlin, where he is a research associate at the research unit in psychological gerontology in the Department of Geronto-psychiatry. He received his MA in psychology from the University of Heidelberg. His current research interests are in the field of geropsychiatric epidemiology and clinical geropsychology, with an emphasis on the definition and assessment of disability and dependency as well as coping processes of the elderly.

Patricia Wisocki, PhD, is a Professor in the Department of Psychology at the University of Massachusetts. A clinical psychologist by training, she has presented her research in behavioral gerontology in three continents and has published over 30 articles on the topic. Her current research interests are grief reactions and worry among the elderly.

Rosemary Yancik, PhD, is Assistant Director of the Centers and Community Oncology, as well as the Division of Cancer Prevention and Control, at the National Cancer Institute. She is a medical sociologist with a longstanding interest in geriatric medicine and care of the chronically ill. Special areas of interest are cancer management problems unique to elderly cancer patients, quality of life assessment of cancer patients, the impact of cancer on the families of cancer patients, and cross-cultural comparisons of health care systems. She is the editor-in-chief of *Perspectives on Prevention and Treatment of Cancer in The Elderly*. Her current research involves examination of the effects of old age on cancer incidence, treatment, and survival as well as the clinical interface between cancer and old age.

Jerome W. Yates, MD, MPH, is Associate Director of the Centers and Community Oncology and the Division of Cancer Prevention and Control at the National Cancer Institute. He is a medical oncologist with an interest in clinical epidemiology. His research activities have addressed home health care, supportive care of cancer patients, influence of aging on treatment choices and outcomes, and economics of health care. He serves on the editorial board of the *Journal of Psychosocial Oncology* and is an associate editor of the *Journal of the National Cancer Institutes*.

Judy M. Zarit, PhD, is an Adjunct Assistant Professor of Psychology at Pennsylvania State University and in private practice with the Child Adult and Family Psychological Center. She is coauthor (with Steven H. Zarit and Nancy K. Orr) of *The Hidden Victims of Alzheimer's Disease*, and has authored two booklets, *How to Talk to Your Doctor* and *How to Talk to Your Doctor About Alzheimer's Disease*. Her research interests focus on neuropsychological assessment of the elderly.

Steven H. Zarit, PhD, is Professor of Human Development and Assistant Director for Research of the Gerontology Center at Pennsylvania State University. He is coauthor (with Nancy K. Orr and Judy M. Zarit) of *The Hidden Victims of Alzheimer's Disease*. He serves on the editorial boards of the *Gerontologist* and *The American Journal of Alzheimer Care*. His research interests include the impact of dementia on the family and community approaches to the care of the elderly.

Sheldon Zimberg, MD, is an Associate Professor of Psychiatry at the Mt. Sinai School of Medicine and Director of Psychiatry, Joint Diseases, North General Hospital in New York. He authored *The Clinical Management of Alcoholism* and was senior editor (with John Wallace, PhD and Sheila Blume, MD) of *Practical Approaches to Alcoholism Psychotherapy*, 2nd Edition.

William W. K. Zung, MD, is a Professor in the Department of Psychiatry at Duke University Medical Center. He is an expert in the area of psychopharmacology and has served as a consultant to the Federal Drug Administration and the National Institute of Mental Health. He is actively engaged in research in the area of affective disorders, including depression and anxiety disorders.